YESTERDAY'S AUTHORS of BOOKS for CHILDREN

YESTERDAY'S AUTHORS of BOOKS for CHILDREN

Facts and Pictures about Authors
and Illustrators of Books for Young People,
from Early Times to 1960

Volume 1

Anne Commire
Editor

Adele Sarkissian
Agnes Garrett
Associate Editors

GALE RESEARCH COMPANY • BOOK TOWER • DETROIT, MICHIGAN 48226

Special thanks to Carolyn Riley.

Assistant Editor: Linda Shedd

Sketchwriters: Rosemary DeAngelis Bridges, Gale Garnett,
Susan Johnson, Jo Ann Tedesco, Ruth Toms

Editorial Assistants: Cathy Coray, Debra Dunthorn,
Elisa Ann Sawchuk, Anna Deavere Smith

Library of Congress Catalog Card Number 76-17501
ISBN 0-8103-0073-3

Introduction

Somewhere in that grab bag of myths otherwise known as the "general consensus of opinion" is one promoting the idea that children's books are written by ladies of egg-shell consistency, who, when not penning prose, drink tea laced with apricot brandy and gasp whenever a door is slammed. Definitely white gloved. This thinking originates from the same source that makes students positive their second-grade teacher sleeps in the cloakroom, else how could she always be there before everybody else. Myth's source: they don't have all the information.

Boom out *The Sun Also Rises* and the author's name echoes back. But who wrote *Bambi* or *Pinocchio* or *Pollyanna*?. . . silence. People still play "Name all Seven Dwarves" on car trips, at ski lodges, or waiting for the salads to arrive. . .but ask the Big Question "who wrote *Undine"* and again there is silence.

Facts Explode "The Myth"

There are two ways to get information—read a book about it or write a book about it. The *YABC* staff did both and were surrounded with lives that certainly exploded the myth. Here came Beatrix Potter who freely loathed Michelangelo and relished her hard-won independence "at seventy." Betty MacDonald and her grandmother who read "bad weather reports" from around the world. Kate Douglas Wiggin's youthful encounter with Charles Dickens, where she told him breathlessly she read every one of his books, although she did "skip some of the dull parts; not the short parts; but the long ones." Hans Christian Andersen was practically illiterate until age seventeen and E. Nesbit led anything but a tidy life.

In writing their life sketches (*life* being the operative word), the staff took delight in their humorous phrasings, abrupt ironies, and well-sanded lines. Like Stephen Vincent Benét on *John Brown's Body*: "When that thing was finished, I felt as if I had given birth to a grand piano." Betty MacDonald's grandmother putting her grandchildren in snowsuits with mismatched owners so they "were so tight in the crotch they had to walk on tiptoe." Joel Chandler Harris' Brer Rabbit stuck in a bucket at well bottom convincing Brer Fox to get in the attached upper bucket. As Brer Rabbit rose and the Fox descended a moot point was made: "Some goes up, en some goes down."

Here writers are illuminated who celebrate LIFE, its ups and its downs. Edna St. Vincent Millay wrote a poem called "Childhood is the Kingdom Where Nobody Dies" and her fellow writers give testimony in their own words. Herein presented is their communal epitaph—the resiliency of the human spirit.

YABC Includes Authors Who Died Before 1961

YABC is a companion series to Gale's *Something about the Author (SATA)*, which now covers approximately 2,500 children's authors who are alive or who have died since 1961. *YABC* will bring together in a similar series information on children's authors who died before 1961 with primary attention given to authors who are still being read by children. *YABC* is intended both for children and for students of children's literature, however, and some attention will also be given to earlier writers who were influential in their time, even though they may not be widely read today. In *YABC,* personal and professional backgrounds are presented chronologically, and thus the listings often illuminate the significant connections between the author's personal and creative lives. Because *YABC* includes only authors whose careers have been terminated by death a number of years ago, it is possible to offer thorough overviews of their life and work. Hence, the listings for authors in *YABC* will be considerably longer than those in *SATA* (with about forty listings per volume in *YABC* compared with over two hundred author listings in each volume of *SATA*). Each *YABC* listing will represent a major research effort, bringing together in one listing diverse kinds of information about the author.

Author's Diaries, Etc., Quoted Extensively

Whenever possible, aspects of the author's personality and creative viewpoint are presented in his or her own words, drawn from autobiographies, diaries, and letters.

Illustrations, also, are chosen to contribute to the comprehensive presentation of the author's life and works. Several illustrations from an author's works (rather than only one, as in *SATA*) will accompany each author's listing. Photographs, portraits, movie stills, etc., are used in addition to book illustrations, making *YABC* interesting to read as well as helpful as a research guide.

Finally, listings feature sections titled, "For More Information See" and "Adaptations," where secondary sources such as books and journal articles as well as films, filmstrips, and recordings relevant to the study of the author's life and work are cited.

Cumulative Indexes in Future Editions

Each volume of *YABC* will include cumulative indexes of authors and illustrations. Listings in *YABC* will also be included in the cumulative indexes to *SATA*.

A partial list of authors about whom material is now being gathered for inclusion in forthcoming volumes of *YABC* is given following this introduction. As always, comments and suggestions concerning additional authors to be included—or any other aspect of the series—are welcome.

A Partial List of Authors
Who Will Appear in Forthcoming Volumes of
Yesterday's Authors of Books for Children

Ainsworth, William Harrison
Alden, Isabella MacDonald
Alger, Horatio
Allee, Marjorie Hill
Allen, Merritt Parmalee
Andrews, Roy Chapman
Anstey, F.
Asbjornsen, Peter
Ashmun, Margaret (Eliza)
Atwater, Richard
Baden-Powell, Lord Robert
Baldwin, James
Ballantyne, Robert Michael
Bannerman, Helen Brodie
Barbour, Ralph Henry
Barne, Kitty
Baum, L(yman) Frank
Baynes, Ernest Harold
Beard, Dan(iel) Carter
Becker, May Lamberton
Beim, Jerrold
Beim, Lorraine
Bell, Robert Stanley Warren
Bevan, Tom
Bewick, Thomas
Bianco, Margery Williams
Birch, Reginald
Blyth, Harry
Boylston, Helen (Dore)
Bridges, Thomas Charles
Brooke, Leonard Leslie
Brooks, Walter R.
Broster, D(orothy) K.
Brown, Margaret Wise
Brown, Paul
Browne, Frances
Brunhoff, Jean de
Brunhoff, Laurent de
Buchan, John
Bulfinch, Thomas
Burgess, Gelett
Burnett, Frances Hodgson
Caldecott, Randolph
Canfield, Dorothy
Carroll, Lewis
Charlesworth, Marie Louisa
Church, Alfred J.
Coblentz, Catherine Cate
Coke, Desmond
Coolidge, Susan
Collingwood, Harry
Collodi, C.
Corkran, Alice
Cox, Palmer
Craik, Mrs.
Crane, Walter
Crew, Helen Coale
Crockett, Samuel Rutherford
Crompton, Frances E(liza)
Cruikshank, George
Dasent, Sir George Webbe
d'Aulnoy, Countess

Dawson, A.J.
Day, Clarence
De La Mare, Walter
De Morgan, Mary
Dickson, Marguerite
Dimmock, Frederick Hayden
Ditmars, Raymond L(ee)
Dodge, Mary Mapes
Dulac, Edmund
Du Soe, Robert C.
Edgeworth, Maria
Evens, George Bramwell
Everett-Green, Evelyn
Ewing, Juliana Horatia
Fabre, Jean-Henri
Falkner, John Meade
Falls, C. B.
Farrar, Frederic William
Farrow, George Edward
Fenn, George Manville
Field, Eugene
Field, Rachel
Finley, Martha
Fischer, Hans Erich
Fitch, Florence Mary
Fitzpatrick, Sir James Percy
Flack, Marjorie
Fraser, Claud Lovat
Freeman, Douglas Southall
Frost, Arthur B.
Frost, Frances
Fyleman, Rose
Gall, Alice
Gatty, Margaret
Gilson, Charles
Golden Gorse
Goodyear, Robert Arthur
Graham, Eleanor
Greenaway, Kate
Greenwood, James
Grey Owl
Grimm, Jakob
Grimm, Wilhelm
Grinnell, George Bird
Gruelle, Johnny
Habberton, John
Hadath, Gunby
Hale, Lucretia Peabody
Hall, James
Handforth, Thomas
Hauff, Wilhelm
Hawthorne, Hildegarde
Hemyng, Bracebridge
Henty, George Alfred
Hoffmann, Heinrich
Holland, Rupert Sargent
Hood, Tom
Hope, Anthony
Hosford, Dorothy
Howard, Edward G. G.
Hughes, Arthur
Hughes, Thomas

Hunt, Clara Whitehill
Ingelow, Jean
Jacobs, Joseph
James, Will
Jefferies, Richard
Jewett, Sarah Orne
Judson, Clara Ingram
Keary, Annie
Kingsley, Charles
Kingston, William Henry Giles
Kipling, Rudyard
Kjelgaard, Jim
Knatchbull-Hugessen, E. A.
Knight, Eric
Knipe, Emilie Benson
Laboulaye, Edouard
Lagerlof, Selma
Lamb, Charles
Lamb, Mary
Lamprey, Louise
Lang, Andrew
Larsson, Carl Olof
Laut, Agnes C.
Lawson, Robert
Leaf, Munro
Lear, Edward
Leeming, Joseph
Lewellen, John
Lewis, Elizabeth F(oreman)
Linderman, Frank B.
Lofting, Hugh
London, Jack
Longfellow, Henry Wadsworth
Lucas, E(dward) V(errall)
MacDonald, George
MacGregor, Ellen
MacKinstry, Elizabeth A.
Marchant, Bessie
Marryat, Frederick
Martineau, Harriet
McNeely, Marian Hurd
Meade, L. T.
Miller, Elizabeth Cleveland
Moe, Jorgen Engebretsen
Molesworth, Mary Louisa
Moon, Carl
Newbery, John
Nordhoff, Charles
O'Brien, Jack
Orton, Helen Fuller
Otis, James
Ouida
Paget, Francis Edward
Parry, David Harold
Parton, Ethel
Patch, Edith M.
Pemberton, Max
Perkins, Lucy Fitch
Perrault, Charles
Phillpotts, Eden
Pogany, William Andrew
Porter, Eleanor Hodgman

Porter, Gene Stratton
Poulsson, Emilie
Pudney, John
Pyle, Howard
Pyle, Katharine
Rackham, Arthur
Rankin, Louise S.
Reed, Talbot Baines
Ried, Mayne
Roberts, Elizabeth Madox
Robinson, Tom
Rossetti, Christina
Sabin, Edwin L.
Salten, Felix
Scoville, Samuel Jr.
Seaman, Augusta
Seton, Ernest Thompson
Sewell, Anna
Sewell, Helen
Shaw, Flora
Sherwood, Mrs. Mary Martha
Sidney, Margaret
Sinclair, Catherine
Snedeker, Caroline Dale
Spring, Howard
Spyri, Johanna
Stables, William Gordon
Stein, Evaleen
Stong, Phil
Street, James
Sublette, C(lifford) M.
Tallant, Robert
Tarkington, Booth
Taylor, Ann
Taylor, Jane
Tenniel, Sir John
Thorne-Thomas, Gudrun
Tippett, James S.
Tucker, Charlotte Maria
Van Loon, Hendrik Willem
Walkey, Samuel
Wallace, Dillon
Walton, Mrs. Octavius Frank
Watts, Isaac
Webb, Marion St. John
Webster, Jean
Welles, Winifred
Westerman, Percy F.
Wetherell, Elizabeth
Weyman, Stanley
White, Eliza Orne
Wilder, Laura Ingalls
Wilkins, Vaughan
Wyss, Johann David
Ylla
Yonge, Charlotte M.
Young, Ella
Zollinger, Gulielma
Zwilgmeyer, Dikken

GRATEFUL ACKNOWLEDGMENT

is made to the following publishers, authors, and artists, for their kind permission to reproduce copyrighted material. ■ **ARTIA PRAGUE.** Illustrations by Jiri Trnka from the Czechoslovakian edition of *Marchen* by Hans Christian Andersen. Copyright 1959. Reprinted by permission of Artia Prague. ■ **A. S. BARNES AND CO., INC.** Illustration by Robin Jacques from *Hans Andersen, Forty-Two Stories,* translated by M. R. Tames. Copyright 1959. Reprinted by permission of A. S. Barnes and Co., Inc. ■ **ERNEST BENN, LTD.** Illustration by H. R. Millar from *The Magic World* by E. Nesbit./ Illustrations by C. E. Brock and H. R. Millar from *Oswald Bastable and Others* by E. Nesbit. First re-issued in this edition 1960. Both reprinted by permission of Ernest Benn, Ltd. ■ **BODLEY HEAD, LTD.** Illustration by Peggy Fortnum from *The Reluctant Dragon* by Kenneth Grahame. Illustration © 1959 The Bodley Head, Ltd. Reprinted by permission of Bodley Head, Ltd. ■ **BRANDT & BRANDT.** Sidelight excerpts from *Anybody Can Do Anything* by Betty MacDonald. Copyright 1950 by Betty MacDonald. Copyright 1950 by The Curtis Publishing Co./ Sidelight excerpts from *The Egg and I* by Betty MacDonald. Copyright 1945 by Betty MacDonald. Copyright renewed 1973 by Donald C. MacDonald, Anne Elizabeth Evans and Joan Keil./ Sidelight excerpts from *The Plague and I* by Betty MacDonald. Copyright 1948 by Betty MacDonald. Copyright renewed 1976 by Anne Elizabeth Evans and Joan Keil./ Sidelight excerpts from *Cross Creek* by Marjorie Kinnan Rawlings. Copyright 1942 by Marjorie Kinnan Rawlings. Copyright 1933 by Scribner's Magazine. Copyright 1942 by *The Atlantic Monthly.* All reprinted by permission of Brandt & Brandt. ■ **CURTIS BROWN, LTD.** Sidelight excerpts from *Kenneth Grahame: Life, Letters and Unpublished Work* by Patrick R. Chalmers./ Sidelight excerpts from *Autobiography (Its Too Late Now)* by A. A. Milne. First published in 1939 by Methuen. Both reprinted by permission of Curtis Brown, Ltd. [*Autobiography (Its Too Late Now)* on behalf of C. R. Milne.] ■ **CHATTO & WINDUS, LTD.** Decorations by Janina Domanska from *The Trumpeter of Krakow* by Eric P. Kelly. Copyright © 1966 by The Macmillan Publishing Co., Inc. Reprinted by permission of Chatto & Windus, Ltd. ■ **CONSTABLE & CO.** Illustration by W. Heath Robinson from "Tommelise," *Hans Andersens Fairy Tales.* Reprinted by permission of Constable & Co. ■ **COUNTRY LIFE BOOKS.** Sidelight excerpts from *Oxford Through a Boy's Eyes* by Kenneth Grahame. Reprinted by permission of Country Life Books. ■ **COWARD, McCANN & GEOGHEGAN, INC.** Illustration by Wanda Gág from *The ABC Bunny* by Wanda Gág. Lettering by Howard Gág. Copyright 1933 by Wanda Gág./ Sidelight excerpts from *Growing Pains: Diaries and Drawings for the Years 1908-1917* by Wanda Gág. Copyright 1940 by Wanda Gág./ Illustrations by Wanda Gág from *Millions of Cats* by Wanda Gág. Copyright 1928 by Coward-McCann Inc. Renewed 1956 by Robert Jansson./ Illustration by Wanda Gág from *Snow White and the Seven Dwarfs* translated by Wanda Gág. Copyright 1938 by Wanda Gág./ Illustration by Wanda Gág from *Tales from Grimm* translated by Wanda Gág. Copyright 1936 by Wanda Gág./ Illustration by James Daugherty from *Uncle Tom's Cabin* by Harriet Beecher Stowe. Copyright 1929 by Coward-McCann, Inc. All reprinted by permission of Coward, McCann & Geoghegan, Inc. ■ **DESCLÉE DE BROUWER.** Illustration by Jacqueline Ide from *Les Contes D'Andersen Ferme-L'Oeil Le Petit Elfe.* Reprinted by permission of Desclée de Brouwer. ■ **DIAL PRESS.** Illustration by Steven Kellogg from *Matilda Who Told Lies and Was Burned to Death* by Hilaire Belloc. Picture copyright © 1970 by Steven Kellogg. Reprinted by permission of the Dial Press. ■ **DOUBLEDAY & CO.** Sidelight excerpts from *A Treasury of the World's Great Diaries* edited by Philip Dunaway and Mel Evans. Reprinted by permission of Doubleday & Co. ■ **E. P. DUTTON & CO., INC.** Illustration by Else Hasselriis from *Shen of the Sea* by Arthur Bowie Chrisman. Copyright © 1925 by E. P. Dutton & Co., Inc. Renewal 1953 by Arthur Bowie Chrisman./ Illustrations by F. I. Bennett from *The Story of Grettir the Strong* by Allen French. Copyright by E. P. Dutton & Co. 1908. Copyright renewal 1936 by Allen French./ Sidelight excerpts from the preface of *The Story of Grettir the Strong* by Allen French. Copyright 1908 by E. P. Dutton & Co. Renewal 1936 by Allen French./ Illustration by Ernest H. Shepard from *The House at Pooh Corner* by A. A. Milne. Copyright 1928 by E. P. Dutton & Co., Inc. Copyright renewal 1956 by A. A. Milne./ Illustration by Ernest H. Shepard from *When We Were Very Young* by A. A. Milne. Copyright

Reprinted by permission of Mary Sarg Murphy./ Illustrations by Arthur Rackham from *Fairy Tales* by Hans Christian Andersen. Reprinted by kind permission of Mrs. Barbara Edwards./ Illustration by Steven Kellogg from *Matilda Who Told Lies and Was Burned to Death* by Hilaire Belloc. Reprinted by permission of Sheldon Fogelman, attorney.

We want to extend special thanks to Ruth Jackson and Naomi Noyes, of the New York Public Library; and to Helen S. Canfield, Salvatrice Schultze and Patricia O'Malley of the Hartford Public Library.

Thanks also to the Performing Arts Research Center of the New York Public Library at Lincoln Center for permission to reprint the following theater stills: "Peter Pan," "Little Women," "Uncle Tom's Cabin," and "Rebecca of Sunnybrook Farm."

ADAMS, Andy   1859-1935

PERSONAL: Born May 3, 1859, in Whitley County, Indiana; died September 26, 1935; son of Andrew and Elizabeth (Elliott) Adams. *Education:* Attended a country school in Indiana. *Home:* Colorado Springs, Colorado.

CAREER: Cowboy in Texas for ten years; miner in Colorado; author.

WRITINGS: The Log of a Cowboy: A Narrative of the Old Trail Days (illustrated by E. Boyd Smith), Houghton, 1903, reprinted, Airmont, 1969, earlier edition illustrated by R. Farrington Elwell, Houghton, 1927; *A Texas Matchmaker* (illustrated by E. Boyd Smith), Houghton, 1904; *The Outlet* (illustrated by E. B. Smith), Houghton, 1905, reprinted, Literature House, 1970; *Cattle Brands: A Collection of Western Camp-Fire Stories,* Houghton, 1906,

(From *Trail Drive* by Andy Adams. Illustrated by Glen Rounds.)

Andy Adams, 1904.

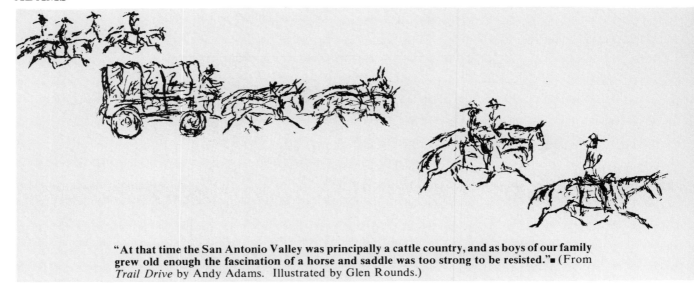

"At that time the San Antonio Valley was principally a cattle country, and as boys of our family grew old enough the fascination of a horse and saddle was too strong to be resisted." ■ (From *Trail Drive* by Andy Adams. Illustrated by Glen Rounds.)

reprinted, Books for Libraries, 1971; *Reed Anthony, Cowman: An Autobiography,* Houghton, 1907; *Wells Brothers: The Young Cattle Kings* (illustrated by Erwin E. Smith), Houghton, 1911; *The Ranch on the Beaver: A Sequel to "Wells Brothers"* (illustrated by Edward Borein), Houghton, 1927; *Why the Chisholm Trail Forks, and Other Tales of the Cattle Country,* edited by Wilson M. Hudson (illustrated by Malcolm Thurgood), University of Texas Press, 1956; *Trail Drive: A True Narrative of Cowboy Life from Andy Adams' "Log of a Cowboy"* (edited and illustrated by Glen Rounds), Holiday House, 1965.

SIDELIGHTS: **May 3, 1859.** Born in a log cabin in Thorncreek Township, Indiana. "I was raised on a stock farm, the youngest of three boys. With Scotch thrift, [my mother] kept bees and won all comers with thick slices of bread and butter and honey. . . . After the corn was planted, the dogwood in bloom, my father allowed his boys a day off, usually going along himself, when we all fished as earnestly

as the Apostles." [Wilson M. Hudson, *Andy Adams: His Life and Writings,* Southern Methodist University Press, 1964.[1]]

Fall, 1866. Entered Thorncreek Township school. "All the schooling I ever had, I picked up at a cross-roads country school house. Now, a grammar was the most uninteresting book to me, because it didn't carry any pictures in it. A history or geography, I could stand, if they had plenty of illustrations. Why, once I studied algebra. I don't know any more about it today than before I first saw the book. Lessons were easy . . . but the dread of whippings, nurturing a vagabond nature to burn the bridges behind me, was ever present."[1]

1873. "As a boy, I early mastered the knack of driving oxen. An innate laziness was one of the marked characteristics of my youth, and my father, conscious of my dilatory ways, always assigned me a yoke of cattle during plow

time, they being about suited to my gait and action. It was heartbreaking to a tired, hungry boy to trudge home from the fields beside a yoke of oxen at meal time, while my older brothers jauntily rode past me on mules and horses.

"One day I was plowing new ground—this was in Indiana, a timbered country—the plow had kicked me repeatedly that morning throwing me from the landside across the furrow, as it struck a root or stump, until at noontime I was worn out and ill tempered. This yoke of oxen with which I was plowing had a habit, when hurrying home to their dinner, of hauling off, that is, not walking upright side by side, but leaning outward. This forenoon they had been very unruly, not responding with alacrity when the plow struck a hidden root, and the plowboy, whom poets sing about, was jerked two ways at once. There was something out of harmony that day—a rift in the lute somewhere—between a stout yoke of oxen, new ground, and a hungry, barefooted plowboy, and at noontime I decided to break that yoke of

cattle from hauling off when going home. Accordingly when the horn blew for dinner, I unhitched with remarkable quickness, and having provided myself with an extra chain, as the oxen placidly stood in the furrow, I took it around their bodies, chaining them closely together.

"All went well for a time. As long as the oxen walked erectly the chain was no restraint. But as I left the clearing and made a tack for home, that yoke of cattle fell to hauling off—and stopped. They did more. Each emitted a blood-curdling bellow and stood transfixed, quivering with fear, while the chains proved their metal by holding their united weight. Never before had I found myself in such a predicament. With fear and trembling, I admonished those oxen to walk up-rightly. I pulled their tails, and still they fell apart, for what could a fourteen-year-old boy do in a physical contest with an eighteen-hundred-pound ox, for reason having fled, at that stage, the contest was reduced to one of brawn. To further disturb my perplexity my brothers rode

"There was a forced effort on the part of the drinkers to appear indifferent to the situation, but with the stranger sitting sullenly in their rear and an iron-gray man standing at the farther end of the line, hungering for an opportunity to settle differences with six-shooters, their indifference was an empty mockery." ■ (From *Trail Drive* by Andy Adams. Illustrated by Glen Rounds.)

Andy Adams, early 1920's. (Photo by Elmo Scott Watson)

up, laughed at me in my dilemma, and passed on, leaving me to work out the embarrassing situation.

'Again left to myself, there seemed no hope. The oxen were frantic and beyond appeal, the chain could be neither broken nor unhooked, and I was at my rope's end. Report, however, had reached my father at the stable, and with an occasional bellow of the oxen, making my location certain, I saw him coming, trimming a whip as he came, and which there could be no doubt was intended for me. Parenthetically—it is hardly necessary to mention that Scotch Presbyterians are rather strict in bringing up their boys. But in such an instance, the brain works quickly, and the thought flashed into my mind to unyoke the team, which was done with alertness, when the oxen, in a brief struggle, freed the chain. Taking the yoke on my shoulder, I escaped through the woods, and thus missed a well merited punishment.''[1]

1874. Ran away from home at fifteen and drifted to Arkansas to work in a lumber camp.

1882-1883. Went to Texas. Helped take a horse herd up the trail to Caldwell, Kansas. In succeeding years he made several trips to Caldwell. His book, *Matchmaker,* was dedicated to a friend he met at this time: "Red, do you remember, once upon a time in the old days, when you and I were at the Randado Rancho, our securing a bottle of rare old Cognac, smuggled goods beyond the peradventure of a doubt, from Tio 'Chino' Chapa. And when on breaking the seal and passing it about in the store to be sampled by those present, you offered the bottle to three strangers, one of whom wore a clerical garb and who courteously declined your proffered hospitality. And when on our riding away from the rancho, I took you to task for offending one of the sacred cloth, you replied in your usual drawl, 'Well, I thought-he-was-a preacher, but - I - didn't - propose - to slight - him - on - that - account.' And in memory of your proven, innate politeness, I dedicate to you these pages."[1]

1889. Quit the trail. Moved to Rockport on Aransas Bay above Corpus Christi, Texas. There, with a partner, he set up a feed and seed store. Because they were "easy-going" and often sold on credit, their money became tied up in uncollected debts and they had to close. "It was like the cowpuncher who started up a restaurant when he retired from the trail. His friends all brought their friends in and after they had finished, airily waved their hands and said; 'Charge 'er up, old man; these men are with me.' The cowpuncher also went out of business."[1]

November, 1893. Headed for Colorado to cash in on the Cripple Creek gold boom. Became a "mining broker." Invested heavily in stocks and lost the rest of his money. "If I hadn't been broke I might never have written."[1]

July 21, 1898. His first effort was a play, "The Corporal Segundo."

He looked every inch a chief, and was a natural born orator. There was a certain easy grace to his gestures, only to be seen in people who use the sign language. ■
(From *The Log of a Cowboy: A Narrative of the Old Trail Days* by Andy Adams. Illustrated by E. Boyd Smith.)

May 23, 1903. *Log of a Cowboy* published. "The cowmen and boys of the trail were a distinct type. Reared in the open, living in the saddle, at maturity they possessed statures equaled only by the Vikings of the sea. Owing to the arid nature of the country the Texas pioneer led a pastoral life, surrounding himself with herds and flocks, which multiplied as the years rolled on. The avarice of modern times was unknown to him, and monarch that he was of all he surveyed covetousness was foreign to his nature.

"Dispensing a hospitality which literally knew no bounds, admitted of no comparison, his open house became a proverb to the wayfaring man. If, unaware in his tents on the Asian plain, Abraham entertained the angels, so did the Texas cowman without question welcome the itinerant preacher, padre or horse thief.

"I never could quite understand that perverseness of human nature which demands that the range man of our West should be depicted, both by pen and pencil, as a drunken vagabond. Artists and writers know better, but public clamor demands that this pastoral character must be represented as picturesque, wild and woolly, bloodthirsty, the embodiment of all that is vicious and immoral. When our range man is so pictured, in painting and story, he gratifies a profane world that never knew him, but why is beyond my comprehension.

"Those who knew the cowboy best, know that amid the prosaic details of his daily life, he often displayed patience, courage, and even heroism, which entitled him to respect and admiration. And when his history shall have been truthfully written, it will show that this man bore his burden among other pioneers in reclaiming the old West."[1]

1904. Ran on the Democratic ticket for sheriff of El Paso County, of which Colorado Springs was the county seat. Lost by 2,994 votes.

1905. Reluctantly began to revise his short stories for *Cattle Brand's* magazine collection. "I can't revise well, . . . and unless what is wanted is pointed out clearly, I would no doubt overlook serious defects. With me, I never feel the same interest in a story after it has gotten cold, and I can never revive any enthusiasm while working it over. Once the frenzy of doing it passes, it is about as palatable as a cold pancake.

"These brands are mere chips that have fallen while hewing to the line of a continued effort. In my trilogy of the cattle they were crowded out, and now find expression in a group by themselves. If the parlance of the range was permissible, we might term this book a round-up of strays, a cutting out of mavericks, in which the smell of smoke from a camp-fire might be detected. A hard day's work or a reminiscent night may be recalled in its pages, wherein the characters around the fire were the men who redeemed the Lone Star State from crime and lawlessness. The cowboy may be met in his own salon, with his back to the wagon wheel or his head pillowed in a saddle, looking up at the stars. In fact, all the characters met in these brands were men—nothing more, just men."[1]

(From *The Log of a Cowboy: A Narrative of the Old Trail Days* by Andy Adams. Illustrated by E. Boyd Smith.)

1916. Ran for sheriff a second time and was again defeated.

June 30, 1935. Became ill. "Tomorrow will be eleven months since I awoke at daybreak fighting for my life. My heart had flunked, which resulted in a congestion of the lungs, and I took the count like a short sport."[1]

September 26, 1935. Died. "It was a privilege to live in and observe our day."[1]

FOR MORE INFORMATION SEE: Wilson Mathis Hudson, *Andy Adams: His Life and Writings,* Southern Methodist University Press, 1964.

Passers-by probably thought them a pair of harmless lunatics for they entirely forgot to hail a bus, and strolled leisurely along, oblivious of deepening dusk and fog. ■ (From *Little Women* by Louisa May Alcott. Illustrated by Jessie Wilcox Smith.)

ALCOTT, Louisa May 1832-1888

PERSONAL: Born November 29, 1832, in Germantown, Pennsylvania; died March 6, 1888, in Boston, Massachusetts; buried in Sleepy Hollow Cemetery, Concord, Massachusetts; daughter of Amos Bronson (an educator and philosopher) and Abigail (May) Alcott. *Education:* Tutored by her father until the age of sixteen; later studied under Henry David Thoreau, Ralph Waldo Emerson, and Theodore Parker.

CAREER: Author of novels, short stories, and poems. In her youth, held a variety of jobs, including teacher, seamstress, and domestic servant; nurse at Union Hospital, Georgetown, District of Columbia, 1861-63; editor of *Merry's Museum* (children's magazine), 1867.

WRITINGS—"Little Women" series: *Little Women; or, Meg, Jo, Beth, and Amy* (illustrated by sister, May Alcott), Roberts Brothers, 1868, Part II (illustrated by Hammatt Billings), added 1869, both reprinted, Dutton, 1972, Part II also published separately as *Good Wives*, Dutton, 1907, reprinted, Penguin, 1965 [other editions illustrated by Frank T. Merrill, Roberts Brothers, 1880; Alice Barber Stephens, Little, Brown, 1902; H. M. Brock, Pearson, 1904; Jessie Willcox Smith, Little, Brown, 1915, reprinted in Centennial Edition, 1968; Clara M. Burd, Winston, 1926; Harvé Stein, Garden City Publishing, 1932; Elinore Blaisdell, Little, Brown, 1946; Hilda Van Stockum, World Publishing, 1946; Louis Jambor, Grosset & Dunlap, 1947; Henry C. Pitz, Limited Editions Club, 1947; Salaman Van Abbé, Dutton, 1951; Barbara Cooney, Crowell, 1955; Betty Fraser, Macmillan, 1962; Tasha Tudor, World Publishing, 1969; dramatizations of *Little Women* include those adaptations by Elizabeth Lincoln Gould (two-act; illustrated by Reginald Birch), Little, Brown, 1900; Marian De Forest (four-act), Samuel French, 1921; Roger Wheeler (three-act), Baker, 1934; John D. Revold (three-act), Samuel French, 1935, later adapted as a three-act opera with lyrics by Frederick Howard and music by Geoffrey O'Hara, 1940; Peter Clapham (three-act), Evans Brothers, 1967; dramatization of *Good Wives* by Peter Clapham, Evans Brothers, 1965].

An Old-Fashioned Girl, Roberts Brothers, 1870, reprinted, Grosset & Dunlap, 1971 [other editions illustrated by Jessie W. Smith, Little Brown, 1902; Elenore Abbott, Little, Brown, 1926; Clara M. Burd, Winston, 1928; Nettie Weber, World Publishing, 1947; dramatization by John D. Ravold (three-act), Samuel French, 1935]; *Little Men: Life at Plumfield with Jo's Boys,* Roberts Brothers, 1871, reprinted, Airmont, 1969 [other editions illustrated by Reginald Birch, Little, Brown, 1901; Clara M. Burd, Winston, 1928; Harvé Stein, Garden City Publishing, 1933; Douglas W. Gorsline, Grosset & Dunlap, 1947; Hilda Van Stockum, World Publishing, 1950; Paul Hogarth, Macmillan, 1963; dramatizations include those adaptations by Elizabeth L. Gould (two-act; illustrated by Reginald Birch), Little, Brown, 1900; Ruth Putnam Kimball (published as *Daisy's Ball*), Baker's Plays, 1970].

Eight Cousins; or, The Aunt-Hill, Roberts Brothers, 1875, reprinted, Grosset & Dunlap, 1971 [other editions illustrated by Harriet Roosevelt Richards, Little, Brown, 1904; Hattie Longstreet Price, Little, Brown, 1927; Clara Burd, Winston, 1931; C. B. Falls, World Publishing, 1948; drama-

Louisa May Alcott, circa 1862.

tization by Ethel H. Freeman (three-act), Samuel French, 1934]; *Rose in Bloom: A Sequel to "Eight Cousins,"* Roberts Brothers, 1876, reprinted, Grosset & Dunlap, 1971 [other editions illustrated by H. R. Richards, Little, Brown, 1904; H. L. Price, Little, Brown, 1927; dramatization by J. D. Ravold (three-act), Samuel French, 1935]; *Under the Lilacs,* Roberts Brothers, 1878, reprinted, Grosset & Dunlap, 1971 [other editions illustrated by Alice B. Stephens, Little, Brown, 1905; Marguerite Davis, Little, Brown, 1928].

Jack and Jill: A Village Story, Roberts Brothers, 1880, reprinted, Grosset & Dunlap, 1971 [other editions illustrated by H. R. Richards, Little, Brown, 1905; Beatrice Stevens, Little, Brown, 1928; Nettie Weber, World Publishing, 1948]; *Jo's Boys and How They Turned Out: A Sequel to "Little Men,"* Roberts Brothers, 1886, reprinted, Grosset & Dunlap, 1971 [other editions illustrated by Ellen Wetherald Ahrens, Little, Brown, 1903; Clara Burd, Little, Brown, 1925; Louis Jambor, Grosset & Dunlap, 1949; Grace Paull, World Publishing, 1957; James Spanfeller, Crowell, 1962; dramatization by Alma Johnson, Row, Peterson, 1940].

Stories and collections: *Flower Fables,* Briggs, 1855; *Hospital Sketches,* Redpath, 1863, reprinted (edited by Bessie Z. Jones), Belknap Press of Harvard University Press, 1960 (also published as *Hospital Sketches [and] Camp and Fireside Stories,* Roberts Brothers, 1869); *The Rose Family: A Fairy Tale,* Redpath, 1864; *On Picket Duty, and other Tales,* Redpath, 1864, reprinted, Mss Information, 1972; *Morning-Glories, and Other Stories,* Carleton, 1867,

"Only don't be hard on Sanch; he's been real good to me, and we're fond of one another." ■ (From *Under the Lilacs* by Louisa May Alcott.)

enlarged edition (illustrated by Miss Greene), Fuller, 1868; *Three Proverb Stories* (illustrated by Augustus Hoppin), Loring, 1868 (contains *Kitty's Class-Day*, *Aunt Kipp*, and *Psyche's Art;* each title was first published separately in the same year); *Nellie's Hospital*, U.S. Sanitary Commission, 1868 (reprinted from *Our Young Folks*, Volume I, [Boston], 1865); *Concord Sketches* (illustrated from drawings by May Alcott), Fields, Osgood, 1869.

Aunt Jo's Scrap-Bag, six volumes, Roberts Brothers, Volume I: *My Boys*, 1872, Volume II: *Shawl Straps*, 1872, Volume III: *Cupid and Chow-Chow*, 1874, Volume IV: *My Girls*, 1878, Volume V: *Jimmy's Cruise in the Pinafore*, 1879, Volume VI: *An Old-Fashioned Thanksgiving*, 1882 (new edition of Volume VI, illustrated by Holly Johnson, Lippincott, 1974), also published as *Aunt Jo's Scrap-Book: A Selection*, one volume (illustrated by Beatrice Stevens), Little, Brown, 1929; *Silver Pitchers [and] Independence: A Centennial Love Story*, Roberts Brothers, 1876, a later edition illustrated by J.W.F. Kennedy, Little, Brown, 1908; *Meadow Blossoms*, Crowell, 1879; *Water Cresses*, Crowell, 1879; *Sparkles for Bright Eyes*, Crowell, 1879.

Proverb Stories, Roberts Brothers, 1882, revised edition, 1897, a later edition illustrated by Ethel Pennwill Brown, Little, Brown, 1908; *Spinning-Wheel Stories*, Roberts Brothers, 1884, a later edition illustrated by William A. McCullough, Little, Brown, 1908; *Lulu's Library*, Roberts Brothers, Volume I, 1886, Volume II, 1887, Volume III, 1889, also published as *Lulu's Library: A Selection*, one volume (illustrated by Gertrude A. Kay), Little, Brown, 1930; *A Garland for Girls* (illustrated by Jessie Mc-Dermott), Roberts Brothers, 1888, reprinted, Grosset & Dunlap, 1971, an earlier edition illustrated by Clara E. Atwood and others, Little, Brown, 1908; *The Spinning-Wheel Series*, four volumes, Roberts Brothers, 1897 (contains *Spinning-Wheel Stories*, *Silver Pitchers*, *Proverb Stories*, and *A Garland for Girls*); *A Round Dozen: Stories* (edited, and with an introduction, by Anne Thaxter Eaton; illustrated by Tasha Tudor), Viking, 1963; *Glimpses of Louisa: A Centennial Sampling of the Best Short Stories by Louisa May Alcott* (edited, and with an introduction and notes, by Cornelia Meigs), Little, Brown, 1968.

Stories taken from collections: *Marjorie's Three Gifts* (illustrated by Albert D. Schmidt), Little, Brown, 1899 (from *My Girls*, Volume IV of *Aunt Jo's Scrap-Bag*); *May Flowers* (illustrated by Schmidt), Little, Brown, 1899 (from *A Garland for Girls*); *A Hole in the Wall* (illustrated by Schmidt), Little, Brown, 1899 (from *Lulu's Library*, Volume I); *The Candy Country* (illustrated by L. Praud), Little, Brown, 1900 (from *Lulu's Library*, Volume I); *Poppies and Wheat* (Illustrated by Praud), Little, Brown, 1900 (from *A Garland for Girls*); *A Christmas Dream* (illustrated by John Ireland), Little, Brown, 1901 (from *Lulu's Library*, Volume I; dramatization by Laure Clair Foucher published as *Effie's Christmas Dream*, Little, Brown, 1912).

Little Button-Rose (illustrated by E. Pollock), Little, Brown, 1901 (from *A Garland for Girls*); *The Dolls' Journey* (illustrated by J. Ireland), Little, Brown, 1902 (from *An Old-Fashioned Thanksgiving*, Volume VI of *Aunt Jo's Scrap-Bag*); *Pansies and Water-Lilies* (illustrated by Ireland), Little, Brown, 1902 (from *A Garland for Girls*); *Mountain-Laurel and Maidenhair* (illustrated by E. Fosbery), Little, Brown, 1903 (from *A Garland for Girls*); *Morning-Glories and Queen Aster* (illustrated by J.W.F. Kennedy), Little, Brown, 1904 (from *Lulu's Library*, Volume II); *A Modern Cinderella, or, The Little Old Shoe*, [Philadelphia], 1904 (from *Hospital Sketches [and] Camp and Fireside Stories*).

Adult novels: *Moods* (illustrated by Frank T. Merrill), Loring, 1865, revised edition, Roberts Brothers, 1882; *The Mysterious Key, and What It Opened* (dime novel), Elliott, Thomes & Talbot, 1867; *The Skeleton in the Closet*, included in Perley Parker's dime novel *The Foundling*, Elliott, Thomes & Talbot, 1867; *Work: A Story of Experience* (illustrated by Solomon Eytinge), Roberts Brothers, 1873; *A Modern Mephistopheles* (first published anonymously), Roberts Brothers, 1877, later published under real name with *A Whisper in the Dark*, 1889.

Other: *Comic Tragedies Written by "Jo" and "Meg" and Acted by the "Little Women,"* Roberts Brothers, 1893; *Thoreau's Flute*, Stylus Press, 1899; *Three Unpublished Poems by Louisa May Alcott*, [Clara Endicott Sears], 1919 (contains *A.B.A.*, *A Little Grey Curl*, and *To Papa*). Also author of "sensational" fiction which appeared in periodicals and dime novels anonymously or under pseudonyms, including "A. M. Barnard." Author of several unproduced melodramas, including *The Bandit's Bride* and *The Moorish Maiden's Vow*.

Contributor to numerous periodicals, including *St. Nicholas, Hearth and Home, Young Folks' Journal, Merry Museum, The Youth's Companion, Atlantic Monthly, Saturday Evening Gazette,* and *Putnam's* Magazine.

ADAPTATIONS—Movies: "Little Women," (feature film), Famous Players, Lasky Corp., 1919, starring Katharine Hepburn (115 min., 16mm, sound, b/w), RKO, 1933, starring Elizabeth Taylor, June Allyson, Margaret O'Brien, and Peter Lawford (122 min., 16mm, sound, b/w, color), Metro-Goldwyn-Mayer, 1949; "Little Men," starring Dickie Moore (80 min., 16mm, sound, b/w), Mascot, 1934, starring Kay Francis (75 min., 16mm, sound, b/w), RKO, 1940; "An Old-Fashioned Girl" (feature film), Pathé Industries, 1949; "Louisa May Alcott" (18 min., b/w), Encyclopaedia Britannica.

Recordings: "Invisible Louisa" (record or cassette, 44:25 min.), Miller-Brody, 1970; "Little Women," read by Julie Harris (record or cassette), Caedmon; "Louisa May Alcott's Little Women," chapters 1 and 2 read by Elinor Basescu (record or cassette), Miller-Brody.

SIDELIGHTS: **November 29, 1832.** Born in Germantown, Pa.

1834. Moved to Boston.

1835. Elizabeth (Lizzie) Alcott born. (Beth of *Little Women*.)

1840. Stayed in Concord where Abba May Alcott was born. (Amy of *Little Women*.) Made first literary contribution with:

"Why Jo, your stories are works of Shakespeare, compared to half the rubbish that is published every day. Won't it be fun to see them in print; and shan't we feel proud of our authoress?" ∎
(From the movie "Little Women," copyright 1949 Metro-Goldwyn-Mayer, starring June Allyson and Peter Lawford.)

TO THE FIRST ROBIN

"'Welcome, welcome, little stranger,
Fear no harm, and fear no danger;
We are glad to see you here,
For you sing ''Sweet Spring is near.''

Now the white snow melts away;
Now the flowers blossom gay;
Come dear bird and build your nest,
For we love our robin best.'

"This gem my proud mother preserved with care, assuring me that if I kept on in this way I might be a second Shakespeare in time. Fired with this modest ambition, I continued to write poems upon dead butterflies, lost kittens, the baby's eyes, and other simple subjects till the storytelling mania set in; and after frightening my sisters out of their wits by awful tales whispered in bed, I began to write down these histories of giants, ogres, dauntless girls, and magic transformations till we had a library of small paper-covered volumes illustrated by the author. Later the poems grew gloomy and sentimental, and the tales more fanciful and less tragic, lovely elves and spirits taking the places of the former monsters.

"One of my earliest recollections is of playing with books in my father's study,—building houses and bridges of the big dictionaries and diaries, looking at pictures, pretending to read, scribbling on blank pages whenever pen or pencil could be found. Many of these first attempts at authorship still remain in Bacon's Essays, Plutarch's Lives, and other works of a serious nature, my infant taste being for solid literature, apparently.

"On one occasion we built a high tower round baby Lizzie as she sat playing with her toys on the floor, and being attracted by something out-of-doors, forgot our little prisoner. A search was made, and patient baby at last discovered curled up and fast asleep in her dungeon cell, out of which she emerged so rosy and smiling after her nap that we were forgiven for our carelessness.

"Another memory is of my fourth birthday, which was celebrated at my father's school-room in Masonic Temple. All the children were there. I wore a crown of flowers, and stood upon a table to dispense cakes to each child as the procession marched past. By some oversight the cakes fell short, and I saw that if I gave away the last one *I* should have none. As I was the queen of the revel, I felt that I ought to have it, and held on to it tightly till my mother said,—'It is always better to give away than to keep the nice things; so I know my Louy will not let the little friend go without.'

"The little friend received the dear plummy cake, and I a kiss and my first lesson in the sweetness of self-denial,—a lesson which my dear mother beautifully illustrated all her long and noble life.

"Running away was one of the delights of my early days;

(From the 1932 Broadway production of *Little Women* starring Jessie Royce Landis.)

and I still enjoy sudden flights out of the nest to look about this very interesting world, and then go back to report.

"On one of these occasions I passed a varied day with some Irish children, who hospitably shared their cold potatoes, salt-fish, and crusts with me as we revelled in the ash-heaps which then adorned the waste lands where the Albany Depot now stands. A trip to the Common cheered the afternoon, but as dusk set in and my friends deserted me, I felt that home was a nice place after all, and tried to find it. I dimly remember watching a lamp-lighter as I sat to rest on some doorsteps in Bedford Street, where a big dog welcomed me so kindly that I fell asleep with my head pillowed on his curly back, and was found there by the town-crier, whom my distracted parents had sent in search of me. His bell and proclamation of the loss of 'a little girl, six years old, in a pink frock, white hat, and new green shoes,' woke me up, and a small voice answered out of the darkness,—'Why, dat's me!'

"Being with difficulty torn from my four-footed friend, I was carried to the crier's house, and there feasted sumptuously on bread-and-molasses in a tin plate with the alphabet round it. But my fun ended next day when I was tied to the arm of the sofa to repent at leisure.

"I became an Abolitionist at a very early age, but have never been able to decide whether I was made so by seeing the portrait of George Thompson hidden under a bed in our house during the Garrison riot, and going to comfort 'the poor man who had been good to the slaves,' or because I was saved from drowning in the Frog Pond some years later by a colored boy. However that may be, the conversion was genuine; and my greatest pride is in the fact that I lived to know the brave men and women who did so much for the cause, and that I had a very small share in the war which put an end to a great wrong.

"I never went to school except to my father or such governesses as from time to time came into the family. Schools then were not what they are now; so we had lessons each morning in the study. And very happy hours they were to us, for my father taught in the wise way which unfolds what lies in the child's nature, as a flower blooms, rather than crammed it, like a Strasburg goose, with more than it could digest. I never liked arithmetic nor grammar, and dodged those branches on all occasions; but reading, writing, composition, history, and geography I enjoyed, as well as the stories read to us with a skill peculiarly his own.

"*Pilgrim's Progress,* Krummacher's *Parables,* Miss Edgeworth, and the best of the dear old fairy tales made the reading hour the pleasantest of our day. On Sundays we had a simple service of Bible stories, hymns, and conversation about the state of our little consciences and the conduct of our childish lives which never will be forgotten.

"Walks each morning round the Common while in the city, and long tramps over hill and dale when our home was in the country, were a part of our education, as well as every sort of housework,—for which I have always been very grateful, since such knowledge makes one independent in these days of domestic tribulation with the 'help' who are too often only hindrances.

"Needle-work began early, and at ten my skillful sister

There was a pleasing inequality in the table, which produced many mishaps to cups and plates; acorns dropped into the milk, little black ants partook of the refreshments without being invited, and fuzzy caterpillars swung down from the tree to see what was going on. ■ (From *Little Women* by Louisa May Alcott. Illustrated by Louis Jambor.)

made a linen shirt beautifully; while at twelve I set up as a doll's dressmaker, with my sign out and wonderful models in my window. All the children employed me, and my turbans were the rage at one time, to the great dismay of the neighbors' hens, who were hotly hunted down, that I might tweak out their downiest feathers to adorn the dolls' headgear.

"Active exercise was my delight, from the time when a child of six I drove my hoop round the Common without stopping, to the days when I did my twenty miles in five-hours and went to a party in the evening.

"I always thought I must have been a deer or a horse in some former state, because it was such a joy to run. No boy could be my friend till I had beaten him in a race, and no girl if she refused to climb trees, leap fences, and be a tomboy.

"My wise mother, anxious to give me a strong body to support a lively brain, turned me loose in the country and let me run wild, learning of Nature what no books can teach, and being led,—as those who truly love her seldom fail to be,—'Through Nature up to Nature's God.'

"I remember running over the hills just at dawn one summer morning, and pausing to rest in the silent woods, saw, through an arch of trees, the sun rise over river, hill, and wide green meadows as I never saw it before.

"Something born of the lovely hour, a happy mood, and the unfolding aspirations of a child's soul seemed to bring me very near to God; and in the hush of that morning hour I always felt that I 'got religion' as the phrase goes. A new and vital sense of His presence, tender and sustaining as a father's arms, came to me then, never to change through forty years of life's vicissitudes, but to grow stronger for the sharp discipline of poverty and pain, sorrow and success.

"Those Concord days were the happiest of my life, for we had charming playmates in the little Emersons, Channings, Hawthornes, and Goodwins, with the illustrious parents and their friends to enjoy our pranks and share our excursions. [*Louisa May Alcott: Her Life, Letters and Journals*, edited by Ednah D. Cheney, Roberts Brothers, 1889.]

The Alcott girls were required to keep journals (read by both parents) of their interior lives—their deepest desires as well as their moral struggles. Her mother wrote inspiring notes to the girls: "I preserve them to show the ever tender, watchful help she gave to the child who caused her the most anxiety, yet seemed to be the nearest to her heart till the end."[1]

1843. Bronson Alcott embarked unsuccessfully on an experiment in communal living at "Fruitlands," near Harvard. She told of this time in her journal: "*Thursday, 14th.*—Mr. Parker Pillsbury came, and we talked about the poor slaves. I had a music lesson with Miss F. I hate her, she is so fussy. I ran in the wind and played be a horse, and had a lovely time in the woods with Anna and Lizzie. We were fairies, and made gowns and paper wings. I 'flied' the highest of all.

"*Sunday, 24th.*—Father and Mr. Lane have gone to [New Hampshire] to preach. It was very lovely. . . . Anna and I got supper. In the eve I read *Vicar of Wakefield*. I was cross to-day, and I cried when I went to bed. I made good resolutions, and felt better in my heart. If I only *kept* all I make, I should be the best girl in the world. But I don't, and so am very bad.

"*October 8th.*—When I woke up, the first thought I got was, 'It's Mother's birthday: I must be very good.' I ran and wished her a happy birthday, and gave her my kiss. After breakfast we gave her our presents. I had a moss cross and a piece of poetry for her.

"We did not have any school, and played in the woods and got red leaves. In the evening we danced and sung, and I read a story about 'Contentment.' I wish I was rich, I was good, and we were all a happy family this day.

"*Thursday, 12th.*—After lessons I ironed. We all went to the barn and husked corn. It was good fun. We worked till eight o'clock and had lamps. . . . Mother and Lizzie are going to Boston. I shall be very lonely without dear little Betty, and no one will be as good to me as mother. I read in Plutarch. I made a verse about sunset:

> "'Softly doth the sun descend
>   To his couch behind the hill,
> Then, oh, then, I love to sit
>   On mossy banks beside the rill.'

"Anna thought it was very fine; but I didn't like it very well."[1]

"*November 29. Eleven years old.* It was Father's and my birthday. We had some nice presents. We played in the snow before school. Mother read *Rosamond* when we sewed. Father asked us in the eve what fault troubled us most. I said my bad temper.

"I told mother I liked to have her write in my book. She said she would put in more, and she wrote this to help me:

"DEAR LOUEY,—Your handwriting improves very fast. Take pains and do not be in a hurry. I like to have you make observations about our conversations and your own thoughts. It helps you to express them and to understand your little self. Remember, dear girl, that a diary should be an epitome of your life. May it be a record of pure thought and good actions, then you will indeed be the precious child of your loving mother.

"*December 10.* I did my lessons, and walked in the afternoon. Father read to us in dear *Pilgrim's Progress*. . . . In the eve father and mother and Anna and I had a long talk. I was very unhappy, and we all cried. Anna and I cried in bed, and I prayed God to keep us all together." [*A Treasury of the World's Great Diaries*, edited by Philip Dunaway and Mel Evans, Doubleday, 1957.[2]]

The lofty experiment of communal living failed. Her relief was frankly stated: "Life is pleasanter than it used to be, and I don't care about dying any more." [Louisa May Alcott, *Little Women*, Roberts Brothers, 1868.[3]]

Their idealism and creativity was encouraged by Bronson Alcott's highly principled friends. The most notable being Ralph Waldo Emerson. "People wondered at our frolics, but enjoyed them, and droll stories are still told of the adventures of those days. Mr. Emerson and Margaret Fuller were visiting my parents one afternoon, and the conversation having turned to the ever interesting subject of education, Miss Fuller said, 'Well, Mr. Alcott, you have been able to carry out your methods in your own family, and I should like to see your model children.'

"She did in a few moments, for as the guests stood on the door-steps a wild uproar approached, and round the corner of the house came a wheelbarrow holding baby May arrayed as a queen; I was the horse, bitted and bridled, and driven by my elder sister Anna; while Lizzie played dog, and barked as loud as her gentle voice permitted.

"All were shouting and wild with fun, which, however, came to a sudden end as we espied the stately group before us; for my foot tripped, and down we all went in a laughing heap; while my mother put a climax to the joke by saying, with a dramatic wave of the hand, 'Here are the model children, Miss Fuller.'"[1]

1845. With money left Mrs. Alcott by her father and an additional five hundred dollars from Emerson, the family was able to buy the home in Concord known as Hillside (later occupied by Nathaniel Hawthorne). It was here that she passed the girlish years so vividly portrayed in *Little Women*. "When cautious friends asked mother how she dared to have such outcasts among her girls, she always

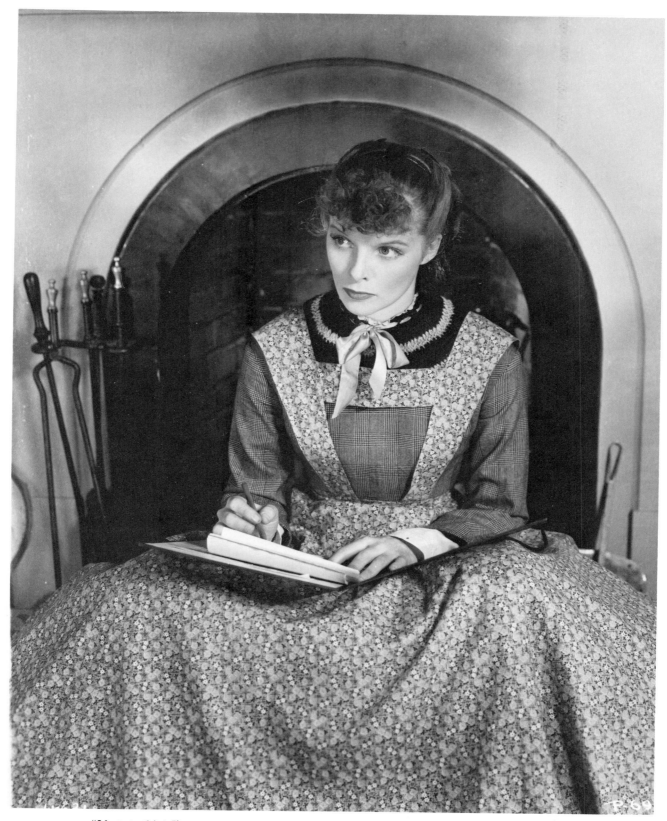

"I hate to think I've got to grow up, and be Miss March, and wear long gowns and look as prim as a China-aster!" ■ (From the movie "Little Women," copyright 1933 by RKO Pictures, starring Katherine Hepburn as Jo.)

Louisa May Alcott, 1876.

answered, with an expression of confidence which did much to keep us safe, 'I can trust my daughters, and this is the best way to teach them how to shun these sins and comfort these sorrows. They cannot escape the knowledge of them; better gain this under their father's roof and their mother's care, and so be protected by these experiences when their turn comes to face the world and its temptations.'

"Once we carried our breakfast to a starving family; once lent our whole dinner to a neighbor suddenly taken unprepared by distinguished guests. Another time, one snowy Saturday night, when our wood was very low, a poor child came to beg a little, as the baby was sick and the father on a spree with all his wages. My mother hesitated at first, as we also had a baby. Very cold weather was upon us, and a Sunday to be got through before more wood could be had. My father said, 'Give half our stock, and trust in Providence; the weather will moderate, or wood will come.' Mother laughed, and answered in her cherry way, 'Well, their need is greater than ours, and if our half gives out we can go to bed and tell stories. So a generous half went to the poor neighbor, and a little later in the eve, while the storm still raged and we were about to cover our fire to keep it, a knock came, and a farmer who usually supplied us appeared, saying anxiously, 'I started for Boston with a load of wood, but it drifts so I want to go home. Wouldn't you like to have me drop the wood here; it would accommodate me, and you needn't hurry about paying for it.'... Mother's motto was 'Hope, and keep busy,' and one of her sayings, 'Cast your bread upon the waters, and after many days it will come back buttered.'"[1]

1847. "My romantic period began at fifteen, when I fell to writing poetry, keeping a heart-journal, and wandering by moonlight instead of sleeping quietly. About that time, in browsing over Mr. Emerson's library, I found Goethe's *Correspondence with a Child,* and at once was fired with a desire to be a Bettine, making my father's friend my Goethe. So I wrote letters to him, but never sent them; sat in a tall cherry-tree at midnight, singing to the moon till the owls scared me to bed; left wild flowers on the doorstep of my 'Master,' and sung Mignon's song under his window in very bad German.

"Not till many years later did I tell *my* Goethe of this early romance and the part he played in it. He was much amused, and begged for his letters, kindly saying he felt honored to be so worshipped. The letters were burnt long ago, but Emerson remained my 'Master' while he lived, doing more for me,—as for many another,—than he knew, by the simple beauty of his life, the truth and wisdom of his books, the example of a great, good man, untempted and unspoiled by the world which he made better while in it, and left richer and nobler when he went.

"The trials of life began about this time, and happy childhood ended. One of the most memorable days of my life is a certain gloomy November afternoon, when we had been holding a family council as to ways and means. In summer we lived much as the birds did, on our fruit and bread and milk; the sun was our fire, the sky our roof, and Nature's plenty made us forget that such a thing as poverty existed."[1]

1848. The Alcotts moved to Boston where she had her own room. "It does me good to be alone, and Mother has made it very pretty and neat for me. My work-basket and desk are by the window, and my closet is full of dried herbs that smell very nice. The door that opens into the garden will be very pretty in summer, and I can run off to the woods when I like.

"I have made a plan for my life, as I am in my teens, and no more a child. I am old for my age, and don't care much for girl's things. People think I'm wild and queer; but Mother understands and helps me. I have not told any one about my plan; but I'm going to *be* good. I've made so many resolutions, and written sad notes, and cried over my sins, and it doesn't seem to do any good! Now I'm going to *work really,* for I feel a true desire to improve, and be a help and comfort, and not a care and sorrow, to my dear mother.

"Since coming to the city I don't seem to have thought much, for the bustle and dirt and change send all lovely images and restful feelings away. Among my hills and woods I had fine free times alone, and though my thoughts were silly, I daresay, they helped to keep me happy and good. I see now what Nature did for me, and my 'romantic tastes,' as people called that love of solitude and out-of-door life, taught me much.

"This summer, like the last, we shall spend in a large house (Uncle May's, Atkinson Street), with many comforts about us which we shall enjoy, and in the autumn I hope I shall have something to show that the time has not been wasted. Seventeen years have I lived, and yet so little do I know, and so much remains to be done before I begin to be what I desire,—a truly good and useful woman.

"In looking over our journals, Father says, 'Anna's is about other people, Louisa's about herself.' That is true, for I don't *talk* about myself; yet must always think of the wilful, moody girl I try to manage, and in my journal I write of her to see how she gets on. Anna is so good she need not take care of herself, and can enjoy other people. If I look in my glass, I try to keep down vanity about my long hair, my well-shaped head, and my good nose. In the street I try not to covet fine things. My quick tongue is always getting me into trouble, and my moodiness makes it hard to be cheerful when I think how poor we are, how much worry it is to live; only it's cowardly to die till you have done something.

"I can't talk to any one but Mother about my troubles, and she has so many now to bear I try not to add any more. I know God is always ready to hear, but heaven's so far away in the city, and I so heavy I can't fly up to find Him.

"We had small-pox in the family this summer, caught from some poor immigrants whom mother took into our garden and fed one day. We girls had it lightly, but Father and Mother were very ill, and we had a curious time of exile, danger, and trouble. No doctors, and all got well."[1]

July, 1850. "I had to take [Anna's] school of twenty in Canton Street. I like it better than I thought, though it's very hard to be patient with the children sometimes. They seem happy, and learn fast; so I am encouraged, though at first it was very hard, and I missed Anna so much I used to

Nat enjoyed an hour or two of genuine happiness, learning the sweet old tunes, and forgetting the hard past in the cheerful present. ■ (From *Little Men* by Louisa May Alcott. Illustrated by Douglas W. Gorsline.)

cry over my dinner and be very blue. I guess this is the teaching I need; for as a *school-marm* I must behave myself and guard my tongue and temper carefully, and set an example of sweet manners.

"I found one of mother's notes in my journal, so like those she used to write me when she had more time. It always encourages me; and I wish some one would write as helpfully to her, for she needs cheering up with all the care she has. I often think what a hard life she has had since she married,—so full of wandering and all sorts of worry! so different from her early easy days, the youngest and most petted of her family. I think she is a very brave, good woman; and my dream is to have a lovely, quiet home for her, with no debts or troubles to burden her. But I'm afraid she will be in heaven before I can do it.

"**August, 1850.** School is hard work, and I feel as though I should like to run away from it. But my children get on; so I travel up every day, and do my best.

"I get very little time to write or think; for my working days have begun, . . . so I have no quiet. I think a little solitude every day is good for me. In the quiet I see my faults, and try to mend them; but, deary me, I don't get on at all.

"I used to imagine my mind a room in confusion, and I was to put it in order; so I swept out useless thoughts and dusted foolish fancies away, and furnished it with good resolutions and began again. But cobwebs get in. I'm not a good housekeeper, and never get my room in nice order. I once wrote a poem about it when I was fourteen, and called it 'My Little Kingdom.' It is still hard to rule it, and always will be I think.

"Anna wants to be an actress, and so do I. We could make plenty of money perhaps, and it is a very gay life. Mother says we are too young, and must wait. A. acts often splendidly. I like tragic plays, and shall be a Siddons if I can. We get up fine ones, and make harps, castles, armor, dresses, water-falls, and thunder, and have great fun."[1]

Orchard House, Concord, Massachusetts. Home of the Alcott Family, 1858.

The other lads sat quietly upon the steps, keeping watch that no newcomer should disturb the house; Franz lingered at his post; and so, soothed, served, and guarded by her boys, poor Mrs. Jo slept at last, and forgot her sorrow for an hour. ■ (From *Little Men* by Louisa May Alcott. Illustrated by Paul Hogarth.)

1852. "*High Street, Boston.* After the small-pox summer, we went to a house in High Street. Mother opened an intelligence office, which grew out of her city missionary work and a desire to find places for good girls. It was not fit work for her, but it paid; and she always did what came to her in the way of duty or charity, and let pride, taste, and comfort suffer for love's sake."[1]

1855. *Flower Fables* published.

June, 1856. Elizabeth and May ill with scarlet fever. This was the beginning of Elizabeth's slow decline. "The long, cold, lonely winter has been too hard for the frail creature, and we are all anxious about her. I fear she may slip away; for she never seemed to care much for this world beyond home.

"*August.*—A sad, anxious month. Betty worse; mother takes her to the seashore. Father decides to go back to Concord; he is never happy far from Emerson, the one true friend who loves and understands and helps him.

"*September.*—An old house near R.W.E.'s is bought with Mother's money, and we propose to move. Mother in Boston with poor Betty, who is failing fast.

"*October.*—Move to Concord. Take half a house in town till spring, when the old one is to be made ready. Find dear Betty a shadow, but sweet and patient always. Fit up a nice room for her, and hope home and love and care may keep her. People kind and friendly, and the old place looks pleasant, though I never want to live in it.

"*November.*—Father goes West, taking Grandma home. We settle down to our winter, whatever it is to be. Lizzie seems better, and we have some plays.

"Twenty-five this month. I feel my quarter of a century rather heavy on my shoulders just now. I lead two lives. One seems gay with plays, etc., the other very sad,—in [Lizzie's] room; for though she wishes us to act, and loves to see us get ready, the shadow is there, and Mother and I see it. [Lizzie] loves to have me with her; and I am with her at night, for Mother needs rest. [Lizzie] says she feels 'strong' when I am near. So glad to be of use.

"*January, 1858.*—Lizzie much worse; Dr. G. says there is no hope. A hard thing to hear; but if she is only to suffer, I pray she may go soon. She was glad to know she was to 'get well,' as she called it, and we tried to bear it bravely for her sake. We gave up plays; Father came home; and Anna took the housekeeping, so that Mother and I could devote ourselves to her. Sad, quiet days in her room, and strange nights keeping up the fire and watching the dear little shadow try to wile away the long sleepless hours without troubling me. She sews, reads, sings softly, and lies looking at the fire,—so sweet and patient and so worn, my heart is broken to see the change.

"*February.* Lizzie makes little things, and drops them out of windows to the school-children, smiling to see their surprise. In the night she tells me to be Mrs. Gamp, when I give her her lunch, and tries to be gay that I may keep us. Dear little saint! I shall be better all my life for these sad hours with you."[1]

"*March 14th,* [1858].—My dear Beth died at three this morning, after two years of patient pain. Last week she put her work away, saying the needle was 'too heavy,' and having given us her few possessions, made ready for the parting in her own simple way. For two days she suffered much, begging for ether, though its effect was gone. Tuesday she lay in Father's arms, and called us round her, smiling contentedly as she said, 'All here!' I think she bid us good-by then, as she held our hands and kissed us tenderly. Saturday she slept, and at midnight became unconscious, quietly breathing her life away till three; then, with one last look of the beautiful eyes, she was gone.

"A curious thing happened, and I will tell it here, for Dr. G. said it was a fact. A few moments after the last breath came, as Mother and I sat silently watching the shadow fall on the dear little face, I saw a light mist rise from the body, and float up and vanish in the air. Mother's eyes followed mine, and when I said, 'What did you see?' she described the same light mist. Dr. G. said it was the life departing visibly.

"For the last time we dressed her in her usual cap and gown, and laid her on her bed,—at rest at last. What she had suffered was seen in the face; for at twenty-three she looked like a woman of forty, so worn was she, and all her pretty hair gone.

"*April.*—Came to occupy one wing of Hawthorne's house (once ours) while the new one was being repaired. Father, Mother, and I kept house together; May being in Boston, Anna at Pratt Farm, and, for the first time, Lizzie absent. I don't miss her as I expected to do, for she seems nearer and dearer than before; and I am glad to know she is safe from pain and age in some world where her innocent soul must be happy.

"Death, never seemed terrible to me, and now is beautiful; so I cannot fear it, but find it friendly and wonderful.

"*May.*—A lonely month with all the girls gone, and Father and Mother absorbed in the old house, which I don't care about, not liking Concord.

"On the 7th of April, Anna came walking in to tell us she was engaged to John Pratt; so another sister is gone. J. is a model son and brother,—a true man,—full of fine possibilities, but so modest one does not see it at once. He is handsome, healthy, and happy; just home from the West, and so full of love he is pleasant to look at.

"I moaned in private over my great loss, and said I'd never forgive J. for taking Anna from me; but I shall if he makes her happy, and turn to little May for my comfort.

"*June.*—The girls came home, and I went to . . . Boston. Saw Charlotte Cushman, and had a stagestruck fit. Dr. W. asked Barry to let me act at his theatre, and he agreed. I was to do Widow Pottle, as the dress was a good disguise and I knew the part well. It was all a secret, and I had hopes of trying a new life; the old one being so changed now, I felt as if I must find interest in something absorbing. But Mr. B. broke his leg, so I had to give it up; and when it was known, the dear, respectable relations were horrified at the idea. I'll try again by-and-by, and see if I have the gift. Perhaps it is acting, not writing, I'm meant for. Nature must have a vent somehow.

(From the movie "Little Men," copyright 1934 by Mascot Pictures Corp.)

Yesterday's Authors of Books for Children   17

"*July*.—Worked off my stage fever in writing a story, and felt better; also a moral tale, and got twenty-five dollars."[1]

1861. Worked in Concord during summer on first two novels, "Moods" and "Success." War declared between North and South.

1862. Taught kindergarten. Volunteered as a nurse for Georgetown Hospital. "*November*.—Thirty years old. Decided to go to Washington as nurse if I could find a place. Help needed, and I love nursing, and *must* let out my pent-up energy in some new way. Winter is always a hard and a dull time, and if I am away there is one less to feed and warm and worry over.

"I want new experiences, and am sure to get 'em if I go. So I've sent in my name, and bide my time writing tales, to leave all snug behind me, and mending up my old clothes,—for nurses don't need nice things, thank Heaven!

"*December*.—On the 11th I received a note . . . telling me to start for Georgetown next day to fill a place in the Union Hotel Hospital. . . . Though a hard place, help was needed. I was ready, and when my commander said 'March!' I marched. Packed my trunk, and reported in B[oston] that same evening.

"[The family] had been full of courage till the last moment came; then we all broke down. I realized that I had taken my life in my hand, and might never see them all again. I said 'Shall I stay, Mother?' as I hugged her close. 'No, go! and the Lord be with you!' answered the Spartan woman; and till I turned the corner she bravely smiled and waved her wet handkerchief on the door-step. Shall I ever see that dear old face again?

"So I set forth in the December twilight, with May and Julian Hawthorne as escort, feeling as if I was the son of the house going to war.

"Friday, the 12th, was a very memorable day, spent in running all over Boston to get my pass, etc., calling for parcels, getting a tooth filled, and buying a veil,—my only purchase. . . . A most interesting journey into a new world full of stirring sights and sounds, new adventures, and an evergrowing sense of the great task I had undertaken.

"I said my prayers as I went rushing through the country white with tents, all alive with patriotism, and already red with blood.

"All went well, and I got to Georgetown one evening very tired. Was kindly welcomed, slept in my narrow bed with two other room-mates, and on the morrow began my new life by seeing a poor man die at dawn, and sitting all day between a boy with pneumonia and a man shot through the lungs. A strange day, but I did my best; and when I put mother's little black shawl round the boy while he sat up panting for breath, he smiled and said, 'You are real motherly, ma'am.' I felt as if I was getting on."[1]

1863. Taken ill and sent home. "Hospital Sketches," based on her wartime experiences, published in the *Commonwealth* magazine. Then as a book.

1865. Sailed for Europe as companion to an invalid. Met Ladislas (Laurie in *Little Women*) in Nevey. . . . "Laddie waiting for me in Paris to take me to my room at Madame Dyne's. A very charming fortnight here; the days spent in seeing sights with my Laddie, the evenings in reading, writing, hearing 'my boy' play, or resting. Saw all that I wished to see in a very pleasant way, and on the 17th reluctantly went to London."[1]

July, 1866. Returned to Concord. "A trip of fourteen stormy, dull, long, sick days, but at last at eleven at night we sailed up the harbor in the moonlight, and I saw dear John waiting for me on the wharf. Slept on board, and next day reached home at noon to find Father at the station, Nan and babies at the gate, May flying wildly round the lawn, and Marmee crying at the door. Into her arms I went, and was at home at last.

"Happy days, talking and enjoying one another. Many people came to see me, and all said I was much improved; of which I was glad, as there was, is, and always will be room for it.

"*August*.—Soon fell to work on some stories, for things were, as I expected, behindhand when the money-maker was away. Found plenty to do, as orders from E., L., 'Independent,' 'U.S.C.S. Magazine,' and several other offers waited for me. Wrote two long tales . . . and got $200 for them. One . . . which paid $75, also a bit of poetry for $5. [E.] wanted a long story in twenty-four chapters, and I wrote it in a fortnight,—one hundred and eighty-five pages,—besides work, sewing, nursing, and company.

"*September*—Mother sick, did little with my pen. Got a girl, and devoted myself to Mother, writing after she was abed. In this way finished a long tale. But E. would not have it, saying it was too long and too sensational!

"*November*—Mother slowly mending. A sensible Western woman 'rubbed' her, and did her a great deal of good. She left her room and seemed more like herself. I never expect to see the strong, energetic Marmee of old times, but, thank the Lord! she is still here, though pale and weak, quiet and sad; all her fine hair gone, and face full of wrinkles, bowed back, and every sign of age. Life has been so hard for her, and she so brave, so glad to spend herself for others. Now we must live for her."[1]

1867. "*September*.—Niles, partner of Roberts, asked me to write a girls' book. Said I'd try.

"F. asked me to be the editor of 'Merry's Museum.' Said I'd try.

"Began at once on both new jobs; but didn't like either.

"The Radical Club met at Sargent's. Fine time. Bartol inspired; Emerson chairman; Alcott on his legs; strong-minded ladies out in full force; aesthetic tea for refreshment.

"*October*.—Agreed with F. to be editor for $500 a year. Read manuscripts, write one story each month and an editorial. On the strength of this engagement went to Boston, took a room—No. 6 Hayward Place—furnished it, and set up housekeeping for myself. Cannot keep well in [Concord], so must try Boston, and not work too hard."[1]

1868. "*May.*—Father saw Mr. Niles about a fairy book. Mr. N. wants a *girls' story*, and I begin *Little Women*.

Marmee, Anna, and May all approve my plan. So I plod away, though I don't enjoy this sort of thing. Never liked girls or knew many, other than my sisters; but our queer plays and experiences might be interesting, though I doubt it."[1]

October, 1868. *Little Women* published. "I never had a study. Any pen and paper do, and an old atlas on my knee is all I want. Carry a dozen plots in my head, and think them over when in the mood. Sometimes keep one for years, and suddenly find it all ready to write. Often lie awake and plan whole chapters word for word, then merely scribble them down as if copying.

"Used to sit fourteen hours a day at one time, eating little, and unable to stir till a certain amount was done.

"Very few stories written in Concord; no inspiration in that dull place. Go to Boston, hire a quiet room and shut myself up in it."[1]

November 25, 1877. Mother died. "[She] kept her bed for three days, lying down after weeks in a chair, and on the 25th, at dusk, that rainy Sunday, fell quietly asleep in my arms.

"She was very happy all day, thinking herself a girl again, with parents and sisters round her. Said her Sunday hymn to me, whom she called 'Mother,' and smiled at us, saying 'A smile is as good as a prayer.' Looked often at the little picture of May, and waved her hand to it, 'Good-by, little May, good-by!'

"We feared great suffering, but she was spared that, and slipped peacefully away. I was so glad when the last weary breath was drawn, and silence came, with its rest and peace.

"On the 27th it was necessary to bury her, and we took her quietly away to Sleepy Hollow. A hard day, but the last duty we could do for her; and there we left her at sunset beside dear Lizzie's dust,—alone so long.

"Quiet days afterward resting in her rest.

"My duty is done, and now I shall be glad to follow her.

"*December.*—I never wish her back, but a great warmth seems gone out of life, and there is no motive to go on now.

"My only comfort is that I *could* make her last years comfortable, and lift off the burden she had carried so bravely all these years. She was so loyal, tender, and true; life was hard for her, and no one understood all she had to bear but we, her children."[1]

December 29, 1879. May died.

Autumn, 1882. Bronson Alcott stricken with paralysis.

March 4, 1888. Bronson Alcott died. Two days later, Louisa May Alcott died. "One person's [writing] method is no rule for another. Each must work in his own way; and the only drill needed, is to keep writing and profit by criticism. Mind grammar, spelling, and punctuation, use short words, and express as briefly as you can your meaning. Young people use too many adjectives and try to 'write fine.' The strongest, simplest words are best, and no *foreign* ones if it can be helped.

"Write, and print if you can; if not, still write, and improve as you go on. Read the best books, and they will improve your style. See and hear good speakers and wise people, and learn of them. Work for twenty years, and then you may some day find that you have a style and place of your own, and can command good pay for the same things no one would take when you were unknown.

"I know little of poetry, as I never read modern attempts, but advise any young person to keep to prose, as only once in a century is there a true poet; and verses are so easy to do that it is not much help to write them. . . . I can say no more, but . . . give you for a motto [Michaelangelo's] wise words: 'Genius is infinite patience.'"[1]

FOR MORE INFORMATION SEE: Ednah D. Cheney, *Louisa May Alcott: The Children's Friend,* Prang, 1888; Cheney, editor, *Louisa May Alcott: Her Life, Letters, and Journals,* Roberts Brothers, 1889, reprinted, Abbotsford Publishing, 1974; Lucile Gulliver, compiler, *Louisa May Alcott: A Bibliography* (with an appreciation by Cornelia Meigs), Little, Brown, 1932, reprinted, B. Franklin, 1973; Katharine S. Anthony, *Louisa May Alcott,* Knopf, 1938; Marion Talbot, "Glimpses of the Real Louisa May Alcott," *New England Quarterly,* December, 1938; Madeleine B. Stern, *Louisa May Alcott,* University of Oklahoma Press, 1950, reprinted, 1971; Marjorie Muir Worthington, *Miss Alcott of Concord: A Biography,* Doubleday, 1958; Aileen Fisher and Olive Rabe, *We Alcotts: The Story of Louisa May Alcott's Family as Seen through the Eyes of "Marmee," Mother of Little Women,* Atheneum, 1968; *Horn Book Magazine,* October, 1968, special issue on the centenary of *Little Women;* M. B. Stern, editor, *Behind a Mask: The Unknown Thrillers of Louisa May Alcott,* Morrow, 1975.

For children: Belle Moses, *Louisa May Alcott, Dreamer and Worker: A Story of Achievement,* Appleton, 1909, reprinted, R. West, 1973; Cornelia Meigs, *The Story of the Author of "Little Women": Invincible Louisa,* Little, Brown, 1933, reprinted (with a new introduction) as *Invincible Louisa: The Story of the Author of "Little Women,"* 1968; Jean B. Wagoner, *Louisa Alcott: Girl of Old Boston,* Bobbs-Merrill, 1943; Elizabeth R. Montgomery, *Story behind Great Books,* McBride, 1946; Catherine Owens Peare, *Louisa May Alcott: Her Life,* Holt, 1954; Pamela Brown, *Louisa,* Crowell, 1955; Joan Howard (pseudonym of Patricia Gordon), *The Story of Louisa May Alcott,* Grosset & Dunlap, 1955.

Martha Robinson, *Young Louisa M. Alcott,* Roy, 1963; Helen Papashvily, *Louisa May Alcott,* Houghton, 1965; Lewis C. Rodd, *Louisa, the Runaway Tomboy: The Story of Louisa M. Alcott,* Cheshire, 1966; Polly Anne Colver Graff, *Louisa May Alcott: Author of "Little Women,"* Garrard, 1969; Laura Benét, *Famous New England Authors,* Dodd, 1970; Cornelia Meigs, *Louisa M. Alcott and the American Family Story,* Walck, 1970.

Joseph A. Altsheler

ALTSHELER, Joseph A(lexander)   1862-1919

PERSONAL: Born April 29, 1862, in Three Springs, Kentucky; died June 5, 1919, in New York City; son of Joseph and Louise (Snoddy) Altsheler; married Sarah Boles, May 30, 1888; children: Sidney. *Education:* Attended Liberty College, Glasgow, Kentucky, and Vanderbilt University. *Home:* New York City.

CAREER: Author of juvenile fiction; began work as newspaperman, briefly with Louisville *Evening Post,* then with *Courier Journal,* 1885-92; became feature writer for New York *World* in 1892, later editor of magazine section.

WRITINGS—All fiction; all published by Appleton, except as indicated: *The Hidden Mine,* Tait, 1896; *The Sun of Saratoga: A Romance of Burgoyne's Surrender,* 1897; *A Soldier of Manhattan, and His Adventures at Ticonderoga and Quebec,* 1897; *A Herald of the West: An American Story of 1811-1815,* 1898; *The Rainbow of Gold,* Continental, 1898.

The Last Rebel, Lippincott, 1900; *In Circling Camps: A Romance of the Civil War,* 1900; *In Hostile Red: A Romance of the Monmouth Campaign* (based on author's short story, "A Knight of Philadelphia"), Doubleday, Page, 1900; *The Wilderness Road: A Romance of St. Clair's Defeat and Wayne's Victory,* 1901; *My Captive: A Novel,* 1902; *Before the Dawn: A Story of the Fall of Richmond,* Doubleday, Page, 1903; *Guthrie of the Times: A Story of Success* (illustrated by F. R. Gruger), Doubleday, Page, 1904; *The Candidate: A Political Romance,* Harper & Brothers, 1905.

The Young Trailers: A Story of Early Kentucky, 1907; *The Forest Runners: A Story of the Great War Trail in Early Kentucky,* 1908; *The Recovery: A Story of Kentucky,* Lovell, 1908; *The Free Rangers: A Story of Early Days along the Mississippi,* 1909; *The Last of the Chiefs: A Story of the Great Sioux War,* 1909; *The Riflemen of the Ohio: A Story of Early Days along "The Beautiful River",* 1910; *The Horsemen of the Plains: A Story of the Great Cheyenne War* (illustrated by Charles Livingston Bull), Macmillan, 1910, reprinted, 1967.

He heard a shock near him and,...saw a huddled mass of wreckage.... The ribs of the plane were driven deep into the earth and he looked away. ■ (From *The Forest of Swords* by Joseph A. Altsheler. Illustrated by Charles Wrenn.)

He advanced a step or two nearer, and the stranger was yet motionless. Another step, and the man spoke in a sharp whisper: "You are John Bedford?" ■ (From *The Quest of the Four* by Joseph A. Altsheler.)

The Quest of the Four: The Story of the Comanches and Buena Vista, 1911; *The Scouts of the Valley: A Story of Wyoming and the Chemung*, 1911; *The Border Watch: A Story of the Great Chief's Last Stand*, 1912; *The Texan Star: The Story of a Great Fight for Liberty*, 1912; *The Texan Scouts: A Story of the Alamo and Goliad*, 1913; *Apache Gold: A Story of the Strange Southwest*, 1913; *The Texan Triumph: A Romance of the San Jacinto Campaign*, 1913; *The Guns of Bull Run: A Story of the Civil War's Eve*, 1914, reprinted, 1966; *The Guns of Shiloh: A Story of the Great Western Campaign*, 1914; *The Sword of Antietam: A Story of the Nation's Crisis* (illustrated by Charles L. Wrenn), 1914; *The Scouts of Stonewall: The Story of the Great Valley Campaign* (illustrated by Wrenn), 1914; *The Forests of Swords: A Story of Paris and the Marne* (illustrated by Wrenn), 1915; *The Guns of Europe* (illustrated by Wrenn), 1915; *The Rock of Chickamauga: A Story of the Western Crisis* (illustrated by Wrenn), 1915; *The Hosts of the Air: The Story of a Quest in the Great War* (illustrated by Wrenn), 1915; *The Star of Gettysburg: A Story of Southern High Tide* (illustrated by Wrenn), 1915.

The Keepers of the Trail: A Story of the Great Woods

(illustrated by D. C. Hutchinson), 1916; *The Shades of the Wilderness: A Story of Lee's Great Stand* (illustrated by Charles L. Wrenn), 1916; *The Tree of Appomattox: A Story of the Civil War's Close* (illustrated by Wrenn), 1916; *The Hunters of the Hills: A Story of the Great French and Indian War* (illustrated by D. C. Hutchinson), 1916; *The Eyes of the Woods: A Story of the Ancient Wilderness* (illustrated by Hutchinson), 1917; *The Rulers of the Lakes: A Story of George and Champlain* (illustrated by Charles L. Wrenn), 1917; *The Shadow of the North: A Story of Old New York and a Lost Campaign* (illustrated by Wrenn), 1917; *The Great Sioux Trail: A Story of Mountain and Plain* (illustrated by Wrenn). 1918; *The Lost Hunters: A Story of Wild Man and Great Beasts* (illustrated by Wrenn), 1918; *The Masters of the Peaks: A Story of the Great North Woods*, 1918; *The Lords of the Wild: A Story of the Old New York Border* (illustrated by Charles L. Wrenn), 1919; *The Sun of Quebec: A Story of a Great Crisis* (illustrated by Wrenn), 1919.

FOR MORE INFORMATION SEE: Stanley J. Kunitz and Howard Haycraft, editors, *Junior Book of Authors*, Wilson, 1934; Obituary—*New York Times*, June 7, 1919.

Late in the afternoon John saw the battle thicken. The earth quivered under his feet with the roll of the cannon, and the German line moved forward much more slowly. ■ (From *Guns of Europe* by Joseph A. Altsheler. Illustrated by Charles L. Wrenn.)

Statue of Hans Christian Andersen, Central Park, N.Y.C. (Photograph by Rosemary DeAngelis Bridges)

ANDERSEN, Hans Christian 1805-1875
(Villiam Christian Walter)

PERSONAL: Born April 2, 1805, in Odense, Denmark; died August 4, 1875, in Copenhagen, Denmark; son of a shoemaker and a washerwoman. *Education:* Schooled but illiterate at the age of fourteen, he began grammar school studies at the age of seventeen and finally attended the University of Copenhagen, passing degree examinations in 1829.

CAREER: Author of fairy tales, playwright, novelist, and writer of travel books. From the age of eleven, worked in a cloth factory, a tobacco factory, and later as an apprentice to a shoemaker; tried unsuccessfully to become an actor, singer, and dancer. *Awards, honors:* Grant from the King of Denmark, 1833-35, for travel in Germany, France, Switzerland, and Italy; Swedish Order of the Knight of the Polar Star, White Falcon of Weimar, Red Eagle of Prussia, Order of Our Lady of Guadalupe, honorary Danish Councillor of State.

WRITINGS—Collected Fairy Tales: *Eventyr* ("Tales"), Reitzel (Copenhagen), 1835, is the first of several collections published between 1835 and 1872. The first illustrated edition was done by Thomas Vilhelm Pedersen, 1850. The complete collection of 168 tales is contained in *Eventyr og historien* ("Tales and Stories"; illustrated by Pedersen), Reitzel, 1862-63, and in *Nye eventyr og historien* ("New Tales and Stories"; illustrated by Lorenz Froelich), Reitzel, 1870-74.

Collected editions in English translation appear in numerous, and variously titled editions, including the following: *Wonderful Stories for Children* (translated by Mary Howitt), Chapman & Hall, 1st series, 1835-37, 2nd series, 1838, 3rd series, 1845; *Danish Fairy Legends and Tales* (translated by Caroline Peachey), 1st edition, Pickering, 1846, 2nd edition, enlarged, Addey, 1852, 3rd edition, enlarged, Bohn, 1861; *A Danish Story-Book* (translated by Charles Boner; illustrated by Count Pocci), Cundall, 1846; *A Poet's Day Dreams* (translated by Anne S. Bushby), Bentley, 1853; *Stories and Tales* (translated by H. W. Dulcken; illustrated by A. W. Bayes), Routledge, 1864 [another edition under the same title illustrated by M. L. Stone, and with the original illustrations by T. V. Pedersen, Hurd & Houghton, 1871]; *Fairy Tales and Stories* (illustrated by A. W. Bayes), Warne, 1865 [other editions under the same title illustrated by Carl O. Larsson, Estes, 1887; Henry M. Brock, Pearson, 1905; Eric Pape, Macmillan, 1921; George Hauman, Macmillan, 1953]; *Wonder Stories Told for Children* (illustrated by M. L. Stone, and with the original illustrations by T. V. Pedersen), Hurd & Houghton, 1871; *Fairy Tales* (illustrated by E.V.B., pseudonym of Eleanor Vere Boyle), Sampson, Low, 1882 [other editions under the same title illustrated by Hans Christian Tegner, Heinemann, 1900; Gordon F. Browne, Wells, Gardner, 1902; Cecile Walton, T. C. Jack, 1911; Dugald S. Walker, Doubleday, 1914; Elenore Plaisted Abbott, Macrae, Smith, 1917; Kay Nielsen, Doran, 1924; W. H. Robinson, Doran, 1924; Harry Clarke, Harrap, 1931; Arthur Rackham, Harrap, 1932; Arthur Szyk, Grosset & Dunlap, 1945; Jean O'Neill, World Publishing, 1946, reissued, 1975; Leonard Weisgard, Junior Deluxe Editions, 1956; translated by Reginald Spink and illustrated by Hans Baumhauer, Dutton, 1958; illustrated by Jiri Trnka, Hamlyn, 1961].

Stories and Fairy Tales (illustrated by Arthur J. Gaskin), G. Allen, 1893; *Hans Andersen's Fairy Tales* (illustrated by John R. Weguelin), Lawrence & Bullen, 1893 [other editions under the same title illustrated by Milo Winter, Rand McNally, 1916, reprinted, 1972; Shirley Hughes, Blackie, 1961; E. H. Shepard, Oxford University Press, 1961, Walck, 1962]; *Danish Fairy Tales and Legends* (illustrated by William H. Robinson), Bliss, Sands, 1897; *Fairy Tales from Hans Christian Andersen* (illustrated by Charles, Thomas H., and William H. Robinson), Dent, 1899 [another edition under the same title illustrated by Tasha Tudor, Oxford University Press, 1945]; *Fairy Tales of Hans Andersen* (illustrated by Helen Stratton), Newnes, 1899; *Twenty Best Fairy Tales by Hans Andersen* (illustrated by Lucy Fitch Perkins), Stokes, 1907; *Fairy Tales from Hans Andersen* (illustrated by Maxwell Armfield), Dutton, 1910; *Three Tales of Hans Andersen* (illustrated by Edward L. Sambourne), Macmillan, 1910; *Stories from Hans Andersen* (illustrated by Edmund Dulac), Hodder & Stoughton, 1912; *Fairy Tales and Wonder Stories* (illustrated by Louis J. Rhead), Harper, 1914.

Forty Stories (illustrated by Christine Jackson), Faber, 1930, new edition published as *Forty-Two Stories* (illustrated by Robin Jacques), 1953; *Andersen's Fairy Tales* (translated by Jean Hersholt; illustrated by Fritz Kredel), Heritage Press, 1942 [other editions under the same title illustrated by Elizabeth MacKinstry, Coward, McCann, 1933; "World Edition," four volumes, edited by Svend Larsen, translated by R. P. Keigwin, and illustrated from the original drawings by T. V. Pedersen, E. Ward, 1951-60; illustrated by Lawrence Beall Smith, Macmillan, 1963]; *Four Tales from Hans Andersen* (illustrated by Gwendolyn Raverat), Cambridge University Press, 1935; *Fairy Tales and Legends* (illustrated by Rex J. Whistler), Oxford University Press, 1936, new edition, Dufour, 1959; *The Complete Andersen*, six volumes (all of the 168 tales; translated and edited by Jean Hersholt; illustrated by Fritz Kredel), Heritage Press, 1952; *Seven Tales* (translated by Eva Le Gallienne; illustrated by Maurice Sendak), Harper, 1959; *Favorite Fairy Tales* (illustrated by Paul Durand), Golden Press, 1974; *The Complete Fairy Tales and Stories* (translated by Erik Christian Haugaard; foreword by Virginia Haviland), Doubleday, 1974.

Single tales published separately or as title stories of collections: *Shoes of Fortune and Other Tales* (illustrated by Otto Speckter and others), Chapman & Hall, 1847, Wiley, 1848; *The Dream of Little Tuk, and Other Tales* (illustrated by Count Pocci), Grant & Griffith, 1848; *The Story Teller, and Other Fairy Tales*, Francis, 1850; *Little Ellie, and Other Tales*, Francis, 1856; *The Sand-Hills of Jutland, and Other Stories* ("En historie fra klitterne"), Ticknor & Fields, 1860; *The Ice Maiden* ("Iisjomfruen"; illustrated by John B. Zwecker), Bentley, 1863; *Little Rudy, and Other Stories*, Miller, 1864; *What the Moon Saw, and Other Stories* (illustrated by Alfred W. Bayes), Routledge, 1866; *The Will-o'-the-Wisp, and Other Stories*, Routledge, circa 1869; *The Marsh King's Daughter, and Other Stories* ("Dyndkongens datter"), Routledge, 1869; *The Snow Man, and Other Stories*, Routledge, circa 1870; *The Wood-Nymph* ("Drayden"), Sampson, Low, 1870; *The Snow Queen* ("Sneedronningen"; illustrated by T. Pym, pseudonym of Clara Creed), Wells, Gardner, 1883 [other editions illustrated by H. R. Millar, Macmillan, 1935; Marcia Brown, Scribner, 1972]; *Little Thumb* ("Tommelise"; illus-

The whole city was talking about the splendid cloth which the Emperor had ordered to be woven at such great cost. ■ (From *The Emperor's New Clothes* by Hans Christian Andersen. Illustrated by Virginia Lee Burton.)

trated by Laura Troubridge), Mansell, 1883, also published as *Thumbelina* (illustrated by Hilda Scott), Holiday House, 1939 [other editions under the latter title illustrated by Oscar Fabrès, Putnam, 1944; Adrienne Adams, Scribner, 1961].

The White Swans, and Other Tales (''De vilde svanen''; illustrated by Alice M. Havers), Hildesheimer, 1885, also published as *The Wild Swans, and Other Stories* (illustrated by Elenore Plaisted Abbott and Edward Shenton), Jacobs, 1922 [another edition of the title story illustrated by Marcia Brown, Scribner, 1963]; *The Little Mermaid, and Other Stories* (''Den lille havfrue''; illustrated by J. R. Weguelin), Lawrence & Bullen, 1892 [other editions of the title story illustrated by Maxwell Armfield, Dutton, 1913; Pamela Bianco, Holiday House, 1935; Dorothy Lathrop, Macmillan, 1939; translated by Eva Le Gallienne, illustrated by Edward Frascino, Harper, 1971]; *The Nightingale* (''Nattergalen''; illustrated by Mary J. Newill), Napier, 1894 [other editions illustrated by Harold Berson, Lippincott, 1962; translated by Eva Le Gallienne, illustrated by Nancy Ekholm Burkert, Harper, 1965], also published as *The Emperor and the Nightingale* (illustrated by Bill Sokol), Pantheon, 1959.

The Old House (''Det gamle hus''; illustrated by Hugh Wallis), Beaver Press, 1904; *Little Klaus and Big Klaus* (''Lille Claus og store Claus''; illustrated by Charles Pears), Gowans & Gray, 1906 [another edition illustrated by Palle Bregnhoei, Van Nostrand, 1971]; *The Ugly Duckling* (''Den grimme aelling''; illustrated by Maxwell Armfield), Dutton, 1914 [other editions illustrated by Johannes Larsen, Macmillan, 1955; Adrienne Adams, Scribner, 1965]; *The Flower Maiden, and Other Stories* (illustrated by Elenore Plaisted Abbott and Edward Shenton), Jacobs,

1922; *The Garden of Paradise, and Other Stories* (''Paradisets have''; illustrated by Dugald S. Walker), Heinemann, 1923; *The Little Fairy Sleepy-Eyes* (''Ole Lukoeje''; illustrated bu Andre Helle), Duffield, 1925; *The Story of a Mother* (''Historien om en moder''; illustrated with the original drawings by Fritz Syberg), V. Christensen, 1929.

The Real Princess (''Prinsessen paa aerten''; illustrated by Hedvig Collin), Whitman, 1932, also published as *The Princess and the Pea, and Other Famous Stories* (illustrated by Jan Balet), Parents' Magazine Press, 1962; *It's Perfectly True! and Other Stories* (translated by Paul Leyssac; with the original illustrations by T. V. Pedersen), Macmillan, 1937 [another edition illustrated by Richard Bennett, Harcourt, 1938]; *The Old Man Is Always Right* (''Hvad fatter goer, en altid det rigtige''; illustrated by Feodor S. Rojankovsky), Harper, 1940; *Tumblebug and Other Tales* (translated by Paul Leyssac; illustrated by Hertha List), Harcourt, 1940; *The Red Shoes* (''De rode skoe''; illustrated by V. G. Messenger), Lapworth, 1943; *The Beetle* (''Skarnbassen''), Sandle Brothers, 1944; *The Little Match Girl* (''Den lille pige med svovlstikkerne''; illustrated by Gustaf Tenggren), Grosset & Dunlap, 1944; *The Fir Tree* (''Grantraeet''; illustrated by Alice Schlesinger), Grosset & Dunlap, 1947 [another edition illustrated by Nancy Ekholm Burkert, Harper, 1970]; *The Emperor's New Clothes* (''Kejserens nye klaeder''; illustrated by Virginia Lee Burton), Houghton, 1949 [another edition translated and illustrated by Erik Blegvad, Harcourt, 1959].

The Steadfast Tin Soldier (''Den standhaftige tinsoldat''; illustrated by Marcia Brown), Scribner, 1953; *The Swineherd* (''Svinedrengen''; translated and illustrated by Erik Blegvad), Harcourt, 1958; *The Magic Suit* (retold by Elizabeth Rose; illustrated by Gerald Rose), Faber, 1966; *The*

Tinder Box ("Fyrtoejet"; illustrated by Cyril Satorsky), Prentice-Hall, 1970; *The Jumping Match* ("Springfyrene"; illustrated by Gaynor Chapman), Hamish Hamilton, 1973; *The Woman with the Eggs* (adapted by Jan Wahl from a poem by Andersen; illustrated by Ray Cruz), Crown, 1974; *Hans Clodhopper* ("Klods-Hans"; retold and illustrated by Leon Shtainmets), Lippincott, 1975; *The Shepherdess and the Chimney Sweep* (illustrated by Fleur Brofos Asmussen), Kaye & Ward, 1975.

Novels and stories: (Under pseudonym Villiam Christian Walter) *Ungdoms-forsoeg*, privately printed, 1822, later published as *Gjenfaerdet ved Palnatokes grav, og Alfsol* "The Ghost of Palnatoke's Grave" and "Alfsol"), Schovelin, 1827; *Improvisatoren*, Reitzel, 1835, translation by Mary Howitt published as *The Improvisatore; or, Life in Italy*, Harper, 1845 [another edition illustrated by Harry C. Edwards, Bonner, 1891]; *O.T.*, Reitzel, 1836, and *Kun en Spillemand*, Reitzel, 1837, both translated by Mary Howitt and published as *Only a Fiddler [and] O.T.; or Life in Denmark*, Harper, 1845; *Billedbog uden billeder*, Reitzel, 1840, translation by Mary Howitt published as *A Picture Book without Pictures*, Francis, 1848; *De to baronesser*, Reitzel, 1848, translation by Charles Beckwith Lohmeyer published as *The Two Baronesses*, Bentley, 1848; *At vaere eller ikke vaere*, Reitzel, 1857, translation by Anne S. Bushby published as *To Be or Not to Be?*, Bentley, 1857; *Lykke-Peer* ("Lucky Peer"), Reitzel, 1870.

Plays: *Kjaerlighed paa Nicolae taarn, eller, Hvad siger parterret: Heroisk vaudeville i een act* ("Love on St. Nicholas Tower"), Reitzel, 1829; *Maurerpigen: Tragedie i fem acter*, privately printed, 1840; *Mulatten: Romantisk drama i fem acter*, [Copenhagen], 1840; *Lykkens blomst: Eventyr-comedie i to acter*, Reitzel, 1845; *Kunstens Dannevirke: Forspil ved kongelige danske Theaters Hundredaars Fest*, Reitzel, 1848; *Meer end perler og guld: Eventyr-comedie i fire acter*, Reitzel, 1849; *Den nye barselstue: Lystspil i een act*, Reitzel, 1850; *En Nat i Roeskilde: Vaudeville-spoeg i een act*, [Copenhagen], 1850; *Liden Kirsten: Romantisk Sygestykke i een act*, [Copenhagen], circa 1850; *Ole Lukoeie: Eventyr-comedie in tre acter*, Reitzel, 1850; *Hyldemoer: Phantasiespil i een act*, Reitzel, 1851; *Nokken: Opera in een act*, [Copenhagen], 1853; *En landsbyhistorie:*

Y el Emperador se estiro aun mas. ■ (From *Cuentos de Hans Andersen*. Illustrated by Arthur Rackham. Translated by Alfonso Nadae.)

(From the Russian edition of *Fairy Tales* by H. Ch. Andersen. Translated from Danish by A. Ganzen. Illustrated by V. Konashevicha.)

Folke-skuespil i fem acter, Reitzel, 1855; *Paa Langebro: Folkekomedie med chor og sange i fire acter*, [Copenhagen], 1864; *Da Spanierne var her: Romantiskt lystspil in tre acter*, Reitzel, 1865; *Ravnen: Eventyr-opera i fire acter*, [Copenhagen], 1865.

Poems: *Digte* ("Poems"), C. H. Robert, 1830; *Samlede Digte* ("Collected Poems"), Reitzel, 1833; *Digte, Gamle og nye* ("Poems, Old and New"), Reitzel, 1847; *Poems* (translated and edited by Murray Brown), Elsinore Press, 1972.

Travel books: *Fodreise fra Holmens Canal til Oestpynten af Amager* ("A Journey on Foot from Holman's Canal to the East Point of Amager"), [Copenhagen], 1829; *Skyggebilleder af en reise til Harzen*, Reitzel, 1831, translation by Charles Beckwith Lohmeyer published as *Rambles in the Romantic Regions of the Hartz Mountains*, Bentley, 1848; *En Digters bazar*, Reitzel, 1842, translation by Lohmeyer published as *A Poet's Bazaar*, Bentley, 1846; *I Sverrig*, Reitzel, 1851, translation by Lohmeyer published as *Pictures of Sweden*, Bentley, 1851; *I Spanien*, Reitzel, 1863, translation by Anne S. Bushby published as *In Spain*, Bentley, 1864; *Et Besoeg i Portugal*, [Copenhagen], 1866, translation published in *In Spain* [*and*] *A Visit to Portugal*, Hurd & Houghton, 1870, new edition, translated and edited by Grace Thornton, published as *A Visit to Portugal, 1866*, Bobbs-Merrill, 1974; *Et Besoeg hos Charles Dickens i sommeren, 1857*, [Copenhagen], 1868, translation published in *Pictures of Travel in Sweden, among the Hartz Moun-*

tains, and in Switzerland, with a visit at Charles Dickens's House, Hurd & Houghton, 1871; *A Visit to Spain and North Africa, 1862*, translated and edited by Grace Thornton, P. Owen, 1975.

Autobiographies: *Levnedsbog: Digterens liv, 1805-1831, nedskrevet 1832* (draft, written in 1832), Aschehoug, 1926; *Mit Eget eventyr uden Digtning* (manuscript that became the basis for the later autobiography), edited by Helge Topsoe-Jensen, Nyt Nordisk Forlag, 1942; *Das Maerchen meines lebens ohne Dichtung: Eine Skizze* (in German; first publication of the completed autobiography), C. B. Lorck, 1847, English translation from the German by Mary Howitt published as *The True Story of My Life: A Sketch*, Monroe, 1847; *Mit Livs eventyr* (Danish translation), Reitzel, 1855, revised version published as *Mit Livs eventyr fortsaettelse, 1855-1867*, translation published as *The True Story of My Life . . . to the Odense Festival of 1867*, Hurd & Houghton, 1871 [other editions include the translation by W. Glyn Jones published as *The Fairy Tale of My Life* (illustrated by Niels Larsen Stevns), British Book Centre, 1951; an abridged translation by Maurice Michael published as *The Mermaid Man*, Library Publishers, 1955; *The Fairy Tale of My Life: An Autobiography* (reprinted from an 1868 edition), Two Continents Publishing, 1975].

Other: *Collected Works*, ten volumes, Hurd & Houghton, 1869-71; *Hans Christian Andersen's Correspondence with the late Grand Duke of Saxe-Weimar, Charles Dickens, etc.*, edited by F. Crawford, Dean & Son, 1891; *Hans Christian Andersen's Visits to Charles Dickens, as Described in His Letters*, edited by Ejnar Munksgaard, Levin & Munksgaard, 1937; *The Andersen-Scudder Letters: Hans Christian Andersen's Correspondence with Horace Elisha Scudder*, edited by Jean Hersholt and Waldemar Westergaard, University of California Press, 1949.

ADAPTATIONS—Plays: Robin Short, *The Red Shoes* (two-act), Samuel French, 1956; George H. Holroyd, *Little Plays from Andersen* (illustrated by Branney Williams), G. Philip, 1963; Alan Broadhurst, *The Tinder Box*, Children's Theatre Press, 1963; Dean Wenstrom, *Big Klaus and Little Klaus* (one-act), Anchorage Press, 1966; Pat Hale, *The Little Mermaid* (two-act; music by Al Bahret), New Plays for Children, 1968.

Movies and filmstrips: "Little Claus and Big Claus," Dania Biofilm Co., 1914; "Christmas Rhapsody," adaptation of *The Fir Tree*, Encyclopaedia Britannica Films, 1948; "The Fir Tree" (filmstrips), Society for Visual Education, 1949 and 1960, Encyclopaedia Britannica Films, 1955; "The Fir Tree" (motion picture), Encyclopaedia Britannica Educational Corp., 1971; "The Red Shoes" (motion pictures), J. Arthur Rank/Eagle Lion Films, starring Moira Shearer, 1948, McGraw-Hill, 1967; "The Red Shoes" (filmstrip in two parts), McGraw-Hill, 1967; "The Princess and the Pea" (filmstrips), Stillfilm, 1949, Cooper Films and Records, 1969; "The Princess and the Pea" (motion picture), McGraw-Hill, 1966; "The True Princess" (filmstrip), BFA Educational Media, 1972.

"The Tinder Box" (filmstrips), Stillfilm, 1949, Encyclopaedia Britannica Films, 1956, Society for Visual Education, 1960; "The Tinder Box" (motion pictures), Graphic Curriculum, 1968, Encyclopaedia Britannica Educational Corp., 1971; "The Little Match Girl" (filmstrips), Society

(From *The Snow Queen* by H. C. Andersen. Illustrated by Marcia Brown.)

Costruirono una barchetta con un vecchio giornale, vi misero il soldatino di piombo e lo fecero navigare nel ruscello. ■ (From *Il Favoloso Andersen.* Illustrated by Maraja.)

for Visual Education, 1949 and 1960, Spoken Arts, 1967, Coronet Instructional Films, 1968; "The Little Match Girl" (motion pictures), Castle Films, 1954, International Communication Films, 1968; "La Pequena vendedora de fosforos" (filmstrip), Spanish adaptation of *The Little Match Girl,* Gessler Publishing, 1965; "Petite fille aux allumettes" (filmstrip), French adaptation of *The Little Match Girl,* Gessler Publishing, 1965; "Das Maedchen mit der Streichhoelzern" (filmstrip), German adaptation of *The Little Match Girl,* Gessler Publishing, 1967.

"The Ugly Duckling" (filmstrips), Stillfilm, 1949, Curriculum Films, 1951, Curriculum Materials Corp., 1957, Society for Visual Education, 1960, Eye Gate House, 1961, Coronet Instructional Films, 1968, Educational Projections Corp., 1968, Popular Science Publishing, 1968, Universal Education and Visual Arts, 1969, Jam Handy School Service Center, 1970, Walt Disney Educational Materials Co., 1970, Carman Educational Associates, 1971, Viewlex, 1972; "The Ugly Duckling" (motion pictures), Coronet Films, 1953, Encyclopaedia Britannica Films (11 min., b/w, color), 1953, Walt Disney Educational Materials Co., 1955, Walt Disney Home Movies, 1968, Encyclopaedia Britannica Educational Corp., 1969, Doubleday Multimedia (13½ min., 16mm), 1970; "Reading Out Loud: Eva Le Gallienne (motion picture), a reading of *The Ugly Duckling,* Westinghouse Broadcasting Co., 1960.

"Thumbelina" (filmstrips), Curriculum Films, 1951, Encyclopaedia Britannica Films, 1956, Curriculum Materials Corp., 1957, Society for Visual Education, 1960, Eye Gate House, 1961, Educational Media Distribution Center, 1967, Educational Projections Corp., 1970, Viewlex, 1972; "Thumbelina" (motion picture), Coronet Instructional Films, 1970; "The Story of Little Thumb" (filmstrip), Encyclopaedia Britannica Films, 1965; "Hans Christian Andersen" starring Danny Kaye (112 min., 16mm, sound, color), RKO, 1952; "The Emperor's New Clothes" (motion pictures), Columbia Pictures Corp., 1953, Brandon Films, 1959, McGraw-Hill, 1966; "The Emperor's New Clothes" (filmstrips), Teaching Aids Service, 1956, Society for Visual Education, 1960; "The Little Mermaid" (filmstrips), Encyclopaedia Britannica Films, 1956 and 1965, Jam Handy School Service Center, 1970.

"The Swineherd" (filmstrips), Encyclopaedia Britannica Films, 1956, Spoken Arts, 1967; "Hans Clodhopper" (filmstrips), Jam Handy Organization, 1954, Encyclopaedia Britannica Films, 1956, Coronet Instructional Films, 1968; "The Steadfast Tin Soldier" (motion pictures), Brandon Films, 1955, McGraw-Hill, 1967; "The Steadfast Tin Soldier" (filmstrips), McGraw-Hill, 1967, Coronet Instructional Films, 1968; "The Constant Tin Soldier" (filmstrip), Spoken Arts, 1968; "The Toy Soldier" (filmstrip), Encyclopaedia Britannica Educational Corp., 1969; "El Soldadito de juguete" (filmstrip), Spanish adaptation of "The Toy Soldier," Encyclopaedia Britannica Educational Corp., 1972; "The Shepherdess and the Chimneysweep" (filmstrip), Encyclopaedia Britannica Films, 1956.

"The Wild Swans" (filmstrips), Encyclopaedia Britannica Films, 1958, Coronet Instructional Films, 1968; "The Emperor's Nightingale" (motion picture), McGraw-Hill, 1967; "The Emperor's Nightingale" (60 min., 16mm, color) narrated by Boris Karloff, Macmillan Audio-Brandon Films; "The Emperor and the Nightingale" (filmstrips),

Universal Education and Visual Arts, 1969, Troll Associates, 1970; "The Nightingale" (filmstrips), Jam Handy School Service Center, 1970, BFA Educational Media, 1972, Doubleday Multimedia, 1973; "Candles" (filmstrip), BFA Educational Media, 1972; "The Flying Trunk" (filmstrip), Jam Handy School Service Center, 1970; "The Snow Queen" (filmstrip), Coronet Instructional Films, 1968; "The Snowman" (filmstrip), BFA Educational Media, 1972.

"The Snow Queen" (Russian, 70 min., 16mm, sound, color, animated, dubbed), Universal, 1960; "The Nightingale" (22:32 mins., cassette with narration, music and sound effects, mini-filmstrip depicting costumes, make-up and set design, teacher's guide, twenty scripts), Doubleday Multimedia, 1973. "Fairy Tales from Hans Christian Andersen" (average frames: 51, sound, four records or cassettes), BFA Educational Media; "The Hans Christian Andersen Series" (color), Scott Education Division; "Hans Christian Andersen Stories" (six filmstrips, 39 frames each), Encyclopaedia Britannica; "The World of Hans Christian Andersen" (80 min., 16mm, color, animated), Macmillan Audio Brandon Films.

Recordings: "Contes De Perrault, d'Andersen Et de Grimm," read by Danielle Darrieux, Caedmon; "The Emperor's New Clothes and Other Tales," read by Michael Redgrave (record or cassette, teacher's guide), Caedmon; "The Emperor's New Clothes; The Constant Tin Soldier," read by Eve Watkinson and Christopher Casson (cassette only), Spoken Arts; "Eva Le Gallienne Reads Hans Christian Andersen" (eight records or cassettes, read-along paperback texts), Miller-Brody Productions; "Great Claus and Little Claus," read by Eve Watkinson and Christopher Casson (cassette only), Spoken Arts; "Hans Christian Andersen: His Poems and the Story of His Life," read by Siobhan McKenna (record or cassette), Caedmon, 1973; "The Little Match Girl and Other Fairy Tales," read by Boris Karloff (record or cassette, teacher's guide), Caedmon; "The Little Match Girl; The World's Fairest Rose; The Flax," read by Eve Watkinson and Christopher Casson (cassette only), Spoken Arts; "The Little Mermaid," read by Cathleen Nesbitt (record or cassette, teacher's guide), Caedmon; "The Red Shoes; The Swineherd," read by Eve Watkinson and Christopher Casson (cassette only), Spoken Arts; "The Snow Queen," read by Cathleen Nesbitt (record or cassette, teacher's guide), Caedmon; "The Snow Queen" (44 min., cassette or tape), Children's Classics on Tape; "Thumbelina," read by Eve Watkinson and Christopher Casson (cassette only), Spoken Arts; "The Tinder Box; The Drop of Water," read by Eve Watkinson and Christopher Casson (cassette only), Spoken Arts; "The Ugly Duckling" (cassette only, teacher's guide), Miller-Brody Productions; "The Ugly Duckling; The Real Princess," read by Eve Watkinson and Christopher Casson (cassette only), Spoken Arts; "The Ugly Duckling and Other Tales," read by Boris Karloff (record or cassette, teacher's guide), Caedmon; "The Wild Swans," read by Eve Watkinson and Christopher Casson (cassette only), Spoken Arts.

SIDELIGHTS: **April 2, 1805.** Born in Odense, Denmark. Six years previously his mother had given birth to an illegitimate daughter. Andersen did his best to prevent anyone

(From the movie, "The Ugly Duckling," copyright by Walt Disney Productions.)

(From the Czechoslovakian edition of *Marchen* by
Hans Christian Andersen. Illustrated by Jiri Trnka.)

(From the Czechoslovakian edition of *Marchen* by Hans Christian Andersen. Illustrated by Jiri Trnka.)

THE·SHEPHERDESS·AND·THE·CHIMNEY·SWEEP

The sky with all its stars was high above, and all the roofs of the town deep below them. They looked far around—far, far out into the world. ■ (From *Fairy Tales* by Hans Andersen. Illustrated by Kay Nielsen.)

ever knowing of his half-sister's existence. His background was low—with an insane grandfather, a grandmother who was a pathological liar, an alcoholic mother, and an aunt who ran a brothel.

"I was the only child, and was extremely spoiled, but I continually heard from my mother how very much happier I was than she had been, and that I was brought up like a nobleman's child. She, as a child, had been driven out by her parents to beg, and once when she was not able to do it, she had sat for a whole day under a bridge and wept.

"My father gratified me in all my wishes. I possessed his whole heart; he lived for me. On Sundays he made me perspective glasses, theatres, and pictures which could be changed; he read to me from Holberg's plays and the "Arabian Tales"; it was only in such moments as these that I can remember to have seen him really cheerful, for he never felt himself happy in his life as a handicraftsman. His parents had been country people in good circumstances, but upon whom many misfortunes had fallen: the cattle had died; the farm-house had been burned down; and lastly, the husband had lost his reason. On this the wife had removed with him to Odense, and there put her son, whose mind was full of intelligence, apprentice to a shoemaker; it could not be otherwise, although it was his ardent wish to attend the grammar school, where he might learn Latin. I recollect that once, as a child, I saw tears in his eyes, and it was when a youth from the grammar school came to our house to be measured for a new pair of boots, and showed us his books and told us what he learned.

THE·ELDER·TREE·MOTHER

"Surely," said he; "and yonder in the corner stood a butt of water; there I swam my boat, ... How it could sail!" ■ (From *Fairy Tales* by Hans Andersen. Illustrated by Kay Nielsen.)

"The mother of my father came daily to our house, were it only for a moment, in order to see her little grandson. I was her joy and her delight. She was a quiet and most amiable old woman, with mild blue eyes and a fine figure, which life had severely tried. From having been the wife of a countryman in easy circumstances she had now fallen into great poverty, and dwelt with her feeble-minded husband in a little house, which was the last, poor remains of their property. She was employed to take care of the garden belonging to a lunatic asylum, and every Sunday evening she brought us some flowers, which they gave her permission to take home with her.

"She burned, twice in the year, the green rubbish of the garden, on such occasions she took me with her to the asylum, and I lay upon the great heaps of green leaves and pea-straw. I had many flowers to play with, and—which was a circumstance upon which I set great importance—I had here better food to eat than I could expect at home.

"All such patients as were harmless were permitted to go freely about the court; they often came to us in the garden, and with curiosity and terror I listened to them and followed them about; nay, I even ventured so far as to go with the attendants to those who were raving mad. A long passage led to their cells. On one occasion, when the attendants were out of the way, I lay down upon the floor, and peeped through the crack of the door into one of these cells. I saw within a lady almost naked, lying on her straw bed; her hair hung down over her shoulders, and she sang with a very beautiful voice. All at once she sprang up, and threw herself against the door where I lay; the little valve

Yesterday's Authors of Books for Children

"...I saw him hasten away with your child: he strides faster than the winds, and never brings back what he has taken away." ■ (From *Fairy Tales* by Hans Andersen. Illustrated by Kay Nielsen.)

through which she received her food burst open; she stared down upon me, and stretched out her long arm toward me. I screamed for terror—I felt the tips of her fingers touching my clothes—I was half dead when the attendant came; and even in later years that sight and that feeling remained within my soul.

"Close beside the place where the leaves were burned the poor old women had their spinning-room. I often went in there, and was very soon a favorite. When with these people, I found myself possessed of an eloquence which filled them with astonishment. And they rewarded my eloquence by telling me tales in return; and thus a world as rich as that of the Thousand and One Nights, was revealed to me.

"I was very much afraid of my weak-minded grandfather. Only once had he ever spoken to me. He employed himself in cutting out of wood strange figures,—men with beasts' heads and beasts with wings. One day, when he was returning to Odense, I heard the boys in the street shouting after him; I hid myself behind a flight of steps in terror, for I knew that I was of his flesh and blood.

"I very seldom played with other boys; even at school I took little interest in their games, but remained sitting within doors. At home I had playthings enough, which my father made for me. I was a singularly dreamy child, and so constantly went about with my eyes shut, . . . to give the impression of having weak sight, although the sense of sight was especially cultivated by me.

"An old woman-teacher, who had an ABC school taught me the letters, to spell, and 'to read right,' as it was called. She made use of a big rod, which she always carried with her. The school consisted mostly of girls. It was the custom of the school for all to spell loudly and in as high a key as possible. The mistress dared not beat me, as my mother had made it a condition of my going that I should not be touched. One day having got a hit of the rod, I rose immediately, took my book, and without further ceremony went home to my mother, asked that I might go to another school, and that was granted me. My mother sent me to Carsten's school for boys.

"The theatre, soon became my favorite place, but, as I could only very seldom go there, I acquired the friendship of the man who carried out the playbills, and he gave me one every day. With this I seated myself in a corner and imagined an entire play, according to the name of the piece and the characters in it. That was my first, unconscious poetizing." [Hans Christian Andersen, *The Fairy Tale of My Life*, Paddington Press, 1975.[1]]

1808-1812. Denmark, as an ally of Napoleon, declared war on Sweden. "The events of the war in Germany, which [my father] read in the newspapers with eager curiosity, occupied him completely. Napoleon was his hero: his rise from obscurity was the most beautiful example to him. At that time Denmark was in league with France; nothing was talked of but war; my father entered the service as a soldier, in hope of returning home a lieutenant. My mother wept, the neighbors shrugged their shoulders, and said that it was folly to go out to be shot when there was no occasion for it.

"The morning on which the corps were to march I heard my father singing and talking merrily, but his heart was deeply agitated; I observed that by the passionate manner in which he kissed me when he took his leave. I lay sick of the measles and alone in the room, when the drums beat, and my mother accompanied my father, weeping, to the city gate.

"That was the first day of real sorrow which I remember."[1]

1814. "The regiment advanced no further than Holstein; peace was concluded, and the voluntary soldier returned to his work-stool. [But] his health had suffered. One morning he woke in a state of the wildest excitement, and talked only of campaigns and Napoleon. He fancied that he had received orders from him to take the command. My father died the third day after that. His corpse lay on the bed; I therefore slept with my mother, A cricket chirped the whole night through. **April 26, 1816.** He was buried in a pauper's grave.

"After my father's death I was entirely left to myself. My mother went out washing. I sat alone at home with my little theatre, made dolls' clothes, and read plays. It has been told me that I was always clean and nicely dressed. I had grown tall; my· hair was long, bright, and almost yellow, and I always went bareheaded. There dwelt in our neighborhood the widow of a clergyman, with the sister of her deceased husband. This lady opened to me her door, and hers was the first house belonging to the educated class into which I was kindly received.

"Here it was that I heard for the first time the word *poet* spoken, and that with so much reverence, as proved it to be something sacred. Here, too, for the first time, I read Shakespeare,—in a bad translation, to be sure, but the bold descriptions, the heroic incidents, witches, and ghosts were exactly to my taste. I immediately acted Shakespeare's plays on my little puppet theatre. I saw Hamlet's ghosts, and lived upon the heath with Lear. The more persons died in a play, the more interesting I thought it. At this time I wrote my first piece; it was nothing less than a tragedy, wherein, as a matter of course, everybody died."[1]

1816. "The son of one of our neighbors worked in a cloth manufactory, and every week brought home a sum of money. . . . I was also now to go to the manufactory, 'not for the sake of the money!' my mother said, 'but that she might know where I was, and what I was doing.'

"My old grandmother took me to the place, therefore, and was very much affected, because, said she, she had not expected to live to see the time when I should consort with the poor ragged lads that worked there.

"Everybody liked me; and in this way the first days in the manufactory passed on very merrily. One day, however, when I was in my best singing vein, and everybody spoke of the extraordinary brilliancy of my voice, one of the journeymen said that I was a girl, and not a boy. He seized hold of me. I cried and screamed. The other journeymen thought it very amusing, and held me fast by my arms and legs. I screamed aloud, and was as much ashamed as a girl; and then, darting from them, rushed home to my mother, who immediately promised me that I should never go there again.

(From the movie "Hans Christian Andersen," copyright 1952, RKO Radio Pictures. Starring Danny Kaye.)

"I was sent, to the charity school, but learned only religion, writing, and arithmetic, and the last badly enough; I could also scarcely spell a word correctly. I never studied my lessons at home; I used to learn them on the way to school and my mother boasting of my good memory at the expense of our neighbor's son said, 'He reads till it hums, but Hans Christian does not need to open his book and yet he knows his lesson.'

"Often I sat dreaming and gazing on the variegated wall, and [the master] gave me a little reprimand because I was absent-minded. I told the boys curious stories in which I was always the chief person, but was sometimes rallied for that. The street lads had also heard from their parents of my peculiar turn of mind, and that I was in the habit of going to the houses of the gentry. I was therefore one day pursued by a wild crowd of them, who shouted after me derisively, 'There runs the play-writer!' I hid myself at home in a corner, wept, and prayed to God.

"My mother said that I must be confirmed, in order that I might be apprenticed to the tailor trade, and thus do something rational. She loved me with her whole heart, but she did not understand my impulses and my endeavors, nor indeed at that time did I myself. The people about her always spoke against my odd ways, and turned me to ridicule.

"We belonged to the parish of St. Knud, and the candidates for Confirmation could either enter their names with the provost or the chaplain. The children of the so-called superior families and the scholars of the grammar school went to the first, and the children of the poor to the second. I, however, announced myself as a candidate to the provost, who was obliged to receive me, although he discovered vanity in my placing myself among his catechists, where, although taking the lowest place, I was still above those who were under the care of the chaplain. I would, however, hope that it was not alone vanity which impelled me. I had a sort of fear of the poor boys, who had laughed at me, and I always felt, as it were, an inward drawing towards the scholars of the grammar school, whom I regarded as far better than other boys. When I saw them playing in the church-yard, I would stand outside the railings, and wish that I were but among the fortunate ones—not for the sake of play, but for the sake of the many books they had, and for what they might be able to become in the world. At the provost's, therefore, I should be able to associate with them, and be as they were; but I do not remember a single one of them now, so little intercourse would they hold with me. I had daily the feeling of having thrust myself in where people thought I did not belong.

"An old female tailor altered my deceased father's great coat into a confirmation suit for me; never before had I worn so good a coat. I had also, for the first time in my life, a pair of boots. My only fear was that everybody would not see them, and therefore I drew them up over my trousers, and thus marched through the church. The boots creaked, and that inwardly pleased me, for thus the congregation would hear that they were new. My whole devotion was disturbed; I was aware of it, and it caused me a horrible pang of conscience that my thoughts should be as much with my new boots as with God. I prayed him earnestly from my heart to forgive me, and then again I thought about my new boots.

"During the last year I had saved together a little sum of money. When I counted it over I found it to be thirteen rix-dollars banco (about thirty shillings). I was quite overjoyed at the possession of so much wealth, and as my mother now most resolutely required that I should be apprenticed to a tailor, I prayed and besought her that I might make a journey to Copenhagen, that I might see the greatest city in the world.

"'What wilt thou do there?' asked my mother.

"'I will be famous,' returned I; and then I told her all that I had read about extraordinary men. 'People have,' said I, 'at first an immense deal of adversity to go through, and then they will be famous.'

"It was a wholly unintelligible impulse that guided me. I wept, I prayed, and at last my mother consented, after having first sent for a so-called wise woman out of the hospital, that she might read my future fortune by the coffee-grounds and cards.

"'Your son will become a great man,' said the old woman, 'and in honor of him Odense will one day be illuminated.'

"My mother wept when she heard that, and I obtained permission to travel. All the neighbors told my mother that it was a dreadful thing to let me, at only fourteen years of age, go to Copenhagen, which was such a long way off, and such a great and intricate city, and where I knew nobody.'"[1]

September 5, 1819. "I saw from the heights of Fredericksberg, Copenhagen for the first time.

"I bought a newspaper, and found among the advertisements that a cabinetmaker was in want of an apprentice. The man received me kindly, but said that before I was bound to him he must have an attestation, and my baptismal register from Odense; and that till these came I could remove to his house, and try how the business pleased me. At six o'clock the next morning I went to the workshop: several journeymen were there, and two or three apprentices; but the master was not come. They fell into merry and idle discourse. I was as bashful as a girl, and as they soon perceived this, I was unmercifully rallied upon it. Later in the day the rude jests of the young fellows went so far, that, in remembrance of the scene at the manufactory, I took the resolute determination not to remain a single day longer in the workshop. I went down to the master, therefore, and told him that I could not stand it; he tried to console me, but in vain; I was too much affected, and hastened away.

"I now went through the streets; nobody knew me; I was quite forlorn. I then bethought myself of having read in a newspaper in Odense the name of an Italian, Siboni, who was the director of the Academy of Music in Copenhagen. Everybody had praised my voice; perhaps he would assist me for its sake; if not, then that very evening I must seek out the master of some vessel who would take me home again. At the thoughts of the journey home I became still more violently excited, and in this state of suffering I hastened to Siboni's house.

"It happened that very day that he had a large party to dinner; our celebrated composer Weyse was there, the poet Bagesen, and other guests. The housekeeper opened the door to me, and to her I not only related my wish to be engaged as a singer, but also the whole history of my life. She listened to me with the greatest sympathy and then she left me. I waited a long time, and she must have been repeating to the company the greater part of what I had said, for, in a while, the door opened, and all the guests came out and looked at me. They would have me to sing, and Siboni heard me attentively. I gave some scenes out of Holberg, and repeated a few poems; and then, all at once, the sense of my unhappy condition so overcame me that I burst into tears; the whole company applauded.

"Siboni promised to cultivate my voice, and that I therefore should succeed as singer at the Theatre Royal. It made me very happy; I laughed and wept; and as the housekeeper led me out and saw the excitement under which I labored, she stroked my cheeks, and said that on the following day I should go to Professor Weyse, who meant to do something for me, and upon whom I could depend.

"I went to Weyse, who himself had risen from poverty; he had deeply felt and fully comprehended my unhappy situation, and had raised by a subscription seventy rix-dollars banco for me. I then wrote my first letter to my mother a letter full of rejoicing, for the good fortune of the whole world seemed poured upon me. The opera singers came daily for practice, and sometimes I was allowed to be present.

"Half a year afterward my voice broke, or was injured, in consequence of my being compelled to wear bad shoes through the winter, and having besides no warm underclothing. There was no longer any prospect that I should become a fine singer. Siboni told me that candidly, and counseled me to go to Odense, and there learn a trade.

1821. "I had now been two years in Copenhagen. The sum of money which had been collected for me was expended, but I was ashamed of making known my wants and my necessities. I had removed to the house of a woman whose husband, when living, was master of a trading-vessel, and there I had only lodging and breakfast. Those were heavy, dark days for me. The lady believed that I went out to dine with various families, whilst I only ate a little bread on one of the benches in the royal garden. Very rarely did I venture into some of the lowest eating-houses, and choose there the least expensive dish. I was, in truth, very forlorn; but I did not feel the whole weight of my condition. Every person who spoke to me kindly I took for a faithful friend.

"I heard it said every day, what a good thing it would be for me if I could study. People advised me to devote myself

He lifted it with a trembling hand, and shouted with a trembling voice: "Gold! Gold!" ■ (From *The Winds Tale and The Emperor's New Clothes* by Hans Christian Andersen. Illustrated by Edmund Dulac.)

to science, but no one moved one step to enable me to do so; it was labor enough for me to keep body and soul together. It therefore occurred to me to write a tragedy, which I would offer to the Theatre Royal, and would then begin to study with the money which I should thus obtain. Within fourteen days I wrote my national tragedy called the 'Robbers in Wissenberg' (the name of a little village in Funen). There was scarcely a word in it correctly written, as I had no person to help me, because I meant it to be anonymous. After an interval of six weeks, I received it back, accompanied by a letter which said that people did not frequently wish to retain works which betrayed, in so great a degree, a want of elementary knowledge.

"It was just at the close of the theatrical season, in **May, 1822,** that I received a letter from the directors, by which I was dismissed from the singing and dancing school, the letter adding also, that my participation in the school teaching could lead to no advantage for me, but they wished some of my many friends would enable me to receive an education, without which talent availed nothing. I felt myself again, as it were, cast out into the wide world, without help and without support."[1]

June, 1822. First story published in a book called *Youthful Attempts,* under pseudonym Villiam Christian.

September 6, 1822. The Royal Theatre agreed to send Andersen to grammar school for three years so he could acquire at least the elements of education. "In a few days I was sent for by the directors of the theatre, [who] gave me back my play as useless for the stage; adding, however, that there were so many grains of corn scattered in it, they hoped that perhaps, by earnest study, after going to school and the previous knowledge of all that is requisite, I might some time, be able to write a work which should be worthy of being acted on the Danish stage.

"In order therefore to obtain the means for my support and the necessary instruction, [I was] recommended to King Frederick VI, who granted to me a certain sum annually for some years; and, the directors of the high schools allowed me to receive free instruction in the grammar school at Slagelse, where just then a new, and, as was said, an active rector was appointed."[1]

October 26, 1822. "On a beautiful autumn day I set off with the mail from Copenhagen to begin my school-life in Slagelse. I boarded with a respectable widow of the educated class, and had a little chamber looking out into the garden and field. My place in the school was in the lowest class, among little boys: I knew indeed nothing at all.

"I had the greatest desire to learn, but for the moment I floundered about, as if I had been thrown into the sea; one wave followed another; grammar, geography, mathematics: I felt myself overpowered by them, and feared that I should never be able to acquire all these. The Rector, who took a peculiar delight in turning everything to ridicule, did not, of course, make an exception in my case. To me he stood there as a divinity; I believed unconditionally every word which he spoke.

"I may freely confess that I was industrious, and I rose, as soon as it was possible, into a higher class; but in proportion as I rose did I feel the pressure upon me more strongly, and that my endeavors were not sufficiently productive. Many an evening, when sleep overcame me, I would wash my head with cold water, or run about the lonely little garden, till I was again wakeful, and could comprehend the book anew. The Rector filled up a portion of his hours of teaching with jest, nicknames, and not the happiest of witticisms. I was as if paralyzed with anxiety when he entered the room, and from that cause my replies often expressed the opposite of that which I wished to say, and thereby my anxiety was all the more increased. What was to become of me?

"In a moment of ill-humor I wrote a letter to the head master, who was one of those who was most friendly inclined to me. I said in this letter that I regarded myself as a person so little gifted by nature, that it was impossible for me to study, and that the people in Copenhagen threw away the money which they spent upon me: I besought him therefore to counsel me what I should do. The excellent man strengthened me with mild words, and wrote to me a most friendly and consolatory letter: he said that the Rector meant kindly by me; that it was his custom and way of acting; that I was making all the progress that people could expect from me; and that I need not doubt of my abilities. The misfortune for me was, that I ought to have been treated differently from the other scholars, but that this could hardly be done in a school; still that things were progressing, and that I stood well both with the teachers and my fellow-students.

"One day after another glided away, but the less there is going on and the more quiet and monotonous one's life is the sooner one thinks of preserving what passes,—of keeping a diary, as it is called. At that time I also kept such a one, of which I have retained a couple of leaves, in which the whole of my strange, childish nature at that time is faithfully reflected. I insert here some passages from it, copying them literally.

"I was then in the upper class but one, and my whole existence and happiness depended on being promoted to the highest class at the approaching examination. I wrote:

"'*Wednesday.*—Depressed in spirit I took up the Bible, which lay before me, for an oracle, opened it, pointed blindly at a place and read, 'O Israel, thou hast destroyed thyself! but in me is thine help!' (Hosea.) Yes, Father, I am weak, but thou lookest into my heart and wilt be my help so that I can be promoted to the fourth class. Have answered well in Hebrew.

"'*Thursday.*—Happened to pull off the leg of a spider; went nicely through in mathematics. O God, God, to thee my heart's entire thanks.

"'*Friday.*—O God, help me! The night is so wintry clear. The examination is well over—to-morrow comes the result. O Moon! to-morrow thou wilt behold either a pale, desperate being or one of the happiest.

"'*Saturday.*—O God, now my fate is decided, but still hidden from me: what may it be? God, my God! do not forsake me! my blood runs so fast through my veins, my nerves tremble with fear. O God, Almighty God, help me—I do not deserve it, but be merciful O God, God!—(Later.) I am promoted—Is it not strange? My joy is not so violent as I supposed it would be.'

. . . **mais un vaisseau magnifique etait devant la maison.** ■ (From *Les Contes D'Andersen Ferme-L'oeil Le Petit Elfe* by Hans Christian Andersen. Illustrated by Jacqueline Ide.)

Yesterday's Authors of Books for Children   39

Hans Christian Andersen in Rome, 1834. (Painting by Albert Kuchler)

"You can see by this what trouble I had in my pious mind, and what degree of development I had reached, although at that time I was already twenty years old. How much better other young men at that age would have written in their diary!"[1]

May, 1826. "The Rector grew weary of his residence in Slagelse; he applied for the vacant post of Rector in the grammar school of Helsingör, and obtained it. He told me of it, and added kindly, that I might ask leave to accompany him thither; that I might live in his house, and could even now remove to his family; I should then in half a year become a student, which could not be the case if I remained behind, and that then he would himself give me some private lessons in Latin and Greek. I, of course, immediately received permission, and removed to the house of the Rector.

"The scenery here made a lively impression upon me, but I dared only to cast stolen glances at it. When the school hours were over, the house-door was commonly locked; I was obliged to remain in the heated school-room and learn my Latin, or else play with the children, or sit in my little room; I never went out to visit anybody. My life in this family furnishes the most evil dreams to my remembrance. I was almost overcome by it, and my prayer to God every evening was, that He would remove this cup from me and let me die. I possessed not an atom of confidence in myself. I never mentioned in my letters how hard it went with me, because the Rector found his pleasure in making a jest of me, and turning my feelings to ridicule.

"During my whole residence in Slagelse I had scarcely written more than four or five poems; two of which, 'The Soul,' and 'To my Mother,' will be found printed in my collected works. In my school-days in Helsingör I wrote only two poems, 'New Year's Night' and 'The Dying Child,' the last one was the first of my poems which gained attention and acknowledgment and was earliest published and translated.

"[The Rector] had heard it said that I had read in company one of my own poems. He looked at me with a penetrating glance, and commanded me to bring him the poem, when, if he found in it one spark of poetry, he would forgive me. I tremblingly brought to him 'The Dying Child,' he read it, and pronounced it to be sentimentality and idle trash. He gave way freely to his anger. If he had believed that I wasted my time in writing verses, or that I was of a nature which required a severe treatment, then his intention would have been good; but he could not pretend this. But from this day forward my situation was more unfortunate than ever; I suffered so severely in my mind that I was very near sinking under it. That was the darkest, the most unhappy time in my life.

"Just then one of the masters went to Copenhagen, and related exactly what I had to bear, and immediately removed me from the school and from the Rector's house. When, in taking leave of him, I thanked him for the kindness which I had received from him, the passionate man cursed me, and ended by saying that I should end my days in a madhouse. I trembled to my innermost being, and left him."[1]

(From *Thumbelina* by Hans Christian Andersen. Illustrated by Vilhelm Pedersen.)

Hans Christian Andersen's house, Odense, 1868.

April 18, 1827. Left Elsinore before finishing school. Tutored in Copenhagen to prepare for *examen artium*. "In September, 1828, I was a student. I was already twenty-three years old, but still much a child in my whole nature and my manner of speaking."[1]

January 2, 1829. *Journey on Foot to Amager* privately published. First edition of 500 copies sold out. The book was well received by the critics and public. Also play "The Forest Chapel" produced briefly at the Royal Theatre. "No publisher had the courage to bring out that juvenile work. I ventured therefore to do it myself, and in a few days after its appearance, the publisher Reitzel bought from me the copyright of the second edition, and after a while he had a third.

"Everybody in Copenhagen read my book; I heard nothing but praise, only a protector of rank gave me a severe lecture but it struck me as rather comical.

"I was now a happy human being, thinking well of all mankind; I possessed the courage of a poet and the heart of a youth. All houses began to be open to me; I flew from circle to circle in happy self-contentment. Under all these external and internal affections, I still however devoted myself industriously to study, so that without my teacher I

passed my second academical examination, *Examen philogicum et philosophicum*, with highest marks."[1]

January, 1830. "At Christmas I brought out the first collected edition of my poems [*Digte*], which met with great praise. I liked to listen to the sounding bell of praise. I had such an overflow of youth and happiness. Life lay bright with sunshine before me."[1]

May 16, 1831. Set out to visit Dresden, Berlin and Hamburg. "The little journey in Germany had great influence upon me, as my Copenhagen friends acknowledged. The impressions of the journey were immediately written down, and I gave them forth under the title of 'Shadow Pictures.' Whether I were actually improved or not, there still prevailed at home the same pretty pleasure in dragging out my faults, the same perpetual schooling of me; and I was weak enough to endure it from those who were officious meddlers. I seldom made a joke of it; but if I did so, it was called arrogance and vanity, and it was asserted that I never would listen to rational people.

"I willingly read for everybody whom I visited what I lately had written that pleased me. I had not yet learned by experience how seldom an author ought to do this, at least in this country. Any gentleman or lady who can hammer on

Then they could see that this was a proper Princess, since she had felt the pea through the twenty mattresses and the twenty eiderdowns. Nobody could possibly have such a tender skin but a real Princess. ■ (From *Hans Andersen: Forty-two Stories* transcribed by M. R. Tames. Illustrated by Robin Jacques.)

a piano or sing a few songs, has no hesitation, in whatever company they may enter, to carry their music-book with them and place themselves before the piano; it is but very seldom that any remark is made on that; an author may read aloud others' poetical works but not his own—that is vanity.

"From the end of the year **1828,** to the beginning of **1839,** I maintained myself alone by my writings. It was difficult for me to pull through,—doubly difficult, because my dress must in some measure accord with the circles into which I went. To produce, and always to be producing, was destructive, nay impossible. I translated a few pieces for the theatre,—and wrote the text for a couple of operas."[1]

April 13, 1833. Given a stipend of 600 rix dollars per annum for two years.

1833-1835. Traveled through Europe. "Nowadays we travel speedily through Germany to Paris, but it was not so in 1833. Then there were no railways, and we crept slowly forward, stowed away night and day in heavy, clumsy stage-coaches.

"There were several of us Danes together that summer in Paris; we all lived in the same hotel, and went in company together to restaurants, cafés, and theatres. Our own home-tongue was always spoken, letters were read by each other, views of home received and talked over, and at last we hardly knew whether we were in a foreign land or our own.

"Everything was seen and had to be seen, for it was on this account we had come abroad. I remember that one of our dear friends one morning returning from museums and palaces almost exhausted, said: 'I cannot help it, they must be

seen; for when I go home again I shall be ashamed to be asked and have to confess that I had not seen this or that; there only remain a few places, and when they are done, I shall have a real good time!' This was the common talk, and will probably very often be repeated. I went out in company with the others and saw and saw, but most of it has long since been effaced from my memory.

"I very seldom received letters from home, and except one or two they were all written with the intent to instruct me, and were often very inconsiderate. They could not help grieving me, and they affected me so much that the Danes whom I liked in Rome, and with whom I associated, always exclaimed: 'Have you got another letter from home? I would not read such letters, and I would give up friends who only pain and plague me!' Well, I needed to be educated and they took me in hand, but harshly and unkindly. They did not reflect how much a thoughtlessly written word could affect me; when enemies smite with scourges, friends' whips are scorpions.

"I felt so depressed by [letters about my new poem, 'Agnete'] and other letters still more painful that I was in despair and on the point of forgetting God, and giving up Him and all mankind. I thought of death in an unchristian manner.

"When I was thus depressed at the judgment passed upon me at home, I received information of the death of my old mother. My first exclamation was: 'O God, I thank thee! Now her poverty is at an end, and I could not relieve her from it!' I wept, but could not familiarize myself with the thought that I now possessed not a single one in the world who would love me because I was of the same kith and kin.

"Italy, with its scenery and the life of its people, occupied my soul, and toward this land I felt a yearning. My earlier life and what I had now seen, blended themselves together into an image—into poetry, which I was compelled to write down, although I was convinced that it would occasion me more trouble than joy, if my necessities at home should oblige me to print it. I had already in Rome written the first chapter, and others afterward in Munich. It was my novel of 'The Improvisatore.'

"My journey was ended. It was in **August** of **1834** that I returned to Denmark. I wrote the first part of the book . . . in Sorö, in a little chamber in the roof, among fragrant lime-trees. I finished it in Copenhagen.

"This book raised my sunken fortunes, collected my friends again around me, nay, even obtained for me new ones. For the first time I felt that I had obtained a due acknowledgment.

"I was very productive, and my writings, in my own country, were now classed among those which were always bought and read; therefore for each fresh work I received a higher payment. [But] I call to my mind how astonished Charles Dickens was at hearing of the payment I had received for 'The Improvisatore.'

"'What did you get?' asked he. I answered, 'Nineteen pounds!'—'For the sheet?' he inquired. 'No,' said I, 'for the whole book.'—'We must be misunderstanding each other,' continued he; 'you don't mean to say that for the whole work, 'The Improvisatore,' you have only nineteen pounds; you must mean for each sheet!' I was sorry to tell him that it was not the case, and that I had only got about half a pound a sheet.

"Already for many years there had existed, under Frederick VI, an institution which does the highest honor to the Danish government, namely, that beside the considerable sum expended yearly for the traveling expenses of young literary men and artists, a small pension shall be awarded to such of them as enjoy no office emoluments. It was my hope and my wish that the same good fortune might be mine—and it was. Frederick VI granted me two hundred rix-dollars banco yearly. I was filled with gratitude and joy. I was no longer *forced* to write in order to live; I had a sure support in the possible event of sickness; I was less dependent upon the people about me.

1841. Wrote play "The Mulatto." "It is characteristic of the people of Copenhagen, that when a new piece is announced, they do not say, 'I am glad of it,' but 'It will probably be good for nothing; it will be hissed off the stage.' That hissing off plays a great part, and is an amusement which fills the house; but it is not the bad actor who is hissed; no, the author and the composer only are the criminals; for them the scaffold is erected. Five minutes is the usual time, and the whistles resound, and the lovely women smile and felicitate themselves, like the Spanish ladies at their bloody bull-fights.

"For a number of years November and December were always the most dangerous time for a new piece, because the young scholars were then made 'Students,' and, having cleared the fence of 'artium,' were very severe judges. All our most eminent dramatic writers have been whistled down, to say nothing of foreign classics, as Moliére.

"And as I had often heard that I did not possess the assiduity sufficient to work my *matériel* well, I resolved to *labor* this drama—'The Mulatto'—from the beginning to the end in the most diligent manner, and to compose it in alternately rhyming verse, as was then the fashion.

"[It] was received with the most triumphant acclamation."[1]

Summer, 1842. "I wrote a little piece for the summer theatre, called 'The Bird in the Pear-tree,' in which several scenes were acted up in the pear-tree. I had called it a dramatic trifle, in order that no one might expect either a great work or one of a very elaborate character. It was a little sketch, which, after being performed a few times, was received with so much applause, that the directors of the theatre accepted it—and then suddenly it was hissed. Some young men, who gave the word to hiss, had said to some others, who inquired of them their reasons for doing so, that the trifle had too much luck, and then Andersen would be getting too mettlesome.

"I was not, on this evening, at the theatre myself, and had not the least idea of what was going on. On the following evening I went to the house of one of my friends. I had headache, and was looking very grave. The lady of the house met me with a sympathizing manner, took my hand, and said, 'Is it really worth while to take it so much to heart! There were only two who hissed, the whole house beside took your part.'

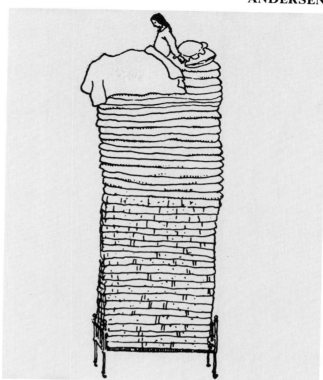

(Illustration by Gilbert James from *The Princess on the Pea.*)

"'Hissed! My part! Have I been hissed?' exclaimed I. It was quite comic; one person assured me that this hissing had been a triumph for me; everybody had joined in acclamation, and 'there was only one who hissed.'

"After this, another person came and I asked him the number of those who hissed. 'Two,' said he. The next person said 'three' and said positively there were no more. One of my most veracious friends, . . . now made his appearance; he did not know what the others had said, and I asked him, upon his conscience, how many he had heard; he laid his hand upon his heart, and said that, at the very highest, there were five.

"'No,' said I; 'now I will ask nobody more; the number grows just as with Falstaff; here stands one who asserts that there was only one person who hissed.'

"Shocked, and yet inclined to set it all right again, he replied, 'Yes, that is possible; but then it was a strong, powerful hiss.'"[1]

1843. "By my last works, and by prudent economy, I had now saved a small sum of money, which I set apart for the purpose of a new journey to Paris. At the end of January, I left Copenhagen.

"I often visited at Victor Hugo's and enjoyed great kindness there. At [his] invitation I saw at the Théâtre Francais his abused tragedy, 'Les Burggraves,' which was every evening hissed and parodied at the smaller theatres. His wife was very handsome, and possessed that amiability so peculiar to French ladies which makes foreigners so entirely at home with them.

"Yes, I will go with thee!" said Tommelise, and she seated herself on the bird's back. ■ (From "Tommelise," *Hans Andersen's Fairy Tales*. Illustrated by W. Heath Robinson.)

"I generally found the jovial Alexandre Dumas in bed, even long after mid-day; here he lay, with paper, pen, and ink, and wrote his newest drama. I found him thus one day; he nodded kindly to me, and said, 'Sit down a minute; I have just now a visit from my muse; she will be going directly.' He wrote on; spoke aloud; shouted a *viva!* sprang out of bed, and said, 'The third act is finished!'

"When the edition of my collection of [children's] stories came out at Christmas, 1843, the reaction began; acknowledgment of my merits was made, and favor shown me in Denmark, and since that time I have no cause for complaint. I have obtained and I obtain in my own land that which I deserve—nay, perhaps much more. [They] have been placed by everyone, without any hesitation, higher than anything else I had hitherto written.

"Only a few months after the 'Improvisatore' appeared, in 1835, I brought out my first volume of *Wonder Stories* which at that time was not so very much thought of. One monthly critical journal even complained that an author who had taken such a step forward in the 'Improvisatore,' would immediately fall back with anything so childish as the tales. I reaped a harvest of blame, precisely where people ought to have acknowledged the advantage of my mind producing something in a new direction. Several of my friends, whose judgment was of value to me, counseled

me entirely to abstain from writing tales, as these were something for which I had no talent. Others were of opinion that I had better, first of all, study the French fairy tale.

"The *Monthly Journal of Literature* paid no attention to the book, nor has it done so since. 'Dannora,' edited and published by J. N. Höst, was in 1836 the only one that gave a notice, which reads amusingly now, though at the time it naturally grieved me. The reviewer says that 'These *Wonder Stories* will be able to amuse children, but they are so far from containing anything instructive that the critic hardly ventures to recommend them as harmless reading; at least nobody will maintain that a child's sense of decency will be sharpened when it reads about a princess who rides in her sleep on a dog's back to a soldier who kisses her, after which she herself, wide-awake, tells of this fine adventure—as a wonderful dream, etc. The story of the 'Princess on Pease,' the reviewer finds, has no wit, and it strikes him 'not only as indelicate but positively without excuse, as putting the notion into a child's head that a lady of such rank must always be excessively refined.' The reviewer concludes with the wish that the author may not waste any more time in writing wonder stories for children. I would willingly have discontinued writing them, but they forced themselves from me.

"In the volume which I first published, I had, like Musäus, but in my own manner, related old stories, which I had heard as a child. The tone in which they still sounded in my ears seemed a very natural one to me, but I knew very well that the learned critics would censure the style of talk, so, to quiet them, I called them *Wonder Stories told for Children,* although my intention was that they should be for both young and old. The volume concluded with one which was original, 'Little Ida's Flowers,' and seemed to have given the greatest pleasure, although it bore a tolerably near affinity to a story of Hoffman's, and I had already given it in substance in my *Foot Journey.* In my increasing disposition for children's stories, I therefore followed my own impulse, and invented them mostly myself. In the following year a new volume came out, and soon after that a third, in which the longest story, 'The Little Mermaid,' was my own invention. This story, in an especial manner, created an interest which was only increased by the following volumes. One of these came out every Christmas, and before long no Christmas-tree could exist without my stories.

"Some of our first comic actors made the attempt of relating my little stories from the stage; it was something new, and a complete change from the declamatory poetry which had been heard to satiety. 'The Constant Tin Soldier,' therefore, 'The Swineherd,' and 'The Top and Ball,' were told from the royal stage, and from those of private theatres, and were well received.

"A refreshing sunshine streamed into my heart; I felt courage and joy, and was filled with a living desire of still more and more developing my powers in this direction,—of studying more thoroughly this class of writing, and of observing still more attentively the rich wells of nature out of which I must create it. If attention be paid to the order in which my stories are written, it certainly will be seen that there is in them a gradual progression, a clearer working out of the idea, a greater discretion in the use of agency, and, if I may so speak, a more healthy tone and a more natural freshness may be perceived.

(From *Fairy Tales* by Hans Christian Andersen. Illustrated by Arthur Rackham.)

"As one step by step toils up a steep hill, I had at home climbed upward, and now beheld myself recognized and honored, appointed a distinct place in the literature of my country. This recognition and kindness at home atoned for all the hard words that the critics had spoken. Within me was clear sunshine; there came a sense of rest, a feeling that all, even the bitter in my life, had been needful for my development and my fortune."[1]

August 4, 1875. Died near Copenhagen. "I often think: if only I were handsome OR rich and had a little office of some kind, then I would get married, I would work, eat and finally lie down in the churchyard—what a pleasant life that would be; but since I am ugly and will always remain poor nobody will want to marry me, for that is what the girls look for, don't you know, and they are quite right. So I shall have to stand alone all my life as a poor thistle and be spat at because it happened to fall to my lot to have thorns."[1]

FOR MORE INFORMATION SEE: Robert Nisbet Bain, *Hans Christian Andersen: A Biography,* Dodd, 1895; Elith Reumert, *Hans Andersen, the Man* (translated from the Danish by Jessie Broechner), Methuen, 1927, reprinted, Gale, 1971; Signe Toksvig, *The Life of Hans Christian Andersen,* Harcourt, 1934; Constance Buel Burnett, *The Shoemaker's Son,* Random House, 1941; Elias Bredsdorff, *Danish Literature in English Translation, with a Special Hans Christian Andersen Supplement,* Munksgaard, 1950, reprinted, Greenwood Press, 1973; *Catalogue of the Jean Hersholt Collection of Hans Christian Andersen,* U.S. Library of Congress Bulletin, 1954; Rumer Godden, *Hans Christian Andersen: A Great Life in Brief,* Knopf, 1955; Bredsdorff, *Hans Christian Andersen and Charles Dickens: A Friendship and Its Dissolution,* W. Heffer, 1956.

Fredrik Book, *Hans Christian Andersen: A Biography* (translated from the Swedish by George C. Schoolfield), University of Oklahoma Press, 1962; Monica Stirling, *The Wild Swan: The Life and Times of Hans Christian Andersen,* Harcourt, 1965; E. L. Bredsdorff, "Hans Christian Andersen: A Bibliographical Guide to His Works," *Scandinavica,* Volume VI, 1967; Svend Larsen, *Hans Christian Andersen* (translated from the Danish by Mabel Dyrup), Flensted, 1967; Frederick J. Marker, *Hans Christian Andersen and the Romantic Theatre: A Study of Stage Practices in the Prenaturalistic Scandinavian Theatre,* University of Toronto Press, 1971; Andersen, *The Fairy Tale of My Life: An Autobiography,* Two Continents Publishing, 1975; Bredsdorff, *Hans Christian Andersen,* Scribner, 1975; Reginald Spink, *Hans Christian Andersen and His World,* Putnam, 1972.

For children: Hedvig Collin, *Young Hans Christian Andersen,* Viking, 1955; Shannon Garst, *Hans Christian Andersen,* Houghton, 1965; Ruth Manning-Sanders, *The Story of Hans Andersen: Swan of Denmark,* Dutton, 1966; Laura Benét, *Famous Storytellers for Young People,* Dodd, 1968; Elizabeth R. Montgomery, *Hans Christian Andersen, Immortal Storyteller,* Garrard, 1968; Eva Moore, *The Fairy Tale Life of Hans Christian Andersen,* School Book Service, 1972; Marion M. Brown, *The Pauper Prince: The Story of Hans Christian Andersen,* new edition, Crescent Publications, 1973.

They all exclaimed, "Oh!" held up their forefingers, and nodded their heads. But the poor fisherman who had heard the real Nightingale sing said, "Yes! It's pretty enough; it's a fairly good imitation, but there's something lacking—I can't explain just what it is!" ■ (From *The Nightingale* by Hans Christian Andersen. Translated by Eva LaGallienne. Illustrated by Nancy Ekholm Burkert.)

Hans Christian Andersen

BARRIE, J(ames) M(atthew)   1860-1937

PERSONAL: Born May 9, 1860, in Kirriemuir, Forfar-shire, Scotland; died June 19, 1937; son of David (a weaver) and Margaret (Ogilvy) Barrie; married Mary Ansell (an actress), 1894 (divorced, 1909). Education: Edinburgh University, M.A., 1882. Home: London, England.

CAREER: Playwright and novelist. Began as a writer and reviewer for the Nottingham Daily Journal, 1883-84; later worked as a free-lance journalist in London, sometimes writing under the pseudonym Gavin Ogilvy. Rector of St. Andrews University, 1919-22; chancellor of Edinburgh University, 1930-37. Member: Society of Authors (president, 1928-37). Awards, honors: Created a baronet, 1913; Order of Merit, 1922; LL.D., Edinburgh and St. Andrews Universities; D.Litt., Oxford and Cambridge Universities.

WRITINGS—Peter Pan books: The Little White Bird; or, Adventures in Kensington Gardens, Scribner, 1902, reprinted, Milford House, 1973; Peter Pan; or, The Boy Who Would Not Grow Up (play; based on an extract from The Little White Bird; first produced in London at Duke of York's Theatre, December 27, 1904), Scribner, 1928 [later editions include those illustrated by Nora S. Unwin, Scribner, 1950; Richard Kennedy, Penguin, 1967; adaptations include those published as The Peter Pan Picture Book (adapted by Daniel O'Connor; illustrated by Alice B. Woodward), G. Bell, 1907; Peter Pan: The Story of the Play (adapted by Eleanor Graham; illustrated by Edward Ardizzone), Scribner, 1961; Walt Disney's Peter Pan and Captain Hook (adapted by Mary Carey from the Disney motion picture), Random House, 1972]; Peter Pan in Kensington Gardens (illustrated by Arthur Rackham), Scribner, 1906, reprinted, Weathervane Books, 1975 [later adaptations include J. M. Barrie's Peter Pan in Kensington Gardens (retold by May Byron; illustrated by Arthur Rackham), Hodder & Stoughton, 1929, Scribner, 1930]; Peter and Wendy (narrative version of the play Peter Pan; illustrated by F. D. Bedford), Scribner, 1911 [later editions include those published as Peter Pan and Wendy (illustrated by Mabel Lucie Attwell), Scribner, 1921; J. M. Barrie's Peter Pan and Wendy (retold by May Byron; illustrated by M. L. Attwell), Scribner, 1926; The Blampied Edition of Peter Pan (illustrated by Edmund Blampied), Scribner, 1940, reissued as Peter Pan: The Original Text of Peter and Wendy, 1967; Peter Pan (edited by Josette Frank; illustrated by Marjorie Torrey), Random House, 1957]; "Peter Pan: An Afterthought, or When Wendy Grew Up" (play; first produced in London, 1908), later published as When Wendy Grew Up: An Afterthought, Nelson (Edinburgh), 1957, Dutton, 1958.

Novels: Better Dead, privately printed, 1887, Sonnen-schein, Lowrey (London), 1888, reprinted as Auld Licht Idylls [and] Better Dead, Books for Libraries, 1970; When a Man's Single: A Tale of Literary Life, Harper, 1889; The Little Minister, Lovell, 1891, new edition, Airmont, 1968 [an earlier edition illustrated by William B. Hole, Cassell, 1893]; Two of Them, Lovell, Coryell, 1893; Sentimental Tommy: The Story of His Boyhood (illustrated by William Hatherell), Scribner, 1896; Tommy and Grizel (sequel to Sentimental Tommy), Cassell, 1900.

Short stories: Auld Licht Idylls, Hodder & Stoughton, 1888, reprinted as Auld Licht Idylls [and] Better Dead, Books for Libraries, 1970; An Edinburgh Eleven: Pen Portraits from College Life, Lovell, Coryell, 1888; A Window in Thrums, Hodder & Stoughton, 1889, reprinted, Scholarly Press, 1969; A Holiday in Bed, and Other Sketches, New York Publishing, 1892, reprinted, Books for Libraries, 1971; An Auld Licht Manse, and Other Sketches, Knox, 1893, reprinted, Books for Libraries, 1970; A Lady's Shoe [and] The Inconsiderate Waiter, Brentano's, 1893; A Tilly-loss Scandal, Lovell, Coryell, 1893, reprinted, Books for Libraries, 1969; Jess (an extract from A Window in Thrums), Estes, 1898; Farewell, Miss Julie Logan, Scribner, 1932, reissued, Hodder & Stoughton, 1970.

Plays—All first produced in London, except as noted: Caught Napping (one-act), [Nottingham, England], 1883; "Becky Sharp" (one-act; adaptation of Thackeray's conclusion to Vanity Fair), first produced at Terry's Theatre, 1891; (with H. B. Marriott Watson) Richard Savage (four-act; first produced at Criterion Theatre, April 16, 1891), published, 1891; Ibsen's Ghost; or, Toole up to Date (one-act; first produced at Toole's Theatre, May 30, 1891), published, 1939; Walker, London (three-act; first produced at Toole's Theatre, February 25, 1892), Samuel French, 1907; The Professor's Love Story (first produced in New York at Star Theatre, December 19, 1892; produced in London at Comedy Theatre, June 5, 1894), published, 1942; (with Arthur Conan Doyle) Jane Annie; or, The Good Conduct Prize (comic opera; music by Ernest Ford; first produced at Savoy Theatre, May 13, 1893), Chappell, 1893; The Little Minister (adapted by the author from his novel of the same title; first produced at Haymarket Theatre, November 6, 1897), published, 1942.

The Wedding Guest (four-act; first produced at Garrick Theatre, September 27, 1900), Scribner, 1900; Quality Street (four-act; first produced in Toledo, Ohio, 1901), Hodder & Stoughton (illustrated by Hugh Thomson), 1913; The Admirable Crichton (first produced at Duke of York's Theatre, November 4, 1902), Hodder & Stoughton (illustrated by Hugh Thomson), 1914, reissued, 1966; Little Mary (first produced at Wyndham's Theatre, September 24, 1903), published, 1942; Alice Sit-by-the-Fire (first produced at Duke of York's Theatre, April 5, 1905), Scribner, 1919; Pantaloon (one-act; first produced at Duke of York's Theatre, April 5, 1905), published in Half Hours, Scribner, 1914 [also see below]; "Josephine," first produced at Comedy Theatre, April 6, 1906; "Punch" (one-act), first produced at Comedy Theatre, April 6, 1906; What Every Woman Knows (first produced at Duke of York's Theatre, September 3, 1908), Hodder & Stoughton, 1918.

Old Friends (one-act; first produced at Duke of York's Theatre, March 1, 1910), published, 1928; The Twelve-Pound Look (one-act; first produced at Duke of York's Theatre, March 1, 1910), published in Half Hours, Scribner, 1914 [also see below]; "A Slice of Life" (one-act), first produced at Duke of York's Theatre, June 7, 1910; Rosalind (one-act; first produced at Duke of York's Theatre, October 14, 1912), published in Half Hours, Scribner, 1914 [also see below]; "The Adored One: A Legend of the Old Bailey," first produced at Duke of York's Theatre, September 4, 1913 (produced in America as "The Legend of Leonora"), revised as Seven Women (one-act; produced in

London at New Theatre, April 7, 1917), published, 1928; *The Will* (one-act; first produced at Duke of York's Theatre, September 4, 1913), published in *Half Hours*, Scribner, 1914 [also see below]; *Half an Hour* (one-act; first produced at the Hippodrome, September 29, 1913), published, 1928; "The Dramatists Get What They Want" (sketch; included in the revue "Hello Ragtime!," first produced, 1913); *Der Tag; or, The Tragic Man* (first produced at the Coliseum, December 21, 1914), Scribner, 1914.

The New Word (one-act; first produced at Duke of York's Theatre, December 11, 1915), published in *Echoes of the War*, Hodder & Stoughton, 1918 [also see below]; "The Fatal Typist," first produced, 1915; "Rosy Rapture, the Pride of the Beauty Chorus" (revue; music by Herman Darewski, Jerome Kern, and John Crook), first produced at Duke of York's Theatre, March 22, 1915; *A Kiss for Cinderella* (first produced at Wyndham's Theatre, March 16, 1916), Hodder & Stoughton, 1920, Scribner, 1921; "Shakespeare's Legacy," first produced, 1916; *The Old Lady Shows Her Medals* (one-act; first produced at New Theatre, April 7, 1917), published in *Echoes of the War*, Hodder & Stoughton, 1918 [also see below]; *Dear Brutus* (three-act; first produced at Wyndham's Theatre, October 17, 1917), Scribner, 1922, reissued, University of London Press, 1962; *A Well-Remembered Voice* (one-act; first produced at Wyndham's Theatre, June 28, 1918), published in *Echoes of the War*, Hodder & Stoughton, 1918 [also see below]; *Barbara's Wedding* (one-act; first produced at Savoy Theatre, August 23, 1927), published in *Echoes of the War*, Hodder & Stoughton, 1918 [also see below]; "La Politesse," first produced, 1918.

The Truth about the Russian Dancers (comic ballet; first produced at the Coliseum, March 16, 1920), Johnson Reprint, 1962; *Mary Rose* (three-act; first produced at Haymarket Theatre, April 22, 1920), Scribner, 1924, reissued, Hodder & Stoughton, 1956; "The Real Thing at Last," first produced, 1920; *Shall We Join the Ladies?* (first act of an unfinished play; first produced at the Royal Academy of Dramatic Art, December 19, 1921, Scribner, 1928; "The Two Shepherds," first produced, 1936; *The Boy David* (three-act; first produced at His Majesty's Theatre, December 14, 1936), Scribner, 1938.

Half Hours, Scribner, 1914 (contains *Pantaloon, The Twelve-Pound Look, Rosalind,* and *The Will*); *Echoes of the War*, Hodder & Stoughton, 1918 (contains *The Old Lady Shows Her Medals, The New Word, Barbara's Wedding,* and *A Well-Remembered Voice*).

Nonfiction: *My Lady Nicotine: A Study in Smoke,* Rand McNally, 1891; *Margaret Ogilvy* (biography of the author's mother), Scribner, 1896, reprinted, Scholarly Press, 1969; *George Meredith, 1909,* Constable, 1909, reprinted, Folcroft, 1974; *Courage: The Rectorial Address Delivered at St. Andrews University,* Scribner, 1922, reissued, Hodder & Stoughton, 1960; *The Entrancing Life: The Address Delivered on Installation as Chancellor of Edinburgh University,* Scribner, 1930; *The Greenwood Hat* (autobiography), privately printed, 1930, P. Davies, 1937, Scribner, 1938; *M'Connachie and J. M. B.: Speeches by J. M. Barrie* (preface by Hugh Walpole), P. Davies, 1938, Scribner, 1939, reprinted, Books for Libraries, 1971.

J. M. Barrie

Also author of *Scotland's Lament: A Poem on the Death of Robert Louis Stevenson, December 3, 1894,* privately printed, 1895.

Collections: *The Novels, Tales, and Sketches of J. M. Barrie,* twelve volumes, Scribner, 1896-1911; *The Works of J. M. Barrie,* Peter Pan Edition, eighteen volumes (definitive edition), Scribner, 1929-41, reprinted, AMS Press, 1975; *The Plays of J. M. Barrie* (edited by A. E. Wilson; definitive edition), Scribner, 1928, revised edition, 1942; *The Letters of J. M. Barrie* (edited by Viola Meynell), P. Davies, 1942, Scribner, 1947.

ADAPTATIONS—Movies and filmstrips: "The Story of the Little Minister" (motion picture), Vitagraph Co. of America, 1912; "The Little Minister" (motion pictures),

(From the stage production of "Peter Pan," which opened on November 6, 1905, starring Maude Adams.)

Vitagraph Co. of America, 1921, starring Katherine Hepburn, RKO Radio Pictures, 1934; "Male and Female" (motion picture), adaptation of *The Admirable Crichton,* Famous Players-Lasky Corp., 1919; "Half an Hour" (motion picture), Famous Players-Lasky Corp., 1920; "The Doctor's Secret" (motion picture), adaptation of *Half an Hour,* Paramount Famous-Players Lasky Corp., 1929; "Sentimental Tommy" (motion picture), Famous Players-Lasky Corp., 1921; "What Every Woman Knows" (motion pictures), Famous Players-Lasky Corp., 1921, Metro-Goldwyn-Mayer, 1934.

"Peter Pan" (motion pictures), Famous Players-Lasky Corp., 1924, Walt Disney Productions, 1952; "Peter Pan" (filmstrips), Encyclopaedia Britannica Films, 1958, Coronet Instructional Films, 1969, Walt Disney Educational Materials, 1973; "A Kiss for Cinderella" (motion picture), Famous Players-Lasky Corp., 1926; "Quality Street" (motion pictures), Metro-Goldwyn-Mayer, 1926, RKO Radio Pictures, starring Katherine Hepburn and Franchot Tone, 1937; "Seven Days Leave" (motion picture), adaptation of *The Old Lady Shows Her Medals,* Paramount Famous Lasky Corp., 1930; "The Courting of Bell" (motion picture), General Television Enterprises, 1949; "Darling, How Could You!" (motion picture), adaptation of *Alice Sit-by-the-Fire,* Paramount Pictures, 1951; "Forever Female" (motion picture), adaptation of *Rosalind,* starring Ginger Rogers and William Holden, Paramount Pictures, 1953; "The Admirable Crichton" (motion picture), Britain, 1957, released in the United States under title "Paradise Lagoon," Columbia, 1958.

Recordings: "The Story of Peter Pan," adapted by Marianne Mantell, music by Dick Hyman, told by Glynis Johns, Caedmon, 1972.

Television: "The Old Lady Shows Her Medals," starring Gracie Fields; "Peter Pan," starring Mary Martin, NBC, 1955, starring Mia Farrow, NBC, 1977.

SIDELIGHTS: **May 9, 1860.** Born in Kirriemuir, Scotland. The most important remembrance of his first six years was his mother: "When you looked into my mother's eyes you knew, as if He had told you, why God sent her into the world—it was to open the minds of all who looked to beautiful thoughts. And that is the beginning and end of literature. Those eyes . . . have guided me through life, and I pray God they may remain my only earthly judge to the last. They were never more my guide than when I helped to put her to earth, not whimpering because my mother had been taken away after seventy-six glorious years of life, but exulting in her even at the grave.

"She told me everything, and so my memories of our little red town are coloured by her memories. I knew it as it had been for generations, and suddenly I saw it change, and the transformation could not fail to strike a boy, for these first years are the most impressionable (nothing that happens after we are twelve matters very much); they are also the most vivid years when we look back, and more vivid the farther we have to look, until, at the end, what lies between bends like a hoop, and the extremes meet. . . .

"We read many books together when I was a boy, *Robinson Crusoe* being the first (and the second), and the *Arabian Nights* should have been the next, for we got it out of the library (a penny for three days), but on discovering that they were 'nights' when we had paid for 'knights' we sent that volume packing, and I have curled my lips at it ever since. *The Pilgrim's Progress* we had in the house (it was as common a possession as a dresserhead), and so enamoured of it was I that I turned our garden into sloughs of Despond, with pea-sticks to represent Christian on his travels and a buffet-stool for his burden, but when I dragged my mother out to see my handiwork she was scared, and I felt for days, with a certain elation, that I had been a dark character.

"Besides reading every book we could hire or borrow I also bought one now and again, and while buying (it was the occupation of weeks) I read, standing at the counter, most of the other books in the shop, which is perhaps the most exquisite way of reading. And I took in a magazine called *Sunshine,* the most delicious periodical, I am sure, of any day. It cost a halfpenny or a penny a month, and always, as I fondly remember, had a continued tale about the dearest girl, who sold water-cress, which is a dainty not grown and I suppose never seen in my native town. This romantic little creature took such hold of my imagination that I cannot eat water-cress even now without emotion. I lay in bed wondering what she would be up to in the next number; I have lost trout because when they nibbled my mind was wandering with her; my early life was embittered by her not arriving regularly on the first of the month.

"I know not whether it was owing to her loitering on the way one month to an extent flesh and blood could not bear, or because we had exhausted the penny library, but on a

He was never more sinister than when he was most polite, which is probably the truest test of breeding. ■ (From the movie, "Peter Pan," copyright Walt Disney Productions.)

day I conceived a glorious idea, or it was put into my head by my mother, then desirous of making progress with her new clouty hearth-rug. The notion was nothing short of this, why should I not write the tales myself? I did write them—in the garret—but they by no means helped her to get on with her work, for when I finished a chapter I bounded downstairs to read it to her, and so short were the chapters, so ready was the pen, that I was back with new manuscript before another clout had been added to the rug. Authorship seemed, like her bannock-baking, to consist of running between two points. They were all tales of adventure (Happiest is he who writes of adventure), no characters were allowed within if I knew their like in the flesh, the scene lay in unknown parts, desert islands, enchanted gardens, with 'knights' (none of your 'nights') on black chargers, and round the first corner a lady selling water-cress." [James M. Barrie, *Margaret Ogilvy,* Scribner, 1940.[1]]

1867. His older brother, David, fractured his skull while away at school ice skating and died hours afterward. "I remember very little about him, only that he was a merry-faced boy who ran like a squirrel up a tree and shook the cherries into my lap. When he was thirteen and I was half his age the terrible news came, and I have been told the face of my mother was awful in its calmness as she set off to get between Death and her boy. We trooped with her down the brae to the wooden station, and I think I was envying her the journey in the mysterious waggons; I know we played around her, proud of our right to be there, but I do not recall it, I only speak from hearsay. Her ticket was taken, she had bidden us good-bye with that fighting face which I cannot see, and then my father came out of the telegraph-office and said huskily 'He's gone!' Then we turned very quietly and went home again up the little brae. But I speak from hearsay no longer; I knew my mother for ever now.

"That is how she got her soft face and her pathetic ways and her large charity, and why other mothers ran to her when they had lost a child. 'Dinna greet, poor Janet,' she would say to them, and they would answer, 'Ah, Margaret, but you're greeting yoursel.' Margaret Ogilvy had been her maiden name, and after the Scotch custom she was still Margaret Ogilvy to her old friends. Margaret Ogilvy I loved to name her. Often when I was a boy, 'Margaret Ogilvy, are you there?' I would call up the stair. She was always delicate from that hour, and for many months she was very ill.[1]

"[My] sister . . . came to me with a very anxious face and wringing her hands, and she told me to go ben to my mother and say to her that she still had another boy. I went ben excitedly, but the room was dark, and when I heard the door shut and no sound came from the bed I was afraid, and I stood still. I suppose I was breathing hard, or perhaps I was crying, for after a time I heard a listless voice that had never been listless before say, 'Is that you?' I think the tone hurt me, for I made no answer, and then the voice said more anxiously 'Is that you?' again. I thought it was the dead boy she was speaking to, and I said in a little lonely voice, 'No, it's no' him, it's just me.' Then I heard a cry, and my mother turned in bed, and though it was dark I knew that she was holding out her arms.

"I sat a great deal on her bed trying to make her forget him, which was my crafty way of playing physician." [Janet Dunbar, *J. M. Barrie: The Man Behind the Image*, Houghton, 1970.[2]]

1868. Attended Glasgow Academy for one year.

(Mia Farrow in the NBC television production of "Peter Pan," 1976.)

1869-1872. Attended Forfar Academy. "At twelve or thereabout I put the literary calling to bed for a time, having gone to a school where cricket and football were more esteemed, but during the year before I went to the university, it woke up and I wrote great part of a three-volume novel. The publisher replied that the sum for which he would print it was a hundred and—however, that was not the important point (I had sixpence): where he stabbed us both was in writing that he considered me a 'clever lady.' I replied stiffly that I was a gentleman, and since then I have kept that manuscript concealed. I looked through it lately, and, oh, but it is dull. I defy any one to read it."[1]

October 30, 1878. Entered University of Edinburgh. "I knew three under-graduates who lodged together in a dreary house at the top of a dreary street; two of them used to study until two in the morning, while the third slept. When they shut up their books they woke number three, who arose, dressed, and studied until breakfast time. Among the many advantages of this arrangement the chief was that, as they were dreadfully poor, one bed did for the three. Two of them occupied it at the one time, and the third at another. Terrible privations? Frightful destitution? Not a bit of it. The Millenium was in those days. If life was at the top of a hundred steps, if students occasionally died of hunger and·hard work combined, if the midnight oil only burned to show a ghastly face 'weary and worn,' if lodgings were cheap and dirty, and dinners few and far between, life was still real and earnest; in many cases it did not turn out an empty dream."[2]

Barrie was concerned over his lack of stature, he was not much over five feet. Young ladies, he was convinced, never looked at short men. "I was in the Scotch express on my way to London and I think it was at Carlisle that five of them boarded my compartment, all husband-high. When their packages had been disposed of and they were comfortably settled in their seats they turned their eyes on me and gave their verdict in the deaf-and-dumb alphabet, which unfortunately I understood. It spelt out the words 'Quite harmless' and they then disregarded me for the rest of the journey. They talked quite openly of the most intimate things as if I were far away in the guard's van. It is a treatment I am used to, but never perhaps have I been so blotted out, I who know that with another face I could be quite harmful. . . .

"They were right, those ladies in the train; 'quite harmless' summed [me] up, however [I] may have writhed. I am not speaking of how [I] appealed to men, but about how [I] did not appeal to women. Observe [me] in that compartment. Though insignificant [I am] not ugly. To be ugly, if you are sufficiently ugly, is said to attract the wayward creatures. If you could dig deep enough into [me] you would find first [my] Rothchildian ambition, which is to earn a pound a day; beneath that is a desire to reach some little niche in literature; but in the marrow you find [me] vainly weltering to be a favourite of the ladies. All the other cravings [I] would toss aside for that; [I am] only striving hard for numbers one and two, because [I] know with an everlasting sinking that number three can never be for [me]."[2]

1882. Earned M.A. "From the day on which I first tasted blood in the garret my mind was made up; there could be no hum-dreadful-drum profession for me; literature was my game. It was not highly thought of by those who wished me

(In 1955, NBC's special telecast of "Peter Pan," starring Mary Martin, attracted 65,000,000 viewers—the largest audience to that date for any television program.)

well. I remember being asked by two maiden ladies, about the time I left the university, what I was to be, and when I replied brazenly, 'An author,' they flung up their hands, and one exclaimed reproachfully, 'And you an M.A.!' My mother's views at first were not dissimilar; for long she took mine jestingly as something I would grow out of, and afterwards they hurt her so that I tried to give them up. To be a minister—that she thought was among the fairest prospects, but she was a very ambitious woman, and sometimes she would add, half scared at her appetite, that there were ministers who had become professors, 'but it was not canny to think of such things.'[1]

"While I was away at college she drained all available libraries for books about those who go to London to live by the pen, and they all told the same shuddering tale. London, which she never saw, was to her a monster that licked up country youths as they stepped from the train; there were the garrets in which they sat abject, and the park seats where they passed the night. Those park seats were the monster's glaring eyes to her, and as I go by them now she is nearer to me than when I am in any other part of London. I daresay that when night comes, this Hyde Park which is so gay by day, is haunted by the ghosts of many mothers, who run, wild-eyed, from seat to seat, looking for their sons.

"But if we could dodge those dreary seats she longed to see

(The musical production of "Peter Pan" starring Veronica Lake opened at the Lyric Theater, Baltimore, Md., October 10, 1951. Music and lyrics by Leonard Bernstein.)

me try my luck, and I sought to exclude them from the picture by drawing maps of London with Hyde Park left out. London was as strange to me as to her, but long before I was shot upon it I knew it by maps, and drew them more accurately than I could draw them now."[1]

1883-1884. First job was as leader-writer for the Nottingham *Journal*. Wrote a column under the pseudonym of "Hippomenes." "Leaders! How were they written? what were they about? My mother was already sitting triumphant among my socks, and I durst not let her see me quaking. I retired to ponder, and presently she came to me with the daily paper. Which were the leaders? she wanted to know, so evidently I could get no help from her. Had she any more newspapers? I asked, and after rummaging, she produced a few with which her boxes had been lined. Others, very dusty, came from beneath carpets, and lastly a sooty bundle was dragged down the chimney. Surrounded by these I sat down, and studied how to become a journalist.

"A devout lady, to whom some friend had presented one of my books, used to say when asked how she was getting on with it, 'Sal, it's dreary, weary, uphill work, but I've wrastled through with tougher jobs in my time, and, please God, I'll wrastle through with this one.' It was in this spirit I fear, though she never told me so, that my mother wrestled for the next year or more with my leaders, and indeed I was always genuinely sorry for the people I saw reading them."[1]

"In my spare hours I was trying journalism of another kind and sending it to London, but nearly eighteen months elapsed before there came to me, as unlooked for as a telegram, the thought that there was something quaint about my native place. A boy who found that a knife had been put into his pocket in the night could not have been more surprised. A few days afterwards I sent my mother a London evening paper with an article entitled 'An Auld Licht Community,' and they told me that when she saw the heading she laughed, because there was something droll to her in the sight of the words Auld Licht in print. For her, as for me, that newspaper was soon to have the face of a friend. To this day I never pass its placards in the street without shaking it by the hand, and she used to sew its pages together as lovingly as though it were a child's frock; but let the truth be told, when she read that first article she became alarmed, and fearing the talk of the town, hid the paper from all eyes. For some time afterwards, while I proudly pictured her showing this and similar articles to all who felt an interest in me, she was really concealing them fearfully in a bandbox on the garret stair. And she wanted to know by return of post whether I was paid for these articles just as I was paid for read articles; when she heard that I was paid better, she laughed again and had them out of the bandbox for re-reading, and it cannot be denied that she thought the London editor a fine fellow but slightly soft."[1]

1885. "I wrote and asked the editor if I should come to London, and he said No, so I went, laden with charges from my mother to walk in the middle of the street (they jump out on you as you are turning a corner), never to venture forth after sunset, and always to lock up everything. (I who could never lock up anything, except my heart in company.) Thanks to this editor, for the others would have nothing to say to me though I battered on all

[Peter Pan] passed under the bridge and came within full sight of the delectable gardens. ■ (From *Peter Pan in Kensington Gardens* by J. M. Barrie. Illustrated by Arthur Rackham.)

their doors, she was soon able to sleep at nights without the dread that I should be waking presently with the iron-work of certain seats figured on my person, and what relieved her very much was that I had begun to write as if Auld Lichts were not the only people I knew of.''[1]

1886. First book published, *Better Dead*. Chronic headaches start.

1890's. Began long and rewarding correspondence with Robert Louis Stevenson. "R.L.S. These familiar initials are, I suppose, the best beloved in recent literature, certainly they are the sweetest to me, but there was a time when my mother could not abide them. She said 'That Stevenson man' with a sneer, and it was never easy to her to sneer. At thought of him her face would become almost hard, which seems incredible, and she would knit her lips and fold her arms, and reply with a stiff 'oh' if you mentioned his aggravating name. In the novels we have a way of writing of our heroine, 'she drew herself up haughtily,' and when mine draw themselves up haughtily I see my mother thinking of Robert Louis Stevenson. He knew her opinion of him, and would write, 'My ears tingled yesterday; I sair doubt she has been miscalling me again.' But the more she miscalled him the more he delighted in her, and she was informed of this, and at once said 'The scoundrel!' If you would know what was his unpardonable crime, it was this, he wrote better books than mine.

"I remember the day she found it out, which was not, however, the day she admitted it. That day, when I should have been at my work, she came upon me in the kitchen, *The Master of Ballantrae* beside me, but I was not reading: my head lay heavy on the table and to her anxious eyes, I doubt not, I was the picture of woe. 'Not writing!' I echoed, no, I was not writing, I saw no use in ever trying to write again. And down, I suppose, went my head once more. She misunderstood, and thought the blow had fallen; I had awakened to the discovery, always dreaded by her, that I had written myself dry; I was no better than an empty ink-bottle. She wrung her hands, but indignation came to her with my explanation, which was that while R.L.S. was at it we others were only 'prentices cutting our fingers on his tools. 'I could never thole his books,' said my mother immediately, and indeed vindictively.

"'You have not read any of them' I reminded her.

"'And never will,' said she with spirit.

"And I have no doubt that she called him a dark character that very day. For weeks too, if not for months, she adhered to her determination not to read him, though I, having come to my senses and seen that there is a place for the 'prentice, was taking a pleasure, almost malicious, in putting *The Master of Ballantrae* in her way. I would place it on her table so that it said good-morning to her when she

(From the stage production of "Peter Pan" at the Civic Repertory Theatre in 1928, starring Eva LeGallienne.)

rose. She would frown, and carrying it downstairs, as if she had it in the tongs, replace it on its book-shelf. I would wrap it up in the cover she had made for the latest Carlyle: she would skin it contemptuously and again bring it down. I would hide her spectacles in it, and lay it on top of the clothes-basket and prop it up invitingly open against her tea-pot.

"And at last I got her, though I forget by which of many contrivances. What I recall vividly is a key-hole view, to which another member of the family invited me. Then I saw my mother wrapped up in *The Master of Ballantrae* and muttering the music to herself, nodding her head in approval, and taking a stealthy glance at the foot of each page before she began at the top. Nevertheless she had an ear for the door, for when I bounced in she had been too clever for me; there was no book to be seen, only an apron on her lap and she was gazing out at the window. Some such conversation as this followed:

"'You have been sitting very quietly, mother.'

"'I always sit quietly, I never do anything, I'm just a finished stocking.'

"'Have you been reading?'

"'Do I ever read at this time of day?'

"'What is that in your lap?'

"'Just my apron.'

"'Is that a book beneath the apron?'

"'It might be a book.'

"'Let me see.'

"'Go away with you to your work.'

"But I lifted the apron. 'Why it's *The Master of Ballantrae!*' I exclaimed, shocked.

"'So it is!' said my mother, equally surprised. But I looked sternly at her, and perhaps she blushed.

"'Well what do you think: not nearly equal to mine?' said I with humour.

"'Nothing like them,' she said determinedly.

"'Not a bit,' said I, though whether with a smile or a groan is immaterial; they would have meant the same thing. Should I put the book back on its shelf? I asked, and she replied that I could put it wherever I liked for all she cared, so long as I took it out of her sight (the implication was that it had stolen on to her lap while she was looking out at the window). My behaviour may seem small, but I gave her a last chance, for I said that some people found it a book there was no putting down until they reached the last page.

"'I'm no that kind,' replied my mother.

"Nevertheless our old game with the haver of a thing, as she called it, was continued, with this difference, that it was now she who carried the book covertly upstairs, and I who replaced it on the shelf, and several times we caught each other in the act, but not a word said either of us."[1]

1891. *The Little Minister* published. First play, "Walker, London," produced.

July 9, 1894. Married Mary Ansell, an actress.

September 1, 1894. His sister, Jane Ann, died. His mother died three days later. "In those last weeks, though we did not know it, my sister was dying on her feet. For many years she had been giving her life, a little bit at a time, for another year, another month, latterly for another day, of her mother, and now she was worn out. 'I'll never leave you, mother,'—'Fine I know you'll never leave me.' I thought that cry so pathetic at the time, but I was not to know its full significance until it was only the echo of a cry. Looking at these two then it was to me as if my mother had set out for the new country, and my sister held her back. But I see with a clearer vision now. It is no longer the mother but the daughter who is in front, and she cries, 'Mother, you are lingering so long at the end, I have ill waiting for you.'

"But she knew no more than we how it was to be; if she seemed weary when we met her on the stair, she was still the brightest, the most active figure in my mother's room; she never complained, save when she had to depart on that walk which separated them for half an hour. How reluctantly she put on her bonnet, how we had to press her to it, and how often, having gone as far as the door, she came back to stand by my mother's side. Sometimes as we watched from the window, I could not but laugh, and yet with a pain at my heart, to see her hasting doggedly onward, not an eye for right or left, nothing in her head but the return. There was always my father in the house, than whom never was a more devoted husband, and often there were others, one daughter in particular, but they scarce dared tend my mother—this one snatched the cup jealously from their hands. My mother liked it best from her. We all knew this. 'I like them fine, but I canna do without you.' My sister, so unselfish in all other things, had an unwearying passion for parading it before us. It was the rich reward of her life.

"The others spoke among themselves of what must come soon, and they had tears to help them, but this daughter would not speak of it, and her tears were ever slow to come. I knew that night and day she was trying to get ready for a world without her mother in it, but she must remain dumb, none of us was so Scotch as she, she must bear her agony alone, a tragic solitary Scotchwoman. Even my mother, who spoke so calmly to us of the coming time, could not mention it to her. These two, the one in bed, and the other bending over her, could only look long at each other, until slowly the tears came to my sister's eyes, and then my mother would turn away her wet face. And still neither said a word, each knew so well what was in the other's thoughts, so eloquently they spoke in silence, 'Mother, I am loath to let you go,' and 'Oh, my daughter, now that my time is near, I wish you werena quite so fond of me.' But when the daughter had slipped away my mother would grip my hand and cry, 'I leave her to you; you see how she has sown it will depend on you how she is to reap.' And I made promises, but I suppose neither of us saw that she had already reaped.

"In the night my mother might waken and sit up in bed, confused by what she saw. While she slept, six decades or more had rolled back and she was again in her girlhood; suddenly recalled from it she was dizzy, as with the rush of the years. How had she come into this room? When she went to bed last night, after preparing her father's supper, there had been a dresser at the window: what had become of the salt-bucket, the meal-tub, the hams that should be hanging from the rafters? There were no rafters; it was a papered ceiling. She had often heard of open beds, but how came she to be lying in one? To fathom these things she would try to spring out of bed and be startled to find it a labour, as if she had been taken ill in the night. Hearing her move I might knock on the wall that separated us, this being a sign, prearranged between us, that I was near by, and so all was well, but sometimes the knocking seemed to belong to the past, and she would cry, 'That is my father chapping at the door, I maun rise and let him in.' . . . Then I would hear—it was a common experience of the night—my sister soothing her lovingly, and turning up the light to show her where she was, helping her to the window to let her see that it was no night of snow, even humouring her by going downstairs, and opening the outer door, and calling into the darkness, 'Is anybody there?' and if that was not sufficient, she would swaddle my mother in wraps and take her through the rooms of the house, lighting them

For long the two enemies looked at one another; Hook shuddering slightly, and Peter with the strange smile upon his face. ■ (From *Peter Pan* by J. M. Barrie. Illustrated by Richard Kennedy.)

one by one, pointing out familiar objects, and so guiding her slowly through the sixty odd years she had jumped too quickly. And perhaps the end of it was that my mother came to my bedside and said wistfully, 'Am I an auld woman?'

"But with daylight, even during the last week in which I saw her, she would be up and doing, for though pitifully frail she no longer suffered from any ailment. She seemed so well comparatively that I, having still the remnants of an illness to shake off, was to take a holiday in Switzerland, and then return for her, when we were all to go to the much-loved manse of her much-loved brother in the west country. So she had many preparations on her mind, and the morning was the time when she had any strength to carry them out. To leave her house had always been a month's work for her, it must be left in such perfect order, every corner visited and cleaned out, every chest probed to the bottom, the linen lifted out, examined and put back lovingly as if to make it lie more easily in her absence, shelves had to be re-papered, a strenuous week devoted to the garret. Less exhaustively, but with much of the old exultation in her house, this was done for the last time, and then there was the bringing out of her own clothes, and the spreading of them upon the bed and the pleased fingering of them, and the consultations about which should be left behind. Ah, beautiful dream! I clung to it every morning; I would not look when my sister shook her head at it, but long before each day was done, I too knew that it could never be. It had come true many times, but never again. We two knew it, but when my mother, who must always be prepared so long beforehand, called for her trunk and band-boxes we brought them to her, and we stood silent, watching, while she packed.

J. M. Barrie, at the time of his marriage.

"The morning came when I was to go away. It had come a hundred times, when I was a boy, when I was an undergraduate, when I was a man, when she had seemed big and strong to me, when she was grown so little and it was I who put my arms round her. But always it was the same scene. I am not to write about it, of the parting and the turning back on the stair, and two people trying to smile, and the setting off again, and the cry that brought me back. Nor shall I say more of the silent figure in the background, always in the background, always near my mother. The last I saw of these two was from the gate. They were at the window which never passes from my eyes. I could not see my dear sister's face, for she was bending over my mother, pointing me out to her, and telling her to wave her hand and smile, because I liked it so. That action was an epitome of my sister's life.

"I had been gone a fortnight when the telegram was put into my hands. I had got a letter from my sister, a few hours before, saying that all was well at home. The telegram said in five words that she had died suddenly the previous night. There was no mention of my mother, and I was three days' journey from home.

"The news I got on reaching London was this: my mother did not understand that her daughter was dead, and they were waiting for me to tell her.

"I need not have been such a coward. This is how these two died—for, after all, I was too late by twelve hours to see my mother alive.

"Their last night was almost gleeful. In the old days that hour before my mother's gas was lowered had so often been the happiest that my pen steals back to it again and again as I write: it was the time when my mother lay smiling in bed and we were gathered round her like children at play, our reticence scattered on the floor or tossed in sport from hand to hand, the author became so boisterous that in the pauses they were holding him in check by force. Rather woeful had been some attempts latterly to renew those evenings, when my mother might be brought to the verge of them, as if some familiar echo called her, but where she was she did not clearly know, because the past was roaring in her ears like a great sea.

"But this night was the last gift to my sister. The joyousness of their voices drew the others in the house upstairs, where for more than an hour my mother was the centre of a merry party and so clear of mental eye that they, who were at first cautious, abandoned themselves to the sport, and whatever they said, by way of humourous rally, she instantly capped as of old, turning their darts against themselves until in self-defence they were three to one, and the three hard pressed. How my sister must have been rejoicing. Once again she could cry, 'Was there ever such a woman!' They tell me that such a happiness was on the daughter's face that my mother commented on it, that having risen to go they sat down again, fascinated by the radiance of these two. And when eventually they went, the last words they heard were, 'They are gone, you see, mother, but I am here, I will never leave you,' and 'Na, you winna leave me; fine I know that.' For some time afterwards their voices could be heard from downstairs, but what they talked of is not known. And then came silence.

"Had I been at home I should have been in the room again

several times, turning the handle of the door softly, releasing it so that it did not creak, and standing looking at them. It had been so a thousand times. But that night, would I have slipped out again, mind at rest, or should I have seen the change coming while they slept?

"Let it be told in the fewest words. My sister awoke next morning with a headache. She had always been a martyr to headaches, but this one, like many another, seemed to be unusually severe. Nevertheless she rose and lit my mother's fire and brought up her breakfast, and then had to return to bed. She was not able to write her daily letter to me, saying how my mother was, and almost the last thing she did was to ask my father to write it, and not to let on that she was ill as it would distress me.

"The doctor was called, but she rapidly became unconscious. In this state she was removed from my mother's bed to another. It was discovered that she was suffering from an internal disease. No one had guessed it. She herself never knew. Nothing could be done. In this unconsciousness she passed away, without knowing that she was leaving her mother.

"When I reached London I did hear how my sister died, but still I was afraid. I saw myself in my mother's room telling her why the door of the next room was locked, and I was afraid. God had done so much, and yet I could not look confidently to Him for the little that was left to do. 'O ye of little faith.' These are the words I seem to hear my mother saying to me now, and she looks at me so sorrowfully.

"He did it very easily, and it has ceased to seem marvellous to me because it was so plainly His doing. My timid mother saw the one who was never to leave her carried unconscious from the room, and she did not break down. She who used to wring her hands if her daughter was gone for a moment never asked for her again, they were afraid to mention her name; an awe fell upon them. But I am sure they need not have been so anxious. There are mysteries in life and death, but this was not one of them. A child can understand what happened. God said that my sister must come first, but He put His hand on my mother's eyes at that moment and she was altered.

"They told her that I was on my way home, and she said with a confident smile, 'He will come as quick as trains can bring him.' That is my reward, that is what I have got for my books. Everything I could do for her in this life I have done since I was a boy; I look back through the years and I cannot see the smallest thing left undone.

"They were buried together on my mother's seventy-sixth birthday, though there had been three days between their deaths. On the last day, my mother insisted on rising from bed and going through the house. The arms that had so often helped her on that journey were now cold in death,

. . . they drew near the Neverland; for after many moons they did reach it, and, what is more, they had been going pretty straight all the time, not perhaps so much owing to the guidance of Peter or Tink as because the island was out looking for them. It is only thus that any one may sight those magic shores. ■ (From *Peter Pan* by J. M. Barrie. Illustrated by Nora S. Unwin.)

(From the movie "The Little Minister," copyright 1934, RKO Radio Pictures. Starring Katherine Hepburn.)

but there were others only less loving, and she went slowly from room to room like one bidding good-bye. . . . All this time there seemed to be something that she wanted, but the one was dead who always knew what she wanted, and they produced many things at which she shook her head.

"They did not know then that she was dying, but they followed her through the house in some apprehension, and after she returned to bed they saw that she was becoming very weak. Once she said eagerly, 'Is that you, David?' and again she thought she heard her father knocking the snow off his boots. Her desire for that which she could not name came back to her, and at last they saw that what she wanted was the old christening robe. It was brought to her, and she unfolded it with trembling, exultant hands, and when she had made sure that it was still of virgin fairness her old arms went round it adoringly, and upon her face

there was the ineffable mysterious glow of motherhood. Suddenly she said, 'Who's bairn's dead? is a bairn of mine dead?' but those watching dared not speak, and then slowly as if with an effort of memory she repeated our names aloud in the order in which we were born. Only one, who should have come third among the ten, did she omit, the one in the next room, but at the end, after a pause, she said her name and repeated it again and again and again, lingering over it as if it were the most exquisite music and this her dying song. And yet it was a very commonplace name.

"They knew now that she was dying. She told them to fold up the christening robe and almost sharply she watched them put it away, and then for some time she talked of the long lovely life that had been hers, and of Him to whom she owed it. She said good-bye to them all, and at last turned her face to the side where her best-beloved had lain, and for over an hour she prayed. They only caught the words now and again, and the last they heard were 'God' and 'love.' I think God was smiling when He took her to Him, as He had so often smiled at her during those seventy-six years.

"I saw her lying dead, and her face was beautiful and serene. But it was the other room I entered first, and it was by my sister's side that I fell upon my knees. The rounded completeness of a woman's life that was my mother's had not been for her. She would not have it at the price. 'I'll never leave you, mother.'—'Fine I know you'll never leave me.' The fierce joy of loving too much, it is a terrible thing. My sister's mouth was firmly closed, as if she had got her way.

"And now I am left without them, but I trust my memory will ever go back to those happy days, not to rush through them, but dallying here and there, even as my mother wanders through my books. And if I also live to a time when age must dim my mind and the past comes sweeping back like the shades of night over the bare road of the present it will not, I believe, be my youth I shall see but hers, not a boy clinging to his mother's skirt and crying, 'Wait till I'm a man, and you'll lie on feathers,' but a little girl in a magenta frock and a white pinafore, who comes toward me through the long parks, singing to herself, and carrying her father's dinner in a flaggon.''[1]

1896. Sailed from Liverpool on the "Campania" to New York.

1897. Play, "The Little Minister," opened in New York with Maude Adams. Returned to London and met the Llewelyn Davies and their five sons, George, Jack, Peter, Michael and Nicholas. Barrie considered them "my boys" and they later became the basis for "Peter Pan."

1898. Honorary degree from St. Andrew's University.

1902. Wrote "The Little White Bird," forerunner of "Peter Pan."

1909. Offered knighthood but declined.

October 13, 1909. Divorced.

1913. Was made baronet: Sir James M. Barrie.

March 15, 1915. George Llewelyn Davies killed in trenches of France during World War I. Barrie was disconsolate.

April, 1920. The play, "Mary Rose," opened at the Haymarket.

June 19, 1937. Died. "A Scotch family are probably better acquainted with each other, and more ignorant of the life outside their circle, than any other family in the world. And as knowledge is sympathy, the affection existing between them is almost painful in its intensity; they have not more to give than their neighbours, but it is bestowed upon a few instead of being distributed among many; they are reputed niggardly, but for family affection at least they pay in gold. In this, I believe, we shall find the true explanation why Scotch literature, since long before the days of Burns, has been so often inspired by the domestic hearth and has treated it with a passionate understanding.''[1]

FOR MORE INFORMATION SEE: John A. Hammerton, *J. M. Barrie and His Books,* H. Marshall, 1900, reprinted, Haskell House, 1974; Henry Mackinnon Walbrook, *J. M. Barrie and the Theatre,* F. V. White, 1922, reprinted, Kennikat Press, 1969; Patrick Braybrooke, *J. M. Barrie: A Study in Fairies and Mortals,* Lippincott, 1925, reprinted, Haskell House, 1972; Thomas Moult, *Barrie,* Scribner, 1928, reprinted, R. West, 1973; Frederick J. H. Darton, *J. M. Barrie,* Nisbet, 1929, reprinted, Haskell House, 1974; J. A. Hammerton, *Barrie: The Story of a Genius,* Sampson, Low, 1929; John Kennedy, *Thrums and the Barrie Country,* Heath, Cranton, 1930; Bradley D. Cutler, *Sir James Barrie: A Bibliography with Full Collations of the American Unauthorized Editions,* Greenberg, 1931, reprinted, B. Franklin, 1967; James A. Roy, *James Matthew Barrie: An Appreciation,* Jarrolds, 1937, Scribner, 1938; Patrick R. Chalmers, *The Barrie Inspiration,* P. Davies, 1938; William A. Darlington, *J. M. Barrie,* Blackie, 1938, reprinted, Haskell House, 1974.

Denis Mackail, *Barrie: The Story of J.M.B.* (authorized biography), Scribner, 1941, reprinted, Books for Libraries, 1972; George Blake, *Barrie and the Kailyard School,* Roy, 1951; Roger L. Green, *Fifty Years of Peter Pan,* P. Davies, 1954; Cynthia Asquith, *Portrait of Barrie,* Dutton, 1955, reprinted, Greenwood Press, 1972; Janet Dunbar, *J. M. Barrie: The Man behind the Image,* Houghton, 1970; Harry M. Geduld, *James Barrie,* Twayne, 1971.

For children: Elizabeth R. Montgomery, *Story behind Great Books,* McBride, 1946; R. L. Green, *J. M. Barrie,* Walck, 1961; Michael Elder, *The Young James Barrie* (illustrated by Susan Gibson), Roy, 1968.

Sir J. M. Barrie

BELKNAP, B. H.
See ELLIS, Edward S(ylvester)

BELLOC, (Joseph) Hilaire (Pierre) 1870-1953

PERSONAL: Surname is accented on the first syllable; born July 27, 1870, in St. Cloud, Paris, France; naturalized British subject, 1902; died July 16, 1953, in Guildford, Surrey, England; son of Louis Swanton (a French lawyer) and Bessie Rayner (Parkes) Belloc; married Elodie Agnes Hogan, 1896 (died, 1914); children: Hilary, Louis (died in World War I), Peter (died in World War II), Eleanor Belloc Jebb, Marie Adelaide Belloc Lowndes. *Education:* Balliol College, Oxford, first class honors in history, 1895. *Religion:* Roman Catholic. *Home:* King's Land, Shipley, Horsham, England.

CAREER: Historian, biographer, novelist, essayist, and poet; began writing for magazines and newspapers after leaving college; member of the House of Commons for Salford, 1906-10; founder, with G. K. and Cecil Chesterton, of the weekly paper *New Witness,* 1911; head of the English department, East London College, 1911-13; writer of a regular column, "A Wanderer's Note-Book," in the London *Sunday Times,* beginning 1938. *Military service:* Served in the French Army, 8th Regiment, as a driver, about 1891-92. *Awards, honors:* Knight Commander of the Order of St. Gregory the Great, 1934, conferred by the Pope; honorary degrees from Glasgow and Dublin Universities.

WRITINGS—Novels: *Emmanuel Burden* (illustrated by G. K. Chesterton), Scribner, 1904; *Mr. Clutterbuck's Election,* Eveleigh Nash, 1908; *A Change in the Cabinet,* Methuen, 1909; *Pongo and the Bull,* Constable, 1910; *The Girondin,* T. Nelson, 1911; *The Green Overcoat* (illustrated by Chesterton), McBride, Nast, 1912, reprinted, Books for Libraries, 1971; *The Mercy of Allah* (linked short stories), Appleton, 1922, reprinted, Christian Classics, 1973; *Mr. Petre* (illustrated by Chesterton), McBride, 1925; *The Emerald of Catherine the Great* (illustrated by Chesterton), Harper, 1926; *The Haunted House* (illustrated by Chesterton), Arrowsmith, 1927, Harper, 1928; *Where Are the Dead?,* [London], 1928; *Belinda: A Tale of Affection in Youth and Age,* Constable, 1928, Harper, 1929; *The Missing Masterpiece* (illustrated by Chesterton), Harper, 1929; *The Man Who Made Gold* (illustrated by Chesterton), Arrowsmith, 1930, Harper, 1931; *The Postmaster General* (illustrated by Chesterton), Lippincott, 1932; *The Hedge and the Horse* (illustrated by Chesterton), Cassell, 1936.

Humorous poems: *The Bad Child's Book of Beasts* (illustrated by B.T.B., pseudonym of Basil T. Blackwell), Alden, 1896, new edition, Knopf, 1965; *More Beasts for Worse Children* (illustrated by B.T.B.), E. Arnold, 1897, new edition, Knopf, 1966 [another edition published as *The Bad Child's Book of Beasts and More Beasts for Worse Children* (illustrated by Harold Berson), Grosset & Dunlap, 1966]; *The Modern Traveller* (illustrated by B.T.B.), E. Arnold, 1899, new edition, Campion Press, 1959; *A Moral Alphabet* (illustrated by B.T.B.), E. Arnold, 1899, new edition, Duckworth, 1973; *Cautionary Tales for Chil-*

Hilaire Belloc by Eric Gill, 1910.

dren (illustrated by B.T.B.), Eveleigh Nash, 1908; *More Peers* (illustrated by B.T.B.), S. Swift, 1911; *New Cautionary Tales* (illustrated by Nicolas Bentley), Duckworth, 1930; *Ladies and Gentlemen: For Adults Only and Mature at That* (illustrated by Bentley), Duckworth, 1932; *Cautionary Verses: Collected Humorous Poems* (illustrated by B.T.B. and N. Bentley), Duckworth, 1940, Knopf, 1941, new edition, Duckworth, 1965; *Matilda Who Told Lies and Was Burned to Death* (illustrated by Steven Kellogg), Dial, 1970; *The Yak, the Python, and the Frog: Three Beast Poems* (illustrated by Kellogg), Parents' Magazine Press, 1975.

Other poems: *Verses and Sonnets,* Ward & Downey, 1896; *Verses,* Duckworth, 1910; *Sonnets and Verse,* Duckworth, 1923, new edition, 1954; *An Heroic Poem in Praise of Wine,* privately printed, 1932; *Songs of the South Country,* London, 1951.

Essays: *The Liberal Tradition,* [London], 1897; *Avril: Essays on the Poetry of the French Renaissance,* Dutton, 1904, reprinted, Books for Libraries, 1969; *On Nothing and Kindred Subjects,* Methuen, 1908, reprinted, Books for Libraries, 1970; *On Everything,* Dutton, 1909, reprinted, Books for Libraries, 1970; *On Anything,* Dutton, 1910, reprinted, Books for Libraries, 1969; *On Something,* Methuen, 1910, reprinted, Books for Libraries, 1968; *First and Last,* Methuen, 1911, reprinted, Books for Libraries, 1969; *This and That and the Other,* Dodd, 1912, reprinted, Books for Libraries, 1968; *At the Sign of the Lion, and Other Essays,* T. B. Mosher, 1916, reprinted, Books for Libraries, 1964.

The Jews, Constable, 1922, new edition, Houghton, 1937; *On, Doran*, 1923, reprinted, Books for Libraries, 1967; *The Contrast between Europe and America*, Arrowsmith, 1923, McBride, 1924, reprinted, Arno Press, 1974; *Short Talks with the Dead, and Others*, Cayme Press, 1926, reprinted, Books for Libraries, 1967; *But Soft, We Are Observed* (illustrated by G. K. Chesterton), Arrowsmith, 1928, published in America as *Shadowed!*, Harper, 1929; *A Conversation with an Angel, and Other Essays*, J. Cape, 1928, Harper, 1929, reprinted, Books for Libraries, 1968; *Survivals and New Arrivals*, Macmillan, 1929; *A Conversation with a Cat, and Others*, Harper, 1931, reprinted, Books for Libraries, 1969; *Essays of a Catholic*, Macmillan, 1931 (published in England as *Essays of a Catholic Layman in England*, Sheed & Ward, 1931), reprinted, Books for Libraries, 1967; *On Translation*, Clarendon Press, 1931; *An Essay on the Restoration of Property*, Distributist League (London), 1936; *The Crisis of Our Civilization* (lectures delivered at Fordham University, 1937), Fordham University Press, 1937, reprinted, Greenwood, 1973; *An Essay on the Nature of Contemporary England*, Sheed & Ward, 1937; *On the Place of Gilbert Keith Chesterton in English Letters*, Sheed & Ward, 1940; *The Silence of the Sea, and Other Essays*, Sheed & Ward, 1940, reprinted, Books for Libraries, 1971.

History: *Paris*, E. Arnold, 1900, 2nd edition, Methuen, 1907; *The Eye Witness*, Eveleigh Nash, 1908; *The French Revolution*, Holt, 1911, 2nd edition, Oxford University Press, 1948, reprinted, 1966; *British Battles*, six volumes, S. Swift, 1911-13 (includes *Blenheim, Malplaquet, Waterloo, Tourcoing, Crécy, Poitiers*), revised edition, in one volume, published as *Six British Battles*, Arrowsmith, 1931; *Warfare in England*, Williams & Norgate, 1912; *The Book of the Bayeux Tapestry*, Putnam, 1914; *A General Sketch of the European War*, T. Nelson, Volume I: *First Phase*, 1915, Volume II: *Second Phase*, 1916; *The Last Days of the French Monarchy*, Chapman & Hall, 1916; *The Principles of War*, [London], 1918.

The Campaign of 1812 and the Retreat from Moscow, T. Nelson, 1924; *Mrs. Markham's New History of England* (satire), Cayme Press, 1926; *A Companion to Mr. Well's Outline of History* (historical criticism), Sheed & Ward, 1926; *History of England*, Putnam, Volumes I and II, 1925, Volume III, 1928, Volume IV, 1932; *Miniatures of French History*, T. Nelson, 1925, Harper, 1926; *How the Reformation Happened*, McBride, 1928; *The Tactics and Strategy of the Great Duke of Marlborough*, Arrowsmith, 1933; *A Shorter History of England*, Macmillan, 1934; *The Battle Ground: A History of Syria to 1187 A.D.*, Lippincott, 1936; *Characters of the Reformation* (illustrated by Jean Charlot), Sheed & Ward, 1936, reprinted, Books for Libraries, 1970; *The Crusades: The World's Debate*, Bruce Publishing, 1937 (published in England as *The Crusade*, Cassell, 1937); *The Great Heresies*, Sheed & Ward, 1938, reprinted, Books for Libraries, 1968; *Louis XIV*, Harper, 1938 (published in England as *Monarchy: A Study of Louis XIV*, Cassell, 1938); *Charles II: The Last Rally*, Harper, 1939 (published in England as *The Last Rally: A Story of Charles II*, Cassell, 1940).

Biography: *Danton*, Scribner, 1899, reprinted, AMS Press, 1969; *Robespierre*, Scribner, 1901, reprinted, Books for Libraries, 1972; *Marie Antoinette*, Doubleday, Page, 1909, reprinted, Books for Libraries, 1972; *James the Second*, Lippincott, 1928, reprinted, Books for Libraries, 1971; *Joan of Arc*, Cassell, 1929; *Richelieu*, Lippincott, 1929, reprinted, Greenwood, 1972; *Wolsey*, Lippincott, 1930; *Oliver Cromwell*, E. Benn, 1931; *Cranmer, Archbishop of Canterbury, 1533-1556*, Lippincott, 1931, reprinted, Haskell House, 1973; *Napoleon*, Lippincott, 1932; *Charles the First: King of England*, Lippincott, 1933; *Becket*, Catholic Truth Society, 1933; *William the Conqueror*, P. Davies, 1933, Appleton-Century, 1934; *Milton*, Lippincott, 1935, reprinted, Greenwood, 1970; *Elizabeth: Creature of Circumstance*, Harper, 1942 (published in England as *Elizabethan Commentary*, Cassell,1942), reprinted under the latter title, Haskell House, 1967.

Travel: *The Path to Rome*, Longmans, Green, 1902; *The Old Road* (illustrated by William Hyde), Constable, 1904; *Esto Perpetua: Algerian Studies and Impressions*, Duckworth, 1906, reprinted, AMS Press, 1969; *The Hills and Sea* (essays), Scribner, 1906, reprinted, Greenwood, 1970; *The Pyrenees* (self-illustrated), Methuen, 1909; *The Four Men: A Farrago*, T. Nelson, 1912; *The Stane Street* (illustrated by W. Hyde), Constable, 1913; *The Cruise of the "Nona,"* Houghton, 1925; *Towns of Destiny* (illustrated by Edmond L. Warre), McBride, 1928 (published in England as *Many Cities*, Constable, 1928), reprinted, AMS Press, 1969; *Return to the Baltic* (illustrated by E. L. Warre), Constable, 1938; *Places* (essays), Sheed & Ward, 1941, reprinted, Books for Libraries, 1971.

Other: *Lambkins Remains* (pastiche), Oxford, 1900; *The Aftermath; or Gleanings from a Busy Life; Called upon the Outer Cover for Purposes of Sale, Caliban's Guide to Letters* (pastiche), Dutton, 1903; *The Historic Thames* (topography), Dutton, 1907; (with Cecil Chesterton) *The Party System* (politics), S. Swift, 1911; *The Servile State* (sociology), T. N. Foulis, 1912, Holt, 1946; *The River of London* (topography), T. N. Foulis, 1912; *The Free Press* (sociology), Allen & Unwin, 1918; *Europe and the Faith* (religion), Paulist Press, 1920, reprinted, Burns & Oates, 1962; *The House of Commons and the Monarchy* (politics), Allen & Unwin, 1920; *Economics for Helen*, Putnam, 1924, also published as *Economics for Young People*, 1925; *Nine Nines; or Novenas from a Chinese Litany of Old Numbers* (illustrated by Thomas Derrick), B. Blackwell, 1931; *The Question and Answer* (religion), Bruce Publishing, 1932; (translator from the French) *The Romance of Tristan and Iseult* (as retold by Joseph Bédier; translation completed by Paul Rosenfeld), Doubleday, 1953, new edition, Pantheon, 1964.

Collections: *A Pickled Company: A Selection from the Writings of Hilaire Belloc*, Methuen, 1915; *Stories, Essays and Poems*, Dent, 1938, new edition, 1957; *On Sailing the Sea: A Collection of Seagoing Writings* (edited by W. N. Roughead), Methuen, 1939, Hart-Davis, 1951; *Hilaire Belloc: An Anthology of His Prose and Verse* (edited by Roughead), Hart-Davis, 1951, reprinted, Mercury Books, 1962; *The Verse of Hilaire Belloc* (edited by Roughead), Nonesuch Press, 1954, new edition published as *The Complete Verse of Hilaire Belloc*, Duckworth, 1970; *The Letters of Hilaire Belloc* (edited by Robert Speaight), Macmillan, 1958; *Belloc: A Biographical Anthology* (edited by Herbert van Thal), Knopf, 1970; *Hilaire Belloc's Prefaces, Written for Fellow Authors* (edited by J. A. De Chantigny), Loyola University Press, 1971.

BELLOC

ADAPTATIONS—Recordings: "Cautionary Tales," read by Joyce Grenfell (six cassettes or individual records), Caedmon.

SIDELIGHTS: **July 27, 1870.** Born in a small chalet in La Celle, St. Cloud, France—a few miles from the center of Paris. Father was a French painter.

1880-1887. Enrolled in the Oratory School at Edgebaston, England. "I felt wretched . . . until I was twelve, after that I felt much better because I began to fight big boys and it did them a lot of good." [*Letters From Hilaire Belloc,* edited by Robert Speaight, Macmillan, 1958.[1]]

"[The faculty] taught me to fear none but God and speak the truth and be in everything an English Gentleman. But it never took. I was and am afraid of any reasonably good woman and of the sea—let alone dentists.

"[But] *all* my generation ought to thank God that they were well whipped into [the classics]—for Latin and Greek are *tasks* for boys and it is as tasks and discipline that they take root. Then in later life they bear a glorious fruit." [Robert Speaight, *The Life of Hilaire Belloc,* Farrar, Straus and Cudahy, 1957.[2]]

1887. Left the Oratory. "When one is quite young then is the time to learn the world. One never learns it later. I have always been glad that I left school at seventeen, learnt to plow, reap and sow, shot a lot, went off to America from east to west, walked all over California and Colorado, went into the French Artillery and got into Balliol all before I was twenty-two. Since then I have done nothing and those are the only years in which one lives; for one has no duties and no accursed conscience."[2]

Went to Manor Farm to learn to be a land agent. Worked, rode, hunted. "[I was] a fairly good shot by nature, but the only thing human I ever shot was a farmer called Halkett. It was his fault, he got out of place in a line on the edge of the wood, and came out suddenly from cover without warning. He leapt high into the air, but suffered no real damage except to his breeches. It stung him up, no doubt, but that did him good."[2]

1889. Half-heartedly tried to have some articles published. "I have for the last week been visiting various people of importance with a view to choosing a profession. I want to be earning soon; I believe that my mathematics and my successful pass at London will help me in engineering—but I never live except when I am on the water.

"As to my writing . . . if you ask why I write as I do, I will tell you this much, that in the circle of newspapers, of criticism, of perfectly turned verses, of madly hunted ideas, I am all at sea. I would have it that no man should write who was not a zealot for something, and *when* I desire, I desire the hills and the sea, I desire the faces of men and women, not some unjust imitation, and I desire above all that free and happy forbearance and that perfection of Charity which this country is absolutely unable to give."[2]

1889. Collaborated with an Oratory friend to found a monthly newspaper, "The Paternoster." "To present to the public a monthly magazine, which . . . shall take care never to help those who are at war with the common ideas

of right and wrong. To present to the public just about as good a sixpenny worth as can be had in the Kingdom."[2] It folded after six issues.

October, 1889. Employed as cycling correspondent in France for *Pall Mall Gazette.* "I have been writing some articles for the *Pall Mall* about the French elections, which articles have brought me in money; I have a cheque uncashed—I am rich. I am now doing them some work on the French Ministry of Agriculture which will give me another cheque—all this is very nice."[2]

1890. Traveled to America.

1891. Enlisted in the French Army.

1892. Accepted at Balliol College at Oxford. "I and four other Balliol men went out on a distant expedition down the Thames last Sunday, and at evening we found ourselves at a place called Cuddeson with no way of getting back to Oxford. We asked the innkeeper for a trap and all he said was: 'Is the trap in the yard yours?' So we went out and saw a trap very neat, and a nice horse with the harness marked with Franklin's initial, the horse dealer in Oxford. We got in and drove back to Oxford and we got out and gave a little boy a shilling to lead it back to Franklin's yard. But who hired the trap and whether he minded our taking it, and how he got home, or indeed whether he got back at all, these and other questions we felt no interest in—and we know nothing of it to this day, but we look askance at the Authorities people and we are frightened. Wasn't it very sporting in a way?"[2]

1895. Tried to get a fellowship to All Souls at Oxford but was turned down. This was a source of embitterment the rest of his life. ". . . I never had any intention of going to the Bar at Oxford. Had I had such an intention I probably could have made a fair success of it, for I have great powers of work, and a precise mind. But what happened was that I determined on a Fellowship, which Dr. Jowett had told me when I first went up to Balliol I was pretty well bound to get. Everybody took it for granted I should have one. I based my life on that calculation. When the time came the religious prejudice was too strong.

"No one minds a man practising the Catholic religion, or any other; but what they do object to is the effect of religion on character and especially upon views of public life, and I think they could not bear the idea of an historical Fellow who would have written and taught history in a fashion clashing with their own. Anyhow, I found that at first one college and then another turned me down though in each one my friends among the Fellows told me I was certain. In this way I wasted the first critical years of my life. It was too late to go to the Bar, and I had no capital upon which to live until briefs should come in. I went to London, and have had to earn my living since then as best I could."[1]

1896. *Bad Child's Book of Beasts* published. Traveled to United States to lecture and visit Elodie Hogan, his bride to be. Broke down because of the strain of the previous five years. "[I] went to pieces, I suppose every man does that once or twice in his life, but I hope never again to suffer from a collapse of the kind. It is worse than drink—one is afraid of delirium."[2]

She died because she never knew
These simple little rules and few.
■ (From *The Yak, The Python, The Frog* by Hilaire Belloc. Illustrated by Steven Kellogg.)

June 11, 1896. Married Elodie Hogan.

By **1898,** had two children. "Eleanor Philippa Mary grins like a pig and grows in weight like a walrus. The Boy Louis is wilful and violent needing taming like a wild boar, but is withal affectionate. He can just make the sign of the Cross."[2]

1899. Applied for a professorship at Glasgow University but was advised that his religion would be a bar to his election. He determined to apply anyway, then his wife received a letter from a friend which warned that by persisting Belloc would make many enemies. "It is very sad . . . I have fits of depression when I consider that there is

no future for me, but again I am merry when I consider the folly, wickedness and immense complexity of the world. It is borne in upon me that before I die I shall write a play or poem or novel, for the sense of comedy grows in me daily."[2]

1899. Published *Danton.* Was awarded twenty five guineas. "[True history writing is] an integration of infinite detail as true sight is. But history differs from mere sight and is nobler in a way, because the acquaintance with the innumerable differentials of it involves labour. . . . There are also many—or at least not few—who deal with an accumulation of detail as rich men with a waggon load of furniture in a new house; careful only to put it into some 'scheme' and ready to consider any 'scheme' into which the whole will fit—but none of these is history. History is to know on one's first vision, but to confirm and build by an immense dual and coincident *work* of research and judgment one's original knowledge: modifying also a little as truth corrects and defines the whole.''[2]

1901. Planned his walk for *Path to Rome*. "I am going to walk on a kind of pilgrimage from Toul (which was my old garrison town) to Rome next Easter and on my way I shall write down whatever occurs to me to write—what proportion will deal with landscape, what with architecture, what with people and what with general subjects I can't yet tell—it will be as the spirit moves me. . . . I don't know if the subject would attract anyone, it will be full of what I think that's recondite, peculiar and often unsympathetic!''[2]

1901. Published *Robespierre*. "When I wrote this book I had not, as I have now considerable and detailed acquaintance with what are called 'representative institutions.' When I wrote this book I was under the common illusion that it was not only possible but natural to combine (principles of revolution) with democracy. I know now what the younger generation has thoroughly learned and experienced, that Parliaments are the negation of democracy, and can never work well in an ancient, complex and highly civilized society save in a senatorial and aristocratic fashion.''[2]

Hilaire Belloc in Rome, June 29, 1901.

1901. Bought his boat the "Nona." "It was in 1901 that she appeared—in one of the East Anglican creeks, a boat worth a hundred oxen at (one pound) an ox. What had been spent on her since then I tremble to think of.''[2]

Belloc would make port with the "Nona" abruptly, tramp through the finest hotels wearing a raincoat fastened with a huge safety pin, and announce himself with a roar: "Send for the manager. I want some telegram forms—send me a boy to take them to the Post Office—bring me a bottle of bubbly. I want a pen and paper.''[2]

1902. Walked 120 miles following the pilgrim's path to Canterbury with friends: "The physical contact with a man's habitat is essential to his history.''[2]

April, 1902. Naturalized a British citizen.

From **June, 1903** to **November, 1904** six books were published. One of which was *Emmanuel Burden*. "I thought it quite on the cards that the middle would never be finished, but the other day, sitting at eleven o'clock in some despair in my room alone without any children in the house or servants, the *Pneuma Hagion* fell upon me, and I wrote rapidly without ceasing till six in the morning.''[2]

1904. Put himself up for adoption as liberal candidate for parliament representing South Salford, near Manchester. Anticipated problems because of his religion. "My religion is of course greater moment to me by far than my politics, or than any other interest could be, and if I had to choose between two policies, one of which would certainly injure my religion and the other as certainly advance it, I would not for a moment hesitate between the two.''[2]

Was adopted. "I was getting tired of being refused in so many places on account of my religion. . . . The chances are against me, but it has already done me a great deal of good that I should be standing. It has helped the sale of my books and has suddenly made the provincial press in the north of England acquainted with my name.''[2]

1905. Contracted pleuro-pneumonia. Convalesced in North Africa. Then moved out of London. "My going out of London in 1905 and keeping no house or flat there was disastrous. And yet I was driven by real—and even dangerous—poverty. I was earning not a quarter of the absolutely minimum income necessary to the meanest household of our sort, and my earnings were decreasing.''[2]

After setting up a new house, and recuperating from pneumonia, he set out to walk the Pyrenees. "It would astonish you to see this place. It is a pity Napoleon did not get there earlier and stay longer; he might have re-invigorated it as he did the valley of the Rhine. As it is, positively *nothing* is done. All the French roads stop dead at the Frontier and even the mule paths up the passes often cease to exist when one gets over on to this Southern side. All the clocks are stopped, all the windows broken and all doors off their hinges.

"Catholicism (or mysticism in excess) has been made to blame for it and it might certainly have such effects, but as a fact it has nothing to do with it. The people are a good deal less Catholic than in France, the Church has more power, or rather it is less attacked politically, but the number of men who go to Mass is less than in France. I think a good deal more Catholicism would wake them up a little.''[2]

1906. The Bellocs bought a house in Sussex, Kings Land. Here Belloc taught his children. "I have renewed my lessons with the boys and find them now clearly developing into mathematics, which they gobble up, and spelling and the other mechanical dull things which bore them horribly. Therefore it is my duty to insist quite for one half upon the latter—but I know my weakness and dread a lapse into the easier part. Meanwhile I find myself enjoying teaching and I shall be proud if I see them later mastering their examinations—which is my object, since examinations are the gates to all the professions still. There is one thing about teaching one's own children, which is that they inherit certain qualities from oneself so that one can often guess what is in their minds. A great part of the difficulty with teaching is the impediment young people have in expressing themselves, and when they are one's own children one can't partly over-ride that by instinct. It is largely only lack of vocabulary, for vocabulary is an acquirement of slow growth. I made Hilary today repeat to me what I had taught him previously of the Parabola. He knew the *facts* exactly; but his exposition of them was 'when the thing to the line is always equal to the other thing on the other side' and that was a definition which sadly lacked precision. . . .''[1]

His favorite domestic pastime was bottling wine. "Having washed my bottles, boiled my corks and set out everything in due order, I began with the aid of the enfeoffed lad and my host of children to fill the bottles and to bang the boiled corks into them, as I have often done before. But Fate was watching with blind eyes and the 203rd bottle broke at the shoulder, it broke in the shape of a long spear of glass which ran up through the ball of the hand into the middle of the palm and up among the knuckle bones making as ugly a wound as any member of a Peace Society would care to see. I shut the wound with a finger and thumb of my other hand, put it under the tap and wondered if I could possibly have missed an artery. It bled like Passover meat for any length of time. The Doctor, summoned with rapidity, arrived in an hour and a half (for he is five miles away), and told me I had missed an artery in the neighbourhood of Palmer's Arch by a small amount. So that makes another Arch to add to the Marble, Trajan's, Orange, and that of Cleopatra's foot. The horrible thing was then sewn up and bandaged, and there I am. So far there are no complications.''[1]

January 13, 1906. Polling day. Belloc elected by majority of 852. "We have pulled it off. Concerning everything in this world worth doing, the first thing is to determine it, and the second thing is to do it. And we have done it.''[2] He declared that he was going to Westminister "on a whole-hearted and well-defined democratic programme, such as that on which Mr. John Burns was returned for Battersea twelve years ago. Liberalism of that kind will spread. It is like lighting a fire that you cannot put out. They cannot put me out of Parliament till Parliament is dissolved, and before that time comes, I intend to let the people at St. Stephen's hear a few truths in the interests of the working classes that will astonish them.''[2]

February, 1906. "I have made my maiden speech. After it I was sick. This is true and not an exaggeration. My maiden speech lasted eight minutes [and] was intensely Radical. . . . The *Morning Post*, naturally trying to hurt the Government, said that I alone of the Liberals had shown courage. The *Times* said in a leader that what I had said was 'dangerous rant.' The Liberal papers keep an ominous silence—being cowardly, but I . . . continue to dance in the sunlight and to sing like the gaslight. For instance, even today I leaped up in my seat and asked a question of the Government which gave them the greatest possible annoyance, to wit, whether it was not a fact that Kaffir labour was increasing steadily until the Chinese labour was brought in, and has since then been decreasing. It is a fact.''[2]

1906-1910. Worked relentlessly, writing and lecturing while in Parliament, always struggling to make enough money. "This week I dictated two articles on Monday morning, lunched in the train, gave an afternoon lecture at Reigate, dined in Norwood with an admirer of *Emmanuel Burden*, and lectured at Dulwich at the same night, wrote another article on Tuesday morning, took the express on Tuesday at 3 o'clock for Chesterfield, lectured in Chesterfield, left Chesterfield before eight on Wednesday, gave two political speeches Wednesday afternoon and evening in my constituency, went out to stop . . . the night in Cheshire, came back to Manchester on Thursday; wrote two notes on the war for 'Outlook' and one note for the Speaker, sent four telegrams and wrote eighteen letters.

Lithograph of Belloc by Daphne Pollen, 1934.

The Big Baboon is found upon
    The plains of Cariboo.
    He goes about
    with nothing on.
(A shocking thing to do).
■ (From *The Bad Child's Book of Beasts* by Hilaire Belloc. Pictures by B.T.B.)

"I received a telegram this morning from Glasgow unsigned saying 'Could you lecture on travel?'. . . I will lecture on the Proper Method of Milking a Cow, which I have never done, or of Mowing a Field which I can do jolly well. I will lecture on the Influence of the Jesuits on Europe, or of the Influence of Europe on the Jesuits. I will lecture in verse, like Milton, or in prose like old Bright of University, or in alternate verse like Apuleius in the theatre of Carthage. I will lecture on anything in any manner for money: and don't you forget it. I can lecture twice a day or three times. I can lecture on my hand, on my head or between my legs or with the dumb alphabet.

"I am doing more work than a man should. But it does not hurt me. What does hurt me is worry and care and debt, especially debt."[2]

Became dissolusioned and impatient with politics. "The House of Commons is hypocritical and dull beyond words, and membership of it is a tremendous price to pay for the little advantages of being able (very rarely) to expose a scandal or to emphasise a point of public interest. Every day that passes makes me more determined to chuck [it]; it is too low for words. The position is ridiculous and the expense is damnable. More than that, it cuts into my life, interferes with my earnings, and separates me from my home—all three irritating."[1]

1907. During a recess from Parliament, walked across the Pyrenees. "Yes, at last! Madrid! But at what a cost! All the way burning deserts from the Pyrenees onwards and my Christ! What cooking! Never again! Next time on a mule, or in a Litter, or even in a train. But never again on foot across those brown Sahara plains and those formless treeless hills. I have added to my knowledge and I am a fuller man."[2]

1909. Elected to a second session in Parliament, although he had not been eager to run again. "I am very dejected about the approaching election. I don't want to stand. I detest the vulgar futility of the whole business and the grave risks to which are attached no proportionate reward. So anxious are most people to get into Parliament that they will do anything to oust an opponent, and I have really no desire to be mixed up with such hatreds, or to see myself placarded on the walls in twenty ridiculous attitudes, and with any number of false statements or suggestions attached to my name. It is a perfectly beastly trace."[2]

1910. Left Parliament, "because it was up to me (A) to make a definite sacrifice of honour for a particular end or (B) to refuse it and work for the same end more round about. It is an *invariable* rule in human life to do (A). [I left] blowing a huge trumpet and banging the door behind. I am relieved to be quit of the dirtiest company it has ever been my misfortune to keep."[2]

1910. Left editorship of *Morning Post* which he had had since 1906. "The *Morning Post* have now played the second trick in the series that I foresaw: the Literary Page being founded they put me on to a lower salary with less frequent attendance in order that I might train to a sufficient degree of competence an assistant."[2]

1911. Unable to find immediate journalism work, Belloc wrote voluminously. "The whole art is to write and write and write and then offer it for sale, just like butter. The more one writes, the more one gets known. The more enormous one's output the more the publishers get to regard you as a reliable milch cow.

"*Don't* sweat up your facts. Out of the abundance of your knowledge, tell the ordinary man generally what you want him to know in a spout, and there comes out a perfect little essay of the length they want. So I did with the French Revolutions, not opening a reference book half-a-dozen times, and dictating the whole thing off-hand, with the result that I have already sold 27,700. If I had worried in the least about it I should not have sold half the number."[2]

The vulture eats between his meals,
    And that's the reason why
He very, very rarely feels
    As well as you and I.
■ (From *More Beasts for Worse Children* by Hilaire Belloc. Illustrated by B.T.B.)

**The whale that wanders round the Pole
Is not a table fish.**
■ (From *The Bad Child's Book of Beasts* by Hilaire Belloc. Illustrated by B.T.B.)

1913. Wrote for *Century* magazine. "Further news is the arrival of an American millionaire who runs the *Century* and who has given me a contract for twelve articles at an enormous price. . . . The millionaire is deaf. He does not use an ear trumpet but a most complicated arrangement consisting of a little black box with a sort of telephone to it. He puts the black box on the table and one talks into it. Conversation thus carried on tends to be mechanical and to lose its subtler graces."[1]

1913. His wife became very ill and was unable to swallow food. "Elodie gets no worse and no better; certain of the symptoms have improved, but others are more distressing and I am bound here very anxiously . . . Elodie is stronger *functionally* i.e. in digestion and nutrition but weaker *nervously*. She eats almost normally but she can see no one, she can read but very little and she sleeps more and more ill. I cry and pray God to take her to the Sun. The doctor won't let her move—not even out of bed—and it will be long, long. Priez pour elle et pour moi."[2]

February 3, 1914. Elodie died. "I am in peril of my intelligence and perhaps through the enormity of what has happened . . . I wish to God it were the body that was in peril."[2]

1914. World War I. Belloc tried in vain to enlist. "Not a sign of a staff for me to go to yet, not even a divisional one. It is an abominable shame, and when I chuck it in disgust and try through the French, it may be too late—they will wonder why I didn't ask before."[2]

Served for a year or so in the Eighth regiment of French artillery at Toul, Meurthe-et-Moselle, as a driver.

1915. Lectured around Britain writing articles for *Land and Water*. Traveled with his daughter in Europe. "The train . . . stopped at Burton where the beer is made and where a Miracle happened. There are three witnesses to it: Eleanor Jebb, Elizabeth Belloc, and me. It was in 1915. We were all in a motor together, I taking them from their convent school at Stone to Derby where I went to lecture. And as we passed through Burton, Eleanor said (being but a child), 'Oh, how I wish I could see some polar bears!' for it was hot weather. Then Elizabeth said, 'Oh! so do I.' At that *same instant* Five Huge Polar Bears came out of a big door and walked down the street. They were men dressed up as Bears for an advertisement. Ever since then I have believed in a God."[1]

1916. Began his *History of England*. "I think the history of England ought to be written, plain simple and short, and I have always wanted to do it; but my real trouble is twofold. (1) I have found by experience in the past that to write such simple condensed history brings one up against one million disputed little points of fact, which involve immense labour in settling.

"(2) No one would read it when I had written it because no one ever reads things which are fundamentally Catholic in tone in this country or in America; and when I say 'no one,' I mean neither Catholics nor Protestants; only here and there an intelligent Jew or an English agnostic of the rare sort. Definite apologetics they will read, but the Catholic standpoint in general history, or economics, or sociology strikes them only as a boring eccentricity.

"After some thought as to the form it ought to take, whether bald statement, take or leave it—or readable stuff fairly persuasive, I have decided on the latter. I think people like nowadays to be let into the secret of how history is written and that the mere statement of the truth would simply fall flat and unheeded. E.g. tell people that men's thoughts turned upon *nothing* during the fifth century except the tremendous struggle between paganism and the Church, and that all the fuss about race and language is beside the mark, and they will not believe you, because race and language are so important today, and because it was so difficult to get into the minds of people who lived a long time ago. But quote sentences and you at once strike their imagination. Not that I think race or language unimportant to such a history; I think it exceedingly important. In order to understand the evidence you must know the state of mind in which the man was who gave the evidence."[1]

1918. End of World War I. His son Louis was reported missing in action and never found.

1919. Belloc visited the battlefields. "The battlefield of the Lys, which I crossed today, is like a white sea. No trees, no houses—nothing. The ground is a mass of shell holes, like waves: and there is complete desolation. It is almost incredible to me that even Protestantism can produce such vile morals as the attempted saving of the authors of such ruin.

"I feel the horror of that destruction more than I did during the war. It is so also with grief; it becomes clearer and more weighty with time. The War overshadowed its own evil. It was a vast activity which filled me with vigour. Now it is over the mind is aghast at what has happened. It has a curiously weird effect upon my mind to approach the battle front *for the first time in four years to hear no sound.* It was as though the world had died."[2]

June, 1920. Given an honorary doctor of law degree by Glasgow University. "My feeling about titles and honours, academic or other . . . is that in the time in which we are living they have become ridiculous. Except the Garter and the Victoria Cross and the regular commissions of the regular Services one has, in such lables, anyone at all as one's colleague. I would not, for instance, accept the Legion of Honour, though it has many material advantages attached to it. Nor would I dream of taking as an old man a Knighthood or anything of that sort or other. In the same way during the war, I would certainly not have accepted one of those disgusting sham titles of Colonels, Admirals, etc."[2]

1920. Visited Morocco. "[The Moroccans] are like children with toys. They adore railways, but cannot believe it just that they should have to pay for tickets. They quite easily learn the telephone and how to drive motors, but they get more easily tired and distracted than do Europeans and they won't work long at a time. They all pick up enough French to get along with—but no more, and all can read a few words of Arabic. They *loathe* the Catholic Church and it will not convert them. But it is now their master which is the next best thing."[2]

1922. Traveled in Europe with his daughter, took her to see the Pope. "Rome is full like an overpacked trunk and bursting. Not a room in any hotel. I fled to the Beda, the English college, where they treat me nobly. I get up at five and have Mass at six and live in a huge whitewashed room with one iron bed and one chair and I am happy. Eleanor I have put into that heavenly convent of the French Nuns just at the back of St. Peter's, hidden away behind the sacristy thereof. It is a place of 'refreshment, light and peace,' with palms and flowers and a postern into Paradise. I do assure you that when I go every morning to take her into town I get a dribbling of faith like a man who feels, or thinks he feels, the first drops of rain upon his head, after too dusty a day. We are to have our Audience tomorrow, I believe. I want to tell the new Pope one or two things. I hope he believes them. The last one doubted me when I told him the Allies were certain to achieve, but this one has wider experience."[1]

1923. Traveled in America and lectured. "I write . . . in the train because it is the only place in which I have five minutes to do anything. No one on this side of the Atlantic has the conception of concentration. They talk to each other incessantly and accompany anyone they choose anywhere. They come into each other's houses without invitation at all moments and when I sit down to write or set out to see a place alone in the rare moments I have, my host, or if I am in a hotel, any stranger, sits down beside me or walks beside me and talks incessantly. It is an extraordinary tradition, born I suppose of Colonial isolation in the pioneer days when the conversation of a human being was priceless. But it has developed into a state of affairs which, to us of Europe, is like living in an amiable and quite pointless lunatic asylum."[1]

1924. Met Mussolini. "I had a long talk with him alone. He has read assiduously and has good judgment on the whole. I bade him not exaggerate the decline of British power, which he is somewhat inclined . . . I have no doubt at all that he means to keep in the middle of the seesaw and advantage whichever side seems to him to be lowest at the moment. . . . He is not ambitious and that is always a great asset in governing men. His driving power is first disgust with Parliamentarianism, which he shares with pretty well everyone in Europe—and next Patriotism. He will do a great deal to confirm the already established religious peace—but I doubt whether he has much faith himself. The point is that his regime will help it to return to the younger generation."[2]

April, 1926. Completed his novel, *Mr. Petre.* "I know how the days go by: largely in reading the Proofs—now finished—of my novel, *Mr. Petre* (which I loathe), largely in making, compelling G. K. Chesterton to finish the drawings, the illustrations of that book. He is marvellous! He is far better with his pencil than his pen. In a line he gives you a whole human being: and it is sane full European stuff. . . . He did eight in an hour and a half. But if I hadn't forced him he'd never have done them at all. I delight in the talents of my fellow men: and his drawing of the human face is amazing.

1926. Criticized H. G. Wells's *Outline of History.* "Wells has written a very strong letter indeed saying that I am a wicked man and an attacker of the innocent which is himself . . . I have made myself unpopular in Charles Street,

Hilaire Belloc, portrait by James Gunn, 1939.

Mount Street, Chesterfield Street and for all I know Farm Street by defending the miners and pointing out that those who run them down are at that very moment swigging champagne.

"I am used to Insult, as I combine in one person three natures, all of them targets for insult . . . A) Poverty. B) Papistry. C) Pugnacity. Any one of the three can just swim, but when all three come together the victim sinks."[1]

June, 1927. "I am in Abbeville. I have long abandoned the sea. It was impossible, or rather the Nona was. Alas! She has lived her life, and all the rest is mere waiting for dissolution and the end. I have loved her well; I love her still. But there is no more sailing in her. Her age is upon her.

With every season she costs more and more to keep her afloat and now her Appel has found her. She takes me out into the salt no more. She leaks very remarkably, decks and all. Her counter breaks at a heavy sea. Her noble lines still lift through it beautifully. A better sea boat never was. But teak and oak are mortal and must pass.

"Do you think I shall find her in the quiet river-mouth of Heaven where the South Wind blows? I doubt it! The theologians would tell me she has no rational soul—yet that is no reason why she should not be preserved on my account and translated, yet wooden—into beatitude—as witness the chariot of Elias and the veils of the Pleiades—material, yet granted immortality. There she lies now alone. But I shall go back to visit her from time to time—unless she sells herself: and she is capable of that. Lord! What times I have had with her! She also enjoyed it, though she never confessed as much (a modest craft) and we understood each other very well. But now that great friendship is interrupted and the end has come."[2]

1927. Went to El Kantara in North Africa to write *James II*. "I wake at six. I get down by 6:30. I write this mud from seven, after coffee, till twelve. I eat till 12:30 (oh! the vile food) very little and read articles in old magazines left behind by tourists of the flood: especially the Revue Hebdomadaire of 1922. I then drink coffee and brandy and smoke. At once I begin again the horrible sing-song of the tenacious and brave—but ill judging—Jacobus. It goes on till four. I then take the air for half-an-hour. Then I write again till seven. Then I eat an ounce or two of nauseating food; then I do nothing for an hour but read or write a letter—as I do now with *empressement*. Then by 8:30 I go to bed and pass the night in dreams of trying to read small print by a bad light. Then I wake at six and start all over again.

"James II . . . is most attractive to me. He was a thruster and loved ships and was sincere. He had 300 affairs with ugly women. He couldn't bear the beauties. They made him weary. What he liked was character, go, wit, buzz, solidity, charm with black tints and affection. He got it."[2]

1928. "I have finished *Belinda*—a fearful sweat—like sawing marble— but worth it. It is the only thing I ever finished in my life and the only piece of my own writing that I have liked for more than forty years. . . .

"I go over it word for word, like a mosaic; changing, fitting in, adapting, dictating, erasing, spatch-cocking, caressing, softening, enlivening, glamouring, suppressing, enhancing and in general divinising this my darling treasure."[2]

1929. Approached old age lonely and in poor health. "After a certain time and experience all life is retrospection and duty. One has to hold on for the sake of the others and one must not long make of any mundane thing a necessity. The end of life, the second half, is a liquidation but of course if they don't reward us afterwards it will be a Bloody Sell. The Little Flower says 'I trust as much in the Justice of God as in his Mercy.'

"Yesterday a man came to see me at the Reform Club by appointment, and began roaring out in the big hall of the Club at the top of his voice all his views on religion and his contemporaries—I had the greatest difficulty in getting him out again. I have just received a threatening postcard warning me of my approaching murder, and a woman's St. John's Ambulance coat sent anonymously! I have also received my usual bi-weekly love-letter from a lunatic woman in Scotland who has sent them faithfully for nearly sixteen years. Altogether I am having quite a pleasant time except for my eyes.

"Isolation after a certain age is profoundly true. . . . I think it is three things combined, and one is the old truth that the faculty of making new relationships is lost. Through most of life one has the power of rapid acquaintance and plastic relationships but at the end these become impossible. For one thing, one knows too much of life. The second cause seems to me to be the simple fact that with the process of time power of meeting people changes. Some drift away, many die, others go and live elsewhere, and so on. At an earlier age this goes on just as much, only we don't care. And the third cause is, I think, though we don't know, that with age the mind acquires greater depth and the essential isolation of this life is apparent to it. It is like seeing the stars at night which you can't see by day. It is not a pleasant thought, but on the other hand it all hangs together for one doesn't appreciate the vile insufficiency of this world till one has nearly done with it. . . ."[1]

1930. "I spent last night at Nantua for memories sake: a town on a dreamy lake in the high jura with mountains all around. It was a Paradise of repose. Today I find it one bestial hell of motors tearing through at thirty miles an hour and motor bicycles in endless intermission making noises like machine guns punctuated by violent explosions. No spot in Europe has more completely changed from Heaven to Hell. Nor is there any refuge, for the great limestone mountains re-echo the din on all sides. The wise man will in future sleep in places where there is no road. How long will it be before some man with brains builds the first hotel designed for sleeping in."[1]

1932. Became very ill. "It was a dreadful thing that happened. I completely lost my memory. I had a very bad night, and when I got up this morning, I was rather dazed and remained so during the morning. I tried to do some work in the library of the Reform Club, and I went on till half past one, and then went off to lunch with my mind quite empty. This sort of thing has happened to me once or twice in the last two or three years. It does not seem to get more frequent, but it is really alarming when it does happen, and distresses me a great deal. It comes of having done more work than I ought to have done at my age." [J. B. Morton, *Hilaire Belloc: A Memoir*, Sheed & Ward, 1955.[3]]

"All my life I have been so strong in body and in mind that with this *defailance* I feel like another person—like a sheep or like a wet rag. I cannot recognise myself for being myself, but all misfortune has this good that it helps one to understand other people and their troubles.

"[A friend] took my place yesterday at a lecture which I was to have given for the Hospital. I was going to lecture on the breakdown of Art and Literature. But on account of my illness I could not do so. He lectured, oddly enough, on me, and I am told, very flatteringly. He read out my poem on Wine and they all began to cry, which is Glory indeed.

But to tell you the truth I am more keen on salvation now, and ultimate repose than Fame, or at any rate, on refreshment, light and peace.

"I would not . . . take the Doctors for more than probability. They can only judge on an average of a mass of people, however intelligent they may be: and most of them, being physical scientists, are fools. But they can tell one *indubitable* facts: and these only. E.g. they x-ray and find a fracture. That is a fact. They auscult and find a 'murmuring' at the heart. That is a fact. But the moment they go beyond that and say that such and such consequences follow on the facts they are in hypothesis. . . .

"My head has been in such a condition that writing with a pen was often illegible and always perilous. I would often have such congestion after finishing quite a short bit with the pen that I was dizzy and ill afterwards. It is a great handicap, especially as the pen thinks for one, and in my trade of writing the machine never has quite the same effect. . . ."[1]

1933. Worked on *A Shorter History of England*. "The task in which I am occupied is a School History of England which is very deplorable rapid hack-work, but the only thing which will provide any ready money, except a novel, for which, though I must write a novel some time before the New Year, I find myself quite without invention. The School History is for England and America. I do not suppose it will have any considerable sale, because the Catholic Schools do not use my work, and my history does not fit in with the regular Protestant examination papers, nor indeed with the kind of history that Catholic teachers have been taught themselves out of Protestant textbooks. It is not so much that what they are taught is untrue as that things are put out of proportion, and the most important things are left out, so that the general effect is a complete falsehood. . . ."[1]

1935. Lectured in Florida. "It is ten miles of villas and gardens in a wide lagoon and the distances from any part to any other part are incredible. And there are no taxis! Everyone has a car—except me—and waddles about all the time. . . ."[1]

1936. Visited Paris. "If people get to know I have a fixed address in Paris I shall get swamped with letters and invitations, and all the rest of it. Perhaps I exaggerate this, but in the last two or three years I have got much better known to the French public and there is danger of my feeling their hot breath on my neck, and hearing the deep bay of the hounds at my very heels. . . .

"When I was young I had a great desire for fame, and I got even a little excitement out of going to other people's houses and being sought after, but now I have lost all that—even the desire for fame. I don't think this is a very healthy sign, because it goes with fatigue. But I do think that, under modern circumstances, the horror of publicity is most legitimate; and it has become almost impossible to distinguish where mere publicity ends, with all its odious vulgarity, and fame or a lot more money if one has publicity than if one has not, but the price to be paid for that money is too high. Meanwhile, the modern methods of publicity throw all values into chaos."[1]

She had refused to take her niece
To hear this entertaining piece!
A deprivation just and wise
To punish her for telling lies.
■ (From *Matilda Who Told Lies and Was Burned to Death* by Hilaire Belloc.   Illustrated by Steven Kellogg.)

1936. Visited Oxford. "Oxford is for me a shrine, a memory, a tomb and a poignant possessing grief. All would have been well if they would have received me in my young days of love and poverty: but they would not. Hence this complaint. There are places in Oxford I will not pass, lest the memories should be too violent. . . ."[1]

1937. "I've been to Hartford, Connecticut, and to Washington, when I had a long private talk with Franklin D. (which makes three of them: the Pope, Mussolini and him: but I've never seen Baldwin, or Blum or Franco or Virginia Woolf, whom, indeed, I keep from the door by my ceaseless labours).

"What was I saying? Oh! yes. I saw the President. I liked him. He is intelligent and well-bred. Also he flattered me, and anyone who flatters me is my friend. I gave him two of my books. In fact the whole interview (which lasted an hour and a half) resembled that between my great grandfather and George Washington. My G.G.F. fawned and slobbered over George at his house in Virginia (1791) and called on him again and again until the President foamed at the mouth with boredom."[1]

Spoke in Washington in favor of Franco. "I am to speak at Washington, as she desires me to do, for the right side in Spain: a ticklish job, but I think I can do it justly and tell *both* sides. There is no danger of some damn fool enthusiast upsetting everything by a mis-comprehending speech, as I shall speak alone, not on a Platform.

"The power of propaganda here—especially of unplanned, instinctive propaganda—is very great. It is less than it was but it is still much of the old world—and even of the past—comes to them through the English language."[1]

1937. Met with Franco in Spain for ten minutes. Described him as "the man who saved us all."[2]

1939. "I flew back from Paris a few days ago in a 'plane as old as Methuselah and the size and shape of a coffin. I got violent vertigo, as I always knew I should if I flew through the air in a flying machine. I shall probably never recover from that foolhardy experiment! How man can half live in the air is more than I can understand.

"As my *Charles II* progresses I wonder what the public will think of the note I have struck all through it, which is the all-importance of Charles's growing conviction about Catholicism. Not many people will read the book, because my books on history have not much circulation, but such as do read this one will, I am afraid, be both puzzled and annoyed!

"The ideal thing is for the historian to write his history and then to have a gang of trained slaves who can go through the proofs from various aspects. That is why, take it all in all, gentlemen have made the best historians."[2]

1939. World War II began. "Of war two things may be said: It is restricted and it is incalculable. This war is more restricted than ever. I was lunching alone with Mary Herbert yesterday in London, and she justly called it an isolationist war. It is petrol that kills me. I am seven miles from my station, four from Mass, an average of two from my close neighbours. Also I have a game leg from a recent slight motor accident, so I can't walk. I can't even drink as heartily as I used to and a thorough drenching quite upsets me. But I have still got some very good wine and can taste it, for which God be praised. . . ."[1]

1939. Met the King of Belgium, and visited his old regiment in France. ". . . At the front I found my old regiment and my old battery, which brought me to the verge of tears, especially when I met my old gun. It had just come out of the front line, and there were all the young men, looking as fresh as daisies and as muddy as an old-fashioned London street. The Colonel made a speech and assembled the officers, so I had to make a speech and then I stood the men huge masses of wine. The regiment gave me champagne, but I gave my piece nothing but gallons and gallons of red wine, which they far prefer. It is an astonishing thing to come back to the same atmosphere and tradition after a gap of just on fifty years. It is the only pleasant accident to mortality I have known, and had an air about it of the immortal."[2]

1940. Belloc became less and less tolerant with the frustrations of illness and depression. "It is all due to Old Age which is, I do assure you, the most horrible lingering (and incurable) disease ever pupped or calved. It's funny that the books lie so horribly about it! To read the books one would think that old age was a lovely interlude between the pleasures of this life and the blaze of Beatitude. The books represent Old Age seated in a fine old comfortable dignified chair, with venerable snowy locks and fine, wise, thoughtful eyes, a gentle but profound smile, and God-knows-what-and-all! But the *reality* is quite other. Old Age is a tangle of Disappointment, Despair, Doubt, Dereliction, Drooping, Debt, and Damnable Deficiency and everything else that begins with a D. Avoid it!"[1]

1941. Son, Peter, killed in Scotland. "The Boy did not fall in action. What happened was this. He went out with the Fleet in the boat to which his Battalion of Marines—the Vth—was attached. When it got back into the Clyde a telegram was sent me saying I should have news. I telephoned at once to Glasgow whether the ship had returned. There was a delay of some hours. When I got through it was only to hear that he was dead. It came thus; in a sort of flash and a stroke of lightning. It was sudden pneumonia. He has been buried here next to his mother. His Battalion sent a detachment and rendered full honours . . ."[2]

1942. Had a stroke plus pneumonia. Ill until his death in 1953. "I used to think (being deceived, like most people, by the poet) that old age came gradually and gently upon a man, like a mist over the Californian mountains; instead of which it attacks one by jumps like a diseased and malignant monkey, snapping and biting and wounding with its yellow teeth. It has the especial disagreeable that there is no cure for it. You cannot say 'I shall be better tomorrow,' for tomorrow one is even older than today."[1]

July 16, 1953. Died in Guildford, Surrey, England. "I said to myself—if you want to be remembered after you are dead, you must get a poet to write about you. But then I said to myself, why would you want to be remembered after you are dead? And to that question I said to myself, I can't imagine."[2]

FOR MORE INFORMATION SEE: C. Creighton Mandell and Edward Shanks, *Hilaire Belloc: The Man and His Work*, Methuen, 1916, reprinted, R. West, 1973; Patrick Braybrooke, *Some Thoughts on Hilaire Belloc: Ten Studies*, Drane's, 1924, reprinted, R. West, 1973; Raymond Las Vergnas, *Chesterton, Belloc, Baring* (translated by C. C. Martindale), Oxford University Press, 1938, reprinted, Folcroft, 1975; Robert Hamilton, *Hilaire Belloc*, D. Organ, 1945; Renee Haynes, *Hilaire Belloc*, Longmans, Green, 1953; Frederick Wilhelmsen, *Hilaire Belloc: No Alienated Man; A Study in Christian Integration*, Sheed & Ward, 1953; Francis J. Sheed, editor, *Born Catholics*, Sheed & Ward, 1954; John B. Morton, *Hilaire Belloc: A Memoir*, Sheed & Ward, 1955, reprinted, Folcroft, 1974; Marie A. Belloc Lowndes, *Young Hilaire Belloc*, Kenedy, 1956; Eleanor Belloc Jebb and Reginald Jebb, *Testimony to Hilaire Belloc*, Methuen, 1956, published in America as *Belloc, the Man*, Newman, 1957; Robert Speaight, *The Life of Hilaire Belloc* (authorized biography), Farrar, Straus, 1957, reprinted, Books for Libraries, 1970; Vincent Brome, *Six Studies in Quarrelling*, Cresset, 1958; Laura Benét, *Famous Poets for Young People*, Dodd, 1964.

Obituaries: *New York Times*, July 17, 1953; *Life*, July 27, 1953; *Newsweek*, July 27, 1953; *Commonweal*, July 31, 1953; *Publishers Weekly*, August 8, 1953; *Wilson Library Bulletin*, September, 1953; *Poetry*, November, 1953; *Britannica Book of the Year 1954*.

BENÉT, Stephen Vincent   1898-1943

PERSONAL: Surname is pronounced Be-*nay;* born July 22, 1898, in Bethlehem, Pennsylvania; died March 13, 1943, in New York City; son of Colonel James Walker (a career Army officer) and Frances Neill (Rose) Benét; brother of the writers, William Rose Benét and Laura Benét; married Rosemary Carr (an author), November 26, 1921; children: Stephanie Jane, Thomas Carr, Rachel Felicity. *Education:* Yale University, B.A., 1919, M.A., 1920; graduate study at the Sorbonne, University of Paris, 1920. *Religion:* Episcopalian. *Home:* New York City.

CAREER: Poet, novelist, short story writer, and dramatist; published his first book of poetry at the age of seventeen and devoted his entire career to writing. *Awards, honors:* Recipient of many, including the Poetry Society of America's prize, 1921 (shared with Carl Sandburg); *Nation* poetry prize, 1923, for *King David;* Guggenheim fellowship, 1926; Pulitzer Prize for Poetry, 1929, for *John Brown's Body;* elected to the National Institute of Arts and Letters, 1929; Shelley Memorial Award, 1932; gold medal from the Roosevelt Memorial Association, 1933; O. Henry Memorial Prize, 1936, for *The Devil and Daniel Webster;* Litt.D., Yale University, 1937; elected to the American Academy of Arts and Letters, 1938; Pulitzer Prize for Poetry, 1944, for *Western Star.*

WRITINGS—Poems: *Five Men and Pompey: A Series of Dramatic Portraits,* Four Seas, 1915; *The Drug Shop; or, Endymion in Edmounstoun* (Yale University prize poem), Yale University Press, 1917; *Young Adventure,* Yale University Press, 1918; *Heavens and Earth,* Holt, 1920; *The Ballad of William Sycamore, 1790-1880,* Brick Row Book Shop, 1923 (illustrated by Brinton Turkle), Little, Brown, 1972; *King David,* Holt, 1923; *Tiger Joy,* Doran, 1925; *The Headless Horseman* (libretto for a one-act opera based on the story by Washington Irving; music by Douglas Moore), Schirmer, 1927; *John Brown's Body,* Doubleday, Doran, 1928 [various later editions include: an edition edited and annotated by Mabel A. Bessey (illustrated by James Daugherty), Farrar & Rinehart, 1941; an edition with an introduction by Douglas Southall Freeman (illustrated by John Steuart Curry), Limited Editions Club, 1948; an edition illustrated by Fritz Kredel and Warren Chappell, Rinehart, 1954; an acting edition (as staged at the Yale Drama School and Off-Broadway, under the direction of Curtis Canfield; music by Fenno Heath), Dramatists Play Service, 1961; and an edition with introduction and notes by Jack L. Capps and C. Robert Kemble, Holt, 1968].

The Litter of the Rose Leaves, Random House, 1930; *Ballads and Poems, 1915-1930,* Doubleday, Doran, 1931; (with wife, Rosemary Carr Benét) *A Book of Americans* (illustrated by Charles Child), Farrar & Rinehart, 1933; *Burning*

Stephen Vincent Benét, photographed in a 16-inch gun (Watervliet, N.Y.).

(From the movie, "Seven Brides for Seven Brothers," copyright 1954, Metro-Goldwyn-Mayer, starring Jane Powell.)

City, Farrar & Rinehart, 1936; *The Ballad of the Duke's Mercy,* House of Books, 1939; *Nightmare at Noon,* Farrar & Rinehart, 1940; *Listen to the People: Independence Day, 1941,* Council for Democracy (New York City), 1941; *Tuesday, November 5, 1940,* House of Books, 1941; *Western Star* (Book I of an unfinished narrative poem), Farrar & Rinehart, 1943.

Novels: *The Beginning of Wisdom,* Holt, 1921; *Young People's Pride* (illustrated by Henry Raleigh), Holt, 1922; *Jean Huguenot,* Holt, 1923; *Spanish Bayonet,* Doran, 1925, reprinted, Scholarly Press, 1971; *James Shore's Daughter,* Doubleday, Doran, 1934.

Short stories: *The Barefoot Saint,* Doubleday, Doran, 1929; *Thirteen O'Clock: Stories of Several Worlds,* Farrar & Rinehart, 1937, reprinted, Books for Libraries, 1971 (among these stories are *By the Waters of Babylon* [also see below], *The Devil and Daniel Webster* [also see below], and *Sobbin' Women*); *The Devil and Daniel Webster* (illustrated by Harold Denison), Farrar & Rinehart, 1937, reprinted, 1965, also published as a one-act play, Dramatists Play Service, 1939, and as a one-act opera (with music by Douglas Moore), Farrar & Rinehart, 1939; *Johnny Pye and the Fool-Killer* (illustrated by Charles Child), Farrar & Rinehart, 1938; *Tales before Midnight,* Farrar & Rinehart, 1939; *Twenty-Five Short Stories,* Sun Dial Press, 1943 (includes *Thirteen O'Clock* and *Tales before Midnight*).

Plays: *A Child Is Born: A Modern Drama of the Nativity* (written for radio), W. H. Baker, 1942; *They Burned the Books* (written for radio), Farrar & Rinehart, 1942; *Stephen Vincent Benét's Stories of America* (adapted for the stage by F. Andrew Leslie), Dramatists Play Service, 1971; *By the Waters of Babylon* (one-act play; adapted by Brainerd Duffield), Dramatic Publishing, 1971.

Essays: *A Summons to be Free,* Farrar & Rinehart, 1941 (includes *We Stand United* [also see below]; *Zero Hour,* and *Nightmare at Noon*), reprinted in a collection of essays by various authors under the title *Zero Hour: A Summons to be Free,* Books for Libraries, 1971; *Dear Adolph,* Farrar & Rinehart, 1942; *America,* Farrar & Rinehart, 1944, reprinted, 1966; *We Stand United, and Other Radio Scripts,* Farrar & Rinehart, 1945.

Collections: *Selected Works of Stephen Vincent Benét,* Volume I: *Poetry,* Volume II: *Prose,* Farrar & Rinehart,

(From the movie, "Seven Brides for Seven Brothers," copyright 1954, by Metro-Goldwyn-Mayer, starring Howard Keel.)

1942, reprinted, 1963, another edition published as *The Stephen Vincent Benét Pocket Book,* edited and with an introduction by Robert Van Gelder, Pocket Books, 1946; *Selected Poetry and Prose,* edited and with an introduction by Basil Davenport, Rinehart, 1942, reprinted, 1960; *The Last Circle: Stories and Poems,* with an introduction by Rosemary Carr Benét, Farrar, Straus, 1946, reprinted, Books for Libraries, 1973.

Screenplays: "The Necessary Evil" (motion picture), adapted from "Uriah's Son" by Benét, First National Pictures, Inc., 1925; "Abraham Lincoln" (motion picture), adaptation by Benét, continuity and dialogue by Benét and Garrit Lloyd, Feature Productions, Inc., 1930; "Love, Honor, and Behave" (motion picture), based on a story by Benét published in the *Saturday Evening Post,* Warner Brothers Pictures, 1938; "All That Money Can Buy" (motion picture), based on *The Devil and Daniel Webster,* screenplay by Benét and Dan Totheroh, RKO Radio Pictures, Inc., 1941, reissued as "The Devil and Daniel Webster," RKO, 1952.

Other writings: *Selected Letters,* edited by Charles A. Fenton, Yale University Press, 1960; *Stephen Vincent Benét on Writing: A Great Writer's Letters of Advice to a Young Beginner,* edited and with a commentary by George Abbe, S. Greene Press (Brattleboro, Vt.), 1964; (author of introduction) Robert Nathan, *The Barly Fields: A Collection of Five Novels,* Knopf, 1967; *The Bishop's Beggar,* St. Teresa's Press (Flemington, N.J.), 1968.

Contributor of articles, stories, and verse to various periodicals, including the *Saturday Evening Post, Yale Review, Century, New Republic, Dial, Bookman, Nation, Harper's, Saturday Review of Literature, Ladies' Home Journal,* and *Collier's.*

Regular reviewer for the *New York Herald Tribune* and for the *Saturday Review of Literature,* beginning 1935; editor of the Yale Series of Younger Poets competition, beginning 1933.

ADAPTATIONS—"Just for You" starring Bing Crosby (motion picture), based on Benét's story *Famous,* Paramount Pictures Corp., 1952; "Seven Brides for Seven Brothers" (motion picture), adapted from *The Sobbin' Women,* starring Jane Powell and Howard Keel, Metro-Goldwyn-Mayer, 1954; "Daniel Webster" (50 min., 16mm, sound, b/w), I.Q. Films, 1965; "John Brown's Body" (filmstrips), Brunswick Productions, 1967, Educational Dimensions Corp., 1968.

Recordings: "A Book of Americans," read by Maureen Stapleton and Pat Hingle (record or cassette), Caedmon; "Nightmare at Noon and Other Poems" (65:02· min.), Caedmon, 1971; "The Poetry of Benét," read by the author and Joseph Wiseman (six cassettes or individual records), Caedmon; "The Poetry of Benét," read by Joseph Wiseman (six cassettes or individual records), Caedmon; "Stephen Vincent Benét Reading His Poems," Caedmon.

SIDELIGHTS: **July 22, 1898.** Born in Bethlehem, Pennsylvania. His brother was William Rose Benét, his sister, Laura Benét. Father, James Walker Benét, was a career officer in the United States Army, by way of West Point. "I cannot agree with those who say that the military mind is narrow and insensitive. . . . [My father] was interested in everything from the Byzantine Emperors to the development of heavy ordnance, and was the finest critic of poetry I have ever known. He taught me many things about the writing of English verse, and tolerance, and independence and curiosity of mind.

"I was born and brought up in the Army—and in an intelligent branch of the army, the ordnance. . . . My grandfather developed the rim-fire cartridge, my father was in charge of the first 16-inch gun ever made in this country, my uncle helped invent one of the earliest light machine guns, the Benét-Mercier. . . . It was an intensely interesting world for a child to grow up in, a world with a code and a flavor all its own. That life produces, at its best, a remarkably fine type of human being. At its best, I know—I have seen the worst of it also.

"I spent my childhood on a series of Regular Army posts. If I were writing stories about that, I would have to explain a few things about the Army. . . . I'd have to give you a sense of being in a world of your own that children have—I'd have to show you that it is quite as natural for an Army child to move to a different Post every few years as for a civilian child to grow up in one town." [*Stephen Vincent Benét, The Life and Times of an American Man of Letters: 1898-1943,* Charles A. Fenton, Yale University Press, 1958.[1]]

At the age of five he read Shakespeare with zest, although without total understanding. That night at dinner he remarked: "I like that man's writing, has he written anything else?"[1]

1910-1911. Attended Hitchcock Military Academy—twenty miles north of San Francisco at Jacinto. His eight months there proved an absolute horror, the boys at the boarding school were merciless in their attacks upon him:

> "A big boy's arm went round him—and a twist
> Sent shattering pain along his tortured wrist,
> As a voice cried, a bloated voice and fat,
> 'Why it's Miss Nancy! Come along, you rat!'"[1]

1911. Family moved to Augusta, Georgia. "The move hardly upset me at all—I was used to moving, being an army child. Wherever we went there was always a post and a striker and a big flag sinking down at evening from a white flagpole. . . . Sometimes there were many children, sometimes only a few—but there was always the same big doherty with the army mules to carry them off to school—and the same line of cleavage between us and the civilian rest of the world."[1]

1913. Began to write constantly. "[I learned that poetry], was not a dead thing or an alien thing or a dry game of words. I knew there were rules and that you could break the rules but that you must never break them unintentionally. I knew [it] was always written by the living, even though the date-line said that the man was dead. . . . The thing, of course, is to make the people come alive. They do, if you can dig them out of the dust. . . . If [the first poet] had merely wanted to tell his friends that he was hungry, or that he had seen a fine herd of deer in the forest, he would not have needed the drum or the cry or that chant. He would have said what he had to say in prose, as we do when we write an ordinary letter about ordinary things. But he wanted to do more than that. He wanted his friends to remember what he said and to think about it. He wanted to excite and stir them as he was excited and stirred. So he made a song in words."[1]

1915. Graduated from Summerville.

May, 1915. Made his first professional sale to the *New Republic.*

July, 1915. Flunked his entrance exam for Yale in Latin prose and mathematics, had a tutor for the summer.

July-August, 1915. Wrote *Five Men & Pompy,* his first book of verse.

September, 1915. Entered Yale.

August 19, 1918. Went to work at the State Department as a clerk.

October, 1918. Transferred to Military Intelligence as a cryptographer. Transferred back to State Department shortly after, his eyes weren't strong enough.

December 21, 1918. Resigned from State Department and returned to Yale.

June, 1919. Graduated from Yale.

June 16, 1920. Received his M.A.

Summer, 1920. Started *The Beginning of Wisdom,* first novel.

November 18, 1920. *Heavens & Earth* published in New York.

November, 1920. Met Rosemary Carr. "[She] would make an anteater burst into madrigals."[1]

He wrote to a friend: "You will love Rosemary when you see her and she will be fond of you. I can't describe her on paper very well—except to say that she is clever, pretty, has a magnificent sense of humor, adventurous, gallant, whimsical, kind, merry, and courageous—and that all these adjectives mean very little when set down that way. As a

There are children lucky from dawn till dusk,
　　But never a child so lucky!
For I cut my teeth on "money musk"
　　In the Bloody Ground of Kentucky!
■ (From *The Ballad of William Sycamore (1790-1871)* by Stephen Vincent Benét. Illustrated by Brinton Turkle.)

scrap of statistics, she was [Phi Beta Kappa] and led her Prom. I don't want to give the impression that she's an Admirable Crichton—but she is so infinitely the finest and most lovely person I have ever known that I am happier than I could ever have imagined. . . . I see everything at present through bright pink spectacles." [*Selected Letters of Stephen Vincent Benét,* edited by Charles Fenton, Yale University Press, 1960.[2]]

1921. Stayed in Scarsdale, N.Y. His parents lived there. "I hate New York literary people, except for a handful. I hate all the literary backbiting and posing and general nervous hurried air of going somewhere faster than anybody else. . . . They remind me of fleas in their attitude toward life and art. Jumping educated fleas. What do they know about Art? They only know the particular prejudices of their clique . . . fraternity politics all over again."[1]

"For if two New Hampshiremen aren't a match for the devil, we might as well give the country back to the Indians." ■ (From the movie "The Devil and Daniel Webster" [also titled "All that Money Can Buy"] copyright RKO Radio Pictures, 1941.)

March 17, 1921. Became engaged. Wrote to his fianceé: "I have done nothing at all but sneeze and typewrite all day—it seems that I *have* hay-fever, a 'touch' of it, though how anything like that can be as gentle as a 'touch' implies, I don't quite see. . . . I will tell you a dreadful secret. The reason I am as far along as I am at 23 is not due to genius or inspiration or anything one-millionth as pleasant—it all boils down to a certain fluency with language and more than that by several cubits and kilos another certain ability which I really ought to take a considerable Moral and Christian Pride in of being able to sit down and work when I don't feel like it. And that is not being modest to have you compliment me, really—that is vérité!

"The doctor came in to see what was the matter. . . . 'Well doctor, is there anything that can be done for hay-fever?' says I amiably. 'There is nothing at all,' says he. 'But, mon médecin, I never had the dam thing before!' I quip and he retorts crushingly 'You never lived in Scarsdale before'

with a nasty smile. 'Go to Cape Cod for a month' says he 'Or Atlantic City—or the great green greasy Limpopo river or ride in triumph through Persepolis or any of a dozen places I can pick out if I blindfold myself and stick my finger on Mercator's projection—and, lo, your hay-fever will cease!' I love certain species of doctors—they are so Really Helpful.

"I think the place for us is Tierra del Fuego. The rain falls there, I understand, all but about three or four days in the year, often so violently as to permanently deafen even old inhabitants who sort of live in the mud like antique crustacea. There you would, doubtless, be almost insanely buoyant and as rain affects me with a delightful twilight-in-Notre Dame sort of painless and mellow gloom—we would be very happy indeed. I would be a rather sleepy shepherd with creaky asthmatic panpipes and a flock of very damp sheep . . . I would carve you necklets from the bones of drowned sailors in odd moments—being naturally of a mortuary turn of mind."[2]

80   **Yesterday's Authors of Books for Children**

August, 1921. Split a $500 prize from The Poetry Society with another author, for year's best volume of poetry, *Heavens and Earth*.

November 26, 1921. Married Rosemary Carr in Chicago. They went abroad for their honeymoon.

Spring, 1922. Returned to New York to live.

April 6, 1924. First child was born, Stephanie Jane.

June, 1925. First glimmer of *John Brown's Body*. "I have a swell idea for a long poem. The only trouble is, it would take about seven years to write and I'd have to read an entire library first."[1]

June, 1925. Accepted offer of a studio for three weeks at MacDowell Colony in Peterborough, N.H. to rewrite "Spanish Bayonet" for *Pictorial*. "I am still very sleepy, and haven't started to work yet. The quiet, of course, appalls me and the birds in the morning sound like airplane engines. I am a city child. I saw a squirrel today and Mr. Novik saw a partridge. Either he has better eyes or a weaker sense of veracity. . . . A strange woman in a white dress has suddenly stationed herself with an enormous black camera out in the road and is taking a picture of this studio and as far as I can see, of my neck. I wonder who *she* is? It is an AliceinWonderland incident—perhaps she will turn into a sheep or a chessman—I would not be surprised."[1]

April, 1926. Received a $2,500 grant from the Guggenheim Memorial Foundation. "What I said in my 'plan,' boiled down to this—that I was sick of writing short-stories and wanted to do a long poem on some American subject. I told them I had several ideas—including the Civil War one—but couldn't say which one I'd take. . . . It would mean a year in which I could write what I want, preferably verse."[1]

Spring, 1926. Went back to France to live and work on his long poem.

September 28, 1926. Son was born, Thomas Carr.

October, 1927. Finished *John Brown's Body*. "When that thing was finished, I felt as if I had given birth to a grand piano."[1]

"You lose the feel of the whole, working on a thing that size for so long, and can see nothing but the parts. But I tried to put America in it—at least some of the America I knew. If I did so, some of it should stand till a better man comes along.

"I feel rather curiously about it myself, I think my best work so far, perhaps, is in it and yet it is more detached from me than anything I have ever done. It seemed to me that a thing of that sort should be tried. A poet of greater faculties would have avoided my failures in it and my superficialities—and there are many of both—but what I have done, I have done to the extent of such capacities as I have. At least I hope it has in it some of the landscapes, the sights, the sounds [and] the people which are American. I

tried to put them there. I am tired—not of criticism of America, for no country can be healthy without self-criticism—but of the small railers, the conventional rebels. We also have a heritage—and not all of it is wooden money."[2]

He was asked to return from France to promote his books. "To tell you the honest truth, I don't think my physical presence in America would do any good. There are some people whose personalities can arouse interest in their work. I am not one of them. My work is the best of me, and I would rather lie behind it, as perdu as possible. And experience has taught me that this is the best course I can follow. Writing should speak for itself—if it cannot, it is lost. And as for me—I am not even a foreign author. I do not speak Czechoslovakian, I never was bitten by a lion or caught a strange species of tortoise while flying over the North Pole. And I've lived in New York long enough for most of the professional literary gang to know who I am without wanting to know any more. You can lionize Trader Horn . . . but you can't do much to me except to raise the remark 'I didn't know he'd been away.'"[2]

March 30, 1928. Benét's father died. "It happened with such suddenness that many of our best friends did not hear till much later. I know the Washington connections were away at the time and unable even to return for the funeral. But I think that everyone who knew me at all, knew what I thought of him. I hope so. Now that is gone. And nothing in life can ever make up for that particular relation or fill that place. He understood me completely. And he was the best man I ever knew or am likely to know. I am glad it was sudden—for him. He would have hated the slow thing so. For me—well, there is no use talking of that."[2]

"I remember my father saying to me, 'We always think of our parents as immortal,' and thinking of it again when I got the news of his death. And yet that is the way we are bound to think of them—especially if we love them. There is no philosophy to soften the shock. He died within twenty-four hours and I have always been very glad of that—

"But work does help, I know. . . . It is the one thing."[1]

1929. Elected to the National Institute of Arts and Letters.

December 2, 1929. Left for Hollywood to write a movie script on Abraham Lincoln for twelve weeks. "Let me recount a little about this madhouse. In the first place Hollywood—Los Angeles, Glendale, Pasadena, etc., etc.—is one loud, struggling Main Street, low-roofed, mainly un-skyscrapered town that straggles along for twenty-five miles or so, full of stop and go lights, automobiles, palm-trees, Spanishy—and God knows what all houses—orange-drink stands with real orange juice—studios—movie-theatres—everything but bookstores. I am the only person in the entire twenty-five miles who walks more than four blocks, except along Hollywood Boulevard in the evening. There are some swell hotels—up in the hills or between Los Angeles and Hollywood—and a few night-clubs. But in general, everything is dead, deserted at 11:30 p.m.

"There is the continual sunlight—the advertised palms—coolness the minute the sun sets—and plenty of people with colds. The boys go around without hats. They look like prize ears of corn. the girls, ditto.

"As for the studio—it's like any office—where I am. People sit around—gossip—smoke—waste time. Outside, of course are the stages and the sets—a perfect reproduction of one corner of a French street—and half of a German castle elsewhere. Occasionally, in the corridors, somebody is wandering dressed as a *gendarme* or an Arab or something. But only occasionally. There isn't much being 'shot' at present.

"The work goes on. I think we're about through and then Mr. Griffith has a new idea. The trouble is—he's generally perfectly right. I continue to like him—and really to think a lot of him, in many ways. He's all right. And he can produce loyalty."[2]

Later he wrote to his agent, Carl Brandt: "The next time you sign me up on a twelve week contract to come out here for any amount of money, there is going to be a good deal of blood flowing around the Brandt office. Happy Lincoln's Birthday and so's your old man!

"Of all the Christbitten places and business[es] on the two hemispheres this one is the last curly kink on the pig's tail. And that's without prejudice to D. W. Griffith. I like him and think he's good. But Jesus, the movies!

"I don't know which makes me vomit worst—the horned toads from the cloak and suit trade, the shanty Irish, or the gentlemen who talk of Screen Art. . . .

"Since arriving, I have written four versions of *Abraham Lincoln*, including a good one, playable in their required time. That, of course, is out. Seven people, including myself, are now working in conferences on the fifth one which promises hopefully to be the worst yet. If I don't get out of here soon I am going crazy. Perhaps I am crazy now. I wouldn't be surprised.

"At any rate, don't be surprised if you get a wire from me that I have broken my contract, bombed the studio, or been arrested for public gibbering. Don't be surprised at all.

". . . There is nothing like the movies, except soap sculpture and zymotic diseases."[2]

Spring and Summer, 1930. Taken ill. A short story he was writing developed into a novelette. "I have had more trouble with this stinking novelette than I've ever had in my life. I now think I've done it from the wrong point of view and ought to do it over again from another, which is always a help when you've written The End and sighed. The trouble with it is that one character in it is too good to throw away, and so are some of the scenes, but the whole thing isn't baked right. Writing is sometimes as enjoyable as prickly heat."[1]

October 22, 1931. Second daughter born, Rachel Carr. "Weight 9 pounds 10 ounces, and quite enterprising."[1]

1930's. Does editing, lecturing and reviewing. "True criticism, creative criticism, is one of the most difficult of all the arts. It must instruct without patronizing, judge without prejudice, know the best of the past and yet know what the new is about."[1]

His critique to Margaret Mitchell: "To return to *Gone with the Wind*—it's a fine book and I hope you write many more

of them. That probably sounds rather portentous to you at the moment, but the wish is sincere. I hope so not only because of your veracity and your ability to get under the skin of a past time and make it live—and I can run up a string of flags for the research you must have done and the way you were able to select—but also because the story moves, and has fire in it, and the reader sits up, wanting to know what happens next.

"There are lots of books like that when you're young—*The Three Musketeers* and *The Cloister and the Hearth* and all the good ones. There aren't so many, now. I admire and respect the serious, high-minded, case histories—the technical jobs in the novel that are like a series of finely-stained slides under the microscope. But fiction is still fiction—and when a book keeps going on in your mind, even when you're not reading it, you don't need anybody to tell you it's good. It was that way with *Gone With the Wind*."[2]

Only occasionally did he render his effective frank judgments: "Most of the authors in this book, write the short story as if they were writing with mittens on."[1]

June, 1933. Accepted editorship of the annual competition called the "Yale Series of Younger Poets," continued this for the rest of his life.

October 24, 1936. "The Devil and Daniel Webster" published in the *Post*. It received the O. Henry Memorial Award as best American short story of the year. "It's always seemed to me, that legends and yarns and folk-tales are as much a part of the real history of a country as proclamations and provisos and constitutional amendments. . . . 'The Devil and Daniel Webster' is an attempt at telling such a legend. . . . I couldn't help trying to show him in terms of American legend; I couldn't help wondering what would happen if a man like that ever came to grips with the Devil—and not an imported Devil, either, but a genuine, homegrown product, Mr. Scratch."[1]

1937. Received an honorary degree from Yale. "I don't know quite what you do with a medal, except carry it around in your upper breast-pocket and hire somebody to shoot you in it, so you can say afterwards that it saved your life—but it is very nice of them and I am pleased to get it."[1]

1937. Collaborated with Douglas Moore on a short operetta, "The Headless Horseman," broadcast by NBC.

1938. Another collaboration on operetta based on "The Devil and Daniel Webster."

1941. Wrote film version of "The Devil and Daniel Webster." Hollywood called it "All that Money Can Buy."

December, 1941. Japan attacked Pearl Harbor.."I guess this is for the record. I was doing a piece on Carl Sandburg on Sunday, December 7 and, as usual, I was late with it. I finished it up about 6 p.m., called a Western Union boy, and sent it down to the *Herald Tribune*. We hadn't had the radio on all day. Then I poured myself a glass of vermouth and sat down to relax. And, ten minutes later, Ellen Barry called up with the news.

"We went over to have dinner with them in their hotel and listen—with that curious thing that comes over you to get together with your close friends when something happens. And, as you listened, you could feel the country harden and come together, like ice forming on a pond. That may seem a curious simile when we were sitting in a warm, well-lighted room on the tenth floor of a New York building. But you knew that that was just what was happening. There wasn't any question about it or any discussion. You just felt it in your skin, like a chemical change.

"All you heard next day in the streets was 'Well, Roosevelt was right.' 'Well, we're in it.' 'Well, anyhow, we've got a great President.' 'Well, anyhow, this has united the country.' And I'm not faking the last sentence. . . .

"I think one of our great troubles has been this idea that 'government' is something high-sounding and far-off and scary that gets after you with a club—that it's outside of and removed from the normal life of the citizen—that it's something you yell to for help in a very bad jam and curse out the rest of the time. It isn't. Government is the people and the people are government. It isn't something some man from Mars called a 'politician' does to you—it's what we do to and for ourselves to get the way of life we want and believe in. If we don't like the men who run it, we can get the men changed—if we don't like the laws they make we can get the laws changed—but we can't do either by sitting back on our rears and remarking, 'The best government is the government that governs least.'

"That never was true of any civilization more complex than that of the free hunter—and while I might like to be a free hunter, I know I can't be. . . . I don't know how you get an ideal government—but I'm perfectly sure you don't get it by regarding it as a dose of salts or an inevitable doom overtaking the innocent taxpayer. To the men who founded this Union, the republic they envisaged and the government they devised meant something—a great and daring experiment and a roof for the people and a flag flung out on the wind. I want to get back to that idea and to the pride that was in that idea. I am tired of apologizing for the American experiment."[2]

1942. Wrote a script for a major official program called "This is War." Did scripts for series called "Dear Adolf."

1942. Served on the grant committee for the National Institute of Arts and Letters. "Money buys the time to do your work well. Recognition by people who know what work is gives you confidence to go ahead. I think we may all be glad that we have done what we have done in this field.

"For, if an institute like ours is to mean anything, it cannot be just a pleasant club or a source of self-gratification to its members. It must help the body of art. It must help the new work coming along and recognize the good work already done, not always widely popular with the public, but done by the enduring people."[2]

February 18, 1943. Struck with heart attack.

March 13, 1943. Died in New York City at forty-four.

He advised young writers: "Do not use up all your shot on the first chipmunk that crosses your path. Or, when an elephant comes along, you'll have an empty gun.

"It is also NOT your business, as a novelist, to draw moral judgments on your characters for the reader's benefit. Particularly at the start of the story. It is your business to show them as they are—by this trait and that, by this incident and that, by this speech and that, to build up the character before your reader. If you want to paint a scoundrel, by all means paint a scoundrel, but do not make him enter with a villainous leer saying what a bad person he is. Thackeray drew a beautiful scoundrel, in the first person, in *Barry Lyndon*. But Barry Lyndon's own approach to himself is that he is an able, abused and much-misunderstood man. It is when, slowly and relentlessly, you begin to realize just the kind of things he is doing and saying, that the horror begins to come over you—a much more genuine horror than if Barry had been labeled a scoundrel in the first place.

"It is a long road—it always is.

"I don't know any short cuts—I don't know any easy way. But, if you are bound and determined to be a writer, you frequently get there."[2]

July, 1943. *Western Star* published. A Book-of-the-Month Club selection, it received the Pulitzer Prize.

FOR MORE INFORMATION SEE: Laura Benét, *Famous American Poets*, Dodd, 1950; E. M. Sickels, "Stephen Vincent Benét," *College English*, May, 1953; Charles A. Fenton, *Stephen Vincent Benét: The Life and Times of an American Man of Letters, 1898-1943*, Yale University Press, 1958; Stephen Vincent Benét, *Selected Letters*, edited by Charles A. Fenton, Yale University Press, 1960; C. A. Fenton, "Writer as Correspondent: The Letters of Stephen Vincent Benét," *Virginia Quarterly Review*, Summer, 1960; Parry E. Stroud, *Stephen Vincent Benét*, Twayne, 1963; Laura Benét, *Famous Poets for Young People*, Dodd, 1964; Laura Benét, *When William Rose, Stephen Vincent and I Were Young*, Dodd, 1976; Obituaries—*New York Times*, March 14, 1943; *Current Biography Yearbook 1943*.

Benét, 1942.

John Bennett

BENNETT, John   1865-1956

PERSONAL: Born May 17, 1865, in Chillicothe, Ohio; died December 28, 1956, in Charleston, South Carolina; son of John Briscoe Henry and Eliza Jane Trimble (Mc-Clintock) Bennett; married Susan D. A. Smythe, April 2, 1902; children: Jane McClintock (Mrs. Forrest Hampton Wells), John Henry van Sweringen, Susan Adger. *Education:* Attended public schools in Chillicothe, Ohio, and the Art Students' League, New York City. *Home:* Charleston, South Carolina.

CAREER: Began as newspaper reporter, *Ross County Register,* 1883; editor, *Chillicothe Daily News,* 1885-1890; later employed as reporter, writer, editor, and correspondent for various newspapers; writer and illustrator of writings for children. Curator, South Carolina Historical Society, and Museum of Charleston, South Carolina. *Member:* Huguenot Society of South Carolina; Historical Society of Jefferson County, Virginia; Historical Society of Ross County, Ohio; Phi Beta Kappa. *Awards, honors:* D.Litt., University of South Carolina.

WRITINGS: Master Skylark: A Story of Shakespeare's Time (illustrated by Reginald B. Birch), Century, 1897, Grosset, 1924, reprinted, 1961, new edition (illustrated by Henry C. Pitz), Century, 1922, adaptation by Kathryn F. Mahoney and Laura E. Preble (illustrated by Mary F. Landrigan), Globe Book, 1953; *Barnaby Lee* (illustrated by Clyde O. De Land), Century, 1902; *The Treasure of Peyre Gaillard,* Century, 1906; *Songs Which My Youth Sung,* Daggett Printing, 1914.

Roger Dawson sat astride a stick of timber in front of Master Geoffrey Thompson's new house, watching Tom Carpenter the carver cut fleur-de-lis and curling traceries upon the front wall beams. He was a tenant-farmer's son, this Roger, and a likely good-for-naught.
■ (From *Master Skylark* by John Bennett. Illustrated by Reginald B. Birch.)

Madame Margot: A Grotesque Legend of Old Charleston, Century, 1921, reprinted, University of South Carolina Press, 1951; *Apothecaries' Hall . . .,* Presses of Southern Printing & Publishing, 1923; *The Pigtail of Ah Lee Ben Loo, with Seventeen Other Laughable Tales and 200 Comical Silhouettes,* Longmans, Green, 1928; *Blue Jacket, War Chief of the Shawnee, and His Part in Ohio's History,* Ross County Historical Society Press, 1943; *The Doctor to the Dead: Grotesque Legends and Folk Tales of Old Charleston,* Rinehart, 1946, reprinted, Negro Universities Press, 1973.

Contributor of poems, fiction, and illustrations to various magazines.

SIDELIGHTS: Even as a young boy Bennett's mind was set on becoming an artist and illustrator. He left high school after two years to pursue his real interests in art school. His writing ability developed from a natural gift for story-telling already evident in his youth.

Bennett's brother, Henry Holcomb Bennett, and his son, John Bennett III, are also writers.

FOR MORE INFORMATION SEE: Stanley J. Kunitz and Howard Haycraft, editors, *Junior Book of Authors*, H. W. Wilson, 1934, 2nd edition, 1951; *Illustrators of Children's Books: 1744-1945*, Horn Book, 1947; M. T. Bennett, "Youth in Pleasant Places," *Horn Book*, June 5, 1960; Obituaries, *New York Times*, December 30, 1956; *Publishers Weekly*, January 14, 1957; *Wilson Library Bulletin*, February, 1957.

BETHUNE, J. G.
See ELLIS, Edward S(ylvester)

BLAND, Edith Nesbit
See NESBIT, E(dith)

BLAND, Fabian (joint pseudonym)
See NESBIT, E(dith)

BROWNING, Robert   1812-1889

PERSONAL: Born May 7, 1812, in Camberwell, London, England; died December 12, 1889, in Venice, Italy; buried in Westminster Abbey; son of a bank clerk; mother's maiden name, Sarah Anna Wiedemann; married Elizabeth Barrett (the poetess), 1846 (died, 1861); children: Robert Wiedemann Barrett (nicknamed Pen). *Education:* Privately tutored at home; attended University College, London, for one year.

CAREER: Poet and playwright. *Awards, honors:* Honorary M.A. and honorary Fellow of Balliol College, Oxford University; Browning Society formed, 1881.

WRITINGS—Poems, except as indicated: *Pauline: A Fragment of a Confession*, Saunders and Otley, 1833; *Paracelsus*, E. Wilson, 1835; *Strafford: An Historical Tragedy* (verse-play; produced in London at Covent Garden, 1837), Longman, Rees, 1837; *Sordello*, E. Moxon, 1840; *Bells and Pomegranates*, E. Moxon, Volume I: *Pippa Passes*, 1841, Volume II: *King Victor and King Charles* (play), 1842, Volume III: *Dramatic Lyrics*, 1842 (includes *Porphyria's Lover, My Last Duchess, Soliloquy in a Spanish Cloister, The Pied Piper of Hamelin* [also see below]), Volume IV: *The Return of the Druses* (play), 1832, Volume V: *A Blot on the 'Scutcheon* (play), 1843, Volume VI: *Colombe's Birthday* (play; produced in London, 1853), 1844, Volume VII: *Dramatic Romances and Lyrics*, 1845 (includes *How They Brought the Good News from Ghent to Aix, The Bishop Orders His Tomb at St. Praxed's Church*), Volume VII: *Luria and A Soul's Tragedy* (plays), 1846.

Christmas Eve and Easter Day, Chapman & Hall, 1850; *Men and Women* (fifty dramatic sketches), Ticknor & Fields, 1855 (includes *An Epistle of Karshish, Cleon, Şaul, A Grammarian's Funeral, In a Balcony, Fra Lippo Lippi, Andrea del Sarto, Bishop Blougram's Apology, Two in the Campagna*); *Dramatis Personae* (collection of dramatic sketches), Ticknor & Fields, 1864, new edition, Collins, 1969 (includes *James Lee, Gold Hair: A Legend of Pornic, The Worst of It, Dis Aliter Visum, Too Late, Abt Vogler, Rabbi Ben Ezra, A Death in the Desert, Caliban upon*

Setibos, Confessions, May and Death, Prospice, Youth and Art, A Face, A Likeness, Mr. Sludge the Medium, Apparent Failure); *The Ring and the Book*, four volumes, Fields, Osgood, 1868-69, new edition, Penguin, 1971; *Balaustion's Adventure, including a Transcript from Euripides*, Smith, Elder, 1871; *Prince Hohenstiel-Schwangau, Saviour of Society*, Smith, Elder, 1871; *Fifine at the Fair*, Smith, Elder, 1872; *Red Cotton Nightcap Country; or, Turf and Towers*, Smith, Elder, 1873.

Aristophanes' Apology, including a Transcript from Euripides; being the last Adventure of Balaustion, Osgood, 1875; *The Inn Album*, Smith, Elder, 1875; *Of Pacchiarotto, and How He Worked in Distemper, with Other Poems*, Osgood, 1876 (includes *At the Mermaid Houses, Shop, Pisgah-Sights, Fears and Scruples, Natural Magic, Magical Nature, Bifurcation, Numpholeptos, Appearances, St. Martin's Summer, Hervé Riel, A Forgiveness, Cenciaja, Fillipo Baldinucci on the Privilege of Burial*); (translator) Aeschylus, *Agamemnon*, Smith, Elder, 1877; *La Saisiaz* [*and*] *The Two Poets of Croisic*, Smith, Elder, 1878; *Dramatic Idyls*, Smith, Elder, first series, 1879 (includes *Martin Relph, Pheidippides, Halbert and Hob, Ivan Ivanovitch, Tray, Ned Bratts*), second series, 1880 (includes *Echetlos, Clive, Muléykeh, Pietro of Abano, Doctor—, Pan and Luna*).

Jocoseria, Houghton, 1883 (includes *Wanting is—What?, Donald, Solomon and Balkis, Cristina and Monaldeschi, Mary Wollstonecraft and Fuseli, Ixlon, Adam, Lilith, and Eve, Jochanan Hakkadosh, Never the Time and the Place, Pambo*); *Ferishtah's Fancies*, Houghton, 1884; *Parleyings*

Robert Browning, from a painting by M. Gordigiani, 1858.

with Certain People of Importance in Their Day, Houghton, 1887; *Asolando: Fancies and Facts,* Houghton, 1890; *Robert Browning's Prose Life of Strafford,* Estes, 1892.

Selected poems for young readers: *The Young Folks Browning* (illustrated by Louis Meynell), Page, 1919; *The Brownings for the Young* (edited by Frederic G. Kenyon), Macmillan, 1896; *The Boys' Browning: Poems of Action and Incident,* Estes, 1899; *Selected Poetry of Robert Browning* (edited by Kenneth L. Knickerbocker), Modern Library, 1951; *Poems of Robert Browning* (edited by Donald Smalley), Houghton, 1956; *Poems of Robert Browning* (edited by Rosemary Sprague; illustrated by Robert Galster), Crowell, 1964.

The Pied Piper of Hamelin (illustrated by Livingston Hopkins), Lyman & Curtiss, 1882 [other editions include those illustrated by Kate Greenaway, Routledge, 1888, Warne, 1910; Hope Dunlap, Rand McNally, 1910; Arthur Rackham, Lippincott, 1934; Roger Duvoisin, Grosset & Dunlap, 1936; Harold Jones, Watts, 1962; Alan Howard, Faber, 1967; Lieselotte Schwarz, Scroll Press, 1970; C. Walter Hodges, Coward, McCann, 1971].

Collections: *The Complete Poetic and Dramatic Works of Robert Browning* (edited by Horace E. Scudder), Houghton, 1895, new edition published as *The Poetical Works of Robert Browning,* 1974; *The Complete Poetical Works of Robert Browning* (edited by Augustine Birrell), Macmillan, 1907, new edition, 1915; *The Complete Works of Robert Browning, with Variant Readings and Annotations,* three volumes (edited by Roma A. King, Jr. and others), Ohio University Press, 1969-72.

The Letters of Robert Browning and Elizabeth Barrett Browning, 1845-1846, Harper, 1899, new edition, edited by Elvan Kintner, Belknap Press of Harvard University Press, 1969; *Letters of Robert Browning* (collected by Thomas J. Wise; edited by T. L. Hood), Yale University Press, 1933; *New Letters* (edited by William Clyde DeVane and K. L. Knickerbocker), Yale University Press, 1950; *How Do I Love Thee? The Love-Letters of Robert Browning and Elizabeth Barrett* (edited by V. E. Stack), Putnam, 1969; *The Brownings: Letters and Poetry* (edited by Christopher Ricks; illustrated by Barnett I. Plotkin), Doubleday, 1970.

ADAPTATIONS—Movies and filmstrips: "The Pied Piper of Hamelin" (motion pictures), Thomas A. Edison, Inc., 1913 and 1917, Macmillan Films, narrated by Eli Wallach, 1966, BFA Educational Media, 1970; "The Pied Piper of Hamelin" (filmstrips), Curriculum Films, 1946, revised, 1951, Stillfilm, 1949, McKeon-Overgard (Spanish-language instruction), 1961, Encyclopaedia Britannica Films, 1966, H. M. Stone Productions, 1972.

"The Ring and the Book" (motion picture), Biograph, 1914; "A Light Woman" (motion picture), American Film Co., 1920; "Poems of Tennyson and Browning" (motion picture and filmstrip versions), McGraw-Hill, 1967; "Andrea del Sarto—Browning" (filmstrip), Educational Record Sales, 1969; "My Last Duchess: A Film Prologue" (motion picture), Universal Education and Visual Arts, 1971.

SIDELIGHTS: **May 7, 1812.** Born in Camberwell, London. Father, Robert Browning Sr. a clerk for the Bank of England. "I have a fancy, to account for some peculiari-

ties in [my father] which connects them with some abominably early experience. [But],—if you question him about it, he shuts his eyes involuntarily and shows exactly the same marks of loathing that may be noticed while a piece of cruelty is mentioned . . . and the *word* 'blood,' even, makes him change colour . . . [Betty Miller, *Robert Browning A Portrait,* Charles Scribner's Sons, 1952.[1]]

"It would have been quite unpardonable in my case, not to have done my best. My dear father put me in a condition most favorable for the best work I was capable of. When I think of the many authors who have had to fight their way through all sorts of difficulties, I have no reason to be proud of my achievements. . . . He secured for me all the care and comfort that a literary man needs to do good work. It would have been shameful if I had not done my best to realize his expectations of me." [*The Poems and Plays of Robert Browning,* edited by Myra Reynolds, Scott, Foresman, 1909.[2]]

"With a touch of ambition, even a spice of vanity, he would assuredly have won a reputation in more ways than one. [But he was the sort of man] who would have stared to hear himself mentioned as remarkable." [William Irvine and Park Honan, *The Book, the Ring, & the Poet,* McGraw-Hill, 1974.[3]]

Browning's mother, Sarah Anna Wiedemann, a religious Scottish gentlewoman, was the unspoken power in the family circle. "In my early boyhood, I had a habit of calling people 'fools' with as little reverence as could be. [It was my mother who] solemnly represented to me after such offences that 'whoso calleth his brother "fool" is in danger &c. for he hath committed murder in his heart already' &c. in short—there was no help for it—I stood there a convicted *murderer* . . . to which I was forced penitently to agree. . . ."[1]

1814. Sister Sarianna was born. It was an unusually serene and happy childhood. His education was conducted at home through his father and private tutors. There was hardly a time when he was not writing in verse. "I desire, to write out certain things which are in me, and so to say my soul. . . .

"(For a new thought sprung up—that it were well
To leave all shadowy hopes, and weave such lays
As would encircle me with praise and love;
So, I should not die utterly—I should bring
One branch from the gold forest, like the knight
Of old tales, witnessing I had been there.)"[1]

While he lived at home, he and his mother shared parallel states of ill-health: "The connection between our ailings is no fanciful one. A few weeks ago when my medical advisor was speaking about the pain and its cause . . . 'Why has anybody to search far for a cause of whatever nervous disorder you suffer from, when *there* sits your mother . . . whom you so absolutely resemble . . . I can trace every feature &c. &c.' to which I did not answer. . . ."[1]

October, 1828. Entered London University.

May 4, 1829. Withdrew from the University feeling the separation from his home and family severely.

Yesterday's Authors of Books for Children

1833. Pressured by his family and friends to pursue a career in some field suitable to earning a living, he made known his feelings: "For my own future way in the world I have always refused to care . . . I had the less repugnance to my father's generosity, that I knew that an effort at some time or other might furnish me with a few hundred pounds which would soon cover my very simple expenses. . . . How can work do dishonour to any man? . . . And what is there in poetry to disqualify one from ordinary duties? . . .

"Well, when they won't pay me for my cabbages, nor praise me for my poems, I may, if I please, say 'more's the shame' . . . and *yet* go very light-hearted back to a garden-full of rose trees, and a soul-full of comforts."[1]

1838. First trip to Naples: "Temples and palaces like fabrics of enchantment piled to heaven."[1]

March, 1840. His book *Sordello,* the product of seven years work, is received with humiliating criticism: "[My] early poems were so transparent in their meaning as to draw down upon [me] the ridicule of the critics, and that, boy that [I] was, this ridicule and censure stung [me] into quite another style of writing. . . .

"How they talk calmly of my throes—my fierce
Aspirings, terrible watchings—each one claiming
Its price of blood and brain; how they dissect
And sneeringly disparage the few truths
Got at a life's cost . . . Wretched crew!"[1]

The conflict grew in his mind as to whether life outside the walls of his family home was worth the risk. The disparity of feelings occupied his thoughts: "About one's family not 'growing' proportionately to one's own growth . . . I meant *symmetrically* rather: for they may grow just as you grow, only—here's the fault—you none of you profit by each other's growth, it is not in your direction, but for somebody else to profit by—much as with a cluster of fruits on a common twig: each may bulge out round and red enough in the sun's eye, but the place where all the clustered knobs touch, where each continues to be known to the other, *that* is hard and green, and as insipid as ever.

"Lovers grow cold, men learn to hate their wives,
And only parents' love can last our lives."

Into the street the Piper stept smiling first a little smile. ■ (From the movie "The Pied Piper," copyright 1971 Paramount Pictures.)

Little hands clapping and little tongues chattering,
And, like fowls in a farm-yard when barley is scattering,
Out came the children running.
■ (From *The Pied Piper of Hamelin* by Robert Browning. Illustrated by Kate Greenaway.)

"[There is the need of every poet to obtain] a free way for impulses that can find vent in no other channel; so instinctively does the Young Poet feel that his desire for this kind of self-enfranchisement will be resisted as a matter of course, that we will venture to say, in nine cases out of ten his first assumption of the license will be made in a borrowed name. . . . Monstrously ambitious thoughts begin to rise like clouds within me. . . . All these disputed questions in the lives of men of genius . . . all these so called calamities of authors—have a common relationship, a connexion so close and inalienable, that they seldom fail to throw important light upon each other.

"It is as old as the world itself, the tendency of certain spirits to subdue each man by perceiving what will master him, by straightway supplying it from their own resources, and so obtaining, as tokens of success, his admiration, or fear, or wonder. . . . [I] really made the most gallant and manly effort of which [my] circumstances allowed to break through the sorry meshes that entangled me. . . . All [my] distress arose out of the impossibility of [my] saying any thing to the real purpose."[1]

1844. Second trip to Naples after the failure of *Sordello:* "My own health is none of the best. I go out but seldom . . . So glides this foolish life away; week by week . . . here everything goes flatly on . . . I make no new friends . . . I am dull, in every sense, this dull evening . . . my *head* which sings and whirls."[1]

"All you gain by travel is the discovery that you have gained nothing, and have done rightly in trusting to your innate ideas—or not done rightly in distrusting them, as the case may be. . . . After this, you go boldly on your own resources, and are justified to yourself, that's all."[1]

The works of Percy Bysshe Shelley had been the greatest single influence on his writing, while in Italy he visiting Shelley's grave: "The lambent flame is—where? Lost from the natural world . . . The Bush is bare."[1]

Upon his return to London he purchased two volumes of poetry that had been published during his absence. They were the *Poems* of Elizabeth Barrett: "[I continued to] read, read, read . . . the fresh strange music, the affluent language, the exquisite pathos and new true brave thought . . . octaves on octaves of quite new golden strings."[1]

He wrote to her:—"I do, as I say, love these books with all my heart—and I love you too. . . . this is no off-hand complimentary letter . . . so into me [have your words] gone, and part of me has it become, this great living poetry of yours."[3]

May 20, 1845. First met Elizabeth Barrett after months of correspondence. "I fancied you just what I found you—I knew you from the beginning . . . [I should like] to shut myself in four walls of a room with you and never leave you and be most all *then* 'a lord of infinite space' . . . the dearest four walls I have ever been enclosed by."[1]

There was an immediate obstacle to this friendship and courtship leading to marriage; Elizabeth (who he called "Ba") had been a confined invalid for many years. Nonetheless he persisted: "From the beginning and at this moment I never dreamed of winning your *love*. . . . Now while I *dream,* let me once dream! I would marry you now and thus—I would come when you let me and go when you bade me—I would be no more than one of your brothers—'no more'—that is, instead of getting tomorrow for Saturday, I should get Saturday as well—when your head ached I would be *here*. Have you not discovered by this time that I go on talking with my thoughts away? . . . There are many things in which I agree with you to such a tremblingly exquisite exactness, so to speak, that I hardly dare cry out lest the charm break.'"[1]

January 27, 1846. He wrote to her: "I claim your promise's fulfillment—say at the summer's end: it cannot be for your own good that this state of things should continue. We can go to Italy for a year or two and be as happy as day and night are long. . . . The ground is crumbling from beneath our feet . . . the spring passes away without the true spring feeling, and then summer itself. . . . All the roses fast going, lilies going . . . autumnal hollyhocks in full blow. . . . Would it be profane, to think of that lament . . . 'the Summer is ended and we are not saved'? . . . therefore think and decide, my Ba! . . . *Now!* jump with me out, Ba!'"[1]

September 12, 1846. They were married and a week later sailed for Italy: "I cannot imagine any condition of life, however full of hardship, which her presence would not render not merely supportable but delicious . . . the divine goodness and infinite tenderness of her heart, that wonderful mind of hers.

"If you take a man from prison and set him free . . . do you not probably cause a single interruption to his previously all engrossing occupation, and sole labour of love, of carving bone-boxes, making chains of cherry stones . . . Does he ever take up that business again with the old alacrity? No! But he begins ploughing, building—(castles he makes, no bone-boxes now).

April 9, 1849. A son Robert was born, nicknamed "Pen." Two weeks later Browning's mother died in England. "[This place] or any other would do me no good of itself, any more than Florence—for apart from the folly and wickedness of the feeling, I am wholly tired of opening my eyes on the world now."[1]

November 17, 1855. *Men and Women* published and greeted with very poor reviews. He continued to be troubled over the reception of his writing: "I can have little doubt that my writing has been in the main too hard for many I should have been pleased to communicate with; but I never designedly tried to puzzle people as some of my critics have supposed. On the other hand, I never pretended to offer such literature as should be a substitute for a cigar or a

Robert Browning (Photo by W. H. Grove.)

game at dominoes to an idle man. So, perhaps, on the whole, I got my deserts, and something over—not a crowd but a few I value more. . . . My stress lay on the incidents in the development of a human soul; little else is worth study. . . . The subtle thing called spirit, the soul's world. . . . I say that man was made to grow not stop. . . . A flying point of bliss remote, a happiness in store afar, a sphere of distant glory. . . . A man's reach should exceed his grasp or what's a heaven for.''[2]

June 29, 1861. Elizabeth Barrett Browning died. He left Italy and returned to London to live: "I hardly know—or care to think—whether I like the things best here, or there, or at the bottom of the sea. . . . Pen, the golden curls and fantastic dress, is gone just as Ba is gone; he has short hair, worn boy-wise, long trousers, is a common boy all at once. . . . I could no more take root in life again, than learn some new dancing step. . . . I shall grow, still, I hope—but my root is taken, [nothing?] remains. . . .''[3]

He became very heavily concerned with the education of his overly-pampered son: "I am quite of your mind about college acquirements and fame, and how little they prove the owner a person of soul's quality: but a race is a race, and whoever tries ought to win. . . . I am always strict upon *rights* in this world, and let generosity and all its derivative virtues and graces show themselves or keep quiet as they please—provided justice is done in the first place. . . . How hard it is for people to get money! I don't wonder they grow misers. It is so terrible to leave all your soul's business and set about getting fifty pounds—even your sorrows you would have to give up. . . . I have ten times the reason to lay up money, and do distasteful things . . . with a son who may want no end of money. . . . There has devolved upon me every sort of sad business that seemed duty, and I am as full as a sponge of vinegar and gall just now.''[1]

1863. *The Poetical Works of Robert Browning* was published in three volumes.

1866. His father died and his sister, Sarianna, came to live with him: "[She has a] habit of repeating all things as on a rosary, as if she did a sacred duty.''[1]

1868. The first three volumes of *The Ring and the Book* were published and received unstinting praise, they were called a spiritual treasure and the most supreme poetical achievement of the time.

1870. His son failed to pass an examination at Oxford and was asked to leave. "All I can do—except to give money—is *done* and done in vain. . . . I am merely the manger at which he feeds, and nothing is more certain than that I could do him no greater good than by dying tonight and leaving him just enough to keep him from starving.''[1]

1881. The Browning Society established.

October 4, 1887. His son married: "You could not do a wiser, better thing, than marry the in every way suitable lady whom you have been fortunate enough to induce to take such a step, and who, you are bound to feel, behaves with the utmost generosity.''[1]

September, 1889. He revisited his favorite Italian town, Asolo: "To think that I should be here again! . . . I shall make the most of the remaining Autumn days,—walk about and enjoy myself.

"Shall I whisper to you my ambition and my hope? It is to write a tragedy better than anything I have done yet. I think of it constantly.''[1]

December, 1889. Caught a chill which developed into bronchitis, this gave way to unmistakable signs of heart failure: "Never say of me that I am dead! . . . Thus I believe, thus I affirm, thus I am certain it is, that from this life I shall pass to another better there where that lady lives of whom my soul was enamoured.''[2]

December 12, 1889. Died at the age of 77.

FOR MORE INFORMATION SEE: Marie A. Molineux, *A Phrase Book from the Poetic and Dramatic Works of Robert Browning,* Houghton, 1896, reprinted, Gale, 1971; G. K. Chesterton, *Robert Browning,* Macmillan, 1903, reprinted, R. West, 1973; Edward Dowden, *Robert Browning,* Dutton, 1904, reprinted, R. West, 1973; Samuel S. Curry, *Browning and the Dramatic Monologue,* Expression, 1908, reprinted, Haskell House, 1969; William Hall Griffin, *The Life of Robert Browning* (completed and edited by Harry C. Minchin), Macmillan, 1910, 3rd edition, revised and enlarged, Methuen, 1938, reprinted, Shoe String Press, 1972; Lilian Whiting, *The Brownings: Their Life and Art,* Little, Brown, 1911, reprinted, Haskell House, 1972; Arthur R. Skemp, *Robert Browning,* Jack, 1916, reprinted, Haskell House, 1974; Fannie Barrett Browning, *Some Memories of Robert Browning,* Marshall Jones, 1928.

Rudolf Besier, *The Barretts of Wimpole Street* (five-act play), Little, Brown, 1930; W. C. DeVane, *A Browning Handbook,* F. S. Crofts, 1935, 2nd edition, Prentice-Hall,

1955; L. N. Broughton, *Robert Browning: A Bibliography, 1830-1950*, Cornell University Press, 1953, reprinted, B. Franklin, 1970; Betty Bergson Miller, *Robert Browning: A Portrait*, Scribner, 1953, new edition, 1973; Katherine H. Porter, *Through a Glass Darkly: Spiritualism in the Browning Circle*, University of Kansas Press, 1958, reissued, Octagon, 1972; Philip Drew, editor, *Robert Browning: A Collection of Critical Essays*, Houghton, 1960; Park Honan, *Browning's Characters: A Study in Poetic Technique*, Yale University Press, 1961, reprinted, Shoe String Press, 1969; N. B. Crowell, *The Triple Soul: Browning's Theory of Knowledge*, University of New Mexico Press, 1963; Boyd Litzinger and K. L. Knickerbocker, editors, *The Browning Critics*, University Press of Kentucky, 1965; Warner Barnes, *The Browning Collection at the University of Texas*, University of Texas Press, 1967; Thomas Blackburn, *Robert Browning: A Study of His Poetry*, Eyre & Spottiswoode, 1967, Rowman & Littlefield, 1974; W. D. Shaw, *The Dialectical Temper: The Rhetorical Art of Robert Browning*, Cornell University Press, 1968; Maisie Ward, *Robert Browning and His World*, two volumes, Holt, 1968-69.

Boyd Litzinger and Donald Smalley, editors, *Browning: The Critical Heritage*, Barnes & Noble, 1970; Clarence Tracy, editor, *Browning's Mind and Art*, Barnes & Noble, 1970; Ioan W. Williams, *Browning*, Arco, 1970; N. B. Crowell, *A Reader's Guide to Robert Browning*, University of New Mexico Press, 1972; Donald S. Hair, *Browning's Experiments with Genre*, University of Toronto Press, 1972; William E. Harrold, *The Variance and the Unity: A Study of Browning's Complementary Poems*, Ohio University Press, 1973; Ian Jack, *Browning's Major Poetry*, Oxford University Press, 1973; William Irvine and Park Honan, *The Ring, the Book, and the Poet: A Biography of Robert Browning*, McGraw-Hill, 1974; Robert B. Pearsall, *Robert Browning*, Twayne, 1974; Isobel Armstrong, editor, *Writers and Their Backgrounds: Robert Browning*, Ohio University Press, 1975; Clyde De L. Ryals, *Browning's Later Poetry, 1871-1889*, Cornell University Press, 1975.

For children: Helen and John Cournos, *Famous British Poets*, Dodd, 1952; Aubrey De Selincourt, *Six Great Poets*, Hamish Hamilton, 1956; Kathleen Wallace, *Elizabeth and Robert* (illustrated by Astrid Walford), Heinemann, 1956; Frances Winwar, *Elizabeth: The Romantic Story of Elizabeth Barrett Browning* (illustrated by Enrico Arno), World Publishing, 1957.

(From the movie "The Pied Piper," adapted by Nevil Shute, copyright 1942, Twentieth-Century Fox, starring Monty Woolley.)

CAMP, Walter (Chauncey) 1859-1925

PERSONAL: Born April 7, 1859, in New Britain, Connecticut; died March 14, 1925; married Alice Graham Sumner; children: Walter, Janet. *Education:* Yale University, A.B., 1880; attended Yale Medical School for two years.

CAREER: New Haven Clock Company, began as a clerk, became president and chairman of the board of directors. Head football coach and director of athletics at Yale University; supervisor of the U.S. Navy's athletic program during World War I; football authority and sports writer.

WRITINGS—Fiction: (With Lilian Brooks) *Drives and Puts: A Book of Golf Stories,* L. C. Page, 1899; *The Substitute: A Football Story,* D. Appleton, 1908; *Jack Hall at Yale: A Football Story,* D. Appleton, 1909; *Old Ryerson,* D. Appleton, 1911; *Danny Fists,* D. Appleton, 1913; *Captain Danny,* D. Appleton, 1914; *Danny the Freshman,* D. Appleton, 1915.

Non-fiction: (Compiler) *Foot Ball Records of American Teams,* Wright & Ditson, 1883; *Foot Ball: How to Coach a Team,* Wright & Ditson, 1886; *American Football,* Harper & Brothers, 1891, new and enlarged edition, 1896; *Base Ball: A Complete History of the College Base Ball from the Year 1886 to the Present Time,* American Sports Publishing, 1893; (compiler) *Football Facts and Figures: A Symposium of Expert Opinions on the Game's Place in American Athletics,* Harper & Brothers, 1894; (with Lorin F. Deland) *Football,* Houghton, 1896; *Walter Camp's Book of College Sports,* Century, 1898; (editor) *Spalding's How to Play Football: A Primer on the Modern College Game with Tactics Brought Down to Date,* American Sports Publishing, 1902; (editor) *Sports and Games* (illustrated by C. M. Relyea), P. Collier, 1903; *Condensed Bridge for the Busy Man,* P. Collier, 1909.

The Book of Football, Century, 1910; *Football for the Spectator,* R. G. Badger, 1911; *Condensed Auction for the Busy Man,* Platt & Peck, 1912; *Auction Up-to-Date, including Nullos: Systems for the Practical Player,* Platt & Peck, 1913; *Keeping Fit All the Way: How to Obtain and Maintain Health, Strength and Efficiency* (illustrated with photographs), Harper & Brothers, 1919; *Athletics All: Training, Organization, and Play,* Scribner, 1919; *Handbook on Health and How to Keep It,* D. Appleton, 1920; *Football without a Coach,* D. Appleton, 1920; *Training for Sports,* Scribner, 1921; *The Daily Dozen for Men and Women,* Reynolds, 1921; (editor) *The Book of Sports and Games,* Crowell, 1923; *A Pocket Bridge Book,* Doubleday, Page, 1923; *Help Yourself,* W. G. Rose, 1925; *Get Ready,* W. G. Rose, 1925.

SIDELIGHTS: **April 7, 1859.** Born in New Britain, Connecticut—a thin boy, not muscular, but spirited. "When we call a boy a thoroughbred, we know he is a boy who is high-spirited, plucky, courageous, and strong. Every boy wants to be the type that is described by these expressions. To make himself fit, he must follow the precepts of health and of morality. Every boy is eager to stand well with his fellows, to be an aid to his team in its sports, to be an individual champion, to play fair and to play well. These things are possible under a course of care and self-discipline not difficult of attainment by any youth.

Walter Camp

"If, however, a boy has *the wish to excel,* he takes on a contract which involves patience, self-control, persistence, and hard work. No boy or man ever made himself a leader in sports, or in life, without doing a great deal of hard work which at times seemed to be drudgery. No one comes to the top without making certain sacrifices. It is not an easy road, but it is an eminently satisfactory road, because it leads to the desired end." [Harford Powell, Jr., *Walter Camp the Father of American Football,* Books for Libraries Press, 1970.[1]]

1867(?) Attended Hopkins Grammar School. Maintained good grades and played football at recess—always keeping fit. "Look at James J. Hill a great grizzly bear of a man who gained his enormous physical strength in railroad construction camps. Look at the man who founded the Vanderbilt family, a sailboat man, accustomed to hoisting sail and handling the tiller in any weather, as part of his ferry business. Collis P. Huntington was a farm hand. Marshall Field grew up on a farm. All were accustomed to hard outdoor labor of some kind, and thus had advantages denied to many of our younger men to-day. The sons and grandsons of men like these are city born and bred. Body-building toil has gone out of their lives."[1]

1876. Entered Yale having been sixth in a class of 35 at Hopkins.

1877. As captain of the Yale football team, he decided a player who had broken training rules was to be dropped from the team. The other players objected. "They told me that this man had learned his lesson, and must be reinstated for the good of the team. I knew that he could not be trusted, and that I had given him every opportunity to deserve confidence. I did not make a hasty decision, and I felt that it must be obeyed. We had a very hot argument, and I resigned the captaincy and left the room. I wanted to play in the coming game, but I did not believe I could give my best efforts in behalf of a team with the members of which I was in such radical disagreement. I spent a very bad night, asking myself if I was doing the right thing, or merely giving way to the spirit of revenge—in which case, I would be both hurting myself and hurting Yale. The happiest moment in my college days came soon afterward, when the men returned and told me that they knew my motives were right, that my decision should stand, and that I was to become their captain again."[1]

Entered Yale Medical School, studying faithfully for two years. Finally decided to drop out. "The fact is that I can't bear the sight of blood."[1]

1896. Wrote *Football* with Lorin Deland.

1905. Invited to attend a football conference at the White House sponsored by Theodore Roosevelt.

1910. Began rewriting football rules for safety and fair play. Became known as "Father of American Football." "In legislating, remember that what a gentleman wants is fair play and the best man to win. When it is possible without losing sight of this, to legislate for improvements in methods, so much the better; but primarily make every rule such that the probability of unfinished, drawn, or disputed contests is reduced to a minimum.

"Football is essentially a game of severe moral and mental standards. No dullard can play the game successfully. Early in his career the football player will find developed in him a degree of self-reliance which probably no other sport in the world would inculcate. He acquired another and an even more valuable quality—self-control. Whatever the provocation, he must never lose his temper, never let his attention be drawn from the play. No game so tries the temper as does football. To promptness of decision and self-restraint the player must also add courage. He must have it to start with, and he will find that he has much more of it as the season advances.

"An army poorly officered becomes a mob; a football team without discipline would be even worse off. The player must bear the biting sarcasm of the coaches without the thought of rebellion. Every order must be unquestioningly obeyed. There are other minor advantages to the player, which must be passed over with a few words. The game requires coolness; it leads to a study of the dispositions of men, and teaches the subordination of strength to will. There is an element in human nature which finds a powerful attraction in personal contest between man and man. We cannot suppress this element, but we may wisely direct it. While in some sports it leads to cheating, it has quite an opposite effect in football. The man who loses his temper will be outplayed. The man who plays an unfair game loses more for his side than he can possibly gain.

"With no disrespect to any other class or condition, I say that the collegian's standard of purity in sports should be the highest. The very fact that he has leisure to devote four years to a higher education should be taken to involve the duty of acquiring a keener perception of right and wrong in matters where right and wrong depend upon delicacy of honor. Gentlemen do not cheat, nor do they deceive themselves as to what cheating is. If you are the captain of a nine, an eleven, or a crew, read over the rules and notice exactly who are allowed to play as contestants by these rules—not merely by the custom of some predecessor, or of your rival, but by the rules themselves. Having done that, do not let a thought enter your head of using some man not clearly and cleanly eligible. It is your duty to know that every one of your men is straight and square. I know what I am talking about when I say that a college captain can, in ninety-nine cases out of a hundred, know the exact truth about every man he thinks of trying.

"It is quite the fashion to say 'sentimental bosh' to anyone who preaches such an old-fashioned thing as honor in sport,

By Walter Camp

Famous Yale Coach's "Daily Dozen" Exercises Now on Phonograph Records

WALTER CAMP
Originator of the Famous "Daily Dozen" System

(A 1922 newspaper article on Walter Camp from the New York Public Library collection.)

but among true gentlemen honor is just as real an article as ever, and it can never ring false. The man who tells you the insufferable rot about being 'practical' and discarding sentiment is not the man you should choose as a friend. He will not stand by you in a pinch. When we come to realities, it is only the man who believes in such things as honor that is worth anything."[1]

He advised spectators: "After winning a match there is no reason why a lot of young men should not do plenty of cheering, but there is every reason why they should not make their enjoyment depend upon insulting those who have lost. You cannot take your hilarity off into a corner and choke it to death. But jeers and jibes at the crestfallen mark you as a man who does not know how to bear victory, a man whose pate is addled by excitement, or whose bringing up has been at fault. When celebrating, do not, I beg of you, do anything because it looks smart. Enjoy yourselves, but do not try to show off. Don't be tough. A little unusual hilarity may upon occasions be overlooked and forgiven, but be ready to appreciate the point beyond which it is carried too far. Show that behind the jolly fun you have the instincts and cultivation of a gentleman's son. If you find you are losing your head, go home; you will not be sorry for it."[1]

1917. Sought for advice on physical exercise for recruits during World War I, he developed the "Daily Dozen." "At the first station I visited, the hospital was a pest house. Lads were in bed with sharp attacks of measles, or sitting around in the throes of mumps, chicken pox, and other children's diseases. Their bodies offered little resistance to the bacteria that carried these minor plagues; and they were in equally poor condition to resist serious contagions like meningitis, scarlet fever, and influenza. The surgeons were keenly alert to prevent the spread of such diseases, but their efforts were largely negatived by the overtiring effect of the setting-up drill. My task was to devise a simple system of movements that would build resistance—not crush it. That was why I worked out the Daily Dozen.

"Twelve simple movements were found to meet the needs, so the young men would resist fatigue as well as contagion. Having worked out these movements, I tried them on classes of men, emphasizing that they were to be done lightly and naturally, more in the spirit of refreshment than with lips compressed, lungs heaving, and muscles tightly flexed."[1]

He declined offers to exploit his "Daily Dozen" commercially. "Promise a boy that you can teach him to chin himself with one hand, and he will pay you for lessons. Promise a middle-aged man or woman that you can melt fat away without too much pain, and you can keep them coming to you for months. The private gymnasium is a gold mine. I expect to see a large industry, presided over by ex-trainers of prizefighters and woolly-headed physical culture 'professors' of one kind and another. But I won't let myself into it. My wife has an entirely proper horror of it. Any attempt on my part to make money out of the Daily Dozen would be regarded as an effort to capitalize [on] my reputation in amateur athletics."[1]

March 14, 1925. Died. "How does happiness come? . . . A sick man has no time to think of anything except his own condition. A well man 'rejoiceth as a strong man to run a race.' Each one of us may have a different picture of happiness. The golfer who has never been under 110 strokes finishes a round, it may be, in 99 strokes. He is happy, but the 99 strokes that brought him happiness would be gall and wormwood to the scratch player. A tennis player who has never before survived the early rounds comes up to the finals and takes the runner-up's prize. And that prize makes him happy, even though he finds himself outclassed by the champion. The man who has no luck all his life in his investments wakes up some morning to find that a stock he had supposed worthless is suddenly running up in leaps and bounds, and his holdings in it may make him free from money troubles again. And he is happy. An unexpected public honor may bring happiness to one, a relief from harassing cares may bring it to another. Someone has said that mere freedom from intolerable pain is the happiness of the aged; but this would mean nothing to the youth who does not know pain. His must be an active, not a passive happiness. His must be success, victory. And these can come only through health and work beforehand."[1]

FOR MORE INFORMATION SEE: Stanley J. Kunitz and Howard Haycraft, editors, *Junior Book of Authors,* Wilson, 1951; J. S. Martin, *Walter Camp and His Gridiron Game,* American Heritage, 1961; Harford Powell, Jr., *Walter Camp: The Father of American Football,* Books for Libraries, 1970.

CANFIELD, Dorothy
See FISHER, Dorothy Canfield

CARLETON, Captain L. C.
See ELLIS, Edward S(ylvester)

CHRISMAN, Arthur Bowie   1889-1953

PERSONAL: Born July 16, 1889, on "Westbrook," a farm near White Post, Virginia; died February 24, 1953, in Shirley, Arkansas; son of Isaac Arthur and Mary Louise (Bryarly) Chrisman. *Education:* Attended a one-room schoolhouse in his youth; Virginia Polytechnic Institute, student, 1906-08. *Religion:* Episcopalian. *Home:* Fox, Arkansas.

CAREER: School teacher for two years; also worked, at various times, as a farmer, draftsman, movie extra, lecturer, and story-teller; writer. *Awards, honors:* Newbery Medal, 1926, for *Shen of the Sea.*

WRITINGS: Shen of the Sea (stories; illustrated by Else Hasselriis), Dutton, 1925, reissued, 1968; *The Wind That Wouldn't Blow: Stories of the Merry Middle Kingdom for Children, and Myself* (illustrated by Else Hasselriis), Dutton, 1927; *Treasures Long Hidden: Old Tales and New Tales of the East* (illustrated by Weda Yap), Dutton, 1941.

SIDELIGHTS: Arthur Bowie Chrisman's favorite books were "action stories of the extreme type, told out of doors, usually up a tree. I thought nothing of dropping ten feet from bough to bough . . . and strange to say there was never so much as a deep scratch received while reciting and chanting and wildly acting the stories of 'Wonderful Peedie the Monkey.'" In bad weather these stories were told in the upper room of the abandoned slave quarters. "Here I kept all of my treasures, clay men and clay jugs, sailing ships, and bows and arrows, sand mills and wind mills, water mills and heat mills, sleds, wagons, fishing poles and many other contrivances, all made by my own hands. I never owned more than a half dozen bought toys in my life, but made my own toys in the thousands.

"I never have written with the idea of making a fortune, I merely decided to write and let fate take care of all subsequent happenings.

"My favorite motto has always been an old Chinese proverb, 'Walk slowly, perhaps the river will have receded when you come to it.'" [Bertha Mahony Miller and Elinor Whitney Field, *Newbery Medal Books: 1922-1955,* Horn Book, 1955.]

FOR MORE INFORMATION SEE: Stanley J. Kunitz and Howard Haycraft, editors, *Junior Book of Authors,* H.W. Wilson, 1934, 1951; Elizabeth C. Reed, "Arthur Bowie Chrisman, 1889-1953," in *Newbery Medal Books, 1922-1955,* edited by Bertha Mahony Miller and Elinor Whitney Field, Horn Book, 1955.

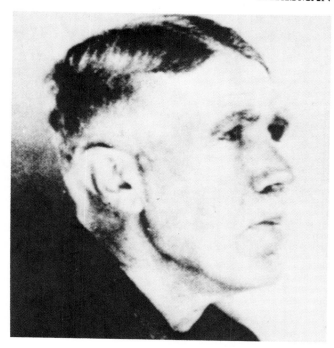

Arthur Bowie Chrisman

(From "Shen of the Sea," Weston Woods filmstrip.)

How could they know that the flapping was caused by a man-made thing, later to be named "feng cheng" (kite)? And how could they know that the eyes were mere bottles, filled with insects called "Bright at night" (fireflies)? ■ (From *Shen of the Sea* by Arthur Bowie Chrisman. Illustrated by Else Hasselriis.)

COPPARD, A(lfred) E(dgar)   1878-1957

PERSONAL: Surname pronounced *Kop*-ard; born January 4, 1878, in Folkestone, Kent, England; died January 13, 1957; son of George (a tailor) and Emily Alma (a housemaid; maiden name, Southwell) Coppard; married Lily Anne, 1906; married second wife, Winifred May deKok; children: one son, one daughter. *Education:* Self-educated after leaving elementary school at the age of nine. *Home:* Dunmow, Essex, England.

CAREER: Held a variety of jobs from the age of nine, including shop boy for a tailor, office boy, professional sprinter, clerk, and accountant for an engineering firm in Oxford, 1907-1919; full-time writer of poems and short stories, beginning 1919.

WRITINGS—All short story collections, except as indicated: *Adam and Eve and Pinch Me,* Golden Cockerel, 1921, Knopf, 1922, reprinted, Books for Libraries, 1970; *Clorinda Walks in Heaven,* Golden Cockerel, 1922; *The Black Dog, and Other Stories,* Knopf, 1923, reprinted, Books for Libraries, 1970; *Fishmonger's Fiddle,* Knopf, 1925, reprinted, Books for Libraries, 1970; *The Field of Mustard,* J. Cape, 1926, Knopf, 1927; *Silver Circus,* J. Cape, 1928, Knopf, 1929.

Pink Furniture: A Tale for Lovely Children with Noble Natures (illustrated by Nancy Bankart Gurney), J. Cape and H. Smith, 1930; *Nixey's Harlequin,* J. Cape, 1931, Knopf, 1932; *Rummy: That Noble Game Expounded in Prose, Poetry, Diagram and Engravings* (game; illustrated by Robert Gibbings), Golden Cockerel, 1932, Houghton, 1933; *Dunky Fitlow,* J. Cape, 1933; (contributor) *The Fairies Return: Or, New Tales for Old,* P. Davies, 1934; *Polly Oliver,* J. Cape, 1935, reprinted, Books for Libraries, 1970; *Ninepenny Flute: Twenty-One Tales,* Macmillan (London), 1937, reprinted, Books for Libraries, 1970; *You Never Know, Do You? and Other Tales,* Methuen, 1939.

Ugly Anna, and Other Tales, Methuen, 1944; *Fearful Pleasures,* Arkham, 1946; *Selected Tales from His Twelve Volumes Published between the Wars,* J. Cape, 1946; *Dark-Eyed Lady: Fourteen Tales,* Methuen, 1947; *The Collected Tales of A. E. Coppard,* Knopf, 1948, reissued, 1966; *Lucy in Her Pink Jacket,* P. Nevill, 1954; *It's Me, O Lord!* (autobiography), Methuen, 1957; *Selected Stories* (introduction by Doris Lessing), J. Cape, 1972.

Stories published separately: *Count Stefan* (illustrated by Robert Gibbings), Golden Cockerel, 1928; *The Higgler,* Chocorua, 1930; *The Man from Kilsheelan* (illustrated by Gibbings), W. Jackson, 1930; *The Hundredth Story of A. E. Coppard* (illustrated by Gibbings), Golden Cockerel, 1931; *Crotty Shinkwin [and] The Beauty Spot* (illustrated by Gibbings), Golden Cockerel, 1932; *Ring the Bells of Heaven,* White Owl, 1933; *Emergency Exit,* Random House, 1934; *Tapster's Tapestry,* Golden Cockerel, 1938.

Poems: *Hips and Haws,* Golden Cockerel, 1922; (editor) *Songs from Robert Burns* (illustrated by Mabel M. Annesley), Golden Cockerel, 1925; *Yokohama Garland, and Other Poems* (illustrated by Wharton Esherick), Centaur, 1926; *Pelagea and Other Poems* (illustrated by Robert Gibbings), Golden Cockerel, 1926; *Collected Poems,* Knopf, 1928; *Cherry Ripe* (illustrated by Valenti Angelo), Hawthorne House, 1935 (published in England with illustrations by Sylvia Marshall, Tintern, 1935).

SIDELIGHTS: **January 4, 1878.** "I was born the son of George the tailor and Emily Alma the housemaid . . . in the county of Kent, Folkestone, the borough with Caesar's Camp and Sugarloaf Hill close by. Nobody specially noted the event except my parents and a doctor who came to [my mother] carrying a black bag. I was often to wonder what that black bag had contained, its blackness being somehow insistent, even sinister. In time I learned from Mother that it had contained me. Somewhat dubious then, I have been dubious since about many other things she told me. Actually there had not been a doctor at all—my mother was always wildly given to romantic fiction—there was not even an old midwife, a friendly neighbour lent a helping hand.

"A registrar had to be told about it. . . . Should you happen to be one of a couple responsible for somebody's birth, it behoves you to go, indeed you are bound to go, and tell a registrar somewhere, personally, about it. In the years to come he will be able to charge you a trifle for telling you again what you then, in the sheer joy of your heart, told him for nothing. I have myself paid . . . a shilling or two for a recapitulation of the agreeable occasion, testifying that it was me who had then occurred.

"Five years . . . was the whole span of my life at Folkestone. I know we were lodgers in two rooms of the house of a man named Winton who was manifestly a carpenter, although my mother swore to me in secret that he was really a policeman, a private un-uniformed sort specially ordained for the apprehension of rude little rascals, of whom she artlessly assured me there were then too many living in our very street. A little girl named Florrie belonged to him and his unpleasant wife; she was their daughter, but she also belonged to me for I adored her and wooed her and we loved each other with an un-innocent abandon that was never discovered, was not even suspected. Our family counted five, for I had two sisters younger than myself, but the two rooms must have been snug enough.

"My father was a radical, all tailors were radicals then, free-thinkers to a man and scoffers at hellfire, and so were all cobblers. I recall him as a nice young man of medium height and lean stature, with a chestnut beard, large reddish nose, and thick disordered dark hair—indeed he was always rather untidy, for a tailor anyway. . . . He never seemed to walk with any objective but just strolled along, as though in meditation, with one hand in his trousers pocket and the other folded behind his back. He loved flowers, birds, the open air, and to go a-roving over the hills for mushrooms, blackberries, nuts, cowslips, whatever was seasonable and free, but being doomed, as he knew, by tuberculosis, he became careless and something of a drinker, and so we were always shockingly poor. I well remember the grace which despite my mother's quite spurious expostations—for she was a bubbling laughter-lover—he would get me to intone with him after our Sunday dinners:

> *We thank the Lord for what we've had,*
> *For a little more we would be glad;*
> *But since our parents are so poor*
> *We must be content for we'll get no more.*

COPPARD

"My mother was exceedingly orderly and tidy, and Father's careless habits were her bane, but she was easy to placate and suffered physically I am sure from her own frenzies of laughter." [A. E. Coppard, *It's Me, O Lord!*, Methuen, 1957.[1]]

1884. "From Folkestone we were rudely impelled by a crisis of which I knew only that papa had deserted us and run away. I never knew what caused him to run off, I was too young to apprehend it, too childish to be told, and ever afterwards too unconcerned ever to inquire; it was seventy years ago and they are long dead now, both of them. But we were in sore straits until he wrote a letter from Brighton, the old home of both my parents. He had walked there, it is a long way, a hundred miles, and there were no bicycles then, no cars, no lifts in those days; you had legs and you used them. And Father had got a new job, we were to join him at Brighton and all was going to be well again. So to Brighton we all went, the four of us, and I myself lived there for the next twenty-five years.

"At Brighton I *attended* the *Board School in Fairlight Place,* a school where you then had to take a penny (or was it twopence—something special for the extra copper?) to pay for your education each week. It was worth that much anyway for the solid grounding you received in the three R's, the third of which, though, was my killjoy, my degradation, my Achilles heel—O indeed it was my whole leg!

"Yet, strange to relate, when I grew up I became an accountant and rather rapid at sums. Despite my miserable scholastiness I never once played truant. I may have wanted to at times, I can't remember, but I am sure I was ever too afraid to do anything so base, so dangerous, having an altogether awful regard for any rule or regulation; such things had almost the warranty of Almighty God and how could I bring myself to challenge that!

"My mother had a deep concern for her children's education, nevertheless my schooling ceased when I was but nine years old. This early cessation did not result from any act of truancy or misbehaviour; far from it, I was a mild meek little boy and no prodigy either; nor were my parents gipsies, bargees, or vagrants; it came about in this way. I was held to have acquired, though I have no recollection of it, an unusual malady that enabled the dispensary doctor to certify my fitness for total exemption from the burden of any more schooling. It is true I had once been sent home because of the lice seen in my hair, a deeply shaming affliction which with a perennial scabbiness despite my enraged endeavours pursued me wellnigh into manhood, but this mysterious ailment of which I seem to have been personally unconscious had some reference to the height, or may it not have been the depth? of my liver which I fancied dangled from a sort of pin in my belly much as the liver of a lamb or a calf is suspended on the shop hooks of a butcher. Whether my ambitious liver had surged or drooped I cannot say, but it is certain that some authority and perhaps a little fate decreed there and then that I should not go to school ever again. This interdiction was accepted almost happily and consolingly by my mother, I never went back, my schooldays were ended."[1]

1887. "My father died [of tuberculosis] when he was only twenty-nine and I had but just left school.

"In her widowhood my mother became something of a martinet; she had no time to be kind, my father's death having sunk us at once into destitution. At times she was subject to fits of wild maniacal laughter, at others to torrents of tears. In between she was always fighting against the persistent outwearing of every piece of clothing or boot we possessed, as well as the inevitable neglect we, her four youngsters, and the domesticity suffered from her twelve-hour daily absence at a laundry where she had had to start out as a plain ironer from eight o'clock to eight o'clock at twenty-seven pence a day, and where she achieved the heaven of her ambition when she was later on promoted to first class at two and six per day.

"Although in my youth time there was no other way for a boy like me to 'see the world,' I never ran away to sea or joined the army as drummer or bugle boy. Within the radius of a dozen miles afoot, north, east, or west of Brighton, I could roam a realm of hills and valleys, had but to travel a mile or so for things to happen and play themselves into my fancy. I was a poet by nature though without any poetic ability; having no means of expression I was dumb, but found content and an exalting pastoral joy on the green hills that were so truly mine.

"I do not remember having any literary flair for anything save for just playing around. At school I was nothing of a scholar; I liked drawing, and I liked the singing lessons although I never mastered tonic-solfa and the old notation remained forever Greek to me—as did the songs we had to sing.

> Hearts of oak are our ships,
> Gallant tars are our men,
> We always are ready,
> Steady, boys, steady.

"What does that mean?

"In the poetic field I had my idols—who has not—although most of them wrote more than I wanted of them, much that nothing could induce me to read again. It is stupid, but tempting, to hold that the poet we adore never stepped awry in his art; it is stupider to assume that there is no virtue in the mind that is excited by work that totally fails to please us, and stupid beyond all to think that art which does not please us has no virtue at all. The mind has facets that shine only by reflected light. I am triple-dyed in this stupidity, am ineradicably guilty on all three counts.

"I love Chaucer, Shakespear, Milton, Wordsworth, Keats, Browning and Whitman. I have always hated Dryden, disliked Donne, and got but a thimbleful of joy from Byron or Shelley. Later there is the matchless early Tennyson, and of my own time I found great treasure in Bridges, Masefield, Houseman, Yeats and Hardy."[1]

1888. "It was always understood that I was to follow my father's calling but he died before I had acquainted myself with the craft, my contact with it being broken at his death. It was resumed, however, twelve months later when I was sent up to the East End of London just at the time of the Jack-the-Ripper murders. . . . It was there I lost childhood, innocence, schooling, and became acquainted with grief, starvation, poor clothes, and slums; with a London City then chock-full [of] horse traffic and little boys in scarlet

Yesterday's Authors of Books for Children

jackets scurrying about Cheapside and Leadenhall Street scooping up eternal horsedung. There was a workshop in Whitechapel kept by a nice agreeable Jew named Alabaster who employed half a dozen women to make men's trousers at one and ninepence a time for the various smart tailoring establishments of the city, one of which bore the classic name of Dombey and Son. I was ten years old. I went to work for Mr. Alabaster. There is a good and truthful vignette of this experience presented in my tale 'The Presser.'"[1]

1890. "I was reft from the arms of Mr. Alabaster and transferred to a pool of messenger boys at Reuter's Telegraph Agency in Old Jewry. I don't know how it happened, indeed I never knew, but I fancy it was by the grace of some effort by a friend of the family. Daily I had to descend an iron spiral staircase into a dim cellar under the office into the growling charge of an unsteady, purple-nosed, pompous impossibility named Krekeler.

"There can have been no telephone system then, no tape machines, or it would not have been necessary to employ messengers to trudge afoot with news to the newspapers, bankers, shippers, and brokers, of the greatest city in the world established mainly around Throgmorton Street and Fleet Street. The Safety bicycle was not yet in being and on all important and urgent messages we had to run, for which special service a bonus of threepence a message was earned. During the Spanish-American war, when all messages relating to the conflict had to be run, I drew astonishing wages."[1]

A. E. Coppard, 1921.

1891. "I [returned to] Brighton again and . . . cast the flutter of London from my heart. I was thirteen years old.

"Brighton was never much of a place to look at; it had no fine architecture, no fine history, no cultural texture. There is the military barracks, a country cricket ground, a racecourse, a couple of piers and a frontage wide and open to the sea, with no cover from the winds that sneak up from their stormy refuge in the Bay of Biscay—or somewhere in that direction.

"For a little while I was out of work, an obstacle being not my age but my pigmy stature."[1]

1894. "My life [was] a sort of kaleidoscope of running, reading, falling in love, and trying to write verse. During this period I changed jobs several times, though not so often as I changed my girls, who liked me well enough, as I thought, and always seemed sad to part but, as I divined, were none the less intent on parting. Often, no doubt, my lamentable appearance was the cause, for my ready-made trousers seldom cost more than five shillings and the rest of me was to match; by their standards (alas) I was not a presentable object; by temperament I was no swashbuckler, there was no more to be said. There came the time when I was able to put some gloss on myself, but that was not to be for some years.

"From [an] auctioneers I had gone to the cheesemongers, from the cheesemongers to the soapery. I liked [that] so well that when I got the sack from the soapery for some reason never imparted to me, I went to Jordans the carriers, with whom I worked very happily until I was twenty-one."[1]

1897. "Now while I was at Jordan's a most wonderful thing happened to me. I was awarded a prize in a literary competition organized by a local newspaper, the first I ever entered. That in itself was encouraging as well as fearfully exciting to me, but the special circumstance was that I had to choose a book for my prize. I chose, and I have no recollection now of what led me to the choice, a one-volume edition of Chaucer. . . . It was a tome of nearly nine hundred pages of small print in language that caused me to blench 'more than somewhat'—the glossary alone runs to a hundred and fifty pages!—but which I felt it imperative to conquer, for it had long seemed to be of special propriety for me to absorb some very long poems.

"In the pursuit of culture and understanding of literature I had no tutor or mentor or fellow-seeker after such righteousness, I continued to follow my instinct. What else could I have done? There were no night schools or evening classes for my purpose, I had to find my own way and my instinct seldom misled me.

"Certainly I was never bored, I have never in my life experienced that so common malaise. Nobody could order me to study some book because it was renowned or esteemed; I was not set to prepare any papers for scholarly or examination reasons on subjects that were of no interest to me; I obeyed no alien direction, my own was good enough always. Assiduously I kept to my instinctive channel and was never conscious of a lack of benevolent guidance. I felt no want of assistance or instruction from anybody and always wanted to be alone in this. I was not thwarted by our family poverty, poverty was the environment I had been born into and I had an admirable adaptability. I shrank from conferring with anybody about my private hobby, for I could not bear to be laughed at.

"My mother, still working at the laundry, was scornful of me because I always had my head in a book. How she abused me, but all the same mended my down-at-heel boots herself! I was tyrannical and ruthless too, for I demanded complete silence for the brief time of an evening when we were all together at home, and the loud-ticking clock whose noise exacerbated my dainty nerves had to be removed from the mantelpiece and put out on the stairs. Such preparation of course left me undisciplined, self-willed, opinionated, and intolerant, but I suppose it nourished whatever spark of original talent I had. I was utterly susceptible to poetry and read it seekingly—that is the only fitting work; although there was no positive goal in my seeking beyond the exalting happiness of entering into the enchanting mood."[1]

1899-1907. "Before the Boer War came to annoy us and dreadfully shame us, . . . I left Jordan's and went to work as a departmental clerk with an engineering firm established in a newly built factory opposite the barracks. It was the work-place of some of my friends in football and cricket employed there, fitters, mechanics, and brass finishers, and it was an important move for me although I was unaware of its significance. The stenographers were all engaged more or less to fellows, but the only one who left to get married while I was there, and I was there for eight years, was the one I was eventually fortunate enough to get myself engaged to. After awhile I was promoted. . . . I was given an office to myself with a big increase of salary, the excitement of which sent me scurrying home to Mother with the injunction that she was to quit at once her dreadful laundry job, straightaway, never go near it again, finished. For a while she believed I was . . . making a fool of her. She was positively flummoxed, and argued that it would not be right to behave quite so quick. O no, O yes. No.

"My mother was extremely old-fashioned, she never went in for aspirins, her nostrum was an antibilious pill; she was also extremely work-proud, having graduated into a first-class ironer able to polish the shirt fronts and collars of people who went in for that kind of wear, and she was properly proud of attaining this summit of the laundry ironer's ambition . . . So now. She was positive she ought to keep the job on for a few weeks longer—in case! In case of what? Why, to make sure. Sure of what? . . . Her hesitation and unfaith in me drove me into a passion and so I had to abuse her as usual, on which she surrendered and we kissed . . . and all was well. How proud I was! All the same I knew my pride was mixed with relief at the removal of a stigma."[1]

January, 1907. "[Lily Anne] and I left Brighton for Oxford where I had a clerking job that was to detain me for twelve years. A good deal besides clerking happened to both of us during this time.

"We arrived in . . . exceedingly cold weather, the canal was frozen over, the fringes of the Thames were iced in Port Meadow; . . . we had to get into lodgings in Jericho, . . . and we were cold and miserable there. . . . Moreover my new job presented difficulties that I had not anticipated

or encountered before. Although I was a cost-keeper and soaked in figures, I had not hitherto kept the account ledgers and finance books of a company and consequently knew very little of the procedure with them. To this drawback there was the added nuisance that my predecessor in the post had absconded and left the books in an unsatisfactory condition. However, our furniture and our whippets soon followed us; L. A. got us a couple of rooms in a house at Iffley, my troubles at the office were smoothed out, and soon all began to be very well and comparatively nice except for the disquieting realization that my new firm was financially in something very much lower than low water.

"L. A. revelled in the architectural charms and academic air of Oxford. So did I, and there was also a lot of sport to be observed, with envy by outsiders who had no chance of participating, and with apparent sadness by undergraduates. On first attending a good soccer match I was appalled to find that miracles of agility and rallies of great glory were approved by no more than a cold-blooded clap of the hand when my own private impulse, so hard to curb, was to clout my neighbour over the head with ecstasy and howl the top of the pavilion clean out of the Parks.

"L. A. and I were unhappy in our rooms, we wanted a house to ourselves and our dogs, somewhere in the country nearby, and shortly L. A. went out and found us one at Islip, a sweet stonebuilt cottage having its back garden emerging on a stream which otter-hunters drew, or cast for, or somehow explored with their hounds in the proper season. We stayed there three or four years and the public events I chiefly recall were the great comet that swept the heavens for many a night, a mad snowfall in May, the loss of the *Titanic* and the death of Edward the Seventh.

"Here at last I began to do some writing, although it was many years yet before I was able to place it with any editors. Among stories and poems I recall 'Piffingcap' and 'Clorinda Walks in Heaven,' in both of which there are vague traces of Combe. I don't know how long we stayed there, two years it might have been, for L. A. had established a sort of principle that we should change the place of our abode fairly often, three years being her limit for any one place. I gave up my railway season-ticket and bought a two-stroke motor-cycle out of some money advanced by the firm.

"I remained working at the Eagle Ironworks for twelve years, until 1919, and although . . . thrice we lived in adjacent villages, my association with Oxford was so close and constant and of such importance to me that I must make a sort of conspectus of that whole period irrespective of our place of dwelling.

"Being the head of my office there was seldom any difficulty about my taking time off during office hours to attend lectures and series of lectures in which I was interested. These were devised mainly for the students but the public were freely admitted. I could always make up for the loss of any time so taken—in truth this was necessary!

"Already, for twenty years then, I had risen day by day to hand myself over punctually to certain other persons and do for them a job I had no mind to be doing but which they were unable or unwilling to do themselves on behalf of themselves. By some powerful ordination such people are in a position to compel your attention to their interests for the better part of the day and every day and so on to the end of life. I had enjoyed this peculiar freedom in London and Brighton for twenty years, practising the ritual that was imposed upon such a freeborn creature and impressed upon him as the doing of his duty in that station of life to which it had pleased God to call him—celestial warrant thus being added to the more mundane pressures. For one does want to eat, and in order to eat it is imperative to have access to the means of life, so one casts his pinch of salt upon the altar and makes the best of a serfdom he cannot afford to ignore. I was to go on doing this, still unreluctantly, for another twelve years.

"But it was just there and then, in Oxford, that I first met the thing I recognized as intellect, and it was being so casually exercised by old and by young, startlingly in the young, austerely in the mature.

"In course of time I came to know many undergraduates who were as keen on poetry and art as I was, although often it was not the same poetry or the same art. How we became friendly I do not remember. There was a marked social gap between town and gown, not the traditional melodramatic antagonism—I never experienced any such thing—but there was simply no medium of intercourse or exchange.

"Over the last third of my Oxford time, from 1914 to 1918, lay the desperate gloom of the First World War, the number one that was to end all wars, and was fought by our entrenched infantry in the charge of cavalry generals. They could not win it, we could not stop it, could neither forget it nor ignore it. Some of my friends, both town and gown, went to the trenches and were lost for ever. The Examination Schools in the High became a hospital for officers. I watched the first convoy of wounded to be brought there; among them were some Germans who, as they were borne in on stretchers from the ambulances, were accorded hisses by some patriots, a manifestation that was at once indignantly suppressed by the great crowd that was silently assembled.

"Because of my thirty-eight years I escaped conscription for a while but at length my age group was called upon, late in **1916,** and I was ordered to report at Cowley Barracks for medical examination. I was graded A1 and normally would have been in the Army within a few days, but the Ironworks was by then solely engaged upon munitions, because of which I had already received an exemption certificate, from the government office."

"At the close of **1918,** the fighting being ended, I was plunged into a state of reluctant and tremulous decision, but none the less decision. Not about what I wanted to do, that was pretty clear to me; I had been shaping myself for a literary vocation and intended now, the war being over, to launch myself upon that career. My dubiety was about *when* I was to knock off my clerical shackles and *how,* in the total absence of any resources, I was to manage without a salary. I was forty years old, long past my youth, was married. 'God above! Has he gone daft, do you think?' was what my seriously agitated mother-in-law asked her likewise dubious daughter. For thirty years, barring two periods each of six weeks when I was out of work, I had received weekly or monthly pay, but now that faithful con-

comitant was abruptly to cease, it and I were about to part company, I was to chance my arm and go live on my wits. In subsequent years and soon, other alarms assailed me, but none to compare with the initial unpleasantness that hovered over my voluntary retreat from the secure fastness of a regular income.

"Tales and poems of mine had already been coming out, not in little unfertile brochures, but in well-known and established magazines and journals who paid; this is a matter of intense concern to anyone intending to earn a living by writing. My sorrow! I was soon to discover that there are many other editors and publishers besides those of the little brochures who have to be written off. Already on my hands were a dozen tales and poems that one would publish. I had no illusions about achieving immediate success; if success came at all it would, I knew, be slow, but in order to justify my presumption, success, true and substantial, would have to come some time; meanwhile I would be content to earn enough to procure me some beer and a few skittles.

"The first of my tales to be published before I left the Ironworks was *Communion* which came out in *The Varisty* in 1916. The first of my poems to get printed were 'The Lock' and 'The Oracle' in *The Egoist* of June 1917 under the editorship of T. S. Eliot. This should not be scored too heavily against him as I believe it occurred in only the first or second week of his appointment as editor. *The Nation* had printed two others. With all these scalps and a number of other tales sufficient to make up a volume I did not think it foolhardy to contemplate a break with my accustomed way of life . . . but all the same I viewed the contemplated change with such trepidation that it was taking a deal of pressure to urge myself over the brink."[1]

A. E. Coppard, 1901.

COPPARD

April, 1919. "I began my career as a professional writer on the meet occasion of All Fools' Day. . . . I know now, as indeed I was to know very soon, that it was a preposterous move, it had such little warrant; All Fools' Day was truly the congenital date of it, and yet, although it was a step I could never recommend to others, I have not regretted it for myself—or not very often, and not for very long."[1]

1919-1922. "I went off to live in a cottage in a field near Oxford and began to become a real writer. . . . The address was Shepherds Pit, Bayswater, Headington, a pleasant spot, although the cottage was skimpy with its one room and a pantry downstairs and two tiny bedrooms up.

"I lived at Shepherds Pit about three years and my recollections of that place and period are most pleasurably concerned with summer days and the summer nights when I slept in a camp-bed outside my cottage door and was truly awakened by birds.

"Sometimes the rural postman would reach me in his rounds before I was up, and mine being his extreme place of call, the very outlier of his morning trudge, he would then sit and rest on the foot of my bed and discourse affably about the weather, the crops, or the goings-on of some scallywags in the neighbourhood. Daily he came and often he lingered when I was itching for him to be gone so that I could open those dreadful letters, rejected manuscripts as I could well tell, that I was too ashamed to open in his presence; I desired no witness of my chagrin and disgrace.

"When I went to Shepherds Pit L. A. and I temporarily parted, she to retain her post at Witney Aerodrome, thus gallantly absolving me from any financial worry about her; I visited her on a bicycle at week-ends. I was well-suited by this living alone, it gave me no feeling of loneliness; I have never experienced loneliness, and hardly ever boredom, I seem to be quite a good companion to myself!

"Towards the close of 1922 a sour disaster dropped upon me; there was to be a drastic change, the farmer was wanting the cottage for a labourer and gave me notice to quit as soon as I could find other accommodation—and not to be too long about *that!* It was reasonable enough, but I did not want to leave at all. Shepherds Pit had done so much for me, as much as Oxford itself. In a way I had been hatched there, feathered there, and I wanted dearly to go on growing there. But go I must, so here was the end of another period. I felt wretchedly forlorn, for I grooved easily and shrank from domestic change, it always tormented me. But L. A., the kind creature, at once gave up her job at the aerodrome and came home to my aid and found us another cottage at Chinnor, which lies on the western fall of the Chilterns some fifteen miles from Oxford."[1]

1920-1950. "Now for more than thirty years this writing of tales has been my means of livelihood, my life, my time. Plenty of reviews of my tales have appeared in all sorts of journals, yet of all these estimates and criticisms I can truthfully declare that not one taught me a single thing about the art of writing a tale, but I certainly soon learned something else that was at first surprising to me, even shocking, to wit: that there are all sorts of differing tastes in the cohorts of readers. I loved writing about the things I wrote about, and in my simplicity thought that a really good tale (and weren't mine all good!) would please any and

every soul that had a capacity for pleasure. This was not so, not at all, it was an altogether fallacious assumption; so far from pleasing everybody I found I could not please even very many, that people with pronounced literary taste were as divergent in their literary leanings as those with none, and were not less vocally emphatic about it. Taking the popular test, there were of course those readers who loved Dickens and loathed Thackeray, just as there were the inexplicable vermin who did the reverse. I fancy there was no middle category then, and though fewer people read either of them nowadays their works remain to be talked about.

"Are not such differences to be found in every sphere? To me rugby is a boring rigmarole—but I own I never played it. I shudder at the mere invitation to swallow an oyster or to eat caviare. I like rice pudding and delight in tinned foods. If you are not like me in this, I fear I must suspect you of something unpleasant, you are alien to me, you are diverse, you are incredible! Therefore—I concluded—the only reliable verdict must be that of time and posterity. But—how comes it—I can hardly breathe in the air of a Thackeray, a Swift, a Dr. Johnson, yet they have undeniably passed the accepted test! It became clear to me that the idea of pure critical judgment with the ability to standardize and compare and add up two and two to make a universal aesthetic four was moonshine, and that Wilde's dictum, 'All criticism is introspection,' was unassailable."[1]

January 13, 1957. Died. "As a lifelong dweller in the comfort of atheism (I was never anything so frozenly credulous as an agnostic), I am not in the least afraid of death or the dying into it. I am dissatisfied and sometimes even annoyed at the inevitability of the farewell to all this comic futility, for I have liked my share of life and had I the choice of a transmigration would almost certainly elect to repeat it, having by no means exhausted the possibilities of enchanting experience in this preposterous world. It was never a 'vale of sorrow' for me, and many things have to be left undone that I have longed to do, unrealizable visions, places unvisited whose beautiful names alone are a potent lure—Andalusia, the Vale of Kashmir, the Pass of Killicrankie—and more unread books to grapple with, *Das Kapital, Ruff's Guide, Little Women,* and perhaps even Carlyle and Trollope."[1]

HOBBIES AND OTHER INTERESTS: "[I] enjoyed a welter of robust sporting activities such as sprinting, cross-country running, boxing, swim-racing, cricket and football. I had no claim to a champion's form in any of these though I was a pretty fair sprinter and might have developed in that field had I not been so enamoured of cross-country running that I could never refrain; it is an ill basis for augmenting speed. Football was my most cherished and long-lasting game; when I was fifty I had to buy fresh football boots, having worn out the previous generation of that gear; at fifty-five I had again to buy another pair."[1]

FOR MORE INFORMATION SEE: Jacob Schwartz, *The Writings of Alfred Edgar Coppard: A Bibliography* (foreword and notes by A. E. Coppard), Ulysses Bookshop, 1931; D. Brewster and A. Burrell, "Short Story and the Novelette: Anton Chekhov, Katherine Mansfield, A. E. Coppard and Others," in *Modern Fiction,* Columbia University Press, 1934; Brian Doyle, *The Who's Who of Children's Literature,* Schocken, 1969.

Obituaries: *Illustrated London News,* January 19, 1957; *New York Times,* January 19, 1957; *New Statesman,* January 26, 1957; *Newsweek,* January 28, 1957; *Time,* January 28, 1957; *Publishers Weekly,* February 11, 1957; *Wilson Library Bulletin,* March, 1957; *Americana Annual 1958.*

CROWFIELD, Christopher
See STOWE, Harriet (Elizabeth) Beecher

CROWNFIELD, Gertrude   1867-1945

PERSONAL: Born October 26, 1867, in Baltimore, Maryland; died June 2, 1945, in New York City; daughter of Herman Frederic and Sophia Henrietta (Ring) Crownfield. *Education:* Earned a professional nursing degree. *Home:* New York City.

CAREER: Elementary school teacher in Ohio and Wisconsin for ten years; practiced nursing in New York City; office assistant to a nerve specialist in New York City, 1906-27; author of stories and historical novels for children.

WRITINGS—All novels, except as indicated: *The Little Tailor of the Winding Way* (illustrated by Willy Pogany), Macmillan, 1917; *Princess White Flame* (illustrated by Anne Merriman Peck), Dutton, 1920; *The Shadow Witch* (illustrated by Peck), Dutton, 1922; *The Blue Swordsman* (illustrated by Peck), Dutton, 1924; *Alison Blair* (illustrated by George M. Richards), Dutton, 1927; *The Feast of Noel: Tales of Provence* (illustrated by Mary Lott Seaman), Dut-

Gertrude Crownfield

ton, 1928; *Joscelyn of the Forts* (illustrated by George M. Richards), Dutton, 1929.

Freedom's Daughter (illustrated by Agnes C. Lehman), Dutton, 1930; *Heralds of the King: The Story of the Nativity* (illustrated by Frances W. Delehanty), Dutton, 1931; *Katherine Gordon: Patriot* (illustrated by Richard H. Rodgers), Dutton, 1932; *Mistress Margaret* (illustrated by Walter Pyle), Lippincott, 1933; *Where Glory Waits: The Romance of Mary Vining and Anthony Wayne,* Lippincott, 1934; *Conquering Kitty: A Romance of the Sassafras River* (illustrated by Albert Kruse), Lippincott, 1935; *Traitor's Torch* (illustrated by Walter Pyle), Lippincott, 1935; *The Decree,* Lippincott, 1937; *King's Pardon* (illustrated by Pyle), Lippincott, 1937; *Strong Hearts and Bold* (illustrated by Marguerite de Angeli), Lippincott, 1938; *Christina of Old New York* (illustrated by de Angeli), Lippincott, 1939; *Diantha's Signet Ring* (illustrated by Ervine Metzl), Crowell, 1939; *Lone Star Rising* (illustrated by Lydia Parmelee), Crowell, 1940; *Angelique* (illustrated by Agnes C. Lehman), Crowell, 1941; *Proud Lady* (illustrated by Lehman), Lippincott, 1942.

Stories; all published by Bouillon-Sanders: *Beezeebees,* 1926; *Catching Up with the Circus,* 1926; *Down the Rabbit Hole,* 1926; *Land of Lollipop,* 1926; *Rain Wagon,* 1926; *Time in Rime,* 1926.

Contributor of stories and verse to magazines, including *St. Nicholas;* also contributor of more than a hundred articles on child hygiene to magazines.

FOR MORE INFORMATION SEE: Stanley J. Kunitz and Howard Haycraft, editors, *Junior Book of Authors,* Wilson, 1934, 1951.

CUMMINS, Maria Susanna   1827-1866

PERSONAL: Born April 9, 1827, in Salem, Massachusetts; died October 1, 1866; daughter of David (a judge) and Mehitable (Cave) Cummins. *Education:* Tutored at home, later attended a private school in Lenox, Massachusetts. *Home:* Boston, Massachusetts.

CAREER: Novelist; began by writing stories for the *Atlantic Monthly* and other magazines.

WRITINGS—Novels: *The Lamplighter,* J. P. Jewett, 1854, reprinted, Garrett Press, 1969; *Mabel Vaughan,* Crosby, Nichols, 1858, new edition, Houghton, 1885; *El Fureidis,* Ticknor & Fields, 1860, new edition, Houghton, 1888. Also author of *Haunted Hearts: A Tale of New Jersey,* published in 1864.

FOR MORE INFORMATION SEE: Stanley Kunitz and Howard Haycraft, editors, *Junior Book of Authors,* H. W. Wilson, 1934; Helen Waite Papashvily, *All the Happy Endings: A Study of the Domestic Novel in America, the Women Who Wrote It, the Women Who Read It, in the Nineteenth Century,* Harper, 1956; Brian Doyle, *The Who's Who of Children's Literature,* Schocken, 1968.

Robert Davis

DAVIS, Robert   1881-1949

PERSONAL: Born July 28, 1881, in Beverly, Massachusetts; died September 25, 1949, in Proctor, Vermont; son of William Henry (a Congregational minister) and Emma (Meacham) Davis; married Kathleen Johnson, circa 1918; children: four sons, three daughters. *Education:* Graduated from Union Theological Seminary, New York City. *Home:* Near Bordeaux, France.

CAREER: Ordained Congregational minister; served as an assistant to Dr. Henry Van Dyke at the Brick Church in New York City and later as pastor of his own church for ten years; American Red Cross commissioner in Europe during World War I, serving in France, Austria, Armenia, Russia, and the Baltic States; chief editorial writer for the *New York Herald Tribune* Paris edition; correspondent and reporter; director of the American Library in Paris, 1932-36; Middlebury College, Middlebury, Vermont, professor of history, 1941-46; farmer in France, raising dairy cattle and growing grapes; author of books for children.

WRITINGS—All published by Holiday House: *Padre Porko, the Gentlemanly Pig* (illustrated by Fritz Eichenberg), 1939, enlarged edition, 1948; *Pepperfoot of Thursday Market* (illustrated by Cyrus LeRoy Baldridge), 1941; *Hudson Bay Express* (illustrated by Henry C. Pitz), 1942; *Gid Granger* (illustrated by Charles Banks Wilson), 1945; *France* (nonfiction; illustrated by Rafaello Busoni), 1947; *Partners of Powder Hole* (illustrated by Marshall Davis), 1947; *That Girl of Pierre's* (illustrated by Lloyd Lózes

Goff), 1948. Also author of *Diary with Denekine,* 1919; *Poem of an Old French Farm,* 1931; *The Wit of Northern Vermont,* 1937; and *A Vermonter in Spain,* 1938.

SIDELIGHTS: "In *Guide of Southern Spain,* edited by Muirhead, reference is made to earliest carvings in stone, nearly obliterated by time, but of *undoubtedly porcine character.* These must antedate the Moorish occupation, as the Mohammedan considered swine unclean. They may even go back beyond the Visigoth and the Roman, to the original Iberic stock, which was Celtic. In Celtic regions the pig is much valued, and is the most important domestic animal. It harmonizes with what we know of Celtic character that there should be a legendary figure of a wise and benevolent spirit, in the form of a pig.

"The first time I heard the words 'Padre Porko' was from a doctor in Cadiz. Referring to a matter which had escaped our control, he remarked, 'We'll have to leave it to Padre Porko.' It had the same significance as though an American had said, 'We'll have to trust to luck.' Without quite remanding the affair to Providence, it yet indicated that a spiritual force, not unfriendly, became responsible.

"In the winter of 1938 means of communication were demoralized in Spain. I was able to assist an elderly lady who was searching for one of her daughters. For forty-eight hours we were fellow-passengers in an overcrowded and dilatory train. This lady had all the Celt's imagination, had lived in the country districts, and herself brought up a large family. She had a great fund of local superstitions and customs, and the legends and fables that children love. By the end of that journey the character and many of the genial exploits of the fabulous pig were distinct in my mind. The main elements of this incongruous fairy were his ability to talk all languages, his humorous good sense, and his belief that all animals could and should work together. She was to the Padre what Uncle Remus was to Br'er Rabbit. I have not seen the lady again, nor did she give me her name. But the tales of the Padre come from a background which is authentic, and the central figure can honestly be believed to have its origins in a far distant past." [Robert Davis, *Padre Porko,* Holiday, 1939, 1948.[1]]

FOR MORE INFORMATION SEE: N. B. Baker, "Robert Davis," *Wilson Library Bulletin,* October, 1949; Stanley J. Kunitz and Howard Haycraft, editors, *Junior Book of Authors,* Wilson, 2nd edition, 1951; Obituaries—*New York Times,* September 26, 1949; *Publishers Weekly,* October 22, 1949; *Wilson Library Bulletin,* November, 1949.

. . . the vulgar foreigner was guzzling down food as fast as the Widow Hedge-Hog, her sisters, and her nine nieces could fetch it out. . . . ■ (From *Padre Porko* by Robert Davis. Illustrated by Fritz Eichenberg.)

"My soul and body," exclaimed the good Padre, "if it isn't Old Century himself." ■ (From *Padre Porko* by Robert Davis. Illustrated by Fritz Eichenberg.)

DAY, Thomas 1748-1789

PERSONAL: Born June 22, 1748, in London, England; died September 28, 1789, in Wargrave, Berkshire, England; married Esther Milnes (an heiress and reformer), 1778. *Education:* Attended Charterhouse School and Corpus Christi College, Oxford. *Home:* Anningsley, Surrey, England.

CAREER: Although admitted to the Bar in 1775, Day never practised law. By means of an inheritance he was able to devote his life to writing, philanthropy, and social reform.

WRITINGS: The History of Sanford and Merton, Volume I originally published in 1783, Volume II, 1787, Volume III, 1789, and since published in numerous editions, including an edition revised and abridged by Thomas Teller (pseudonym of George Tuttle), published as *Sandford and Merton,* S. Babcock, 1845; an edition illustrated by the Dalziel Brothers, Ward & Lock, 1860; and an edition revised by Cecil Hartley, Hurd & Houghton, 1864; also published in an abridged version in *Three Sentimental Novels* (edited, and with an introduction, by Albert J. Kuhn), Holt, 1970 (also contains Laurence Sterne's *A Sentimental Journey through France and Italy* and Henry Mackenzie's *The Man of Feeling*).

The History of Little Jack (illustrated by John Bewick), Stockdale, 1797 (originally published in Stockdale's *Children's Miscellany,* 1788), later edition published as *The Entertaining and Instructing History of Little Jack,* J. Lumsden, 1820; reprinted in *The History of Little Jack and Other Stories,* McLoughlin Brothers, 1906.

Poetry: (With John Bicknell) *The Dying Negro: A Poetical Epistle, Supposed to be Written by a Black, Who Lately Shot Himself on Board a Vessel in the River Thames, to His Intended Wife,* [London], 1773, 3rd edition, W. Flexney, 1775; *The Devoted Legions,* J. Ridley, 1776, reprinted in *The Magazine of History* (Tarrytown, New York), 1925; *The Desolation of America,* G. Kearsley, 1777; *The Poetical Works of Thomas Day* (edited by Thomas Park), J. Sharpe, 1809.

Other writings: *Reflections upon the Present State of England, and the Independence of America,* Stockdale, 1782; *The Letters of Marius: Or, Reflections upon the Peace, the East-India Bill, and the Present Crisis,* Stockdale, 1784; *A Letter from ***, in London, to His Friend in America, on the Subject of the Slave-Trade,* printed by S. Loudon, 1784, also published as *Fragment of an Original Letter on Slavery of the Negroes,* Francis Bailey, 1784; *A Dialogue between a Justice of the Peace and a Farmer,* Stockdale, 1785; *Four Tracts,* Stockdale, 1785; *A Letter to Arthur Young, Esq. on the Bill Now Depending in Parliament to Prevent the Exportation of Wool,* Stockdale, 1788; *The Speech of Thomas Day, Esq. on the Necessity of a Reform in Parliament,* D. I. Eaton, 1794.

Possible author, under pseudonym Joel Collier, of *Musical Travels through England,* 4th edition, G. Kearsley, 1776.

SIDELIGHTS: Thomas Day was essentially a philosopher and teacher of moral principles—inspired by Rousseau. "Rousseau alone, with a perspicuity more than mortal, has

Thomas Day

been able at once to look through the human heart, and discover the secret sources and combinations of the passions. Every page is big with truth." [Sir Samuel Haslam Scott, *The Exemplary Mr. Day 1748-1789,* Putnam, 1935.[1]]

1766. Having graduated from Oxford at eighteen, he sought to live a life of virtue: "I have opposed as criminal, habitual acquiescence in sorrow which renders us unfit for the discharge of our duties."[1]

The gentleness of Day's nature is exemplified by his sensitivity to all forms of life. When a friend asked him to kill a spider, Day said: "Suppose when you are going in your coach to Westminster, a superior being who perhaps may have as much power over you as you have over that spider, should say to his companion: 'kill that lawyer, kill that lawyer,' how should you like that. . . . And, to some people, a lawyer is more obnoxious than a spider."[1]

Day held the general view that women were not as well developed intellectually and spiritually as men, but he also believed that the proper environment would produce "a paragon among women," who would be "some female wiser than all the rest of her sex, who would feel for him the most romantic and everlasting attachment—a paragon who should forget the follies and vanities of her sex for him."[1]

He even went so far as to enter into a Rousseau-inspired experiment raising two orphan girls in the hopes of "creating" one of these "paragons." He sought to flesh-out the Pygmalion legend by bringing up his future "perfect" wife. Believing that ". . . women were endowed with capacities which had atrophied through misuse. It arises less from nature than from education."[1]

He was realistic in assessing the degree of patient effort required in achieving his goal of training the two girls, Sabrina and Lucretia: "Do we not see, in trifling habits of body and speech that long attention is required to change them? Why then should we imagine those of the mind less obstinate or subject to different laws, so why despair if first experiments do not succeed?"[1]

1769. He took the girls to Avignon where he wrote to his friend Richard Edgeworth: "I am alive, and what is more, tolerably well. . . . Were I to relate the stage-coaches I have traveled in, the post-boys I have talked to (nay I have gone so far as to say sacre Dieu), the Inns I have lain at, the rivers I have passed with no more than a three-quarters of an inch plank between me and destruction, I should make you shudder!

"I think it will be of some advantage to me to have been in France. I flatter myself, that by going into company here, . . . I shall have upon my return (or at least know how to assume) sufficient impertinence, loquacity, vanity and fine clothes, to set up with some degree of success for the character of a *polite* man.

"You inquire after my pupils. I am not disappointed in any one respect. I am more attached to, and more convinced of the truths of my principles than ever. I am very sure that the company of these children has preserved me from a great many melancholy hours. I have made them in respect to temper two such girls as, I may perhaps say without vanity, have never been seen at the same age. They have never given me a moment's trouble throughout the voyage, are always contented; and think nothing so agreeable as waiting upon me (no moderate convenience for a lazy man). . . ."[1]

1772. He was momentarily attracted to Honora Sneyd, to whom he submitted a written proposal of his plan for an ideal marital existence through his friend, Edgeworth. But only after seeking his advice on the matter. "Tell me, have you sufficient strength of mind to totally subdue love, that cannot be indulged compatibly with peace or honor or virtue?"[1]

Edgeworth was invited to Day's house in order to more carefully study the situation while actually "in company with the dangerous object."[1] Honora declined the offer on the grounds that Day's vision excluded some of women's basic rights.

Within the year, however, he was again in love. This time in the frail form of Honora's younger and more romantic sister, Elizabeth. She agreed much more passively to Day's "program," but also managed to convince him that his total disdain for the graces and manners of society was not totally to his advantage. He, therefore, embarked upon a journey to France in order to acquaint himself with the proprieties of the day and acquire the polish necessary to elevate himself in Elizabeth's eyes. She in turn spurned her frivolous social life and began some serious reading.

His attempt was in vain, the social graces which he acquired on his journey were in too sharp a contrast with his ungainliness. The effect was comic and Elizabeth only laughed.

(From *The History of Sandford & Merton* by Thomas Day. Illustrated by Thomas Bewick.)

After this latest rebuff, he rejoined Edgeworth in France, and again took up the pursuits "of higher aim, more congenial to [my] talents and former principles."[1] But he despondently showed "an indifference to all human affairs, an aversion to restraint and engagement and embarrassment."[1]

That same winter of 1772, Day's romantic interest was revived and focused upon Mlle. Panckcoucke, a French woman.

At this same time Edgeworth's wife died, freeing him from an unhappy marriage. He immediately sought out Honora Sneyd to whom he had always openly been attracted. Day said: "My dear friend, while virtue and honor forbade you to think of her, I did everything in my power to separate you; but now that you are both at liberty, I have used the utmost expedition to reach you on your arrival in England, that I might be the first to tell you that Honora is in perfect health and beauty; improved in person and mind, and, though surrounded by lovers, still her own mistress."[1]

By this time one of Day's "experiments," Sabrina, had sufficiently matured and developed into a beautiful, finished woman. There was genuine affection on both parts and marriage seemed imminent, until Sabrina erred socially regarding proper dress and Day "consider[ed] this circumstance as a criterion of her attachment, and as a proof of her want of strength of mind."[1]

He left her as a lover but remained a faithful guardian. Admitting the failure of his *Plan,* he spoke of it later as one of the "extravagancies of a warm heart and a strong imagination."[1]

Toward the end of **1777,** Day wrote a poem entitled "The Desolation of America" depicting the flight of the Colonists in the face of the invading British. "All the beauty and prosperity of America are now ruined. The air resounds with the cries of Mothers lamenting their slaughtered children; the mangled infants' wails meet with no pity. In vain had England's child labored to provide treasure for a luxurious, pompous and proud Mother Country."[1]

Once the Sabrina episode was finally laid to rest, he was introduced to a woman who seemed ideally suited to him, Esther Milnes. Not altogether impervious to physical charms, Day inquired: "But has she white and large arms? Does she wear long petticoats?"[1]

He was relieved to discover that her petticoats were, in fact, "uncommonly long."[1]

Still hurt by his previous failures at love, he was much more cautious about a union. "I know and feel her merit, and nothing but her large fortune prevents me from wishing that I had it in my power to effect such an union: for the plan of life which I have laid down for myself is too remote from common opinion to admit of flattering myself with the expectation of so much conformity from a person of her affluent circumstance."[1]

They were married. Esther became the "perfect wife" abiding by all her philosopher husband's requests, even his more exasperating ones. She was made to give up music: "We have no right to luxuries while the poor want bread."[1]

In spite of his now contented state in life, he could still identify and sympathize with those less fortunate than he and in **1783** wrote: "How hard is the lot of the poor in sickness. How intolerable do we find bodily disorder with every convenience and alleviation. How pitiable is a fellow-creature tortured by sickness and surrounded by a family wanting the necessities of life if he intermits labor for a day.

"There is not much difference between one human being and another. If there is, the most valuable are those who cultivate the ground and provide necessaries for the rest."[1]

1783. The first volume of *Sandford and Merton* was published. It has become one of the most famous of the "didactic" children's books of the period.

September 28, 1789. Day was still writing the *Sandford and Merton* books when he died. His death was an ironic outgrowth of one of his theories. Of the opinion that any animal would respond to human kindness, he insisted that was all that was necessary to turn the most ferocious beast into a purring pet. He owned a rather spirited colt which he was sure he could handle armed only with his theory and a gentle heart. The unbroken colt threw Day onto his head, and he died within the hour, never having regained consciousness. He was forty-one years of age and never lived to see the enormous success of the completed *Sandford and Merton.*

FOR MORE INFORMATION SEE: James Keir, *An Account of the Life and Writings of Thomas Day,* Stockdale, 1791, reprinted, Garland, 1970; Michael E. Sadler, *Thomas Day, an English Disciple of Rousseau,* Cambridge University Press, 1928; George W. Gignilliat, *The Author of Sandford and Merton: A Life of Thomas Day, Esq.,* Columbia University, 1932; Muriel Jaeger, "Child of Nature," in *Adventures in Living: From Cato to George Sand,* Morrow, 1932; Samuel H. Scott, *The Exemplary Mr. Day, 1748-1789, Author of "Sandford and Merton",* Faber, 1935; A. E. Newton, "Books of My Boyhood," in *Carrousel for Bibliophiles,* edited by William Targ, Duschnes, 1947; V. S. Pritchett, "The Crank," in *The Living Novel and Later Appreciations,* Random House, 1964; Hesketh Pearson, *Extraordinary People,* Harper, 1965; Frank Swinnerton, "Philosopher Day," in *A Galaxy of Fathers,* Doubleday, 1966.

DUNCAN, Norman 1871-1916

PERSONAL: Born July 2, 1871, in Brantford, Ontario, Canada; died October 18, 1916, in Fredonia, New York; buried in Brantford, Ontario; son of Robert Augustus and Susan (Hawley) Duncan. *Education:* University of Toronto, student, 1891-95. *Home:* Willoughby, Ohio.

CAREER: Newspaper reporter with the *Bulletin,* Auburn, New York, 1895, and with the New York *Evening Post,* 1897-1901; correspondent for *McClure's Magazine,* 1900, and for *Harper's Magazine,* 1907-08, and 1912-13, serving

Norman Duncan

"Then you want credit?" said he. "Look here, dad!" Archie burst out, "of course, I want credit. I'll tell you all about it," he rattled anxiously. "We want . . . to charter the *On Time* . . . and trade the ports of White Bay and the French Shore." ■ (From *Billy Topsail & Co.* by Norman Duncan.)

in the Middle East, Australia, and the Dutch East Indies; Washington and Jefferson College, Washington, Pennsylvania, professor of rhetoric, 1902-06; University of Kansas, Lawrence, adjunct professor of English, 1908-10; author of travel and adventure stories. *Awards, honors:* Litt.D., University of Pittsburgh, 1912.

WRITINGS: Soul of the Street: Correlated Stories of the New York Syrian Quarter, McClure, Phillips, 1900; *The Way of the Sea* (short stories), McClure, Phillips, 1903, reprinted, Books for Libraries, 1970; *Doctor Luke of Labrador* (novel), Revell, 1904, reprinted, 1934; *The Mother,* Revell, 1905; *Dr. Grenfell's Parish: The Deep Sea Fishermen,* Revell, 1905; *The Adventures of Billy Topsail: A Story for Boys,* Revell, 1906; *The Cruise of the Shining Light* (novel), Harper & Brothers, 1907; *Every Man for Himself,* Harper & Brothers, 1908; *Going Down from Jerusalem: The Narrative of a Sentimental Traveller* (illustrated by Lawren S. Harris), Harper & Brothers, 1909; *Higgins: A Man's Christian,* Harper & Brothers, 1909; *The*

Suitable Child (illustrated by Elizabeth Shippen Green), Revell, 1909.

Billy Topsail & Company: A Story for Boys, Revell, 1910; *The Measure of a Man: A Tale of the Big Woods,* Revell, 1911; *The Best of a Bad Job: A Hearty Tale of the Sea,* Revell, 1912; *Finding His Soul,* Harper & Brothers, 1913; *The Bird-Store Man: An Old-Fashioned Story* (illustrated by C. H. Taffs), Revell, 1914; *Australian Byways: The Narrative of a Sentimental Traveler* (illustrated by George Harding), Harper & Brothers, 1915; *Christmas Eve at Swamp's End,* Revell, 1915; *Billy Topsail, M.D.: A Tale of Adventure with Doctor Luke of Labrador,* Revell, 1916; *Battles Royal Down North* (short stories), Revell, 1918, reprinted, Books for Libraries, 1970; *Harbor Tales Down North,* Revell, 1918, reprinted, Books for Libraries, 1970.

FOR MORE INFORMATION SEE: Stanley J. Kunitz and Howard Haycraft, editors, *Junior Book of Authors,* Wilson, 1934, 2nd edition, 1951.

A cheer broke from the crew. The men ran forward to their stations at the winch. "Ha!" the captain repeated with intense satisfaction, his ruddy face wreathed in smiles. "Did you see me? Ha-a-a-a! It is a dead w'ale." ■ (From *The Adventures of Billy Topsail* by Norman Duncan.)

EASTMAN, Charles A(lexander) 1858-1939

PERSONAL: Indian name was "Ohiyesa"; born in 1858 in Redwood Falls, Minnesota; died January 8, 1939; son of Many Lightnings (who took the name Jacob Eastman) and Nancy Eastman; married Elaine Goodale (a social worker), June, 1891; children: Dora Winona, Irene Taluta (deceased), Virginia, Ohiyesa II, Eleanor, Florence. *Education:* Dartmouth College, B.S., 1887; Boston University, M.D., 1890. *Home:* North Hampton, Massachusetts.

WRITINGS: Indian Boyhood (autobiography; illustrated by E. L. Blumenschein), McClure, Phillips, 1902, reprinted, Dover, 1971; *Red Hunters and the Animal People* (stories), Harper, 1904, reprinted, ÁMS Press, 1976; *Old Indian Days* (stories; illustrated by Dan Sayre Groesbeck), McClure, 1907, reprinted, Fenwyn Press, 1970; (with wife, Elaine Goodale Eastman) *Wigwam Evenings: Sioux Folk Tales Retold* (illustrated by Edwin Willard Deming), Little, Brown, 1909; (with E. G. Eastman) *Smoky Day's Wigwam Evenings: Indian Stories Retold*, Little, Brown, 1910; *The Soul of the Indian: An Interpretation*, Houghton Mifflin, 1911, reprinted, Johnson Reprint, 1971; *Indian Child Life* (illustrated by George Varian), Little, Brown, 1913; *Indian Scout Talks: A Guide for Boy Scouts and Campfire Girls*, Little, Brown, 1914, reprinted as *Indian Scout Craft and Lore*, Dover, 1974; *The Indian To-Day: The Past and the Future of the First American*, Doubleday, Page, 1915, reprinted, AMS Press, 1975; *From the Deep Woods to Civilization: Chapters in the Autobiography of an Indian*, Little, Brown, 1916; *Indian Heroes and Great Chieftains* (biography), Little, Brown, 1918. Also author of *Lectures on Indian Life and History*.

SIDELIGHTS: **1858.** Born in Redwood Falls, Minnesota in the lodge of "Many Lightnings." "What boy would not be an Indian for a while when he thinks of the freest life in the world? This life was mine. Every day there was a real hunt. There was real game. Occasionally there was a medicine dance away off in the woods where no one could disturb us, in which the boys impersonated their elders, Brave Bull, Standing Elk, High Hawk, Medicine Bear, and the rest. They painted and imitated their fathers and grandfathers to the minutest detail and accurately too, because they had seen the real thing all their lives.

"Of course I myself do not remember when I first saw the day, but my brothers have often recalled the event with much mirth; for it was a custom of the Sioux that when a boy was born his brother must plunge into the water, or roll in the snow naked if it was winter time; and if he was not big enough to do either of these himself, water was thrown on him. If the new-born had a sister, she must be immersed. The idea was that a warrior had come to camp, and the other children must display some act of hardihood.

"I was so unfortunate as to be the youngest of five children who, soon after I was born, were left motherless. I had to bear the humiliating name of 'Hakadah,' meaning 'the pitiful last,' until I should earn a more dignified and appropriate name. I was regarded as little more than a plaything by the rest of the children.

"My mother, who was known as the handsomest woman of all the Spirit Lake and Leaf Dweller Sioux, was dangerously ill, and one of the medicine men who attended her said: 'Another medicine man has come into existence, but the mother must die. Therefore let him bear the name "Mysterious Medicine."' But one of the bystanders hastily interfered, saying that an uncle of the child already bore the name, so, for the time, I was only 'Hakadah.'

"My beautiful mother, sometimes called the 'Demi-Goddess' of the Sioux, who tradition says had every feature of a Caucasian descent with the exception of her luxuriant black hair and deep black eyes, held me tightly to her bosom upon her death-bed, while she whispered a few words to her mother-in-law. She said: 'I give you this boy for your own. I cannot trust my own mother with him; she will neglect him and he will surely die.'

"The woman to whom these words were spoken was below the average in stature, remarkably active for her age (she was then fully sixty), and possessed of as much goodness as intelligence. My mother's judgment concerning her own mother was well founded, for soon after her death and old lady appeared, and declared that Hakadah was too young to live without a mother. She offered to keep me until I died, and then she would put me in my mother's grave. Of course my other grandmother denounced the suggestion as a very wicked one, and refused to give me up.

"In [an] upright cradle I lived, played and slept the greater part of the time during the first few months of my life. Whether I was made to lean against a lodge pole or was suspended from a bough of a tree, while my grandmother cut wood, or whether I was carried on her back, or conveniently balanced by another child in a similar cradle hung on the opposite side of a pony, I was still in my oaken bed.

"This grandmother, who had already lived through sixty years of hardships, was a wonder to the young maidens of the tribe. She showed no less enthusiasm over Hakadah than she had done when she held her first-born, the boy's father, in her arms. Every little attention that is due to a loved child she performed with much skill and devotion. She made all my scanty garments and my tiny moccasins with a great deal of taste. It was said by all that I could not have had more attention had my mother been living.

"As a motherless child, I always regarded my good grandmother as the wisest of guides and the best of protectors. [A] story of her was related to me by my father. My grandfather, who was a noted hunter, often wandered away from his band in search of game. In this instance he had with him only his own family of three boys and his wife. One evening, when he returned from the chase, he found to his surprise that she had built a stockade around her teepee.

"She had discovered the danger-sign in a single foot-print, which she saw at a glance was not that of her husband, and she was also convinced that it was not the foot-print of a Sioux, from the shape of the moccasin. This ability to recognise footprints is general among Indians, but more marked in certain individuals.

"This courageous woman had driven away a party of five Ojibway warriors. They approached the lodge cautiously, but her dog gave timely warning and she poured into them from behind her defences the contents of a double-barrelled gun, with such good effect that the astonished braves thought it was wise to retreat.

"The Indian women, after reaching middle age, are usually heavy and lack agility, but my grandmother was in this also an exception. She was fully sixty when I was born; and when I was seven years old she swam across a swift and wide stream, carrying me on her back, because she did not wish to expose me to accident in one of the clumsy round boats of bull-hide which were rigged up to cross the rivers which impeded our way, especially in the springtime. Her strength and endurance were remarkable. Even after she had attained the age of eighty-two, she one day walked twenty-five miles without appearing much fatigued.

"Indian children were trained so that they hardly ever cried much in the night. This was very expedient and necessary in their exposed life. In my infancy it was my grandmother's custom to put me to sleep, as she said, with the birds, and to waken me with them, until it became a habit. She did this with an object in view. An Indian must always rise early. In the first place, as a hunter, he finds his game best at daybreak. Secondly, other tribes, when on the warpath, usually make their attack very early in the morning. Even when our people are moving about leisurely, we like to rise before daybreak, in order to travel when the air is cool, and unobserved, perchance, by our enemies.

"As a little child, it was instilled into me to be silent and reticent. This was one of the most important traits to form in the character of the Indian. As a hunter and warrior it was considered absolutely necessary to him, and was thought to lay the foundations of patience and self-control. There are times when boisterous mirth is indulged in by our people, but the rule is gravity and decorum.

"After all, my babyhood was full of interest and the beginnings of life's realities. The spirit of daring was already whispered into my ears. The value of the eagle feather as worn by the warrior had caught my eye. One day, when I was left alone, at scarcely two years of age, I took my uncle's war bonnet and plucked out all its eagle feathers to decorate my dog and myself. So soon the life that was about me had made its impress, and already I desired intensely to comply with all of its demands.

"It is commonly supposed that there is no systematic education of their children among the aborigines of this country. Nothing could be farther from the truth. All the customs of this primitive people were held to be divinely instituted, and those in connection with the training of children were scrupulously adhered to and transmitted from one generation to another.

"Very early, the Indian boy assumed the task of preserving and transmitting the legends of his ancestors and his race. Almost every evening a myth, or a true story of some deed done in the past, was narrated by one of the parents or grandparents, while the boy listened with parted lips and glistening eyes. On the following evening, he was usually required to repeat it. If he was not an apt scholar, he struggled long with his task; but, as a rule, the Indian boy is a good listener and has a good memory, so that the stories were tolerably well mastered. The household became his audience, by which he was alternately criticized and applauded.

Dr. Charles A. Eastman

"It is wonderful that any children grew up through all the exposures and hardships that we suffered in those days! The frail teepee pitched anywhere, in the winter as well as in the summer, was all the protection that we had against cold and storms. I can recall times when we were snowed in and it was very difficult to get fuel. We were once three days without much fire and all of this time it stormed violently. There seemed to be no special anxiety on the part of our people; they rather looked upon all this as a matter of course, knowing that the storm would cease when the time came.

"I could once endure as much cold and hunger as any of them; but now if I miss one meal or accidentally wet my feet, I feel it as much as if I had never lived in the manner I have described, when it was a matter of course to get myself soaking wet many a time. Even if there was plenty to eat, it was thought better for us to practice fasting sometimes; and hard exercise was kept up continually, both for the sake of health and to prepare the body for the extraordinary exertions that it might, at any moment, be required to undergo. In my own remembrance, my uncle used often to bring home a deer on his shoulder. The distance was sometimes considerable; yet he did not consider it any sort of a feat.

"The usual custom with us was to eat only two meals a day and these were served at each end of the day. This rule was not invariable, however, for if there should be any callers, it was Indian etiquette to offer either tobacco or food, or both. The rule of two meals a day was more closely observed by the men—especially the younger men—than by the women and children. This was when the Indians recognized that a true manhood, one of physical activity and endurance, depends upon dieting and regular exercise. No such system is practised by the reservation Indians of to-day.'' [Charles Eastman, *Indian Boyhood*, Phillips, 1902.[1]]

1862. As a result of winning a sporting contest, Eastman was renamed Ohiyesa. ''In memory of this victory, the boy would now receive his name. A loud 'Ho-o-o' of approbation reverberated from the edge of the forest upon the Minnesota's bank. Half frightened, the little fellow was now brought into the circle, looking very much as if he were about to be executed. Cheer after cheer went up for the awe-stricken boy. Chankpee-yuhah, the medicine man, proceeded to confer the name.

'''Ohiyesa' (or Winner) shall be thy name henceforth. Be brave, be patient and thou shalt always win! Thy name is Ohiyesa.

''The Indians are a patient and a clannish people; their love for one another is stronger than that of any civilized people I know. If this were not so, I believe there would have been tribes of cannibals among them. White people have been known to kill and eat their companions in preference to starving; but Indians—never!

''In times of famine, the adults often denied themselves in order to make the food last as long as possible for the children, who were not able to bear hunger as well as the old. As a people, they can live without food much longer than any other nation.

''I once passed through one of these hard springs when we had nothing to eat for several days. I well remember the six small birds which constituted the breakfast for six families one morning; and then we had no dinner or supper to follow! What a relief that was to me—although I had only a small wing of a small bird for my share! Soon after this, we came into a region where buffaloes were plenty, and hunger and scarcity were forgotten.

''During the summer, when Nature is at her best, and provides abundantly for the savage, it seems to me that no life is happier than his! Food is free—lodging free—everything free! All were alike rich in the summer, and, again, all were alike poor in the winter and early spring. However, their diseases were fewer and not so destructive as now, and the Indian's health was generally good. The Indian boy enjoyed such a life as almost all boys dream of and would choose for themselves if they were permitted to do so.

''The raids made upon our people by other tribes·were frequent,.and we had to be constantly on the watch. I remember at one time a night attack was made upon our camp and all our ponies stampeded. Only a few of them were recovered, and our journeys after this misfortune were effected mostly by means of the dog-travaux.''[1]

Adopted into the family of his uncle. ''The second winter after the massacre, my father and my two older brothers, with several others, were betrayed by a half-breed at Winnipeg to the United States authorities. As I was then living with my uncle in another part of the country, I became separated from them for ten years. During all this time we believed that they had been killed by the whites, and I was taught that I must avenge their deaths as soon as I was able to go upon the war-path.

''I must say a word in regard to the character of [my] uncle, my father's brother, who was my adviser and teacher for many years. He was a man about six feet two inches in height, very erect and broad-shouldered. He was known at that time as one of the best hunters and bravest warriors among the Sioux in British America, where he still lives, for to this day we have failed to persuade him to return to the United States.

''He is a typical Indian—not handsome, but truthful and brave. He had a few simple principles from which he hardly ever departed.

''Sometimes my uncle would waken me very early in the morning and challenge me to fast with him all day. I had to accept the challenge. We blackened our faces with charcoal, so that every boy in the village would know that I was fasting for the day. Then the little tempters would make my life a misery until the merciful sun hid behind the western hills.

''I can scarcely recall the time when my stern teacher began to give sudden war-whoops over my head in the morning while I was sound asleep. He expected me to leap up with perfect presence of mind, always ready to grasp a weapon of some sort and to give a shrill whoop in reply. . . . Often he would vary these tactics by shooting off his gun just outside of the lodge while I was yet asleep, at the same time giving blood-curdling yells. After a time I became used to this.

''When Indians went upon the war-path, it was their custom to try the new warriors thoroughly before coming to an engagement. For instance, when they were near a hostile camp, they would select the novices to go after the water and make them do all sorts of things to prove their courage. In accordance with this idea, my uncle used to send me off after water when we camped after dark in a strange place. Perhaps the country was full of wild beasts, and, for aught I knew, there might be scouts from hostile bands of Indians lurking in that very neighborhood.''[1]

1873. ''I was scarcely old enough to know anything definite about the 'Big Knives,' as we called the white men, when the terrible Minnesota massacre broke up our home and I was carried into exile. I have already told how I was adopted into the family of my father's younger brother, when my father was betrayed and imprisoned. We all supposed that he had shared the fate of those who were executed at Mankato, Minnesota.

''Now the savage philosophers looked upon vengeance in the field of battle as a lofty virtue. To avenge the death of a relative or of a dear friend was considered a great deed. My uncle, accordingly, had spared no pains to instill into my young mind the obligation to avenge the death of my father and my older brothers. Already I looked eagerly forward to the day when I should find an opportunity to carry out his teachings. Meanwhile, he himself went upon the war-path and returned with scalps every summer. So it may be imagined how I felt toward the Big Knives!

"On the other hand, I had heard marvelous things of this people. In some things we despised them; in others we regarded them as *wakan* (mysterious), a race whose power bordered upon the supernatural. I learned that they had made a 'fire-boat.' I could not understand how they could unite two elements which cannot exist together. I thought the water would put out the fire, and the fire would consume the boat if it had the shadow of a chance. This was to me a preposterous thing! But when I was told that the Big Knives had created a 'fire-boat-walks-on-mountains' (a locomotive) it was too much to believe.

"'Why,' declared my informant, 'those who saw this monster move said that it flew from mountain to mountain when it seemed to be excited. They said also that they believed it carried a thunder-bird, for they frequently heard his usual war-whoop as the creature sped along!'

"Several warriors had observed from a distance one of the first trains on the Northern Pacific, and had gained an exaggerated impression of the wonders of the pale-face. They had seen it go over a bridge that spanned a deep ravine and it seemed to them that it jumped from one bank to the other. I confess that the story almost quenched my ardor and bravery.

"Two or three young men were talking together about this fearful invention.

"'However,' said one, 'I understand that this fire-boat-walks-on-mountains cannot move except on the track made for it.'

"Although a boy is not expected to join in the conversation of his elders, I ventured to ask: 'Then it cannot chase us into any rough country?'

"'No, it cannot do that,' was the reply, which I heard with a great deal of relief.

"I had seen guns and various other things brought to us by the French Canadians, so that I had already some notion of the supernatural gifts of the white man; but I had never before heard such tales as I listened to that morning. It was said that they had bridged the Missouri and Mississippi rivers, and that they made immense houses of stone and brick, piled on top of one another until they were as high as high hills. My brain was puzzled with these things for many a day. Finally I asked my uncle why the Great Mystery gave such power to the *Wasbicbu* (the rich)—sometimes we called them by this name—and not to us Dakotas.

"'For the same reason,' he answered, 'that he gave to Duta the skill to make fine bows and arrows, and to Wach-esne no skill to make anything.'

"'And why do the Big Knives increase so much more in number than the Dakotas?' I continued.

"'It has been said, and I think it must be true, that they have larger families than we do. I went into the house of an *Easshicba* (a German), and I counted no less than nine children. The eldest of them could not have been over fifteen. When my grandfather first visited them, down at the mouth of the Mississippi, they were comparatively few; later my father visited their Great Father at Washington, and they had already spread over the whole country.'

"'Certainly they are a heartless nation. They have made some of their people servants—yes, slaves! We have never believed in keeping slaves, but it seems that these *Wasbicbu* do! It is our belief that they painted their servants black a long time ago, to tell them from the rest, and now the slaves have children born to them of the same color!

"'The greatest object of their lives seems to be to acquire possessions—to be rich. They desire to possess the whole world. For thirty years they were trying to entice us to sell them our land. Finally the outbreak gave them all, and we have been driven away from our beautiful country.'

"'They are a wonderful people. They have divided the day into hours, like the moons of the year. In fact, they measure everything. Not one of them would let so much as a turnip go from his field unless he received full value for it. I understand that their great men make a feast and invite many, but when the feast is over the guests are required to pay for what they have eaten before leaving the house. I myself saw at White Cliff (the name given to St. Paul,

(From *Indian Boyhood* by Charles A. Eastman. Illustrated by E. L. Blumenschein.)

Minnesota) a man who kept a brass drum and a bell to call people to his table; but when he got them in he would make them pay for the food!'

"'I am also informed,' said my uncle, 'but this I hardly believe, that their Great Chief (President) compels every man to pay him for the land he lives upon and all his personal goods—even for his own existence—every year!' (This was his idea of taxation.) 'I am sure we could not live under such a law.'

"'When the outbreak [Civil War] occurred, we thought that our opportunity had come, for we had learned that the Big Knives were fighting among themselves, on account of a dispute over their slaves. It was said that the Great Chief had allowed slaves in one part of the country and not in another, so there was jealousy, and they had to fight it out. We don't know how true this was.'

"'There were some praying-men who came to us some time before the trouble arose, [continued the uncle]. They observed every seventh day as a holy day. On that day they met in a house that they had built for that purpose, to sing, pray, and speak of their Great Mystery. I was never in one of these meetings. I understand that they had a large book from which they read. By all accounts they were very different from all other white men we have known, for these never observed any such day, and we never knew them to pray, neither did they ever tell us of their Great Mystery.'

"'In war they have leaders and war-chiefs of different grades. The common warriors are driven forward like a herd of antelopes to face the foe. It is on account of this manner of fighting—from compulsion and not from personal bravery—that we count no *coup* on them. A lone warrior can do much harm to a large army of them in a bad country.'

"It was this talk with my uncle that gave me my first clear idea of the white man.

"I was almost fifteen years old when my uncle presented me with a flint-lock gun. The possession of the 'mysterious iron,' and the explosive dirt, or 'pulverized coal,' as it is called, filled me with new thoughts. All the war-songs that I had ever heard from childhood came back to me with their heroes. It seemed as if I were an entirely new being—the boy had become a man!

"'I am now old enough,' said I to myself, 'and I must beg my uncle to take me with him on his next war-path. I shall soon be able to go among the whites whenever I wish, and to avenge the blood of my father and my brothers.'

"I had already begun to invoke the blessing of the Great Mystery. Scarcely a day passed that I did not offer up some of my game, so that he might not be displeased with me. My people saw very little of me during the day, for in solitude I found the strength I needed. I groped about in the wilderness, and determined to assume my position as a man. My boyish ways were departing, and a sullen dignity and composure was taking their place.

"The thought of love did not hinder my ambitions. I had a vague dream of some day courting a pretty maiden, after I had made my reputation, and won the eagle feathers.

"One day, when I was away on the daily hunt, two strangers from the United States visited our camp. They had boldly ventured across the northern border. They were Indians, but clad in the white man's garments. It was as well that I was absent with my gun.

"My father, accompanied by an Indian guide, after many days' searching had found us at last. He had been imprisoned at Davenport, Iowa, with those who took part in the massacre or in the battles following, and he was taught in prison and converted by the pioneer missionaries. . . . He was under sentence of death, but was among the number against whom no direct evidence was found, and who were finally pardoned by President Lincoln.

"When he was released, and returned to the new reservations upon the Missouri river, he soon became convinced that life on a government reservation meant physical and moral degradation. Therefore he determined, with several others, to try the white man's way of gaining a livelihood. They accordingly left the agency against the persuasions of the agent, renounced all government assistance, and took land under the United States Homestead law, on the Big Sioux river. After he had made his home there, he desired to seek his lost child. It was then a dangerous undertaking to cross the line, but his Christian love prompted him to do it. He secured a good guide, and found his way in time through the vast wilderness.

"As for me, I little dreamed of anything unusual to happen on my return. As I approached our camp with my game on my shoulder, I had not the slightest premonition that I was suddenly to be hurled from my savage life into a life unknown to me hitherto.

"When I appeared in sight my father, who had patiently listened to my uncle's long account of my early life and training, became very much excited. He was eager to embrace the child who, as he had just been informed, made it already the object of his life to avenge his father's blood. The loving father could not remain in the teepee and watch the boy coming, so he started to meet him. My uncle arose to go with his brother to insure his safety.

"My face burned with the unusual excitement caused by the sight of a man wearing the Big Knives' clothing and coming toward me with my uncle.

"'What does this mean, uncle?'

"'My boy, this is your father, my brother, whom we mourned as dead. He has come for you.'

"My father added: 'I am glad that my son is strong and brave. Your brothers have adopted the white man's way; I came for you to learn this new way, too; and I want you to grow up a good man.'

"He had brought me some civilized clothing. At first, I disliked very much to wear garments made by the people I had hated so bitterly. But the thought that, after all, they had not killed my father and brothers, reconciled me, and I put on the clothes.

What boy would not be an Indian for a while when he thinks of the freest life in the world? ■ (From *Indian Boyhood* by Charles A. Eastman. Illustrated by E. L. Blumenschein.)

"In a few days we started for the States. I felt as if I were dead and traveling to the Spirit Land; for now all my old ideas were to give place to new ones, and my life was to be entirely different from that of the past.

"Still, I was eager to see some of the wonderful inventions of the white people. When we reached Fort Totten, I gazed about me with lively interest and a quick imagination.

"My father had forgotten to tell me that the fire-boat-walks-on-mountains had its track at Jamestown, and might appear at any moment. As I was watering the ponies, a peculiar shrilling noise pealed forth from just beyond the hills. The ponies threw back their heads and listened; then they ran snorting over the prairie. Meanwhile, I too had taken alarm. I leaped on the back of one of the ponies, and dashed off at full speed. It was a clear day; I could not imagine what had caused such an unearthly noise. It seemed as if the world were about to burst in two!

"I got upon a hill as the train appeared. 'O!' I said to myself, 'that is the fire-boat-walks-on-mountains that I have heard about!' Then I drove back the ponies.

"My father was accustomed every morning to read from his Bible, and sing a stanza of a hymn. I was about very early with my gun for several mornings; but at last he stopped me as I was preparing to go out, and bade me wait.

"I listened with much astonishment. The hymn contained the word *Jesus*. I did not comprehend what this meant; and my father then told me that Jesus was the Son of God who came on earth to save sinners, and that it was because of him that he had sought me. This conversation made a deep impression upon my mind.

"Late in the fall we reached the citizen settlement at Flandreau, South Dakota, where my father and some others dwelt among the whites. Here my wild life came to an end, and my school days began."[1]

1887. Graduated from Dartmouth College.

1890. Won diploma at Boston University.

1891. Married Elaine Goodale.

1890-1893. Government physician at Pine Ridge Agency in South Dakota.

1894-1897. Private practice of medicine in Saint Paul, Minnesota. Indian secretary for Y.M.C.A.

1897-1900. Advocate for Santee Sioux tribe in Washington, D.C.

1900-1903. Government physician in Crow Creek, South Dakota.

1903-1909. Assigned task of renaming the Sioux Indians.

1914. Director of Brooks-Bryce Foundation.

1914-1925. With wife, established and operated girls camp in Munsonville, New Hampshire.

Charles A. Eastman

1922-1939. National councilman, Boy Scouts of America.

1925. Appointed U.S. Indian Inspector.

January 8th, 1939. Died.

FOR MORE INFORMATION SEE: John T. Faris, "Out of an Indian Teepee (C. A. Eastman)," in *Men Who Conquered*, Revell, 1922, reprinted, Books for Libraries, 1968; Henry C. Tracy, "Ohiyesa (Charles Alexander Eastman)," in *American Naturists*, Dutton, 1930; Stanley J. Kunitz and Howard Haycraft, editors, *Junior Book of Authors*, Wilson, 2nd edition, 1951; Robert Patterson and others, editors, *On Our Way*, Holiday House, 1952.

ELLIS, Edward S(ylvester) 1840-1916 (B. H. Belknap, J. G. Bethune, Captain L. C. Carleton, Colonel H. R. Gordon, Captain R. M. Hawthorne, Lieutenant R. H. Jayne, C. E. Lassalle, Seward D. Lisle, Billex Muller, Lieutenant J. H. Randolph, Seelin Robins, Emerson Rodman, Captain Wheeler)

PERSONAL: Born April 11, 1840, in Geneva, Ohio; died June 20, 1916, at Cliff Island, Maine; son of Sylvester and Mary (Alberty) Ellis; married Anna M. Dean, December 25, 1862 (died, 1900); married Clara Spalding Brown, November 20, 1900; children: (first marriage) one son. *Education:* Attended State Normal School of New Jersey. *Home:* Upper Montclair, New Jersey.

CAREER: Worked as teacher, principal, school trustee, and superintendent of schools in Trenton, New Jersey, 1875-86, although devoting most of his time to writing after 1881. *Awards, honors:* Honorary M.A. from Princeton University, 1887.

WRITINGS—Fiction: *Seth Jones: or, The Captives of the Frontier*, Beadle, 1860, also published as *Seth Jones of New Hampshire*, Dillingham, 1907, and as *Seth Jones [by] Edward S. Ellis, and Deadwood Dick on Deck [by] Edward L. Wheeler*, edited by Philip Durham, Odyssey Press, 1966; *Kent, the Ranger; or, The Fugitives of the Border*, Beadle, 1863; *Oonomoo, the Huron*, Beadle, 1863; *The Hunter's Escape: A Tale of the Northwest in 1862*, Beadle, 1864; *Indian Jim: A Tale of the Minnesota Massacre*, Beadle, 1864; *Nathan Todd; or, The Fate of the Sioux' Captive*, Beadle, 1864; *The Rangers of the Mohawk: A Tale of Cherry Valley*, Beadle, 1864; *The Mystic Canoe: A Romance of One Hundred Years Ago*, Beadle, 1865; *The Rival Scouts; or, The Forest Garrison*, Beadle, 1865; *The Haunted Wood: A Legend of the Mohawk in 1778*, Chapman, 1866; *Monowano, the Shawnee Spy*, Beadle, circa 1866; *Prairie Trail*, Irwin, 1867; *Phantom Horseman*, Beadle, 1869; *Chewacho*, Munro, 1870; *Fugitives of the Chatachoochie*, Munro, 1870.

Jack's Horseshoe; or, What the Waugroo Bitters Did, National Temperance Society, 1883; *Ned in the Blockhouse: A Tale of Early Days in the West*, Porter & Coates, 1883; *Life on the Mountain and Prairie*, Munro, 1884; *The Lost Trail*, Porter & Coates, 1884; *Ned in the Woods: A Tale of the Early Days in the West*, Porter & Coates, 1884; *Ned on the River*, Porter & Coates, 1884; *Campfire and Wigwam*, Porter & Coates, 1885; *Up the Tapajos; or, Adventures in Brazil*, Cassell, 1886; *Down the Mississippi*, Cassell, 1886; *Lost in the Wilds*, Cassell, 1886; *Footprints in the Forest*, Porter & Coates, 1886; *The Last War Trail*, Porter & Coates, 1887; *The Hunters of the Ozark*, Porter & Coates, 1887; *The Camp in the Mountains*, Porter & Coates, 1887; *Adrift in the Wilds; or, the Adventures of Two Shipwrecked Boys*, Burt, 1887; *Wyoming*, Porter & Coates, 1888; *The Star of India*, Munsey, 1888; *A Young Hero; or, Fighting to Win*, Burt, 1888; *Storm Mountain*, Porter & Coates, 1889; *A Jaunt through Java: The Story of a Journey to the Sacred Mountain by Two American Boys*, Burt, 1889.

The Cabin in the Clearing: A Tale of the Frontier, Porter & Coates, 1890; *Arthur Helmuth*, United States Book Co., 1891; *Tad; or, "Getting Even" with Him* (illustrated by John Schonberg), Cassell, 1891; *Through Forest and Fire*, Porter & Coates, 1891; *Lost in Samoa: A Tale of Adventure in the Navigator Islands* (illustrated by Gordon Browne), Cassell, 1891; *Check 2134*, United States Book Co., 1891; *On the Trail of the Moose*, Porter & Coates, 1892; *From the Throttle to the President's Chair: A Story of American Railway Life*, Cassell, 1892; *The River Fugitives*, Price-McGill, 1893; *The Campers Out; or, The Right Path and the Wrong*, Penn, 1893; *The Wilderness Fugitives*, Price-McGill, 1893; *Lena-Wingo, the Mohawk*, Price-McGill, 1893; *Across Texas*, Porter & Coates, 1893; *Among the Esquimaux; or, Adventures under the Arctic Circle*, Penn, 1894; *The Great Cattle Trail*, Porter & Coates, 1894; *Righting the Wrong*, Merriam, 1894; *Honest Ned*, Merriam, 1894; *Brave Tom; or, The Battle That Won*, Merriam, 1894.

Edward S. Ellis

The Young Ranchers; or, Fighting the Sioux, H. T. Coates, 1895; *The Young Scout: The Story of a West Point Lieutenant*, Burt, 1895; *Comrades True; or, Perseverance versus Genius*, Penn, 1895; *Jack Midwood; or, Bread Cast upon the Waters*, Merriam, 1895; *The Path in the Ravine*, Porter & Coates, 1895; *Four Boys; or, The Story of a Forest Fire*, Merriam, 1896; *The Phantom of the River*, H. T. Coates, 1896; *Shod with Silence: A Tale of the Frontier*, H. T. Coates, 1896; *Uncrowning a King: A Tale of King Philip's War*, New Amsterdam Book Co., 1896, also published as *An American King: A Story of King Philip's War*, H. T. Coates, 1903; *Young Conductor*, Merriam, 1896; *True to His Trust* (illustrated by J. Steeple Davis), Penn, 1897; *Eye of the Sun*, Rand McNally, 1897; *A Strange Craft and Its Wonderful Voyage*, H. T. Coates, 1897; *In the Days of the Pioneers*, H. T. Coates, 1897.

Cowmen and Rustlers: A Story of the Wyoming Cattle Ranges in 1892, H. T. Coates, 1898; *Lost in the Rockies*, Burt, 1898; *Two Boys in Wyoming: A Tale of Adventure*, H. T. Coates, 1898; *Klondike Nuggets, and How Two Boys Secured Them* (illustrations after Orson Lowell), Doubleday & McClure, 1898, also published as *The Young Gold Seekers of the Klondike* (illustrated by F. A. Carter), Penn, 1899; *Captured by Indians: A Tale of the American Frontier; [and] Daughter of the Chieftain: Story of an Indian Girl*, Cassell, 1899; *Tales Told out of School*, Bardeen, 1899; *Through Jungle and Wilderness*, Mershon, 1899; *Dorsey, the Young Inventor*, Fords. Howard, 1899; *Iron Heart, War Chief of the Iroquois*, H. T. Coates, 1899;

The Land of Wonders, Mershon, 1899; *Secret of Coffin Island*, H. T. Coates, 1899.

The Boy Patriot: A Story of Jack, the Young Friend of Washington (illustrated by J. Watson Davis), Burt, 1900; *Blazing Arrow: A Tale of the Frontier*, H. T. Coates, 1900; *A Waif of the Mountains*, Mershon, 1900; *Red Plume*, Mershon, 1900; *Our Jim; or, The Power of Example*, Estes, 1901; *Red Eagle: A Tale of the Frontier*, H. T. Coates, 1901; *Lucky Ned* (illustrated by J. W. Kennedy), Estes, 1902; *Jim and Joe, Two Brave Boys*, H. T. Coates, 1902; *Limber Lew, the Circus Boy! or, The Battle of Life*, H. T. Coates, 1903; *Old Ironsides, the Hero of Tripoli and 1812, and Other Tales and Adventures on Sea and Land*, Hurst, 1903; *The Jungle Fugitives: A Tale of Life and Adventure in India, including Also Many Stories of American Adventure, Enterprise and Daring*, Hurst, 1903; *True Blue: A Story of Luck and Pluck* (illustrated by J. W. Kennedy), Estes, 1903; *The Last Emperor of the Old Dominion*, H. T. Coates, 1904; *Patriot and Tory* (illustrated by

"Hugh! 'Pache ober dere," was the reply, accompanied by a pointing of his dusky finger at the ridge. ■ (From *The Young Scout* by Edward S. Ellis.)

Kennedy), Estes, 1904; *The Telegraph Messenger Boy; or, The Straight Road to Success*, Mershon, 1904; *The Cromwell of Virginia: A Story of Bacon's Rebellion*, H. T. Coates, 1904.

Plucky Jo (illustrated by J. W. Kennedy), Estes, 1905; *Deerfoot on the Prairies* (illustrated by J. Steeple Davis), Winston, 1905; *Deerfoot in the Mountains* (illustrated by Davis), Winston, 1905; *Deerfoot in the Forest* (illustrated by Davis), Winston, 1905; *Among the Redskins*, Street & Smith, 1906; *The Hunt of the White Elephant* (illustrated by Edwin J. Prittie), Winston, 1906; *From Low to High Gear* (illustrated by J. W. Kennedy), Estes, 1906; *A Hunt on Snow Shoes* (illustrated by E. J. Prittie), Winston, 1906; *Lost in the Forbidden Land* (illustrated by Prittie), Winston, 1906; *River and Jungle* (illustrated by Prittie), Winston, 1906; *Tracked through the Wilds*, Street & Smith, 1906; (with William P. Chipman) *The Cruise of the Firefly* (illustrated by Prittie), Winston, 1906.

Fighting to Win: The Story of a New York Boy (illustrated by J. Watson Davis), Burt, 1907; *The Forest Messengers* (illustrated by E. J. Prittie), Winston, 1907; *Low Twelve: "By Their Deeds Ye Shall Know Them." A Series of Striking and Truthful Incidents Illustrative of the Fidelity of Free Masons to One Another in Times of Distress and Danger*, Niglutsch, 1907; *Princess of the Woods*, Cassell, 1907; *The Queen of the Clouds* (illustrated by E. J. Prittie), Winston, 1907; *The Mountain Star* (illustrated by Prittie), Winston, 1907; *Brave Billy* (illustrated by Carl Strehlan), Winston, 1907; *The Lost Dragon* (illustrated by J. W. Kennedy), Estes, 1907; *Plucky Dick: Or, Sowing and Reaping* (illustrated by J. W. Gruger), Winston, 1907; *Tam: or, Holding the Fort* (illustrated by Gruger), Winston, 1907.

Fire, Snow and Water; or, Life in the Lone Land (illustrated by Louis R. Dougherty) Winston, 1908; *The P.Q. & G.; or, "As the Twig Is Bent the Tree's Inclined"* (illustrated by J. W. Kennedy), Estes, 1908; *The Phantom Auto* (illustrated by L. R. Dougherty), Winston, 1908; *Off the Reservation; or, Caught in an Apache Raid* (illustrated by E. J. Prittie), Winston, 1908; *The Story of Red Feather: A Tale of the American Frontier*, McLoughlin Brothers, 1908; *The Young Pioneers; or, Better to Be Born Plucky Than Rich* (illustrated by J. Watson Davis), Burt, 1908; *The Round-up; or, Geronimo's Last Raid* (illustrated by E. J. Prittie), Winston, 1908; *Alden among the Indians; or, The Search for the Missing Pony Express Rider* (illustrated by Prittie), Winston, 1909; *Alden, the Pony Express Rider; or, Racing for Life* (illustrated by Prittie), Winston, 1909; *Boy Hunters of Kentucky*, Cassell, 1909; *Unlucky Tib* (illustrated by L. J. Bridgman), Estes, 1909; *Upside Down: An Automobile Story for Boys*, Winston, 1909.

Catamount Camp (illustrated by E. J. Prittie), Winston, 1910; *Captain of the Camp; or, Ben the Young Boss* (illustrated by Prittie), Winston, 1910; *The Frontier Angel: A Romance of Kentucky Rangers' Life*, Hurst, 1910; *The Forest Spy: A Tale of the War of 1812*, Hurst, 1910; *Work and Win: Story of a Country Boy's Success*, Burt, 1910; *The Ranger; or, The Fugitives of the Border*, Hurst, 1911; *Irona; or, Life on the Southwest Border*, Hurst, 1911; *The Hunter's Cabin: An Episode of the Early Settlements of Southern Ohio*, Hurst, 1911; *The Flying Boys to the Rescue* (illustrated by E. J. Prittie), Winston, 1911; *The Flying Boys in the Sky* (illustrated by Prittie), Winston,

1911; *Adrift on the Pacific: A Boys Story of the Sea and Its Perils* (illustrated by J. Watson Davis), Burt, 1911.

Riflemen of the Miami, Hurst, 1912; *The Worst Boy*, American Tract Society, 1912; *The Launch Boys' Adventure in Northern Waters* (illustrated by Burton Donnel Hughes), Winston, 1912; *The Launch Boys' Cruise in the Deerfoot* (illustrated by Hughes), Winston, 1912; *High Twelve*, Macoy Publishing & Masonic Supply Company, 1912; *The Boy Patrol around the Council Fire* (illustrated by E. J. Prittie), Winston, 1913; *"Remember the Alamo"* (illustrated by Prittie), Winston, 1914; *The Three Arrows* (illustrated by Prittie), Winston, 1914.

Under pseudonym B. H. Belknap: *Peleg Smith: A Tale*, Irwin, 1866.

Under pseudonym J. G. Bethune: *Hands Up! or, The Great Bank Burglary*, United States Book Co., 1890; *The "F" Cipher*, Price-McGill, 1892; *The Great Berwyck Bank Burglary*, Collier, 1893; *The Third Man*, Cassell, 1893.

Under pseudonym Captain L. C. Carleton; all published by Munro, except as noted: *The Hunter*, Beadle, circa 1863; *The Trapper's Retreat: A Sequel to "The Hunter,"* Beadle, 1863; *Scar-Cheek: The Wild Half-Bred*, 1864; *The Three Daring Trappers*, 1865; *Old Norte the Hunter; or, Adventures in Texas*, 1866; *Buffalo Jack*, 1866; *Hank Wiggins, Esq.*, 1867; *Cooney Bush, Trapper and Scout*, 1867; *Spotted Day*, 1867; *Marksman the Hunter*, 1867; *Hunter Scouts*, 1869; *Hunters and Redskins*, 1869; *Brimstone Jake*, 1869; *Small-Pox Dave*, 1869; *Red Hand*, 1870; *Club-Foot*, 1879; *Mysterious Hunter; or, The Man of Death*, 1885; *The Wild Man of the Woods*, 1892.

Under pseudonym Colonel H. R. Gordon; all published by Dutton: *Pontiac, Chief of the Ottawas: A Tale of the Siege of Detroit*, 1897; *Tecumseh, Chief of the Shawanoes: A Tale of the War of 1812*, 1898; *Osceola, Chief of the Seminoles*, 1899; *Red Jacket, the Last of the Senecas*, 1900; *Logan the Mingo: A Story of the Frontier*, 1902; *Black Partridge; or, The Fall of Fort Dearborn*, 1906.

Under pseudonym Captain R. M. Hawthorne: *Hurricane Gulch: A Tale of the Aosta and Bufferville Trail*, Collier, 1892.

Under pseudonym Lieutenant R. H. Jayne: *Perils of the Jungle: A Tale of Adventure in the Dark Continent*, Munsey, 1888; *The White Mustang: A Tale of the Lone Star State*, Lovell, 1889; *The Land of Mystery*, Lovell, 1889; *On the Trail of Geronimo; or, In the Apache Country*, Lovell, 1889, also published as *Trailing Geronimo; or, Campaigning with Crook* (illustrated by E. J. Prittie), Winston, 1908; *Lost in the Wilderness*, Price-McGill, 1892; *Through Apache Land*, Price-McGill, 1893; *The Cave in the Mountain*, Merriam, 1894; *In the Pecos Country*, Merriam, 1894; *The Golden Rock*, American Publishers Corp., 1896.

Under pseudonym C. E. Lassalle; all published by Beadle: *Buffalo Trapper*, 1870; *Burt Bunker, Trapper*, 1870; *Forest Monster*, 1870.

Under pseudonym Seward D. Lisle: *Teddy and Towser: A*

Away his horse careered, as swift as the wind—now thundering up some swell in the prairie, now plunging headlong through the bushes.... ■ (From *Nathan Todd* by Edward S. Ellis.)

Story of Early Days in California, H. T. Coates, 1904; *Up the Forked River; or, Adventures in South America*, H. T. Coates, 1904.

(Under pseudonym Billex Muller) *River Rifles*, F. Starr, 1870; (under pseudonym Lieutenant J. H. Randolph) *Buck Buckram*, F. Starr, 1869; (under pseudonym Seelin Robins) *The Phantom Chief*, Irwin, 1867; (under pseudonym Emerson Rodman) *Mad Anthony's Scouts*, F. Starr, 1870; (under pseudonym Captain Wheeler) *The Track of Fire; or, A Cruise of the Pirate Semmes*, Beadle, 1864.

Nonfiction—Biography: *The Life and Times of Colonel Daniel Boone, the Hunter of Kentucky*, Beadle, 1860; *The Life and Times of Christopher Carson, the Rocky Mountain Scout and Guide*, Beadle, 1861, also published as *The Life of Kit Carson, Hunter, Trapper, Guide, Indian Agent, and Colonel U.S.A.*, New York Publishing, 1899; *The Life of Pontiac, the Conspirator, Chief of the Ottawas*, Beadle, 1861; *The Life and Adventures of Colonel David Crockett*, Beadle, 1862; *Makers of Our Country: Biographical Stories from United States History*, Potter, 1894; *Lives of the Presidents of the United States*, Flanagan, 1897; *Alexander Hamilton: A Character Sketch*, University Association (Chicago), 1898; *Thomas Jefferson: A Character Sketch*, University Association, 1898, revised edition published as *The Life of Thomas Jefferson, Third President of the United States, 1801-1809*, Laird & Lee, 1913; *Dewey and*

If there was a man in Arizona who exulted in the baffling of the murderous miscreants that man was Juan Morelos. ▪ (From *The Round-Up* by Edward Ellis. Illustrated by Edwin J. Prittie.)

Other Naval Commanders, Hovendon, 1899; *From Tent to White House; or, How a Poor Boy Became President*, Street & Smith, 1899, reprinted as *The Life of William McKinley, the Twenty-Fourth President of the United States*, 1901; *The Life Story of Admiral Dewey*, [Philadelphia], 1899; *From the Ranch to the White House: The Life of Theodore Roosevelt, Author, Legislator, Field Sportsman, Soldier, Reformer and Executive*, Hurst, 1906, new edition (with additional chapters by W. Montgomery Major), Whitman, 1927.

History: *The Eclectic Primary History of the United States*, American Book Co., 1884; *The Camp-Fires of General Lee, from the Peninsula to Appomattox Court-House*, H. Harrison, 1886; *The Youths' History of the United States from the Discovery of America by the Northmen to the Present Time*, four volumes, Cassell, 1886-87; *The Indian Wars of the United States, from the First Settlement at Jamestown, in 1607, to the Close of the Great Uprising of 1890-91*, Cassell, 1892; *Complete School History of the United States*, Porter & Coates, 1892; *Epochs in American History*, Flanagan, 1896; *Stories from American History*, Flanagan, 1896; *The People's Standard History of the United States, from the Landing of the Norsemen to the Present Time*, five volumes, Woolfall,

1896-97, later editions published under various titles, including *Ellis's History of the United States*, *Twentieth Century History of the United States*, *Library of American History*, and *The History Americana*; *Young People's History of Our Country*, Lee & Shephard, 1898; (with others) *The Standard History of All Nations and Races*, ten volumes (illustrated by W. H. Lippincott and others), Landis Brothers, 1899.

Popular History of the World, from the Dawn of Information to the Present Time (illustrated by George Spiel), [Chicago], 1900; *Young People's History of France*, Altemus, 1901; *Young People's History of Germany*, Altemus, 1901; *Young People's History of Greece*, Altemus, 1901; *Young People's History of Rome*, Altemus, 1901; *Young People's History of the United States*, Altemus, 1901; *Young People's History of England*, Altemus, 1901; (with Charles F. Horne) *The Story of the Greatest Nations*, nine volumes, Niglutsch, 1901-03; *Historical Readings Illustrative of American Patriotism*, Silver, Burdett, 1903; *The Wonderful Story of Old, Told for Boys and Girls*, M. W. Hazen, 1904; *The United States: An Historical Sketch*, Werner, 1904; *True Stories of the American Indians*, [Philadelphia], 1905, reprinted as *Thrilling Adventures among the American Indians*, World Bible House, 1905; (with Henry Snyder) *A Brief History of New Jersey*, American Book Co., 1910; (editor) *A Grandfather's Historic Stories of Our Country from Its Discovery to the Present Time*, ten volumes, Hartley-Thomas, 1911; (editor with Augustus R. Keller) *History of the German People from the First Authentic Annals to the Present Time*, fifteen volumes (Volumes XII-XV edited by Keller and Charles F. Horne), International Historical Society, 1916.

Other: *The Continental Primary Physiology; or, Good Health for Boys and Girls*, D. Van Winkle, 1885, also published as *Ellis's Primary Physiology*, Taintor Brothers, 1889; *Standard Complete Arithmetic, combining Oral and Written Exercises*, Standard School Book Co., 1886, also published as *Standard Elementary Arithmetic*, 1886; *Common Errors in Writing and Speaking: What They Are and How to Avoid Them*, Woolfall, 1894; (editor and author of introduction) *The Youth's Dictionary of Mythology for Boys and Girls*, Woolfall, 1895, also published as *1000 Mythological Characters Briefly Described*, Hinds & Noble, 1899, and as *A Classical Dictionary*, Penn, 1900; *Outdoor Life and Indian Stories*, G. F. Lasher, 1912.

Also author of the following: *Astray in the Forest, Bear Cavern, Lost River, River and Forest*, and *Wolf Ear the Indian*, all published by Cassell; *Boy Captive, Lone Wolf Cave*, and *Ned in the Mountains*, all published by C. C. Thompson; *Haunted Hunter, Jack Darcy, My Plucky Boy Tom*, and *Two Scouts*, all published by Street & Smith; *The Singular Escape; or, Kit Carson among the Indians*, published by Donohue; *Young People's Imitation of Christ* (based upon the work of Thomas à Kempis), published by the American Baptist Publishing Society; *The Story of South Africa*, 1899; *School History of New York*, 1899.

Editor of *Public Opinion* (daily newspaper), 1874-75, and of *Golden Days* (juvenile magazine), 1878-81.

FOR MORE INFORMATION SEE: Brian Doyle, *The Who's Who of Children's Literature*, Schocken, 1968; Obituary: *New York Times*, June 21, 1916.

FILLMORE, Parker H(oysted) 1878-1944

PERSONAL: Born September 21, 1878, in Cincinnati, Ohio; died June 5, 1944, in Amherst, Virginia; son of William Aden and Adelaide Martha Susan (Molloy) Fillmore; married Louise Dutton; children: Rose. *Education:* University of Cincinnati, B.A., 1901. *Home:* New York City.

CAREER: School teacher in the Philippine Islands, 1901-1904; member of the banking firm of W. H. Fillmore & Co., Cincinnati, Ohio, 1904-18; author of books for children.

WRITINGS: The Hickory Limb (illustrated by Rose Cecil O'Neill), John Lane, 1910; *The Young Idea: A Neighborhood Chronicle* (illustrated by O'Neill), John Lane, 1911; *The Rosie World* (illustrated by Maginel Wright Enright), Holt, 1914; *A Little Question in Ladies' Rights* (an extract from *The Young Idea;* illustrated by O'Neill), John Lane, 1916; (reteller) *Czechoslovak Fairy Tales* (illustrated by Jan Matulka), Harcourt, 1919; (reteller) *The Shoemaker's Apron: A Second Book of Czechoslovak Fairy Tales and Folk Tales* (illustrated by Matulka), Harcourt, 1920.

"I am sure I can cure you," Danilo told her, "provided you confess to me all your misdeeds and hand over to me whatever you have that belongs to someone else." ■ (From *The Laughing Prince* by Parker Fillmore. Illustrated by Jay Van Everen.)

The Laughing Prince: A Book of Jugoslav Fairy Tales and Folk Tales (illustrated by Jay Van Everen), Harcourt, 1921; *Mighty Mikko: A Book of Finnish Fairy Tales and Folk Tales* (illustrated by Van Everen), Harcourt, 1922; *The Wizard of the North: A Tale from the Land of Heroes* (illustrated by Van Everen), Harcourt, 1923; *Fillmore Folk Tales* (selections from *Mighty Mikko* and *The Laughing Prince;* edited by Wilhelmina Harper; illustrated by Van Everen), Harcourt, 1926; *The Stuffed Parrot* (illustrated by Phyllis Britcher), Harcourt, 1931; *Yesterday Morning,* Century, 1931; (reteller) *The Shepherd's Nosegay: Stories from Finland and Czechoslovakia* (edited by Katherine Love; illustrated by Enrico Arno), Harcourt, 1958.

FOR MORE INFORMATION SEE: Stanley J. Kunitz and Howard Haycraft, editors, *Junior Book of Authors,* Wilson, 2nd edition, 1951.

Parker Fillmore

Dorothy Canfield, age six.

FISHER, Dorothy Canfield 1879-1958
(Dorothy Canfield)

PERSONAL: First name was originally Dorothea; born February 17, 1879, in Lawrence, Kansas; died November 9, 1958; buried at St. James Church, Arlington, Vermont; daughter of James Hulme (an educator) and Flavia (an artist; maiden name, Camp) Canfield; married John Redwood Fisher, May 9, 1907; children: Sarah, James. *Education:* Ohio State University, Ph.B., 1899: Columbia University, Ph.D., 1904. *Home:* Arlington, Vermont.

CAREER: Author, critic, and translator. Secretary of the Horace Mann School, New York City, 1902-05; spent three years in France doing war work during First World War; served on editorial board of Book-of-the-Month Club for 25 years; served on State Board of Education, Vermont, 1921-23. *Awards, honors:* D.Litt. from Middlebury College, Vermont, 1921, Dartmouth College, 1922, University of Vermont, 1922, Columbia University, 1929, Northwestern University, 1931, Ohio State University, 1935, Williams College, 1935, University of Nebraska, 1937, Swarthmore College.

WRITINGS—Many under name Dorothy Canfield; children's books: (Contributor) *What Shall We Do Now? Five Hundred Games and Pastimes,* F. A. Stokes, 1907; *Understood Betsy* (novel; illustrated by Ada C. Williamson), Holt, 1917, revised edition (illustrated by Martha Alexander), 1972; (with Sarah Fisher Scott) *On a Rainy Day* (games; illustrated by Jessie Gillespie), A. S. Barnes, 1938; *Tell Me a Story: A Book of Stories to Tell Children* (illustrated by Tibor Gergely), University Publishing, 1940; *Something Old, Something New: Stories of People Who*

Are America (illustrated by Mary D. Shipman), W. R. Scott, 1949; *Paul Revere and the Minute Men* (illustrated by Norman Price), Random House, 1950; *Our Independence and the Constitution* (illustrated by Robert Doremus), Random House, 1950; *A Fair World for All: The Meaning of the Declaration of Human Rights* (foreword by Eleanor Roosevelt; illustrated by Jeanne Bendick), Whittlesey House, 1952; *And Long Remember: Some Great Americans Who Have Helped Me* (illustrated by Ezra Jack Keats), Whittlesey House, 1959.

Adult fiction: *Gunhild: A Norwegian-American Episode,* Holt, 1907; *The Squirrel Cage* (illustrated by John Alonzo Williams), Holt, 1912; (with Sarah N. Cleghorn) *Hillsboro People* (poems and stories), Holt, 1915; *The Bent Twig,* Holt, 1915, reprinted, 1958; *The Real Motive* (poems and stories), Holt, 1916; *Home Fires in France* (short stories), Holt, 1918; *The Day of Glory* (short stories), Holt, 1919; *The Brimming Cup* (novel), Harcourt, 1921; *Rough-Hewn* (novel), Harcourt, 1922; *Raw Material* (novel), Harcourt, 1923; *The Home-Maker* (novel), Harcourt, 1924; *Made-to-Order Stories* (illustrated by Dorothy P. Lathrop), Harcourt, 1925; *Her Son's Wife,* Harcourt, 1926; *The Deepening Stream* (novel), Harcourt, 1930; *Basque People* (short stories; illustrated by Robert Ball), Harcourt, 1931; *Bonfire* (novel), Harcourt, 1933; *Fables for Parents,* Harcourt, 1937; *Seasoned Timber* (novel), Harcourt, 1939 [also see below]; *The Election on Academy Hill* (an excerpt from *Seasoned Timber*), Harcourt, 1939; *Four-Square* (short stories), Harcourt, 1949, reprinted, Books for Libraries, 1971; *A Harvest of Stories: From a Half Century of Writing,* Harcourt, 1956. Also author of short story with Willa Cather, "The Fear That Walks by Noonday," published in *The Sombrero,* Lincoln, Nebraska, 1894.

Nonfiction: *Corneille and Racine in England: A Study of the English Translations of the Two Corneilles and Racine, with Especial Reference to Their Presentation on the English Stage,* Macmillan, 1904, reprinted, AMS Press, 1966; (with George R. Carpenter) *Elementary Composition,* Macmillan, 1906; *A Montessori Mother,* Holt, 1912, later published as *Montessori for Parents,* Bentley, 1965; *The Montessori Manual,* W. E. Richardson, 1913, later published as *The Montessori Manual for Teachers and Parents,* Bentley, 1964; *Mothers and Children,* Holt, 1914; *Self-Reliance: A Practical and Informal Discussion of Methods of Teaching Self-Reliance, Initiative, and Responsibility to Modern Children,* Bobbs-Merrill, 1916, reprinted, Holt, 1929; (translator from the Italian) Giovanni Papini, *Life of Christ,* Grosset, 1921; *What Grandmother Did Not Know,* Pilgrim, 1922; *Why Stop Learning?,* Harcourt, 1927; (translator from the Italian) Adriano Tilgher, *Work: What it Has Meant to Man through the Ages,* Harcourt, 1931, later published as *Homo Faber: Work through the Ages,* Regnery, circa 1965; *Tourists Accommodated: Some Scenes from Present-Day Summer Life in Vermont* (a play), Harcourt, 1934; (with Sarah N. Cleghorn) *Nothing Ever Happens and How It Does: Sixteen True Stories* (illustrated by Esther Boston Bristol), Beacon Press, 1940; *Our Young Folks,* Harcourt, 1943; *American Portraits* (illustrated by Enit Kaufman), Holt, 1946; (with Eunice Katherine Crabtree and LuVerne Crabtree Walker) *Highroads and Byroads* (illustrated by Mary Royt and George Buctel), University Publishing, 1948; *Vermont Tradition: The Biography of an Outlook on Life,* Little, Brown, 1953; *Memories of Arlington, Vermont,* Duell, Sloan, 1957.

Dorothy Canfield in Paris, 1917.

ADAPTATIONS—Movies: "The Homemaker," 1925; "Two Heads on a Pillow" (based on the story *Eternal Masculine*), Liberty, 1934.

SIDELIGHTS: **February 17, 1879.** Born in Lawrence, Kansas. Father a professor at the State University. Mother a painter. As a child she read of the persecutions new settlers in America inflicted upon one another because of personal beliefs. She shouted up to the trees: "Lookey-here, lookey-here! You're doing just what you left England for, so people wouldn't do it to you. Stop it!" Her father explained it to her: "The Pilgrim Fathers wanted the same sort of 'freedom of thought' that everybody wants—freedom to bully everybody else into thinking as they do." [Elizabeth Yates, *Pebble in a Pool*, Dutton, 1958.[1]]

Trips to her grandparents in Arlington, Vermont were the greatest source of joy in her childhood years. "Arlington is exactly the same, only more beautiful. I haven't had a cold since I've been here and my feet have been wet every day.... [But] the reckless way these people talk of years is perpetually astonishing to me. 'How long ago did that happen, Uncle Zed?' I asked him yesterday. 'Oh, a few years, fourteen or fifteen maybe.' Why, that's more than my whole life!"

1897. Went to Europe, for two years to continue her study of languages. "I may be only eighteen, but I've lived long enough to know that life is a thing that can be saved or spent, but that it has value only as it's spent! It only has worth and dignity if we *do* something with it, and isn't the doing what makes people of more value than machines? For every person in the world there must be something he can do a little better than anyone else. If he doesn't do it it will be left undone, and that would be a pity.... That's what Mother does to people when she talks to them about art! That's what Father does when he encourages his students to see that education can quicken every avenue of their lives! Why—life is to know you are needed for work that belongs to you, just because you are you, work that nobody else can do."[1]

1902. Went to Columbia University to work on her doctorate for teaching. Also worked as a secretary and collaborated with her father on an article called "The Three Greatest Libraries" (London, Paris and Russia). Met John Fisher, who was also a student at the university.

June, 1904. Received her degree at Columbia University, Doctor of Philology.

1905. Sold enough stories to think of writing as a career.

June, 1905. She and John Fisher made indefinite plans to marry. She recalled a childhood country saying: "Never marry a man just because you think you could manage to live with him. Don't do it unless you are dead sure you couldn't live without him."[1]

July 30, 1905. From Norway she wrote her family: "I can't remember that I have ever spent four happier weeks—Father sends a warning note in his last letter 'Not to keep too much company with yourself. It is dangerous.' Well, it must be dangerous on the Puritan principle that whatever you enjoy you shouldn't have too much of—for

I've enjoyed my own company immensely. Don't laugh—too hard, that is, I expect you to laugh some—I honestly have. I never knew there were so many lovely things to think about if one only had time. I take long walks, or I clamber over the mountains, towering above the fjord, as I lie on a peak of rock in the sun and I think such interesting and lovely things and imagine such moving scenes that I am never ready to stop.

"I haven't written much ... but I've thought a lot more about my Norwegian story. If I could write that as I now conceive it, it would be something I'd not be ashamed of. But of course, I can't. I expect a fearful set-back, when I begin work on it—the method will have to be so different from any written-at-one-spurt short stories. I have it pretty well planned—fourteen chapters, scene here and in Christiania, but oh, my hero is so frightfully complicated a person. It wears me out to follow him in and out of the labyrinth of motives he gets himself tied up in. The old aunt is Aunt Phebe with a sense of humor added. She's the only one from life—every scrap of the rest is pure make-up—'made out of my own head' as the young wife told the old professor of the pudding. I'm afraid I've set myself too hard a task in managing so many people; but it won't do any harm to be thinking about it.

"Did I tell you I had a long letter from Mr. Sedgwick (*Leslie's* Editor, you know) very warm and friendly and unexpectedly serious. He says that my 'talent heaven be praised, lies outside the ordinary channels of magazine literature. Don't try to make it run in those shallow ways. You can write stories with big ideas and true ones, back of them. *Do* it! Don't be willing to be amusing when you can do more.' etc., etc. He winds up by saying he doesn't want to spoil my holiday with over-earnest exhortation but I am to bear in mind that 'we in the office are following your work with the greatest interest and belief'—

"I wrote Mr. Sedgwick that his letter came most opportunely when I was just getting up the nerve to take my writing more seriously. I said 'big ideas' as he put it weren't exactly in my line but I did mean to try honestly to have the ideas I was trying to express true ones, and to try and move people to more than a passing interest in a certain verbal dexterity. I was ashamed to send the letter for a while after I'd written it. It's all very well to say to my family whatever 'biggety' idea is in my head but I was afraid to him it might sound pretentious. I sent it all the same. I'm getting up a fine strong variety of 'literary nerve' if you know what I mean by that."[1]

May 9, 1907. Married John Fisher. Given a house in Arlington, Vermont for a wedding present. "Living in the country is like being married to humanity for better or worse, not just being on speaking terms with it, as one is in the city."[1]

October, 1907. First novel *Gunhild* published. Continued writing short stories for American magazines, *Good Housekeeping, Ladies Home Journal* etc. Sometimes used the nom de plume, "Stanley Cranshaw." When asked to write a particular story for a particular date, she replied: "Why, I couldn't write a story to order! An article yes, but not a story. It would be like being asked to fall in love next Friday."[1]

Dorothy and John Fisher, portrait by Norman Rockwell.

Yesterday's Authors of Books for Children   125

July, 1909. First child, Sally, was born.

1913. Son, James, was born. Morning hours were dedicated to her writing, the rest of the day was given over to family and household. "I owe a *debt to my children.* . . . Having brought them into the world, their father and I owe it to them to furnish them a happy, free life of physical health, cheerful industry, intellectual growth, and moral dignity and sanity. To pay my part of this debt I have at my command a certain amount of money, physical strength, intellectual vigor, nervous energy and spiritual force. If I am to keep my honor untarnished I must, as every honest debtor does, use my resources *first of all* to keep up the payments on my debt."

When most people stated that they thought of God as a glorified human father she replied: "I never had much of that feeling about my father, for all I loved him so dearly. Even as a very little girl, I knew perfectly well that I was the one who had to stand the pain of the tooth-pulling, no matter who held my hand. And I feel that way now a good deal; that I must stand on my own feet and bear my own burdens and have plain, sheer endurance for a daily ingredient in my life, and mustn't try to throw the responsibility upon anybody else—not even on God—even if I had that personal idea of God, which I haven't at all. . . .

"I haven't a bit of the mystic in me, you know, and I get dizzy at the very idea of contemplation. . . . I used to depend entirely on what the Quakers call 'the inner light' (what the rest of us call conscience) and just try to do the best I could from day to day. . . . But a question of little Sally's brought home to me what that inner light really means to me. Haven't you noticed how the children are always making you go to the heart of things? Sally came to me one day when she was about four years old, with her great friend and playmate, Lillian. She said, 'Mother, what is God? Lillian says he's an old man with a white beard who lives up on top of Red Mountain and looks down on us.'

"Well, there I was, face to face with the question I'd been dodging all my life. Sally looked up at me confidently and I had to answer. And in trying to make it simple enough for a four-year-old child to understand, I made it, for the first time, simple enough so that I could understand. I said right away, as though I'd had that answer ready for years, 'Why, little daughter, I think that God is the feeling in our hearts that makes us want to do what's right. . . .'

"And ever since then I've realized that I trust the inner light because I really believe, even in my blackest moments, that there is something immortal and eternal in it."[1]

August, 1916. Sailed to France to be with her husband who was stationed there during the first world war. "I am going to France, . . . for the very simple, elemental reason that my husband is there, and that we are the kind of husband-and-wife who find it almost intolerable to be separated. Life's too short to miss any of that perfect companionship!

"I'm going to establish a quiet little French home in a suburb of Paris, near the American Ambulance in Neuilly where my husband will be, for the most part, in service, and just live there through the winter to come, instead of on

They were feeling rather cross, for they hadn't any sauce
To eat with their pudding or their pie
■ (From *Tirra Lirra* by Laura E. Richards. Illustrated by Marguerite Davis.)

cause I've written a great deal this last year, and I want to give myself time to do a lot of thinking and living before undertaking anything new. And I hope our two children will enjoy their French winter as much as a Vermont one. . . .

"It all seems quite simple and natural to me, my husband giving up a year of his life to France, and I going to live near my dear French friends in this very dark moment of their lives—like going to help out one's cousins in need. I think we'll both be happier all our lives to have done this. I hate war . . . but like nearly all of my generation I'm terribly, tragically bewildered by the complexity of the situation. And it will ease an aching heart to do the simple, obvious, human thing, even if it is not very deep or far-reaching, establish a home near my husband who is alleviating pain, and fill my house, small though it will be, with a succession of homeless Belgian and French children who can share in the mothering I give to my own. . . ."[1]

She visited the cathedral at Chartres. "I hadn't more than stepped in before the unearthly beauty and impressiveness of that nave swept my mind clear of everything but the thought, '*Men* did this! The same men who are making the war. They did this and they will do it again, when this war is a forgotten bad dream.' After a while Sally whispered, 'Why Mother, what is that on your cheek?' and I saw I was crying . . . very happy tears.

"Discussions in this world of 1916 are not apt to be very cheerful, especially if one member of the party is John, who is not very cheerful about the war and its meaning. Well, I'm not myself, but I have more of a willful determination to see the hopeful side of things. John calls it just bull-headed on my part, but I have a feeling, deep-rooted as the necessity to breathe, that if we just hold on hard now, through this time, the eternal elements will come into view again. John says sceptically, maybe they aren't so durned eternal as we have been thinking."[1]

1917. She had earlier suffered a loss of hearing, which grew worse and then stabilized. She wrote her family from France: "My throat and ear don't get better as they ought to . . . If it weren't for my fear of deafness I think I'd worry along without specialists. . . . [But] he sees no reason to think my deafness will greatly increase *if* I keep my general health good. Same old story, you see. As to the intense pain in my throat and ears, that is due, he thinks, to pressure from the nerve on the enlarged gland on my neck, which has become considerably larger in the last few months. He thinks that must be treated at once, and sends me to another doctor whom I am to see on Monday. . . . No more time, dear, *dear* folks! John is fearfully homesick and awfully tired of his devouring job. But *very* proud of the number of volunteers who make it devouring, and both of us very happy to be here—'happy!' That's too big a word for 1917—you know what I mean."[1]

Later: "I have been to see two specialists since I last wrote you, and have come away considerably lighter in purse and not very much wiser than I was before, because they told me nothing new. . . . I remember . . . when Sally was a little thing . . . Dr. Cochrane's giving me some advice and saying that what I needed more than anything else was to say about other people's affairs and things: 'I don't give a damn about that.' The French specialist put in very elegant French precisely the same advice, so that, even as he talked, I burst into a fit of laughter, remembering the homely Anglo-Saxon vigor of Cochrane's previous counsel! The upshot of it is that they neither of them will undertake to do anything for me, that I have got to take charge of myself. . . . I now promise solemnly to follow all the good advice that has been given me at such a high price, until I am quite restored.

"Well, that is enough of a not very important topic. . . . John foams and frets about the Ford chassis that won't come up from Bordeaux when they are promised and about the impossibility of getting men out to the Front as fast as they ought to go. . . . I spend so much time compressing articles for Braille publication and figuring out . . . exactly how many lines to put on a page, and how many words to a line, in order to fit the matter neatly on to the brass plaques, that, as so often happens in real life, I quite lose myself in the mass of details and it comes to me once in a while, with a start and with such a sense of sudden happiness as you can imagine, that, after all, I am really doing something useful for the war blind!"[1]

Awarded a silver medal for "great service rendered" but wondered, "whatever can anybody *do* with a medal!"[1]

With all her war work there was little time for writing and she began to feel "like a bottle of cider that has 'worked' and is all ready to explode if somebody doesn't pull the cork and pour it out in a glass!"[1]

The Armistice was signed and the Fishers returned to Arlington, Vermont. She resumed her writing. "I have no idea whence this tide comes, or where it goes, but when it begins to rise in my heart, I know that a story is hovering in the offing. It does not always come safely to port. The daily routine of ordinary life kills off many a vagrant emotion. Or if daily humdrum occupation does not stifle it, perhaps this saturated solution of feeling does not happen to crystalize about any concrete fact, episode, word or phrase. It seldom crystallizes from an actual happening offered by friends who are sure that such an interesting event 'ought to go in a story.'

"The beginning of a story is then for me in more than usual sensitiveness to emotion. If this encounters the right focus . . . I get simultaneously a strong thrill of intense feeling, and an intense desire to pass it on. . . . *Flint and Fire* thus hovered vaguely in a shimmer of general emotional tensity, and thus abruptly crystallized itself about a chance phrase and the cadence of the voice which pronounced it. For several days I had been almost painfully alive to the beauty of an especially lovely spring, always so lovely after the long winter in the mountains. One evening going on a very prosaic errand to a farmhouse of our region, I walked along a narrow path through dark pines, beside a brook swollen with melting snow, and found the old man I came to see, sitting silent and alone before his blackened small old house. . . . The old man said quietly, 'Seems to me I never heard the brook sound so loud as it has this spring.' . . .

"My daily routine continued as usual, gardening, telling stories, music, sewing, dusting, motoring, callers, . . . and as usual with my story-making, this plot was sprouting out in a dozen places, expanding, opening up, till I perceived that I had enough material for a novel. In fact, a novel was seriously thought of but for a number of considerations was discarded. As it was, the material had to be compressed drastically. . . .

"[One day] I 'went' almost as precipitately as skis go down a long white slope, scribbling as rapidly as my pencil would go, indicating whole words with a dash and a jiggle, filling page after page with scrawls.

"The next morning, back at the desk, I looked over what I had written, conquered the usual sick qualms of discouragement at finding it so infinitely flat and insipid compared to what I had wished to make it, and with a very clear idea of what remained to be done, plodded ahead doggedly, and finished the first draught before noon. It was almost twice too long.

"After this came a period of steady deskwork, every morning, of rewriting, compression, more compression, and the more or less mechanical work of technical revision. . . . The first thing to do each morning was to read a part of it over aloud, sentence by sentence, to try to catch clumsy, ungraceful phrases, overweights at one end or the other. . . . When I begin to suspect that my ear is dulling, I turn to other varieties of revision, of which there are plenty to keep anybody busy . . . revision to explain facts . . . revision for suggestiveness . . . for ordinary sense . . . for movement . . . for sound, sense proportion, even grammar . . . and always interwoven with these mechanical revisions recurrent intense visualizations of the scenes. This is the mental trick which can be learned, I think, by practice and effort. Personally, although I never used as material any events in my own intimate life, I can write nothing if I cannot achieve these very definite, very complete visualizations of the scenes. . . . I can write nothing at all about places, people or phases of life which I do not intimately know. . . ."[1]

On reading her finished copy, she wondered why she "had the presumption to try to translate into words, and make others feel a thrill of sacred living human feeling. . . . I heard again the incommunicable note of profound emotion in the old man's voice, suffered again with his sufferings; and those little black marks on white paper lay dead, dead in my hands. . . . I would never write again. All that effort, enough to have achieved a masterpiece it seemed at the time . . . and this, *this* for a result! . . .

"From the subconscious depths of long experience came up the cynical, slightly contemptuous consolation, 'You know this never lasts. You always have this same fit, and get over it.' So, suffering from really acute humiliation and unhappiness, I went out hastily to weed a flower-bed.

"And sure enough, the next morning, after a long night's sleep, I felt quite rested, calm, and blessedly matter-of-fact. *Flint and Fire* seemed already very far away and vague, and the question of whether it was good or bad, not very important or interesting, like the chart of your temperature in a fever now gone by."[1]

Her neighbor, Robert Frost, laughed at her concern: "You're just like a person walking through a field of burdocks—when you want a story you reach down to your skirt and pick off a burdock. There are always plenty of them."[1]

Other concerns took precedence over her writing: "This period of life is absorbingly filled with the small domestic cares of running a large and various family, with young and very old people in it, who all have perfectly good claims on my thought and vitality . . . they get sick and have to be nursed; they aren't able to plan for their own lives yet and have to have plannings made for them . . . and then patiently carried out through an infinity of details; they must be thought about and cared for, in the tiny unimportant always recurring ways which make up homelife. . . .

"I don't pretend to know whether it is a good thing or not, whether homelife ought to be something different, but this is the way mine seems to be in these years. In the summer, when the children are home from school and a house has to be run, it does not leave me breathing space. . . . I'm the most *terre-a-terre* housekeeper these days you can imagine, good for nothing but to plan for the next dinner, to read aloud to grandmothers and nurse little boys through the mumps. . . . I don't deserve the name of a woman of letters, but then there are innumerable people who were always quite sure I never did. . . ."[1]

"The writer is not born (as is his boast) with more capacity than other people for seeing color and interest and meaning in life. He is born merely with an irrepressible desire to tell everybody what he sees and feels."[1]

When asked why she lived in Vermont, where life was fraught with so many hardships, she replied: "But life everywhere is full of hardships and discomforts. In the country I can get more of what I like and dodge more of what I don't like. I like to fuss with an open fire. And I can't be bothered waiting in restaurants for expensive food when there's so much else I'd rather do. Plain food is always more enjoyable to me than a stalled ox eaten against a background of steam-heated air, too little sleep, and no physical activity. Elegance is something I don't want; or fashion as fashion; or Bohemia—I saw too much of it in my childhood around Latin Quarter studios.

"Country life is crammed for me with physical delights. Take clothes: there's joy in wearing clothes constructed to fit the body instead of trying to remake the body to fit the latest style. I like to wear clothes I can forget once I've put them on, that bother me as little as my skin, that give me bodily ease and freedom. Shoes that are loose, flexible and heelless, leaving my feet as alive and muscular as my hands, making walking or running as brisk a pleasure as dancing. Lyric foot comfort for me in the summer is in Basque canvas sandals with twine soles; or in the winter in those felt socks and moccasins worn by lumbermen.

"I detest mild wishy-washy air and delight in keen mountain air—just to smell ploughed land, wild grapes, wet forests, wood fires—is keen enjoyment. Too many people take too little bodily enjoyment and that 'little brother the body' takes it out of them in the end for not giving him his fair share of the fun.

"I've always been keenly sensitive to the joy of bodily rhythm and equilibrium—dancing, skating. Living in the country I can stand up from my desk; strap on my skis, and from my very door go skimming down a snow slope. Every nerve tingling in the excitement of flight, or in a few moments walk I can be at the Cut-off and there leave the laborious stub-stub of one foot after another for the long effortless suavity of skating . . . in the summer I can lay down my pen whenever tired of sitting still, struggling with my brains, and in three minutes step out on to a tennis court for an exhilarating struggle with mind and nerve. And all year round I walk on living feet not over flat monotonous sidewalks but over interesting mountain paths, varying between rocks which make every step an enchanting problem in balance, and mossy leaf mold which springs under the foot like velvet.

"I like to sit down with a book in a quiet room, sure of uninterrupted time in which to savor its wisdom, beauty, gaiety, sadness. . . . Music I love, but we can go to the city for a concert or two when we feel the hunger, and now the radio is bringing music into our homes. As for the theater, I'm deaf enough to find it a vexation rather than a pleasure.

Again Paul Revere's back hairs crawled on his neck as his taut body expected a shot from behind. But his mind knew no fear. ■ (From *Paul Revere and the Minute Men* by Dorothy Canfield Fisher. Illustrated by Norman Price.)

In the country I am unharried by unimportance. There are no calls to make or receive with their exchange of straw-like conversation, or gossip which is only fiction produced by non-professionals: but there are hours of leisure and the heart's wide welcome in which to enjoy real visits from real friends and conversation that is the ripe expression of mature and interesting minds.

"It's all a matter of personal taste, but country life leaves me more time and strength for my work, and I like to like my fellow man. I can like him better if I don't constantly have too large a dose of him. I can stand a week in New York, survive a fortnight, but longer, I'm dazed, deafened, beaten down by the terrific concentration on material possessions, I run back to Vermont. . . . I don't like to live in New York because I can't 'live' there. It doesn't feel like life to me. It feels like being trampled under·foot by the herd."[1]

1930. Mother died.

June, 1933. Daughter, Sally, married.

July, 1933. Visited Austria with her son, James.

December 7, 1941. For the second time she witnessed her country in a world war. "As much as tanks and ammunition, do we need the backing of farseeing, gifted, sincere writers and poets and artists, whose occupation is always to try to see through the surface confusion of mixed-up details to the clear, enduring, immortal pattern of which each detail is a part. . . . The function of the 'real' writer . . . is to keep us from just pawing facts over and over aimlessly, like a discouraged person pawing over the pieces of a jigsaw puzzle. It is the creative writer who makes us feel the eager certainty that those facts can make sense."[1]

March, 1943. Husband suffered a heart attack, but recovered. "And one of the preparations I made for a trial of strength and endurance, as instinctively as a student drinks a cup of strong hot coffee before starting to take a long hard examination, was to send for a reproduction of Goya's *The Forge.*

". . . Nobody needs to give more than one look at that masterpiece to understand the first and most obvious reason for this choice. Just to glance, as you hurry by, at the tremendous outgoing strength of the man with upraised sledge-hammer, is as challenging as a sudden bugle-call. Vitality gushes out of that throb of creative human power, sweeping away fatigue, nervous tension and the poisonous stirrings of half-subconscious self-pity which sap our ability to endure. The terrific energy of that upswung sledge-hammer, the magnificent line of strength from the foot gripping the earth so stoutly, all along up the man's muscular body to the great arm at the top of its swing—they make self-pity seem laughable. They call out wordlessly a summons to take joy in putting out all the effort that can be summoned up. . . .

"Nothing is more contagious than vitality, you think, stopping before the picture for a moment to drink in another draught of it. . . .

"So much you see in the very first look at the masterpiece of this great Spanish painter. But as your eye grows more familiar with it, you begin to notice other beauties, other strengths, which also have meaning for one's everyday existence. . . . You reflect, looking with pleasure at that uncluttered wall and floor, that any objects there, no matter how beautiful in themselves, would spoil the pure concentration of your gaze on what the artist is telling you. You can hardly help thinking, more or less consciously, 'Why, that principle holds true also in the ordering and composition of one's life. Each day, as we wake in the morning, is laid in our hands for us to make shapely and useful,—or the opposite. When we clutter our lives up with too many accessories—no matter how desirable any one of them is—too many clothes or shoes or hats, too much furniture, too many committees and Leagues and athletic clubs and Lodges and Associations or too many good causes, too many parties and social doings, too much attention to eating—we are spoiling the composition of our lives.' To decide what is the chief business of our lives, and then to concentrate our powers on that—such an admonition speaks from Goya's mastery of the principles of composition. . . ."[1]

1943. Son, James, now a first lieutenant in the U.S. Army Medical Corps.

1945. Supported the formation of the United Nations. "We are starting well ahead of time, to try to reach a much wider American public. Everybody realizes that one of the great difficulties for the lack of support of the League of Nations idea was that only intellectuals or near-intellectuals were kept informed about it. The filling-station man and his brother were left out. This time we are trying to make it a popular movement in the French and Italian meaning of the word 'popular' as belonging to the people. . . . The cause of peace is an emotional one and must be approached, I think, through the emotions just as much as war. . . .

January, 1945. She wrote to her son: "Dear dear *dear* son, so much love goes out to you from this snowheaped old home of yours—love and pride, and—now!—real hopes that I'm going to live to see you return to us."[1]

January 31, 1945. James was killed in action. Months later she wrote to a friend: "We are struggling with what strength we have to reconstruct our lives without Jimmy. . . . To the eye I am the same gray-haired, deaf writer as ever, bent over the desk, the weary old hand still driving the old pen."[1]

August 6, 1945. Atomic bomb dropped on Hiroshima. "Six miles away from the trail of the first atomic bomb, the impact of the explosion knocked men down as though by a blow from a giant fist. All of us, by the same fist, have been knocked down, spiritually and mentally, by that terrific event.

"Yet those six-miles-away observers, felled to the ground, were not killed. Not yet. Shaken and trembling, they were able to rise and face human life once more. *Once* more. And we too must face human life once more, appalled by the collective remorse, and fear of the future which after two examples of the horrible destructiveness of the bomb, lies crushingly on the heart of every responsible man and woman.

"It is not true that the atomic bomb is something new to man, and hence something of which our experience teaches us nothing. It is new only in degree. It is no more than a development of the clubs of the first men who fought each other. Then the man with a club could conquer the man without a club. . . ."[1]

1946. Visited Boston and spoke to a gathering of teachers. "And anybody who thinks that a good home can be produced by a human being immature and undeveloped in character, insults the sacred name of home. . . .

"And that final axiom, 'A man doesn't want a career-woman with interests to conflict with his, when he gets home after a hard day's work. He wants a wife.' What are you teachers doing, I wonder, to protect growing American girls and boys from the poisonous false reasoning in this familiar exhortation?. . .

"He wants a wife runs the rest of the fish-hook phrase, I'll say he does! He *wants* a wife, in the old meaning of the word, of *need*. Only what do you mean, 'wife?' I think you ought to show you mean a woman, full grown, capable through experience, of understanding what steady effort is needed for earning a living, a woman, with that sense of the true proportion of things which can only grow out of experience of reality. . . .

"Just add to that condition some honest realization that men and women can love each other all the more if they respect each other fully."[1]

Boston held memories of her son, James. Here he had gone to medical school, been an intern, lived as a married man. "Luckily Boston is a big city, and nobody pays any attention to anybody's looks in big cities, so nobody noticed a small, gray-haired woman trying to see her way here and there through tears."[1]

She visited with her daughter, Sally, and her four children in Bar Harbor, Maine: "It is rather a complicated trip from here to Bar Harbor, as trips are apt to be in country which was settled long before the railroads were thought of. The steel rails don't exactly run where you would like to have them. I left home at eleven in the morning last Sunday, went by bus to Bennington, changed there for Williamstown, got off the bus there and took a taxi to the railway station, took a train to Boston, changed there (with a three-hour wait) went on by sleeper to Ellsworth, Maine arriving there at seven in the morning, took a bus from there to Bar Harbor, and arrived at the bus terminal station there where Sally met me with their car. . . .

"**The oatmeal's in that kettle on the stove and the milk is in the blue pitcher. If you want a piece of bread and butter, here's a new loaf just out of the oven and the butter's in that brown crock.**" ■ (From *Understood Betsy* by Dorothy Canfield.)

"Like any other country woman, I snatched up just before I left the house, a fresh roasting fowl which had just come in from the neighbor of whom we buy our poultry, wrapped it up in a paper bag and took it along under my arm with me. . . .

"I also took along, as I always do, some Book-of-the-Month proof-sheets to read, since that work goes on incessantly every day of my life. . . . I can't read very well on the train because my eyes are none too good in these years, but I can read at every station when the train is standing still. This is not a bad way, because as soon as the train begins to move and jiggle the page, I shut my eyes and think over what I have been reading. By the time I had been to Bar Harbor and back, I had fully made up my mind about those two books!

". . . The train was late and Sally and Vivian had been up as long as I had in the train, to be sure to be awake and dressed by the time I arrived. So they had had their breakfast, but Sally sat down for another visit with me while I had my coffee—very welcome after that long trip. I had seen the children so lately that the younger ones, David and John Paul, recognized me and there was no period of shyness to get over.

Jean and Vivian were off in a very few minutes for their school, looking bright-eyed and rosy-cheeked as everybody does in that cool, moist, seaside climate. . . .

"The evening meal—or indeed any meal in Sally's household—reminds one a little of one of the Jordaen pictures, you remember how jovial and noisy they are, with somebody playing a horn and with the rest of the people singing and the younger children playing with the dog, and such an atmosphere of hearty appetite for food and living bursting from the canvas. The dog and the cat whom you always see in the Jordean pictures are there too, roaming around the table, very well-mannered but quite present. Jean furnishes the music, for—at least while I was there—practically every moment she was in the house when she was not upstairs reading, she was at the piano playing fluently one Christmas song after another. . . . Since the piano is just on the other side of the open door to the dining room, the noise of her spirited playing comes through clearly and makes everybody at the table raise his voice—this suits a deaf grandmother very well indeed, as you can imagine. And just the noise is inspiriting you know if it is good natured noise—John Paul raising his voice to a shout to make himself heard, little David who doesn't speak a word of English yet but who is very fluent in his own baby talk, contributing his share, and the grown-ups making themselves understood as best they can.

"In the midst of this cheerful turmoil, I suddenly had a thrust to the heart such as comes to all of us in the later years after sorrow has reached us. For Jean began to play loudly and cheerfully as she played all the other things, the French carol of the three kings, a song which in my mind and memory is intimately connected with Jimmy, since it was the first song he ever learned to sing. It was while Sally was so sick with typhoid fever in Paris. . . . Every morning I raced over along the Boulevard de Clichy to take Jimmy to his nursery school, and this morning he came out to me calling out that he had learned to sing a song and sang the

Dorothy Canfield Fisher, 1954.

first phrases 'Ce matin, j'ai rencontre les Mages,' and then in an instant, those of you who are old enough and experienced enough know how this is, everything around me melted away and I stood again on that cold, ugly, cheerless, French boulevard, looking down into my little son's beautiful, soft, brown eyes and hearing his voice exactly as though he stood there again beside me.

"And then the struggle, familiar to all . . . older people . . . I am sure, quickly to repress the tears, not to darken the cheerful present moment by one's own sadness, the effort—vain as always—not to go on to the inevitable next picture to see those same soft brown eyes closing in death, half-way around the globe, his tall soldier comrades weeping around him, his voice sending the last touching message, 'Tell-tell them I always tried to do my best.' And then the slow fading of that like a Bach air heard in the midst of a lively Haydn symphony fading away—and the happy, vital family around me seen again—the interval having been so brief that not a sentence had been finished, not a gesture had been completed, and the piano sounding loudly in my ears something quite different 'God rest ye merry, gentlemen.'"[1]

1949. Celebrated her 70th birthday. "When you get to be my age you take whatever comes without fussing."[1]

She addressed herself to her reading audience and their letters to her concerning her books: "Of course I don't profit from every one. Sometimes it is apparent that a reader dislikes my work because it is not something I could never make it—that is, the work of another kind of person. Nothing to be done about that. Once in a while my fear is that a reader likes something in a story which I didn't know was there and wouldn't have left in, if I had seen it. But often a considered criticism accurately casts a light on a place which can be improved. And how heart-warming and reassuring is a reader's perception of an inner meaning I was not sure I had succeeded in writing between the line. . . .

"I don't share the feeling of those writers who say they write solely for themselves. It doesn't seem to me that I am unlike people who read my books—how should I be? What I write is an invitation to those with whom time has proved that I have much in common to join me in reflecting on the human life we all lead. . . . Here is the place to acknowledge with comradely appreciation the spoken explicit, and unspoken implicit co-operation given me by readers in the revision and re-writing of these stories."[1]

December 1, 1953. Suffered a stroke of paralysis. "Here it is now a week after New Year's, and I am downstairs walking around (slowly and cautiously but without a cane and without limping), looking around happily at the heaps of bright cards, and the flowers (always so miraculous in Vermont in December) and the Christmas candy-boxes and the pretty knitted things, Christmas presents not yet put away, and the dear, welcome, loving letters. . . . I'm well enough now to dictate into my invaluable electric dictation machine with no manual fatigue.

"Here is the chronology of what happened;—The last of November my nephew and his wife were at the brick farm-house. . . . John and I went down to spend the evening with them. . . . I never felt better in my life. When we came home, I went cheerfully to bed and had a fine night's sleep.

"The next morning I woke, feeling just as usual (I think it is worth setting down how suddenly that interruption to the brain nerve center can happen), got up, staggered a little, thought I must be still half asleep, went on into the bathroom, tried to take a shower, couldn't seem to manage the faucets or the curtain, decided to get dressed, had unconquerable difficulties with hooks and eyes and buttons, dragged some clothes on, sideways, began to realize there was really something the matter with me, managed to take a few steps to the couch in John's study just across the landing from the bathroom, and lay down on that. Laddie, the big young collie dog, delighted to see somebody awake, leaped joyfully up beside me and, with collie enthusiasm, started to lick my face. I tried to raise my left hand to push him back, and found I couldn't lift that arm at all. It just lay dead on the bed and so did my left leg.

"Then I knew what had happened—probably more accurately than some of you would. For a stroke of paralysis (as it is picturesquely called in ordinary language up here) is not only a common enough occurrence with elderly people, but extra familiar among Canfields. . . . The inert left arm and leg told me the story clearly. . . .

"So when John got Dr. Russell here (he's been our doctor for more than 40 years and knows the family history), we had some data to talk over. His medical examination showed cerebral hemorrhage without any doubt. But which kind? My great-grandmother's variety or Uncle Zed's? There was no high blood pressure at all. I've always been just about normal in blood pressure and I still was. And I could move the toes on my left foot. So there was a pretty good chance, both the doctor and I thought. . . . Dr. Russell's guess was that I'd be bedridden at least six weeks or two months. . . ."[1]

June, 1954. Well enough to appear in public at Smith College, where she was made Doctor of Letters.

1957. Spoke with a group of foreign-exchange students at Bennington College: "I hope that you will all be writers—in your notebooks, in your letters home. Tell people in the countries you come from what your reactions are to situations here. Don't keep everything to yourself. Share it. That's the only way ignorance can be dealt with, and it's ignorance that keeps us apart."[1]

"The Dorothy Canfield Fisher Children's Book Award" was established. "These years are almost too happy, too fulfilled, but there is so little time left, so little vitality, I don't want to waste it."[1]

November 9, 1958. Died. "The writer is not born (as is his boast) with more capacity than other people for seeing color and interest and meaning in life. He is born merely with an irrepressible desire to tell everybody what he sees and feels."[1]

FOR MORE INFORMATION SEE: M. R. Parkman, "Adventures in Everyday Living: Dorothy Canfield Fisher," in *High Adventurers,* Appleton-Century, 1931; Winifred M. Kirkland and Frances Kirkland, "Dorothy Canfield Fisher: At Home and Abroad," in *Girls Who Became Writers,* Harper, 1933; Harlan H. Hatcher, *Creating the Modern American Novel,* Farrar, 1935; Margaret Lawrence, *School of Femininity,* Stokes, 1936; Percy Holmes Boynton, "Two New England Regionalists," in *American Contemporary Fiction,* University of Chicago Press, 1940; D. L. Mann, "Educator and Novelist," in *Careers in the Making,* second series, edited by I.M.R. Logie, Harper, 1942; D. Baumgardt, "Dorothy Canfield Fisher on Her Seventieth Birthday," *Educational Forum,* November, 1950; Harry Redclay Warfel, *American Novelists of Today,* American Book, 1951; E. C. Wagenknecht, "Dorothy Canfield: The Rhythm of the Permanent," in *Cavalcade of the American Novel,* Holt, 1952; Elizabeth Yates, *Pebble in a Pool: The Widening Circles of Dorothy Canfield Fisher's Life,* Dutton, 1958; Elizabeth Yates, *Lady from Vermont: Dorothy Canfield Fisher's Life and World,* Stephen Greene Press, 1971.

Obituaries: *New York Times,* November 10, 1958; *Newsweek,* November 17, 1958; *Publishers Weekly,* November 17, 1958; *Time,* November 17, 1958; *Saturday Review,* November 29, 1958; *Wilson Library Bulletin,* January, 1959; *Britannica Book of the Year 1959*; *Americana Annual 1959.*

Allen French

FRENCH, Allen   1870-1946

PERSONAL: Born November 28, 1870, in Massachusetts; died October 6, 1946; son of John James and Frances Maria (Stratton) French; married Ellen R. Dorrance, April 14, 1898 (died April, 1918); married Aletta A. Lillibridge, June 17, 1922; children: (first marriage) Maude Dorrance, Frances Stratton, Ellen. *Education:* Massachusetts Institute of Technology, S.B., 1892; University of Boston, student, 1892-93; Harvard University, A.B., 1894. *Home:* Concord, Massachusetts.

CAREER: Harvard University, instructor in English, 1908-13, 1919-20; author of children's books and historical works. *Member:* National Thoreau Society (vice-president).

WRITINGS—All novels, except as indicated: *The Junior Cup* (illustrated by Bernard J. Rosenmeyer), Century, 1901; *Sir Marrok: A Tale of the Days of King Arthur,* Century, 1902; *The Colonials: Being a Narrative of Events Chiefly Connected With the Siege and Evacuation of the Town of Boston in New England,* Doubleday, Page, 1902; *The Story of Rolf and the Viking's Bow* (illustrated by B. J. Rosenmeyer), Little, Brown, 1904, new edition (illustrated by Henry Pitz), 1924, also published as *Rolf and the Viking*

Bow, Walker, 1964; *The Barrier,* Doubleday, Page, 1904; *Heroes of Iceland* (adapted from Dasent's translation of *The Story of Burnt Njal*), David Nutt, 1905; *The Reform of Shaun* (illustrated by Philip R. Goodwin), Little, Brown, 1905; *Pelham and His Friend Tim* (illustrated by Charles Grunwald), Little, Brown, 1906; *The Story of Grettir the Strong* (adapted from the translation of William Morris and Eirikr Magnusson), Dutton, 1908, 11th edition, 1962, new edition (illustrated by Bernard Blatch), Bodley Head, 1961.

The Runaway (illustrated by C. M. Relyea), Century, 1914; *The Golden Eagle* (illustrated by Relyea), Century, 1917; *The Hiding-Places,* Scribner, 1917; *The Drama of Concord: A Pageant of Three Centuries* (play; first produced by the Concord Players in Concord, Massachusetts, September 11, 1935), Production Committee, 1935; *The Red Keep: A Story of Burgundy in the Year 1165* (illustrated by N. C. Wyeth and Andrew Wyeth), Houghton, 1938; *The Lost Baron: A Story of England in the Year 1200* (illustrated by A. Wyeth), Houghton, 1940.

Nonfiction: *The Book of Vegetables and Garden Herbs: A Practical Handbook and Planting Table for the Vegetable Gardener,* Macmillan, 1907, also published as *How to Grow Vegetables and Garden Herbs,* 1911; *The Siege of Boston,* Macmillan, 1911, reprinted, Reprint Co. (Spartan-

His eye still fixed on Berengar, he seemed to meditate upon his own words, as reviewing his exact meaning. ■ (From *The Red Keep* by Allen French. Illustrated by N. C. Wyeth and Andrew Wyeth.)

FRENCH

When Grettir saw he was in earnest he rose up and defended himself with his shield, but he did not draw his sword. ■ From *The Story of Grettir the Strong* by Allen French. Illustrated by F. I. Bennett.)

burg, South Carolina), 1969; *The Beginner's Garden Book: A Textbook for the Upper Grammar Grades,* Macmillan, 1914; *Old Concord* (illustrated by Lester G. Hornby), Little, Brown, 1915; *At Plattsburg,* Scribner, 1917.

The Day of Concord and Lexington: The Nineteenth of April, 1775, Little, Brown, 1925, reprinted, Reprint Co.,

1969; (editor) *A British Fusilier in Revolutionary Boston: Being the Diary of Lieutenant Frederick Mackenzie, Adjutant of the Royal Welsh Fusiliers, January 5-April 30, 1775,* Harvard University Press, 1926, reprinted, Books for Libraries, 1969; *The Taking of Ticonderoga in 1775: The British Story; a Study of Captors and Captives,* Harvard University Press, 1928; *The First Year of the American Revolution,* Houghton, 1934, reprinted, Octagon, 1968; *General Gage's Informers: New Material Upon Lexington and Concord,* University of Michigan Press, 1932, reprinted, Greenwood Press, 1968; *Historic Concord: A Handbook of Its Story and Its Memorials, with the Story of the Lexington Fight,* Riverside Press, 1942; *Charles I and the Puritan Upheaval: A Study of the Causes of the Great Migration,* edited by Aletta French, Houghton, 1955.

SIDELIGHTS: "Among Icelandic sagas there are two which, from their human interest and literary perfection, deserve to be classed with world-literature. The first of these is the Njal's Saga, the second the Grettir's Saga; both of them have been in English form for about forty years, but because the translations faithfully followed the originals they never became popular, especially since this branch of literature, of great importance in illustrating the development of the northern races, has in our schools been neglected in favor of the poetry and mythology of the Greeks and Romans.

"Valuable as are the classic tales, there is to be drawn from them no such lesson of manliness as the northern stories teach. If I wished a lad to learn from his reading the quality of steadfast courage, I would put into his hands these two Icelandic sagas, with the Morte d'Arthur and even the Niebelungen Lied, rather than the Iliad, the Odyssey, or the Æneid. There is only one book whose tales surpass these northern stories in teaching the lesson of manly self-dependence, and that book is the Bible." [Allan French, *The Story of Grettir the Strong,* Dutton, 1901.[1]]

FOR MORE INFORMATION SEE: Stanley J. Kunitz and Howard Haycraft, editors, *Junior Book of Authors,* Wilson, 2nd edition, 1951; Obituaries—*American Historical Review,* January, 1947; *New York Times,* October 7, 1946; *School & Society,* October 12, 1946; *Wilson Library Bulletin,* December, 1946.

And bobbing on their surface, well outside the line of surf, a little skimming dish, a saucer nearly as wide as it was long, held a boy and a girl. ■ (From *The Lost Baron* by Allen French. Illustrated by Andrew Wyeth.)

GÁG, Wanda (Hazel)   1893-1946

PERSONAL: Last name rhymes with "cog"; born March 11, 1893, in New Ulm, Minnesota; daughter of Anton (an artist) and Lissi (Biebl) Gág; married Earle Marshall Humphreys, 1930. Sister, Flavia, was also an author/illustrator. *Education:* Studied art in Minnesota at the St. Paul Institute of Arts and the Minneapolis School of Art, and in New York City at the Art Students League. *Home:* "All Creation," in the Muscanetcong Mountain region of New Jersey.

CAREER: Author and illustrator; began working as a teenager, illustrating for the children's section of the Minneapolis *Journal;* teacher in a country school for one year after high school graduation; held a variety of jobs in commercial art, including fashion designing. Her works were first exhibited at the Weyrhe Gallery, New York City, in 1926. Permanent exhibitions of her work are now in many institutions throughout the world, including the Metropolitan Museum of Modern Art, British Museum, Bibliotheque Nationale (Paris), Kupferstich Kabinett (Berlin), Library of Congress, Whitney Museum of Art, and the Art Institute of Chicago. *Awards, honors: Millions of Cats,* 1928, was runner-up for a John Newbery medal, 1929 and won the Lewis Carroll Shelf Award, 1958; first prize in Philadelphia Lithograph Show, 1930; *A B C Bunny,* 1933, was runner-up for a John Newbery medal, 1934; *Snow White and the Seven Dwarfs,* was runner-up for a Randolph Caldecott medal, 1939; *Nothing at All,* 1941, was runner-up for a Randolph Caldecott medal, 1942; purchase prizes for lithographs, Metropolitan Museum of Modern Art, 1942, and Library of Congress, 1944.

WRITINGS—All self-illustrated; all published by Coward-McCann: *Millions of Cats,* 1928, reprinted, 1960; *The Funny Thing,* 1929, reprinted, 1960; *Snippy and Snappy,* 1931, reprinted, 1960; *Wanda Gág's Story Book,* 1932; *The A B C Bunny* (with hand-lettering by her brother, Howard Gág, and music by her sister, Flavia Gág), 1933, reprinted, 1960; *Gone Is Gone: The Story of a Man Who Wanted to Do Housework* (retold), 1935, reprinted, 1960; *Growing Pains: Diaries and Drawings for the Years 1908-1917,* 1940; *Nothing-at-All,* 1941, reprinted, 1960.

So there she stayed, and washed and sewed and knitted, and kept house for the kindly little men. ■ (From *Snow White and the Seven Dwarfs* translated and illustrated by Wanda Gág.)

Wanda Gág, December, 1916.

Illustrator and translator of works by Jakob L. K. Grimm and Wilhelm K. Grimm: *Tales from Grimm,* Coward-McCann, 1936, reprinted, Faber, 1973; *Snow White and the Seven Dwarfs,* Coward-McCann, 1938; *Three Gay Tales from Grimm,* Coward-McCann, 1943; *More Tales from Grimm,* Coward-McCann, 1947, reprinted, Faber, 1962.

Illustrator: Michael Wigglesworth, *Day of Doom* (poems), Spiral Press, 1929. Also illustrator of *A Child's Book of Folklore.* Contributor of illustrations and articles to various magazines, including *Horn Book.*

ADAPTATIONS—Movies, filmstrips: "Millions of Cats" (filmstrip; also in Spanish, "Milliones De Gatos"), Weston Woods; "The Fisherman and His Wife" (motion picture-20 min.), Weston Woods.

Recordings: "Tales from Grimm" (tape cassette), Weston Woods.

SIDELIGHTS: **March 11, 1893.** Born in New Ulm, Minnesota. First of seven children.

1897. Moved to new house at Washington Street and Third North "on a bare corner lot only recently wrested from the surrounding prairie. It was the type of building much in fashion during McKinley's administration and one which by present-day standards would be looked upon as over-trimmed and even somewhat amusing. But in those days it was considered beautiful and we children, reveling in its turrets and gables and gingerbread decorations, regarded it with pride. We loved it, especially the front porch, a round two-storied affair with twirled posts and banisters which offered excellent opportunities for climbing.

"Not many children's books were there. A book of recitations, *Grimm's Fairy Tales,* and *Struwwel Peter* in German, and a set of seven books entitled *Birds and All Nature* which were illustrated in color and of which we never tired. All these were read and reread, but there were other books, huge tomes, which served mainly as picture books. There were, for example, three volumes with awesome illustrations by Doré: Dante's *Inferno,* Milton's *Paradise Lost,* and *The Doré Bible Gallery.* Only a little less awesome were *Don Quixote, Les Miserables,* a big German Bible illustrated by Carl von Schnorensfeld, *The Life of Grant,* and an Indian and pioneer book called *Down the Great River.*

"Don Quixote, especially, held a troublesome fascination for me. Here was this thin man with feverish eyes whose mind because of too much reading was peopled with strange, terrifying visions. Realizing that I also read too much, I worried lest I too, like 'Donkey-hoty,' would become queer. Yet I read on until there came a time when my eyes became so watery that they were pasted shut every morning." [Wanda Gág, *Growing Pains,* Coward, 1940[1]]

1898. Sent to Turner School in New Ulm. "I was forbidden to get any more library books for the time being, but although I tried hard to obey, every Friday something drew me to the few shelves of books in the school corridor (which was all New Ulm had at that time in the way of a library) and always, against my better judgment, I came away with a book. And in order to escape the much deserved scolding from Papa, I read the book behind my geography book at school, or smuggled it into the house to be read in a dark corner of the attic. Needless to say, the books read in this furtive fashion were doubly interesting, and needless to say, too, reading in the dark corners didn't help my eyes a bit! Finally I was ordered to bed in a dark room by the doctor and after a bookless week my eyes were as good as ever."[1]

January, 1908. Because of father's illness, forced to quit high school and give her time to care of house and baby sister.

May 21, 1908. Father died of tuberculosis. Family left with $1,200 insurance and an allowance from the county of $8.00 a month.

January, 1909. Returned to high school part-time. Family very low in funds. Contributed to *Journal Junior,* a juvenile supplement to the *Minneapolis Journal.* Took over household as mother was too low-spirited and overwhelmed. She started diary. "Fern Fischer was here yesterday and she said that somebody told her that I don't do anything but read and draw. I guess so! I wonder if washing dishes, sweeping about six times a day, picking up things the baby and Howard throw around are reading. And I've never heard of taking care of babies, combing little sisters, cleaning bedrooms & attics as drawing! I wonder what else people will say about me.

"**May 15, 1909, Saturday.** Things do look a little brighter now, for as I only want to write of the brighter sides of every day, things haven't gone near as smooth as they look written out on these pages. The buzzing in mama's ears has quite stopped, tho of course she is not well yet; her nerves are still weak, nevertheless she can sleep better than usual. I think it is because she goes out in the fresh air so much.

"**August 30, 1909, Monday.** Feel splendid tonight. First day of school and I'm really going to High School again. Could almost jump some twenty odd feet in the air for joy. Am going to take five subjects. . . . I'm sure I don't know what to do tho, because I need two books, and one costs $1.25 and the other $.75.

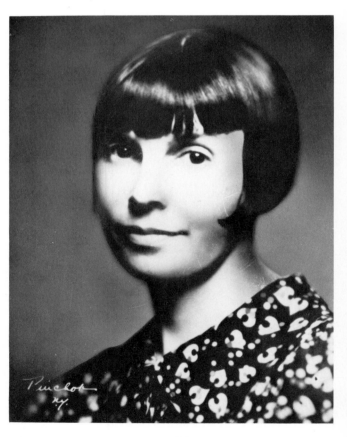

Wanda Gág

"September 11, 1909, Saturday. . . . I sorted drawings tonight for the Fair. I haven't hardly any that I made this year. That's because I did more painting and drawing for other people. Oh dear, I wish I could earn a pile of money so that I could draw a little for myself, and so that I could go to school without having to think of quitting. I can't see why some kids don't like school. I can scarcely wait for the Monday's.

"I have often wondered whether I had a style of my own, in drawing. The other day a lady told me they could always tell when they saw my pictures that I drew them. I wonder if other people think so too. I wonder why all people can't draw.

"December 5, 1909, Saturday. . . . I made some rules regarding painting and reading. As I've said before, I generally read while I'm waiting for the paint to dry. Now the rule is:—When I've finished one picture I may read two pages, with exceptions in case the drawing is not dry by that time, and get this book out of the way when somebody's coming up the steps, (sometimes you're in danger of getting a lecture, especially when Stella or Tussy come with their 'fire-and-flames'!) But I don't care, I didn't really read much to-day. I worked pretty hard and had a little cry after supper, don't care if I do say it, because it's true. Snow outdoors, whiteness, brilliancy, anything you please; inside—well, scrubbing doesn't help much unless you scrub about two times.

"April 14, 1910, Thursday. Oh glory! if I feel as if I were anywhere I feel as if I were in the seventh heaven of delight! Honestly, I feel as if I had had a grand splendid dream, only it wasn't a dream at all. Lucy and Daisy asked me to go up to the art exhibit. Mr. Koehler speeched. And then President Cyrus Northrop (of the State University) read the list of prizes and of course I didn't get any because I didn't expect any anyway. And when he was done he said something about an extra prize awarded to a young girl of New Ulm, and he meant me, just think of it! Really I had such a queer feeling, I was so awfully surprised. And then all the people turned around and looked at me. And then he said my name and asked if I was there and if I were I should come up and get my prize of $5.00 and Oh hum! I didn't want to go up there until they said, 'Go on, Wanda,' so I had to go. Gee (excuse this) I wonder how I looked stumbling up there (I suppose I *did* stumble) and then President Northrop shook my hand and talked ever so much. I don't remember half he said because I was quite certain it was only a dream or one of my flights of fancy. And then he pressed the five silver dollars into my hand and said 'if it wasn't too heavy.' The money, you know. I thanked him and went back to my seat as red as a beet I suppose.

"I got about thirty congratulations that evening, and all the while I couldn't see why so many people complimented me on such a few little drawings. President Northrop asked, 'Since when have you been doing this work?' and I told him ever since I remembered. And then he said that I ought to be sent to drawing school and Mr. Jolliffe and Professor Koehler said they thought so too. Anyway I think this is about the happiest day of my life, and I'm not sentimentally happy to-day; it's just a pure, real, material happiness and it's grand.

"June 4, 1910. Fun in school all week except exams. About half the Bookkeeping kids got zero in the state exam, and

Their bustles were puffed, their bodies stuffed, their skirts were ruffled and tufted with bows; their sleeves were muffled with furbelows. They wore bells that tinkled, and glittering rings; and rubies and pearls and little birds wings! ■ (From *Tales from Grimm* translated and illustrated by Wanda Gág.)

naturally I was one of the unlucky 'schluckers.' It seems to me bookkeepers were 'born and not made' as well as poets. I can never, never hope to be a decent bookkeeper, and I'm mighty glad too.

"Monday was Decoration Day. Daisy and I watched the parade. At first I wanted to go [to] the cemetery but I didn't anyway. . . . Bawled in the evening, I was so discouraged I could have cried quarts of tears, I guess. I wish papa were living so that there would at least be somebody who can understand me. People may think I am queer, I think myself that I am queer, sometimes; but I'm sure I can't help it. One who is an artist, or one who wants to be one (like me) has to dream and think, and that's all there is to it.

"I felt blue to-day, I don't know why. People may say I have talent and they may say they wished they had it, but I'm sure if I have any talent at all, I have to pay for it; I do not have it for nothing. But I know I wouldn't want to exchange places with anyone else; there is always the talent (?).

"August 14, 1910, Sunday—at grandma's. . . . When I read stories about artists I get to thinking about art more than ever. This morning it was deliciously cozy in bed so I looked over my drawings to see if I couldn't criticize them a little myself. I could; I found some mistakes which I knew how to correct—to some extent, I mean. It strikes me so queer that every one who does any drawing or painting, whether he is an artist, or hopes to be one (as it is in my case) has a style of his own. One would think there weren't enough styles to supply them all! And just think of all the scores of artists still waiting to become famous; where *will* they find enough individuality in their work? I'm sure I don't know, but I suppose they will when the time comes.

(From *The ABC Bunny* by Wanda Gág. Illustrated by the author.

"**December 3, 1910, Saturday.** People positively don't understand me, that's all there's to it. Here they even tell me to stop drawing and painting altogether. Goodness knows I *couldn't,* and if I could, I shouldn't, I'm too much in love with art for that. I wasn't made to be a bookkeeper or a store clerk or anything like that. If I had been, I would be better off than I am now perhaps. I can't help it that I've got to draw and paint forever; I cannot stop; I cannot, *cannot,* CANNOT! They say it doesn't pay to draw, that it is not appreciated, that I do not get for my work what it is worth. That is only too true but it isn't my fault. Besides, I earn more than some other girls. I wish we were rich, so rich that I could draw and paint for people and not charge anything. I hate to ask people for the money for my work.

"I am not as prosaic as some people think I am. I wish I were a little more prosaic sometimes. If I do dream they think I'm posing for effect or am wasting time; when, in truth, I'm dreaming very sensible things. I mostly dream sensible things; I have to If I could, I would sit and dream,

just delicious, idle meditations, but I have too many other things to think about that simply must have thought."[2]

June, 1912. Graduated from high school. Although she wanted desperately to go to art school, instead studied and got certificate to teach in a county school so she could help her brother and sisters.

"**July 24, 1912. At home.** . . . I've just finished writing my applications and the effect is still upon me. I believe I told you I applied for a school. Well, they never answered, so this morning I stepped up to the County Superintendent and informed him of my 'unsuccess.' He gave me two other schools to write to. I told him I'd like very much to have a school because I wished to send my sisters thru High School. Somehow that *utterance* had a very pathetic effect on me and I believe my eyes became misty. They *felt* very appealing as I looked at him. I hope they looked it. He certainly is nice. I do wonder what I'll do if I don't get a school. I don't know of a single way to earn money, and

Stella and Tussy are going to High School if I can help it. Am wearing my new shirt waist to-day because I wanted to look somewhat 'severe' up at the superintendent's.'' [Alma O. Scott, *Wanda Gág: The Story of an Artist*, University of Minnesota Press, 1949.[2]]

October, 1912. Assigned to "District 59." Taught class of nineteen pupils.

"November 14, 1912, Thursday. Springfield. Well, I got a school and have taught nine days. I came out here November 4—that is, I came to Springfield first. It was a little after 9 a.m. when I arrived at the depot where I whiled away three happy (?) hours, the reason being that no one cared enough for me to get me. Well, it was getting rather tiresome. When it was nearly twelve I grabbed my unbrella, suitcase, and papa's guitar (I admit I can't play a note on it but I was scared I'd come to a place where I'd have no music and one can always learn) and stepped along Main Street. I tried to look as composed and 'un-lost' as I could but whether I succeeded is another matter. I finally came to the conclusion that I'd better hire an auto out. It cost me $1.50 but it had to be. Anyway the livery man was nice and gave me some advice. But think of it, no one wanted to board me. I wished with all my heart that I were so fascinating that they couldn't help but say, 'Certainly, come in, we'll make room for you.' Only I wasn't. I was on the verge of tears (the genuine kind too, not the coaxing variety) when I prevailed on Klinger's to keep me at least for a day or two. I have been here since, and even tho it is a mile to my school house, I'll stay here if they'll let me.

"March 1, 1913, Saturday. I guess if I would not have to teach school, I would get a drawing mood. It cannot be properly encouraged here, and there is absolutely no time to draw at school. Goodness knows, I have trouble enough keeping them moderatley settled even when I am constantly on the alert. The whole trouble of the matter is that I am too absolutely good to them. How I wish I could be hopping mad once, so angry that I could wallop every single one soundly. Nearly every night I think, 'Now tomorrow I'm going to be strict. I'll give it to them good and proper' but it's the old story over and over again—and if I ever was near crying, it was yesterday.

"If I teach school next year I'll know better. How well I remember when Mr. harrington advised me to 'put my foot down.' And there were bits of advice of a similar nature from other people. I smiled complacenly and planned out a brilliant system of 'no whipping and no scolding' rules. It was to be almost ideal, the children were to be educated in morals, in politeness, and the main feature (Ye gods and little fishes!) was to be discipline by kindness. It is now nondiscipline by kindness. My pupils can absolutely twirl me around their little fingers—anyway the seven big ones. Why wasn't I stern in the beginning—inspiring them with awe and respect, why didn't I give them a smack once in a while?"[2]

June, 1913. Friend of her father's (Charles Weschke) decided to support her in art school.

"June 21, 1913, Saturday, 3:22 p.m. Well, it's over. Mr. Weschke's visit, I mean, and I'm to go to Art School. And such charming arrangements! I don't even have to work for my board. I shall probably stay at the Y.W.C.A. and be

independent. Have a definite amount of money put in the bank by someone or a number of someones and not do anything but 'Do the things I was meant to do' as he expresses it. He impressed it fully upon us that his was no charity work but that he was predestined—so to speak—to do what he was doing. He is doing it for art's sake and for humanity's sake. He thinks (oh, how can he) that I will repay humanity a thousandfold for what is being done for me. He knows just how I feel about things, simply taking words out of my mouth.''[2]

September, 1913. Started at St. Paul School of Art.

"September 27, 1913, Saturday, 9:05 p.m. I am finally at St. Paul, and in my room at the Y.W.C.A.—its number is 412. It's the darlingest little room—it has cream-tinted walls and the woodwork is plain and stained brown. . . . I am tickled stiff that I have a good mirror in my dresser so that when I have a drawing streak I can at least draw myself.

"October 13, 1913. . . . There was a Geneva party that Theresa wanted me to attend. I told her I couldn't stop drawing but she begged me to come all the time. I told her, 'Theresa, you don't *know* what it is to have a drawing streak.' She came in my room and sat down beside me on my bed where I was drawing away for dear life. She said, 'Oh, I think you're a little too much that way,' and I said, 'Perhaps I am. Not thru any fault of mine, however.' And she said, '*I* think so.' and oh it hurt my feelings so much that I could have wept right then and there—and I *don't* cry *easily*. She inferred that I was just doing that to show off or as an excuse for not attending the Geneva party. If people who have never had drawing moods would get one once they would see that showing off was the last thing they would think of.

"I can see easily enough how it would be hard for people to understand drawing moods. They are a grand and beautiful mystery to me. I am glad that I have been able to analyze them as much as I have. It comes very unexpectedly (the drawing fit) and still you don't know it's there at first. All at once you find yourself drawing with that gratifying fervor that always distinguishes a drawing streak. Now I think there is scarcely a time (if any at all) that I don't look at things without thinking of how it would look drawn, or trying to figure out how I would get to work at it if I were to draw it. I really wonder how people who don't draw, look at things. But when I have a drawing streak things seem much more beautiful than they do at other times, and I see something all the time which I'm wild to draw.

"September 20, 1914, Sunday. . . . They (people) have been in a most terrible suspense all the time for fear that I wouldn't get to the point where I would earn money. (I forgot to say that I am getting $5.00 a week now.) Paula reminded me of the time she had told me to draw magazine covers and said that was the result of hearing some remarks.

"They expect me to make a great deal of money and, sort of along the side, to become famous. And when I want neither fame nor money. Ding it, ding it, ding it. I wish I had iron to bite or wood to gnaw or logs to chop. I know I need the money but I can't sit here serenely listening while they lose sight of the—of *the* thing.

"I am afraid I shall have to disappoint them. If I were to become a popular magazine illustrator they would undoubtedly say, 'Wanda has made good,' whereas if I turn my art over to Life and win no fame, they will say, 'She had talent but she didn't use it in the right way.'

"There are some whom I do not include here. They are the ones who say least but do most. If I ever do anything for New Ulm, it will be for these people (for them I respect and love and appreciate more than they will ever know perhaps) and for its woods and brooks and flowers."[2]

November, 1914. *Minneapolis Journal* offered to pay expenses to Minneapolis School of Art.

"**December 11, 1914, Friday.** Monday I came over to Minneapolis. About the first thing I did after I came to my room was to arrange my furniture more aesthetically. Its former arrangement had hurt my vision. I have a screen covered with green burlap, and I conceived the brilliant idea of pinning some of my drawings to it. I call it my art gallery, and when people ask to see some of my sketches I simply unfold the screen, saving myself the trouble of *wühling* all thru my drawers first. I have a good mirror in my dresser too, bigger than those at the Y.W. As a consequence I have some seven or eight sketches of myself since I am here.

"**January 16, 1915.** I think I really do my best most of the time, altho it may seem to all outward appearances that I am at times rather negligent. For instance, I talk a great deal in Still Life and draw part of the time only. Usually I talk to Mr. Dehn.

"One of the girls, who works like a beaver, looks at me every once in a while as if to say, 'That girl might do otherwise than talking so much.' But ding, when I draw, *I draw.* When I don't draw, I am studying character or other things and I am sure the time is not wasted. Someone will say, 'Yes, but my dear girl, you can only reach your end by hard work.' I know that too, thank you. I may be working hard as the dickens when I seem to be doing nothing at all. Aside from that, I am not losing sight of the drudgery part of art. The fact is that I enjoy the drudgery part. I love to sit in Life and study out the lines and proportions and muscles and bones. Stacks of fun.

"I think there are some people who learn best by drawing and plugging whether they are inspired or not, but I stick to my old theory that in order to do something worth while *I* at least have to be inspired and *see* things unveiled. People may rake me over the coals if they wish, for having moods, drawing moods and others, but I maintain that—Oh well, I've said it often enough.

"I stick to my old idea, that's all.

"THAT'S ALL, I SAY.

"If others want to draw away without inspiration and produce master pieces, let them do so, *I* don't care. I'll get along as fast as they anyway. I learn as much in one evening from 8 p.m. to 1 a.m. (that time stands for a drawing fit) than they do in a week. I learned more about life drawing one morning last week than I have in three weeks.

"Then there is my arrogance which is very useful. Some of the other students may have it, but they are afraid to be frank about it and are therefore unable to make use of it. I don't suppose I ought to call it arrogance for it isn't ordinary, everyday arrogance. My arrogance is mostly for self-defense—or rather for Myself-defense. I refuse to let any one get ahead of me. If they do, I do my double best not to let them. Not because I don't like to see others do things. It's an incentive, that's all.

"It's cowardly to be overly modest. In fact I think many artists are modest for just that reason. For instance a man would be afraid to say, 'If I want, I can make people sit up and notice my work.' He's afraid that he can't live up to it—he's afraid of facing *ignominious defeat.* Ding, what if you don't succeed! You at least don't have to be ashamed of your *Aim.* My *aim* is limitless. That I will never reach it I know, but I'm going to get as near there as I can. That will keep me running all the rest of my life, believe me.

"**January 20, 1915, Wednesday.** Yesterday was an event in my life—I started painting in oils. I am rather timid about handling my brush for I am not at all used to the medium, so my study is abominally smooth and insipid. It looks something like the work of that eternal aunt or sister or cousin of everyone you meet 'who does beautiful oil studies and has never taken a lesson in all her life.' But ding, I have a long road to travel in oil painting. It seems that Emma Brock (a former student who did some good illustrations last year) has returned. They say she doesn't care about eating either."[2]

February, 1917. Mother died of tuberculosis.

"**February 14, 1917.** I will not tell the details of my stay home. I could see that mama was very ill. She had become very thin and was too weak to even sit up in bed alone. My premonition continued to grow and when, a week after I had come home, Mrs. Diel told me that she was afraid mama would never recover, I was not shocked. It was only a confirmation of my fears. After that I had to keep myself well under control. I tried to be cheerful with the kids, for I told no one of the matter, and I had to be careful not to be over-solicitous towards dear mama lest she should suspect something. I could write pages of all the silent grief I carried about with me, etc., but I won't. I worked so hard that I soon felt I couldn't stand it any longer, notwithstanding the fact that under the circumstances there was nothing I liked better to do than work from morning to night. It was bitterly cold. We froze a good deal altho we nearly ran our legs off keeping the furnace and kitchen fires going.

"Tuesday night when I was all alone with the four younger children, mama became decidedly worse. The doctor and Mrs. Diel and Mrs. Spenz were with me when she died, at 4:45 Wednesday morning. I was the only one in the family who saw our dear, brave mother die.

"She was unconscious for the most part of the last three hours, but she became conscious twice during that time for a few minutes. Each time she called me. The first time she had already returned to unconsciousness when I reached her bedside (I had gone down to the children for a few minutes) and the second time she told me that it was warm. She was not warm, poor mama—her breath was coming shorter and shorter and she felt the need of air. The doctor told me, as I was watching her during her last hours struggling for breath, that she was not suffering any to speak of, and of course I was glad for that.

"And then came the funeral. All the responsibility rested upon me, for of course now I am the head of the family. The neighbors were very kind to us all, and other folks farther away were also kind. I held out until a few hours before the funeral. I got shaky in the knees and I just flopped together and wept.

"Well, and now I am back at Minneapolis. I came February 10. I am quite surprised at myself. I never thought I would be so stoical in a thing like this. I thought, for instance, that when I would meet [my friends] I would just drop into their arms and cry. But I did nothing of the sort. All my crying happens after I am in bed. Everybody tells me that I am so brave. The trouble is that I am too brave for my own good. It is very wearing to hold yourself in check. The responsibility resting on my shoulders is just about too much for me, and during the last few days I have come nearer to being utterly discouraged than ever before, I think."[2]

September 26, 1917. Set out for New York to study under scholarship awarded by New York Art Students League.

"Undated Entry. Adolphe [Dehn], and I have each been awarded a scholarship at the Art Students League in New York! We are two out of twelve of the entire United States, and I believe this is the first time that this honor has been conferred on any member of our school. It is the biggest honor either of us have won. . . . I haven't dared to write home about it. They will say, 'Yes but you have no money to live on, and what is to become of us?' "[2]

September, 1918. Because of family financial needs, did not go back to Art Students League but began to free-lance in New York: "lamp shading," batik-dying, toy designing, then fashion drawings.

1918-1920. Lived in Greenwich Village.

1920. Moved to upper Eastside, 78th St.

1921. Spent summer drawing in Ridgefield, Ct.

1926. Work exhibited to acclaim in one-man show at Weyhre Gallery.

Summer, 1927. Moved to "Tumble Timbers," near Glen Gardner, N.J. Spent summers there drawing.

"We ate some of the squashes, but most of them rotted in the process of being drawn. You see, I'm not exactly the

He climbed over the sunny hills. He trudged through the cool valleys. He walked a long, long time and at last he came to a hill which was quite covered with cats. ■ (From *Millions of Cats* by Wanda Gág. Illustrated by the author.)

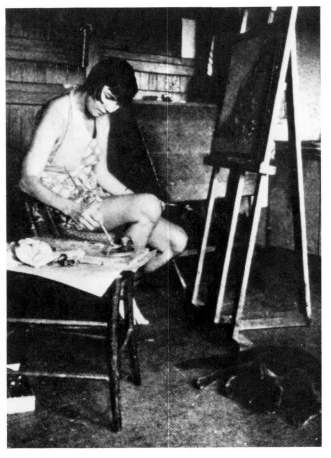

In the studio on the hill at "All Creation."

easiest person in the world to live with at times. I'm forever having things stand around that can't be moved because I want to draw them. At Tumble Timbers this situation was particularly bad. At the end of dinner I might see a lamp making interesting shadows, so that the dishes had to be postponed. Sometimes I wouldn't allow anyone to touch a certain chair or table for weeks!

"Once we got a new aluminum canning kettle—we mean to can—but when someone set the kettle down on a rag rug beside some gourds, tomatoes, and peppers, it reflected them so beautifully that the canning had to be postponed until I had painted a picture of the accidental still life. And the worst of it was that the kettle and vegetables had to be placed right in the middle of the floor, because I had the best light there for painting, and everyone had to walk around both vegetables and kettle for *days* until the painting was finished."[1]

1928. *Millions of Cats* published, followed quickly by *The Funny Thing,* and *The ABC Bunny.*

"I aim to make the illustrations for children's books as much a work of art as anything I would send to an art exhibition. I strive to make them completely accurate in relation to the text. I try to make them warmly human, imaginative, or humorous—not coldly decorative—and to make them so clear that a three-year-old can recognize the main objects in them."[1]

1930. Married Earle Humphreys, a salesman. With husband, syndicated "Wanda's Wonderland" for a year. Bought 100-year-old farm in the Muscanetcong Mountains on the banks of the Quequacommissicong Creek. Named it "All Creation."

"A hundred and twenty-five acres, all around the place—think of what wonderful insulation that will be against distractions!"[1]

1936. *Tales from Grimm* published. "I am translating the original and authentic Grimm's Fairy Tales (about fifty of them). These I plan to distribute among about three volumes, *Profusely Illustrated* as the old Story Books used to say. I find this very interesting and, in many cases, difficult, because what can one do with such words as *Kindlein, Weibchen, Käppchen,* etc? Little child, small wife, wee cap—are just not the same. Some words lend themselves to the *kin, ken,* or *let* ending, but all too few have that form. Well, I do the best I can. Mine is to be a *free* translation, true to the spirit rather than the letter, because I want to show just what *Märchen* meant to *me* as a child."[1]

1938. *Snow White* and *Nothing-at-All* published. "[*Nothing-at-All*] is a story I've had in my head for so long a time that I can't even remember when the idea germinated (probably soon after *Millions of Cats*) but while I tried this and that, I could never make it jell.

"This winter Rose [Dobbs] wanted me to do another single Grimm tale in the same format as 'Snow White,' but while I have four or five translated ones to choose from, I somehow couldn't get into the swing of things, so I began poking around among my own half-begun stories. I worked for a week on another fairy story (a wild one!) which I've picked up off and on for years, but I couldn't solve it. So I went back to my little *Nothing-at-All,* and lo! the story worked itself out in one day.

"After two weeks of work on it, I feel it is still very rough in spots, but the big thing is to find out how much (or little!) the main idea, as well as the various devices in it, appeal to children.

"How I've worked on that *Nothing-at-All!* I . . . draw it all on glass and it's a very lengthy process. For months I've been working ten to fourteen hours a day on it and it is finally all drawn and the plates and proofs made. I think it looks very good. Naturally, since this is my first book in color I was pretty nervous about it, wondering whether I had visualized the different weights and textures correctly. You see I draw all three plates in *black,* and it's pretty hard to know for instance, how heavy a drawing will look when it's translated into green or red, or worse still, how it will look with green superimposed on the red! Well, it's all over but the final printing now and since it does look good, I don't mind so much having been a prisoner and a slave all these months."[1]

1931-1939. Exhibitions of her work in Mexico, Russia, Sweden, and all over U.S.

1938. "I am taking a sort of 'vacation' this summer—that is, a vacation from *deadlines* and such. It's a working vacation, of course, but it's what I've long wanted to do:

working in water color and doing just what suits my fancy with no effort to make something which will be sold or shown.

"It is possible that a few pictures will fall into that category, but I'm painting *to learn*, not to make a finished picture. Naturally this isn't the first time I've done water colors. I did quite a lot about ten years ago, but there were many things I didn't like about my way of seeing color at that time, and so I hope to improve on my former *vision.* Also I've lived for so many years among nature, during which time I've studied the ever-changing color schemes, and so I'm at it. Well, it's devilish hard at times, because I am doing the things 'I do not yet know how to do' as Van Gogh says—it would be no trick to do well the things I *know* how to do. . . ."[1]

February, 1945. An exploratory operation showed she had cancer of the lung. She wasn't told.

"The subject of fairy tales is very soothing for someone who is convalescing. For a long time I wasn't able to sit up and draw, but about two months ago I found that my hand was steady enough to do some preliminary sketches, and lately I have even been able to sit up at the drawing table for several hours at a time. The result is I have all my illustrations *planned,* all but about ten solved, and about eighty drawn in ink, although these are still 'preliminaries.' Most of these, though, are in next to the final stage. Rose [Dobbs of Coward-McCann] hasn't the *glimmering* of an idea of how much I have done, so don't mention it to her. I would like to surprise her with it."[1]

Christmas Day, 1945 to late Spring, 1946, went to Florida. "Florida has been very good for me because merely being saved from fighting cold weather is an advantage. . . . I have actually accomplished things. I made eight illustrations for *East of the Sun and West of the Moon* for the new edition of *The Book of Knowledge.* Then, with Earle's help, I got thirty-three Grimm translations typed, corrected, and in good shape to be sent to Rose. I also did some work on the illustrations for these stories, *and* I've done quite a few rough studies in water colors. I wish I could have done some finished water colors but I don't seem to have the sustaining strength to carry that through. . . . I have to try to be patient (which is hard, often) and only do color studies when I'd just love to plunge in and turn out a raft of finished, completely solved pictures.

"Isn't it maddening that people . . . who would be willing to work ourselves to a frazzle, always have to be limited by our strength or lack of it, while so many others have a lot of vitality and don't need it. That's a pretty trite observation, but there's this about trite statements, there's usually an overwhelming amount of truth in them."[1]

June 27, 1946. Died at "All Creation."

FOR MORE INFORMATION SEE—Books: Winifred M. Kirkland and Frances Kirkland, "Wanda Gág, Who Followed Her Own Way," in *Girls Who Became Artists,* Harper, 1934; Gág, *Growing Pains: Diaries and Drawings for the Years 1908-1917,* Coward-McCann, 1940; Carl Zig-

(From *Millions of Cats* by Wanda Gág. Illustrated by the author.)

rosser, *Artist in America: Twenty-Four Close-Ups of Contemporary Printmakers,* Knopf, 1942; Bertha E. Mahony, "Two Artists," *Horn Book,* September, 1946; Elizabeth R. Montgomery, *Story behind Great Stories,* Dodd, 1947; Karl Kup, "Wanda Gág and Her Work," *American Artist,* February, 1947; Rose Dobbs, "Wanda Gág, Fellow-Worker," *Horn Book,* May, 1947; Ernestine Evans, "Wanda Gág as Writer," *Horn Book,* May, 1947, reprinted in *A Horn Book Sampler,* edited by Norma R. Fryatt, Horn Book, 1959; E. Humphreys, editor, "Letters from Children to Wanda Gág," *Horn Book,* May, 1947; Anne C. Moore, "Art for Life's Sake," *Horn Book,* May, 1947; Alma O. Scott, "Wanda Gág," *Horn Book,* May, 1947; Lynd Ward, "Wanda Gág, Fellow-Artist," *Horn Book,* May, 1947; Carl Zigrosser, "Wanda Gág, Artist," *Horn Book,* May, 1947; *Illustrators of Children's Books: 1744-1945,* Horn Book, 1947; Alma O. Scott, *Wanda Gag: The Story of an Artist,* University of Minnesota Press, 1949.

Junior Book of Authors, edited by Kunitz & Haycraft, H. W. Wilson, 2nd edition, 1951; R. M. Walker, "Wanda Gág: The Story of an Artist," *Horn Book,* January, 1951; B. J. Hurley, "Wanda Gág—Artist, Author," *Elementary English,* October, 1955; *A Treasury of the World's Great Diaries,* edited by Philip Dunaway and Mel Evans, Doubleday, 1957; *More Junior Authors,* edited by Muriel Fuller, H. W. Wilson, 1963; Nancy E. Duin, *Wanda Gág, Author and Illustrator of Children's Books,* SamHar Press, 1973; Norah Smaridge, *Famous Author-Illustrators for Young People,* Dodd, 1973; Virginia Haviland, *Children and Literature: Views and Reviews,* Lothrop, 1974; Margery Fisher, *Who's Who in Children's Books,* Holt, 1975.

Obituaries: *New York Times,* June 28, 1946; *Publishers Weekly,* July 6, 1946; *Art Digest,* August, 1946; *Wilson Library Bulletin,* September, 1946; *Current Biography Yearbook 1946.*

GORDON, Colonel H. R.
 See ELLIS, Edward S(ylvester)

Kenneth Grahame, portrait by John Singer Sargent, 1912.

GRAHAME, Kenneth   1859-1932

PERSONAL: Born March 3 (or March 8, according to some sources), 1859, in Edinburgh, Scotland; died July 6, 1932, in Pangbourne, England; buried in Holywell Churchyard, Oxford; son of J. C. Grahame (a lawyer) and Bessie Grahame; married Elspeth Thomson, 1899; children: Alistair (died, 1920). *Education:* Attended schools in England. *Home:* London, later Blewbury, Berkshire, and Pangbourne, England.

CAREER: Bank of England, London, began as a clerk, 1878, and became Secretary of the Bank, 1898-1907; essayist, poet, and writer for children, beginning in the 1880's. *Member:* New Shakespeare Society.

WRITINGS—Essays and stories: *Pagan Stories,* Stone & Kimball, 1894, reprinted, Books for Libraries, 1972; *The Golden Age,* Stone & Kimball, 1895, new edition (illustrated by Maxfield Parrish), John Lane, 1900, later editions illustrated by R. J. Enraght-Moony, 1915, and by Ernest H. Shepard, 1928, Dodd, 1929; *The Headswoman,* Bodley Head, 1898, new edition (illustrated by Marcia Lane Foster), John Lane, 1921; *Dream Days* (sequel to *The Golden Age*), John Lane, 1898, new edition (illustrated by Maxfield Parrish), 1902, later editions illustrated by Lois Lenski, 1922, and by Ernest H. Shepard, 1930, Dodd, 1931; *The Reluctant Dragon* (story from *Dream Days;* illustrated by E. H. Shepard), Holiday House, 1938, reissued 1966, later editions illustrated by Peggy Fortnum, Dufour Editions, 1959, and by Gregorio Prestopino, Grosset, 1968, stage adaptation for children written by Harcourt Williams and

published by Samuel French, 1934; *The Golden Age and Dream Days* (illustrated by Charles Keeping), Dufour Editions, 1965.

The Wind in the Willows (story), Scribner, 1907, later editions illustrated by Paul Bransom, 1913, Nancy Barnhart, 1922, Wyndham Payne, Ernest H. Shepard, 1933, reprinted 1965, Arthur Rackham, Limited Editions Club, 1940, reprinted, Heritage Press, 1966, Tasha Tudor, World Publishing, 1966, Dick Cuffari, Grosset, 1966, Roberta Carter Clark, Grosset, 1966, David K. Stone, Golden Press, 1968, Alex Tsao, New American Library, 1969; stage adaptation of *The Wind in the Willows,* written by A. A. Milne, published as *Toad of Toad Hall,* Scribner, 1929, reprinted, 1965; motion picture adaptation, *Ichabod and Mr. Toad* (based on *The Wind in the Willows* and Washington Irving's *The Sketch Book*), produced by Walt Disney, 1949; books based on the Disney motion picture, adapted by John Hench, published as *Walt Disney's The Adventures of Mr. Toad,* Simon & Schuster, 1949, and as *Walt Disney's Magnificent Mr. Toad,* Grosset, 1949.

The First Whisper of "The Wind in the Willows," (edited and with an introduction by the author's wife, Elspeth Grahame), Methuen, 1944, Lippincott, 1945 (contains the author's letters to his son on which *The Wind in the Willows* was based, and a previously unpublished story, "Bertie's Escapade"); *Bertie's Escapade* (illustrated by Ernest H. Shepard), Lippincott, 1949.

Editor: Eugene Field, *Lullaby-Land: Songs of Childhood* (illustrated by Charles Robinson), John Lane, 1898; *The Cambridge Book of Poetry for Children* (illustrated by Maud Fuller), Putnam, 1916, new edition (with a contribution by Grahame; illustrated by Gwen Raverat), Cambridge University Press, 1932, Putnam, 1933.

Collected Editions: *The Kenneth Grahame Book,* Methuen, 1932 (contains *The Golden Age, Dream Days,* and *The Wind in the Willows*).

Contributor to newspapers and magazines, including *St. James Gazette, National Observer,* and the *Yellow Book.*

ADAPTATIONS—Movies, filmstrips: *The Reluctant Dragon,* Walt Disney Productions, 1941; *The Adventures of Ichabod and Mr. Toad* (based on *The Wind in the Willows* and Washington Irving's *The Sketch Book*), Walt Disney Productions, 1949; *The Adventures of Mr. Toad* (filmstrip based on Disney's *The Adventures of Ichabod and Mr. Toad*), Encyclopaedia Britannica Films, 1958; *The Wind in the Willows,* motion picture by Richard Slote, Universal Education and Visual Arts, 1970; "The Wind in the Willows" (8 color filmstrips with 8 12" 33 rpm records or cassettes), Miller-Brody Productions.

Recordings: "A Graveyard of Ghost Tales" (cassette only), Caedmon; "The Reluctant Dragon" (cassette only), Caedmon; "The Wind in the Willows" (cassette only), Caedmon; "The Wind in the Willows," Listening Library; "The Wind in the Willows" (two records or cassettes), Miller-Brody Productions; "The Wind in the Willows," read by Christopher Casson, (parts 1 & 2, cassettes only), Spoken Arts; "The Wind in the Willows," Teaching Resources Films.

SIDELIGHTS: **1859.** Born in Edinburgh, third of four children.

April 4, 1864. Mother died of scarlet fever. Grahame caught infection the same day, and was close to death. The disease weakened him permanently with chronic bronchial condition. Because their father was an alcoholic, the children were sent to live with their maternal grandmother. "Looking back to those days of old, ere the gate shut to behind me, I can see now that to children with a proper equipment of parents these things would have worn a different aspect." [Kenneth Grahame, *The Golden Age,* Stone & Kimball, 1895.[1]]

1868-1876. Attended St. Edward's School, Oxford. ". . . I cannot help noticing that when a distinguished general, a famous statesman, or other deservedly successful and popular personage, honours a school by consenting to give away the Prizes, he is fond of informing his admiring audience that he, for his part, strange to say, never reached any giddy pre-eminence in his school lists, was rather an idle dog than otherwise, and ranked very low in the opinion of all the masters. 'And look at me now!' he seems to say, though of course he does not use those actual words. For my part, I have always thought this mental attitude of Distinguished Person not exactly a prudent one, to put it mildly. Dr. Johnson, who was a very sensible man, says somewhere or other—at least I think it was Dr. Johnson—that a man should never tell a story, however witty and amusing it may be, of which the point, the ultimate point, is against himself. Because, he adds shrewdly, though people may be greatly amused, and laugh heartily, at the time, yet—yet—they *remember it against you.*

"Now, how would it be, just as an experiment, next time such a person addresses you on those lines, telling you perhaps that, for his part, he never rose beyond the Lower Third, you were to remark blandly, 'Why, of course not!' or 'What about it? Where did you expect to be?' or words to that effect. This would not exactly please the general or statesman, of course, in fact it would probably annoy him very much. But what of that? You are not there to amuse him. It's his business to amuse you—if he can. And it might do him good.

"Those of you who are determined to become great generals or statesmen, by the sheer process of remaining doggedly in the Junior Second, should pause and remember that we cannot all be great statesmen or generals. There aren't enough of such jobs to go round. Turn your thoughts elsewhere. There is many a hard-working, honest—at least fairly honest—millionaire, many a fashionable physician, prominent barrister, or successful dramatist, who is only waiting to resign his position to you as soon as you have gently but firmly signified your intention of occupying it. And of course the first question he will ask you will be, whether you ever succeeded in getting out of the Fourth Form. Moreover, strange as it may seem, it is not so easy as you may think for the most ambitious youth to attain his ends by sticking to the bottom of the form.

"Let me give you a little reminiscence of my own, which dates from the first few days of my arrival at this school—the old school, I mean, of New-Inn-Hall Street days. The Junior form, or class, was in session, so to speak, and I was modestly occupying that position, at the

At this very moment, perhaps, Toad is busy arraying himself in those singularly hideous habiliments so dear to him, which transform him from a (comparatively) good-looking Toad into an Object which throws any decent-minded animal that comes across it into a violent fit. ■ (From the movie "The Wind in the Willows," copyright by Walt Disney Productions.)

very bottom, which seemed to me natural enough, when the then Headmaster entered—a man who had somehow formed an erroneous idea of my possibilities. Catching sight of me, he asked sternly, 'What's that thing doing down there?' The master in charge could only reply that whether it was crass ignorance or invincible stupidity, he wotted not, but there it was. The Headmaster, who was, I was persuaded, a most illogical man, and could not really have studied that immortal work, the *Republic of Plato,* in which the principles of ideal Justice are patiently sought out, merely remarked that if the thing—meaning me—was not up there or near it, pointing to the head of the form, before the close of work, it was to be severely caned: and left the room.

"Well, you can imagine my feelings. I was a very little chap—not yet ten. I was not accustomed to be caned—that is, beaten. I never had been beaten. I had been doing my best, and at home I had not been considered an absolute fool. And there I was, up against it in the fullest sense of the word! It was not surprising, perhaps, that I shed some bitter tears. But what happened? Not one of my colleagues started forth, as I half expected, to champion the cause of youth and innocence. Instead, they all proceeded to display an ignorance and a stupidity, on even the simplest matters, which seemed unnatural, even for them. The consequence was, that I presently found myself, automatically it really seemed, soaring, soaring—till I stood, dazed and giddy, at the top of the form itself, and was kept there till my friendly colleagues thought the peril was safely past, when I was allowed to descend from that bad eminence to which merit had certainly not raised me. It was from that moment, I think, that I first began to realize that I was never very likely to become either a successful general or a leading statesman.

"You see therefore that the path to success is not easy, even by a steady neglect of the educational side of school life. Some of you may therefore say, 'I will try other methods. Hang it all, why shouldn't I try and get into the Sixth!' Well, it is a great thing to have arrived at the Sixth, even if you are unable to maintain your position there for as much as a whole term. But you must remember, that the Sixth are very great men. To hope to reach the giddy height of the Sixth is like wanting to begin life as a Cabinet Minister. No, it might be more prudent to have a modest aim—say about the middle of the Fourth. The advantage of that is, that nobody will be jealous of you, and as people will think you more stupid even than you really are, they will always be ready to lend you a helping hand.

"Let us suppose, then, that Jones, as we will call him, goes forth into the world from the giddy eminence of the Lower Fourth. He looks round for somebody to give him a leg up, and he sees Smith, whom he remembers in the Sixth, and who, of course, by now holds some distinguished position. He writes to Smith, Smith says, condescendingly, 'Ah yes, Jones! I remember him well. Such a good fellow, Jones. Not a genius, of course, like some fellows. Poor Jones! We must give him a leg up.' He does so, and in due course Jones finds himself occupying a position not very inferior to that of Smith. And soon, by giving his mind to it, Jones succeeds in doing Smith out of his job, and wangling it for himself. That is one way of doing it, almost as good as the general's way of dodging education altogether." [Patrick Chalmers, *Kenneth Grahame: Life, Letters and Unpublished Work*, Methuen, 1933.[2]]

"The main difficulty that confronts me in setting down these random recollections of a now very distant past is to avoid the excursions, the tempting bypaths, that start into sight and appeal to me at every stop of my progress. For instance, I tried to begin in brisk and strictly historical fashion by stating that on or about Michaelmas Day, 1868, a bright and eager (sullen, reluctant, very ordinary-looking) youth of nine summers sprang lightly (descended reluctantly, was hauled ignominiously) on to the arrival platform of the Great Western Railway Station at Oxford.

"We were distributed in bedrooms, five or six or thereabouts apiece. There was also a master's sitting-room, a cheerful bow-windowed room, overlooking the playground. Thither I was shortly summoned, and met a round and rosy young man with side-whiskers, who desired, he said, to record my full name for some base purpose of his own. When he had got it he tittered girlishly, and murmured, 'What a *funny* name!' His own name was—but there! I think I won't say what his own name was. I merely mention this little incident to show the sort of stuff we bright lads of the late 'sixties sometimes found ourselves up against.

"The canings came along in due time. But after I had seen my comrades licked, or many of them, the edge of my anticipation was somewhat dulled. We used to play cricket under difficulties on Port Meadow (this must have been in the following year). The sole advantage of Port Meadow as

a cricket pitch was the absence of boundaries. If an ambitious and powerful slogger wanted to hit a ball as far as Wolvercote, he could do so if he liked; there was nothing to stop him, and the runs would be faithfully run out. The chief drawback was that the city burgesses used the meadow for pasturage of their cows—gramnivorus animals of casual habits. When fielding was 'deep,' and frenzied cries of 'Throw her up!' reached one from the wicket, it was usually more discreet to feign a twisted ankle or a sudden faintness, and allow some keener enthusiast to recover the ball from where it lay." [Kenneth Grahame, "Oxford through a Boy's Eyes," *Country Life*.[3]]

New Years' Eve, 1874. Older brother Willie died at sixteen.

1876. Deeply disappointed because he couldn't afford Oxford, became clerk in Uncle's office in Westminster. Moved to London.

January 1, 1879. Entered Bank of England as gentleman-clerk.

February 27, 1887. Father died.

1888. Transferred to Chief Cashier's office, Bank of England.

1889. Transferred to Secretary's office, remained there until his retirement.

1890-96. Wrote for magazines and journals.

1893. Collection of essays, "Pagan Papers," published in book form.

1894. Bought house at No. 5 Kensington Crescent.

1898. Became Secretary of the Bank of England at age 39. One of the youngest in history. *Dream Days* published which included the story, "The Reluctant Dragon." "Vitality—that is the test; and, whatever its components, more truth is not necessarily one of them. A dragon, for instance, is a more enduring animal than a pterodactyl. I have never yet met anyone who really believed in a pterodactyl; but every honest person believes in dragons—down in the back-kitchen of his consciousness." [P. J. Billinghurst's introduction to *A Hundred Fables of Aesop*, 1899.[4]]

April 3, 1899. Took seriously ill with pneumonia and emphysema.

July 22, 1899. Entered into a disastrous marriage with Elspeth Thomson. Bought house in Campden Hill.

May 12, 1900. Alastair Grahame was born with congenital cataract completely blinding the right eye and a squint in the other. Throughout his youth he received letters from his father about the Toad. "10 May, 1907. This is a birthday letter to wish you very many happy returns of the day. I wish we could have been all together, but we shall meet again soon and then we will have *treats*. I have sent you two picture-books, one about Brer Rabbit, from Daddy, and one about some other animals, from Mummy.

"Have you heard about the Toad? He was never taken prisoner by brigands at all. It was all a horrid low trick of his. He wrote that letter himself—the letter saying that a

It was a golden afternoon; the smell of the dust they kicked up was rich and satisfying. ■ (From *The Wind in the Willows* by Kenneth Grahame. Illustrated by Arthur Rackham.)

"...When you talk of settling down, and the neighbours, and so on, I can't help feeling that you don't quite realize your position. You're an enemy of the human race, you see!"
"Haven't got an enemy in the world," said the dragon, cheerfully. "Too lazy to make em, to begin with. And if I *do* read other fellows my poetry, I'm always ready to listen to theirs!" ▪ (From *The Reluctant Dragon* by Kenneth Grahame. Illustrated by Ernest H. Shepard.)

hundred pounds must be put in the hollow tree. And he got out of the window early one morning and went off to a town called Buggleton and went to the Red Lion Hotel and there he found a party that had just motored down from London and while they were having breakfast he went into the stable-yard and found their motor-car and went off in it without even saying Poop-poop! And now he has vanished and every one is looking for him, including the police. I fear he is a bad low animal.''[2]

May, 1906. Moved out of London to Cookham Dene.

June, 1908. Resigned from bank.

October, 1908. *Wind in the Willows* published to poor reviews. A letter from a reader asked who cleaned Mole End in Mr. Mole's absence and fed his goldfish. Grahame's reply deals with "the fabric of a fairytale." "Dear Sir,—The very natural inquiries contained in your kind letter which reached me this morning are probably best answered by a simple reference to the hopelessly careless and slipshod methods of the author whose work you are criticizing. But it may perhaps be pointed out in his defence, that Mole, though unmarried and evidently in rather poor circumstances, as incomes go nowadays, could probably have afforded some outside assistance say twice a week or so, indeed, living as he did, it would be almost a necessity. He probably then had a char-mouse in for a few hours and her dinner on certain days, and the animal would have cleaned up his white-washing mess in a perfunctory sort of way; then, finding that her weekly pittance was no longer forthcoming, quite naturally and properly would have taken her services elsewhere, though from kindness of heart she might have continued to give an occasional eye to the goldfish.

"In support of his theory, I would ask you to observe that our author practises a sort of 'character economy' which has the appearance of being deliberate. The presence of certain characters may be indicated in or required by the story, but if the author has no immediate use for them, he simply ignores their existence. Take this very question of domestic service—however narrow poor Mole's means may have been, it is evident that Rat was comfortably off—indeed I strongly suspect him of a butler-valet and cook-housekeeper. Toad Hall, again, must have been simply crawling with idle servants eating their heads off.

"But the author doesn't happen to want them, so for him they simply don't exist. He doesn't say they are *not* there; he just leaves them alone. To take another instance—the wretched fellow, ignorant as he is, must have known perfectly well that the locomotive on which Toad escaped required the services of a stoker as well as an engine-driver, but he didn't happen to *want* a stoker, so he simply ignored him.

"I think you will find that this same character-economy runs through all the classic old fairy-tales and our author probably thought that he was sinning (if sinning at all) in very good company. The modern method leaves so little to the imagination of the reader that it describes with insistent particularity the appearance of the taxi-driver who did *not* say 'Thank you' to the heroine when she gave him 3*d*. Our author would have treated a taxi exactly as he would treat a Magic Carpet (which indeed is just what it is) and would not have given the taxi a driver at all. And this is right, for not one passenger in a hundred is ever conscious of the presence of a driver at all. They only see at the end a paw thrust out into which they drop something, and the taxi vanishes with a snort. Probably Magic Carpets had drivers too, but the authors of old saw that they were unessential to their stories, and ignored them.''[2]

January, 1910. Bought house in village of Blewbury, near Didcot. "We live in a small clearing in a forest of books and furniture, striving vainly to reduce things to some appearance of order. Blewbury is perhaps the most beautiful of a string of pretty and very primitive villages stretched along the northern edge of the Berkshire Downs. It is only about 54 miles from London, but 5,400 years remote from it in every way.

"This is the heart of King Alfred's Country, 'Alfred the Great' who beat the Danes, close by here, about 860, and nothing has really happened since. True, a tiresome innovator, called William the Conqueror, came along some years later, and established a thing called the Curfew Bell, which still rings here during the winter months, to the annoyance

I'm not half happy in my own mind, thinking of that poor animal lying up there, without a bit o'hot supper or anyone to change the news with. ▪ (From *The Reluctant Dragon* by Kenneth Grahame. Illustrated by Peggy Fortnam.)

"When I've grown up, big, and have money of my own, and a full-sized walking stick, I will set out early one morning, and never stop till I get to that little walled town." ∎ (From *Dream Days* by Kenneth Grahame. Illustrated by Maxfield Parrish.)

(From the animated movie "The Reluctant Dragon," copyright 1941, Walt Disney Productions.)

of the more conservative inhabitants, who say they used to get on very well before these newfangled notions; but this is all that divides us from Saxon times. We are some twelve miles from Oxford, but its culture does not permeate to us; if we penetrate as far as Abingdon or Wallingford we are mighty travellers and have seen great and distant cities.

"The village is really a charming one—a mixture of orchards and ancient timbered cottages and clear little streams, and the people are simple and friendly and dignified. The downs lie a mile or two to the south—splendid bare grassy spaces with (so-called) Roman or British 'Camps' and 'Barrows'. The villages along the edge are all beautiful with fine old churches—ours is a beauty, and not much spoilt. We went to a memorial service for King Edward there to-day and the simplicity and genuineness of it all was very touching. As for this little house, it is a plain Berkshire farmer's house, 'unfaked' and unaltered, with no special architectural features, with its orchard on one side and its farm buildings on the other."[2]

1915. World War I. "Our little village has played up well, sending some seventy men out of a total population of less than 500 souls. I think there has been a certain amount of

nonsense talked about the recruiting. From all I have seen I should say that men have come in splendidly—and are still coming in; and good stuff too. . . . I don't go into Oxford as of old. One misses the boys, and it's sad to see the river deserted, and have nobody playing the garden-ass or the giddy-goat. Oxford has played up well and no mistake.

"The 'veterans' of Blewbury have started a Volunteer Defence Corp, and we drill, in the evenings, in a beautiful great timber-framed thatched barn—like my own, only three times as big. The rats run in and out of the thatch along the rafters, and the barn cat, who ought to be attending to them, sits on wheat sacks and reviews us with great delight. He is having the time of his life, for he thinks that these drills are specially got up for him, to brighten the monotony of his long dull evenings. The corps have elected me their Commanding Officer—the cat concurring—because they said I was the most martial-looking of the crowd, and there I agree with them; they were careful to add, however, that it wasn't for any other reason whatever, and that also I can fully understand."[2]

May 7, 1920. Son, Alastair, found lying across railroad tracks, run over by a train. Coroner reported "accidental death" but some suspected suicide.

October 30, 1920-1924. Sailed to Italy. "I doubt very much if I shall ever write another book. A certain amount of . . . *life* must go into the making of any page of prose.

"A sentence that is easy to read may have been difficult to put together. Perhaps the greater the easiness in reading, the harder that task in composition. Writing is not easy. There is always a pleasure in the exercise; but also there is always an agony in the endeavour. If we make a formula of these two motives, I think we may define the process. It is, at its best, a pleasurable agony.

"I am not a professional writer. I never have been, and I never will be, by reason of the accident that I don't need any money. I do not care for notoriety; in fact, it is distasteful to me. If I should ever become a popular author, my privacy would be disrupted and I should no longer be allowed to live alone.

"What, then, is the use of writing, for a person like myself? The answer might seem cryptic to most. It is merely that a fellow entertains a sort of hope that, somehow, some time, he may build a noble sentence that might make Sir Thomas Browne sit up once again in that inhospitable grave of his in Norwich."[2]

1924. Made last home at Pangbourne. "Granted that the average man may live for seventy years, it is a fallacy to assume that his life from sixty to seventy is more important than his life from five to fifteen. Children are not merely people; they are the only really living people that have been left to us. Any child will agree with [the] American poet, Walt Whitman, when he says: 'To me every hour of the day and night is an unspeakably perfect miracle.'

"In my tales about children, I have tried to show that their simple acceptance of the mood of wonderment, their readiness to welcome a perfect miracle at any hour of the day or night, is a thing more precious than any of the laboured acquisitions of adult mankind.

"As for animals, I wrote about the most familiar in *The Wind in the Willows* because I felt a duty to them as a friend. Every animal, by instinct, lives according to his nature. Thereby he lives wisely, and betters the tradition of mankind. No animal is ever tempted to deny his nature. No animal knows how to tell a lie. Every animal is honest. Every animal is true—and is, therefore, according to his nature, both beautiful and good."[2]

July 6, 1932. Died of cerebral hemorrhage. He had earlier written an essay for his old school magazine. "He was born at the pleasant town of Abingdon, that sits among its lush water-meadows and almost catches the chimes down the stream from the not so distant Oxford towers; and he 'went to Oxenforde to scole,' as of course a good saint should; and many a time he must have ridden out over Grandpont and along the old raised 'Cawsy'—still there under the road—to visit his home and his good mother who was thought worthy to have inscribed on her tomb that she was the 'flower of widows.' Also he 'dwellyd long after at Oxenforde' and 'Teddy,' the last of the old Halls, is said to perpetuate his name. But specially we should envy him his white vision in the meadow; for which he should be regarded as the patron saint of all those who of set purpose choose to walk alone, who know the special grace attaching

(Robert Benchley acted in and narrated the animated movie version of "The Reluctant Dragon," copyright 1941, Walt Disney Productions.)

to it, and ever feel that somewhere just ahead, round the next bend perhaps, the White Child may be waiting for them.

"For Nature's particular gift to the walker, through the semi-mechanical act of walking—a fit no other form of exercise seems to transmit in the same high degree—is to set the mind jogging, to make it garrulous, exalted, a little mad maybe—certainly creative and suprasensitive, until at last it really seems to join in, sun and the wind, the white road and the dusty hedges, the spirit of the season, whichever that may be, the friendly old earth that is pushing forth life of every sort under your feet or spell-bound in death-like winter trance, till you walk in the midst of a blessed company, immersed in a dream-talk far transcending any possible human conversation. Time enough, later, for that—across the dinner table, in smoking-room armchairs; here and now, the mind has shaken off its harness, is snorting and kicking up heels like a colt in a meadow. Not a fiftieth part of all your happy imaginings will you ever, later, recapture, note down, reduce to dull inadequate words; but meantime the mind has stretched itself and had its holiday. But this emancipation is only attained in solitude, the solitude which the unseen companions demand before they will come out and talk to you; for, be he who may, if there is another fellow present, your mind has to trot between shafts.

"A certain amount of 'shafts' indeed, is helpful, as setting the mind more free; and so the high road, while it should always give way to the field path when choice offers, still has this particular virtue, that it takes charge of you—your body, that is to say. Its hedges hold you in friendly steering-reins, its milestones and finger-posts are always on hand, with information succinct and free from frills; and, it always gets *somewhere,* sooner or later. So you are nursed along your way, and the mind may soar in cloudland and never need to be pulled earthwards by any string. But this is as much company as you ought to require, the comradeship of the road you walk on, the road which will look after you and attend to such facts as must not be overlooked. Of course the best sort of walk is the one on which it doesn't matter twopence whether you get anywhere at all at any time or not; and the second best is the one on which the hard facts of routes, times, or trains give you nothing to worry about. And this is perhaps the only excuse for the presence of that much-deprecated Other Fellow—that you can put all that sort of thing on to him. For the world is fortunately well-furnished with fellows who really like looking up Bradshaw, and paying bills, and taking charge generally; and it is wise to keep some such a man within easy hail. But spiritually he will be of little use, even if he were the angel that walked with Tobias.

"Much converse will he have, too, with shy bird and furtive little beast, the fellow that walks alone. I seem to have noticed a different expression in the eye of bird or animal at one's solitary approach, from the way it looks at you when there are two or three of you about. In the first case it seems to say wistfully, 'This *may* be a pal!' In the second, 'This is certainly a conspiracy!' and acts accordingly. As for adventures, if they are the game you hunt, everyone's experience will remind him that the best adventures of his life were pursued and achieved, or came suddenly to him unsought, when he was alone. For company too often

Kenneth Grahame, about age sixty.

means compromise, discretion, the choice of the sweetly reasonable. It is difficult to be made in company; yet but a touch of lunacy in action will open magic doors to rare and unforgettable experiences.

"But all these are only the by-products, the casual gains, of walking alone. The high converse, the high adventures, will be in the country of the mind." [Peter Greene, *Kenneth Grahame: A Biography,* World, 1959.[5]]

1933. *The Cambridge Book of Poetry for Children* published. "In the output of those writers who have deliberately written for children, it is surprising how largely the subject of *death* is found to bulk. Dead fathers and mothers, dead brothers and sisters, dead uncles and aunts, dead puppies and kittens, dead birds, dead flowers, dead dolls—a compiler of Obituary Verse for the delight of children could make a fine fat volume with little difficulty. I have turned

I had a dove and the sweet dove died;
    And I have thought it died of grieving;
O, what could it grieve for? It's feet were tied
    With a silken thread of my own hands' weaving.
■ (From *The Cambridge Book of Poetry for Children* edited by Kenneth Grahame. Illustrated by Gwen Raverat.)

(From *Dream Days* by Kenneth Grahame. Illustrated by Maxfield Parrish.)

The barge-horse was not capable of any very sustained effort, and its gallop soon subsided into a trot, and its trop into an easy walk; but Toad was quite contented with this, knowing that he, at any rate, was moving, and the barge was not. ▪ (From *The Wind in the Willows* by Kenneth Grahame. Illustrated by Ernest H. Shepard.)

... he dressed as quickly as possible in the smartest suit he could lay hands on at the moment, filled his pockets with cash which he took from a small drawer in the dressing-table, and next, knotting the sheets from his bed together and tying one end of the improvised rope round the central mullion of the handsome Tudor window which formed such a feature of his bedroom, he scrambled out .... ▪ (From *The Wind in the Willows* by Kenneth Grahame. Illustrated by Ernest H. Shepard.)

Book, April, 1954; G. Macy, "Arthur Rackham and 'The Wind in the Willows'," in *A Horn Book Sampler on Children's Books and Reading,* Horn Book, 1959; N. Braybrooke, "Kenneth Grahame, 1859-1932," *Elementary English,* January, 1959; Peter Green, *Kenneth Grahame: A Biography,* World Publishing, 1959; H.P.B. Smith, "Kenneth Grahame: The Piper at the Gates of Dawn," *Canadian Library Association Bulletin,* July, 1959.

Eleanor Graham, *Kenneth Grahame,* Walck, 1963; K. A. Smith, "Kenneth Grahame and the Singing Willows," *Elementary English,* December, 1968; Laura Benét, *Famous Storytellers for Young People,* Dodd, 1968; N. Braybrooke, "A Note on Kenneth Grahame," *Horn Book,* October, 1970.

off this mournful tap of tears as far as possible, preferring that children should read of the joy of life, rather than revel in sentimental thrills of imagined bereavement.

"There exists, moreover, any quantity of verse for children, which is merely verse and nothing more. It lacks the vital spark of heavenly flame, and is useless to a selector of Poetry. And then there is a whole corpus of verse—most of it of the present day—which is written *about* children, and this has even more carefully to be avoided. When the time comes that we send our parents to school, it will prove very useful to the compilers of their primers." [Kenneth Grahame, *The Cambridge Book of Poetry,* Putnam, 1933.⁶]

FOR MORE INFORMATION SEE: Patrick R. Chalmers, *Kenneth Grahame: Life, Letters, and Unpublished Work,* Methuen, 1933, Kenikat, 1972; Elizabeth Rider Montgomery, *Story behind Great Books,* McBride, 1946; Roger L. Green, *Tellers of Tales,* Ward, 1953; Ernest H. Shepard, "Illustrating 'The Wind in the Willows'," *Horn*

What the Boy chiefly dabbled in was natural history and fairytales, and he just took them as they came, in a sandwichy sort of way, without making any distinctions; and really his course of reading strikes one as rather sensible. ▪ From *The Reluctant Dragon* by Kenneth Grahame. Illustrated by Ernest H. Shepard.)

HARRIS, Joel Chandler   1848-1908

PERSONAL: Born December 9, 1848, near Eatonton, Georgia; died July 3, 1908, in Atlanta, Georgia; son of Mary Harris; married Esther LaRose, April 21, 1873; children: nine. *Education:* Attended local private schools until the age of thirteen. *Home:* "Wren's Nest," Atlanta, Georgia.

CAREER: Printer's apprentice to Joseph Addison Turner, editor of the weekly *Countryman*, 1860-62; writer for newspapers in Macon and Savannah, Georgia, and in New Orleans, Louisiana; *Atlanta Constitution* (newspaper), Atlanta, Georgia, began as a staff writer, became editor, 1876-1900; editor of *Uncle Remus Magazine* (later merged with *Home Magazine*), 1907-08; humorist, author of short stories and novels.

WRITINGS—"Uncle Remus" series: *Uncle Remus, His Songs and His Sayings: Folklore of the Old Plantation* (illustrated by Frederick S. Church and James H. Moser), D. Appleton, 1880, revised edition (illustrated by Arthur Burdett Frost), 1895, reprinted, Shocken Books, 1965, later editions illustrated by A. B. Frost and Edward W. Kemble, 1920, by Fritz Eichenberg, Peter Pauper Press, 1937, and by Seong Moy (with introduction by Marc Connelly), Heritage Press, 1957; *Nights with Uncle Remus: Myths and Legends of the Old Plantation*, Houghton, Mifflin, 1883, new edition (illustrated by Milo Winter), 1917; *Daddy Jake the Runaway, and Short Stories Told after Dark by "Uncle Remus,"* Century, 1889, reprinted, Books for Libraries, 1972; *Uncle Remus and His Friends: Old Plantation Stories, Songs, and Ballads* (illustrated by A. B. Frost), Houghton, Mifflin, 1892.

The Tar-Baby, and Other Rhymes of Uncle Remus (illustrated by A. B. Frost and E. W. Kemble), D. Appleton, 1904; *Told by Uncle Remus: New Stories of the Old Plantation* (illustrated by A. B. Frost, J. M. Condé, and Frank Verbeck), McClure, Phillips, 1905, reprinted, Books for Libraries, 1972; *Uncle Remus and Brer Rabbit*, F. A. Stokes, 1907; *Uncle Remus and the Little Boy* (illustrated by J. M. Condé), Small Maynard, 1910; *Uncle Remus Returns* (illustrated by A. B. Frost and J. M. Condé), Houghton, Mifflin, 1918; *The Witch Wolf: An Uncle Remus Story* (illustrated by W. A. Dwiggins), Bacon & Brown, 1921.

Seven Tales of Uncle Remus, edited by Thomas H. English, Emory University Library, 1948; *The Favorite Uncle Remus*, edited by George Van Santvoord and Archibald C. Coolidge (illustrated by A. B. Frost), Houghton, Mifflin, 1948 (published in England as *The Essential Uncle Remus*, J. Cape, 1949, reprinted, 1960); *The Complete Tales of Uncle Remus*, edited by Richard Chase (illustrated by A. B. Frost), Houghton, Mifflin, 1955.

"Uncle Remus" adaptations: *Brer Rabbit: Stories from Uncle Remus*, adapted by Margaret Wise Brown (illustrations of A. B. Frost redrawn by Victor Dowling), Harper & Brothers, 1941; *Walt Disney's Uncle Remus*, retold by Marion Palmer (illustrations by Bob Grant adapted from the Walt Disney movie, "Song of the South"), Simon & Schuster, 1947; *Walt Disney's Uncle Remus Stories*, retold by Marion Palmer (illustrations by Al Dempster and Bill Justice adapted from the Walt Disney movie, "Song of the

Joel Chandler Harris, 1877.

South"), Simon & Schuster, 1947, reprinted, Golden Press, 1966; *The Wonderful Tar-Baby, Told by Uncle Remus: Retold for Little Children* (illustrated by Dellwyn Cunningham), Wonder Books, 1952; *Animal Stories: Tales of the Old Plantation* (illustrated by Ezra Jack Keats), Junior Deluxe Editions, 1954; *Brer Rabbit and His Tricks*, adapted by Ennis Rees (illustrated by Edward Gorey), Young Scott Books, 1967; *More of Brer Rabbit's Tricks*, adapted by Rees, Young Scott Books, 1968; *Livin' de Life: A Play for Young People*, adapted by Edward Graczyk, Anchorage Press, 1970.

Other writings for children—All illustrated by Oliver Herford and published by Houghton, Mifflin, except as noted: *Little Mr. Thimblefinger and His Queer Country: What the Children Saw and Heard There*, 1894; *Mr. Rabbit at Home: A Sequel to Little Mr. Thimblefinger and His Queer Country*, 1895; *The Story of Aaron (So Called), the Son of Ben Ali, Told by His Friends and Acquaintances*, 1896; *Aaron in the Wildwoods*, 1897; *Wally Wanderoon and His Story-Telling Machine* (illustrated by Karl Moseley), McClure, Phillips, 1903; *The Bishop and the Boogerman* (illustrated by Charlotte Harding), Doubleday, Page, 1909.

Novels and novellas: *On the Plantation: A Story of a Georgia Boy's Adventures during the War* (autobiographical; illustrated by E. W. Kemble), D. Appleton, 1892 (published in England as *A Plantation Printer*, Osgood, McIlvaine, 1892); *Sister Jane, Her Friends and Acquaintances: A Narrative of Certain Events and Episodes Transcribed from the Papers of the Late William Wornum*, Houghton, Mifflin, 1896; *Gabriel Tolliver: A*

Yesterday's Authors of Books for Children

Story of Reconstruction, McClure, Phillips, 1902, reprinted, Gregg Press, 1967; *A Little Union Scout* (illustrated by George Gibbs), McClure, Phillips, 1904, reprinted, Books for Libraries, 1972; *The Shadow between His Shoulder-Blades* (illustrated by George Harding), Small, Maynard, 1909; *Qua: A Romance of the Revolution,* edited by Thomas H. English, Emory University Library, 1946.

Short stories: *Mingo, and Other Sketches in Black and White,* J. R. Osgood, 1884, reprinted, Books for Libraries, 1970; *Free Joe, and Other Georgian Sketches,* Scribner, 1887, reprinted, Gregg Press, 1967; *Balaam and His Master, and Other Sketches and Stories,* Houghton, Mifflin, 1891, reprinted, Books for Libraries, 1969; *Tales of the Home Folks in Peace and War,* Houghton, Mifflin, 1898, reprinted, Books for Libraries, 1969; *The Chronicles of Aunt Minervy Ann* (illustrated by A. B. Frost), Scribner, 1899, reprinted, Garrett Press, 1969; *Plantation Pageants* (illustrated by E. Boyd Smith), Houghton, Mifflin, 1899, reprinted, Books for Libraries, 1970; *On the Wing of Occasions: Being the Authorized Version of Certain Curious Episodes of the Late Civil War, including the Hitherto Suppressed Narrative of the Kidnapping of President Lincoln,* Doubleday, Page, 1900, reprinted, Books for Libraries, 1969, also published as *The Kidnapping of President Lincoln, and Other War Detective Stories,* Doubleday, Page, 1909; *The Making of a Statesman, and Other Stories,* McClure, Phillips, 1902, reprinted, Books for Libraries, 1970.

Nonfiction: *Stories of Georgia,* American Book Co., 1896, reprinted, Gale, 1976, also published as *Georgia from the Invasion of DeSoto to Recent Times,* D. Appleton, 1896; *Joel Chandler Harris, Editor and Essayist: Miscellaneous Literary, Political, and Social Writings,* edited by daughter-in-law, Julia Collier Harris, University of North Carolina Press, 1931.

Editor: *Joel Chandler Harris' Life of Henry W. Grady including His Writings and Speeches,* Cassell, 1890, reprinted as *The Life of Henry W. Grady, including His Writings and Speeches,* Haskell House, 1972; *The Book of Fun and Frolic,* Hall & Locker, 1901, reprinted as *The Merry Maker,* Auxiliary Educational League, 1954. Editor-in-chief, with Edwin Anderson Alderman, *Library of Southern Literature,* Martin & Hoyt, 1908-13, reprinted, Johnson Reprint, 1970; member of board of editors, *The World's Wit and Humor: An Encyclopedia of the Classic Wit and Humor of All Ages and Nations,* Review of Reviews Co., 1905-06, reprinted, Mini-Print Corp., 1973.

ADAPTATIONS—Movies and filmstrips—All by Walt Disney Productions, except as noted: "Song of the South," 1946; "Br'er Rabbit and the Tar Baby" (filmstrip), Curriculum Films, 1947, revised version, Curriculum Materials, 1960; "Brer Rabbit Runs Away" (filmstrip), Encyclopaedia Britannica Films, 1960; "Brer Rabbit and the Laughing Place" (filmstrip), 1973; "Brer Rabbit Meets the Tar Baby" (filmstrip), 1973; "Brer Rabbit Runs Away" (filmstrip), 1973.

Den de Little Gal, she ax' im won't he dance, en Brer Rabbit, he 'spon' how in de name er goodness kin a man dance w'iles he all tie up dis a-way, en den de Little Gal, she say she kin ontie 'im, en Brer Rabbit, he say he ain't keerin ef she do. ■ (From *Nights with Uncle Remus* by Joel Chandler Harris. Illustrated by Frederick Church.)

Recordings: "Brer Rabbit and His Tricks," read by Ennis Rees (cassette only), Spoken Arts; "Brer Rabbit and More Brer Rabbit," Miller-Brody Productions; "Brer Rabbit and More Brer Rabbit," read by Ennis Rees (cassette only), Spoken Arts; "Brer Rabbit and the Tar Baby" (11:30 min., record and cassette), Walt Disney; "Uncle Remus," Miller-Brody Productions.

SIDELIGHTS: **December 9, 1848.** Born in Eatonton, Georgia. Father deserted shortly after his birth. Took his unwed mother's last name. "It is a great blessing for a young fellow in the clutches of poverty to be raised among such people as those who lived in Eatonton when I was a boy, and whose descendants still live there. I have not the slightest difficulty in the world in referring all that I have ever done or hope to do to the kindly interest which the people of Eatonton took in my welfare when I was too young to know of the troubles which inhabit the world by right of discovery and possession." [Atlanta *Daily News*, October 10, 1900.[1]]

"My desire to write—to give expression to my thoughts—grew out of hearing my mother read *The Vicar of Wakefield*. I was too young to appreciate the story, but there was something in the style or something in the humor of that remarkable little book that struck my fancy, and I straightway fell to composing little tales, in which the principal character, whether hero or heroine, silenced the other characters by crying 'Fudge!' at every possible opportunity. None of these little tales have been preserved, but I am convinced that since their keynote was 'Fudge!' they must have been very close to human nature." [Julia Collier Harris, *Joel Chandler Harris,* Houghton, 1918[2]]

March, 1862. At age thirteen went to work as typesetter apprentice for editor, Joseph Addison Turner of *The Countryman*. Lived on Turner's Turnwold Plantation, 1862-66. Contributed articles and reviews. "Eatonton was not a newspaper office, and I had to leave there in order to stick my head in an ink fountain. There came a time when I had to be up and doing, as the poet says, and it so happened that I was in the post office at Eatonton reading the Milledgeville papers when the first member of *The Countryman* was deposited on the counter where all the newspapers were kept. I read it through, and came upon an advertisement which announced that the editor wanted a boy to learn the printer's trade. This was my opportunity, and I seized it with both hands. I wrote to the editor, whom I knew well, and the next time he came to town he sought me out, asked if I had written the letter with my own hand, and in three words the bargain was concluded." [Harris, *On the Plantation,* D. Appleton & Co., 1892[3]]

"As you may well believe, it was a great and saving experience for a youngster of that age. It was just lonely enough to bring me face to face with myself and yet not lonely enough to breed melancholy. I used to sit in the dusk and see the shadows of all the great problems of life flitting about, restless and uneasy, and I had time to think about them. What some people call loneliness was to me a great blessing, and the printer's trade, so far as I learned it, was in the nature of a liberal education; and, as if that wasn't enough, Mr. Turner had a large private library, containing all the best books."[2]

November, 1864. Detachment of Sherman's Federal troops

Dar he swung, en he fear'd he gwineter fall, en he fear'd he wer'n't gwineter fall. ■ (From *Uncle Remus: His Songs and Sayings* by Joel Chandler Harris. Illustrated by A. B. Frost.)

invaded Turnwold; ransacked and burned part of it. "That the Federal army should be plunging through that peaceful region after all that [I] had seen in the newspapers about Confederate victories, seemed to [me] to be an impossibility. The voices of the men, and their laughter, sounded vague and insubstantial." [Paul M. Cousins, *Joel Chandler Harris,* Louisiana State University Press, 1968 [4]]

May, 1866. Publication of *The Countryman* suspended. Returned home at seventeen, then moved to Macon for job as typesetter on Macon *Telegraph*. Also reviewed books and magazines.

Fall, 1866. Moved to New Orleans. Became private secretary to William Evelyn, publisher of the *Crescent Monthly*. "[I] was in a city far from home, and not at all happy in [my] new surroundings. [I] hung up [my] stocking, nevertheless, and woke to find it empty, and no wonder! Santa Claus could not have found [me] without a map of the town, and even then he would have needed a guide to show him the way to [my] small room in the top of a French boarding-house under the shadow of a great cathedral." [*Uncle Remus's Home Magazine,* XXIV, December, 1908.[5]]

May, 1867. Decided to return to Eatonton. "Whether you go from the city, or from the plantations, you are inevitably impressed with a sense of the attractiveness of the place; you fall under the spell of the old town—it was old even in the old times of the sixties. And yet if you were called upon to define the nature of the spell, what could you say? What name could you give to the transient beauty that hovers about and around the place, when the fresh green leaves of the great trees are fluttering in the cool wind and everything is touched and illumed by the tender colors of spring? Under what heading in the catalogue of things would you place the vivid richness which animates the town and the landscape all around when summer is at its height? And how could you describe the harmony that time has brought about between the fine old houses and the setting in which they are grouped?'' (Joel Chandler Harris, *Gabriel Tolliver*[6])

June, 1867. Joined staff of *Monroe Advertiser* in Forsyth, Ga. Then ''left Forsyth with much regret—and only after the most serious deliberation. If I had consulted my desires—my personal feelings, I mean—I would have remained on the ''Advertiser''; but in this miserable world, personal predilections are often sacrificed for gain. It is a sad confession to make, but, in my case at least, it is true. The personal relations between Mr. Harrison and myself have been, throughout, of the kindest and most intimate character. There have been occasions, undoubtedly, when his impatient temper rendered me uncomfortable, because I am extremely sensitive; but I dare say that *my* shortcomings, together with the thousand and one imperfections which, through some bitter destiny, are a part of my nature, have to an infinite degree overbalanced everything. The cause of my leaving Forsyth was a matter of business simply, and had nothing to do with my friendship or personal feelings.

''I was offered a position as associate editor on the 'News' at a salary which I could not refuse—and I therefore concluded to accept. I talked long and seriously with Mr. Harrison, and there was perfect confidence between us on the subject. I spoke fully and freely of my hopes and prospects and asked his advice on this matter. If there was any restraint at all—which I do not believe—it was altogether on his side. The position of associate editor on a leading paper like the ''News' is not often tendered to a person as young and as inexperienced as myself—and I could not refuse.

''I never knew what a real friend was until I went to Forsyth, and it is no wonder that I look back upon my life there with the tenderest and most sincere regrets—regrets that I was compelled to give it up. My history is a peculiarly sad and unfortunate one—and those three years in Forsyth are the very brightest of my life.''[2]

Fall, 1870. Accepted position as associate editor of the Savannah *Morning News.* Began daily column, ''Affairs in Georgia,''—which won him reputation as Georgia's foremost newspaper humorist. ''I don't expect to make any friends here—for the simple reason that I shall not try. I haven't room in my heart for them. My love, my friendship, and my esteem are exhausted on the few friends I already have. You see, I am conservative in my disposition and suspicious of new faces. I wouldn't give even the *memory* of *my* friends for the balance of the world. I have an *absolute horror* of strangers, and as for making friends of them now, it is not to be thought of. I am determined to put myself to the test at once—so that I may know exactly what is in me. In order to do this, I will have to trust entirely to merit for success, instead of depending upon the biased judgment of friends. By this means my capabilities—if I have any—will show themselves.

''The truth is, I am morbidly sensitive. With some people the quality of sensitiveness adds to their refinement and is quite a charm. With me it is an affliction—a disease—that has cost me more mortification and grief than anything in

the world—or everything put together. The least hint—a word—a gesture—is enough to put me in a frenzy almost. The least coolness on the part of a friend—the slightest rebuff tortures me beyond expression, and I have wished a thousand times that I was dead and buried and out of sight. You cannot conceive to what an extent this feeling goes with me. It is *worse* than death itself. It is *horrible.* My dearest friends have no idea how often they have crucified me. Of course no one can sympathize with such an inexplicable disposition. I can see how foolish it is, but the feeling is there, nevertheless, and I can no more control it than I can call into life the 'dry bones' or bid the moon to stand still 'over the valley of Ajalon.'

''Do you really think it is a merit to be different from other people—to have different thoughts and ideas about everything? I have a suspicion sometimes that it is the result of some abnormal quality of the mind—a peculiarity, in fact, that lacks only *vehemence* to become downright insanity. I have been convinced for many years that the difference between lunacy and extreme sensitiveness is not very clear. Like the colors of the prism, they blend so readily that it is difficult to point out precisely where the one begins and where the other leaves off. I have often thought that my ideas were in some degree distorted and tinged with a coloring of romance fatal to any practical ambition. But if it be so, so be it.

W'iles he wuz lookin' roun', he year some un laffin' fit ter kill, en he looked over de fence fer ter see who 'twuz. Dar wuz Brer Rabbit des a-rollin' in de grass en laffin' hard ex he kin.
Brer Fox, he say, "Tain nobody in de roun' worril but Brer Rabbit, en ef I ain't mighty much mistooken, he done gone en got a case er de highstericks." ▪ (From *The Favorite Uncle Remus* by Joel Chandler Harris. Illustrated by A. B. Frost.)

"You may be sure that I shall cling to my idiosyncrasies; they are a part of me and I am a part of them. They are infinitely soothing, and I would not be without them for the world. Why, sometimes—do you know?—I give myself up to the sweet indolence of thinking for hours at a time, and at such times I am supremely and ineffably happy—happy whether my thoughts are tinged with regret or flushed with hope. Not the least of my pleasures is the pleasure of melancholy. Sorrow is sometimes sweet—always sweet when it brings back to us, through the unexplorable caverns of the nights that have fled, some dear dead face—the touch of some vanished hand—the tone of some silent voice. Those who have not been wrapped about with the amber fogs of sorrow—have not experienced the grandest developments of this life, and from my soul I pity them."[2]

April 20, 1873. Married Esther LaRose, a fellow rooming-house boarder in Savannah.

1873-76. Two children born, Julian LaRose and Evelyn. "I am fond of children, but not in the usual way, which means a hug, a kiss, and a word in passing. I get down to their level, think with them and play with them."[2]

"**Den ole Miss Goose ax Brer Rabbit w'at she gwine do, en Brer Rabbit he up en tell Miss Goose dat she mus' go home en tie up a bundle er de wite folks' cloze, en put um on de bed, en den she mus' fly up on a rafter, en let Brer Fox grab de cloze en run off wid um.**" ■
(From *Nights with Uncle Remus* by Joel Chandler Harris. Illustrated by J. H. Beard.)

August, 1876. Outbreak of yellow fever in Savannah. Harris escaped with family to Atlanta.

September, 1876. Accepted employment on Atlanta *Constitution*. Began to write dialect stories at request of Evan P. Howell, editor-in-chief.

October 26, 1876. Dialect sketch appeared in Atlanta *Constitution*. "Jeems Rober'son's Last Illness" contained old Negro named Uncle Remus. Child born—Evan Howell. "*The Countryman* was published on a plantation and it was on this and neighboring plantations that I became familiar with the curious myths and animal stories that form the basis of the volumes accredited to 'Uncle Remus.' I absorbed the stories, songs and myths that I heard, but had no idea of their literary value until, sometime in the seventies, *Lippincott's Magazine* published an article on the subject of negro folklore, containing some rough outlines of some of the stories. This article gave me my cue, and the legends told by 'Uncle Remus' are the result. . . .

"This was the accidental beginning of a career that has been accidental throughout. It was an accident that I went to *The Countryman,* an accident that I wrote 'Uncle Remus,' and an accident that the stories put under that name struck the popular fancy." [*Lippincott's Magazine*[7]]

"He was not an invention of my own, but a human syndicate, I might say, of three or four old darkies whom I had known. I just walloped them together into one person and called him 'Uncle Remus.' You must remember that sometimes the negro is a genuine and an original philosopher."[2]

March 7, 1878. First novel serialized in Atlanta *Constitution*.

April, 1878. Son, Evan Howell, died of measles.

November, 1880. *Uncle Remus: His Songs and His Sayings* published. Immediate success. "Let us have the folktales told as they were intended to be told, for the sake of amusement—as a part of the art of literary entertainment. Then, if the folklorists find in them anything of value to their pretensions let it be picked out and preserved with as little cackling as possible.

"To be frank, I did not know much about folklore, and I didn't think that anybody else did. Imagine my surprise when I began to receive letters from learned philologists and folklore students from England to India, asking all sorts of questions and calling upon me to explain how certain stories told in the rice-fields of India and on the cottonfields of Georgia were identical, or similar, or at least akin. Then they wanted to know why the folklore had been handed down for centuries and perhaps for thousands of years. They wanted to know, too, why the negro makes Brer Rabbit so cunning and masterful. These letters came from royal institutes and literary societies, from scholars and from travelers. What answer could I make to them? None—none whatever. All that I know—all that we Southerners know—about it, is that every old plantation mammy in the South is full of these stories. One thing is certain—the negroes did not get them from the whites: probably they are of remote African origin."[2]

1881. *Nights with Uncle Remus* is published. "In the introduction to the first volume of 'Uncle Remus' occurs this

Joel Chandler Harris, painting by Lucy Mary Stanton.

Some goes up en some goes down. ■ (From *The Favorite Uncle Remus* by Joel Chandler Harris. Illustrated by A. B. Frost.)

statement: Curiously enough, I have found few negroes who will acknowledge to a stranger that they know anything of these legends; and yet to relate one is the surest road to their confidence and esteem.

"This statement was scarcely emphatic enough. The thirty-four legends in the first volume were comparatively easy to verify, for the reason that they were the most popular among the negroes, and were easily remembered. This is also true of many stories in the present volume; but some of them appear to be known only to the negroes who have the gift of story-telling,—a gift that is as rare among the blacks as among the whites. There is good reason to suppose, too, that many of the negroes born near the close of the war or since, are unfamiliar with the great body of their own folklore. They have heard such legends as the 'Tar Baby' story and 'The Moon in the Mill-Pond,' and some others equally as graphic; but, in the tumult and confusion incident to their changed condition, they have had few opportunities to become acquainted with that wonderful collection of tales which their ancestors told in the kitchens and cabins of the Old Plantation. The older negroes are as fond of the legends as ever, but the occasion, or the excuse, for telling them becomes less frequent year by year.

"With a fair knowledge of the negro character, and long familiarity with the manifold peculiarities of the negro mind and temperament, the writer has, nevertheless, found it a difficult task to verify such legends as he had not already heard in some shape or other. But, as their importance depended upon such verification, he has spared neither pains nor patience to make it complete. The difficulties in the way of this verification would undoubtedly have been fewer if the writer could have had an opportunity to pursue his investigations in the plantation districts of Middle Georgia; but circumstances prevented, and he has been compelled to depend upon such opportunities as casually or unexpectedly presented themselves.

"One of these opportunities occurred in the summer of 1882, at Norcross, a little railroad station, twenty miles northeast of Atlanta. The writer was waiting to take the train to Atlanta, and this train, as it fortunately happened, was delayed. At the station were a number of negroes, who had been engaged in working on the railroad. It was night, and, with nothing better to do, they were waiting to see the train go by. Some were sitting in little groups up and down the platform of the station, and some were perched upon a pile of cross-ties. They seemed to be in great good-humor, and cracked jokes at each other's expense in the midst of boisterous shouts of laughter. The writer sat next to one of the liveliest talkers in the party; and, after listening and laughing awhile, told the 'Tar Baby' story by way of a feeler, the excuse being that someone in the crowd mentioned 'Ole Molly Har .' The story was told in a low tone, as if to avoid attracting attention; but the comments of the negro, who was a little past middle age, were loud and frequent. 'Dar now!' he would exclaim, or, 'He's a honey, mon!' or, 'Gentermens! git out de way, an' gin 'im room!'

"These comments and the peals of unrestrained and unrestrainable laughter that accompanied them, drew the attention of the other negroes, and before the climax of the story had been reached, where Brother Rabbit is cruelly thrown into the brier-patch, they had all gathered around and made themselves comfortable. Without waiting to see what the effect of the 'Tar Baby' legend would be, the writer told the story of 'Brother Rabbit and the Mosquitoes,' and this had the effect of convulsing them. Two or three could hardly wait for the conclusion, so anxious were they to tell stories of their own. The result was that, for almost two hours, a crowd of thirty or more negroes vied with each other to see which could tell the most and the best stories. Some told them poorly, giving only meagre outlines, while others told them passing well; but one or two, if their language and their gestures could have been taken down, would have put Uncle Remus to shame.

"Some of the stories told had already been gathered and verified, and a few had been printed in the first volume; but the great majority were either new or had been entirely forgotten. It was night, and impossible to take notes; but that fact was not to be regretted. The darkness gave greater scope and freedom to the narratives of the negroes, and but for this friendly curtain it is doubtful if the conditions would have been favorable to story-telling. But however favorable the conditions might have been, the appearance of a notebook and pencil would have dissipated them as utterly as if they had never existed. Moreover, it was comparatively an easy matter for the writer to take the stories away in his memory, since many of them gave point to a large collection of notes and unrelated fragments already in his possession." [Joel Chandler Harris, *Nights with Uncle Remus*, Houghton, 1881[8]]

1882. Bought house "The Sign of the Wren's Nest"; so named because a wren had built its nest in the mailbox at the end of the walk. Summer—"The weather is warm, and we have a profusion of roses. La France seems to be outdoing herself this year, giving us some buds larger than I have ever seen from a hot house, and delightfully fragrant. I trimmed the bushes very close in March, and now they are paying me back. I never saw so many buds. But for the cold weather and high winds, the flowers would have been more perfect, but they are perfect enough for me. I'm not grumbling—which reminds me that J. C. has placed a

"Dey wuz times . . . w'en de creeturs 'ud segashuate tergedder des like dy aint had no fallin out." ■
(From the movie "Song of the South," copyright 1946, by Walt Disney Productions.)

'grumble-box' on the dinner table. Whoever grumbles must place a copper in the box.

Winter—"The thermometer and the mercury caught hold of each other's hands and went down nearly to zero. I hope they liked it; I'm sure I didn't. If I had the tropic zone here I'd sleep with it tonight, much as I dislike to sleep with strangers.

"We have had so much house cleaning lately that it is too nice to believe in, but we can't help ourselves. We are obliged to live in it or camp out next door to the street, but this would be an invitation to burglars. And so mamma prefers to sleep in the mansion, though really, the dust and dirt are horrible. Nobody knows where they come from. Chloe carries out seven bale-fuls every Friday and mamma sweeps out seven bale-fuls every Saturday. I suppose this is the way to enjoy life, but as for me, I'd prefer to live in a house that didn't have to be swept but once every fifteen years.

"Mamma is enthusiastic, and I am glad of it. When we lose enthusiasm, appreciation goes with it and then the joy of living is taken away."[2]

1882. First daughter, Mary Esther, died.

May, 1882. Met Mark Twain in New Orleans for proposed joint readings. Then declined because of attack of overwhelming shyness.

1882. Lillian born.

1883. Linton born.

1885. Mildred born.

1889. Joel C. Jr. born. Periodic illness confined him to his home—still associate editor of Atlanta *Constitution*.

1890. Linton died at age seven. "At the funeral services of little Linton Harris, in West End, yesterday, the floral offerings were less remarkable for their quantity than their quality. The rarest bloom that the season affords were there, sent by those who knew the little fellow in life. With him the love of flowers was something more than fancy—it was a passion that gave to his young life a beautiful ardor and a delicate refinement that are not to be acquired by artificial aid.

"In the early spring it was a favorite remark of his that he proposed to hide in the bushes and watch the roses bloom. That he discovered this secret there can be no doubt, for he carried the knowledge of it in the wise, mysterious, and unfathomable depths of his beautiful eyes. But the secret was inviolate. Whether told him by the singing birds, the droning bees, or the very grand wind, it went no farther. But it was not alone the secret of the rose that he learned. There was no flower of the woods or fields so shy that it hid from him. At his timid but familiar knock Nature opened wide the door of her vast storehouse.

"Didn't the fox never catch the rabbit, Uncle Remus?" asked the little boy the next evening. "He come mighty nigh it, honey, sho's you born—Brer Fox did." ▪ (From the movie "Song of the South" copyright 1946, by Walt Disney Productions.)

"It is natural that the hand that pens these lines should permit itself to be swayed by partiality in touching on the characteristics of the little boy that is dead; and yet an old man, a distinguished writer, and one of the most accomplished scholars the South has produced, was so attracted by the rare personal characteristics of the lad that he wrote him long and affectionate letters."[2]

March 30, 1891. Harris' mother dies.

1895. New edition of *Uncle Remus: His Songs and His Sayings* is published. Illustrated by A. B. Frost.

September 5, 1900. Resigned from *Constitution* after twenty-four years. "Please don't make a splutter about it. I am too old to relish the brief notoriety that is the result of a newspaper article. Just say, in your kindly way, that an old family hoss, grown tired of stopping before the same doors every day, has kicked out of the harness and proposes to keep the flies off in his own way."[4]

June, 1902. Emory College conferred honorary degree of Doctor of Literature.

1902. Winter and spring. Suffered long illness, slow recovery in Warm Springs, Ga.

1905. Son Julian and others founded monthly literary magazine, "Uncle Remus Magazine." Harris reluctantly took an editorship. May 15, 1905. Elected to membership of American Academy of Arts and Letters.

November, 1907. Invited to White House as guest of Teddy Roosevelt. "Thar's one thing about the White House that'll astonish you ef ever you git thar while Teddy is on hand. It's a home; it'll come over you like a sweet dream the minnit you git in the door, an' you'll wonder how they sweep out all the politics an' keep the place clean an' wholesome. . . ."[2]

July 3, 1908. Died of acute nephritis but also suffered from cirrhosis of the liver. Was baptized in the Catholic faith a week before his death. "Do not say, when a man dies, that he is no more, but rather that *he is forever.*

"If this illness takes me off, and they try to start any monument business, don't let them do it. A statue will stand out in the rain and the cold or dust-covered, useless and disfiguring, will soon be forgotten except by the sparrows in nesting-time. If what little I have done is found worthy of commendation, tell the people of the South to let the Magazine succeed. And if it is not too much trouble, run a little line somewhere—'Founded by Joel Chandler Harris.'"[2]

Movies and filmstrips—All by Walt Disney Productions, except as noted: "Song of the South," 1946; "Br'er Rabbit and the Tar Baby" (filmstrip), Curriculum Films, 1947, revised version, Curriculum Materials, 1960; "Brer Rabbit Runs Away" (filmstrip), Encyclopaedia Britannica Films, 1960; "Brer Rabbit and the Laughing Place" (filmstrip), 1973; "Brer Rabbit Meets the Tar Baby" (filmstrip), 1973; "Brer Rabbit Runs Away" (filmstrip), 1973.

FOR MORE INFORMATION SEE: Julia Collier Harris, *The Life and Letters of Joel Chandler Harris,* Houghton, Mifflin, 1918; Alvin F. Harlow, *Joel Chandler Harris, Plantation Storyteller,* Messner, 1941; Stella Brewer Brookes, *Joel Chandler Harris, Folklorist,* University of Georgia Press, 1950; David E. Estes, *The Joel Chandler Harris Collection,* Emory University, 1966; Bruce Jackson, editor, *The Negro and His Folklore in Nineteenth-Century Periodicals,* University of Texas Press for the American Folklore Society, 1967; Paul M. Cousins, *Joel Chandler Harris: A Biography,* Louisiana State University Press, 1968; C. A. Ray, compiler, "Joel Chandler Harris," in *Bibliographical Guide to the Study of Southern Literature,* Louisiana State University Press, 1969.

HAWTHORNE, Captain R. M.
See ELLIS, Edward S(ylvester)

HEYLIGER, William 1884-1955
(Hawley Williams)

PERSONAL: Born March 22, 1884, in Hoboken, New Jersey; died January 15, 1955; married Catherine McDermott, 1906; children: eight. *Education:* Attended public and parochial schools in Hoboken, New Jersey.

CAREER: Author; began as a newspaper reporter with the *Hudson Observer* (later the *Jersey Observer*); associate editor with Westminster Press, beginning 1944.

WRITINGS—Stories for boys; all published by D. Appleton, except as noted: *Bartley: Freshman Pitcher*, 1911; *Bucking the Line*, 1912; *The Captain of the Nine*, 1912; *Against Odds*, 1913; *Strike Three!*, 1913; *Off Side* (illustrated by George Varian), 1914; *Captain Fair-and-Square* (illustrated by W. W. Clarke), 1916; *Don Strong of the Wolf Patrol* (illustrated by Norman P. Rockwell), 1916;

William Heyliger

The County Pennant (illustrated by W. W. Clarke), 1917; *Don Strong: Patrol Leader* (illustrated by Walt Louderback), 1918; *Fighting for Fairview* (illustrated by W. W. Clarke), 1918; *High Benton* (illustrated by J. Scott Williams), 1919.

Don Strong: American, 1920; *High Benton: Worker*, 1921; *Dan's To-morrow*, 1922; *The Spirit of the Leader*, 1923; *Quinby and Son*, 1925; *Dorset's Twister*, 1926; *The Fighting Captain, and Other Stories*, 1926; *The Macklin Brothers*, 1928; *The Builder of the Dam*, 1929; *Jerry Hicks and His Gang* (illustrated by Bert Salg), Grosset, 1929; *Jerry Hicks: Ghost Hunter* (illustrated by Salg), Grosset, 1929; *Yours Truly: Jerry Hicks* (illustrated by Salg), Grosset, 1929.

Bean-Ball Bill, and Other Stories (illustrated by Salg), Grosset, 1930; *Bill Darrow's Victory* (illustrated by Salg), Grosset, 1930; *Jerry Hicks: Explorer* (illustrated by Salg), Grosset, 1930; *Hot-Dog Partners* (illustrated by Howard L. Hastings), Grosset, 1931; *Johnny Bree* (illustrated by Ferdinand E. Warren), 1931; *Quarterback Hot-Head* (illustrated by W. B. Grubb), Grosset, 1931; *Boys Who Became President* (illustrated by Leslie Thomas), Thomas Nelson, 1932; *The Gallant Crosby: A Baseball Story* (illustrated by James C. McKell), 1933.

Stories published by Appleton-Century, except as noted: *Ritchie of the News* (illustrated by F. E. Warren), 1933; *Backfield Comet* (illustrated by George M. Richards), 1934; *The Silver Run: A Story of the Sardine Industry* (illustrated by Richards), 1934; *Detectives, Inc.: A Mystery Story for*

As lightly as a cat the giant leaped aside. ■ (From *The Mill in the Woods* by William Heyliger. Illustrated by Wilfred Jones.)

Boys, Goldsmith Publishing, 1935; *Steve Merrill: Engineer* (illustrated by Richards), 1935; *The Big Leaguer,* Goldsmith Publishing, 1936; *Fighting Blood,* Goldsmith Publishing, 1936; *The Mill in the Woods* (illustrated by Wilfred Jones), 1936; *The Loser's End,* Goldsmith Publishing, 1937; *Backfield Play* (illustrated by James MacDonald), 1938; *River Man* (illustrated by W. Jones), 1938.

Gridiron Glory (illustrated by G. M. Richards), 1940; *Son of the Apple Valley* (illustrated by Robb Beebe), 1940; *You're on the Air* (illustrated by Neil O'Keeffe), 1941; *Gasoline Jockey* (illustrated by R. Beebe), 1942; *S O S Radio Patrol,* Dodd, 1942; *Top Lineman* (illustrated by Scott Lusby), 1943.

Under pseudonym Hawley Williams; all published by D Appleton: *Batter Up!,* 1912; *Quarterback Reckless,* 1912; *Five Yards to Go!,* 1913; *Johnson of Lansing* (illustrated by George Avison), 1914; *The Winning Hit,* 1914; *Fair Play!,* 1915; *Straight Ahead!,* 1917.

Novels: *The Making of Peter Cray,* D. Appleton, 1927; *Dark Conquest,* Appleton-Century, 1936; *Brave Years,* Appleton-Century, 1937; *Wildcat* (illustrated by Gordon Grant), Appleton-Century, 1937; *Home Is a One-Way Street,* Westminster Press, 1945.

"I know, Brandon, for I was one of them".

(From *Wildcat* by William Heyliger. Illustrated by Gordon Grant.)

"Great stuff," said Ted when the warm-up was over. "Sting them in like that during the game and they'll be nothing to it." ■ (From *Don Strong Patrol Leader* by William Heyliger. Illustrated by Walt Louderback.)

SIDELIGHTS: "If I have a philosophy of writing it is this: there is no such thing as writing down to the boy; a man is fortunate indeed if he can write up to him. For he represents an audience in the world.

"I am out of all patience with those superior persons—often writing folk—who seem to think that boys' books are a sort of literary poor relation to be sent around to the back door. True, the book of fiction for the adolescent lacks the tradition that surrounds the novel. Nevertheless, it has its own dignity, fine and stalwart, and need not lower its head in the best of literary company. Give it time. The man who writes a real book for a boy has written a book that has no age limitation. He has fashioned a piece of art. No writing man can do more than that—very few have achieved that much." [*Catholic Authors,* edited by Matthew Hoehn, J. J. Little & Ives, 1948.]

FOR MORE INFORMATION SEE: Stanley J. Kunitz and Howard Haycraft, editors, *Junior Book of Authors,* Wilson, 2nd edition, 1951; Obituaries—*Publishers Weekly,* March 19, 1955; *Wilson Library Bulletin,* May, 1955.

JAYNE, Lieutenant R. H.
See ELLIS, Edward S(ylvester)

KELLY, Eric P(hilbrook) 1884-1960

PERSONAL: Born March 16, 1884, in Amesbury, Massachusetts; died January 3, 1960; son of Edward Lowell and Massalena Hadley (Philbrook) Kelly; married Katherine Collins Merrill, July 2, 1924. *Education:* Dartmouth College, A.B., 1906, A.M., 1929. *Religion:* Episcopalian. *Home:* Youngtown, Arizona (winter); Chebeague Island, Maine (summer).

CAREER: Reporter on various newspapers in Massachusetts and New Jersey, 1906-18, and summers, 1922-24; Dartmouth College, Hanover, New Hampshire, instructor in English, 1921-29, professor of journalism, 1929-54, professor emeritus, 1954-60. Kosciuszko Foundation scholar and lecturer at University of Krakow, 1925-26; vice-president of Paderewski Commission in New England, 1942-43; sent to Mexico by the Office of Foreign Relief, U.S. State Department, 1943, to assist Polish refugees; chairman, Pulitzer Prize committee on the novel, 1951, 1952, and 1954. *Member:* Modern Language Association of America, Polish Roman Catholic Union (Chicago), Polanie Club (Minneapolis). *Awards, honors:* Newbery Medal, 1929, for *The Trumpeter of Krakow;* Gold Cross of Merit (Poland); Order of Polonia Restituta, Chevalier, 1934, Commander, 1945; Kosciuszko Foundation, gold medal, 1956, medal of achievement, 1957.

WRITINGS: The Trumpeter of Krakow: A Tale of the Fifteenth Century (illustrated by Angela Pruszynska), Macmillan, 1928, new edition (illustrated by Janina Domanska), 1966; *The Blacksmith of Vilno: A Tale of Poland in the Year 1832* (illustrated by Angela Pruszynska), Macmillan, 1930; *The Golden Star of Halich: A Tale of the Red Land in 1362* (illustrated by Angela Pruszynska), Macmillan, 1931; *The Christmas Nightingale: Three Christmas Stories from Poland* (illustrated by Marguerite de Angeli), Macmillan, 1932; *Three Sides of Agiochook: A Tale of the New England Frontier in 1775* (illustrated by LeRoy Appleton), Macmillan, 1935; *Treasure Mountain* (illustrated by Raymond Lufkin), Macmillan, 1937; *At the Sign of the Golden Compass: A Tale of the Printing House of Christopher Plantin in Antwerp, 1576* (illustrated by Raymond Lufkin), Macmillan, 1938; (with Clara Hoffmanowa) *A Girl Who Would Be Queen: The Story and the Diary of the Young Countess Krasinska* (illustrated by Vera Bock), A. C. McClurg, 1939.

On the Staked Plain (illustrated by Harvé Stein), Macmillan, 1940; (contributor) Stephen P. Mizwa, editor, *Great Men and Women of Poland,* Macmillan, 1941; *The Land of the Polish People,* F. A. Stokes, 1943, 2nd edition, revised, Lippincott, 1952, 3rd edition, revised (with Dragos D. Kostich) published as *The Land and People of Poland,* 1964, 4th edition, revised (by Kostich), 1972; *From Star to Star: A Story of Krakow in 1493* (illustrated by Manning de V. Lee), Lippincott, 1944; *The Hand in the Picture: A Story of Poland* (illustrated by Irena Lorentowicz), Lippincott, 1947; *The Amazing Journey of David Ingram,* Lippincott, 1949; (contributor) Herschel Brickell, editor, *Writers on Writing,* Doubleday, 1949; *In Clean Hay* (illustrated by Maud and Miska Petersham), Macmillan, 1953; *Polish Legends and Tales,* Polish Publication Society of America, 1971.

Eric P. Kelly

Also author of the booklet, *The Hope of All Poles in the World,* 1940; editor of *Best Short Stories for Children,* 1939. Contributor of articles and stories to various magazines, including *Youth's Companion, St. Nicholas,* and *Horn Book.* Co-editor of *Youngtown Record and Desert Call,* 1959.

SIDELIGHTS: "In the years since 1926 when I wrote the *Trumpeter of Krakow* the hectic rush of American existence has flung me headlong into its tide. Immediately from that book it seems as if pen were never tranquil nor typewriter silent. The subject matter of the *Trumpeter* had launched me into the destiny of a new nation. I was at one with those who were building Poland into a very miracle of a nation, though at the same time, the call for writing, for production, for the creation of new images accompanied the other demand. . . . I was teaching as well, sharing experience in the writing world with students, gaining from that more than I ever thought possible.

"Thus it went, book after book, story after story, the technique once attained,—I think I did some ten books at least in those years of the decade after the Newbery Award, for the most part Polish, though two or three with Indian backgrounds, and one Belgian. Those were really happy years in work, my working backgrounds were extant, a real tolerance seemed to be growing up in the world (one should have known better), a positive desire everywhere for peaceful living (seemingly), a demand in publishing for a type of romantic tale of which I was capable.

"Then at once,—Crash! My world, and for that matter everyone's world flew into splinters. Poland needed all our help, we served on boards, commissions for relief,—then finally, I was picked out by the U.S. Department of State, to settle Polish refugees in Mexico. With the aid of expert people, I built a refuge for homeless Poles, half of them children, in an old abandoned hacienda in Leon, Mexico. With all these people coming to a strange land, most of them suffering from malaria, undernourished, mentally distressed at separation from the other members of their families whom many were never to see again; I really am rejoiced in this, that I brought them all through without losing a single soul. The Hacienda Santa Rosa, today in Mexico, is a 'model village' and has become something of a national show-place.

"War over, I came back to Dartmouth. The distress that had been growing upon me that Poland would never be restored began to make me bitter, I think. The country that had lain on the flank of Europe for centuries, taking the shock of all Eastern invasions, the country that had defied Hitler and brought appeasement to an end,—I never can express my anguish at seeing it broken almost in two, occupied by the hostile forces of its old enemy Russia, and surrendered as if in appeasement to the Soviets at Yalta and what followed. I wrote a book when I came back,— *The Hand in the Picture,*—endeavoring to show what Poland had been, through the ages, but somehow in that period Poland had lost its hold upon people's imagination. It was now a Satellite State. But I would ask both England and America whose fault was it that it was a Satellite State? I did some more writing. My little story, *The Christmas Nightingale,* dramatized went on playing in more than a dozen places each Christmas. . . . I had been working at *David Ingram* for many years, chiefly through material in the Dartmouth Library, and that, with a revised edition of *The Land of the Polish People,* with its sequel to the *Trumpeter of Krakow,* completed the books.

Krakow was flooded with a golden sunlight. Joseph, who saw for the first time a large city, gaped in very astonishment as he glanced left and right about him. ∎ (From the *Trumpeter of Krakow* by Eric P. Kelly. Decorations by Janina Domanska.)

There were sleighs laden with small trees for the holiday; traveling booths that would open for the sale of gifts and goodies; platform sleighs whereon players would enact scenes from the life of Our Lord. ∎ (From *The Christmas Nightingale: Three Christmas Stories from Poland* by Eric P. Kelly. Illustrated by Marguerite deAngeli.)

". . . I retired from Dartmouth in June, 1954, moved back to my island Chebeague, in Casco Bay, and planned to go over the work I had done in those years. I found that I had amassed a vast amount of material, not completed or at least not worked over, some three or four books, masses of curious verse, stories by the dozens, and an attempt at an epic. Will these ever be finished? Who knows? I did find one piece of work, a book, that pleased me, and might be reworked, a story of Webster in his earlier years. I brought some of it back here, to Ojo Caliente in New Mexico, where I hope to spend my winters,—the island is for spring, summer, and early fall, despite the alarming tendencies in later years of hurricanes to move north. What this will bring, I don't know, but outside the changes and the loss of many whose generation is my generation, I am really quite happy in the existence which is mine." [*Newbery Medal Books: 1922-55,* edited by Bertha Mahony Miller and Elinor Whitney Field, Horn Book, 1955.]

FOR MORE INFORMATION SEE: Eric P. Kelly, "Autobiographical Note," in *Newbery Medal Books, 1922-1955,* edited by Bertha E. Mahony Miller and Elinor Whitney Field, Horn Book, 1955; "The Calendar," January-April, 1974; Obituaries— *New York Times,* January 4, 1960; *Publishers Weekly,* January 18, 1960; *Wilson Library Bulletin,* March, 1960.

LASSALLE, C. E.
See ELLIS, Edward S(ylvester)

LISLE, Seward D.
See ELLIS, Edward S(ylvester)

MacDONALD, Betty (Campbell Bard) 1908-1958

PERSONAL: Given name was Anne Elizabeth; born March 26, 1908, in Boulder, Colorado; died February 7, 1958; daughter of Darsie Campbell (a mining engineer) and Elsie Tholimar (sanderson) Bard; married Robert E. Heskett (an insurance salesman, later a chicken farmer), 1927 (divorced); married Donald Chauncey MacDonald, April 24, 1942; children: (first marriage) Anne Elizabeth, Joan Sydney. *Education:* Attended the University of Washington in Seattle. *Home:* Carmel Valley, California.

CAREER: With her first husband operated a small chicken farm in the Olympic Mountain region of Washington State until 1931; later held various positions with the U.S. Government, including labor adjuster in the National Recovery Administration, 1931-33, staff member of the procurement division of the Treasury Department, supervisor of publicity for the National Youth Administration, 1939-42, and assistant purchasing agent for the Office of Emergency Management; writer, beginning 1942. *Member:* Theta Sigma Phi.

WRITINGS—For children: *Mrs. Piggle-Wiggle* (illustrated by Richard Bennett), Lippincott, 1947, new edition (illustrated by Hilary Knight), 1957; *Mrs. Piggle-Wiggle's Magic* (illustrated by Kurt Wiese), Lippincott, 1949, new edition (illustrated by Hilary Knight), 1957; *Nancy and Plum* (illustrated by Hildegarde Hopkins), Lippincott, 1952;

Betty MacDonald

"It's just that I guess I, uh, sort of forgot that I sort of loosened the screws in the bed this morning. I mean I was testing out the screwdriver on my pocket knife to see if it was any good." ■ (From *Mrs. Piggle-Wiggle's Farm* by Betty MacDonald. Pictures by Maurice Sendak.)

Mrs. Piggle-Wiggle's Farm (illustrated by Maurice Sendak), Lippincott, 1954; *Hello, Mrs. Piggle-Wiggle* (illustrated by Hilary Knight), Lippincott, 1957.

For adults—All Autobiographical: *The Egg and I* (partially serialized before publication in the *Atlantic Monthly*), Lippincott, 1945; *The Plague and I* (partially serialized before publication in *Good Housekeeping*), Lippincott, 1948; *Anybody Can Do Anything,* Lippincott, 1950; *Onions in the Stew,* Lippincott, 1955, adapted for the stage by William Dalzell and Anne Coulter Martens, Dramatic Publishing, 1956; *Who Me?,* Lippincott, 1959 (contains portions of *The Egg and I, The Plague and I, Anybody Can Do Anything,* and *Onions in the Stew*).

*ADAPTATIONS—*Movies: "The Egg and I," starring Claudette Colbert and Fred MacMurray (108 min., 16mm, sound, b/w), Universal, 1947; "Ma and Pa Kettle," starring Marjorie Main and Percy Kilbride (72 min., 16mm, sound, b/w), Universal, 1949; "Ma and Pa Kettle Go to Town" (82 min., 16mm, sound, b/w), Universal, 1950; "Ma and Pa Kettle Back on the Farm" (80 min., 16mm, sound, b/w), Universal, 1951; "Ma and Pa Kettle at the Fair" (80 min., 16mm, sound, b/w), Universal, 1952; "Ma and Pa Kettle on Vacation" (74 min., 16mm, sound, b/w), Universal, 1953; "Ma and Pa Kettle at Home" (81 min., 16mm, sound, b/w), Universal, 1954; "Ma and Pa Kettle at Waikiki" (79 min., 16mm, sound, b/w), Universal, 1955; "The Kettles in the Ozarks" (81 min., 16mm, sound, b/w), Universal, 1956; "Kettles on Old Macdonald's Farm" (82 min., 16mm, sound, b/w), Universal, 1957.

SIDELIGHTS: **March 26, 1908.** Born in Boulder, Colorado. Her father, a mining engineer, died when she was eleven of streptococcic pneumonia but he left an indelible scar on her memory and personality. He was a firm believer in LESSONS—ballet, singing, piano, French dramatics, body-building, cooking, roof-painting and shooting.

"After tennis we had breakfast and then went down for our gym and swimming lessons. I think my innate hatred for all exercise and all gym teachers was bred in those early years at the Y.W.C.A. The teachers were always big mannish women with short hair and sadistic tendencies.''

The household also contained three sisters, Mary, Alison, and Dede, a brother, Cleve, a mother who "gobbled up one book and several magazines a day" and Gammy "who wore her corset upside down, her shoes on the wrong feet and married a gambler with yellow eyes."

"Gammy was my father's mother who lived with us and consistently undermined his health program. She was a tireless reader-alouder, doll-clothes sewer, storyteller and walk-taker, but she was a pessimist, the kind of pessimist who gives every cloud a pitch black lining.

"[She] would pick up the morning paper and read aloud bad news. 'I see that the Huns are cutting off all the Belgian women's breasts,' she would remark pleasantly as she took a sip of Postum. Or, 'Well, here's a poor careless little child who played on the railroad tracks and the train came along and cut off both his legs at the hip. Poor little legless creature'.... When she had exhausted all the sad news about people, she would read bad weather reports from all over the world.

Mrs. Piggle-Wiggle laughed and said, "Isn't it a shame that children can't be all evened up? I mean some are show-offs and some are shy and some are quiet and some are noisy and some laugh too much and some cry too much . . . but children are wonderful and I love them all."

"Gammy . . . stuffed us into each other's clothes. . . . She was completely indifferent to backs and fronts, rights and lefts and sizes. She matched garments and children by the simple expedient of grabbing the nearest at hand of each and forcing them to mesh. . . . We creaked along in the snow for half a block before we became aware that Mary had on Cleve's leggings which were so tight in the crotch that she had to walk on tiptoe." [Betty MacDonald, *The Plague and I*, Lippincott, 1948.[1]]

1914. "I started to . . . school and because of a shyness so terrible that I was unable to speak above a faint whisper, it took them several months to discover that I could read and write and really belonged in the second grade."

Her older sister, Mary, added strongly to her education. She knocked out her teeth with a pole, and convinced her she should jump from a hayloft into an armful of straw which disguised an upturned rake. When Betty was ten, Mary suggested she "stand naked in the window of [their] bedroom and wave to the President of the Milwaukee Railroad, who with his wife was being shown the garden by Mother and Daddy."

1917. Family moved to Seattle where she later attended Roosevelt High School and was immortalized in her yearbook as an "honor roll student and true friend." [Betty MacDonald, *Anybody Can Do Anything*, Lippincott, 1950.[2]]

1927. Entered the University of Washington to major in art but abruptly ended her collegiate days when she fell in love and married Robert Eugene Heskett. Heskett dropped his job as an insurance salesman and with their wedding money, savings, and a small legacy bought a chicken farm in the Olympic Mountain area. "It was the little old deserted farm that people point at from car windows, saying, 'Look at that picturesque old place!' Then quickly drive by toward something not quite so picturesque but warmer and nearer to civilization.

"So do I," said Phillip's mother. "And actually, Mrs. Piggle-Wiggle, Phillip's showing off doesn't bother me. But his daddy says he is obnoxious and his sister Connie says he is disgusting." ■ (From *Hello, Mrs. Piggle-Wiggle* by Betty MacDonald. Pictures by Hilary Knight.)

"That first spring and summer I alternated between delirious happiness and black despair. . . . And then winter settled down and I realized that defeat, like morale, is a lot of little things.

"[The following spring and summer] it rained and rained and rained and rained. It drizzled-misted-drooled-spat-poured and just plain rained. . . . Along about November I began to forget when it hadn't been raining and became as one with all the characters in all of the novels about rainy seasons, who rush around banging their heads against the walls, drinking water glasses of straight whiskey and moaning, 'The rain! The rain! My God, the rain!'

"[The nearest neighbors were the Kettles.] Mrs. Kettle had pretty light brown hair, only faintly streaked with gray and skinned back into a tight knot, clear blue eyes, a creamy skin which flushed exquisitely with the heat, a straight delicate nose, fine even white teeth, and a small rounded chin. From this dainty pretty head cascaded a series of busts and stomachs which made her look like a cookie jar shaped like a woman. Her whole front was dirty and spotted and she wiped her hands continually on one or the other of her stomachs.

"[She] began most of her sentences with Jeeeeesus Keyrist and had a stock disposal of everything of which she did not approve, or any nicety of life which she did not possess. 'Ah she's so high and mighty with her 'lectricity,' Mrs. Kettle sneered. 'She don't bother me none—I just told her to take her old vacuum cleaner and stuff it.' Only Mrs. Kettle described in exact detail how this feat was to be accomplished.

"Even with the continual rain, July, August, September, and even October were bad fire months in the mountains. If you were unfortunate enough to live on a ranch near the Kettles, any month was dangerous. It was said that the Kettles set the original peat fires in the valleys and that one summer, Paw, to save himself the effort of mowing the lawn, set fire to the grass and burned off the front porch.

"[They had two daughters that managed to survive that primitive life but the chickens were less fortunate, they kept dying.] I kept the vital statistics in a 'Death and Food Record Book'—causes Chicken Pox, Eggzema, and suicide—opinions which my husband changed to 'not determined.' [Difference of opinion was uncommon, as the couple rarely talked.] "Another year or two and we probably won't even use first names. . . . Husband and wife teamwork is just fine except when it reaches a point where the husband is more conscious of the weight his wife's shoulder carries than of the shoulder itself." [Betty MacDonald, *The Egg and I*, Lippincott, 1945.[3]]

1931. "[She wrote her family that she] hated chickens . . . was lonely, and . . . seemed to have married the wrong man." She returned to Seattle with her daughters.

"The best thing about the depression was the way it reunited our family and gave my sister, Mary, a real opportunity to prove that anybody can do anything, especially Betty. . . . As time went on I became more and more convinced that Mary was right and that anybody could do anything, but I had sense enough to realize that it was a hell of a lot harder for some people than for others.

"Ow, ow, the pain is awful!" Harbin said to himself as he looked down and saw his leg caught clear to the thigh in the shell of a giant clam. "I will have to cut off my leg but it is worth it because I have found the famous pink pearl and. . ."
"Harbin Quadrangle!" Sylvia yelled right in his ear. "You've probably made Daddy miss his train." ■
(From *Hello, Mrs. Piggle-Wiggle* by Betty MacDonald. Pictures by Hilary Knight.)

February, 1931. "[The depression] was a terrible time to be out of a job. . . . Every day found a little better class of people selling apples on street corners and even tips about jobs from friends were embarrassingly unreliable, I learned when I applied for a supposedly excellent secretarial job and was coldly informed, to my horror, that they weren't quite ready to interview new applicants as the former secretary had only just jumped out the window.

"I wanted some sort of very steady job with a salary, and duties mediocre enough to be congruent with my mediocre ability. I had in mind sort of a combination janitress, slow typist and file clerk. Not for a moment did Mary entertain any such humble idea. She had in mind for me any job up to and including the President of the United States.

"If you are the type of person who remembers your second grade teacher's pinching you on the neck because you exhibited a doll dress your mother had made as your own handiwork at the school carnival; who buys brown print dresses that are too short in the waist and are unbecoming anyway, because you are afraid of the saleswoman; . . . then the chances are you would be the next to worst salesman in the world. I was the worst.

"When I was first married I was neat and clean and tried to keep my house and my kids clean. . . . [Then] I says to myself, 'I can't make Paw change and be neat, so I'll have to change and be dirty, or it'll be fight, fight, fight all our lives, and so I got easier and easier and found it don't really matter one way or the other.' " ■ (From "Ma and Pa Kettle Go to Town," copyright 1948 by Universal Pictures Co., Inc.)

"There is no getting around the fact that being poor takes getting used to. You have to adjust to the fact that it is no longer a question of what you eat but if you eat. . . . I went to work in a credit bureau [and] one day when my boss was out of his office I sneaked over and looked up our family's credit. We took up almost a whole drawer and from what I read it sounded as if the credit bureau not only wouldn't recommend us for credit, they wouldn't even let us pay cash.

"[I shortly found out] a bill collector is a man with a loud voice who hates everybody. [And that] a collection agency is a collection of bill collectors with loud voices who hate everybody and always know where she works. [These experiences also taught me that] all bankers [were] little Emilys. The only time they untwist their little striped bags and take out a jelly bean or two is after you have proved conclusively that you already have plenty of jelly beans of your own and aren't hungry anyway. . . . And no matter how many times we had macaroni and cheese there was always somebody left over."[2]

1931-35. Attended nightschool for shorthand to increase her job potential. "My shorthand teacher, an old lady who wore black patent Mary Jane slippers and a hat with a long black tassel that swung when she dictated like the hand on a metronome, was very excitable and when she dictated over one-hundred words a minute she ran all her words together, tore out the pages of her book and dropped her pencils. One evening, when she got up to 150 words per minute, she became so hysterical she dropped her glasses on the floor and crushed them under the heel of one of the large Mary Janes.

"She was a dreadful teacher . . . but I reasoned that if I could take down and transcribe her dictation, 'Dissa (dear sir) Weareinreceiptofyoursofthethirdandwewishtostatethat wedonothaveanymorehorseshoesinstockbutwewillshipthem toyouassoonaswereceivethem.' I could work anywhere. Also I liked the atmosphere of the shorthand class because all of us students were obvious failures of one kind or another but I was the youngest and the prettiest or, more truthfully, the least old and the least repulsive."

"Sure he tracks in manure and he don't clean the barn and last week the cheese factory sent us a warnin' about dirt in the cream, but he's real good-natured and he's never lifted a hand to one of the kids. . . ." ■ (From "Ma and Pa Kettle on Vacation" copyright 1953 by Universal Pictures Co., Inc.)

During these years she worked for a mining engineer, lumberman, rabbit grower, lawyer, florist, dentist, gangster. She also sold advertising, was a public stenographer, and photograph tinter.

1931-33. Was hired as labor adjuster for the U.S. Government. "One of the first things I learned and loved about the government was that I wasn't the only bonehead working for it. There were thousands of us who didn't know what we were doing but were all doing it in ten copies. [The first day I was given a] paper knife and a stack of mail and I set to work at the first job I had ever had that really fitted my capabilities, lift, slit, take out, unfold, lift, slit, take out, unfold, lift, slit. . . .''

September, 1938. "Getting tuberculosis in the middle of your life is like starting downtown to do a lot of urgent errands and being hit by a bus. When you regain consciousness you remember nothing about the urgent errands. You can't even remember where you were going. The important things now are the pain in your leg; the soreness in your back; what you will have for dinner; who is in the next bed.

"The ironic thing is that, although I knew nothing about tuberculosis and never entertained the thought that I might have the disease, for two years I had been very concerned about a co-worker of mine in the Government service, who looked like a cadaver and coughed constantly, with a dry little hacking cough, much of the time in my face. 'I think that man has tuberculosis,' I finally told my boss excitedly. 'Who don't?' was his laconic reply.

"From Gammy's training, the movies I had seen and the books I had read, I thought that the only real symptom of tuberculosis was a . . . cough and a clean white linen handkerchief delicately touched to pale lips and coming away blood-flecked.

"Because our family motto was 'People are healthy and anybody who isn't is a big stinker,' [I] tried to adjust myself to the fact that I might be at [Firland] for the rest of my life. At least I will go through menopause under medical supervision.

"[On the first day the Charge nurse], Florence Nightingale,

Mrs. Piggle-Wiggle's cure for children who won't take baths: All you have to do is buy one package of radish seeds. The small red round ones are the best, and don't get that long white icicle type. Then, let Patsy strictly alone as far as washing is concerned, for several weeks. When she has about half an inch of rich black dirt all over her and after she is asleep at night, scatter radish seeds on her arms and head. Press them in gently and then just wait. I don't think you will have to water them because we are in the rainy season now and she probably will go outdoors now and then. When the little radish plants have three leaves you may begin pulling the largest ones." ■ (From *Mrs. Piggle-Wiggle* by Betty MacDonald. Drawings by Hilary Knight.)

leaned over the counter and directed us with her pen down one of the dark corridors to a waiting room. She undoubtedly was impersonal but she was also the most thoroughly disagreeable woman I had ever met and I didn't see why [they] didn't rent her out to England to threaten India with.

"The staff . . . had but one motivating factor—to get the patients well. This motivating factor, like a policeman's nightstick, was twirled over our heads twenty-four hours a day. And by necessity too, because a tuberculosis sanatorium is a paradox. It should be a place where the patients are striving to get well, aided by the doctors and nurses, but is actually a place where the patients are trying to kill themselves but are prevented in many cases, by the doctors and nurses. . . . One thing to be said in favor of [Firland] it was going to make dying seem like a lot of fun.

"I like people but not all people. I'm neither Christian enough nor charitable to like anybody just because he is alive and breathing. I want people to interest or amuse me. I want them fascinating and witty or so dull as to be different. I want them either intellectually stimulating or hundred percent stinker. I like my chosen companions to be distinguishable from the undulating masses and I don't care how. . . . From my stay at the [sanatorium] I learned that a stiff test for friendship is: 'Would she be pleasant to have tb with?'

"[One of my roommates] was so damned happy all the time, so well adjusted. She loved the institution and the institution loved her. She loved all the nurses and all the nurses loved her. She loved all the other patients and all the patients, but one, loved her. That one used to lie awake in the long dark cold winter nights and listen hopefully for her breathing to stop.

"[The wards were freezing.] I pulled the clammy sheet up around my neck, stuck my feet timidly down into the icy regions at the foot of the bed and thought longingly of delightful hot climate diseases like leprosy, cholera, and jungle rot. . . . How I envied the lucky patient in the private room who . . . was burning up with fever.

"[They continued to freeze uncomplainingly. Then Eileen was brought in.] She took off her robe, which was pale blue and leaned far from the required warm sensible bathrobe and heavily toward a peignoir. She had on sleeveless, backless, black satin pajamas and an anklet. Granite eyes [the nurse] took her by the bare arm disdainfully as though she were holding her up in two fingers and disposing of her. Eileen, not at all disturbed, leapt nimbly into the bed, but as she slid down between the icy sheets she let out a yell. 'Jeeeeeesus God, this bed's cold!' like a shout in any empty church the yell bounded against the walls of the completely quiet bedrest hospital."[1]

June, 1939-1942. Returned to the business world as the publicity supervisor for the National Youth Administration.

April, 1942. Married Donald MacDonald and moved to Vashon Island in Puget Sound. "Anyone contemplating island dwelling must be physically strong and it is an added advantage if you aren't too bright. . . . Vashon is a medium sized island . . . being approximately fifteen miles from shoulder to calf and five miles around the hips. . . . South of us is Mt. Rainier, that magnificent, unbelievably shy moun-

Mother had taught me that a husband must be happy in his work and if Bob wanted to be happy in the chicken business I didn't care. I knew how to make mayonnaise and mitre sheet corners and light candles for dinner, so, chickens or insurance, I could hold up my end. That's what I thought. ■ (From the movie "The Egg and I," copyright 1947 by Universal Pictures, Inc.)

tain who parts her clouds and shows her exquisite face only after she has made sure Uncle Jim and Aunt Helen are really on their way back to Minneapolis.

"Vashon is not a geranium-planted-in-the-wheelbarrow, wagon-wheel-against-the-fence, Ye Olde Tea Shoppe community . . . a typical western crossroads settlement, [it] is small, flourishing, friendly, adequate and tacky."

1945. First book, *Egg and I,* is published. Moved to Carmel Valley, California.

February 7, 1958. Died of cancer.

FOR MORE INFORMATION SEE: "Life Goes Calling on the Author of The Egg and I," *Life,* March 18, 1946; R. Thompson, "In and Out of Books," *New York Times Book Review,* December 5, 1948; "Life in MacDonald Manor," *Saturday Evening Post,* June 17, 1950; B. B. MacDonald, "Important Authors of the Fall, Speaking for Themselves," *New York Herald Tribune Book Review,* October 8, 1950; "Betty MacDonald Cleared in West Coast Libel Action," *Publishers Weekly,* March 17, 1951; "Funny Lady," *Newsweek,* May 16, 1955.

Obituaries: *New York Times,* May 16, 1958; *Current Biography Yearbook 1958; Britannica Book of the Year 1959.*

MILNE, A(lan) A(lexander)   1882-1956

PERSONAL: Surname rhymes with "kiln"; born January 18, 1882, in London, England; son of John Vine Milne; married Dorothy Daphne de Selincourt (a writer), 1913; children: Christopher Robin (a writer). *Education:* Graduated from Trinity College, Cambridge, 1903. *Home:* Cotchford Farm, Hartfield, Sussex, England.

CAREER: Free-lance journalist in London, 1903-06; *Punch* magazine, London, assistant editor, 1906-14; essayist, dramatist, novelist, and writer for children. *Military service:* British Army, Royal Warwickshire Regiment, 1915-19. *Awards, honors:* The World of Pooh, was given the Lewis Carroll Shelf Award, in 1960, *The World of Christopher Robin,* 1962.

WRITINGS—For children: *Make Believe* (one-act play; produced, 1918), revised edition in three acts, with music by Georges Dorlay and lyrics by C. E. Burton, published by Samuel French, 1925 [also see below]; *When We Were Very Young* (poems; illustrated by Ernest H. Shepard), Dutton, 1924, reprinted, 1961; *Winnie-the-Pooh* (story; illustrated by Shepard), Dutton, 1926, new edition (including reproduction of the original manuscript), 1971, later edition (illustrated by Helen Page), John Martin's House, 1946, miniature edition in 4 volumes published as *Pooh's Pot o' Honey,* Dutton, 1968; selections from *Winnie-the-Pooh,* all published by Dutton in 1947: *Introducing Winnie-the-Pooh and Other Selections, The King's Breakfast and Other Selections, The Old Sailor and Other Selections, Sneezles and Other Selections.*

Adaptations of *Winnie-the-Pooh: Winnie-the-Pooh and Eeyore's Tail* and *Winnie-the-Pooh and the Bees* (pop-up picture books), both adapted by A. Schenk, Dutton, 1952; stage adaptation by Kristin Sergel, Dramatic Publishing, 1957, later adapted as a musical comedy by Alan Jay Friedman and Kristin Sergel, 1964; *Walt Disney's Winnie-the-Pooh: A Tight Squeeze,* edited by Al White, Western Publishing, 1962; *Walt Disney's Winnie-the-Pooh and Eeyore's Birthday,* edited by Norman McGary and Bill Lorencz, Western Publishing, 1964; *Winnie-the-Pooh Meets Tigger* (illustrated by Peter Adby), adapted by Jocelyn Phillips, Purnell, 1969.

Now We Are Six (poems; illustrated by Ernest H. Shepard), Dutton, 1927, reprinted, 1961; *The House at Pooh Corner* (illustrated by Shepard), Dutton, 1928, reprinted, 1961; *Toad of Toad Hall* (play adapted from Kenneth Grahame's *The Wind in the Willows*), Scribner, 1929, reprinted, 1965, acting edition (with music by Harold Fraser-Simson), Samuel French, 1932; *The Magic Hill, and Other Stories* (illustrated by Helen Sewell), Grosset, 1937; *The Princess and the Apple Tree, and Other Stories* (illustrated by Helen Sewell), Grosset, 1937; *The Ugly Duckling* (one-act play), Samuel French, 1941; *Prince Rabbit [and] The Princess Who Could Not Laugh* (illustrated by Mary Shepard), Dutton, 1966.

The Hums of Pooh (verses by Milne set to music by Harold Fraser-Simson), Methuen, 1929, revised edition, 1972 [also see below]; *The Pooh Song Book* (music by H. Fraser-Simson; illustrated by Ernest H. Shepard), Dutton, 1961 (contains *The Hums of Pooh, The King's Breakfast,* and fourteen songs from *When We Were Very Young*).

Collections—All illustrated by E. H. Shepard: *The Christopher Robin Story Book* (also published as *The Christopher Robin Reader*), Dutton, 1929, reprinted, 1961; *The Tales of Pooh,* Methuen, 1930; *The Christopher Robin Birthday Book,* Methuen, 1930, Dutton, 1931; *The Christopher Robin Verses,* Dutton, 1932, new edition published as *The World of Christopher Robin,* 1958; *The World of Pooh,* Dutton, 1957; *Pooh's Birthday Book,* Dutton, 1963; *The Pooh Story Book,* Dutton, 1965; *The Christopher Robin Book of Verse,* Dutton, 1967 (published in England as *The Christopher Robin Verse Book,* Methuen, 1969); *Pooh's Alphabet Book,* Dell, 1975; *Winnie-the-Pooh's Calendar Book,* Dell, 1976.

For adults—Plays; all light comedies: *First Plays,* Chatto & Windus, 1919, Knopf, 1930 (contains *Wurzel-Flummery, The Lucky One* [also produced as *Let's All Talk about Gerald*], *The Boy Comes Home* [also produced as *Hallo, America!*], *Belinda,* and *The Red Feathers*); *Second Plays,* Chatto & Windus, 1921 (contains *Make Believe, Mr. Pim Passes By, The Camberley Triangle, the Romantic Age,* and *The Stepmother*); *Three Plays,* Putnam, 1922 (contains *The Dover Road, The Truth about Blayds,* and *The Great Broxopp*); *The Man in the Bowler Hat: A Terribly Exciting Affair,* Samuel French, 1923; *The Artist: A Duologue,* Samuel French, 1923.

Four Plays, Chatto & Windus, 1926 (contains *To Have the Honour* [produced in America as *To Meet the Prince*], *Ariadne, or Business First, Portrait of a Gentleman in Slippers,* and *Success* [produced in America as *Give Me Yesterday*]); later edition of *Four Plays,* Putnam, 1932 (contains *Michael and Mary, To Meet the Prince, The Perfect Alibi* [produced in England as *The Fourth Wall*], and *Por-*

Ecce Eduardus Ursus scalis nunc tump-tump-tump occipite gradus pulsante post Christophorum Robinum descendens. ■(From *Winnie Ille Pu: A Latin Edition of Winnie-the-Pooh* by A. A. Milne. Translated by Alexander Lenard. Illustrated by E. H. Shepard.)

trait of a Gentleman in Slippers); *The Ivory Door*, Putnam, 1928; *Other People's Lives*, Samuel French, 1935 (produced in America as *They Don't Mean Any Harm*); *Miss Elizabeth Bennet* (based on Jane Austen's *Pride and Prejudice*), Chatto & Windus, 1936; *Miss Marlowe at Play*, Samuel French, 1936; *Sarah Simple*, Samuel French, 1939; *Before the Flood*, Samuel French, 1951.

Novels: *Once on a Time* ("a fairy tale for grown ups"; adapted from an earlier play), Hodder & Stoughton, 1917, later editions illustrated by Charles Robinson, 1925, and Susan Perl, New York Graphic Society, 1962; *Mr. Pim* (adapted from his play, *Mr. Pim Passes By*), G. H. Doran, 1922; *The Red House Mystery*, Dutton, 1922, new edition, 1936, reprinted, 1959, stage adaptation by Ruth Sergel, Dramatic Publishing, 1956; *Four Days' Wonder*, Dutton, 1933, reprinted, University Microfilms, 1971; *Chloe Marr*, Dutton, 1946.

Short stories: *The Secret and Other Stories*, Fountain Press, 1929; *The Birthday Party, and Other Stories*, Dutton, 1948; *A Table Near the Band*, Dutton, 1950.

Essays and sketches: *The Day's Play*, Methuen, 1910; *The Holiday Round*, Methuen, 1912; *Happy Days*, G. H. Doran, 1915; *Not That It Matters*, Dutton, 1920; *If I May*, Methuen, 1920, Dutton, 1921; *The Sunny Side*, Methuen, 1921, Dutton, 1922; *Once a Week*, Dutton, 1925; *A Gallery of Children* (illustrated by Saida, pseudonym of H. Willebeek LeMair), David McKay, 1925, new edition (illustrated by A. H. Wilson), 1939; *Those Were the Days*, Dutton, 1929 (contains *The Day's Play, The Holiday Round, Once a Week,* and *The Sunny Side*), selections from *Those Were the Days* published as *The Pocket Milne*, 1941; *By Way of Introduction*, Dutton, 1929; *A. A. Milne: An Anthology of His Humorous Work*, Methuen, 1933; *Year In, Year Out* (illustrated by Ernest H. Shepard), Dutton, 1952.

Poems: *For the Luncheon Interval: Cricket, and Other Verses*, Methuen, 1925; *Behind the Lines*, Dutton, 1940; *The Norman Church*, Methuen, 1948.

Nonfiction: *When I Was Very Young* (illustrated by E. H. Shepard), Fountain Press, 1930; *Autobiography*, Dutton, 1939 (published in England as *It's Too Late Now: The Autobiography of a Writer*, Methuen, 1939); (contributor) Edward C. Wagenknecht, editor, *When I Was a Child: An Anthology* (introduction by Walter de la Mare), Dutton, 1946.

Peace with Honour: An Enquiry into the War Convention, Dutton, 1934, new edition (with an introduction by Sylvia Strauss), Garland Publishing, 1972; *War with Honour*, Macmillan, 1940; *War Aims Unlimited*, Methuen, 1941.

Contributor of essays, stories, and verse to various periodicals, including *Punch, Merry-Go-Round, Nation, Spectator, Country Life, Living Age,* and *Saturday Review*.

ADAPTATIONS—Movies, filmstrips: "The Perfect Alibi" (based on the play of the same title), RKO Radio Pictures, 1931; "Michael and Mary" (based on the play of the same title), Gainsborough Pictures, 1932; "Where Sinners Meet," 1934; "Winnie-the-Pooh and the Honey Tree" (motion picture), Walt Disney Productions, 1965; "Winnie-the-Pooh and the Honey Tree" (filmstrip; both captioned and sound versions, each with teacher's guide), Walt Disney Productions, 1970; "Winne-the-Pooh and the Blustery Day" (filmstrip; both captioned and sound versions, each with teacher's guide), Walt Disney Productions, 1971; "Mr. Shepard and Mr. Milne" (29 min. movie with selected readings by Christopher Robin Milne), Weston Woods; "Winnie the Pooh on the Way to School" (a series of 6 color filmstrips with discs or cassettes) includes: "Pooh Rides the Bus," "Tigger Becomes a Pedestrian," "Rabbit Has a Bicycle Ride," "Eeyore Takes a Walk," "Tigger Finds an Almost-Built House," "Pooh Meets a Stranger," Walt Disney Educational Media, 1976.

Recordings: "Winnie-the-Pooh," read and sung by Carol Channing, music by Harold Fraser-Simson and Julian Slade, Caedmon Records, 1972, read by Norman Shelley, Miller-Brody Productions; "When We Were Very Young," Caedmon; "Prince Rabbit," read by Tammy Grimes, Caedmon.

SIDELIGHTS: **January 18, 1882.** Born in London. Youngest of three boys. "Ken was sixteen months older than I and fifteen months younger than Barry, so he could be as young as the one or as old as the other, whichever he preferred. Fortunately he chose me for contemporary. We were inseparable; sometimes, when fighting, so mixed up as to be indistinguishable. We never ceased to quarrel with each other, nor to feel the need of each other. Save for the fact that he hated cheese, we shared equally all belief, all knowledge, all ambition, all hope and all fear.

A. A. Milne

"Yet I still say that he was nicer than I; kinder, larger-hearted, more lovable, more tolerant, sweeter tempered—all of that or none of that, it doesn't matter, he was just 'nicer.' If you knew us both, you preferred Ken. I might be better at work and games; even better-looking, for he had been dropped on his nose as a baby (or picked up by it, we never could decide which); but 'poor old Ken' or 'dear old Ken' had his private right of entry into everybody's heart.

"On his fourth birthday [he] was given his first real book, *Reynard the Fox*. We both read it. When, forty years later, I wrote a book called *Winne-the-Pooh,* and saw Shepard's drawing of Pooh, the bear, standing on the branch of a tree outside Owl's house, I remembered all that *Reynard the Fox* and *Uncle Remus* and the animal stories in *Aunt Judy's Magazine* had meant to us. Even if none of their magic had descended on me, at least it had inspired my collaborator; and I had the happy feeling that here was a magic which children, from generation to generation, have been unable to resist.

They came round the corner, and there was Eeyore's house, looking as comfy as anything. ■ (From *The House at Pooh Corner* by A. A. Milne. Illustrated by Ernest H. Shepard.)

"On a day towards the end of July, 1891 Ken and I were photographed together—for the first and last time. We are wearing rather tight brown knicker-bocker suits with lace collars. Ken is holding an open book, which the two of us are reading, I with my head resting lovingly on his shoulder. The photograph commemorates an occasion of great happiness to him, of great unhappiness to me. Ken, for the first time in his life, is leaving me. He is going to have his hair cut.

"It shows how completely I had identified myself with him that I had always assumed our hair to be one and indivisible. . . . But no. Ken was too old now for long hair; and I, who thought of myself always as his contemporary, must bear my burden alone.

"Childhood is not the happiest time of one's life, but only to a child is pure happiness possible. Afterwards it is tainted with the knowledge that it will not last, and the fear that one will have to pay for it." [A. A. Milne, *Autobiography,* Dutton, 1939.[1]]

January, 1894. Student at Westminster School. "[My report] in the summer of 1894 . . . said: 'Has done ill, showing little or no ambition, even in mathematics.' When he read this, Father turned his face to the wall, and abandoned hope. I, on the other hand, turned my face to the lighter side of life, and abandoned work.

"Ken, however, remained the writer of the family. It is time that something was said about this business of writing. When I read other people's autobiographies, and learn that . . . the thoughts of Mr. John Merryweather were turned to the stage by the presence of a toy theatre on his fourth birthday, and that before *he* left school, he had written half-a-dozen plays, mostly on the backs of envelopes: then it is brought home to me, that whatever sort of writer I am, I am not (alas!) a 'born writer.' It is comforting, but not

And then she danced . . . . ■ (From *Once On a Time* by A. A. Milne. Illustrated by Susan Perl.)

conclusively so, to remember that probably Shakespeare wasn't either.

"It was in the Christmas holidays of 1899 that I discovered the itch for writing which has never quite left me. I know how I discovered it, but I know not how it came to be there.

"[Ken wrote] . . . a set of verses which surprised me. . . . I had had no idea that he could do it. At the end of them he had written: 'All my own unaided work—and I bet yours wasn't.' . . . Just to show what I could do on my own, I enclosed a set of disparaging odes to all the four children. . . . Ken wrote back, in surprise equal to mine, 'Good Heavens, you can do it too'; to which came the obvious corollary, 'Let's bofe.' So for two years we wrote light verse together.

1900. Graduated from Westminster. "In seven years what had Westminster done for me, or failed to do? It is difficult to say. When I read that Shelley was despised and persecuted at Eton, I reflect that he still came out Shelley. . . .

"So if I am to estimate my debt to Westminster, it is not enough to reckon up my assets and liabilities on leaving. As the landlady suggested when the lodger complained of the fleas, I may have brought them with me."[1]

1900-1903. Undergraduate, Trinity College, Cambridge, editor of *Granta*. "I had no beard; I was twenty and very young for that; but 'people in London' were talking about me. I was thrilled.

"How easy I have found it to go through the world making on equal terms friends, acquaintances, enemies, and to have the persistent feeling that the only side of the equation which matters is my own. I meet Smith, I like Smith; that is all there is about Smith. I meet Jones, I detest Jones; that goes for Jones. What do they, in return, feel about me? That is their own concern. But for some reason which I cannot explain I assume that their feelings are not so definite as mine, nor so well considered. Is this because they feel less deeply than I, or because I am less worth consideration than they? I have never answered that question.

"My last year at Cambridge was sacrificed to the Mathematical Tripos. The sacrifice was in vain. I had hoped that I might just get a Second, but it was not to be. As I wrote later, summing up my life:

> The work we did was rarely reckoned
>   Worthy a Tutor's kindly word,
> For when I said we got a Second,
>   I really meant we got a third. . .

"Oh!" said Pooh, for he had never seen an animal like this before. "Does Christopher Robin know about you?" ■ (From the movie "Winnie the Pooh and the Blustery Days," copyright MCMLXVIII by Walt Disney Productions.)

"It sounds well to say that one has got an Honours Degree; it looks well to write B.A. (Maths. Honours) after one's name; to a maiden aunt one can explain how well her nephew has done. But one cannot explain a Third Class to one's father. Father was so bitterly disappointed that for a week he did not talk to me.

"I had been happy at Cambridge, and I had edited *The Granta*. The only cloud over my happiness had been the Tripos. If I never did examinations again, then I could go on being happy. I turned over another page of history and closed my eyes. Somehow I didn't see myself getting into the Civil Service.

"It had always been held over us, I don't know why, this threat of servitude in a bank. Other sons might be told that they would have to enlist, or emigrate, if they failed in their chosen profession; even to sweep a crossing; but from childhood we had been taught that it was in banks that human driftwood ultimately grounded. What qualifications were necessary for a bank-clerk other than that of being a disappointment to his father we never discovered."[1]

1903. Free-lance journalist. First articles published in *Vanity Fair* and others, and finally in *Punch*. "September saw the end of my first year as a writer. I had earned twenty pounds, and spent the whole of my patrimony."[1]

February, 1906. Appointed assistant editor of *Punch*. Contributed and edited until 1914. "Just as it had seemed wonderful to be editing *The Granta* after so short a struggle, so it seemed wonderful now to be, at twenty-four, Assistant Editor of *Punch*. In fact I had no need to be so surprised at myself. My real achievement in either case was to be not wholly the wrong person, in the right spot at the right moment.

"Being now a man of means (or so it seemed to me) I moved from Wellington Square to a flat which had the high-sounding address 'St. James' Park, Chambers, Queen Anne's Gate,' but which was more easily identifiable by cabmen as '31 Broadway, Westminster.' It had its inconveniences. In order to get to the long living-room in front, it was necessary to pass through either of the two rooms at the back; which gave visitors an immediate acquaintance with one's bedroom or one's bathroom, as preferred. In these days this might be supposed to strike the right note of intimacy at the start, but in those days one kept something in reserve. I decided, therefore, to sleep in the bathroom, or, as I chose to put it, to have the luxury of a completely fitted bath in my bedroom.

"The world was not then the damnable world which it is today; it was a world in which imaginative youth could be happy without feeling ashamed of its happiness. I was very young, very light-hearted, confident of myself, confident of the future. I loved my work; I loved not working; I loved the long week-ends with the delightful people of other people's delightful houses. I loved being in love, and being out of love and free again to fall in love. I loved feeling rich again, and having no responsibilities but only the privileges of a benevolent uncle. I loved hearing suddenly that some Great Man, full of serious purpose, had loved my last article. And if anybody says that all this is a misuse of the much misused word 'love,' well, it is, but I like misusing it, for it conveys my simple happiness."[1]

1913. Married Dorothy de Selincourt. "In 1913 Owen Seaman's god-daughter, Dorothy de Selincourt (Daphne to friends), was persuaded to marry me. Owen had taken me to her coming-out dance, and we had gone about together in a way common enough now, but less usual in those days. When I wanted a present for a sister-in-law or a new suit for myself, I would summon her to help me; when she wanted a man to take her to a dance she would ring me up. She laughed at my jokes, she had my contributions to *Punch* by heart before she met me, she had (it is now clear) the most perfect sense of humour in the world; and I, in my turn, had a pianola to which she was devoted, and from which I could not keep her away."[1]

1914. World War I. Joined Royal Warwickshire Regiment and served in France. "I should like to put asterisks here, and then write: 'It was in 1919 that I found myself once again a civilian.' For it makes me almost physically sick to think of that nightmare of mental and moral degradation, the war. . . .

"To people like myself the Great sacrifice was not the sacrifice of our lives but of our liberties. Ever since I had left Cambridge I had been my own master. I fixed my own hours, I was under no discipline; no bell rang for me, no bugle sounded. Now I was thirty-two, married, with a happy home of my own and engaged happily in work which I loved. To be a schoolboy again, to say 'Yes, sir' and 'No, sir' and 'Please, sir' and 'May I, sir?' was no hardship to schoolboys, no hardship to a million men in monotonous employment, but it was hell itself to one who had been as spoilt by good-fortune as I."[1]

1915. Wrote first children's book, during service, *Once On a Time;* also began playwriting. "It was a reserve battalion, into which the Colonel had persuaded many . . . personal friends, some of whom were married. After six experimental weeks in which I learnt to be just a little, but not much, like a soldier, Daphne joined the married strength, and from then on, whenever it was possible, she shared the war with me. Through a variety of accidents I became Signalling Officer. . . .

"Mrs. Williams, the Colonel's wife, mother of five children and the regiment, only to be described as a 'perfect dear,' became great friends with Daphne. They put their heads together and organized an entertainment for the troops, one of the features of which was to be (whether the troops liked it or not) a little play in which Daphne and the Colonel's children would act. The play would be written by the Signalling Officer. My collaborator was detailed to break the news to me. I said that I was much too tired in the evenings to write anything. She said that she would do the writings; all I had to do was lie in an armchair and tell her what to write. Easy work. So we wrote a 'little play': about a Prince and Princess and a Wicked Countess (Daphne) and a magic ring.

"Some of the dialogue seemed to us rather funny, and my collaborator said, as she has so often said, 'You mustn't waste this.' But there seemed to be nothing to do with it, since it was no more than one scene in a children's play. 'Write a book round the people in it,' said my collaborator. 'I've never written a book,' I protested, 'not straight off.' 'Well, now's the time to begin,' she said.

(From the movie "Mr. Shepard and Mr. Milne," Weston Woods.)

"So after I had come back from my signalling course, and rejoined the battalion which had now moved to Sandown, and we had taken the prettiest cottage in the town with lilacs and cherry-trees in the garden, I dictated the book: a long fairy-story called *Once on a Time*. There are, I think, some good things in it, but few people have read it, and nobody knows whether it is meant for children or for grown-ups. I don't know myself. But it was the greatest fun to do."[1]

"I am very sure of this: that no one can write a book which children will like, unless he writes it for himself" [A. A. Milne, *Once on a Time*, New York Graphic Society, 1962.[2]]

1919. Returned to *Punch*. "When I said, 'I've come back,' and Owen, instead of falling on my neck, said coldly, 'Oh!' and when i +ppeared the Proprietors had neither expected nor wanted me back, being not only very well satisfied with my elderly substitute, but also a little annoyed that I had written plays, not *Punch* articles, in my spare time; when, in short, it became clear that I was free to do whatever I liked, which is what I have always wanted to do, I said bitterly and ungratefully to myself, 'Kicked out!' But I did know that within a few hours I should be delighted."[1]

August 21, 1920. Only son born, Christopher Robin Milne. "In August of that year my collaborator produced a more personal work. We had intended to call it *Rosemary,* but decided later that *Billy* would be more suitable. However, as you can't be christened William—at least, we didn't see why anybody should—we had to think of two other names, two initials being necessary to ensure him any sort of copyright in a cognomen as often plagiarized as Milne. One of us thought of Robin, the other of Christopher; names wasted on him who called himself Billy Moon as soon as he could talk, and has been Moon to his family and friends ever since. I mention this because it explains why the publicity which came to be attached to 'Christopher Robin' never seemed to affect us personally, but to concern either a character in a book or a horse which we hoped at one time would win the derby.

1923. "When he was three, we took a house in North Wales for August with the Nigel Playfairs. It rained continuously. In the one living-room every morning there were assembled [a large group of people to whom a friend] had issued casual invitations in London before starting north for what he supposed to be his Welsh castle. In a week I was screaming with agoraphobia. Somehow I must escape. I pleaded urgent inspiration, took a pencil and an exercise-book and escaped to the summer-house. It contained a

8. Christopher Robin as seen by E. H. Shepard, drawing for *The House at Pooh Corner*.

9. Christopher

(From *The Enchanted Places* by Christopher Milne.)

chair and a table. I sat down on the chair, put my exercise-book on the table, and gazed ecstatically at a wall of mist which might have been hiding Snowdon or the Serpentine for all I saw or cared. I was *alone*. . . .

"About six months earlier, while at work on a play, I had wasted a morning in writing a poem called 'Vespers.' I gave it to Daphne, as one might give a photograph or a valentine, telling her that if she liked to get it published anywhere she could stick to the money. She sent it to Frank Crowninshield of *Vanity Fair* (N.Y.) and got fifty dollars. Later she lent it to me for the Queen's Doll's House Library, and later still collected one-forty-fourth of all the royalties of *When We Were Very Young*, together with her share of various musical and subsidiary rights. It turned out to be the most expensive present I had ever given her."[1]

"Rose Fyleman was starting a magazine for children. She asked me, I have no idea why, to write some verses for it. I said that I didn't and couldn't, it wasn't in my line. As soon as I had posted my letter, I did what I always do after refusing to write anything: wondered how I would have written it if I hadn't refused. One might, for instance, have written:

There once was a Dormouse who lived in a bed
Of delphiniums (blue) and geraniums (red),
And all the day long he'd a wonderful view
Of geraniums (red) and delphiniums (blue).

"After another wasted morning I wrote to Miss Fyleman to say that perhaps after all I might write her some verses. A poem called *The Dormouse and the Doctor* was the result. It was illustrated by Harry Rountree; proofs had come to me in Wales; and with them came letters from both illustrator and editor saying: 'Why don't you write a whole book of verses like these?'

"So there I was with an exercise-book and a pencil, and a fixed determination not to leave the heavenly solitude of that summer-house until it stopped raining . . . and there in London were two people telling me what to write . . . and there on the other side of the lawn was a child with whom I had lived for three years . . . and here within me unforgettable memories of my own childhood . . . what was I writing? A child's book of verses obviously. Not a whole book, of course; but to write a few would be fun—until I was tired of it. Besides, my pencil had an india-rubber at the back; just the thing for poetry."[1]

1924. Began to publish verse regularly in *Punch*. Collected in first children's book of verses, *When We Were Very Young*, which was immediately successful in the U.S. and Britain, and was dedicated to Billy Moon.

1925. Milne family moved from London to Cotchford Farm, the setting for the Pooh stories.

1926-28. Wrote books and verses which established him as a major contributor to children's literature: *Winnie the Pooh* (1926); a second book of verse, *Now We Are Six* (1927); *The House at Pooh Corner* (1928). "It is inevitable that a book which has had very large sales should become an object of derision to critics and columnists. We all write books, we all want money; we who write want money from our books. If we fail to get money, we are not so humble, nor so foolish, as to admit that we have failed in our object. Our object, we maintain, was artistic success.

"It is easy to convince ourselves that the financial failure of the book is no proof of its artistic failure; and it is a short step from there to affirm that artistic success is, in fact, incompatible with financial success. It must be so; for how else could we be the artists we are and remain in our first editions? If any other artist goes into twenty editions, then he is a traitor to the cause, and we shall hasten to say that he is not one of Us.

"All this is commonplace. What has been particularly irritating about the sales of the Christopher Robin books (even though the irritation has produced no more intimidating retort than the writing of the name 'Kwistopher Wobin') is that the books were written for children. When, for instance, Dorothy Parker, as 'Constant Reader' in *The New Yorker*, delights the sophisticated by announcing that at page five of *The House of Pooh Corner* 'Tonstant Weader fwowed up' (sic, if I may), she leaves the book, oddly enough, much where it was.

"It is easier in England to make a reputation than to lose one. I wrote four 'Children's books,' containing altogether,

I suppose, 70,000 words—the number of words ·in the average-length novel. Having said good-bye to all that in 70,000 words, knowing that as far as I was concerned the mode was outmoded, I gave up writing children's books. M wanted to escape from them as I had once wanted to escape from *Punch;* as I have always wanted to escape. In vain. England expects the writer, like the cobbler, to stick to his last. As Arnold Bennett pointed out: if you begin painting policemen you must go on painting policemen, for then the public knows the answer—Policemen.

"It has been my good fortune as a writer that what I have wanted to write has for the most part proved to be saleable. It has been my misfortune as a business man that, when it has proved to be extremely saleable, then I have not wanted to write it any more."[1]

1943. Wrote *The Ugly Duckling,* one-act play for children. "I gratify myself by taking as much time and trouble over stage directions which may never be seen as I should over an inscription in stone on an inescapable monument. This is due, not entirely to that, pride or self love which makes a woman wear pretty knickers even if nobody is going to discover them, but to a laziness which at times approximates to torpor. I hate writing, by which I mean that I hate the business of putting down words with a pen. Unless I can get some sort of 'kick' out of them I can hardly bring myself to the drudgery of inking them in.

"The most exciting form of writing is the writing of plays. There is, however, this to be said against it; that, when once the play is written, the author is never really happy again until it has been taken off.

"One writes a play; no manager is waiting for it, the play may be sold this year, next year, sometime, never. Being bought, it may be produced this year, next year, sometime, never. If produced, it will not be produced, exact to the last eyebrow, as the author saw it, for the reason that its characters live in the author's imagination, and that, even if they have autotypes in real life, it is extremely unlikely that these will be actors and actresses by profession, available for this production. Finally, when some version of the play has been launched, a puff of foul criticism, a week of fog, a few days of crisis, a 'bus strike, the sudden indisposition of the leading man may be enough to sink it for ever. Even if the play runs, every visit to it brings to the author the realization that this is not the play which he had thought he was writing. Oh, well—next time perhaps. The play comes off, and he loses himself happily in a world of his own imagination, peopled by characters for whom no alien flesh and blood need be sought; he writes a novel.

"Writers are often asked if they force themselves to write every day or if they 'wait for inspiration.' It is not suggested (as far as I know) that they say to their wives at breakfast: 'If I am not inspired by eleven o'clock, dear, I shall want the car'; nor that, being in the middle of a novel, they sit with closed eyes at their desks, waiting for assistance before they start the fifth chapter. It is in the details of conception that the layman is interested, not in the pangs of labour, nor the nourishment of the child when born. In short, is the baby ever accidental?

"For myself I have now no faith in miraculous conception. I have given it every chance. I have spent many mornings at Lord's hoping that inspiration would come, many days on golf courses; I have even gone to sleep in the afternoon, in case inspiration cared to take me completely by surprise. In vain. The only way in which I can get an 'idea' is to sit at my desk and dredge for it. This is the real labour of authorship, with which no other labour in the world is comparable."[1]

January 31, 1956. Died in Hartfield, Sussex.

FOR MORE INFORMATION SEE: Junior Book of Authors, edited by Kunitz & Haycraft, H. W. Wilson, 1934, 2nd edition, 1951; A. A. Milne, *Autobiography,* Dutton, 1939; Elizabeth Rider Montgomery, *Story Behind Great Stories,* McBride, 1947; Frank A. Swinnerton, *The Georgian Literary Scene,* Farrar, Straus, 6th edition, 1951; "The World of Pooh Lives On," *Life,* February 27, 1956; H. Breit, "Milne," *New York Times Book Review,* March 18, 1956; "Magic from Generation to Generation: Alan Alexander Milne, 1882-1956," *New York Herald Tribune Book Review,* May 13, 1956.

Milne, *Once On a Time,* New York Graphic Society, 1962; Frederick C. Crews, *The Pooh Perplex: A Freshman Casebook,* Dutton, 1963; Laura Benét, *Famous Poets for Young People,* Dodd, 1964; *Famous Modern Story-Tellers for Young People,* Dodd, 1969; R. Cowley, "The Man Who Drew Pooh," *McCall's,* August, 1970; Thomas B. Swann, *A. A. Milne,* Twayne, 1971; Christopher Robin Milne, *Enchanted Places,* Dutton, 1975; Margery Fisher, *Who's Who in Children's Books,* Holt, 1975.

And I'd say to myself as I looked so
   lazily down at the sea:
"There's nobody else in the world and the
   world was made for me."
■ (From *When We Were Very Young* by A. A. Milne. Illustrated by Ernest H. Shepard.)

L. M. Montgomery

MONTGOMERY, L(ucy) M(aud)   1874-1942

PERSONAL: Born November 30, 1874, in Clifton, Prince Edward Island, Canada; died April 24, 1942, in Toronto, Ontario, Canada; daughter of Hugh John and Clara Woolner (Macneill) Montgomery; married Ewan Macdonald (a Presbyterian minister), 1911; children: Chester, Hugh. *Education:* Teacher's certificate, Prince of Wales College; also attended Dalhousie University. *Home:* Toronto, Ontario.

CAREER: School teacher for three years; writer for local newspapers; novelist and author for children. *Member:* Royal Society of Arts, Canadian Authors Association, Canadian Women's Press Association. *Awards, honors:* Order of the British Empire, 1935; Fellow of the Royal Society of Authors.

WRITINGS—"Anne" series: *Anne of Green Gables* (illustrated by M. A. and W. A. Claus), Page, 1908, reprinted, Grosset & Dunlap, 1970, other editions illustrated by Sybil Tawse, Page, 1933, by Robert Patterson, Grosset & Dunlap, 1961, and by Hilton Hassell, Ryerson Press, 1964; dramatization by Wilbur Braun published under the same title, Samuel French, 1937; musical adaptation by Donald Harron (with lyrics by Harron, Norman Campbell, and others); presented yearly at the Charlottetown Summer

Festival, Prince Edward Island, 1965—) published under the same title, Samuel French, 1972; *Anne of Avonlea,* 1909, reprinted, Grosset & Dunlap, 1961; *Chronicles of Avonlea, in Which Anne Shirley of Green Gables and Avonlea Plays Some Part* (short stories), Page, 1912, reprinted, Ryerson Press, 1967; *Anne of the Island,* Page, 1915, Grosset & Dunlap, 1970; *Anne's House of Dreams,* Stokes, 1917, reprinted, Grosset & Dunlap, 1961; *Further Chronicles of Avonlea,* Page, 1920, reprinted, Ryerson Press, 1968; *Anne of Windy Poplars,* Stokes, 1936, reprinted, Grosset & Dunlap, 1961, also published as *Anne of Windy Willows,* Angus & Robertson, 1966; *Anne of Ingleside,* Stokes, 1939, reprinted, Grosset & Dunlap, 1961.

Other novels, except as noted: *Kilmeny of the Orchard* (illustrated by George Gibbs), Page, 1910, reprinted, Ryerson Press, 1968; *The Story Girl,* Page, 1911, reprinted, Ryerson Press, 1966; *The Golden Road,* Page, 1913, reprinted, Ryerson Press, 1967; *The Watchman, and Other Poems,* Stokes, 1917; *Rainbow Valley,* Stokes, 1919; *Rilla of Ingleside,* Stokes, 1921; *Emily of New Moon,* Stokes, 1923; *Emily Climbs,* Stokes, 1925; *Emily's Quest,* Stokes, 1927; *The Blue Castle,* Stokes, 1926, reprinted, McClelland & Stewart, 1972; *Magic for Marigold,* Stokes, 1929; *A Tangled Web,* Stokes, 1931, reprinted, McClelland & Stewart, 1972; *Pat of Silver Bush,* Stokes, 1933; (with Mary E. MacGregor under pseudonym Marian Keith, and Mabel Burns McKinley) *Courageous Women* (biography), McClelland & Stewart, 1934; *Mistress Pat: A Novel of Silver Bush,* Stokes, 1935; *Jane of Lantern Hill,* Stokes, 1937; *The Green Gables Letters, from L. M. Montgomery to Ephraim Weber, 1905-1909,* edited by Wilfrid Eggleston, Ryerson Press, 1960; *The Road to Yesterday* (short stories), McGraw-Hill, Ryerson, 1974.

ADAPTATIONS—Movies and filmstrips: "Anne of Green Gables" (motion picture), Realart Pictures, 1919; "Anne of Green Gables" (motion picture), RKO Radio Pictures, 1934; "Anne of Windy Poplars" (motion picture) starring Anne Shirley, RKO Radio Pictures, 1940; "Anne of Green Gables" (filmstrip), National Film Board of Canada, 1953.

Television: Adaptation by Julia Jones of *Anne of Green Gables,* BBC-1, 1972; sequel based on *Anne of Avonlea* and *Anne of the Island,* 1975.

SIDELIGHTS: **November 30, 1874.** Born in Clifton, Prince Edward Island. Her given name was Lucy Maud. "I was never in my life called 'Lucy Maud.' My friends called me 'Maud' and nothing else." [Mollie Gillen, *The Wheel of Things,* Fitzhenry & Whiteside, 1975.[1]]

September 14, 1876. Mother died of tuberculosis. Sent to live with her maternal grandparents. "I spent my childhood in an old-fashioned Cavendish farmhouse, surrounded by apple orchards. I had in my imagination, a passport to fairyland.

"Everything was invested with a kind of fairy grace and charm, emanating from my own fancy, the trees that whispered nightly around the old house where I slept, the woodsy nooks I explored, the homestead fields, each individualized by some oddity or fence or shape, the sea whose murmur was never out of my ears—all were radiant with 'the glory and the dream' . . . amid all the commonplaces of life, I was very near to a kingdom of ideal beauty. Between

(The musical version of "Anne of Green Gables" is produced annually at the Confederation Centre of the Arts, Charlottetown, Prince Edward Island, Canada.)

it and me hung only a thin veil. I could never draw it quite aside, but sometimes a wind fluttered it and I caught a glimpse of the enchanting realm beyond—only a glimpse—but those glimpses have always made life worth while.''[1]

1879. Burning her hand on a red-hot poker resulted in a violent headache which was incorrectly diagnosed as typhoid fever. ''For the time being, I was splendidly, satisfyingly important.''[1]

1881. ''I was shut out from all social life, even such as this small country settlement could offer, debarred from the companionship of other children, and in early youth, other young people. I had no companionship except that of books and solitary rambles in wood and fields. This drove me in on myself and early forced me to construct for myself a world of fancy and imagination very different indeed from the world in which I lived.

''In material respects [my grandparents] were good and kind to me and I am sincerely grateful to them, but in many respects they were unwise in their treatment of me.''[1]

She mentally rebelled against her grandparents' religious strictness. On one occasion she was forced to kneel for hours as penance for a childhood prank. ''Something inside me was outraged. . . . To force a human soul to utter words of prayer and contrition when not in a fit state to do so—when stormy rebellion and bitterness filled it!

''[The result] manifests itself in a *feeling* which lurks under all the beliefs and conclusions of my reason—that religion and all connected with it was something which—like sex—it is necessary to have but made one feel ashamed for all that.''[1]

Spring, 1882. Her father went to Saskatchewan on one of several trips and settled there. She felt his absence.

April, 1887. Went to live with father and new wife in Prince Albert, Saskatchewan.

1890. Half-sister Kate is born.

November 26, 1890. At age sixteen, ''Cape Le Force,'' a long narrative poem was printed on the front page of the *Patriot,* Charlottetown's newspaper. ''It was the first sweet bubble on the cup of success and of course it intoxicated me.''[1]

1890-1891. Several articles and verses are picked up by Winnipeg and Montreal papers. ''It is a start and I mean to keep on. Oh, I wonder if I shall ever be able to do anything worth while in the way of writing. It is my dearest ambition.

''When people say to me, as they occasionally do, 'Oh, how I envy you your gift, how I wish I could write as you do,' I am inclined to wonder, with some inward amusement, how much they would have envied me on those dark, cold, winter mornings of my apprenticeship.''[1]

February, 1891. Half-brother Bruce is born. Her stepmother could not cope with her. Disagreements plus staying out of school to help at home, caused further un-

happiness. ''I am ready to cut my throat in despair. Oh I *couldn't* live another year in this place if I were paid a thousand dollars an hour.''[1]

Summer, 1891. Returned home to live in Cavendish.

1893. Entered Prince of Wales College.

1894. Received second class certificate in teaching. Taught for a year at Bideford.

July 23, 1895. Received first class license. Taught for two years at Belmont Lot 16 and Lower Bedeque. Continued writing. ''[I] grubbed away industriously . . . and ground out stories and verses on days so hot that I feared my very marrow would melt and my gray matter be hopelessly sizzled up. But oh, I love my work! I love spinning stories, and I love to sit by the window of my room and shape some 'airy fairy' fancy into verse.

''The kind of juvenile story I like best to write—and read, too, for the matter of that—is a good, jolly one, 'art for art's sake,' or rather 'fun for fun's sake,' with no insidious moral hidden away in it like a pill in a spoonful of jam!''[1]

March, 1898. Grandfather died. She gave up teaching, returned to Cavendish to assist her grandmother, who was appointed postmistress of the town.

January 16, 1900. Father died of pneumonia. Another half-brother, Carlyle, and half-sister, Ila, had been added to his family. ''I loved my father very very deeply. He was the most lovable man I ever met.''[1]

1901. Began to sell material to U.S. journals.

Fall, 1901-June, 1902. Went to Halifax and became a proofreader and general handy man on the *Daily Echo.* ''All my spare time here I write, and not such bad stuff either, since the *Delineator,* the *Smart Set* and *Ainslies'* have taken some of it. I have grown accustomed to stopping in the middle of a paragraph to interview a prowling caller, and to pausing in full career after an elusive rhyme, to read a lot of proof, and snarled-up copy.''[1]

June, 1902. Returned to Cavendish to live with grandmother. Wrote and did daily chores of housecleaning, painting, sewing, etc. *To work at once, stick to it,* write something *every day,* even if you burn it up after writing it.'' [*Canadian Children's Literature,* vol. 1, no. 3, Canadian Children's Press, Autumn, 1975.[2]]

March, 1902. Began lifetime correspondence with Ephraim Weber, a teacher, and George Boyd MacMillan, a writer. She met each only briefly. ''There is something I want to say right here, if our correspondence is to be really a help and inspiration to each other it is necessary above all else that it should be perfectly frank and sincere. We must feel that we are perfectly free to write as we will, without fear of shocking the other by heresy in any views, spiritual or temporal. You may ask me any question you wish on any subject and I will answer as freely and frankly as there may be light in me to do. Only thus, I think, can a correspondence between people personally unknown be mutually helpful and interesting. In personal intercourse conventional disguises may serve a good and kindly purpose in promoting harmony but I hold them unnecessary in such a friendship as ours.''[1]

1903. ''Six years ago I began to inflict my scribblings on a public that suffereth long and is kind. I have got on well and make a comfortable living for one small girl by my pen, besides finding a vast deal of pleasure in my work.

''But I am frankly in literature to make my living out of it. My prose sells and so I write it, although I prefer writing verse. I know that I can never be a really great writer. My aspiration is limited to this—I want to be a good *workman* in my chosen profession. I cannot be one of the masters but I hope to attain to a recognized position among the everyday workers of my time.

''Apart from my literary bent I am small, said to be very vivacious, and am very fond of fun and good times generally . . . I am interested in many things and *love living*. I have a camera and enjoy taking photos [did her own pro-cessing] . . . I love *fancy-work,* cats, horses, pretty dresses and feminine things generally. Revel in books. Don't go in for athletics but love out-of-doors.

''When I grew up out of that strange dreamy childhood of mine and went out into the world of reality, I met with experiences that bruised my spirit. . . . The outward circumstances of my life are at present miserably circumscribed and carking—owing in great measure to poor old Grandmama's set ways of age and rapidly increasing childishness. . . .

''I am sometimes lonely in the house or when walking with uncongenial company, but I have never known a moment's loneliness in the woods and fields. I have ripe, rich, rare good company there. . . .

''As a rule, I am very careful to be shallow and conventional where depth and originality are wasted. When I get very desperate I retreat into realms of cloudland. . . . I learned that that world and the real world clashed hope-

"I am sorry to see a pupil of mine displaying such a temper and such a vindictive spirit," he said in a solemn tone, as if the mere fact of being a pupil of his ought to root out all evil passions from the hearts of small imperfect mortals. "Anne, go and stand on the platform in front of the blackboard for the rest of the afternoon." ■ (From the movie "Anne of Green Gables," copyright RKO Radio Pictures.)

lessly and irreconcilably, and I learned to keep them apart so that the former might remain for me unspoiled. . . . I learned to hide my thoughts and dreams and fancies that had no place in the strife and clash of the market place. I found that it was useless to look for kindred souls in the multitude. . . .

"The trials of an uncongenial environment should be regarded as discipline. I have been led to this conclusion by the marked influence my external surroundings and the life I have had to live for the past eight years has had upon my character. I see now plainly that I *needed* the training very much and that it has done me much good in many ways but chiefly in enabling me to form habits of self-control. I used to be a most impulsive, passionate creature. I do not use the word passionate in the sense of temper, for that is not one of my besetting sins. But I used always to *rush to extremes* in any emotion, whether of hatred, affection, ambition, or what not, that came uppermost. It was a very serious defect and injurious to me in many ways, mentally, morally, physically. . . . I cannot certainly say that it has been eradicated. I fear that, given favorable circumstances, it might blaze up as strongly as ever. But it certainly has been much modified and as a consequence I am a much more comfortable person to others and to myself. . . .

"I *do* think that we are *always* justified . . . in doing what comes easiest and best for us to do. Do not fear that it is selfish to embark in a life that 'brings the greatest good to yourself alone.' . . . Any life that brings good to yourself must bring good first to other people—and that is enough, even if it be only the good of a laugh, a smile, a moment's relief from the cark and care of existence. . . .

"I think I would have made a good *preacher*. Only, when I got up in the pulpit, and saw facing me rows upon rows of dull, unresponsive faces, unlit by a single flame . . . of feeling, all my fine sentiments would probably collapse like a punctured balloon and I would come down flat.

"There are two distinct sides to my nature. When I go to the woods the dreamy, solitary side comes uppermost and I love the woods best. But when I mingle with other people quite another aspect rules me. I am very fond of society, sparkling conversation, the good *human* times of life. . . . But as to being only 'two of me' . . . there's a hundred of me . . . some of the 'me's' are good, some *not*. It's better than being just two or three, I think—more exciting, more interesting.

"I think the majority of people are prosaic and unideal. . . . The other evening, sitting by myself at the window of my den in the twilight . . . I amused myself by counting up the number of people I knew whom I thought to be really happy. The number was fearfully small—so small that it quite reconciled me to being myself, although a few moments before that I had been full of rebellious discontent, questioning of why and wherefores.

"In *general* company I'm really a dull mortal—having nothing to say and saying it flatly. It is only in a circle where I feel thoroughly at home that I can sparkle at all. I could not . . . 'speak' in public if I died for it . . . to get up and *say* anything—horrors, I should die on the spot . . . I just sit like a log while the others are talking eloquently. If I were to get up on my feet I wouldn't have an idea in my head. The worst of it is people won't believe I *can't*. They know I can write slickly and read well and they think that it is just sheer obstinacy that I won't speak in a discussion. But I simply *cannot* I would stammer and and grope and make grammatical errors that would make the flesh creep on my bones in cold-blooded thought afterwards.

". . . I teach a Sunday School class—but I don't like it much. . . . I have to follow the old traditional paths of thought & expression or I would get into hot water immediately. I don't think I have really any belief in any particular kind of a future life. I believe that there is life after death, that's all. [I] *cannot* accept the *divinity* of Christ.

"I have been sizzling over a hot stove all the afternoon making lemon pies—for we have a houseful of company at present—and just getting madder all the time. Then I went out to water my garden and found that some mysterious grub is eating off all my verbenas. That turned my comparative into superlative and I was just *maddest*.

"I have fled up here to my den where the cares of garden and the deceitfulness of lemon pies cannot enter in. I have got my window wide open and a big jar of garden heliotrope on my table before me. It is mellowing my temper very quickly. I am drinking in its exquisite odor like a cup of aerial wine—and—and—dog-days will pass—and the lemon pies turned out very well—and I'm not over fond of verbenas anyhow and it's a pretty good old world after all!

"*Oh, I hope heaven will be all flowers. One could be good if one lived in a lily. . . . I've known roses I expect to meet in heaven. . . . I hope next time I'm born I'll be a Madonna lily. . . . My sweet-peas are lovely—I think they must be the souls of good butterflies. . . . I have a lovely 'mum out—seven or eight great fluffy pale pink flowers out on it. The 'mum is a society lady, all frills and chiffons and languid grace. . . . Still—'wouldn't you rather be a rose for a fortnight than a 'mum forever?'*"[1]

1906. Secretly engaged to Reverend Ewan Macdonald. "*Love* is a subject we haven't referred to much in our letters, but I see no reason why we should not discuss it frankly, like any other psychological problem. . . . You ask me if I believe that there is an affinity somewhere for everyone. Well, that depends on what is meant by an affinity. If you mean one who is in perfect sympathy with one's whole nature I don't think I do. I did once in the salad days of my teens but I do so no longer. I think we must take our affinities as we do our happiness—not in one long, uninterrupted stretch as I once fondly believed, but in bits here and bits there, thankful if there be no positive friction or disagreement in the natures of those we meet and mingle with. In an ideal world we might expect to meet with our ideal affinity. But in this real world, whose ragged corners rub the bloom off so many beautiful theories we can hardly expect to."[1]

April 8, 1907. *Anne of Green Gables* is accepted by L. C. Page Co. of Boston—her first publisher. By mid-September, 1908, it was through its fourth edition.

"If you want to find out just how much *envy* and *petty spite* and *meanness* exists in people, even people who call themselves your friends, just write a successful book or do something they can't do, and you'll find out! . . . A certain class of people will take it as a personal insult to themselves, will belittle you and your accomplishment in every way and will go out of their way to make sure that you are informed of their opinions. I could not begin to tell you all the petty flings of malice and spite of which I have been the target of late, even among some of my own relations.

"One thing surprised me in the reviews and one thing disappoints me, I am surprised that they seem to take the book so seriously—as if it were meant for grown-up readers and not merely for girls. The disappointment comes in this:—I had hoped to learn something from the reviews. I knew that the book must have faults which its author could not perceive, and I expected the reviews to point them out. But there is no agreement. What one critic praises as the most attractive feature in the book another condemns as its greatest fault—and there am I, no wiser than before. I gave up trying to fathom the mentality of reviewers years ago. . . . They are a series of contradictions.''[1]

1908. Mark Twain (then seventy-three) sent her a personal note. "He wrote me that in *Anne* I had created 'the dearest, and most lovable child in fiction since the immortal

Anne's beauty-loving eyes lingered on it all, taking everything greedily in; she had looked on so many unlovely places in her life, poor child; but this was as lovely as anything she had ever dreamed. ■ (From *Anne of Green Gables* by L. M. Montgomery. Illustrated by Hilton Hassell.)

Alice.' Do you think I wasn't *proud* of Mark's encomium? Oh, perhaps not!''[1]

At this period in her life she was under heavy emotional stress. "[There is] morbid brooding over certain worries and troubles that have been ever present in my life for the past six years. They are caused by people and circumstances over which I have no control, so I am quite helpless in regard to them. . . .''[1]

September, 1909. Sequel, *Anne of Avonlea*, is published by Page. "If the thing takes, they'll want me to write her through college. The idea makes me sick. I feel like the magician in the Eastern story who became the slave of the 'jinn' he had conjured out of a bottle. If I'm to be dragged at Anne's chariot wheels the rest of my life, I'll bitterly repent having 'created' her.''[1]

November, 1910. Visited Boston as a guest at the home of her publisher, Mr. & Mrs. L. C. Page. "I lived more, learned more, and enjoyed more in those fourteen days than I had done in the previous fourteen years.''[1]

While in Boston she was interviewed by a local paper. "As for the woman suffrage question, I feel very little interest in it, but I do believe that a woman with property of her own should have a voice in making the laws. Am I not as intelligent and capable of voting for my country's good as the Frenchman who chops my wood for me, and who may be able to tell his right hand from his left, but cannot read or write.

"So you wish married women everywhere were real companions to their husbands. So do I—as heartily as I wish that married men everywhere were real companions for their wives. You can't, as Emerson says, cut this matter off with only one side. It has to have two. As for 'spheres,' I believe anyone's sphere—whether man or woman—is where they can be happiest and do the best work. The majority of women are happiest and best placed at home, just as the majority of men are in the world. But there are exceptions to *both*. Some women are born for a public career, just as some men are *born* to *cook* in a restaurant. Yes, they are! Sex seems to me to enter very little into the question.

"It is not a very long time, as time goes in the world's history, since the idea of educating a girl beyond her 'three r's' would have been greeted with uplifted hands and shocked countenances. . . . Could she dream of opposing her weak feminine mind to the mighty masculine intellect which had been dominating the world of knowledge from a date long preceding the time when Hypatia was torn to pieces by the mob of Alexandria?

"'Never,' was the approved answer. Girls . . . were taught reading and writing and a small smattering of foreign languages; they 'took' music and were trained to warble pretty little songs and instructed in the mysteries of embroidery and drawing. . . . The larger proportion of them, of course, married. . . . But there was always a certain number of unfortunates—let us call them so since they would persist in using the term—left to braid St. Catherine's tresses for the term of their natural lives; and a hard lot truly was theirs in the past. If they did not live in meek dependence with some compassionate relative, eating the bitter bread of unappreciated drudgery, it was because they could earn a meagre and precarious subsistance in the few and under-paid occupations then open to women. . . . Their education had not fitted them to cope with any and every destiny. . . .

"But nowadays . . . a girl is no longer shut out from the Temple of Knowledge simply because she is a girl; she can compete, and has competed successfully with her brother in all his classes. . . ."[1]

March 10, 1911. Grandmother died. "On March 5th my dear old grandmother, who has been the only mother I knew, became ill with pneumonia and five days later passed peacefully away. . . . I knew I could not hope to have her with me very much longer. But that does not make the parting any easier. . . .

"It hurts me so to think of the old house left desolate and forsaken, with no life in its rooms, no fire glowing on its hearth. Yet I am thankful that dear grandma did not suffer and that she died in her own home surrounded by beloved and familiar faces."[1]

July 5, 1911. Married Macdonald. "After all, this is a prac-tical world and marriage must share in its practicalities. If two people have a mutual affection for each other, don't bore each other, and are reasonably well mated in point of age and social position, I think their prospects of happiness together would be excellent, even if some of the highest up-flashings of the 'flame divine' are missing."[1]

Honeymooned in England and Scotland. On their return they settled in Leaskdale. "Leaskdale is a very pretty country place—would be almost as pretty as Cavendish if it had the sea. . . . It is a farming settlement . . . only fifty miles from Toronto. I find the people here nice and kind. Yes, I like Leaskdale very much. But as yet I do not love it. . . . We have a nice brick manse, prettily situated though too close to the other houses and backyards in the village to suit my love of solitude and retirement. . . ."[1]

July, 1912. First child, a son, Chester Cameron was born. "A dear chubby rosy little fellow. . . . I can't imagine life without him now."[1]

August, 1914. Second son, Hugh Alexander, was stillborn. World War I had just begun and weighed heavily upon her. "Oh, is it not hideous—unbelievable—unthinkable! . . . Oh, surely, surely, Germany cannot win! . . . It is no joke but a simple fact that I have not had one decent dinner since the war began. Our *dinner* hour is one. The mail comes in at 12:30. If the news is good it excites me, if it is bad it upsets me and I can eat little. While if I decide to exert all my will-power and refuse to look at the papers until after dinner the suspense is worst of all and I can eat absolutely nothing. When I tell this to our comfortable, stolid country people who, from a combination of ignorance and lack of imagination, do not seem to realize the war at all, they laugh as if they thought I was trying to be funny. Those who perceive that I am in earnest think I am crazy.

"In Uxbridge, our little market town seven miles away a regiment is billeted for the winter, and about seventeen of our finest boys have enlisted right here in our little rural community. Our church on Sunday is full of khaki uni-forms, and oh, the faces of the poor mothers! The church is full of stifled sobs as my husband prays for the boys at the front and in training.

"I shall never forget the agony of those two weeks when it seemed likely that the Germans were going to smash their way through! It was just when everything here was at its worst—E's illness and my own break-down. I couldn't eat or sleep. I *grew old* in that fortnight."[1]

July, 1915. *Anne of the Island* published.

October, 1915, Third and last son, Ewan Stuart, born.

1916. Frederick Stokes & Co. became her publisher due to serious problems with Page Co. "Next year they're likely to publish a 'new' book by me, but be not deceived. It is a collection of old short stories which they held for years under the old contract but would never publish as long as they could get anything better."[1]

1919. Initiated lawsuit against L. C. Page Co.

May, 1919. Husband's illness diagnosed as nervous prostra-tion.

Mid-1919. Her cousin Frederica Campbell MacFarlane died. "The most terrible blow I ever had to bear in all my life. I only know that I am left desolate, bereft . . . whither has she gone? Across the gulf of separation there comes no response. . . . She took away with her the laughter of life for me."[1]

Canada 8

Lucy Maud Montgomery Anne of Green Gables Anne de Green Gables

Canadian stamp commemorating L. M. Montgomery.

1919. First of two film versions of *Anne of Green Gables* was released. *Rainbow Valley* is completed. "Then I hope to say farewell to Anne forever. [It was to be] positively the last of the Anne series. I have gone completely 'stale' on Anne and *must* get a new heroine. Six books are enough to write about any girl."[1]

1920. *Rilla of Ingleside* published. "In it I definitely and for all time conclude the Anne series, I swear it by the nine gods of Clusium. . . . [Anne] weighed on me like an incubus when she ceased to be an inspiration."[1]

1922. Expressed her ideas on youth and education to a fellow teacher. "Youth is the same in every century. In some it is more rigorously repressed than in others but—underneath the repression it is *the same*—foolish until years teach it bitter wisdom, rebellious until life teaches the futility of rebellion, cocksure until innumerable mistakes have humbled it, selfish and indulgent and hungry—until when—alas, I fear till the grave closes over it. We do not change much; we only grow weaker and wearier.

"You see youth *en masse,* in the raw, with all its disagreeable qualities intensified by the companionship and backing of its mates. I see it only in my rural environment, toned down by the older people among it and bridled by the conventions that are always to a certain extent in force wherever many older people are. When you meet your pupils out in the society of older people, are they quite as crude and crass and raw and bumptious as they are taken in bulk in your classroom?

"I have worked for twelve years in our Young People's Guild here and I can honestly say that I see no difference between the boys and girls of Leaskdale and the boys and girls I mingled with in my teens. Some of them are stupid and silly and crass. So were some thirty years ago.

"I think teaching all down through the ages has been pretty much the same. Only, of course, there are *more* students now when everybody goes to High School. And equally of course I *don't* believe this universal 'education' of everybody is the blessing in practice that it is in theory. To me much of the 'education' of today is like an inadequate spoonful of wine in a glassful of water. The miracle of Cana is not repeated, and the good common thirst-quenching water is spoiled.

"Why ask 'how can we get our pupils to *see* their faults?' You can't. Nobody can. One of the troubles of present day education is that (it) isn't education . . . *a-tall.* It's simply a pouring-in. And why worry because one jug holds a quart and another only a pint. And that most receptacles are sieves, holding nothing at all. Be wise. Just keep on pouring, since pour you have to—and be thankful you have something to pour. Think of the teachers (hundreds of them) who haven't.

"I think 'examinations' are outworn relics of mediaevalism. . . . Why not let everyone go on through every grade? When they get out into the world *it* will examine them very thoroughly and grade them accurately and with no chance of appeal. It may grade (and rightly) some who would have failed to 'pass' the examinations. It may cast out (equally rightly) some who would have made high marks.

Maud Montgomery, age about twenty-five.

"And an Ontario law *compels* all children to go to school until they are sixteen! It is to laugh."[1]

1926. Moved to Norval, Ontario.

August, 1926. Having already authored fourteen books, her first adult novel, *The Blue Castle,* was published. She was constantly torn between her duties as wife, mother, church worker, and author—plus her private beliefs, which were in many ways contradictory to her role as minister's wife. "I had to sit there till two in the morning and talk to scores of the women who were sitting in rows around the room, until I felt like a machine that just talked ever on without any volition. My head ached, my back ached, my mind and soul ached [listening to chatter] and all the other entrancing subjects of 'conversation' which prevail hereabouts—at least when 'the minister's wife' is present.

"[I suspect they talk] racy and malicious and *interesting* gossip, and enjoy themselves much better, but alas, ministers' wives dare not meddle with gossip, else would their tenure in the land be short and troubled.

"I never knew a 'good mixer' yet that was worth a brass farden. [The only really worthwhile people were] cats who walked by themselves, rejoicing in their own peculiar brand of cathood and never pretending to be Maltese if they were tortoise shell. . . . The mixer has no real influence at all—like a *catalyzer* (or is it catalyst?) in chemistry, helping but not influencing.

"What agonies I have endured betimes when I was dying to laugh, but dared not because I was the minister's wife.

"It is really only because of the inroads they make on my time that I rise up and howl occasionally. I have lost the art of living entirely. . . . It isn't right. We weren't meant to live like that. Whatever *real* life I have lived has been in the realm of the spirit.

"I call myself a Christian, in that I believe in Christ's teachings and do my poor best to live up to them. I am a member of the church believing that with all its mistakes and weakness it is the greatest power for good in the world and I shall always do what I can to help its cause. The idea that Christ must have been a wilful impostor if he were not divine does not disturb me . . . it does not disturb me to believe that he, in common with most great teachers and reformers, had an element of fanaticism—for want of a better word—in his character.

"I don't number public prayers as necessary. I don't care for any kind of public prayers, not even in a church. These are nearly always farces and generally unpleasing farces. Perhaps a *little* evil is necessary to give spice to existence—like the dash of cayenne that brings out the flavours of a salad and saves it from vapidity? Wouldn't it be a frightfully tasteless world if there were absolutely *no* evil?"[1]

1927. Husband had increasing moods of melancholia and a belief that he was predestined for hell. "Those whom the gods wish to destroy they make ministers' wives!"[1]

July, 1928. Visited Prince Edward Island again. "A blissful month. . . . I have never been away. And oh, how lovely—and lovelier—and loveliest—it was. How satisfying. . . . Past little hollows full of scented fern, past little 'pole' gates under spruce trees, past stone dykes hung with wild strawberries, and over looping blue rivers and through valley where amber brooks called—and always the fragrance of dead fir coming is as the wine of old romance to me and always opens some floodgate in my soul."[1]

Fall and Winter, 1928. Besieged with influenza, a fall down the church stairs, a sprained arm, a bad cold, intestinal flu, a facial rash and tonsilitis. All of which left her feeling like "a demoralized dishrag."[1]

February, 1929. The long court battles were finally over. She told all to a friend. "And now I am going to expound a dark secret which I promised should be revealed to you in the fulness of time. You remember your surprise when you found on Harrap's list of my books a certain one *Further Chronicles of Avonlea* which you never knew existed. Well, 'thereby hangs a tale'—a tale that would fill a volume but must be condensed into a few pages. For the past *nine years* my existence has been to a certain extent a nightmare because of *Further Chronicles*.

"As you know L. C. Page Co. of Boston were my first publishers. . . . When they accepted *Anne of Green Gables* (because a P.E.I. girl on their staff gave them no peace till

they did) they asked me if I would prefer a royalty or a certain sum outright. I know now they thought I would jump at 'the certain sum' in which case I would have got $500 for *Green Gables*. But green as I was I was not so green as that so I said 'a royalty.' The contract was a hard one even for a beginner and one clause in it was that I must give them all my books on *the same lines* for a period of five years. I did not think this mattered because I never dreamed *Green Gables* was going to be a big success so I willingly signed up.

"In 1912 I had no new book ready so the Pages asked me to send them all my short stories for a volume to fill in. I sent them all I had of any value at all. They selected the best and *Chronicles of Avonlea* were published. They sent back the rest but *unknown to me kept copies of them*. I destroyed the MSS they returned as I did not think they would ever be needed again. I may say that I had rewritten all the stories largely and added a good deal of new material mostly description. These new descriptive bits I kept and used them from time to time in various books that followed—*The Golden Road, Anne of the Island* etc., etc. This is an important point—keep it in memory.

"By 1916 I found it impossible to carry on with the Page Co. any longer. All their authors had left them and I was compelled to do so too. The time limit had now expired so I went to Stokes. Page was furious and threatened lawsuits to no end but in the end he did nothing because he hadn't the shadow of a claim anywhere.

"The next year he kept back $1,000 out of my royalties on the ground that I had been overpaid previously. I needn't go into these details. Page's record is full of these things when dealing with his women writers. He . . . knew most women would submit to anything rather than go to law. But I came of a different breed of cats. I got the Authors League of America to find me a good Boston lawyer, and I entered suit in 1919 and *won it*. The judge gave me the $1000 dollars.

"Page had now found out there was no chance of bulldozing me and his lawyer . . . (a very fine man by the way) approached me with an offer to buy my rights in the books entirely out. I was as anxious to get rid of them as they were to be rid of me, so I named a sum which would bring me in as much income every year if permanently invested as the royalties on the books were. After long dickering they came up to my price but on one condition. They asked me to allow them to publish another volume of short stories—those stories they had returned in 1912. This is where I made my mistake. I should never have done it. But I was terribly worried at the time, having just got word of the fatal illness of my dear friend Frede [MacFarlane] in Montreal and I wanted to get away at once and be free, as I fondly fancied of the Page Co. for evermore. Besides they insinuated a vague threat that they could get those stories from the original magazines and publish them any time they liked—the very year I was bringing out a new book perhaps. So, as the stories were poor stuff, I agreed. I was to send copies of the stories. Of course being bound to Stokes I had to get their consent which they freely gave on *condition that there would be no mention of Anne in the book*. So the contract was drawn up and the Pages given the right to publish the book in 1920. I went home, sent them copies of the stories and thought no more about them.

"Then in the fall of 1919 Page wrote me that they had 'discovered in their vaults copies of the stories I had sent in 1912 and were going to publish *them* as the contracts gave them the right to do.' I was aghast. Not only were there pages of description in those old MS that by this time had been used in succeeding books but there were several appearances of *Anne* in them—inserted when I was preparing them for possible inclusion in the first *Chronicles*. This meant a breach of contract suit from them if they wanted to be nasty. Also I would be made absurd by a book coming out under my name containing no end of paragraphs and descriptions which were to be found in my other books.

"I got my lawyer to notify Page that they had no right to publish the 1912 versions and I would bring suit against them if they did. But they did it and brought out *Further Chronicles* in March, 1920. I at once brought suit for an injunction against the book and damages to my literary reputations. The case came up in May, 1920. I went down to Boston for it. Page's lawyer thought the case would be over in *two days*. My lawyer was not so optimistic and thought it would take three. *It took nearly nine years*.

"Page's regular lawyer would not take the case so they got [another one]. . . . By the time two days were over it became evident that it was going to be longer than they thought so it went before a 'Master.' This Master hears the evidence at leisure, gives his opinion thereon and hands it to the judge who decides accordingly.

"*I had to stay in Boston until the Middle of July*. I was on the witness stand for *three weeks* on end, being cross-examined by the ablest lawyer at the Boston bar. Can you fancy a more nerve-wracking ordeal. But I was telling the truth and not afraid to tell it and he could not break me down. You have heard no doubt of 'the maddening delays of the law.' Well, I know all about them. The hardest thing was their lawyer's 'trick' questions. But, 'though I say it as hadn't orter' he never trapped me once. And when it came to *my* lawyer's turn to grill the Page brothers *we* got some fun out of it—for they . . . would get all tangled up and contradict themselves and each other.

"Of course the whole thing hinged on the interpretation of the contract and their lawyer dragged in something every day to befog the issue. One day my lawyer got George Page to admit a certain thing and after the session he said to me 'We've won our case. I was afraid we couldn't get him to admit that.'

"But we were a long way from winning it. The lawyers would spend *hours* wrangling over the admissibility of certain questions or evidence and for days we would make no progress at all that I could see. Just think of my worry. And one of my boys ill at home! And yet that battle of wits between trained intellects was amazingly fascinating and if I had not been the toad under the harrow I would have enjoyed it.

"*One whole day* those three grave lawyers and myself wrangled over the exact color of *Anne's* hair and the definition of 'Titian' red. Ye gods, it *was* funny. The big table was snowed under with literature and prints to disprove or prove. They had two 'art experts' on the stand who flatly contradicted each other. Years before when I sat down in that old house in Cavendish one rainy spring evening and dowered Anne with red tresses I did not dream that a day would come when it would be fought over in a Boston courtroom. Their lawyer was determined to prove that Titian hair was dark red and that I knew it was dark red. I didn't. I always supposed it was a sort of flame-red and I stuck to it through all his badgerings. One expert said it was 'bright golden-auburn' and the other said it was the color of burnished copper. And so on!

"The raison d'etre of all this was the picture of the red-headed girl on the cover which was a part of our case.

"By the end of June the Pages evidently thought that the case was not going to be over as soon as they had hoped and decided to hurry it up a bit by scaring me into dropping it. They handed me a writ, suing me for $30,000 damages for libel because of the statements in my 'bill of complaint.' This was absurd of course. A bill of complaint is privileged and they had no case. But the trouble is in the States you have to pay your own fees and costs whether you win or lose and the wealthy Page Co. could afford that better than I could. But my fighting blood was up and I determined to ignore their threat and fight to the end. Still, you can imagine the worry and vexation this inflicted on me.

"Then a Page witness swore to a flat lie—a most damaging lie to our case and my lawyer lost his grit. He said it was such damaging testimony that he thought we'd better offer to settle. I would *not* knuckle down to the Pages after the way they had behaved and said so. So on we went.

"I came home in mid-July a perfect wreck. But the case went on.

"In September Page's lawyer filed his damage suit for the libel. Then the Master took *nearly a year* to make up his report. In September, 1921 it came—and it was decidedly adverse to us. I had never expected anything else, of course, after the lies. . . . The report was sent to the judge but it is a *very* rare thing that a judge does not follow the Master's findings. As for the libel suit in August 21 it was thrown [out] of the Massachusetts court on the ground that it was illegal. Then Page appealed it to the Supreme Court of the State. In six months it was thrown out there. Then he carried it to the Supreme Court of the United States!

"As for the Master's report, handed in in September, 1921 would you believe it was *April, 1923* before the judge gave his decision. Such a thing was never heard of I believe. But—perhaps it was as well for me because what happened was that the judge discarded the Master's report and examined all the evidence himself. There was about a trunkful of typewritten evidence and he told my lawyer he had never met such an interesting case in his life. *And he gave decision in my favour!* I got my injunction against the book and *all* the profits.

"Oddly enough the very same day word came that the Page appeal had been thrown out by the Supreme Court of the U.S.

"Do you think my worry was over then? Not by a jugful! Of course the Pages at once appealed from the judge's decision.

"And in December, 1923 they filed the same old libel suit in the courts of *New York State* and attached my royalties due from Stokes to compel me to fight the case over again there. A New York lawyer had to be engaged also!

"In June, 1924 the New York suit was dismissed. Then Page appealed to the Supreme Court of New York.

"On March 4, 1925, the appeal in my case was decided in my favour.

"Then they had to begin the 'accounting' to find out what the 'profits' really were. In October, 1925 the New York libel case was finally thrown out and my long withheld royalties paid to me. My N.Y. lawyer wrote me that, since I was not a resident of N.Y. State, I had a clear case against the Page Co. for the repayment of all the N.Y. suit had cost me. It had cost me $2000. So I thought I would show Page I had plenty of fight left in me yet and I at once entered suit in New York against *him!*

"In June, 1927 the judge gave decision on the profits in my favor. The Pages appealed the amount. In March, 1928 I won my New York suit and got back my money.

"And *finally* in October, 1928 the Page appeal was refused. *At last* there was nothing more they could do by hook or crook. They paid me $18,000 of profits and the thing was ended after nearly nine years of worry and expense. The suit cost me $15,000. So I had for recompense $3000, my injunction against the book—*and* the satisfaction of having whipped the Pages to a finish!

"The suit cost the Pages about $75,000 in all. And for the past four years they and their lawyer have not been on speaking terms, though he continued to act for them.

"Those are just the *outlines!* The details would fill a library!...."[1]

February, 1931. Published her second adult book, *A Tangled Web* (Canadian title). "Some day I shall try to write a book that satisfies me wholly. I do not think I'll ever be able to write stories for mature people."[1]

September, 1933. Son, Stuart, won the national gymnastic championship; began his medical training.

March-December, 1934. Husband besieged by influenza and insomnia and finally by a complete breakdown. Recuperated for four months in a sanatorium, two months at home and a month on the Island. As a result she could not sleep, eat or work for six weeks.

End of 1935. Husband resigned from the ministry and they retired to Toronto. She was then invested with the insignia of the Order of the British Empire.

1936. A national park, embracing Cavendish and *Green Gables* was opened.

1937. Her latest cat, Good Luck, died. "For the greater part of five thousand nights and days my inseparable companion. . . . I loved other cats *as cats,* I loved Lucky as a human being. He was the most beautiful! and uniquely marked cat I have ever seen, with *human* eyes. . . . Whatever Luck was he was *not* a cat. A cat's body, true! But it was not a cat soul that inhabited it . . . I buried him under a little pine tree in my rock garden and no cat was ever more deeply missed or sincerely mourned."[1]

Mid-1937. Ewan's health deteriorated. "It was more than nerves this time—for about two months in the summer he was a mental case, and among other symptoms, lost his memory completely. I could not bear to have him go to any institution for I knew no one could understand him as I did, for I have nursed him through so many of these attacks."[1]

Winter, 1937-38. Had a nervous breakdown. "For four months I lived in a sort of hell on earth. I shall never forget the terrible nights."[1]

Mid-1940. Again victim of a breakdown following a bad fall and depressing war news. "Intolerable distress. . . . I really think I have turned the corner. . . . Several things including my fall came all at once with the breaking of France and caused [my breakdown]. But now I really have some hope of recovering, things do not look so black. But even yet I very often wonder what God can be thinking about!!!"[1]

End of December, 1940. She wrote to Weber. "Dear Friend . . . I do not think I will ever recover. . . . Let us thank God for a long and true friendship."[1]

1941. "I am no better. . . . I have had a very bad year. . . . We have lived to see beauty vanish from the world. . . . Am no better dear friend and never will be. You do not know the blows that have fallen on my life for years. I tried to hide them from my friends. I feel my mind is going. . . . I am very ill and still not able to write.

"My husband is very miserable. I have tried to keep the secret of his melancholic attacks for twenty years, as people do not want a minister who is known to be such, but the burden broke me at last, as well as other things. And now the war. I do not think I will ever be well again."[1]

April 24, 1942. Died and was buried at Cavendish Cemetery.

HOBBIES AND OTHER INTERESTS: Crocheting, knitting, sewing, designing needlepoint lace, astronomy, reading detective novels, and psychic phenomena.

FOR MORE INFORMATION SEE: Arthur L. Phelps, *Canadian Writers,* McClelland & Stewart, 1951; Hilda M. Ridley, *The Story of L. M. Montgomery,* Ryerson Press, 1956; L. M. Montgomery, *The Green Gables Letters, from L. M. Montgomery to Ephraim Weber, 1905-1909,* edited by Wilfrid Eggleston, Ryerson Press, 1960; E. Waterston, "Lucy Maud Montgomery," in *Clear Spirit,* edited by Mary Quayle Innis, University of Toronto Press, 1966; Obituary—*New York Times,* April 25, 1942.

MULLER, Billex
See ELLIS, Edward S(ylvester)

NESBIT, E(dith) 1858-1924
(Edith Nesbit Bland; joint pseudonym, Fabian Bland)

PERSONAL: Born August 15 (or 19, according to some sources), 1858, in London, England; died May 4, 1924, at Jesson St. Mary's, New Romney, Kent, England; daughter of John Collis Nesbit (an agricultural chemist and head of an agricultural college); married Hubert Bland (a journalist), 1880 (died, 1914); married Thomas Terry Tucker (a marine engineer), 1917; children: five, including adopted Rosamund (Mrs. Clifford Sharp). *Education:* Attended private schools in England, France, and Germany. *Home:* The Longboat, Jesson St. Mary's, New Romney, Kent, England.

CAREER: Novelist, poet, and writer for children. *Member:* Fabian Society (founder-member).

WRITINGS—Stories for children, except as noted: *The Voyage of Columbus: Discovery of America* (verse; illustrated by Will and Frances Brundage and J. Pauline Sunter), Tuck, 1892; *Grim Tales,* Innes, 1893; *Something Wrong,* Innes, 1893; *The Girls' Own Birthday Book,* Drane, 1894; (editor) *Poets' Whispers: A Birthday Book,* Drane, 1895; *Pussy Tales* (illustrated by Lucy Kemp-Welch), Ward, 1895; *Doggy Tales* (illustrated by Kemp-Welch), Ward, 1895; *As Happy as a King* (story in verse), Ward, 1896; *Tales Told in the Twilight,* Tuck, 1897; (re-teller) *The Children's Shakespeare,* Tuck, 1897, reprinted (illustrated by Rolf Klep), Random House, 1938; *The Royal Children of English History* (nonfiction; illustrated by Frances Brundage and M. Bowley), Tuck, 1897; *A Book of Dogs* (nonfiction), Dutton, 1898; *The Story of the Treasure Seekers: The Adventures of the Bastable Children in Search of a Fortune* (illustrated by Gordon Browne and Lewis Baumer), Stokes, 1899, British Book Center, 1974 [other editions illustrated by C. Walter Hodges, Benn, 1947, Coward-McCann, 1948; Cecil Leslie, Penguin, 1958].

The Book of Dragons (magic stories; illustrated by H. R. Millar), Harper, 1900, also published as *The Complete Book of Dragons* (with the addition of "The Last of the Dragons" from *The Five of Us and Madeline* [see below]; illustrated by Erik Blegvad), Hamish Hamilton, 1972, Macmillan, 1973; *Nine Unlikely Tales for Children* (illustrated by H. R. Millar and others), Fisher Unwin, 1901, reprinted, Coward-McCann, 1960; *The Would-be-Goods* (illustrated by Reginald Birch), Harper, 1901, reprinted, British Book Center, 1974 [other editions illustrated by Arthur Buckland, John Hassall, and others, Fisher Unwin, 1958; C. Walter Hodges, Benn, 1947, Coward-McCann, 1948; Cecil Leslie, Penguin, 1965]; *The Revolt of the Toys; or, What Comes of Quarrelling* (illustrated by Ambrose Dudley), Nister, 1902; *Five Children and It* (illustrated by H. R. Millar), Fisher Unwin, 1902, Dodd, 1905, reprinted, British Book Center, 1974, an earlier edition illustrated by John Strickland Goodall, Benn, 1948, Coward-McCann, 1949; *The Rainbow Queen, and Other Stories* (illustrated by E. and M. F. Taylor, M. Bowley, and others), Tuck, 1903; *The Phoenix and the Carpet* (sequel to *Five Children and It;* illustrated by H. R. Millar), Macmillan, 1904, reprinted, British Book Center, 1974, an earlier edition illustrated by J. S. Goodall, Benn, 1948, Random House, 1949; (with daughter Rosamund Bland) *Cat Tales* (illustrated by

E. Nesbit, age forty-seven.

Isabel Watkin), Nister, 1904; *The New Treasure-Seekers* (illustrated by G. Browne and L. Baumer), Fisher Unwin, 1904, reprinted, British Book Center, 1974, an earlier edition illustrated by C. Walter Hodges, Benn, 1948, Coward-McCann, 1949.

Oswald Bastable and Others (illustrated by C. E. Brock and H. R. Millar), Wells, Gardner, 1905, reprinted, British Book Center, 1974; *Pug Peter: A Dog Story* (illustrated by Harry Rountree and John Hassall), Cooke, 1905; *The Railway Children* (illustrated by C. E. Brock), Macmillan, 1905, reprinted, British Book Center, 1974 [other editions illustrated by J. B. Long, Collins, 1959; Shirley Hughes, Heinemann, 1961; Lynton Lamb, Coward-McCann, 1961]; *The Story of the Amulet* (illustrated by H. R. Millar), Fisher Unwin, 1906, Dutton, 1907, reprinted, Penguin, 1975, an earlier edition illustrated by J. S. Goodall, Random House, 1949, dramatization by Marie Overton published as *The Time Explorers [and] The Phoenix and the Carpet,* Heinemann, 1966; *The Enchanted Castle* (illustrated by H. R. Millar), Fisher Unwin, 1907, Harper, 1908, reprinted, British Book Center, 1974 [other editions illustrated by Cecil Leslie, Dutton, 1964; Betty Fraser, Platt & Munk, 1966]; *The Old Nursery Stories* (illustrated by W. H. Margetson), Oxford Press, 1908; *The House of Arden* (illustrated by H. R. Millar), Fisher Unwin, 1908, reprinted (illustrated by Clarke Hulton), Dutton, 1968, an earlier edition illustrated by Desmond Walduck, Benn, 1949; *These Little Ones* (illustrated by Spencer Pryse),

"You've got a face as long as a fiddle." ■ (From *Oswald Bastable and Others* by E. Nesbit. Illustrated by C. E. Brock and H. R. Millar.)

Alden, 1909; *Harding's Luck* (illustrated by H. R. Millar), Hodder & Stoughton, 1909, Stokes, 1910, reprinted British Book Center, 1974, an earlier edition illustrated by D. E. Walduck, Benn, 1949; *Cinderella: A Play with Twelve Songs to Popular Airs*, Sidgwick & Jackson, 1909.

The Magic City (illustrated by H. R. Millar), Macmillan, 1910, reprinted, Coward-McCann, 1958; (with George Manville Fenn) *My Sea-Side Story Book* (illustrated by W. Rainey, A. Webb, and others), Nister, 1911; *The Wonderful Garden; or, The Three C's* (illustrated by H. R. Millar), Macmillan, 1911, reprinted, British Book Center, 1974; *The Magic World* (illustrated by H. R. Millar and S. Pryse), Macmillan, 1912, reprinted, British Book Center, 1974; *Our New Story Book* (illustrated by Elsie Wood, Louis Wain, and others), Nister, 1913; *Wet Magic* (illustrated by H. R. Millar), Werner Laurie, 1913, reprinted, Coward-McCann, 1958; (with Doris Ashley) *Children's Stories from English History* (nonfiction; illustrated by John H. Bacon, A.R.A., Howard Davie, and others), Tuck, 1914; *The Five of Us—and Madeline* (edited by Rosamund Bland Sharp; illustrated by Norah S. Unwin), Fisher Unwin, 1925, reprinted (illustrated by Peter Freeman), Coward-McCann, 1958.

The Bastable Children (preface by Christopher Morley), Coward-McCann, 1928 (contains *The Story of the Treasure Seekers, The Would-be-Goods,* and *The New Treasure Seekers* (published in England as *The Complete History of the Bastable Family,* Benn, 1928); *The Five Children,* Coward-McCann, 1930 (contains *The Five Children and It, The Phoenix and the Carpet,* and *The Story of the Amulet*); *The Bastables: The Story of the Treasure Seekers* [*and*] *The Would-be-Goods* (introduction by Noel Streatfeild; illustrated by Susan Einzig), Nonesuch, 1965, Watts, 1966; *The Island of the Nine Whirlpools* (an excerpt from *The Book of Dragons;* illustrated by Faith Jaques), Kaye & Ward, 1970; *Conscience Pudding* (a Bastable story; illustrated by Erik Blegvad), Coward-McCann, 1970.

Contributor of stories or verse to the following illustrated children's books: *Our Friends and All about Them, Listen Long and Listen Well, Sunny Tales for Snowy Days, Told by the Sunbeams and Me,* all published by Tuck, 1893; *Hours in Many Lands, Tales That Are True for Brown Eyes and Blue, Tales for Delight from Morning till Night, Fur and Feathers, Tales for All Weathers, Lads and Lassies,* all published by Tuck, 1894; *Dulcie's Lantern,* Griffith, Farran, 1895; *Treasures from Storyland,* Tuck, 1895.

Adult writings—Poems: *Lays and Legends,* Longmans, Green, 1st series, 1886, 2nd series, 1892; *The Better Part, and Other Poems,* Drane, 1888; *Leaves of Life,* Longmans, Green, 1888; *A Pomander of Verse,* Lane, 1895; *Songs of Love and Empire,* Constable, 1898; *The Rainbow and the Rose,* Longmans, Green, 1905; *Jesus in London* (illustrated by S. Pryse), Fifield, 1908; *Ballads and Lyrics of Socialism, 1883-1908,* Fifield for the Fabian Society, 1908; *Ballads and Verses of the Spiritual Life,* Mathews, 1911; (editor) *Battle Songs,* Goschen, 1914; *Many Voices,* Hutchinson, 1922. Also author of *Garden Poems,* published by Collins.

Poetry booklets: (Editor with Robert Ellice Mack, and contributor) *Spring, Summer, Autumn, Winter Songs and Sketches* (four booklets), Griffith, Farran, 1886; *The Lily and the Cross,* Griffith, Farran, 1887; *The Star of Bethlehem,* Griffith, Farran, 1887; (with Caris Brooke) *Easter-Tide,* Dutton, 1888; (with Brooke and others) *The Time of Roses,* Drane, 1888; *By Land and Sea,* Drane, 1888; *Landscape and Song,* Drane, 1888; *The Message of the Dove,* Drane, 1888; (with Helen J. Wood) *The Lilies Round the Cross,* Nister, 1889; *Corals and Sea Songs,* Nister, 1889; (with others) *Life's Sunny Side,* Nister, 1890; *Songs for Two Seasons,* Tuck, 1890; *Sweet Lavender,* Nister, 1892; (under name E. Bland) *Flowers I Bring and Songs I Sing,* Tuck, 1893; (with Norman Gale and Richard le Gallienne) *Holly and Mistletoe: A Booklet of Christmas Verse,* Ward, 1895; (with Clifton Bingham) *Dinna Forget,* Nister, 1897.

Novels: (With husband Hubert Bland under joint pseudonym Fabian Bland) *The Prophet's Mantle,* Drane, 1885; *The Secret of Kyriels,* Hurst & Blackett, 1899; *Thirteen Ways Home,* Treherne, 1901; *The Red House* (illustrated by A. I. Keller), Harper, 1902; *The Incomplete Amorist* (illustrated by Clarence F. Underwood), Doubleday, Page, 1906; *Daphne in Fitzroy Street,* Doubleday, Page, 1909; *The House with No Address* (illustrated by S. Pryse), Doubleday, Page, 1909 (published in England as *Salome and the Head,* Alston Rivers, 1909); *Dormant,* Methuen,

1911; *The Incredible Honeymoon,* Harper, 1916; *The Lark,* Hutchinson, 1922.

Short stories: (With Oswald Barron) *The Butler in Bohemia,* Drane, 1894; *In Homespun,* Roberts Brothers, 1896; *The Literary Sense,* Macmillan, 1903; *Man and Maid,* Fisher Unwin, 1906; (reteller) *Twenty Beautiful Stories from Shakespeare: A Home Study Course* (edited by E. T. Rose; illustrated by Max Bihn), Hertel, Jenkins, 1907; *Fear,* Stanley Paul, 1910; *To the Adventurous,* Hutchinson, 1923.

Nonfiction: *Wings and the Child; or, The Building of Magic Cities,* Hodder & Stoughton, 1913; (editor) Hubert Bland, *Essays,* Goschen, 1914; *Long Ago When I Was Young* (introduction by Noel Streatfeild; illustrated by Edward Ardizzone), Watts, 1966.

Contributor of stories and verse to numerous periodicals, including *Sunday Magazine, Pall Mall Gazette, Windsor Magazine, Strand Magazine, Good Words, Girls' Own Paper,* and *Illustrated London News.*

ADAPTATIONS—Motion picture: "The Railway Children," written and directed by Lionel Jeffries, was produced by E.M.I. Film Productions (London), 1970.

Recordings: "The Railway Children," excerpts from the sound track of the film with additional narration by Lionel Jeffries, Caedmon Records, 1974; "The Book of Dragons," read by Dame Judith Anderson, Caedmon Records, 1974.

SIDELIGHTS: **August 15, 1858.** Edith, nicknamed "Daisy," Nesbit was born at 38 Lower Kennington Lane, London. Youngest of six children. "When I was a little child I used to pray fervently, tearfully, that when I should be grown up I might never forget what I thought, felt, and suffered then." [Doris Langley Moore, *E. Nesbit: A Biography,* Chilton, 1966.[1]]

1861 or **1862.** Father died. Like all sensitive children, she was a victim of too much imagination and recalled once encountering her father playing "wild beasts" with her brothers. "He wore his great fur travelling coat inside out, and his roars were completely convincing. I was borne away screaming. . . .

"One used to lie awake in the silence, listening, listening to the pad-pad of one's heart, straining one's ears to make sure that it was not the pad-pad of something else, something unspeakable creeping towards one in the horrible dense dark. One used to lie quite, quite still, I remember, listening, listening. . . .

"My nurse—ah, how good she was to me!—never went downstairs to supper after she found out my terrors, which she very quickly did. She used to sit in the day nursery with the door open 'a tiny crack' and that light was company, because I knew I had only to call out, and someone who loved me would come and banish fear."[1]

Her brothers, sometimes terrified her, chasing her round the garden with a "terrible object"—the double head of a malformed calf which their father kept as a curiosity. "But

"Teacher says there ain't no bounds to the wonders of science. Blest if this ain't one of 'em."
■ (From *The Magic World* by E. Nesbit. Illustrated by H. R. Millar.)

one of my father's pupils to whom I owe that and many other kindnesses, one day seized me under his arm and the two-headed horror in the other, and thus equipped, pursued my brothers. They fled shrieking. . . . I never feared it again.''[1]

A kind teacher helped her confront another terror—an emu. ''He took me on his shoulder, where I felt quite safe, reluctant but not resisting, to within a couple of yards of the emu.

'''Now,' he said, 'will you do what I tell you?'

'''Not any nearer,' I said evasively.

'''Now, you know it won't hurt you. . . . Will you stroke it, if I do first?'

''I didn't want to.

'''To please me.'

''That argument was conclusive, for I loved him. Then we approached the black feathers, I clinging desperately to his neck, sobbing convulsively.

So they all sat down on a great flat grey stone that had pushed itself up out of the grass; . . . and when Mother came out to look for them at eight o'clock, she found them deeply asleep in a contented, sun-warmed bunch. ■ (From *The Railway Children* by E. Nesbit. Illustrated by C. E. Brock.)

'''No—no—no—not any nearer!' But he was kind and wise, and insisted. His big hand smoothed down the feathers.

'''Now, Daisy. You know you promised. Give me your hand.' I shut my eyes tight, and let him draw my hand down the dusty feathers. Then I opened my eyes a little bit.

'''Now you stroke it. Stroke the poor emu!' I did so. 'Are you afraid now?' Curiously enough, I wasn't. [But the poor man] paid dearly for his kindness. For several weeks I gave him no peace, but insisted on being taken, at all hours of the day and night, to 'stroke the poor emu.''[1]

1865. Sent to a boarding school. Only stayed one term. ''I used to go home on Saturdays, and then all the bitterness was so swallowed up in the bliss of my home-returning, that I actually forgot the miseries of my school life, but I was very unhappy there.

''I have often wondered what it is that keeps children from telling their mothers these things—and even now I don't know. I only know I might have been saved many of these little-big troubles if I had only been able to explain.''[1]

1866-1867. Sent to a ''select boarding establishment for young ladies and gentlemen at Stamford, and I venture to think that I should have preferred a penal settlement.

''Long division set in again. . . . Day after day, I sat lonely in the schoolroom—now like a furnace—and ate my dry bread and milk and water in the depths of disgrace. . . . Night after night I cried myself to sleep in my bed—whose coarse home-spun sheets were hotter than blankets—because I could not get the answers right.

''[When my mother came] I clung about her neck, and with such insistence implored her not to leave me—not to go without me, that I think I must have expressed my trouble without uttering it, for when, after three delicious days of drives and walks, in which I had always a loving hand to hold, my mother left Stamford, she took me, trembling with joy like a prisoner reprieved, with her. And I have never seen—or wished to see Stamford again.''[1]

1867. Because of older sister Mary's illness, Mrs. Nesbit took her daughters abroad. During the crossing from Newhaven to Dieppe, ''Daisy'' had been exhaustingly seasick. ''My mind was, I suppose, a little upset by my soul's sorrows at Stamford and my body's unspeakable discomforts on board the channel boat, and I was seized with a horror of the words *Debit de Tabac* which I had noticed on our way from the station; I associated them with the gravestone of my father, I don't know why. I can only conjecture that the last syllable of *Débit* being the same as that of our name may have had something to do with it.''[1]

In Bordeaux they decided to see some mummies at the Church of Saint Michel. ''I was consumed by a fever of impatience for the three days which had to go by before the coming of the day on which the treasure might be visited. My sisters, who were to lead me to these delights, believed too that the mummies would be chiefly interesting on account of their association with Bloomsbury.

"Well, we went—I in my best blue silk frock, which I insisted on wearing to honour the occasion, holding the hand of my sister and positively skipping with delicious anticipation. There was some delay about keys, during which my excitement was scarcely to be restrained.

". . . We went through an arched doorway and along a flagged passage, the old man who guided us explaining volubly in French as we went.

"'What does he say?'

"'He says they are natural mummies.'

"'What does that mean?'

"'They are not embalmed by man, like the Egyptian ones, but simply by the peculiar earth of the churchyard where they were buried.'

". . . The passage began to slope downward. A chill air breathed on our faces, bringing with it a damp earthy smell.

Then we came to some narrow stone steps. Our guide spoke again.

"'What does he say?'

"'We are to be careful, the steps are slippery and mouldy.'

"I think even then my expectation still was of a long clean gallery, filled with the white light of a London noon, shed through high skylights on Egyptian treasures. But the stairs were dark, and I held my sister's hand tightly. Down we went, down, down!

"'What does he say?'

"'We are under the church now; these are the vaults.'

"We went along another passage, the damp mouldy smell increasing, and my clasp of my sister's hand grew closer and closer. We stopped in front of a heavy door barred with iron, and our guide turned a big reluctant key in a lock that grated. 'Les voilá,' he said, throwing open the door and drawing back dramatically.

They did not guess then how they would grow to love the railway, and how soon it would become the centre of their new life nor what wonders and changes it would bring to them. ■ (From the movie "The Railway Children" released through MGM-EMI distributors.)

It fell to Jane's lot to waken the grown-up Lamb. She did it gently by tickling his nose with a twig of wild honeysuckle. He said, "Bother the flies!" twice, and then opened his eyes. ■ (From *Five Children and It* by E. Nesbit. Illustrated by J. S. Goodall.)

"We were in the room before my sisters had time to see cause for regretting that they had brought me. The vision of dry boards and white light and glass cases vanished, and in its stead I saw this:

"A small vault, as my memory serves me, about fifteen feet square, with an arched roof, from the centre of which hung a lamp that burned with a faint blue light, and made the guide's candle look red and lurid. The floor was flagged like the passages, and was as damp and chill. Round three sides of the room ran a railing, and behind it—standing against the wall with a ghastly look of life in death—were about two hundred skeletons, hung on wires, like the one you see at the doctor's, but skeletons with their flesh hardened on their bones, with their long dry hair hanging on each side of their brown faces, where the skin in drying had drawn itself back from their gleaming teeth and empty eyesockets. Skeletons draped in mouldering shreds of shrouds and grave-clothes, their lean figures still clothed with dry skin, seemed to reach out towards me. There they stood, men, women, and children, knee-deep in loose bones collected from the other vaults of the church, and heaped around them. On the wall near the door I saw the dried body of a little child hung up by its hair.

"I don't think I screamed or cried, or even said a word. I think I was paralysed with horror, but I remember presently going back up those stairs, holding tightly to that kindly hand, and not daring to turn my head lest one of those charnel-house faces should peep out at me from some niche in the damp wall.

"The mummies of Bordeaux were the crowning horror of my childish life. It is to them, I think, more than to any other thing that I owe nights and nights of anguish and horror, long years of bitterest fear and dread. All the other fears could have been effaced, but the shock of that sight branded it on my brain, and I never forgot it."[1]

In Pau, France they went to a charity bazaar. "Here let me make a confession, I had never really loved any doll. My affections up to that time had been lavished on a black and white spotted penny rabbit, bought at a Kentish fair; but when I saw Renée, it seemed to me that if I could love a doll, this would be the one. . . .

"The bazaar pleased me. It was got up by English residents, and their fancy-work was the fancy-work of the church bazaars in England, and I felt at home among it, and when my eyes rested on Renée I saw the most delightful object I had seen for many weeks. I looked and longed, and longed and looked, and then suddenly in a moment one of the great good fortunes of my life happened to me. That beautiful doll was put up to be raffled, and my sister won her. I trembled with joy as she and her wardrobe were put into my hands.

"I took her home. I dressed and undressed her twenty times a day. I made her play the part of heroine in all my favourite stories. I told her fairy tales and took her to bed with me at night for company, but I never loved her. I have never been able to love a doll in my life."[1]

1867. Arrangements were made for Edith to live with a girl her own age in a French family. "I learned French in three months. All day I was with Mme. Lourdes or Marguerite. . . . It was French or silence, and any healthy child would have chosen French as I did. They were three happy months. I adored Marguerite, who was, I think, the typical good child of French story books. . . .

"I do not think we ever got into wilful mischief. For instance, our starving the cat was quite unintentional. We were playing bandits . . . and it occurred to us that Mimi would make an excellent captive princess, so we caught her and put her in a hamper at the end of the cellar, and when my mother called to take us home to tea with her, we rushed off and left the poor princess still a prisoner.

"[Two nights later] I started up in bed about midnight and pulled Marguerite's yellow pigtail wildly. 'Oh Marguerite,' I cried, 'poor Mimi!' I had to pull at the pigtail as though it was a bell-rope. . . . Then she sat up in bed rigid with a great purpose.

"'We must go down and fetch her,' she said.

"It was winter; the snow was on the ground. Marguerite thoughtfully put on her shoes and her dressing-gown, but I, with some vague recollection of bare-footed pilgrims, and some wild desire to make expiation for my crime, went down bare-footed in my nightgown. The crime of forgetting a cat for three days was well paid for by that expedition.

"I remember so well the feeling of her soft warm fur against my cold little legs. I caught the cat in my arms, and as I turned to go back to the house, my half-frozen foot struck against something on the floor. It felt silky, I picked it up. It was Renée. . . . She also had been shut up here all this time, and I had never missed her!

"We took the cat and my doll back to bed with us and tried to get warm again. Marguerite was soon asleep, but I lay awake for a long time kissing and crying over the ill-used cat.

"I didn't get up again for a fortnight. My bare-footed pilgrimage cost me a frightful cold and the loss of several children's parties to which we had been invited. Marguerite, throughout my illness, behaved like an angel."[1]

Winter, 1868. Joined her mother and sisters in Biarritz, Spain. She had knit a pair of cuffs as a present for her mother. "They were of a size suitable to the wrist of a man of about eight feet, and the irregularities at the edge where I had forgotten to slip the stitch were concealed by stiff little ruchings of blue satin ribbon. I thought of them with unspeakable pride.

"We reached Bagnères after dark, and my passion of joy at seeing my mother again was heightened by the knowledge that I had so rich a gift to bestow upon her.

". . . I went happy to bed. When I was lying between the sheets, I heard one of my sisters laughing in the next room. She was talking, and I knew she was speaking of my precious cuffs. 'They would just fit a coal-heaver,' she said.

"She never knew that I heard her, but it was years before I forgave that unconscious outrage to my feelings."[1]

July, 1868-1870. Family returned to England. Mother found a house at La Haye near Dinan in Brittany. "The small material objects that surround one's daily life have always influenced me deeply. Even as a child I found that in a familiar entourage one could be contented, if not happy; but hotels and boarding-houses and lodgings have always bored me to extinction. . . . I have a cat-like fondness for things I am accustomed to. . . ."[1]

The house at La Haye was adjacent to a farm on one side and a large walled garden on the other. "There never was such another garden, there never will be! Peaches, apricots, nectarines, and grapes of all kinds, lined the inside walls; the avenue that ran down the middle of it was of fig trees and standard peach-trees. . . . Along the end of the garden was a great arcade of black, clipped yews, so thick and strong that a child could crawl on the outside of it without falling through. Above the dairy and coach-house was an immense hay-loft, a straw-loft over the stable and cowhouse. What play-rooms for wet days!

"My mother, with a wisdom for which I shall thank her all my days, allowed us to run wild; we were expected to appear at meals with some approach to punctuality, and with hands and faces moderately clean. . . . But, as a rule, we were left to go our own way, and a very happy way it

E. Nesbit at age twenty-nine.

was. I don't mean that we were neglected; my eldest sister was always a refuge on wet days when a fairy story seemed to be the best thing to be had.

"In the midst of all the parties, picnics and gaieties in which our elders were plunged, my other sister found time to read aloud to us, and to receive such confidence as we deemed it wise to make concerning our plans and our plays. . . .

"A part of the infinite charm of those days lies in the fact that we were never bored, and children are bored much more often and much more deeply than their elders suppose."[1]

Spring, 1869. Attended an Ursuline Convent in Germany. Her German schooling was unsuccessful and included at least three run-away attempts. The war between Germany and France began. "God! Let the Germans be suppressed so that Europe at last may have a rest."[1]

1870. Left Germany to travel to France than England.

1871. Her sister, Mary, who at 18 was engaged to a young blind poet named Philip Bourke Marston, died of consumption.

1872. Family finally settled down at Halstead Hall, in the Kentish village of Halstead in England. "'The Hall' it was called, but the house itself did not lend itself to the pretensions of its name. A long, low, red-brick house, that might have been commonplace but for the roses and the ivy that clung to the front of it, and the rich, heavy jasmine that covered the side. There was a smooth lawn with chestnut trees round it, and a big garden, where flowers and fruit and vegetables grew together, as they should, without jealousy or class-distinction. . . . From a laburnum tree in a corner of the lawn we children slung an improvised hammock, and there I used to read and dream, and watch the swaying gold of leaf and blossom.

". . . There were nooks among the laburnums and lilacs that grew thickly round the pond, nooks where one could hide with one's favourite books, and be secure from the insistent and irritating demands so often made on one's time by one's elders. For grown-up people never thought of spoiling their clothes by penetrating the shrubbery. Here, on many a sunny day, have I lounged away the morning, stifling conscience with Mrs. Ewing's tales, and refusing to remember the tangle of untidiness in which I had left my room involved. For I had a little room of my own, a little, little room with a long, low window and a window-ledge, where bright plants in pots, encouraged by the western sun, withstood the intermittence of my attentions, and blossomed profusely.

"My bookcase stood by this window, an old mahogany bookcase with a deep top drawer that let down to form a writing-table. Here I used to sit and write—verse, verse, always verse—and dream of the days when I should be a great poet like Shakespeare, or Christina Rossetti! Ah me, that day is long in coming. But I never doubted then that it would come.

"Besides the desk and the well-oiled key that formed so excellent a defence against 'the boys'—for what young poet could ever set down a line with the possibility of even the best-loved brothers looking over her shoulder?—my little room had another feature, by turns a terror and a charm. A little trap-door in the ceiling led to that mysterious and delightful region between the roof and the beams, a dark passage leading all round the house, and leading too—oh, deep and abiding joy! to the door that opened on the roof itself. This, until the higher powers discovered it, was a safer haven even than the shrubbery.

"Enclosed by four pointed roofs of tiles was a central space—safe, secluded—whence one could see the world around, oneself invisible, or at least, unseen. Another trap-door, from the linen-closet by the boys' bedroom, afforded them an equal access to this paradise. We kept a store of books and good things in the hollow of the roof, and many a pleasant picnic we enjoyed there.

"Happy, vanished days, when to be on the roof and to eat tinned pineapple in secret constituted happiness!"[1]

1873-75. ". . . When I was fifteen I ventured to show some verses to my mother. She showed them to . . . the editor of *Good Words* and the *Sunday Magazine,* and never shall I forget the rapture of delight and of gratitude with which I received the news that my verses had been accepted. By-and-by they were printed, and I got a cheque for a guinea, a whole guinea, think of it!

"The first poem I ever had published was a non-committal set of verses about dawn, with a moral tag. It was printed in the *Sunday Magazine.* When I got the proof I ran round the garden shouting 'Hooray!' at the top of my voice, to the scandal of the village, and the vexation of my family.

"The next poem came out in *Good Words.* Then I sent a poem to another magazine. I asked my mother to tell me what to say in the covering letter to the editor. She dictated a suitable exercise in propriety, and I wrote it out very fair. But I thought it sounded cold and unconvincing. So I wrote at the end 'P.S.—Do, *please* take this!' He did, too.

"I was seventeen then."[1]

1879. Family moved to London. She became engaged to Hubert Bland. "Mr. Bland and I went to Halstead and had *no end* of a 'nice-time'—we went into the woods—sat about—caught (and kissed) a chaffinch—had lunch in the kitchen of a funny old-fashioned Inn—came back to the station through the grounds of the Oakleys house, home by train and a sumptuous drive in a hansom cab to conclude the most charming day I have ever spent. The country was *fresh young* and *jolly.* So were we."[1]

Her letters at this time were filled with youthful philosophizing. "I'm worried with trying to *understand* things. What good is my life to me? What good can I do with it? *Can* I do *anything?*

"Is life a dream, and death a reality?—Or is *death* the substance?

"I think on—and on—and I *nearly* get an answer and then—just as I think I am attaining to what I so desire, it slips—and I lose my chance and then—I have only to 'dry my eyes and laugh at my fall' and humbly begin my train of thought all over again—I shall never be answered—I think still and from my thoughts *gain* nothing—*attain* nothing, *see* nothing of all that my soul longs to grasp.

> 'Only I discern
> Infinite passion, and the pain
> Of finite hearts that yearn.'

"I'd better stop, I think, I shall only sink into a veritable miry slough, represented by my own ridiculous system of bad metaphysics . . . In my thoughts I sink or swim—alone."[1]

April 22, 1880. Married Hubert Bland. She was seven months pregnant at the time.

1880. Son, Paul, was born.

1880. Husband came down with smallpox. Recovered to learn that his partner in a brush factory investment had defrauded him and left him penniless with wife and newborn son.

1881. Started writing, more or less regularly for the *Weekly Dispatch.* Husband collaborated with her on some of the articles and stories. Met Alice Hoatson at the office of *Sylvia's Home Journal.* After helping Edith sell her first article, they became good friends. Alice Hoatson threw in her lot with the Blands and was a member of their household for over thirty years.

Then the dragon opened her jaws wider and wider and wider. Edmund shut his eyes close, for though his master *was* in the town, yet the amiable Edmund shrank from beholding the awful sight. ■ (From *The Complete Book of Dragons* by E. Nesbit. Illustrated by Erik Blegvad.)

1882. Daughter, Iris, born. Became aware that her husband was still under promise of marriage to a young girl he knew before their marriage. Upon meeting the girl, she also found out the girl had a child by him. The two women became friends. From this time on, she was aware of her husband's weakness for other women and began to suffer them uncomplainingly.

1884. Helped to found the Fabian Society with husband. "[The Fabian Society's] aim is to improve the social system—or rather to spread its news as to the possible improvement of the said S.S. There are about thirty members—some of whom are working men. We meet once a fortnight—and then someone reads a paper and we all talk about it. . . .

"There are two distinct elements in the F.S., the practical and the visionary—the first being much the strongest—but a perpetual warfare goes on between the parties which gives to the Fabian an excitement which it might otherwise lack. We belong—needless to say—to the practical party, and so do most of our intimate friends."[1]

1885. A new member joined the society. "The said Society is getting rather large now and includes some very nice people, of whom Mr. Stapleton is the nicest and a certain G. B. Shaw the most interesting. G.B.S. has a fund of dry Irish humour that is simply irresistible. He is a very clever writer and speaker—Is the grossest flatterer (of men, women and children impartially) I ever met, is horribly untrustworthy as he repeats everything he hears, and does not always stick to the truth, and is *very plain* like a long corpse with a dead white face—sandy sleek hair and a loathsome small straggly beard, and yet is one of the most fascinating men I ever met. Everyone rather affects to despise him 'Oh it's only Shaw.' That sort of thing you know, but everyone admires him all the same. Miss Hoatson pretends to hate him, but my own impression is that she is over head and ears in love with him."[1]

1885. "I am not doing any painting just now, I am sorry to say—so I try to write as many stories as I can—but it is uphill work—writing when you don't feel a bit inclined. I hope the *Weekly Dispatch* will give me some more work later on in the year. We have just sent a joint story to *Belgravia*—of whose acceptance I feel some faint hopes. I still write poems for the *Weekly Dispatch*. . . .

". . . I am writing nothing now by myself except poems[.] In all stories Hubert and I 'go shares'—I am sure it is much better when we write together than when we write separately.

"To-day I have washed my hair and have not been out. I have done two sheets 'sides into middle,' written some paragraphs for a newspaper—cooked the dinner, nursed Iris for a whole hour in the vain hope of getting her to sleep."[1]

1885. Their first book, *The Prophet's Mantle,* published under the pseudonym, "Fabian Bland." It was quickly forgotten.

1885. Son, Fabian, born.

1886. Husband took over editorship of the paper *To-day*.

1886. She gave birth to a stillborn baby.

1886. *Lays and Legends,* first volume of poetry published. One fan wrote:

> 9 Gunterstone Road,
> West Kensington.
> 5 September 1886.

"My dear Madam,
"I hope that you will forgive me for doing a thing (which honestly I never have done before) namely writing to you to express my admiration of your poetry and the great pleasure which it has given me to read it. The immediate occasion which prompts me to write this is the reading of your poem in this month's *Longmans* but I have been a humble admirer of your poetic power ever since I read "Absolution" now some years ago.

"Of course opinions differ about poetry, and I am the last to pretend that any value is to be attached to mine. But as one who writes himself I do know what is calculated to stir our human sympathy, and I must say that for sweetness and strength and beauty of imagery I know no verses from the pen of a modern writer of poems which appeal to me so much as your own. This then must be my excuse for writing to you as one very grateful for shade in the desert land of contemporary verse. Hoping to see some more from your pen before long, and also that I may some day have the pleasure of making your personal acquaintance, believe me dear Madam.

Very truly yours
H. Rider Haggard."[1]

1888. Alice Hoatson became pregnant. Edith decided to adopt the child to raise as her own, then discovered her husband was the father. Still adopted the baby, Rosamund.

1889. Moved to Three Gables, Grove Park (their first home).

1892. First children's book, *The Voyage of Columbus,* published.

1895. Brother, Alfred, died.

1899. *The Story of the Treasure Seekers* published. She had Oswald, the narrator, say: "The best part of books is when things are happening. . . . This is why I shall not tell you in this story about all the days when nothing happened. You will not catch me saying, 'thus the sad days passed slowly by'—or 'the years rolled on their weary course,' or 'time went on'—because it is silly; of course time goes on—whether you say so or not. So I shall just tell you the nice, interesting parts—and in between you will understand that we had our meals and got up and went to bed, and dull things like that. It would be sickening to write all that down, though of course it happens. I said so to Albert-next-door's uncle, who writes books, and he said 'Quite right, that's what we call selection, a necessity of true art.' And he is very clever indeed."[1]

1899. Their money problems over, the family moved to Well Hall at Eltham, Kent—known to readers of her books as the Red House and the Moat House. H. G. Wells spoke of it as "a place to which one rushed down from town at the week-end to snatch one's bed before anyone else got it."[1] Now followed a series of griefs which were among the worst she ever endured.

1899. Gave birth to another stillborn baby.

October, 1899. Alice Hoatson had a son, John, by Bland. Edith again raised this one as her own.

October, 1899. Saretta Deakin, her half-sister, died.

October, 1900. Fabian had to have his tonsils removed, lost consciousness during the operation and died. He was 15. She miserably recalled how he had been locked in a room to repent of one of his mischiefs: "The house is very quiet, because all the other children grew up long ago, and went out into the world. The lamp has just been lighted, but the blinds are not drawn down now. Outside the winter dusk is deepening the shadows in the garden where, in the days when the sun shone, you used to shout and play. Do you remember, understand, forgive? I do not think that you forgive or do not forgive. I do not believe that you remember now that quiet room which was your prison. . . . But you remember, perhaps, hours when your mother was not your goaler; when she held you not in prison, but in her arms that loved you—hours when you were not alone. These other things . . . it is your mother who has them to remember."[1]

December, 1902. Her mother died.

1904. Took a trip to Paris.

February, 1907. Daughter, Iris, married John Austen Philips. "Not auspiciously as it turned out."[1]

1907. Became joint editor with three others of periodical, "The Neolith." It was a critical success, but became too much of a burden financially. For the next five years, contributed time and money advocating the theory that Bacon wrote the works of Shakespeare. Only four issues were published.

Autumn, 1909. Rosamund married Clifford Sharp.

1910. Started writing a weekly article for children in the *Daily Chronicle.*

January, 1910. Goes to Looe in Cornwall for husband's health.

Early, 1914. Because of a disease of the retina of both eyes, husband became blind. She wrote to her brother: "Things are pretty black for us—Hubert has practically lost his sight—he is undergoing a very expensive treatment which *may* do some good, but so far has done very little, if any. I am getting very tired of work, and the expenses of life don't seem to get less. I wish everyone had a small pension at 50—enough to live on. I have had a novel in hand for some time, but I have been too worried to get on with it."[1]

And to Lady Dunsary: "I am very glad you like 'Wings and the Child.' I enjoyed writing it. Indeed I am getting very tired of writing stories, and wish I need only write verse, and set down the things I think. Any success my stories have had is due I think to a sort of light-hearted outlook on life—and now that Hubert's eyes have failed him a steam-roller seems to have gone over all one's hopes and ambitions, and it is difficult to remember how it felt to be lighthearted.

"I am down at Crowlink trying to get well and to do a little work. It is a lonely little house on the downs, not a sound all day but the wind and the sea, and on sunny days, the skylarks. The quiet is like a cool kind hand on one's forehead. . . . I am alone here except for the dogs, and my new secretary, a quiet youth who types what I write and in the evenings plays chess with me. Neither of us are chess-players, so it is quite a pleasant amusement—and not the weighty business that your real chess-player makes of the game."[1]

April, 1914. World War I began. Husband Hubert died. "Hubert wrote as he spoke and he spoke as he thought. He never did for money or for fame sell himself. He had, in the highest degree, the quality of intellectual honesty. He would not deceive himself, nor would he suffer others to be deceived. . . . He hated the Pharisees, the Prigs, and the Puritans. All men else he loved."[1]

She wrote to her brother: "I am much better in health—but I do not find I can take much interest in life. Without Hubert everything is so unmeaning. I don't do much writing, though I am always hoping I shall be able to again. I have taken in paying guests since last October—If I could get a few more I should get on all right. Also I sell flowers out of the garden, and apples and vegetables. In the last eight weeks I have made by that alone 25/-a week. Then there is the pension. If I could live without writing, I should like never to write another line. The War makes everything more miserable. It seems too horrible to be true. . . ."[1]

1914. Suffered from a duodenal ulcer. Underwent an operation, came through it badly, but eventually recovered.

February 20, 1917. Married Thomas Terry Tucker, a marine engineer, known as "Skipper." "He is the soul of goodness and kindness and he never blunders in matters of sentiment or emotion. He doesn't blunder in anything, for the matter of that, but you know in those matters how fatally easy it is to go wrong. After the cold misery of the last three years I feel as though someone had come and put a fur cloak round me. Or like one shipwrecked on a lonely island, and I have found another shipwrecked mariner to help me to build a hut and make a fire. He is a widower and I knew his wife and he knew Hubert, so we can talk about *them.* . . . His whole life seems to have been spent in doing good. Also he is fond of laughter, and likes the same kind of jokes that please me. . . . I feel as though I had opened another volume of the book of life (the last volume) and it is full of beautiful stories and poetry.

"I feel peaceful and contented in my new life with him. . . . He has a philosophy of life which makes all things easy to him. He never worries and he never lets me worry. So, though we are pinched for money, and hard put to it to keep going I am quite at ease. He cares absolutely nothing for material things and *possessions,* though he enjoys life and is very merry and jolly. He has been all over the world as ship's engineer, and is a born *observer.* Also he has words to clothe his thoughts and observations. If we had time I am sure we could do some writing work together."[1]

Spring, 1922. Sold Well Hall and bought a bungalow at Jesson St. Mary's, Kent. Well Hall was razed a few years after her death.

1922. *The Lark,* her last novel and *Many Voices,* her last book of poetry, were published.

1923. Taken fatally ill with bronchiestasis. She wrote to a friend: "I suppose I shall not get well again, but, like Charles II, I take an unconscionable time over the business. You would not know me—I am so thin. Once a Rubens Venus in figure but now more like a pre-Raphaelite Saint Simeon."[1]

And to another: "Alas, your poor E. Nesbit lies dying and it is a long business and very tiresome. I fear the last of the Oswald Saga has been sung.

"I fear I shall never write anything again though I feel now as though I had never written anything comparable in importance and interest to what I could write now if I could hold a pen."[1]

May 4, 1924. Edith Nesbit died of a bronchial illness and cardiac dilatation.

"Poetry . . . is really what I should naturally have done, that and *no* prose, if I had not had to write for a living."[1]

FOR MORE INFORMATION SEE: Doris Langley Moore, *E. Nesbit: A Biography,* Benn, 1933, revised and augmented edition, Chilton, 1966; Roger L. Green, *Tellers of Tales,* Ward, new edition, 1953; E. F. Walbridge, "E. Nesbit," and P. Lynch, "Remembering E. Nesbit," both in *Horn Book,* October, 1953; Noel Streatfeild, *Magic and the Magician: E. Nesbit and Her Children's Books,* Benn, 1958; Edward Eager, "Daily Magic," Eleanor Graham, "Places of Enchantment," M. E. Strange, "E. Nesbit as I Knew Her," and Noel Streatfeild, "An Excerpt from 'Magic and the Magician,'" all in *Horn Book,* October, 1958.

Anthea Bell, *E. Nesbit,* Bodley Head, 1960; Charles G. L. DuCann, *The Loves of George Bernard Shaw,* Funk & Wagnalls, 1963; Muriel Fuller, editor, *More Junior Authors,* Wilson, 1963; E. Nesbit, *Long Ago When I Was Young,* Whiting & Wheaton, 1966; Brian Doyle, editor, *The Who's Who of Children's Literature,* Schocken Books, 1968; Laura Benét, *Famous Storytellers for Young People,* Dodd, 1968; Marcus Crouch, *The Nesbit Tradition: The Children's Novel, 1945-70,* Rowen & Littlefield, 1976.

"Isn't there someone you'd like to hurt if you were as strong as they are, and they were as weak as you?" ■ (From *Oswald Bastable and Others* by E. Nesbit. Illustrated by C. E. Brock and H. R. Millar.)

At last, the animal gathered his forces for a supreme effort, rose plunging and rearing high in the air, then with blood gushing from his nostrils fell to the ground. ■ (From *The Boys' Life of Washington* by Helen Nicolay. Illustrated by W. M. Berger.)

NICOLAY, Helen   1866-1954

PERSONAL: Born March 9, 1866, in Paris, France; died September 12, 1954; daughter of John George (private secretary to Abraham Lincoln) and Therena (Bates) Nicolay. *Education:* Tutored by her father and private teachers. *Religion:* Unitarian. *Home:* Washington, D.C.

CAREER: Author of books for children; historian. *Awards, honors:* Honorary A.M., George Washington University, 1922.

WRITINGS—Biography: The Boys' Life of Abraham Lincoln (illustrated by Jay Hambidge and others), Century, 1906; *The Boys' Life of Ulysses S. Grant*, Century, 1909; *Personal Traits of Abraham Lincoln*, Century, 1912; *The Boys' Life of Lafayette*, Harper, 1920; *The Boys' Life of*

Alexander Hamilton, Century, 1927; *Andrew Jackson, the Fighting President*, Century, 1929; *The Boys' Life of Washington* (illustrated by W. M. Berger), Century, 1931; *The Boys' Life of Thomas Jefferson* (illustrated by Berger), Century, 1933; *The Boys' Life of Benjamin Franklin* (illustrated by Berger), Century, 1935; *Wizard of the Wires: The Boys' Life of Samuel F. B. Morse* (illustrated by Edward Caswell), 1938; *Decatur of the Old Navy* (illustrated by Norman Price), Appleton-Century, 1942; *MacArthur of Bataan*, Appleton-Century, 1942; *China's First Lady*, Appleton-Century, 1944; *Born to Command: The Story of General Eisenhower*, Appleton-Century, 1945; *Lincoln's Secretary: A Biography of John G. Nicolay*, Longmans, Green, 1949, reprinted, Greenwood Press, 1971.

History: *Our Nation in the Building*, Century, 1916; *The Book of American Wars*, Century, 1918; *Our Capital on the Potomac*, Century, 1924; *The Bridge of Water: The Story of Panama and the Canal* (illustrated by Chichi Lasley), Appleton-Century, 1940.

Other: *Peter and Paul and Their Friends: A Manual for Religious Instruction*, Beacon Press, 1922; *Our Perennial Bible*, Appleton-Century, 1937.

FOR MORE INFORMATION SEE: Stanley J. Kunitz and Howard Haycraft, editors, *Junior Book of Authors*, Wilson, 2nd edition, 1951; Obituaries—*New York Times*, September 14, 1954; *Newsweek*, September 27, 1954; *Time*, September 27, 1954; *Publishers Weekly*, October 9, 1954; *Wilson Library Bulletin*, November, 1954; *American Historical Review*, January, 1955.

Benjamin's stock was almost as varied as that of a twentieth-century drug-store. ■ (From *The Boys' Life of Benjamin Franklin* by Helen Nicolay. Illustrated by W. M. Berger.)

POTTER, (Helen) Beatrix   1866-1943

PERSONAL: Born July 28 (or 6, according to some sources), 1866, in London, England; died December 22, 1943, in Sawrey, England; daughter of Rupert Potter (a barrister and amateur photographer); married William Heelis (a lawyer), 1913. *Education:* Tutored by governesses at home; except for some brief private instruction, was self-taught in art. *Home:* Castle Farm, Sawrey, England.

CAREER: Author and illustrator of books for children; sheep farmer in the Lake District after her marriage; as a conservationist, she acquired almost 4,000 acres of land near her home and left it to the National Trust for preservation after her death.

WRITINGS—All self-illustrated stories for children, except as noted: *The Tale of Peter Rabbit,* privately printed, 1901, Warne, 1902, Altemus, 1903, reprinted, Dover, 1972 (also published as *Peter Rabbit* and *The Story of Peter Rabbit*), [later editions illustrated by Florence Nosworthy, Hall & McCreary, 1918; Keith Ward, Whitman, 1935; Jo Musial, Whitman, 1936; Ruth Easthill, Whitman, 1937; Masha, Grosset & Dunlap, 1942; Julian Wehr (animation), Grosset & Dunlap, 1943; Dirk (pseudonym of Richard H. Gringhius), Fideler, 1946; Phoebe Erickson, Childrens Press, 1947; Theresa Kalab, Whitman, 1948; Anne Sellers Leaf (retold by Wallace C. Wadsworth), Rand McNally, 1953; Beth Wilson, Whitman, 1954; Bill Lohse, Winston, 1955; Leonard Weisgard, Grosset & Dunlap, 1955; Florence Sarah Winship, Whitman, 1955; and by Bonnie and Bill Rutherford and Eulalie, Platt & Munk, 1961]; dramatization by Catherine M. Turk published as *Peter Rabbit* (one-act), Samuel French, 1936; musical adaptations—Dudley Glass, *The Songs of Peter Rabbit,* Warne, 1951, reprinted, 1969; Glass, *The Operetta of Peter Rabbit,* Warne, 1962; *Peter Rabbit's Painting Book,* 1911, reprinted, 1954; *Peter Rabbit's Almanac for 1929,* Warne, 1928.

The Tailor of Gloucester, privately printed, 1902, Warne, 1903, reprinted, Dover, 1973, dramatization by E. G. Harcourt Williams published under the same title, Warne, 1929; *The Tale of Squirrel Nutkin,* Warne, 1903, reprinted, Dover, 1972; *The Tale of Benjamin Bunny,* Warne, 1904, reprinted, 1965; *The Tale of Two Bad Mice,* Warne, 1904, reprinted, Dover, 1974; *The Tale of Mrs. Tiggy-Winkle,* Warne, 1905, reprinted, Dover, 1973; *The Pie and the Patty-Pan,* Warne, 1905, reprinted as *The Tale of the Pie and Patty-Pan,* 1964; *The Tale of Mr. Jeremy Fisher,* Warne, 1906, reprinted, Dover, 1974; *Jeremy Fisher's Painting Book,* Warne, 1954; *The Story of a Fierce Bad Rabbit,* Warne, 1906, reprinted, 1964; *The Story of Miss Moppet,* Warne, 1906, reprinted, 1964; *The Tale of Tom Kitten,* Warne, 1907, reprinted, 1965; *Tom Kitten's Painting Book,* 1917, reprinted, 1954; *The Tale of Jemima Puddle-Duck,* Warne, 1908, reprinted, 1965; *Jemima Puddle-Duck's Painting Book,* Warne, 1925; *The Roly-Poly Pudding,* Warne, 1908, reprinted as *The Tale of Samuel Whiskers; or, The Roly-Poly Pudding,* Warne, 1965, dramatization by Theron H. Butterworth published as *Mr. Samuel Whiskers,* Warne, 1933; *The Tale of the Flopsy Bunnies,* Warne, 1909, reprinted, 1962; *Ginger and Pickles,* Warne, 1909, reprinted as *A Tale of Ginger and Pickles,*

Beatrix Potter at age fifteen.

1964, dramatization by E. G. Harcourt Williams published as *Ginger and Pickles* (one-act), Warne, 1930.

The Tale of Mrs. Tittlemouse, Warne, 1910, reprinted, 1964; *The Tale of Timmy Tiptoes,* Warne, 1911, reprinted, 1964; *The Tale of Mr. Tod,* Warne, 1912, reprinted, 1964; *The Tale of Pigling Bland,* Warne, 1913, reprinted, 1964; *Appley Dapply's Nursery Rhymes,* Warne, 1917, reprinted, 1963; *The Tale of Johnny Town-Mouse,* Warne, 1918, reprinted, 1964; *Cecily Parsley's Nursery Rhymes,* Warne, 1922, reprinted, 1964; *The Fairy Caravan,* privately printed, 1929, McKay, 1929, reprinted, Warne, 1951; *The Tale of Little Pig Robinson,* McKay, 1930, reprinted, Warne, 1958; *Sister Anne* (novel; illustrated by Katharine Sturges), McKay, 1932; *Wag-by-Wall* (decorated by J. J. Lankes), Horn Book, 1944; *The Tale of the Faithful Dove,* Warne, 1956, 2nd edition (illustrated by Marie Angel), 1970; *Beatrix Potter's Painting Book,* Warne, 1962; *The Journal of Beatrix Potter from 1881-1897* (transcribed from her code writing by Leslie Linder; with an appreciation by H. L. Cox), Warne, 1966; *Letters to Children,* Walker, 1967; *The Sly Old Cat,* Warne, 1971; *The Tale of Tuppeny* (illustrated by Marie Angel), Warne, 1973; *Beatrix Potter's Birthday Book,* edited by Enid Linder, Warne, 1974.

Also illustrator of *Tales of Uncle Remus* by Joel Chandler Harris, of *Alice in Wonderland* by Lewis Carroll (pseudonym of Charles L. Dodgson), and of *A Happy Pair* (poems) by F. E. Weatherly, Hildesheimer C Faulkner, 1890.

ADAPTATIONS—Filmstrips: "Peter Rabbit," Curriculum Films, 1946, revised version, Curriculum Materials Corp., 1957, other filmstrips by Stillfilm, 1949, Museum Extension Service (New York), 1965, and Educational Projections Corp., 1968; "The Tale of Benjamin Bunny," Weston Woods, 1967; "The Tale of Mr. Jeremy Fisher," Weston Woods, 1967; "The Tale of Peter Rabbit," Weston Woods, 1967; "The Tale of Tom Kitten," Weston Woods, 1967; "The Tale of Two Bad Mice," Weston Woods, 1967; "Treasury of Animal Stories, Parts I & II," read by Frances Sternhagen (six filmstrips, four records or cassettes), Miller-Brody Productions.

Movies: "Peter Rabbit and the Tales of Beatrix Potter," E.M.I. (British, 98 min., 16mm, sound, color), Films Incorporated, 1971.

Recordings: "Beatrix Potter Nursery Rhymes and Tales," read by Claire Bloom (record or cassette), Caedmon; "Peter Rabbit and His Friends—The Favorite Tales of Beatrix Potter," read by Elinor Basescu (record or cassette), Miller-Brody Productions; "Peter Rabbit & Tales of Beatrix Potter," Angel Records; "The Tailor of Gloucester and Other Stories," read by Claire Bloom (record or cassette), Caedmon; "The Tale of the Flopsy Bunnies and other Beatrix Potter Stories" (record or cassette), Caedmon; "The Tale of Little Pig Robinson," read by Claire Bloom (record or cassette), Caedmon; "The Tale of Peter Rabbit" (cassette only), Scholastic; "The Tale of Peter Rabbit and Other Stories" (record, side 1—21:30 min., side 2—16:25 min), Caedmon, 1970; "The Tale of Peter Rabbit and other Stories," read by Claire Bloom (six cassettes, teacher's guide), Caedmon; "The Tale of Squirrel Nutkin and Other Tales," read by Claire Bloom (record or cassette), Caedmon; "Treasury of Animal Stories, Volume I," Spoken Arts; "Treasury of Animal Stories, Volume II," read by Frances Sternhagen, Spoken Arts; "World of Animal Stories," (four cassettes, forty books; or one cassette, ten books), Spoken Arts.

Television: "Beatrix Potter: A Private World."

SIDELIGHTS: **July 28, 1866.** Born at Bolton Gardens, Kensington. Had one younger brother, Bertram. Her father described himself as a barrister who had never practised, that is to say he had no need to work. Beatrix was a well-to-do child of the 1870's, brought up in the confines and loneliness of a Victorian household. She wrote of it in old age as "my unloved birthplace," when she heard it had been destroyed by bombing in 1940.

"Thank goodness, my education was neglected; I was never sent to school . . . The reason I am glad I did not go to school—it would have rubbed off some of the originality (if I had not died of shyness or been killed with over pressure). I fancy I could have been taught anything if I had been caught young; but it was in the days when parents kept governesses, and only boys went to school in most families." [Margaret Lane, *The Tale of Beatrix Potter,* Warne, 1946.[1]]

Spent enjoyable summers in the country with her grandparents at Camfield Place. She had two favorite rooms. "There was not much furniture in these two rooms. Some dwarf elbow chairs, and a stumpy low table on which we made sand-pies without damage, and sailed therein as in a boat when wrong side up, which reminds me there was a drugget very tight stretched. There was also a rocking chair, we had none at home.

"There was a book-shelf hanging on ropes which swayed about when you replaced anything. A work-box banished for its old fashioned ugliness. American cloth on the round table which became sticky when we rested our chins on it. How short we were in those days.

"The green curtains slid on a long brass pole. I have reason to know it was hollow, for once we took it down to extract a tame fieldmouse." [*The Journal of Beatrix Potter,* transcribed from her code writing by Leslie Linder, Warne, 1966.[2]]

1881-1897. From approximately fourteen through thirty she kept a journal in her own private code. "There is something so sad in deliberately writing for the time when these things shall have utterly passed away from me. To me all is bound up together in fact and fancy, my dear grandmother, the place I love best in the world and the sweet balmy air where I have been so happy as a child.

"**Wednesday, February 28th, 1883**—Mr. Whistler is holding an Exhibition somewhere, termed an *Arrangement in white and yellow.* The furniture is painted yellow and the footman is dressed in white and yellow, someone said he looked like a poached egg. Mr. Whistler sent the Princess of Wales and the fine ladies yellow butterflies which they wore at a private view. What a set of yellow butterflies! It's quite disgusting how people go on about these Pre-Raphaelite aesthetic painters.

"**Saturday, March 3rd, 1883**—Been to the Academy again this afternoon with a much better light, more pleased than before, I *will* do something sooner or later.

"Looked particularly at Reynold's pictures. They are very different when one compares them, but the least beautiful is wonderful, in fact, the less worked-up pictures, as with every great master, show the most power.

"**Tuesday, March 6th, 1883**—Two or three Sundays ago there was a seabird at the Round Pond. It was smaller than the common black-backed gull, almost the only kind I know by sight. Slightly hooked bill, dark narrow black head, rather lighter on the back, grey breast and wings, white patch over tail, tail I am not sure forked, only Bertram said so. It kept flying over and over the pond fishing, and came quite close—there were a good many people watching it but there does not seem to be any remark on it in the papers.

"**Monday, May 28, 1883**—I had my first drawing lesson with Miss Cameron in November '78, and my last May 10, '83. I have great reason to be grateful to her, though we were not on particularly good terms for the last good while. I have learnt from her freehand, model, geometry, perspective and a little water-colour flower painting.

"Painting is an awkward thing to teach except the details of the medium. If you and your master are determined to look at nature and art in two different directions you are sure to stick.

(From the movie "Peter Rabbit and Tales of Beatrix Potter," copyright 1971, EMI Films Incorporated, released by MGM.)

"**Wednesday, November 21st, 1883**—Am going to Mrs. A's for the first time tomorrow, two hours, Monday and Thursday, for twelve lessons. Can have no more because Mrs. A's charge is high. . . .

"Of course, I shall paint just as I like when not with her. It will be my *first* lessons in oil or figure drawing. Of the latter I am supposed to be perfectly ignorant, never having shown my attempts to any one.

"I may probably owe a good deal to Mrs. A as my first teacher. I did to Miss Cameron, but I am convinced it lies chiefly with oneself. Technical difficulties can be taught, and a model will be an immense advantage. We shall see.

"**Thursday, November 22nd** [1883]—Refrain to give an opinion till I have been again.

"**Saturday, November 24th, 1883**—Have been to Mrs. A's. Am uncertain what to say about it. Believe, though I would not tell any one on any account, that I don't much like it, which is rather disappointing. Wish it did not cost so much, is the money being thrown away, will it even do me harm? Don't much like the colours, why should I not use English ones. Linseed oil horrid sticky stuff, she actually used bitumen in her big picture.

"She seems to have had three stages in her painting. 1st. German, her best, strong though somewhat hard. 2nd. French, sentimental and rather contemptible (I don't like French art as a rule). 3rd. A development of the French by which it has become woolly! with pinkiness of the English school super-added. I don't mean to say but that she draws and paints pretty well, but I don't like it, it's as smooth as a plate, colour, light and shade, drawing, sentiment.

"It is a risky thing to copy, shall I catch it? I think and hope my self-will which brings me into so many scrapes will

Little Benjamin sat down beside his cousin, and assured him that Mr. McGregor had gone out in a gig . . . . ▪ (From *The Tale of Benjamin Bunny* by Beatrix Potter. Illustrated by the author.)

First he ate some lettuces and some French beans; and then he ate some radishes;
▪ (From *The Tale of Peter Rabbit* by Beatrix Potter. Illustrated by the author.)

guard me here—but it is tiresome, when you do get some lessons, to be taught in a way you dislike and to have to swallow your feelings out of considerations at home and there. Mrs. A. is very kind and attentive, hardly letting me do anything.

"There has been a violent domestic explosion . . . in the lower regions, several small eruptions up here. I have a cold, my temper has been boiling like a kettle, so that things are as usual. I do wish these drawing lessons were over so that I could have some peace and sleep of nights.

"**Thursday, November 29th**—Things are going on worse. Do not like my drawing lessons. She speaks of nothing but smoothness, softness, breaking the colours, and the lightness of the shadows, till there is nothing left.

"**Saturday, December 8th, 1883**—An awful tragedy was discovered Sat. 8th., the whole Bill family, old Bill and Mrs. Little Bill, and ditto Grimes and Sextus Grimes his wife, Lord and Lady Salisbury, Mr. and Mrs. Camfield, Mars and Venus, and three or four others were every one dead and dried up. We have had old Bill more than a year. I am very much put out about the poor things, they have such a surprising difference of character, and besides it was partly our fault, but they were all asleep in bed and it seemed so cruel to water them. [Believed to be a family of garden snails.]

"**Saturday, December 15th, 1883**—Went to four Exhibitions. Hablot Browne's [Phiz] drawings at Fine Arts; Doré Gallery, water colour; Pall Mall; and McLean's. I think the first was by far the most interesting.

"I was much surprised at the extent of the *Phiz* collection, which included oils and water-colours as well as drawings in black and white. The most interesting pencil drawings

Beatrix Potter in 1943.

were the originals of *Dombey & Son, Bleak House* and *David Copperfield.* These drawings and some others of the same kind were simply marvellous. They were drawn for the most part on scraps of paper, blue very often, scribbled in pencil. I do not think the engravings, good as they are, do them justice. There is a wonderful difference of expression in the faces, however small.

"Of the landscapes I was most struck by one of the City, called I believe, *Tom's All Alone.* Some for *Bleak House* were very good, but that one was most striking, equal to Doré's finest illustrations. It was probably done in a few minutes, only soft pencil scribblings on a bit of paper, but what a sense of lone, dismal solitude the artist has given it, what a sermon that little drawing preaches.

"The originals of the *Old Curiosity Shop* were not there. I was sorry, I should have like to have seen the real little Nell. I wonder why Phiz made such a mess of some of his ladies, most in *Dombey & Son.* His young girls were natural and simple, but he could not draw a well-bred lady.

"Next across the road, we went to the Doré Gallery, which I had never seen before. What a contrast! I consider Doré one of the greatest of artists in black-and-white, but I never had any idea of his pictures before, except that they were big, which some of them certainly are.

"Perhaps coming straight from the unpretending little *Phiz* exhibition made me notice it more, but all along I kept being irritated by something vulgar in his exhibition. No doubt the great crimson dome and hangings, the peculiar light, and the sudden introduction to numerous pictures round dark corners may add to the impressiveness thereof, but it suggests an appeal to vulgar fancy, which a noble work of art does not at all require to be appreciated.

"**Friday, January 18th, 1884**—It is a year today since I wrote I had got the dumps. How are my prospects compared with last year. I am not, not in high spirits tonight, something unpleasant having happened, so my opinion should be bended as regards height. This time last year I hadn't tried oils, don't think I've done badly considering all things. Am going to do a group of fruit etc. to compare with last years. If I get on as much every year I may be well satisfied.

"**Saturday, February 9th, 1884**—I notice one thing not quite right in the *News from the Sea;* children who habitually go barefoot always have the toe joint larger, and, I am afraid, are generally flat-footed. Very few artists notice this. Mr. C. Woodville goes to the other extreme and gives his hideous, ill-drawn arabs cloven-feet.

"**Friday, March 28th, 1884**—A shocking rumour is about that Prince Leopold has died today at Nice. He and the Duke of Connaught were the most popular of the Queen's sons. He was looked up to as a very respectable, good man, whatever may be said of two of his brothers. It seems doubtful how the Queen will stand the death of her favourite son. No one says much of it, but for some months it has been suspected that all is not right with her. Some say she is mad, not that that is anything uncommon, half the world is mad when you come to enquire.

"Have been very unsettled this week, first mamma said I should go to Manchester, then that I could not, then I was to stop at home with the girls then it was decided I should

She thought that it looked a safe quiet spot. ■ (From *The Tale of Jemima Puddle-Duck* by Beatrix Potter. Illustrated by the author.)

go to Camfield, but now I am to go to Manchester to-morrow. I am afraid grandmamma Potter will be disappointed, and I very much wished to go, but it is the last chance of seeing the old house. Not that I look forward to that as an unmixed pleasure.

"I have a very pleasant recollection of it, which I fear may be changed. I have now seen longer passages and higher halls. The rooms will look cold and empty, the passage I used to patter along so kindly on the way to bed will no longer seem dark and mysterious, and, above all, the kind voice which cheered the house is silent for ever.

"It is six or seven years since I have been there, but I remember it like yesterday. The pattern of the door-mat, the pictures on the old music-box, the sound of the rocking-horse as it swung, the engravings on the stair, the smell of the Indian corn, and the feeling on plunging ones hands into the bin, the hooting of the turkeys and the quick flutter of the fantails' wings. I would not have it changed.

"**Sunday, April 20th, 1884**—*Judy,* the little lizard we brought from Ilfracombe, died on Sunday 20th. I have had a great deal of pleasure from that little Creature."[2]

Father had rented Dalguise House from 1871 to 1881 for the fishing, where from the age of five, she spent some of her happiest childhood days.

"**Thursday, May 8th, 1884**—Mamma back 8th. Quite uncertain for this summer, I am afraid there is a chance of going back to Dalguise. I feel an extraordinary dislike to this

From the tailor's shop in Westgate came a glow of light.... ■ (From *The Tailor of Gloucester* by Beatrix Potter. Illustrated by the author.)

idea, a childish dislike, but the memory of that home is the only bit of childhood I have left. It was not perfectly happy, childhood's sorrows are sharp while they last, but they are like April showers serving to freshen the fields and make the sunshine brighter than before.

"The place is changed now, and many familiar faces are gone, but the greatest change is in myself. I was a child then, I had no idea what the world would be like. I wished to trust myself on the waters and sea. Everything was romantic in my imagination. The woods were peopled by the mysterious good folk. The Lords and Ladies of the last century walked with me along the over grown paths, and picked the old fashioned flowers among the box and rose hedges of the garden.

"Half believing the picturesque superstitions of the district, seeing my own fancies so clearly that they became true to me, I lived in a separate world. Then just as childhood was beginning to shake, we had to go, my first great sorrow. I do not wish to have to repeat it, it has been a terrible time since, and the future is dark and uncertain, let me keep the past. The old plum tree is fallen, the trees are felled, the black river is an open hollow, the elfin castle is no longer hidden in the dark glades of Craig Donald Wood.

"I remember every stone, every tree, the scent of the heather, the music sweetest mortal ears can hear, the murmuring of the wind through the fir trees. Even when the thunder growled in the distance, and the wind swept up the valley in fitful gusts, oh, it was always beautiful, home sweet home, I knew nothing of trouble then.

"I could not see it in the same way now, I would rather remember it with the sun sinking, showing, behind the mountains, the purple shadows creeping down the ravines into the valley to meet the white mist rising from the river. Then, an hour or two later, the great harvest-moon rose over the hills, the fairies came out to dance on the smooth turf, the night-jar's eerie cry was heard, the hooting of the owls, the bat flitted round the house, roe-deer's bark sounded from the dark woods, and faint in the distance, then nearer and nearer came the strange wild music of the summer breeze.

"**Saturday, June 28th, 1884**—Mamma and papa went to Eastbourne to see Bertram. He is top of third Class. Papa seems to think him rather quiet, better that than talk nonsense. I wonder how he will turn out? Sometimes I am hopeful, sometimes I am feared. He has an absorbing interest, which is a very great help in keeping anyone straight. The best upbringing has sometimes failed in this family, and I am afraid that Bertram has *it* in him. Heaven grant it is not so, but I am afraid sometimes.

"It is a most terrible thing about the Ashworths, she was leaning down with her hands on her ears while he shot at a cat in the garden. She thought it was over, and looked up just in time to get the bullet through her head, and died instantly.... Then Mr. Sumner of Glossop had a very sudden end, being found dead in bed at the Midland Hotel. He had over two millions and left no will. One of his nearest relations, though a very distant one, is a Gloucestershire farmer....

(From the movie "Peter Rabbit and Tales of Beatrix Potter," copyright 1971, EMI Films Incorporated, released by MGM.)

"The cholera has got firm hold and is spreading in France. There was even a report yesterday that it had got to Paris, but this is not confirmed.

"**Friday, July 25th, 1884**—Bertram came home from school Friday 25th. He has got a prize for being top of the third Class. He seems very well, only rather inclined to say path, grāss.

"**Tuesday, September 16th, 1884**—Bertram went back to school September 16th leaving me the responsibility of a precious bat. It is a charming little creature, quite tame and apparently happy as long as it has sufficient flies and raw meat. I fancy bats are things most people are pleasingly ignorant about. I had no idea they were so active on their legs, they are in fact provided with four legs and two wings as well, and their tail is very useful in trapping flies.

"**Saturday, October 4, 1884**—It is all the same, drawing, painting, modelling, the irresistible desire to copy any beautiful object which strikes the eye. Why cannot one be content to look at it? I cannot rest, I must draw, however poor the result, and when I have a bad time come over me it is a stronger desire than ever, and settles on the queerest

things, worse than queer sometimes. Last time, in the middle of September, I caught myself in the back yard making a careful and admiring copy of the swill bucket and the laugh it gave me brought me round.

"**Monday, October 27, 1884**—There's no word about my painting just now, and I don't want any except for more time. I don't want lessons, I want practice. I hope it is not pride that makes me so stiff against teaching, but a bad or indifferent teacher is worse than none. It cannot be taught, nothing after perspective, anatomy and the mixing of paints with medium, which last experience will do best, but I do wish I knew if there is not some non-greasy, pasty article called *mun*.

"I am certain there is a liquid, colourless, non-transparent medium which goes on easily for the dead ground colours, and allows the paint above to stick easily. What are the canvasses primed with? What is drying oil? but that sounds greasy.

"**Saturday, November 15, 1884**—Went to the National Gallery. I have only been there once before, when a child, and had totally forgotten the building. though I have a vivid

**"And what are you dipping into the basin of starch?"
"They're little dicky shirt-fronts belonging to Tom
Titmouse—most terrible particular!"** ■ (From *The
Tale of Mrs. Tiggy-Winkle* by Beatrix Potter. Illustrated by the author.)

recollection of some of the pictures. It is strange how
deeply the mind is impressed when excited. I was just beginning to take interest in pictures then. We only had about
half-an-hour this afternoon, and went into the cellar to see
the Turner drawings, for which we had principally come.

"They are wonderfully clever and brilliant some of them,
but others are enigmas to every eye but their author. The
originals of the *Liber Studiorum* are beautifully designed
and executed, how remarkably like the originals the prints
are. I think Turner is the greatest landscape painter that
ever has lived, far superior to Claude or the Dutch
painters.

"There are some good De Wints in a dark back place and
Cattermole. I think our landscape school has gone off very
much. Went upstairs for a few minutes, looked at the old
Italian pictures. No one will read this. I say fearlessly that
the Michelangelo is hideous and badly drawn; I wouldn't
give tuppence for it except as a curiosity.

"**Friday, November 28th, 1884**—Went out with papa. First
to the French Gallery in the Tate, where there is a very fair
collection of pictures with very little rubbish, chief being
landscapes. . . .

" [Then] went on to the National Gallery . . . Swarms of
young ladies painting, frightfully for the most part, O dear,
if I was a boy and had courage! We did not see a single
really good copy. They are as flat and smooth as ditchwater. The drawing as a rule seems pretty good, but they
cannot have the slightest eye for colour. I always think I do
not manage my paint in that respect, but what I have seen
today gives me courage, in spite of depression caused by
the sight of the wonderful pictures.

"What I am troubled by is the inability to control my medium, but these copyists, content to work greasily with
camel hair brushes, paint with the greatest facility, and yet
can't colour in the least. If I could govern my paint I'd go
better. Age imparts to pictures a peculiar glow and mellowness, varying in different pictures from green or yellow to

orange, the first being the commonest, but, the stronger the
green tint of age, the more persistently do these young ladies
apply a kind of sickly chocolate which they seem to have
caught from one another. Their works certainly would be
the better for going up the chimney a bit. I cannot understand it, and they have such perfect self reliance, uncertainty always makes the colours muddy.

"**Wednesday, May 6th, 1885**—Exhibition opened. . . . Very
interesting though unfinished. How is it these high-heeled
ladies who dine out, paint and pinch their waists to deformity, can racket about all day long, while I who sleep
o'nights, can turn in my stays, and dislike sweets and dinners, am so tired towards the end of the afternoon that I
can scarcely keep my feet? It is very hard and strange, I
wonder if it will always be so?

"**Friday, July 10, 1885**—My education finished 9th. July.
Whatever moral good and general knowledge I may have
got from it, I have retained no literal rules. I don't believe I
can repeat a single line of any language. I have liked my
last governess best on the whole—Miss Carter had her
faults, and was one of the youngest people I have ever
seen, but she was very good-tempered and intelligent.

"I regret German very much, history I can read alone,
French is still going on, the rules of geography and
grammar are tiresome, there is no general word to express
the feelings I have always entertained towards arithmetic.

"**Thursday, December 31st, 1885**—New Years Eve, or
rather the last hours of 1885. How awful it seems at the end
of a year to think it has actually passed into space never to
return! Gone except its memories! Much bitterness and a
few peaceful summer days. Oh life, wearisome, disappointing, and yet in many shades so sweet, I wonder why one is
so unwilling to let go this old year? not because it has been
joyful, but because I fear its successors—I am terribly
afraid of the future. Some fears will inevitably be fulfilled,
and the rest is dark—Peace to the old year, may the seed
sown therein bear no bitter fruit!

"**December, 1886**—Bertram came up from school on July
29th. . . . We being in difficulties as to where to pass the
holidays, and my grandmother being quite unable to move
to Damfield, it was decided we should go there, taking our
own servants. This plan was not without drawback, but
succeeded on the whole. We stopped six weeks. The
weather was not however hot for August.

"Having always from childhood looked upon Camfield as a
palatial residence, it was a little startling to look behind the
scenes, not to mention into the drains, which were still
partially open. They had been found in a shocking state,
why no one ever had a fever, passes me.

"For the first ten days the house was wrong side up, with
plumbers and carpenters and painters. They were country
workmen who laid down a London system of pipes which
they apparently did not understand. I wonder why water
pipes always burst on Sunday? All the time we were there,
there was a periodical downpour through the ceiling of one
of the closets. The plumbers returned several times and
mended up the pipe with putty (!), which thawed gradually
during the week and gave way at precisely half past eight
on Sunday morning (one on Monday). . . .

"When the family are away the house is looked after by Mrs. Newberry, an aged woman who has someway got over my grandmother. Her dirtiness and general character were so nasty that I refrain from describing them. The first evening the maid-servants sat upon the kitchen table, the floor being in possession of inconceivable quantities of cockroaches.

"During the night [the butler] was nearly devoured by fleas, but that was easily explained by the discovery that Mrs. Newberry had used the butler's bed: but the most serious complaint was that of Jim the groom, who announced that in the small hours of the night, he had been set upon and awoke by B flats [bugs]. This being unfortunately true, the little room above the saddle room was sprayed with Keating's powder and shut up.

"However, it is ill complaining about a house that is lent to one, and I never, all things considered, passed a pleasanter summer. We had not two wet days during the six weeks we stayed there.

"On **October 18th, 1887** occurred the death of *Poor Miss Mouse,* otherwise *Xarifa.* I was very much distressed, because she had been so sensible about taking medicine that I thought she would get through, but the asthma got over her one night, and she laid herself out in my hand and died. Poor little thing, I thought at one time she would last as long as myself.

"I believe she was a great age. Her nose and eyebrows were white, and towards the end of her life she was quite blind, but affectionate and apparently happy. I wonder if ever another doormouse had so many acquaintances. . . .

Thursday, May 3rd, 1888—Went to see the Marton Hall pictures at Christie's. A splendid collection, selected with admirable taste, no rubbish and nothing vulgar. I understand this sale comprises only a third of the late Dr. Bolckow's Gallery, whether the cream of it I know not, if only an average, it is singularly high.

"The collector seems to have had a preference for animal painters, one of the leading pictures being Landseer's *Braemar.* It is of enormous size (177 inches x 99 inches) and very thinly painted, rather like scene-painting. At first, disappointed by the thinness of the colour, it struck me as less pleasing than the well-known engraving, but it looks better at a distance, when one gets accustomed to the size.

"I naturally fell to comparing this and the other Landseer with the great stag picture by Rosa Bonheur, charitably placed in another room. I think the Landseers come out badly. Setting apart the large Millais which is so different, to take in composition, Rosa Bonheur's Deer at Fontainebleau was the finest thing in the collection. This picture was not disfigured as were the other two Landseers by hotness of colour, and a certain horrible metallic green, as brilliant as ever pre-Raphaelite painted, but just as conventional as the old-fashioned drab that does duty in most pictures for grass. In the large Fontainebleau the colour if not striking was unobtrusive, the energy of the drawing marvellous.

"Landseer has painted a buck in the fangs of the hounds, but in the death-struggle it does not give one half the idea of fright that is conveyed in those unmolested animals slowly crossing the waste. It will lob over, and its eyes become glazed without an attempt to use its horns, and as to its heels, they are haunches of venison very different to the twitching nervous hinds whose legs seem half drawn back to strike.

"To any person who has handled a dead deer, especially a few hours after it has been shot, when rigid stiffening has to some extent supplied the tense resistance of life, the prevailing impression is of the wooden impracticability of the wiry legs. It is far more like an arrangement of walking-sticks than steaks.

"Our English artists, after Landseer's example, are so absorbed by the grace and suppleness of hoofed animals' legs, that they rather lose sight of the circumstances that the legs are primarily wooden pegs to support the body, the balanced springs superadded to give ease in motion. Not that I deny the great stag in *Braemar* stands on his feet. On the contrary, they are splayed out like a garden chair.

"**May, 1890**—[Bertram and I] decided that I should make a grand effort in the way of Christmas Cards, and if they fell flat, as usual, we would take the matter into our own hands. The cards were put under the plates at breakfast and proved a five minutes wonder. I referred to them the other day and found my uncle had forgotten their existence, but he added with laughable inconsistency that any publisher would snap at them. All the same I might have waited till doomsday before he would have moved a finger. He is a provoking person. Also we wanted a printing machine, price £16 which he regarded with even more languid interest.

"So in the beginning of February I began privately to prepare Six Designs, taking for my Model that charming rascal

"This is getting tiresome, I think I should like some lunch," said Mr. Jeremy Fisher. ■ (From *The Tale of Mr. Jeremy Fisher* by Beatrix Potter. Illustrated by the author.)

Benjamin Bouncer our tame Jack Hare—I may mention (better the day better the deed) that my best designs occurred to me in chapel—I was rather impeded by the inquisitiveness of my aunt, and the idiosyncrasies of Benjamin who has an appetite for certain sorts of paint, but the cards were finished by Easter, and we provided ourselves with five Publishers' addresses. I was prepared, at great expenditure of stamps, to send them all round the trade, but it was a shock, particularly to [Bertram], when they came back from Marcus Ward's by return of post. I had set upon Marcus Ward partly from patriotic grounds (nothing like fine motives), partly because I had toned the colours from one of their Almanacs. I said we would try Raphael Tuck last, it is such an absurd name to be under obligations to."

[Bertram] inclined to Hildesheimer & Faulkner, so we sent them there secondly, when he passed through town for his Oxford Exam. I wrote to him on Tuesday evening, advising him to lower the price to £4 and try De La Rue, *if,* as I had a presentiment, we saw the Cards again, so you see I did not *feel my property coming,* 'like her chops.'

"However, it came the following evening (May 14th) in a fat letter. . . . The envelope contained a cheque for £6 which I had to return to [Bertram] because he had omitted to sign it, and a very civil letter under the misapprehension that I was a gentleman, requiring me to send some more sketches.

"My first act was to give Bounce (what an investment that rabbit has been in spite of the hutches), a cupful of hemp seeds, the consequence being that when I wanted to draw him next morning he was partially intoxicated and wholly unmanageable.

"Then I retired to bed, and lay awake chuckling till 2 in the morning, and afterwards had an impression that Bunny came to my bedside in a white cotton night cap and tickled me with his whiskers.

"**Saturday, August 20th, 1892**—. . . Somewhat indisposed. After breakfast taking Mr. Benjamin Bunny to pasture at the edge of the cabbage bed with his leather dog-lead, I heard a rustling, and out came a little wild rabbit to talk to him, it crept half across the cabbage bed and then sat up on its hind legs, apparently grunting. I replied, but the stupid Benjamin did nothing but stuff cabbage. The little animal evidently a female, and of a shabby appearance, nibbling, advanced to about three straps length on the other side of my rabbit, its face twitching with excitement and admiration for the beautiful Benjamin, who at length caught sight of it round a cabbage, and immediately bolted. He probably took it for Miss Hutton's cat.

"**Sunday, August 21st, 1892**—Went into garden immediately after breakfast, but saw nothing of the wild rabbit except its tracks. Benjamin's mind has at last comprehended gooseberries, he stands up and picks them off the bush, but has such a comical little mouth, it is a sort of bob cherry business.

"Wrote picture-letters to the little Moores. There was a squirrel in the laburnum under the window mobbed by about thirty sparrows and some chaffinches, its fierce excited little movements reminded me of a monkey, but it did not get a spring at them.

"**Saturday, October 1st, 1892**—I trudged up the road at the back with the hand camera, in hopes of getting a harmless shot at the pretty roe-deer. The previous Thursday afternoon, being unprovided with the machine, I saw first a buck which bounced out of the fern 'cursing and swearing' as the local report hath it, like a collie dog with a sore throat. It walked leisurely up the road grunting and repeatedly uttering its hoarse indignant bark.

"I thought it had not gone far, and following cautiously, got another sight of it when it ran off. It had but poor horns and was as red as a fox.

"Finding this deer-stalking a pleasing excitement, I went on up the road stepping from clump to clump of moss, and taking an observation with every step. I was rewarded by the sight of the hind quarters of a roe feeding in a patch where the fern had been cut. It was a good way up on my left. . . .

"I stalked it with delightful success, getting across a hollow and up again, when suddenly I trod upon a stick: the roe's head being behind a tree I had time to become rigid before it looked up, and out came two hinds, lippity, lippity, like rabbits, startled by the noise, but not much frightened, and completely vague as to the point whence it came.

"They came straight at me and stopped in full view. The front one, perhaps in the line of the wind, walked up the wood suspiciously, though without seeing me.

"It is singular how defective the eyes, or more probably the minds of wild animals are for a stationary object. The slightest movement—but if you are motionless they will come close up, certainly not without seeing, but perhaps without focussing their observer.

"I often consider what an important factor the arrangement of the eyes must be in determining the amount of intellect in different animals. If a man examines any object intently, he stares straight at it, seeing it at once, and equally (as regards scope), with both eyes, but in a considerable proportion of animals, the two spheres of sight do not overlap at all, and in certain species, such as bats and rabbits, there is an absolute gap between the two planes of vision.

"Such a state of affairs would be a strain upon a human intellect, and, unless animal minds are more comprehensive than ours, they must either concentrate their attention on one eye at a time, or get a very superficial impression from both, the latter is probably the case. When preoccupied with feeding, they rely on their ears. It would follow logically that those whose eyes are most sideways would rely most on their ears, an interesting subject to work out. The overlapping in human sight is say 15° + 15° out of 60°.

"Whatever may have been the explanation of its behaviour, the hind was very pretty and curious, running about in the fern like a rabbit. It was much plagued with midges, (so was I), totally unprovided with tail which the fallows are always wagging. It flapped its ears and scratched itself with its tiny hind feet.

"When it went back to feed I crept up nearer, but overdid it at last, and it looked up, with a mouthful of wild sage. The plant hung out like a lettuce-leaf in a rabbit's mouth, and it would munch a moment and then stare, and munch again. When its mouthful was finished, it stretched its neck straight out and uttered a long single bleat, which it repeated presently, pumping up the sound from its flanks to judge by the way it heaved, then it took a header over the bank of fern disappearing into the wood with a twinkle of red and white.

"**Thursday, October 13th, 1892**—Account of Lord Tennyson's funeral. I should think no man ever had a more beautifully complete end. It has made a deep impression. There is only one person living whose death would cause the same universal, uncontradicted grief, may it be long distant, I mean the Queen. Or in a less degree, the Princess of Wales or Princess May.

"Mr. James Payne touching the subject with questioning taste in 'The Illustrated,' says Tennyson was one of the three greatest men, the other two being Bismarck and Gladstone. I once in print read a statement of the same sort which had the advantage of not being contradictable, namely, that these three were the only celebrities surviving whose obituary notices would overflow a page of *The Times*, I suppose new stars will arise.

"**Monday, October 24th, 1892**—To photograph Miss Culbard's cat, and had an experience I trust unique in the annals of photography, for when I was in the very act, the patient was overcome by sickness.

"**Sunday, October 30th, 1892**—I am ashamed to say I photographed in the wood. Perhaps it may have been atoned by an act of mercy after breakfast. When I was walking out Benjamin I saw Miss Hutton's black cat jumping on something up the wood. I thought it was too far off to interfere, but as it seemed leisurely I went up in time to rescue a poor little rabbit, fast in a snare.

"The cat had not hurt it, but I had great difficulty in slackening the noose round its neck. I warmed it at the fire, relieved it from a number of fleas, and it came round. It was such a little poor creature compared to mine. They are regular vermin, but one cannot stand by to see a thing mauled about from one's friendship for the race. Papa in his indignation pulled up the snare. I fancy our actions were much more illegal than Miss Hutton's.

"After dinner I was half amused, half shocked, to see her little niece . . . hunting everywhere for the wire. I just had enough sense not to show the stranger to Benjamin Bounce, but the smell of its fur on my dress was quite enough to upset the ill-regulated passions of that excitable buck rabbit.

"Whether he thought I had a rival in my pocket, or like a Princess in a Fairy Tale was myself metamorphosed into a white rabbit I cannot say, but I had to lock him up."[2]

1893. She had a prolific correspondence with children. One of her favourites was Noel Moore, the five year old son of one of her former governesses. To entertain him while he was ill, she sent many stories and illustrations. Her last letter began: "I don't know what to write to you, so I shall tell you the story about four little rabbits, whose names were Flopsy, Mopsy, Cottontail, and Peter. . . ."

Beatrix Potter in her pony carriage, 1889.

This, of course, became her first book. "It seems a long time ago and in another world that *Peter Rabbit* was written. Though after all the world does not change much in the country, where the seasons follow their accustomed course—the green leaf and the sere—and where Nature, though never consciously wicked, has always been ruthless. In towns there is change. People begin to burrow underground like rabbits. The lame boy for whom Peter was invented more than forty years ago is now an air warden in a bombed London parish.

"I have never quite understood the secret of Peter's perennial charm. Perhaps it is because he and his little friends keep on their way, busily absorbed with their own doings. They were always independent. Like Topsy—they just grow'd. Their names especially seemed to be inevitable. I never knew a gardener named 'McGregor.' Several bearded horticulturists have resented the nickname; but I do not know how it came about; nor why 'Peter' was called 'Peter.' There is great difficulty in finding or 'inventing' names void of all possible embarrassment. A few of the characters were harmless skits or caricatures; but 'Mr. McGregor' was not one of them, and the backgrounds of Peter Rabbit are a mixture of locality.

"'Squirrel Nutkin' lived on the shore of Derwentwater Lake near Keswick, and 'Mrs. Tiggywinkle' in the nearby valley of Newlands. 'Jemima Puddleduck,' 'Jeremy Fisher' and others lived at Sawrey in the southern part of the English Lake District. The earlier books, including the later printed *Pig Robinson*, were written for real children in picture letters of scribbled pen and ink. I confess that afterwards I painted most of the little pictures to please myself. The more spontaneous the pleasure, the happier the result.

"I do not remember a time when I did not try to invent pictures and make for myself a fairyland amongst the wildflowers, the animals, fungi, mosses, woods and streams, all the thousand objects of the countryside; that pleasant unchanging world of realism and romance, which in our northern climate is stiffened by hard weather, a tough ancestry, and the strength that comes from the hills." [From *The Horn Book* for March-April, 1944. Reprinted from a letter of Beatrix Potter's to *The Horn Book,* early in 1941 with permission of the Trustees of the Estate of Beatrix Potter.[3]]

"**Sunday, February 5th, 1893**—I went to the Pagets somewhat guilty. This comes of borrowing other people's pets. Miss Paget has an infinite number of guinea-pigs. First I borrowed and drew *Mr. Chopps.* I returned him safely. Then in an evil hour I borrowed a very particular guinea-pig with a long white ruff, known as *Queen Elizabeth.* This PIG—offspring of *Titwillow the Second,* descendant of the *Sultan of Zanzibar* and distantly related to a still more illustrious animal named the *Light of Asia*—this wretched pig took to eating blotting paper, paste-board, string and other curious substances, and expired in the night.

"I suspected something was wrong and intended to take it back. My feelings may be imagined when I found it extended a damp–very damp disagreeable body. Miss Paget proved peaceable, I gave her the drawing.

"**Tuesday, July 28, 1896**—I am thirty this day. I felt a certain irritation upon receiving congratulatory letters from the Hutton girls, for one thing I can never remember theirs. . . . I feel much younger at thirty than I did at twenty; firmer and stronger both in mind and body.

"**Tuesday, November 17, 1896**—I remember I used to half believe and wholly play with fairies when I was a child. What heaven can be more real than to retain the spiritworld of childhood, tempered and balanced by knowledge and commonsense, to fear no longer the terror that flieth by night, yet to feel truly and understand a little, a very little, of the story of life."[2]

1901. She enlarged the story of *Peter Rabbit* and sent it to Warne. They, along with several other firms turned it down. So she had it privately printed. After selling 250 copies, Warne changed their mind and agreed to publish the book if she would do color illustrations instead of the black and white drawings.

"Rabbits are creatures of warm volatile temperament but shallow and absurdly transparent. It is this naturalness, one touch of nature, that I find so delightful in Mr. Benjamin Bunny, though I frankly admit his vulgarity. At one moment amiably sentimental to the verge of silliness, at the next, the upsetting of a jug or tea-cup which he immediately takes upon himself, will convert him into a demon, throwing himself on his back, scratching and spluttering. If I can lay hold of him without being bitten, within half a minute he is licking my hands as though nothing has happened.

"He is an abject coward, but believes in bluster, could stare our old dog out of countenance, chase a cat that has turned tail.

"Benjamin once fell into an Aquarium head first, and sat in the water which he could not get out of, pretending to eat a piece of string. Nothing like putting a face upon circumstances.

1905. Became engaged to Norman Warne (of the publishing family) despite her parents opposition. Purchased her beloved farm "Hill Top" in the north country. Three days before Christmas, her fianceé died suddenly of pernicious anemia.

She signed herself "your affectionate sister" to Mildred Warne (Norman's sister) and wrote: "I am sending you a copy of the sketch I did the last evening in the barley field at Llanbehdr. [It was there Warne's marriage proposal had reached her.] I try to think of the golden sheaves, and harvest: he did not live long, but he fulfilled a useful happy life. I must try to make a fresh beginning next year."[1]

1913. Married William Heelis, a lawyer (solicitor). "I am very happy, and in every way satisfied with Willie. It is best now not to look back."[1]

As time passed, her prestige grew. To her American following she responded in an open and friendly manner: "Never, does anyone outside your perfidiously complimentary nation write to tell me that I write good prose . . . I think I write carefully because I enjoy my writing, and enjoy taking pains over it. I have always disliked writing to order; I write to please myself. . . . My usual way of writing is to scribble, and cut out, and write it again and again. The shorter and plainer the better. And read the Bible (unrevised version and Old Testament) if I feel my style wants chastening."[1]

Her father died at eight-one after a "miserable illness. . . . He was never patient of discomfort and his trials were very great."[1]

1918. Brother Bertram died quite suddenly. "I shall miss my brother sadly, we seldom met, but we wrote regularly . . . and we could help one another. I don't think I yet realize that Bertram is gone—in his prime, and in his usefulness . . . I do think he found true happiness in hard useful manual work. . . . He is buried like the Grasmere folk in the bend of a stream—a flowery graveyard with a ruined ivy-grown church, and graves of the Covenanters."[1]

As Mrs. William Heelis of Sawrey she became president-elect of the Herdwick Association (for the preservation of the ancient Herdwick breed of sheep) and one of the shrewdest farmers in the Lake Country. "You would laugh to see me, amongst the other old farmers, usually in a tavern, after a sheep fair."[1]

1932. Mother died. "My mother's life was a link with times that are passed away, though still vivid in our memory—the old leisurely pleasant days of stately carriage horses, and of the Keswick coach. Latterly she has lived so retired that modern changes have not much affected her. Her chief interests were her canaries, her needlework and her little dog. She was wonderfully clear in mind, but . . . I am glad that she is at rest."[1]

1936. "I do not resent older age, if it brings slowness it brings experience and weight. . . . It is a pity the wisdom and experience of old age are largely wasted.

Beatrix Potter's home, Hill Top, Sawrey.

"I mind it little—with one or two reservations. For one thing (to quote a friend) 'Thank God I have the seeing eye'—that is to say, as I lie in bed I can walk step by step over the fell and rough lands, seeing every stone and flower and patch of bog and cotton-grass where my old legs will never carry me again.

"Also . . . it is rather pleasing to be so much 'wiser' than quantities of young idiots.

"I began to assert myself at seventy. Work not ease was the secret of contentment; keeping the tools in one's hand. I would rather keep going till I drop—early or late—never mind what the work is, so long as it is useful and well done.

"I am sometimes surprised at myself, being contented, . . . I lift my eyes to the hills, and I am content to look at them from below. I married very happily. . . . What are the words in *The Tempest*? 'Spring come to you at the farthest, in the very end of the harvest . . .'"[1]

December 22, 1943. Beatrix Potter died at the age of seventy-seven: "The vastness of the fells covers all with a mantle of peace."[1]

FOR MORE INFORMATION SEE: Junior Book of Authors, edited by Kunitz and Haycraft, H. W. Wilson, 1934; Margaret Lane, *The Tale of Beatrix Potter: A Biography*, Warne, 1946, revised edition, 1968; Marcia Dalphin, "The Tale of Beatrix Potter," *Horn Book*, December, 1946; M. Lane, "On the Writing of Beatrix Potter's Life Story," *Horn Book*, December, 1946; Elizabeth R. Montgomery, *Story behind Great Books*, McBride, 1947; *Illustrators of Children's Books: 1744-1945*, Horn Book, 1947; Stanley J. Kunitz and Howard Haycraft, editors, *Junior Book of Authors*, Wilson, 2nd edition, 1951; (for children) Carolyn Sherwin Bailey, *A Candle for Your Cake*, Lippincott, 1952; Roger L. Green, *Tellers of Tales*, Ward, new edition, 1953, Watts, 1965; Beatrix Potter, *The Art of Beatrix Potter* (with an appreciation by Anne Carroll Moore and notes by Enid and Leslie Linder), Warne, 1955, 5th edition, revised, 1972; E. H. Stevens, "A Visit to Mrs. Tiggy-Winkle," *Horn Book*, April, 1958; A. Deksnis, "Beatrix Potter," *Elementary English*, November, 1958; Bertha Mahony Miller, "Beatrix Potter and Her Nursery Classics," reprinted in *A Horn Book Sampler on Children's Books and Reading*, edited by Norma R. Gryatt, Horn Book, 1959.

Marcus Crouch, *Beatrix Potter* (Bodley Monograph), Walck, 1961, revised edition, Bodley Head, 1969; Leslie Linder, "Beatrix Potter's Code Writing," *Horn Book*, April, 1963; Rumer Godden, "Imaginary Correspondence," *Horn Book*, August, 1963; Potter, *The Journal of Beatrix Potter from 1881-1897*, Warne, 1966; Potter, *The Beatrix Potter Centenary Catalog*, Warne, 1966; R. Godden, "Beatrix Potter," *Horn Book*, August, 1966; Maurice Sendak, "The Journal of Beatrix Potter," *Publishers Weekly*, July 11, 1966; M. Lane, *Purely for Pleasure*, Knopf, 1967; Brian Doyle, editor, *The Who's Who of Children's Literature*, Shocken Books, 1968; Lee Kingman and others, compilers, *Illustrators of Children's Books, 1957-1966*, Horn Book, 1968; P. B. Messner, "Beatrix Potter: Classic Novelist of the Nursery," *Elementary English*, March, 1968; (for children) Dorothy Aldis, *Nothing Is Impossible: The Story of Beatrix Potter*, Atheneum, 1969; Graham Greene, "Beatrix Potter," in *Collected Essays*, Viking, 1969.

L. Linder, *A History of the Writings of Beatrix Potter*, Warne, 1971; *The Linder Collection of the Works and Drawings of Beatrix Potter*, National Book League (London), 1971; R. Godden, *The Tale of the Tales: The Beatrix Potter Ballet* (with illustrations by Beatrix Potter and photographs from the film "The Tales of Beatrix Potter"), Warne, 1971; (for children) Norah Smaridge, *Famous Author-Illustrators for Young People*, Dodd, 1973; Ann M. Mayer, *Beatrix Potter*, Creative Educational Society, 1974; Margery Fisher, *Who's Who in Children's Books*, Holt, 1975.

RANDOLPH, Lieutenant J. H.
See ELLIS, Edward S(ylvester)

RAWLINGS, Marjorie Kinnan 1896-1953

PERSONAL: Born August 8, 1896, in Washington, District of Columbia; died December 14, 1953, in St. Augustine, Florida; buried in Antioch Cemetery; daughter of Frank R. (a patent attorney) and Ida May (Traphagen) Kinnan; married Charles Rawlings, 1919 (divorced, 1933); married Norton Sanford Baskin, October, 1941. *Education:* University of Wisconsin, A.B., 1918. *Home:* Cross Creek, Hawthorn, Florida.

CAREER: Publicity writer for Young Women's Christian Association (Y.W.C.A.), National Headquarters, 1918-19; assistant service editor of *Home Sector* magazine, 1919; newspaper writer with the *Louisville Courier-Journal,* Louisville, Kentucky, and the *Rochester Journal,* Rochester, New York, 1919-23; verse writer for United Features Syndicate, 1925-27; author, beginning 1931. Also owner and manager of a 72-acre orange grove in Florida. *Member:* Kappa Alpha Theta, Phi Beta Kappa.

AWARDS, HONORS: O. Henry Memorial Award, 1933, for the short story "Gal Young Un"; Pulitzer Prize, 1939, for *The Yearling;* LL.D., Rollins College, 1939; L.H.D., University of Florida, 1941; runner-up for the Newbery Medal, 1956, for *The Secret River;* Lewis Carroll Shelf Award, 1963, for *The Yearling.*

WRITINGS—All published by Scribner, except as noted: *South Moon Under* (novel), 1933; *Golden Apples* (novel), 1935; *The Yearling* (novel; illustrated by Edward Shenton), 1938, reissued with a study guide by Mary Louise Fagg and

...to feel the mystery of a seclusion that yet has shafts of light striking through it. This is the essence of an ancient and secret magic. It goes back, perhaps, to the fairy tales of childhood to Hansel and Gretel, to Babes in the Wood, to Alice in Wonderland, to all half-luminous places that pleased the imagination as a child. ■ (From *Cross Creek* by Marjorie Kinnan Rawlings. Illustrated by Edward Shenton.)

Marjorie Kinnan Rawlings

Edith Cowles, 1966, new edition (illustrated by N. C. Wyeth), 1939, reissued, 1968; *When the Whippoorwill—* (short stories), 1940, reprinted, N. S. Berg (Dunwoody, Georgia), 1973; *Cross Creek* (autobiographical sketches; illustrated by Edward Shenton), 1942, new edition (with introduction by Shirley Ann Grau), Time, 1966; *Cross Creek Cookery* (illustrated by Robert Camp), 1942 (published in England as *The Marjorie Kinnan Rawlings Cookbook: Cross Creek Cookery,* Hammond, 1960).

Jacob's Ladder (novella; illustrated by Jessie Ayers), University of Miami Press, 1950; *The Sojourner* (novel), 1953; *The Secret River* (novel; illustrated by Leonard Weisgard), 1955; *The Marjorie Rawlings Reader,* edited and with an introduction by Julia Scribner Bigham, 1956.

ADAPTATIONS—Movies: "The Yearling," starring Gregory Peck and Jane Wyman (135 min., 16mm, sound, b/w), Metro-Goldwyn-Mayer, 1946.

Recordings: "The Yearling," read by David Wayne, Eileen Heckart and Luke Yankee (two records or two cassettes), Caedmon.

SIDELIGHTS: **August 8, 1896.** Born in Washington D.C. (one brother). Father attorney in U.S. Patent office. Wintered in Washington, summered on family farm in Maryland. "I had known my maternal grandfather's Michigan farm, but there I was both guest and child, and the only duties were to gather the eggs from the sweet-smelling hayloft. I had known my father's Maryland farm, but that farm was his love, his escape from Washington governmental routine, and we lived there only in the too few summers. I had no duties there at all. There was only delight; the flowering locust grove; the gentle cows in pasture; Rock Creek, which ran, ten miles away from its Washington park, at the foot of the hill of the locusts, where my brother and I learned to swim and to fish for tiny and almost untakable fishes; long walks with my father through the woods where he hoped some day to build a home; jaunts with him behind Old Dan in the carriage, to the county seat of Rockville, or to buy mules at Frederick." [Marjorie Kinnan Rawlings, *Cross Creek,* Scribner's, 1942[1]]

1913. Father died. Moved to Madison, Wis.

1918. B.A. Degree from University of Wisconsin. Studied under William Ellery Leonard.

1919. Went to New York City. Worked for National Headquarters of YMCA as publicity writer. Married Charles Rawlings (college sweetheart). Moved to Rochester, N.Y.

1920-24. Wrote advertising and special articles for Louisville *Courier-Journal* and Rochester (N.Y.) *Journal.*

1928. Left husband, bought a 72-acre orange grove with 4,000 trees at Cross Creek, Hawthorn, Florida with her inheritance. Settled in to write. "Cross Creek is a bend in a country road, by land, and the flowing of Lochloosa Lake into Orange Lake, by water. We are four miles west of the small village of Island Grove, nine miles east of a turpentine still, and on the other sides we do not count distance at all, for the two lakes and the broad marshes create an infinite space between us and the horizon. We are five white families; 'Old Boss' Brice, the Glissons, the Mackays and the Bernie Basses; and two colored families; Henry Woodward and the Mickenses. People in Island Grove consider us just a little biggety and more than a little queer.

"We have chosen a deliberate isolation, and are enamored of it, so that to the sociable we give the feeling that St. Simeon Stylites on top of his desert pillar must have given the folk who begged him to come down and live among them. He liked the pillar or he would not have been there. Something about it suited his nature. And something about Cross Creek suits us—or something about us makes us cling to it contentedly, lovingly and often in exasperation, through the vicissitudes that have driven others away.

"There is of course an affinity between people and places. 'And God called the dry land Earth; and the gathering together of waters called He Seas; and God saw that it was good.' This was before man, and if there be such a thing as deeper in the core of us than any knowledge of our fellow beings. We were bred of earth before we were born of our mothers. Once born, we can live without mother or father, or any other kin, or any friend, or any human love. We cannot live without the earth or apart from it, and something is shrivelled in a man's heart when he turns away from it and concerns himself only with the affairs of men.

"And along with our deep knowledge of the earth is a preference of each of us for certain different kinds of it, for the earth is various as we are various. One man longs for the mountains, and does not even need to have been a child of the mountains to have this longing; and another man yearns for the valleys or the plains. A seaman I know said that he was making a great effort to assure himself of going to Hell, for the Bible says that in Heaven 'there shall be no more sea,' and Heaven for him is a place of great waters.

"We at the Creek need and have found only very simple things. We must need flowering and fruiting trees, for all of us have citrus groves of one size or another. We must need a certain blandness of season, with a longer and more beneficient heat than many require, for there is never too much sun for us, and through the long summers we do not complain. We need the song of birds, and there is none finer than the redbird. We need the sound of rain coming across the *hamaca,* and the sound of wind in trees—and there is no more sensitive Aeolian harp than the palm. The pine is good, for the needles brushing one another have a great softness, and we have the wind in the pines, too.

"We need above all, I think, a certain remoteness from urban confusion, and while this can be found in other places, Cross Creek offers it with such beauty and grace that once entangled with it, no other place seems possible to us, just as when truly in love none other offers the comfort of the beloved.

"For myself, the Creek satisfies a thing that had gone hungry and unfed since childhood days. I am often lonely. Who is not? But I should be lonelier in the heart of a city. . . . I walk at sunset, east along the road. There are no houses in that direction, except the abandoned one where the wild plums grow, white with bloom in springtime. I usually walk halfway to the village and back again. No one goes, like myself, on foot, except Bernie Bass perhaps, striding firmly in rubber boots with his wet sack of fish over

The tree that nourished me in a lean time is still here and will be as long as I can protect it from everything short of lightning. ■ (From *Cross Creek* by Marjorie Kinnan Rawlings. Illustrated by Edward Shenton.)

Old Julia made no protest. She had known claws before. ■ (From "The Yearling," copyright 1947 by Metro-Goldwyn-Mayer. Starring Jane Wyman and Gregory Peck.)

his shoulder. Sometimes black Henry passes with a mule and wagon, taking a load of lighter'd home to Old Boss; sometimes a neighbor's car, or the wagon that turns off toward the turpentine woods to collect the resin, or the timber truck coming out from the pine woods. The white folks call 'Hey!' and children wave gustily and with pleasure. A stranger driving by usually slows down and asks whether I want a lift. The Negroes touch a finger to their ragged caps or pretend courteously not to see me. Evening after evening I walk as far as the magnolias near Big Hammock, and home, and see no one.

"Folk call the road lonely, because there is not human traffic and human stirring. Because I have walked it so many times and seen such a tumult of life there, it seems to me one of the most populous highways of my acquaintance. I have walked it in ecstasy, and in joy it is beloved. Every pine tree, every gallberry bush, every passion vine, every joree rustling in the underbrush, is vibrant. I have walked it in trouble, and the wind in the trees beside me is easing. I have walked it in despair, and the red of the sunset is my own blood dissolving into the night's darkness. For all such things were on earth before us, and will survive after us, and it is given to us to join ourselves with them and to be comforted.

"When I first came to the Creek, I had for facilities one water faucet in the kitchen, a tin shower adjoining the Kohler shed and an outhouse. For the water faucet in the kitchen I was always grateful, for waterpumps at the Creek are all placed in relation to the well and with little or no concern with distance from the house. When Martha lived in the Mackay house she had no well, but had to carry water from the Creek itself. My outside shower was acceptable enough in summer, though it meant going damp over the sand to the house afterward. In cold weather—and you may believe the Chamber of Commerce that we have none or you may believe me that on occasion bird-baths have been frozen solid—in cold weather the outside shower was a fit device for masochistic monks. The icy spray that attacked the shoulders like splinters of fine glass was in the nature of a cross. I shall not forget the early Christmas afternoon, with six men gathered for dinner, the turkey savory in the oven, the pies cooling, the vegetables ready, the necessity if not the desire for the bath borne in on me, and the temperature at thirty-eight and dropping. I emerged shivering and snarled at the indifferent heavens, 'The first time I get my hands on cash money, so help me, I shall have a bathroom.'

"Because of the cold shower, open at the front to a wan-

A second wind seemed now to reach long muscular fingers through the wall of rain and scoop up everything in its path. It reached down his shirt and into his mouth and eyes and ears and tried to strangle him. ▪ (From *The Yearling* by Marjorie Kinnan Rawlings. Decorations by Edward Shenton.)

dering world, an unfriendly shower, I took to watching for rain like a tree-toad. For when the soft sluiceways of the skies opened and the lichened shingle roof shed the waters in a surge down the northwest sheltered corner of the house, I could strip and accept the benediction. When the day was hot the rain was cool. When the day was cool the rain was many degrees warmer, and as bland as perfumed bath powder. The water faucet and the shower, then, could be endured. It seemed to me that I had done nothing in all my life to deserve the outhouse.''[1]

1933. Divorced Charles Rawlings. First book, *South Moon Under* published. ''In the spring I knew that I should have the manuscript of a book completed by August. I wanted to take it my self to New York to consult over it with my editor. I had a hundred dollars with which to make the trip. I knew that if I did not put the hundred dollars in a place more difficult of access than a bank, August would find it gone. I converted it into five twenty-dollar gold pieces—this was before even the government began to bury

gold—and I went furtively along the fence toward the lakeside hammock in search of a hiding place. Under a fence post seemed a proper spot. I lined up one of the posts with a cedar tree, a palm and a pecan tree and dug deep. I put the gold in a covered jelly glass and the glass in a covered coffee tin. I filled in the hole, patted down the earth, scattered grass over the top, and went away as contented as a dog who has done an especially good job with a choice bone.

''The summer passed, the manuscript was finished, I was ready to go. I was to be driven in the grove truck to the village to catch my train. Somehow, things went wrong that morning, and I was busy until dangerously late. I decided to bathe and dress, then make a quick dash to dig up my buried treasure. The day was hot and steaming. The sun beat down mercilessly and the sand gnats swarmed and stung. I thrust my spade deep beside the fence post that lined up with a cedar tree, a palm and a pecan. I dug

(Claude Jarman, Jr. on the set of "The Yearling."
Copyright © 1971 by Metro-Goldwyn-Mayer, Inc.)

deeper. There was nothing there. I backed off and studied the terrain. Five posts lined up with a cedar tree, a palm and a pecan. I excavated all five in a frenzy. There was no coffee tin, there was no jelly glass, there was no gold. I stood dripping and frustrated in my best clothes. Then I began digging all over again, three times as deep as I had remembered doing the burying. Under a fence post that did not appear to line up with anything at all, my spade struck the disintegrated coffee tin and the jelly glass, full of water and tarnished gold pieces. I swung on the train at the last possible instant and paid for my ticket with money that to all appearances had been buried during the Civil War, held tightly in a grimy paw. I was wet, dirty and dishevelled, and neat passengers stared at me.

"I longed to say haughtily, 'My good people, you have no conception of the difficulties I have encountered in being here at all.'"[1]

1938. *The Yearling* published. Won Pulitzer Prize the following year.

1941. Married Norton Sanford Baskin, a Florida hotel man and moved to St. Augustine, Florida.

1953. *The Sojourner* published. Suggested by memories of her grandfather. Began work on biography of Ellen Glasgow.

December 4, 1953. Died in St. Augustine of a cerebral hemorrhage. "It is more important to live the life one wishes to live, and to go down with it if necessary, quite contentedly, than to live more profitably but less happily."[1]

HOBBIES AND OTHER INTERESTS: "Cookery is my one vanity and I am a slave to any guest who praises my culinary art. This is my Achilles heel. Dorothy Parker has a delightful verse dealing with the abuse she is willing to take from her beloved, and ending, 'But say my verses do not scan, and I get me another man.' For my part, my literary ability may safely be questioned as harshly as one wills, but indifference to my table puts me in a rage.

"My recognition of cookery as one of the great arts was not an original discovery, but it is as important a one for the individual woman as the discovery of love. My mother and her mother had been famous cooks. When I read Della Lutes' *A Country Kitchen,* I wept in nostalgia for my Michigan grandmother's dinner table. My mother was as great a cook, but there was a taint on her art, for she did not consider it a notable accomplishment and she refused to teach me. Also, she worked so hard at it, with so little joy, no matter how capable a maid stood at her side, that she was exhausted, with a migraine headache, when a special feast was ready, and could not touch any of the magnificent dishes.

"I watched her in the kitchen with utter fascination, and since she apparently used no recipes, but combined her inherited knowledge with her own natural gift, I came to the secret conclusion that cooking was a matter of instinct, and that surely it must be in my blood. This belief was as fatuous as the belief of most people that they could write if they cared to take the time for it.

"My instinctive cooking proved, in my maturity, a thing of horror. It bore no relation to that of my mother and my grandmother. The climax was dual, two shocks following closely on each other. One night at dinner a plate of tomato mayonnaise salad was heaved at my head. There was nothing wrong with the salad, but every other dish on the table was inedible. I began to wonder if heredity might not be a snare and a delusion. A week later my mother-in-law came to visit, and while she ate my meals gracefully, courageously and without comment, she had no sooner returned to her home than there came to me in the mail a copy of the

It seemed to Jody that he was alone with his father. ■ (From *The Yearling* by Marjorie Kinnan Rawlings. Illustrated by N. C. Wyeth.)

Boston Cook Book, even ahead of the conventional bread and butter letter.

"I was not offended, but grateful, and I studied Fanny Farmer as a novitiate the prayer book. Lo and behold, my memories of my mother's dishes suddenly fitted in with the new exactness and I could duplicate her secret recipes, her heart-melting egg croquettes, her chicken in aspic, her potato puffs, her white almond cake. Science, art and instinct joined hands in a happy ring-around-the-rosy. I had solid rock under me. I have often thought that if I should be quite destitute, provided I had a modicum of health, I should enjoy making my living as a cook, but it would have to be in an establishment where the cream and butter and cooking sherry were not stinted, for life at the Creek with Jersey cows has unfitted me for skimmed milk and margarine. And I should buy cooking sherry with my last dollar.

"The new foods that I found in Florida were a challenge and I have learned more about cookery in my years at the Creek than in those that preceded them. Some of my best dishes are entirely native and local and I shiver with delight when a stranger pokes at something and asks dubiously, 'What is it?' then, urged to taste, is wreathed with smiles and says, 'It's good, even if it's rattlesnake.' Rattlesnake is of course eaten as a delicate hors d'oeuvre, but of all the queer things I have served or eaten, this alone is not among them. It is sheer prejudice, no doubt, but I know too well the heavy, rolling black and yellow bodies to relish a morsel from their midriffs."[1]

FOR MORE INFORMATION SEE: Marjorie Kinnan Rawlings, *Cross Creek,* Scribners, 1942; Robert Van Gelder, *Writers and Writing,* Scribner, 1946; "Marjorie Kinnan Rawlings Wins Important Case in Florida Courts, *Publishers Weekly,* June 29, 1946; Elizabeth Rider Montgomery, *Story behind Modern Books,* Dodd, 1949; John Cournos and H.S.N.K. Cournos, *Famous Modern American Novelists,* Dodd, 1952; L. Nichols, "A Talk with Mrs. Rawlings," *New York Times Book Review,* February 1, 1952; G. E. Bigelow, "Marjorie Kinnan Rawlings' Wilderness," *Sewanee Review,* Spring, 1965; Bigelow, *Frontier Eden: The Literary Career of Marjorie Kinnan Rawlings,* University of Florida Press, 1966; Bigelow, compiler, "Marjorie Kinnan Rawlings," in *Bibliographical Guide to the Study of Southern Literature,* edited by Louis D. Rubin, Jr., Louisiana State University Press, 1969; de Montreville and Hill, editors, *Third Book of Junior Authors,* H. W. Wilson, 1972.

Obituaries: *New York Times,* December 16, 1953; *Publishers Weekly,* December 26, 1953; *Newsweek,* December 28, 1953; *Time,* December 28, 1953; *Saturday Review,* January 16, 1954; *Wilson Library Bulletin,* February, 1954; *Americana Annual,* 1954; *Britannica Book of the Year 1954; Current Biography Yearbook 1954.*

RICHARDS, Laura E(lizabeth Howe) 1850-1943

PERSONAL: Born February 27, 1850, in Boston, Massachusetts; died January 14, 1943; daughter of Samuel Gridley Howe (author, teacher, and philanthropist) and Julia (Ward) Howe (author of "The Battle Hymn of the Republic"); married Henry Richards (an architect and illustrator), June 17, 1871; children: Alice Maude, Rosalind, Henry Howe, Julia Ward, Maud, John, Laura Elizabeth. *Education:* Tutored at home by private teachers, later attended local schools. *Home:* Gardiner, Maine.

CAREER: Author of books for children; poet; biographer. *Awards, honors:* Pulitzer Prize for biography (shared with sister, Maude Howe Elliott), 1917, for *Julia Ward Howe.*

WRITINGS—Stories for children: *The Little Tyrant,* Estes, 1880; *Our Baby's Favorite,* Estes, 1881; *Sketches and Scraps* (illustrated by husband, Henry Richards), Estes, 1881, reprinted, University Microfilms, 1967; *The Joyous Story of Toto* (illustrated by E. H. Garrett), Roberts Brothers, 1885; (editor) *Four Feet, Two Feet, and No Feet; or, Furry and Feathery Pets, and How They Live* (nonfiction), Estes and Lauriat, 1886; (reteller) *Beauty and the Beast* (illustrated by G. Browne), Roberts Brothers, 1886; (reteller) *Hop o' My Thumb* (illustrated by Browne), Roberts Brothers, 1886; (with H. Baldwin) *Kasper Kroak's Kaleidoscope* (illustrated by A. Hochstein), H. B. Nims, 1886; *Tell-Tale from Hill and Dale* (illustrated by Hochstein), H. B. Nims, 1886; *Toto's Merry Winter,* Roberts Brothers, 1887; *Queen Hildegarde: A Story for Girls,* Estes, 1889.

Captain January, Estes & Lauriat, 1891, new edition (illustrated by Frank T. Merrill), 1893, later published with *The Little Colonel* by Annie Fellows Johnston (illustrated from the motion pictures featuring Shirley Temple), Random House, 1959; *Hildegarde's Holiday: A Sequel to Queen Hildegarde,* Estes & Lauriat, 1891; *Hildegarde's Home,* Estes & Lauriat, 1892; *Glimpses of the French Court: Sketches from French History* (nonfiction), Estes & Lauriat, 1893; *Melody: The Story of a Child,* Estes & Lauriat, 1893; *Narcissa; or, The Road to Rome [and] In Verona,* Estes & Lauriat, 1894; *Marie,* Estes & Lauriat, 1894; *Five Minute Stories* (illustrated by A. R. Wheelan, E. B. Barry, and others), Estes & Lauriat, 1895; *Hildegarde's Neighbors,* Estes & Lauriat, 1895; *Jim of Hellas; or, In Durance Vile [and] Bethesda Pool,* Estes and Lauriat, 1895; *Nautilus,* Estes & Lauriat, 1895.

Isla Heron (illustrated by Frank T. Merrill), Estes & Lauriat, 1896; *Some Say [and] Neighbours in Cyrus,* Estes & Lauriat, 1896; *Hildegarde's Harvest,* Estes & Lauriat, 1897; *Three Margarets* (illustrated by E. B. Barry), Estes & Lauriat, 1897; *Love and Rocks,* Estes & Lauriat, 1898; *Margaret Montfort* (illustrated by E. B. Barry), Estes, 1898, reprinted, 1968; *Rosin the Beau: A Sequel to "Melody" and "Marie,"* Estes & Lauriat, 1898; *Chop-Chin and the Golden Dragon,* Little, Brown, 1899; *The Golden-Breasted Kootoo,* Little, Brown, 1899; *Peggy* (illustrated by E. B. Barry), Estes, 1899; *Quicksilver Sue* (illustrated by W. D. Stevens), Century, 1899.

For Tommy, and Other Stories, Estes, 1900, reprinted, Books for Libraries, 1970; *Snow-White; or, The House in the Wood,* Estes, 1900; *Rita* (illustrated by E. B. Barry), Estes, 1900; *Fernley House* (illustrated by Barry), Estes, 1901; *Geoffrey Strong,* Estes, 1901; *The Hurdy-Gurdy,*

Estes, 1902; *Mrs. Tree*, Estes, 1902; *The Golden Windows: A Book of Fables for Young and Old*, Little, Brown, 1903; *The Green Satin Gown* (illustrated by E. B. Barry), Estes, 1903; *More Five Minute Stories* (illustrated by Wallace Goldsmith), Estes, 1903; *The Merryweathers* (illustrated by daughter, Julia Ward Richards), Estes, 1904; *The Armstrongs* (illustrated by J. W. Richards), Estes, 1905; *Mrs. Tree's Will*, Estes, 1905; *The Silver Crown: Another Book of Fables*, Little, Brown, 1906; *Grandmother: The Story of a Life That Never Was Lived*, Estes, 1907; *The Pig Brother, and Other Fables and Stories*, Little, Brown, 1908; *The Wooing of Calvin Parks*, Estes, 1908.

A Happy Little Time: A Partly-True Story for Children of Betty's Age, Estes, 1910; *Up to Calvin's* (illustrated by F. T. Merrill), Estes, 1910; *On Board the Mary Sands* (illustrated by Merrill), Estes, 1911; *The Little Master*, Estes, 1913, also published as *Our Little Feudal Cousin of Long Ago, Being the Story of the Little Master, Alan of Morven, a Boy of Scotland, in the Time of Robert the Second*, Page, 1922; *Miss Jimmy*, Estes, 1913; *Three Minute Stories* (illustrated by Josephine H. Bruce), Page, 1914; *The Pig Brother Play-Book*, Little, Brown, 1915; *Fairy Operettas* (illustrated by Mary Robertson Bassett), Little, Brown, 1916; *Pippin: A Wandering Flame*, Appleton, 1917; *A Daughter of Jehu*, Appleton, 1918.

Honor Bright: A Story for Girls (illustrated by F. T. Merrill), Page, 1920; *In Blessed Cyrus*, Appleton, 1921; *The Squire*, Appleton, 1923; *Seven Oriental Operettas*, W. H. Baker, 1924; *Honor Bright's New Adventure* (illustrated by Elizabeth R. Withington), Page, 1925; *Star Bright: A Sequel to "Captain January"* (illustrated by F. T. Merrill), Page, 1927; *Harry in England; Being the Partly-True Adventures of H. R. in the Year 1857* (illustrated by Reginald Birch), Appleton, 1937.

Verse: *Five Mice in a Mouse-Trap. By the Man in the Moon. Done in the Vernacular, from the Lunacular* (illustrated by Kate Greenaway, Addie Ledyard, and others), Estes, 1880; *In My Nursery*, Roberts Brothers, 1890; *Sun Down Songs*, Little, Brown, 1899; *The Piccolo*, Estes, 1906; *To Arms! Songs of the Great War*, Page, 1918; *Tirra Lirra: Rhymes Old and New* (Junior Literary Guild selection; foreword by May Lamberton Becker; illustrated by Marguerite Davis), Little, Brown, 1932, later edition with foreword by May Hill Arbuthnot, 1955; *Merry-Go-Round: New Rhymes and Old* (preface by Margaret Widdemer; illustrated by Winifred E. Lefferts), Appleton-Century, 1935; *I Have a Song to Sing You: Still More Rhymes* (illustrated by Reginald Birch), Appleton-Century, 1938; (author of lyrics and music) *The Hottentot and Other Ditties* (piano accompaniments by Twining Lynes), Schirmer, 1939.

Biography: *When I was Your Age* (autobiographical), Estes & Lauriat, 1894; *Florence Nightingale, Angel of the Crimea: A Story for Young People*, Appleton, 1909, later edition edited by Rowena Keith Keyes, 1931; *Two Noble Lives: Samuel Gridley Howe and Julia Ward Howe*, Estes, 1911; *Elizabeth Fry: The Angel of the Prisons*, Appleton, 1916, dramatic adaptation by Rosalie Regen published as *The Seven Sisters* (one-act play based on *Elizabeth Fry* by Laura E. Richards and on *Elizabeth Fry* by Janet Whitney), Friends Publication Board (Richmond, Indiana), 1956; (with sister, Maud Howe Elliott) *Julia Ward Howe, 1819-*

Laura Richards, early 1870's.

1910, Houghton, 1915, reprinted, N. S. Berg, 1970; *Abigail Adams and Her Times*, Appleton, 1917, reprinted, Plutarch Press, 1971; *Joan of Arc*, Appleton, 1919; *Laura Bridgman: The Story of an Opened Door*, Appleton, 1928; *Stepping Westward* (autobiography), Appleton, 1931; *Samuel Gridley Howe*, Appleton-Century, 1935; *E.A.R.* (Edward Arlington Robinson), Harvard University Press, 1936, reprinted, Russell & Russell, 1967.

Other: (Editor) *The Letters and Journals of Samuel Gridley Howe*, Estes, Volume I, 1906, Volume II, 1909; *Acting Charades*, W. H. Baker, 1924; *What Shall the Children Read?* (illustrated by C. B. Falls), Appleton-Century, 1939; (edited by others) *Laura E. Richards and Gardiner* (papers by the author), Gannett Publishing, 1940. Also editor of *The Greek Revolution*, 1906.

Contributor of stories and verse to various periodicals, including *St. Nicholas*, *Atlantic Monthly*, and *Century Magazine*.

ADAPTATIONS—Movies: "Captain January," starring Baby Peggy (60 min., 16mm, silent, b/w), Principal, 1924, starring Shirley Temple (75 min., 16mm, sound, b/w), Twentieth-Century Fox, 1936.

SIDELIGHTS: "I was born in Boston, Massachusetts, on the 27th of February, 1850, being the fourth child and third daughter of Samuel Gridley and Julia Ward Howe. My father was Director . . . of the Perkins Institution and Massachusetts School for the Blind. . . . My mother, an earnest student of literature and philosophy, was preparing her first volume of poems, *Passion Flowers,* which appeared a few years later. She had not at this time taken up the active public service which characterized her later years, but was devoted to study and reflection.

"My eldest sister, Julia Romana (so named from having been born in Rome) was six years old when I was born; Florence, the namesake and god-daughter of Florence Nightingale, was four; Henry Marion was two.

It was New Year's Eve, but the tramp did not know that. He was tired and hungry. ■ (From *For Tommy and Other Stories* by Laura E. Richards. Illustrated by F. T. Merrill.)

"In order to give some idea of this growing family, it may be well to begin by describing the various domiciles that held it. The first was Green Peace (so named by my mother) in South Boston. . . . This was the original house round which my earliest recollections centre. Sometime in the Fifties my father found it insufficient for his growing family, and built the New Part; it remained . . . until a Street Commission swept house garden and all out of existence. I linger about Green Peace, loth to leave it. I have been describing it ever since I began to write, first in *Five Mice in a Mouse-trap,* again in *When I was Your Age.*" [Laura E. Richards, *Stepping Westward,* Appleton and Co., 1931.[1]]

"My father had a passion for change, and we were wisked about from place to place, often from motives that we never knew. Between moves, we were apt to spend weeks or months at the Perkins Institution for the Blind. . . . In the Institution one wing was set apart for my father's use and was known as the Doctor's Part; here we children lived from time to time, a rather breathless sort of life, I seem to think, never exactly taking root, floating, rather like joyous little sea-creatures, on the full tide of Institution life.

"[An] Institution friend was Laura Bridgman, for whom I was named. As a child, I did not think of the wonder of her, any more than of that of sunrise, or a tree, or any other miracle. She was Laura; she was blind, deaf and dumb; Papa had brought her out of prison, into communication with her fellow-beings, the first blind deaf-mute ever so brought. What then? It was the kind of thing Papa did.

"When one went into his office—wonderful room, full of delights and mysteries—and said, 'May I have a shock, please, Papa?' the bright blue eyes looked up, the smile broke, brightening the whole room; the Affairs of Importance—State Charities, Perkins Institution, Prison Discipline, Free Soil, Deaf-Mutes, Feeble-minded, or whatever—were laid aside; one was given a handle; Papa turned the knob; the lightning leaped—oh, terror! oh, joy!—but the numbing thrill of the Leyden jar brought no surprise that I can recall. Nature: Papa: both were primal forces: one saw little difference between them. So in the case of Laura! I did not realize that the opening of that door was a step onward and upward in the history of education.

"[The blind] could do so infinitely many things that I could not. As my fingers fumbled awkwardly over the piano keys, I could hear them playing brilliantly in the next practising room. They read so well, their fingers passing as swiftly (or so it seemed) along the raised letters of their printed page as my eyes along the black and white of mine. They sewed so beautifully; such tiny, even stitches! and to see a blind girl thread a needle, with just a touch of the tip of her tongue! talk of miracles! Even in the matter of stringing beads, they far excelled me; witness the fairy-like baskets, chains, purses, my envy and admiration."[1]

The Howe Children had governesses, masters, and later went to school, but they always delighted in the teachings of their parents. "My mother's singing formed an important part in our education. She had a beautiful soprano voice. . . . When we gathered delightedly round the piano at Green Peace and in all the other houses we came to know and love, we soon began to sing with her [German, French,

(From the movie "Captain January," copyright 1936, Twentieth-Century Fox. Starring Shirley Temple.)

and Italian songs]. We never knew we were studying French, German and Italian; that we were acquiring a vocabulary. . . . When we went to school our teachers realized it as I have been given to understand, as did those of our children in their turn. We all sang more or less . . . except my dear father, who had but two songs, 'Hail to the Chief' and 'Oh Susanna.' We could tell by words and *tempo* which he was singing.

"My mother has often told me that one day, when I was about four years old she found me lying on the floor with a book before me, turning the pages carefully and reciting the ballad of 'Fair Annie of Lochroyan.' On being interrogated, I said I was reading. I have been reading ever since. . . . I would rather read poetry than eat my dinner any day. It has been so all my life. . . .

"My general idea, as I look back through the years, seems to have been, if you see a book read it, especially if it is poetry! My education would seem to stand on a solid foundation of fairy stories, romance and poetry with more or less history tucked in here and there by way of mortar. Pondering these things, I seem to hear the kind voice of my good brother-in-law, the learned Professor saying 'My dear Laura, mathematics, chemistry and physics are the tripod

on which modern education stands.' Alas! But what a good time I had!

1861. Brother, Sam, died of diphtheria.

"It must have been in 1861 that we moved to 13 Chestnut Street. [Then to 19 Boylston Place. Where] I recall . . . the fire, a terror by night which narrowly escaped being a serious disaster. I remember clearly how, when it was well under way, and my father, looking exactly like a figure out of *The Tale of Two Cities* with a striped nightcap over one ear (I cannot imagine why he wore a nightcap, his hair was thick and heavy as a youth's), was hewing away with an axe at the charred and smoking timbers, there came a ring at the front doorbell. I opened the door, and there was my dear brother-in-law to be, George Richards, in irreproachable evening dress, saying with calm courtesy, 'I beg your pardon! Have you a fire here?'

"'Yes, I said, 'won't you come in?'

"And in he came, and in came his four brothers, and set to work valiantly to extinguish the conflagration, which but for their help might have proved serious enough.

White wings over the water,
Fluttering ever farther away.
Dark clouds shrouding the sunbeams,
Sullen and cold and gray.
Back I go in my calico gown,
Back to the hut in the fishing town
And oh! but the night shuts darkly down
After the summer day.

(From *Sketches and Scraps* by Laura E. Richards.
Illustrated by Henry Richards.)

"The Richards brothers were objects of interest to us all;
stalwart, handsome, always perfectly dressed, coming and
going, silent, aloof, mysterious. . . . Harry, the youngest,
had been at dancing school with me . . . but he was shy,
and so was I. I knew he had rosy cheeks and bright blue
eyes, and that he was tall and broad-shouldered, like the
others. I knew no more about him, till I met him on the
upper stairs, he carrying a silver cup, I with my arms filled
with my Christmas presents. It has always seemed to me
curious that he and I occupied adjoining rooms in the two
houses. Had we but known it, he could have bored a hole
from his closet to mine, and we could have played Pyramus
and Thisbe.''[1]

"In March of **1867,** my father sailed for Europe, taking
with him my mother, my sister Julia, and me.

"In the winter of **1869,** Henry Richards and I became engaged. We were young; we had no special prospects, financially speaking. . . . We waited two years before thinking of
marriage. . . . We came to know each other very well. Finally, we were married on **June 17th 1871,** and the Boston
bells rang, and cannons were fired on the Boston Common,
and there were fireworks in the evening. [It was Bunker
Hill Day]''[1]

1871. The newlyweds sailed for Europe. "And when the
pleasant pilgrimage was over, what next? My first housekeeping; my first loaf of bread; my first quince marmalade;
my first Baby. Here begins a whole library of volumes,
bound for the most part in lively colors; how condense
them? Four years saw the birth of the first three of my
seven children, Alice, Rosaline and Henry Howe; saw,
contemporary with these births, the acquisition of my
hurdy gurdy. Ballads and songs and the like, early assimi-
lated, had given me a good ear for metre and rhythm (say
jingle, woman, and have done with it!). I had always
rhymed easily; now, with the coming of the babies, and the
consequent weeks and months of quiet, came a prodigious
welling up of rhymes, mostly bringing their tunes (or what
passed for tunes; the baby, bless it, knew no better!) with
them. I wrote, and sang, and wrote, and could not stop.
The first baby was plump and placid, with a broad, smooth
back which made an excellent writing desk. She lay on her
front, across my lap; I wrote on her back, the writing pad
quite as steady as the writing of jingles required.

"I may as well say at once that my elder sisters called me
'Donkey-fingers.' I could set fine stitches; yes, and make
good button-holes; further than this I never went, except
once. By and by, when my first baby came, I felt that every
canon of duty and propriety demanded that I should make
her a dress; cut and make it all myself. I did, and she wore
it, poor lamb, being unable to defend herself; but after that
I said to myself, 'Whatever your hands were made for, it
was not this!' I laid down the scissors and took up the pen.

"There was much merrymaking at Green Peace in those
days. . . . My mother was studying Greek, and beginning to
be interested in Women's Suffrage—which she had until
then regarded with aversion—and in Peace Congresses. . . .

"In spite of all the laughter and singing, the shadows were
gathering round Green Peace. . . . [My father] laid down
his arms a few weeks before the birth of my eldest boy. He
had done justice, loved mercy, and walked humbly with his
God, close upon seventy-five years; the blade was worn
through, and snapped quietly.''[1]

1876. Her husband's architectural business flourished
during this time, however—"The Finger, having written,
moved on. There came one of those periodic depressions
which now and then mysteriously occur in the profession of
Architecture; and coincident herewith, an urgent request
. . . that my husband should leave Boston and join . . . in
the management of the family paper mill. . . . The decision—a momentous one for the young couple with their
three little children—was made. In the summer of 1876 we
moved to Gardiner, Maine.

"With all my love of the country, with all my passion for
Green Peace and the Valley, and the sea, I was still a city
child. I had—in some ways—the prying mind, but not 'the
waking eye'; *e.g.,* I knew that 'the soodspurge hath a cup
of three,' because Rossetti told me so, not because I had
ever recognized it. My daughter finds a four-leaved clover
whenever she looks down; I have never found one, and
never shall. I saw a butterfly; saw it brilliant, lovely, a
marvel for poets to sing and painters to paint; I did not
know the number of spots on those shining wings, nor the
kind of chrysalis it came out of, nor the time and season of
its hibernation. I saw a bird, and rejoiced in its swift grace
and beauty; it sang, and my heart was lifted up. But I did

not know the shape and position and color of every feather, from crest to tail; or the number or color of its eggs; no, nor the precise range and quality of its notes.

"Is that a song sparrow, dear? I still ask, humbly yet hopefully. I am *so* pleased if the answer is 'Yes!' but it may just as well be, 'No, dear! it is a robin!' "[1]

Moved to the Yellow House in Gardiner. "It was clear that a young and growing family could not continue indefinitely to 'visit round' (we call it 'bange' in Maine) among relations however delightful. We must find a nest of our own. This was not so easy; our requirements were many, and did not always 'conjingle,' to use another Maine word which explains itself. We must be 'on the river,' we must have plenty of space, indoors, and out; we must have this and that and the other. In short, we were like most other young people, demanding the moon, and the stars to boot. At long last we found this house in which I write—and lucky we were to do so—a square 'Colonial' house, with ell and barn, large chimneys, and open fireplace in every room, and even more important an acre of lawn and garden for our delight. We bought the house; and painted it yellow. After the first painting, I was stepping along the bordering street one day, casting side glances of pleasurable pride at the warm, friendly pumpkin-color which brightened the Corner.

" 'Look at the color they've put on that house!' said one of two men walking in front of me. 'Ain't that disgustin'!' And I learned about colors from him.

"In those early years of the Yellow House, I hardly made more than a beginning, and that a feeble one, of knowing anything about the town itself. This was owing chiefly to the advent, and thereafter the care of the children. My husband was busy all day long at the Paper Mill, a mile away, making paper; my babies were coming and growing; life became with every year more wonderful and entrancing. Moreover, the hurdy gurdy turned ever faster and faster, each new baby requiring a new output of jingles. I began to write stories, too; first for children, later for girls, later still for grown people."[1]

"Then it can fit none but you, Senorita Perfecta!" cried Rita." ■ (From *Three Margarets* by Laura E. Richards. Illustrated by Ethelred B. Barry.)

He was conscious only of a friendly feeling of compassion for the fair young creature, built for vigour and an active life, now condemned for months, it might be years, of weariness and pain. ■ (From *Geoffrey Strong* by Laura E. Richards. Illustrated by Frank T. Merrill.)

1880. "All this time I had been writing books. My first book was published . . . *Five Little Mice in a Mouse Trap*, a book which I am glad to find children still reading. The children in it were for the most part as imaginary as the Man in the Moon, who in his own fantastic way (I was nothing if not fantastic in those days) tells the story: yet there may be traces here and there of my own children's words and ways, possibly of those of myself and Brother Harry, twenty-odd years before.

"This was followed in **1881** by *Sketches and Scraps*, the only one in which [my husband] and I worked together, he illustrating the rhymes as I wrote them. In a moment of folly, now hardly credible to me, I consented, some years later to the destruction of the plates of this book, and have regretted it ever since. The pictures were in bright colors, and had a quality of their own which endeared them to children.

Laura E. Richards

"Next came, in **1885**, the editing and largely the writing, of *Four Feet, Two Feet, and No Feet,* a venture into the realm of natural history, where I did not really belong. In the same year I wrote *The Joyous Story of Toto;* and the year after, *Toto's Merry Winter.* These books, which I count among the best I have written, have a special little sad interest for me.

"Not long before that, my baby died, my little Maud, a creature so bright and sweet that her sudden departure—less than two days from rosy health to the last breath drawn in my arms—left a blank that at first nothing could fill. H. R., my tower of strength, did not fail me; the other children were dearer than ever. . . . All would not do; I must have work. So I wrote—I hardly know how—these two little merry tales. It was a great relief and a great help.

1889. ". . . I began upon the series of so-called 'girls' books,' which were to occupy a good deal of my time for the next fifteen years. The 'Hildegarde' books, the 'Margaret' books; I do not know that I have anything special to say about these. The later ones are better written than the earlier ones; if I were twenty years younger, I would write *Queen Hildegarde* over again.

"[A friend] asked me to make her a visit. I well remember how one day during the visit, sitting on the rocks below the house, and looking out to sea, I saw a distant lighthouse, and began dreaming and wondering as to what life might be in such a place. So, up out of the sea, as it were, came to me the little story called *Captain January.* I wrote it quickly, and was rather pleased with it, but when I took it to my publishers, they would have nothing to say to it. It was too short for a long story, too long for a short story; very sorry, but not in their line. I think this story went to every reputable publisher, or to all that I knew about, in this country, and to several in England. No one would have it. Instructed, and rather sorrowful, I put the little manuscript away in a drawer, still feeling that it had some elements of possible success. A year or two later, I chanced to meet Mr. Dana Estes, Sr., with whom I had a pleasant personal acquaintance. He asked me what I had been writing.

"'Nothing,' I said, 'except the little story that you refused.'

**Oh! blithe and merrily sang the shark,
As he sat on the house-top high.**
■ (From *Tirra Lirra* by Laura E. Richards. Illustrated by Marguerite Davis.)

"And then, perhaps seeing some interest or sympathy in his kind face, I said, '"Mr. Estes, would you be willing to read that little story yourself and give me your personal opinion of it?'

"It was much to ask of a publisher, but he kindly consented. That was forty years ago, and *Captain January* still heads my list of sales.

"I tell this for the encouragement of young writers whose manuscripts come fluttering home to them, unwelcome fledglings, not wanted in the nest.

"Not long ago I went to see the film version of *Captain January*. I was displeased at the interpolations and adaptations, but the child actress, Baby Peggy, won my heart. At one point, sitting alone in the friendly darkness, I laughed aloud. It was where, after a truly beautiful representation of the storm, the lighthouse, the old seaman with the rescued child in his arms, the scene suddenly changed, and showed the lighthouse in broad sunlight, the sea at its feet calm and sparkling and covered with—pelicans! The scene, which in tempest might perfectly well have been the coast of Maine, had had its fair weather rehearsals, at least, in Florida.

"All this time, while the songs and stories were coming faster than I could write them, I was engaged on a work of far different nature, and one of deep importance to me; the work of editing the letters and journals of my father. I began to prepare for this work the year after his death, in 1876. The first volume appeared in 1906; the second in 1909, when I gave it to my mother on her ninetieth birthday.

"**1886** began for me a great pleasure which has lasted almost until to-day. My son Hal being then ten years old, it seemed well to gather some of his school and playmates together and make their acquaintance. I formed a little club, and named it the Howe Club, for my father. The boys—an exceptionally interesting group—came to the Yellow House on Saturday evenings for an hour and a half. I read to them—first a poem, then Scott or Dickens for half the time; then there were apples—or—peanuts—and games in many varieties, all with the pill of Information heavily sugar-coated. To give the boys something that school in its crowded curriculum could not give; to enlarge first their vocabulary and then their horizon; to show them the fair face of poetry; first and last to give them a *good time;* this was my ardent desire. If the boys enjoyed their Saturday evenings half as much as I did, I am content. Nine o'clock came all too soon for me.

"Give the children *the best there is!* Give them the great ballads, the Norse sagas, the *Iliad* and the *Odyssey,* the *Lays of Ancient Rome.* Above all, give them *Shakespeare* and the *Bible.*

"I am convinced that in nine cases out of ten the child ought to have the original. He may not understand it all; what if he does not? He has all his life in which to grow to the understanding of it; and once and for all, let me say with my whole heart that I do not believe in confining children to things they understand. I have no doubt there were plenty of people who advised Columbus to stay in Genoa, because he knew his way about there.

(From *Sketches and Scraps* by Laura E. Richards. Illustrated by Henry Richards.)

"When my mother was ninety, she was asked to 'express the aim of life.' After a moment's thought she said: '"To learn; to teach; to serve, to enjoy!'

"This utterance comes more deeply home to me with every year; I realize more and more how these four aspects of life are linked together: how, whenever I have tried to teach, I have been the chief learner; and whenever I have tried to serve, the chief pleasure has been mine."[1]

June 17, 1921. "We celebrated our Golden Wedding. It was a lovely festival: sunshine, children, grandchildren, friends flowers, all to hearts' content. Four of the original guests were here. . . . We danced on the lawn, H. R. and I leading off the Virginia Reel; the music was made by [two Howe Club boys]."[1]

1930's. "What more is there to say? The Eighties find my husband and me still active ever more and more deeply thankful. . . . We have been young and have seen visions; we are old and have dreamed dreams; and the best of the dreams have come true."[1]

January 14, 1943. At ninety-two, died of complications of a cold.

FOR MORE INFORMATION SEE: R. H. Viguers, "Laura E. Richards, Joyous Companion," in *Horn Book,* April-June and October-December, 1956; Laura Benét, *Famous Poets for Young People,* Dodd, 1964.

ROBINS, Seelin
See ELLIS, Edward S(ylvester)

RODMAN, Emerson
See ELLIS, Edward S(ylvester)

ROURKE, Constance (Mayfield) 1885-1941

PERSONAL: Born November 14, 1885, in Cleveland, Ohio; died March 23, 1941, in Grand Rapids, Michigan; daughter of H. B. and Constance E. (Davis) Rourke. *Education:* Vassar College, A.B., 1907; graduate study at the Sorbonne, University of Paris, 1908 and 1909. *Home:* Grand Rapids, Michigan.

CAREER: Vassar College, Poughkeepsie, New York, instructor in English, 1910-15; biographer, historian. *Awards, honors:* Recipient of the Borden Fund for Foreign Travel

Constance Rourke

and Study, with which she studied at the Sorbonne, 1908 and 1909, and was a reader at the Bibliotheque Nationale in Paris and at the British Museum in London, 1908-10; runner-up for the Newbery Medal, 1935, for *Davy Crockett,* and 1937, for *Audubon.*

WRITINGS: Trumpets of Jubilee: Henry Ward Beecher, Harriet Beecher Stowe, Lyman Beecher, Horace Greeley, P. T. Barnum, Harcourt, 1927, reprinted, 1963; *Troupers of the Gold Coast: The Rise of Lotta Crabtree,* Harcourt, 1928; *American Humor: A Study of the National Character,* Harcourt, 1931, reprinted, 1971; *Davy Crockett* (illustrated by James MacDonald), Harcourt, 1934, reprinted, 1962, new edition (illustrated by Walter Seaton), Junior Deluxe Editions, 1956; (contributor) Elisabeth R. Hamilton, editor, *How They Started: Nine Famous Men Begin Their Careers,* Harcourt, 1937; *Charles Sheeler: Artist in the American Tradition* (illustrated with works of Charles Sheeler), Harcourt, 1938, reprinted, Kennedy Galleries, 1969; *Audubon* (illustrated by James MacDonald and with works by J. J. Audubon), Harcourt, 1938, reprinted, F. Watts, 1964; *The Roots of American Culture and Other Essays,* edited, and with a preface, by Van Wyck Brooks, Harcourt, 1942, reprinted, Kennikat, 1965.

Contributor of numerous biographical and critical essays to journals and magazines. Editor of *Index of American Design* (Federal Art Project), 1937.

ADAPTATIONS—Filmstrips: "Davy Crockett, Part 1—Frontiersman, Part 2—Politician" (two filmstrips of a four filmstrip set, average running time; 16½ min., average number of frames: 112, records or cassettes), Walt Disney.

Movies: "Davy Crockett, Indian Scout," starring George Montgomery (71 min., 16mm, sound, b/w), United Artists, 1950; "Davy Crockett and the River Pirates," starring Fess Parker (81 min., 16mm, sound, color), Walt Disney, 1955; "Davy Crockett, King of the Wild Frontier," starring Fess Parker (93 min., 16mm, sound, color), Walt Disney, 1955.

Recordings: "Three Adventures of Davy Crockett" (fourteen records, book containing synopses of the stories and song lyrics), Walt Disney.

Television: "Davy Crockett" series, starring Fess Parker.

FOR MORE INFORMATION SEE: Stanley E. Hyman, *Armed Vision: A Study in the Methods of Modern Criticism,* Knopf, 1948; Muriel Fuller, editor, *More Junior Authors,* Wilson, 1963; Obituaries—*New York Times,* March 24, 1941; *Nation,* March 29, 1941; *Publishers Weekly,* April 5, 1941.

SARG, Anthony Frederick
See SARG, Tony

Tony Sarg, with his "Ali Baba" puppets.

SARG, Tony 1880-1942
(Anthony Frederick Sarg)

PERSONAL: Surname is pronounced with a hard "g"; born April 24, 1880 (or 1882, according to some sources), in Guatemala; came to the United States in 1915, naturalized in 1921; died March 7, 1942 in New York City; son of Francis Charles (an owner of coffee and sugar plantations) and Mary Elizabeth (Parker) Sarg; married Bertha Eleanor McGowan, 1910; children: Mary Eleanor Sarg Norcliffe. *Education:* German Military School, Lichterfelde, Germany. *Home:* New York City and Nantucket, Massachusetts.

CAREER: Author and artist; illustrator for magazines and books; designer of window displays and of handicrafts, furnishings, and toys for children; marionette-maker. *Military service:* Served as an officer in the German Army until 1905.

WRITINGS—All self-illustrated; all published by Greenberg, except as noted: *Tony Sarg's Book for Children from Six to Sixty,* 1924; *Tony Sarg's Book of Animals,* 1925; *Tony Sarg's Wonder Zoo,* 1925; *Tony Sarg's New York,* 1926; (with Anne Stoddard) *Book of Marionette Plays,* 1927; *Tony Sarg's Book of Tricks,* 1928; *Where's Tommy?* (poems), 1932; *Tony Sarg's Wonder Book,* 1941; (with B. F. Jay) *Surprise Book,* Jay, 1941; (compiler) *Tony Sarg's Play-a-Tune Song Book,* Jay, 1942; *Baby's Book,* 1943; *Tony Sarg's Alphabet,* 1945; *Savings Book: A Trip to Golden City,* World, 1946. Also author of *How to Make and Operate a Marionette Theatre* published by Samuel French.

Illustrator: Irvin Shrewsbury Cobb, *"Speaking of Operations—,"* G. H. Doran, 1915; Cobb, *Fiddle, D. D.,* G. H. Doran, 1916; (and contributor) Montrose Jonas Moses, editor, *A Treasury of Plays for Children,* Little, Brown, 1921; (and contributor) M. J. Moses, editor, *Another Treasury of Plays for Children,* Little, Brown, 1926; Felicite Lefevre,

Sarg contributed his talents to Macy's "Christmas Day" parade.

Soldier Boy, Greenberg, 1926; G. R. Mills, Zaida Nelson, and Anne Stoddard, *Talking Dolls,* Greenberg, 1930; Carveth Wells, *Jungle Man and His Animals,* McBride, 1935; Nelson Munson, *Who's Who in Tony Sarg's Zoo,* McLoughlin Brothers, 1937; Sigmund G. Spaeth, *Maxims to Music: Traditional Proverbs, Mottoes, and Maxims of the World Fitted to Music for the Well-Tempered Piano-Child,* McBride, 1939; Carlo Lorenzini, *Pinocchio,* edited by Watty Piper, Platt & Peck, 1940; Elizabeth Mifflin Boyd, *All about David,* Winston, 1940; Felicite Lefevre, *The Cock, the Mouse and the Little Red Hen: An Old Tale Retold,* MacRae, 1945, new edition, Richard's Press, 1959.

ADAPTATIONS—Movies: "Almanac," 1921; "The Tooth Carpenter," 1921.

SIDELIGHTS: **April 24, 1880.** Born in Guatemala. "My father had a theory that it was a good thing for a boy to have a regular duty to perform. The task imposed in my case was to feed the chickens at six-thirty every morning.

"To circumvent this early-morning rising, I rigged up a couple of pulleys, and ran a line from my bedroom window to the sliding drop-door of the chicken house. I spread the grain in the yard the evening before, and when my father knocked on the door in the morning I released the chickens by pulling on the rope.

"Half an hour later my father came back. 'Did you feed the chickens?' he demanded.

"'Yes, sir.'

"'I didn't see you go down.'

"When I showed him my scheme he was so pleased to think that his son had used his head to solve a simple problem that he absolved me from further responsibility toward the chickens." [*Tony Sarg: Puppeteer in America,* T. Hunt, University of Michigan Microfilms, 1976.[1]]

"[When] I made my first marionette it was not particularly

successful, but I had the general idea. I proceeded to get ready a little show which I called *The Music Lesson,* since repeated many times. My first private audiences include Clunn Lewis, the old English marionette showman; Phil May, the caricaturist, and George Bernard Shaw. This was in my studio in the building called Dickens' Old Curiosity Shop. Buses used to stop there and I noticed that Mrs. Hawkins, who had a curio shop on the first floor under my studio, did a good trade in souvenirs. This good Cockney woman had pointed out on more than one occasion, 'Ladies and Gentlemen, that hold room over'ead was Little Nell's bedroom.' I had an idea. I bought some things of the Dickens period, a four-poster bed, old prints and knick-knacks, and recreated the atmosphere of the room as it is described in the novel. Then I persuaded Mrs. Hawkins to let me put up a sign in her shop, 'See Little Nell's bedroom upstairs.'" [Address given by Tony Sarg at a puppeteer's convention, recorded in 1922 edition of *The Grapevine,* the official news organ of the Puppeteers of America.[2]]

1915. Started working with marionettes in the United States. "When I did my first professional show . . . my marionettes were built with many improvements over the first figure I had attempted. One of the twenty-four actors in the production had a small pet monkey which she brought to rehearsals. We decided to put it in the show, and created an Italian organ-grinder marionette to go with it. Little pieces of sugar were strewn over the stage, and while the organ-grinder performed, the monkey would scramble about, its tail curling and uncurling, gathering up the sugar as if it were coins. . . . On another occasion, for the fifth anniversary of the Roxy Theatre, I built a complete stage show in miniature, ballet dancers and orchestra, just like the regular Roxy entertainment.

"[Today] is a far cry from the day . . . of the few marionette showmen, when I was obliged to watch shows lying on my back before the front row to find out how puppets were worked."[2]

"I think every artist is interested in things in miniature, which explains my liking for marionettes. As to my other activities, I love to have a great many irons in the fire. But I advise everyone who expects to do creative work of any kind to build up a healthy constitution in youth.

"I think the most interesting thing about me is the fact that I can do so many things. . . . You see, when I am not illustrating, I am designing new puppets and planning new productions, designing wall paper for children's rooms, note paper for children, silks, pottery, window displays, murals and decorations for grill and night clubs, children's barber shops—and once in a while I enjoy giving a lecture." [Columbia University's Institute of Arts and Sciences *Institute Magazine,* July, 1928.[3]]

"I have never yet been able to use up all the energy for a day's work. . . . If I go to an artists' ball and go home at six-thirty in the morning I am at my drawing board at nine."[1]

Sarg's correspondence with children continued throughout his career: "I am always sending puppets to total little strangers. Many of them have read my book on marionettes, have built a mimic stage of their own, and have got

Tony Sarg with a Macy's balloon of his own design.

into difficulties with the strings. I try to straighten them out."[1]

Speaking of what made puppet theatre "different" and "special": "The puppets transcend the ability of the ordinary actor in several ways. In a puppet theater you can introduce ships that sail, animals, and magical effects which in the legitimate theater could not possibly be worked out save by very cumbersome apparatus. Our puppets can be made to change their shapes, can be devoured by dragons and pop into view again, and can literally carry out many of the fairy stories of our childhood."[3]

"I like stories which make people believe in fairies. . . . It is fun to have children see fairies fluttering about in beautiful, gleaming gauze robes, admonishing peasant folk about things which will bring them happiness and good fortune. The marionette play must be a vehicle to display the accomplishments of the puppets."[1]

"Long sentences of dialogue are necessary because the spoken words must be long enough to cover the marionette's movement. A short bit of repartee would leave an action half finished. Every movement is conspicuous and must mean something directly attached to the furtherance of the story. And, when lines are spoken, the character speaking the lines must be the only marionette in action. Otherwise, confusion would be caused the audience. Out front one centers one's interest naturally on the puppet in movement and instantly connects the dialogue spoken off the stage with this particular character." [*Shadowland Magazine,* September, 1919.[4]]

Hark! I hear them coming. ■ (From *A Treasury of Plays for Children* edited by Montrose J. Moses. Illustrated by Tony Sarg.)

The toymaker of Nuremburg. ■ (From *A Treasury of Plays for Children* edited by Montrose J. Moses. Illustrated by Tony Sarg.)

Of specific character portrayals he was deliberate in his approach: "If your actor is to be a villain, he must look like the most villainous creature that ever existed. If your figure is to represent a beautiful lady, it must appear so extravagantly beautiful that it will take your breath away."[1]

One such figure he recalled was an oriental dancer—this puppet was a challenge and satisfaction to his perfectionist standards: "I doubt if so complicated a figure had ever been used before on the marionette stage. I rehearsed her and rehearsed her. Gradually she grew lovely and graceful. And when two highly trained puppeteers and thirty-seven strings had done their best, she was so seductive that the evil old man never saw she had a knife until it was too late."[1]

He explained the mechanical differences in puppets: "There are three kinds of marionettes. One type consists of a head and empty dress slipped upon the hand of an operator, who animates the puppet with his thumb and two fingers. It is to this type that Punch and Judy belong.

"Another type is the doll operated from below by means of rods. The third type, the true marionette, is a puppet operated from above by means of strings or wires.

"To this third type belong my own dolls and virtually all modern marionettes which astonish their audiences so by imitating practically all the movements of human beings, even to opening and closing their eyes and mouths; by walking, dancing and fighting, by visibly breathing, by picking up and carrying small objects and by seemingly smoking, with real smoke coming from their mouths." [*Ladies' Home Journal,* December 19, 1927.[5]]

July, 1922. He wrote an article for *Theatre Arts Magazine* entitled, "The Revival of Puppet-Play In America:"

"Ten or twelve years ago, few people in this country were even familiar with the word 'marionette.' A bewildered lady at one of my first public performances, back in 1916, referred to the dolls as 'Marie Antoinettes.' (It is interesting, in this connection, to remember that the word 'marionette' was originally derived from the images of the Virgin, carried through the streets of the Italian cities in religious processions during the Middle Ages. 'Little Mary's' these images were called, hence 'Marionette,' for puppets played their part in early church drama and had their own connection with the beginnings of the legitimate stage.) But, if the public was unfamiliar with marionettes in 1916, the same cannot be said today.

"An interesting experience illustrates the difference which ten years have made in the popularity of the dolls in America. A truckman came to my studio, ten or twelve years ago, delivering goods, and was interested by the manikins which he saw in the work-shop. He told me that the Bradley Studios had some trunks full of marionettes which they were anxious to sell. That was an alluring prospect. I went to the Bradley Studios and learned that they had bought at a dock sale five trunks full of Spanish puppets which had been lying unclaimed for years, apparently a puppet show which some one had brought to America with the intention of producing here—and had abandoned for what reason we shall never know. As there was no interest in puppets in America—I seemed to be the only possible purchaser. They offered me the lot for a thousand dollars.

"And then I saw the dolls. There were a hundred marionettes, museum pieces, exquisitely made, each one a work or art. Each doll had two or three changes of costume, some of them, however, devoured by moths. They were worth a small fortune, but a thousand dollars looked like a great deal of money in those days. I went away, but I could not forget those beautiful little figures, and went back from time to time, to try for a better price. In the end I bought the entire outfit for fifty dollars—a windfall which could not occur today, when there is so much interest in the little actors. I still have these charming dolls, brave in their exquisitely embroidered and spangled costumes. Some of them appeared in my production of *Don Quixote*.

"It is encouraging to see that puppet-play has undergone as lively a recrudescence in Europe as in the United States. It would appear that the interest in marionettes in not merely a fad, but a reaction of human nature to an ancient stimulus." [*Theatre Arts Magazine*, July, 1922.[6]]

FOR MORE INFORMATION: Shadowland Magazine, September, 1919; Clayton Meeker Hamilton, "In Praise of Puppet Theatres: Tony Sarg," in *Seen on the Stage,* Holt, 1920; *Theatre Arts Magazine,* July, 1922; Columbia's *Institute Magazine,* July, 1928; Willis Birchman, "Tony Sarg," in *Faces and Facts by and about Twenty-six Contemporary Artists,* Edward P. Judd, 1937; Mary Cass Canfield, "Reflections on Tony Sarg's Marionettes," in *Grotesques and Other Reflections,* Harper, 1941; Robert Spiers, editor, *I Am an American, by Famous Naturalized Americans,* Alliance Book, 1941; Stanley J. Kunitz and Howard Haycraft, editors, *Junior Book of Authors,* Wilson, 1951; T. Hunt, *Tony Sarg: Puppeteer in America,* University of Michigan Microfilms, 1976; Obituary—*New York Times,* March 8, 1942.

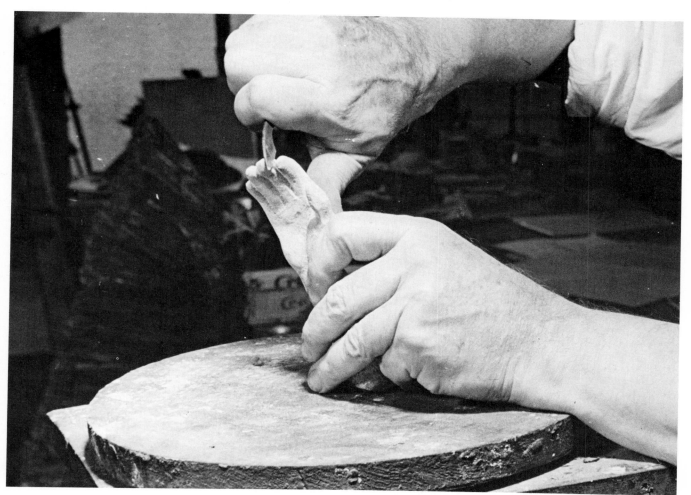

Sarg at work.

SCHULTZ, James Willard 1859-1947

PERSONAL: Named Apikuni (means "Far-Off White Robe") by Blackfeet Indians; born August 26, 1859, in Boonville, New York; died June 11, 1947; son of Philander B. and Frances A. (Joslin) Schultz; married Mutsi Ahwotan Ahki (means "Beautiful Shield Woman") of the Pikuni tribe of the Blackfeet Indians, 1879 (died, 1903); married Celia B. Hawkins, 1907; married third wife, Jessie L. Donaldson, 1931; children: (first marriage) Hart Merriam ("Lone Wolf"; an artist). *Education:* Studied under private tutors and at a private school in New York State.

WRITING—All published by Houghton, except as noted: *My Life as an Indian: The Story of a Red Woman and a White Man in the Lodges of the Blackfeet* (illustrated with photographs by George Bird Grinnell and others), Doubleday, Page, 1907, reprinted, Fawcett, 1968, adaptation by Robert E. Gard (illustrated by David Humphreys Miller), Duell, Sloan, 1957 [*My Life as an Indian* was originally published serially in *Forest and Stream* as "In the Lodges of the Blackfeet" under the pseudonym W. B. Anderson]; *With the Indians in the Rockies* (illustrated by George Varian), 1912, later editions illustrated by Harold Brett, 1925, and by Lorence Bjorklund, 1960, revised and enlarged edition published in England as *Boy Trappers in the Rockies* (illustrated by George Varian and Patten Wilson), Harrap, 1914; *The Quest of the Fish-Dog Skin* (illustrated by Varian), 1913, later edition illustrated by Lorence Bjorklund, 1960; *Sinopah, the Indian Boy* (illustrated by E. Boyd Smith), 1913; *On the Warpath* (illustrated by G. Varian), 1914.

Apauk, Caller of Buffalo, 1916; *Blackfeet Tales of Glacier National Park,* 1916; *The Gold Cache* (illustrated by G. Varian), 1917; *Bird Woman (Sacajawea), the Guide of Lewis and Clark,* 1918; *Lone Bull's Mistake: A Lodge Pole Chief Story* (illustrated by G. Varian), 1918; *Rising Wolf, the White Blackfoot: Hugh Monroe's Story of His First Year on the Plains* (illustrated by Frank E. Schoonover), 1919; *Running Eagle, the Warrior Girl,* 1919.

The Dreadful River Cave: Chief Black Elk's Story (illustrated by Harold Cue), 1920; *In the Great Apache Forest: The Story of a Lone Boy Scout,* 1920; *The War-Trail Fort: Further Adventures of Thomas Fox and Pitamakan* (illustrated by G. Varian), 1921; *Seizer of Eagles* (illustrated by F. E. Schoonover), 1922; *The Trail of the Spanish Horse* (illustrated by G. Varian), 1922, later edition illustrated by Lorence Bjorklund, 1960; *The Danger Trail* (illustrated by G. Varian), 1923; *Friends of My Life as an Indian,* 1923; *Plumed Snake Medicine* (illustrated by G. Varian), 1924; *Sahtaki and I,* 1924; *Questers of the Desert* (illustrated by F. E. Schoonover), 1925; *William Jackson, Indian Scout: His True Story Told by His Friend,* 1926; *Signposts of Adventure: Glacier National Park as the Indians Know It,* 1926; *Sun Woman: A Novel,* 1926; *Red Crow's Brother: Hugh Monroe's Story of His Second Year on the Plains* (illustrated by F. E. Schoonover), 1927; *A Son of the Navahos,* 1927; *In Enemy Country,* 1928; *Skull Head the Terrible* (illustrated by F. E. Schoonover), 1929.

(With Jessie Louise Donaldson) *The Sun God's Children* (illustrated with portraits by Winold Reiss), 1930; *The White Beaver* (illustrated by Rodney Thomson), 1930; *Alder Gulch Gold* (illustrated by Albin Henning), 1931;

Friends and Foes in the Rockies (illustrated by Stockton Mulford), 1933; *Gold Dust* (illustrated by Mulford), 1934; *The White Buffalo Robe* (illustrated by F. E. Schoonover), 1936; *Stained Gold* (illustrated by Schoonover), 1937; *Short Bow's Big Medicine* (illustrated by S. Mulford), 1940; *Blackfeet and Buffalo: Memories of Life among the Indians* (edited, and with an introduction, by Keith C. Seele), University of Oklahoma Press, 1962; *Why Gone Those Times? Blackfoot Tales* (edited by Eugene Lee Silliman; illustrated by Charles M. Russell), University of Oklahoma Press, 1974.

Contributor to periodicals, including *Forest and Stream* and *American Boy-Youth's Companion.*

SIDELIGHTS: August 26, 1859. Born in Boonville, New York. Educated at Peekskille Military Academy in preparation to enter West Point.

1877. Received permission from mother and guardian to go to Montana to hunt buffalo. Promised to return in time for fall entrance to West Point. "From my earliest youth I was happy only when out in the great forest which lay to the north of my home, far beyond the sound of church and school bell and the whistling locomotives. My visits to those grand old woods were necessarily brief, only during summer and winter vacations. But a day came when I could go where and when I chose, and one warm April morning long ago I left St. Louis on a Missouri River steamboat, bound for the Far West.

"The sturdy flat-bottomed, shallow-draft, stern-wheel boat was tied to the shore every evening at dusk, resuming her way at daylight (in the morning), so I saw every foot of the Missouri's shores, 2,600 miles, which lay between the Mississippi and our destination, Fort Benton, at the head of navigation. . . .

"What seemed to me most remarkable . . . was the vast number of buffalo we passed. All through Dakota and through Montana clear to Fort Benton they were in evidence on the hills, in the bottoms, swimming the river. Hundreds and hundreds of them, drowned, swollen, lay on the shallow bars where the current had cast them, or drifted by us down the stream. I believe that the treacherous river, its quicksands, and its unevenly frozen surface in winter played as great havoc with the herds as did the Indian tribes living along its course.

"After we entered the buffalo country there were many places which I passed with regret; I wanted to stop off and explore them. But the captain of the boat would say: 'Don't get impatient; you must keep on to Fort Benton; that's the place for you, for there you'll meet traders and trappers from all over the Northwest, men you can rely upon and travel with, and be reasonably safe. Good God, boy, suppose I should set you ashore here? Why, in all likelihood you wouldn't keep your scalp two days.

"Foolish 'tenderfoot,' innocent 'pilgrim' that I was, I could not bring myself to believe that I, I who thought so much of the Indians, would live with them, would learn their ways, would be a friend to them, could possibly receive any harm at their hands. But one day, somewhere between the Round Butte and the mouth of the Musselshell River, we came upon a ghastly sight. On a shelving, sandy slope of shore,

James Willard Schultz (Apikuni), as a young man.

by a still-smoldering fire of which their half-burned skiff formed a part, lay the remains of three white men. We stopped and buried them, and it is needless to say that I did not again ask to be set ashore.

"Ours was the first boat to arrive at Fort Benton that spring. Long before we came in sight of the place the inhabitants had seen the smoke of our craft and made preparations to receive us. When we turned the bend and neared the levee, cannon boomed, flags waved, and the entire population assembled on the shore to greet us. Foremost in the throng were the two traders who had sometime before bought out the American Fur Company, fort and all.

"Back of the whites were a number of Indians, men and youths from a nearby camp, and women married to the resident and visiting whites.

"I had already learned from what I had seen of the various tribes on our way up the river that the everyday Indian of the plains is not the gorgeously attired, eagle-plume-bedecked creature various prints and written descriptions had led me to believe he was. Of course, all the Indians possessed fancy attire, but it was worn only on state occasions. Those I now saw wore blanket or cow (buffalo) leather leggings, plain or beaded moccasins, calico shirts, and either blanket or cow-leather togas. Most of them were bareheaded, their hair neatly braided, and their faces were painted with reddish-brown ochre or Chinese vermilion. Some carried a bow and a quiver of arrows; some had flintlock fukes, a few the more modern cap-lock rifle. The women wore dresses of calico; a few 'wives' of the traders and clerks and skilled laborers even wore silk, and gold chains and watches, and all had the inevitable gorgeously hued and fringed shawl thrown over their shoulders.

"All this motley crowd had been assembling for days and weeks, impatiently awaiting the arrival of the steamboats. The supply of provisions and things brought up by the boats the previous year had fallen far short of the demand.

"I went ashore and put up at the Overland Hotel, which was a fair-sized log cabin with a number of log-walled additions. For dinner we had boiled buffalo boss ribs, bacon and beans, 'yeast-powder' biscuit, coffee with sugar, molasses, and stewed dried apples.

"I had letters of introduction to the firm which had bought out the American Fur Company. They received me kindly and one of them took me around introducing me to the various employees, residents of the town, and to several visiting traders and trappers. Of the latter I met one, a man only a few years older than myself, who I was told was the most successful and daring of all the traders of the plains. He spoke a number of Indian languages perfectly, and was at home in the camps of any of the surrounding tribes. We somehow took to each other at once, and I passed the balance of the afternoon and evening with him.

"Eventually we became great friends. The Indians called him the Berry. . . . Tall, lean, long-armed, and slightly stoop-shouldered, he was not a fine-looking man, but what splendidly clear, fearless dark brown eyes he had—eyes that could beam with the kindly good nature of those of a child, or fairly flash fire when he was aroused to anger.

Berry taught him wilderness etiquette at a fort dance that evening. "'This,' Berry told me, 'is a traders' and trappers' dance. . . . I can't introduce you to the women, for they do not speak English. However, you must dance with some of them.'

"'But if they do not speak our language, how am I to ask them to dance with me?'

"'You will walk up to one of them, the one you choose, and say, *"ki-tak-stai pes-ka"*—will you dance?'

"I never was what you may call bashful or diffident. A quadrille had just ended. I boldly walked up to the nearest woman, repeating the words over and over that I might not forget them, bowed politely, and said, *'Ki-tak-stai pes-ka?'* The woman laughed, nodded her head, replied, 'Ah,' which I later learned was yes, and extended her hand; I took it and led her to a place for another quadrille just forming. While we were waiting she spoke to me several times, but I could only shake my head and say: 'I do not understand.' Whereupon she would laugh merrily and say a lot more in her language to her neighbor, another comely young woman, who would also laugh and look at me with amusement in her eyes.

"The music struck up and I found that my partner was a light and graceful dancer. I forgot my embarrassment and enjoyed the quadrille, my strange partner, the strange music, and strange surroundings immensely. And how those long-haired, buckskin-clad, moccasined plainsmen did caper and cut pigeon wings, and double shuffle, and leap and swing in the air! I wondered if I could ever, since that seemed to be the style, learn to do likewise. I determined to try it anyhow, but privately at first.

"The quadrille ended, I started to lead my partner to a seat, but instead she led me over to Berry, who had also been dancing, and spoke rapidly to him for a moment.

"'This,' said he to me, 'is Mrs. Sorrel Horse. She invites

us to accompany her and her husband home and have a little feast.'

"Of course we accepted, and after a few more dances we departed. I had been introduced to Sorrel Horse. He was a very tall, slender man, sorrel-haired, sorrel-whiskered, with blue eyes; a man, as I afterward learned, of extremely happy temperament under the most adverse conditions, a sincere and self-sacrificing friend to those he liked but a terror to those who attempted to wrong him.

"Sorrel Horse's home was a fine large Indian lodge of eighteen skins, set up beside his two canvas-covered wagons near the riverbank. His wife built a little fire, made some tea, and presently set before us the steaming beverage with some Dutch-oven baked biscuits, broiled buffalo tongue, and stewed bull berries.

"It was all very new and very delightful to me, and when after a smoke and a chat Sorrel Horse said: 'You had better camp here for the night, boys,' my happiness was complete. We went to sleep on the soft couch covered with soft blankets and listening to the soft murmur of the river's current. This, my first day on the plains, had been, I thought, truly eventful.

"It was agreed that I should join Berry in the autumn, when he would begin the season's trade with the Indians. He owned a large bull train, with which he hauled freight down from Fort Benton to the mining camps in summer, finding in that much more profit than in trading for the deer, elk, and antelope skins which were about the only things of value the Indians had to barter at that season. Buffalo robes were valuable only from animals killed from November to February inclusive. I did not wish to remain in Fort Benton; I wanted to hunt and travel about in this land of glorious sunshine and dry, clear air, so I bought a roll of bedding, large quantities of tobacco, and .44 rimfire cartridges for my Henry rifle, a trained buffalo horse and saddle, and pulled out of the town with Sorrel Horse and his outfit.

"Sorrel Horse's wagons, a lead and a trail, drawn by an eight-horse team, were heavily loaded with provisions and trade goods, for he was going with a band of the Piegans, the Small Robes, on their summer hunt. And this was what had made me accept his invitation to accompany him; I would have an opportunity to study the people.

"Sorrel Horse's brother-in-law, Lis-sis-tsi, Wolverine, and I became great friends. I soon learned to use the sign language, and he helped me in my studies of the Blackfoot language, so difficult that few white men ever did become proficient in it.

"How I enjoyed that summer, part of which we passed at the foot of the Belt Mountains and part on Warm Spring Creek and the Judith River. I joined in the frequent buffalo runs, and on my swift and well-trained horse managed to kill my share of the great animals. I hunted antelope, elk, deer, bighorn, and bear with Wolverine. I would sit for hours on a mountain slope or the summit of some lone butte, and watch the herds and bands of game about me, gaze at the grand mountains and the vast and silent plain, and pinch myself to realize that I was really I, and that it was all real and not a dream. . . .

Here, now, was the most anxious moment and the greatest danger. ■ (From *Sinopah: The Indian Boy* by James Willard Schultz. Illustrated by E. Boyd Smith.)

"I enjoyed myself hugely in that great camp of seven hundred lodges. Some thirty-five hundred people. I attended the dances, and even participated in the one that was called 'Assin-ah-pes-ka'—Assiniboin dance. Remember that I was less than twenty years of age, just a boy, but perhaps more foolish, more reckless than most youths.

"In this Assinboin dance only young unmarried men and women participate. Their elders, their parents, and relatives beat the drums and sing the dance song, which is certainly a lively one, and of rather an abandoned nature. The women sit on one side of the lodge, the men on the other.

"The song begins, everyone joining in. The dancers arise, facing each other, rising on their tiptoes, and then sinking so as to bend the knees. Thus they advance and meet, then retreat, again advance and retreat a number of times, all singing, all smiling, and looking coquettishly into one another's eyes. The dance continues, perhaps for several hours, with frequent pauses for rest, or maybe to feast and smoke. But all the fun comes in toward the close of the festivities; the lines of men and women have advanced; suddenly a girl raises her robe or toga, casts it over her own and the head of the youth of her choice, and gives him a hearty kiss. The spectators shout with laughter, the drums are beaten louder than ever, the song increases in intensity. The lines retreat, the favored youth looking very much embarrassed, and all take their seats. Payment for this kiss must be made on the morrow. If the young man thinks a great deal of the girl, he may present her with one or two horses; he must give her something, if only a copper bracelet, or a string of beads.

"I believe that I was an 'easy mark' for those lively and, I fear, mercenary maidens, for I was captured with the toga and kissed more often than anyone else. And the next morning there would be three or four of them at the trading post with their mothers; and one must have numerous yards of bright prints; another some red trade cloth and beads; still another a blanket. They broke me, but still I would join in when another dance was given.

"But if I danced, and gambled, and raced horses, my life in the camp was by no means a continual round of foolishness. I spent hours and hours with the medicine men and old warriors, learning their beliefs and traditions, listening to their stories of the gods, their tales of war and the hunt. Also I attended the various religious ceremonies; listened to the pathetic appeals of the medicine men to the Sun as they prayed for health, long life, and happiness for the people. It was all exceedingly interesting.

"'Why don't you get a woman?' Weasel Tail abruptly asked one evening as Talks-with-the-buffalo and I sat smoking with him in his lodge.

"'Yes,' my other friend put in. 'Why not? You have the right to do so, for you can count a coup; yes, two of them. You killed a Cree, and took a Cree horse in the fight at the Hairy Cap.'

"'I took a horse,' I replied, 'and a good one he is; but you are mistaken about the Cree; you will remember that he escaped by running into the pines on Hairy Cap.'

"'Oh!' said Talks-with-the-buffalo, 'I don't mean that one; we all know he got away, I mean one of those who first fell when we all fired into them. That tall one, the man who wore a badger-skin cap; you killed him. I saw the bullet wound in his body; no ball from any of our rifles could have made such a small hole.'

"This was news to me; I remembered well having shot several times at that particular warrior, but I never had thought that my bullet had ended his career. I did not know whether to feel glad or sorry about it, but finally concluded that it was best to feel glad, for he would have killed me if he could have done so. I was turning the matter over in my mind, recalling every little incident of that memorable day, when my host aroused me from my reverie. 'I said, Why don't you take a woman? Answer.'

"'Oh!' I replied. 'No one would have me. Isn't that a good reason?'

"'Kyai-yo!' exclaimed Madam Weasel Tail, clapping her hand to her mouth, the Blackfoot way of expressing surprise or wonder. 'Kyai-yo! What a reason! I well know that there isn't a girl in this camp but would like to be his woman.'

"'Mah-kah-kan-is-tsi!' I exclaimed, which is a flippant and slangy term, expressing doubt of the speaker's truthfulness,

"'Mah-kah-kan-is-tsi yourself,' she rejoined. 'Why do you think you are asked to all these Assiniboin dances, where all the young women wear their best clothes, and try to catch you with their robes? Why do you think they put on their best things and go to the trading post with their mothers or other relatives every chance they get? What? You don't know? Well, I'll tell you: they go, each one, hoping that you will notice her, and send a friend to her parents to make a proposal.'

"'It is the truth,' said Weasel Tail.

"'Yes, the truth,' Talks-with-the-buffalo and his woman joined in.

"After that evening I looked more closely at the various young women I met in the camp or at the trading post, saying to myself: 'Now, I wonder what kind of woman that would make? Is she neat, good-tempered, moral?' All the time, however, I knew that I had no right to take one of them. I did not intend to remain long in the West; my people would never forgive me for making an alliance with one. They were of old, proud Puritan stock, and I could imagine them holding up their hands in horror at the mere hint of such a thing.

"You will notice that thus far in this part of my story I have substituted the word women for wife. A plainsman always said 'my woman' when speaking of his Indian better half; the Blackfoot said the same: 'Nit-o-ke-man,' my woman. None of the plainsmen were legally married, unless the Indian manner in which they took a woman, by giving so many horses, or so much merchandise for one, could be considered legal.

"In the first place there was no one in the country to perform the marriage service except occasionally a wandering Jesuit priest. There was no law.

"'No,' I said to myself time and again; 'no, it will not do; hunt, go to war, do anything but take a woman, and in the fall go home to your people.'

"But one morning the Crow Woman and I were sitting out under a shade she had constructed of a couple of travois and a robe or two. She was busy, as usual, embroidering a moccasin with colored quills, and I was thoroughly cleaning my rifle, preparatory to an antelope hunt. A couple of women came by on their way to the trade room with three or four robes. One of them was a girl of perhaps sixteen or seventeen years, not what one might call beautiful, still she was good-looking, fairly tall, and well formed, and she had fine, large, candid, expressive eyes, perfect white, even teeth, and heavy braided hair which hung almost to the ground. All in all, there was something very attractive about her. 'Who is that?' I asked the Crow Woman. 'That girl, I mean.'

"'Don't you know? She comes here often; she is a cousin of Berry's woman. Her name is Nat-ah-ki.'

"I went away on my hunt, but it didn't prove to be very interesting. I was thinking all the time about the cousin. That evening I spoke to Berry about her, learned that her father was dead; that her mother was a medicine-lodge woman and noted for her unswerving uprightness and goodness of character. 'I'd like to have the girl,' I said. 'What do you think about it?'

"'We'll see,' Berry replied. 'I'll talk with my old woman.'

"A couple of days went by and nothing was said by either of us about the matter, and then one afternoon Mrs. Berry told me that I was to have the girl, providing I would promise to be always good and kind to her. I readily agreed to that.

"'Very well, then,' said Mrs. Berry; 'go into the trade room and select a shawl, some dress goods, some bleached muslin—no, I'll select the outfit and make her some white women's dresses like mine.'

"Well, I got the girl. It was an embarrassing time for us both when she came in one evening, shawl over her face, while we were eating supper. Sorrel Horse and his woman were there, and with Berry and his madam they made things interesting for us with their jokes, until Berry's mother put a stop to it.

"We were a pretty shy couple for a long time, she especially. 'Yes' and 'no' were about all that I could get her to say. But my room underwent a wonderful transformation; everything was kept so neat and clean, my clothes were so nicely washed, and my 'medicine' was carefully taken out every day and hung on a tripod. I had purchased a war bonnet, shield, and various other things which the Blackfoot regard as sacred, and I did not say to anyone that I thought they were not so. I had them handled with due pomp and ceremony.

"As time passed this young woman became more and more of a mystery to me. I wondered what she thought of me, and if she speculated upon what I might think of her. I had no fault to find, she was always neat, always industrious about our little household affairs, quick to supply my wants. But that wasn't enough. I wanted to know her, her thoughts and beliefs. I wanted her to talk and laugh with me, and tell stories, as I could often hear her doing in Madam Berry's domicile. Instead of that, when I came around the laugh died on her lips, and she seemed to freeze, to shrink within herself.

"The change came when I least expected it. I was down in the Piegan camp one afternoon and learned that a war party was being made up to raid the Crows. Talks-with-the-buffalo and Weasel Tail were going, and asked me to go with them. I readily agreed, and returned to the post to prepare for the trip. 'Nat-ah-ki,' I said, bursting into our room, 'give me all the moccasins I have, some clean socks, some pemmican. Where is my little brown canvas bag? Where have you put my gun case? Where—'

"'What are you going to do?'

"It was the first question she had ever asked me.

"'Do? I'm going to war; my friends are going, they asked me to join them—'

"I stopped, for she suddenly arose and faced me, and her eyes were very bright. 'You are going to war!' she exclaimed. 'You, a white man, are going with a lot of Indians sneaking over the plains at night to steal horses, and perhaps kill some poor prairie people. You have no shame!'

"'Why,' I said, rather faintly, 'I thought you would be glad. Are not the Crows your enemies? I have promised. I must go.'

The bear was kicking and writhing in the snow, and my partner was showering blows on its head. I delivered a blow or two myself before it ceased to struggle. ■ (From *With the Indians in the Rockies* by James Willard Schultz. Illustrated by Lorence Bjorklund.)

"'It is well for the Indians to do this,' she went on, 'but not for a white man. You, you are rich; you have everything you want. You should be ashamed to go sneaking over the plains like a coyote. None of your people ever did that.'

"'I must go,' I reiterated. 'I have given my promise to go.'

"Then Nat-ah-ki began to cry, and she came nearer and grasped my sleeve. 'Don't go,' she pleaded, 'for if you do, I know you will be killed, and I love you so much.'

"I was never so surprised. All these weeks of silence, then, had been nothing but her natural shyness, a veil to cover her feelings. I was pleased and proud to know that she did care for me, but underlying that thought was another one: I had done wrong in taking this girl, in getting her to care for me, when in a short time I must return her to her mother and leave for my own country.

"I readily promised not to accompany the war party, and then, her point gained, Nat-ah-ki suddenly felt that she had been overbold and tried to assume her reserve again. But I would not have it that way. I grasped her hand and made her sit down by my side. I pointed out to her that she was wrong; that to laugh, to joke, to be good friends and companions were better than to pass our days in silence, repressing all natural feeling. After that, the sun always shone." [James Willard Schultz, *My Life as an Indian*, edited by Robert E. Gard, Duell, Sloan, 1957.[1]]

1880. "The long summer days went one by one, lingeringly, peacefully, happily. No war parties attacked us, and the young men who went out to war upon other tribes returned spoil-laden, without loss to their numbers. One thing troubled me, the insistent letters from home, commanding me to return. They were several months old when I got them, as were my New York *Tribunes* and other papers. I ceased reading any more than the headlines of the papers; they held no more interest for me, but I could not help worrying about the contents of the letters. Many an unpleasant half-hour I passed after breaking their seals, and then, consigning them to the flames of the lodge fire, I would go out with Nat-ah-ki for a ride, or to some feast or social gathering.

"It was interesting to note the extreme care with which my mail was handled. It was securely bunched up by my Fort Benton friends, and then those to whom it was entrusted rewrapped and rebound it in various coverings. The Blackfoot regarded the arts of writing and reading as the greatest of accomplishments. Some of them would sit for hours inspecting the pictures in my magazines and papers, and although they persisted in holding them sideways, or even upside down, they seemed, nevertheless, to grasp their significance.

"Nat-ah-ki came early to know my mother's handwriting, and when I received letters from others written in characteristically feminine style, she would watch me closely as I read them and then question me as to the writers. 'Oh,' I would carelessly answer, 'they are from relatives, women of our house, just telling me the news and asking if I am well and happy.'

"And then she would shake her head doubtfully and exclaim: 'Relatives! Oh, yes, relatives! Tell me truly how many sweethearts you have in your homeland.'

"Then I would truthfully answer, swearing by the Sun, calling upon him to bear witness that I had but the one sweetheart, she there present, and she would be content—until I received another bundle of letters. As the summer wore on these letters became more frequent, and I realized with ever-increasing regret that my days of happy, irresponsible wandering were about over, that I must go home and begin the career which was expected of me.

"I was beginning to feel pretty blue. I showed [Sorrel Horse and Berry] my letters, told them what was expected of me, and declared that I must return East. They both laughed long, loudly, uproariously, and slapped each other on the back, and I gazed solemnly, reproachfully at them. I could not see that I had joked or said anything funny.

"'He's goin' home,' said Sorrel Horse, 'and he's goin' to be a good, quiet little boy ever after.'

"'And go to church,' said Berry.

"'And walk the straight and narrer path, world without end, and so forth,' Sorrel Horse concluded.

"'Well, you see how it is,' I said. 'I've got to go—much as I would like to remain here with you; I simply must go.'

"'Yes,' Berry acquiesced; 'you have to go, all right, but you'll come back. Oh, yes! you'll come back, and sooner than you think. These plains and mountains, the free life have you, and they'll never let go. Mind you, I've been back there myself; went to school there, and all the time old Montana kept calling me, and I never felt right until I saw the sun shining on her bare plains once more and the Rockies looming up sharp and clear in the distance.'

"'And then,' Sorrel Horse put in, speaking Blackfoot, which was as easy to him as English, 'and then, what about Nat-ah-ki? Can you forget her, do you think?'

"He had, indeed, touched the sore spot. That was what was worrying me. I couldn't answer. . . .

"We ate our evening meal: dried meat and back fat (o-sak-i), stewed dried apples, and yeast-powder bread. I went to bed, finally, and for hours I rolled and tossed. 'Nat-ah-ki,' I finally asked, 'are you awake?'

"'Ah.'

"'I want to tell you something: I must go away for a time; my people call me.'

"'That is not news to me. I have long known that you would go.'

"'How did you know?' I asked. 'I told no one.'

"'Have I not seen you read the little writings? Have I not watched your face? I could see what the writing told you. I know that you are going to leave me. I have always known that you would. You are no different from other white men. They are all unfaithful, heartless. They marry but for a day.'

"She began to cry; not loud, just low, despairing heart-broken sobs. Oh, how I hated myself! But I had opened the subject. I felt that I must carry it through, and I began to lie to her, hating myself more and more every moment. I told her that I was now twenty-one, at which time a white youth becomes a man. There were papers about the property which my father had left that I must go home to sign. 'But,' I said, and I called on the Sun to witness my words, 'I will return; I will come back in a few moons, and we will once more be happy. While I am away Berry will look out for you and your good mother. You shall want for nothing.'

"And thus, explaining, lying, I drove away her fear and sorrow, and she fell peacefully asleep. But there was no sleep for me. In the morning I again rode in to the fort and talked long with Berry. He agreed to look after the girl and her mother and keep them supplied with all necessary food and clothing, until such a time, I explained, 'as Nat-ah-ki will forget me and become some other man's woman.' I nearly choked when I said it.

"Berry laughed quietly. 'She will never be another man's woman,' he said. 'You will be only too glad to return. I shall see you again inside of six months.'

"And so, in the morning, Nat-ah-ki and I parted, and I shook hands with everyone and went on board. The boat swung out into the stream, turned around, and we went flying down the swift current, over the Shokin Bar, and around the bend. The old fort, the happy days of the past year were now but a memory.

"There were a number of passengers aboard, mostly miners from Helena and Virginia City, returning to the States with more or less dust.

"They gambled, and drank, and in a vain effort to get rid of my thoughts I joined in their madness. I remember that I lost three hundred dollars at one sitting, and that the bad liquor made me very ill. Also, I nearly fell overboard near Cow Island. We had run into a large herd of buffalo swimming the river, and I tried to rope a huge old bull from the bow of the boat. The loop settled fairly over his head, but we had not counted on such a shock as I and the three others helping me got when the rope tightened. In an instant it was jerked from our hands. I lost my balance and would have followed it into the water had not the next man behind happened to catch me by the collar and draw me back.

"We tied up to the shore each night. There were constant head winds after we entered Dakota, and when early in October we arrived at Council Bluffs, I was glad to leave the boat and board a train of the Union Pacific. In due time I arrived in the little New England town that was my home.

"I saw the place and the people with new eyes; I cared for neither of them any more. It was a pretty place, but it was all fenced up, and for a year I had lived in the beyond, where fences were unknown. The people were good people, but oh! how narrow-minded. Their ways were as prim and conventional as the hideous fences that marked the bounds of their farms. And this is the way most of them greeted me: 'Ah, my boy, so you've come home, have you? Been a hull year in the Indian country. It's a wonder you wasn't scalped. Those Indians are terrible bad people, so I've heard. Wall, you've had your fling; I suppose you'll steady down now and go into business of some kind.

"There was not a moment of my waking hours in which I did not think of Nat-ah-ki and the wrong I had done her. The days passed for me in deadly monotony, and I was in constant strife with my relatives. Not with my mother, I am thankful to say. I think that she rather sympathized with me. But there were uncles and aunts, and others, of old friends of my long-dead father, all well meaning, of course, who thought that it was incumbent on them to advise me, and shape my future. And from the start we were antagonistic.

"There came a certain night when all the well-meaning ones were gathered at our home. They had decided that I should buy out a retiring merchant who, in the course of forty or fifty years, had acquired a modest competency. That was the last straw. I arose in my wrath, and tried to tell them what I thought of the narrow life they led; but words failed me, and seizing my hat, I fled from the house.

"It was past midnight when I returned, but my mother was waiting for me. We sat down by the fire and talked the matter out. I reminded her that from earliest youth I had preferred the forests and streams, rifle and rod, to the so-called attractions of society, and that I felt I could not bear to live in a town or city, nor undertake a civilized occupa-

tion of any kind, especially one which would keep me confined in a store or office. And she, wise woman, agreed that as my heart was not in it, it would be useless to attempt anything of the kind. And she also admitted that, since I had come to love the plains and mountains so well, it was best that I should return to them.

"I said nothing about Nat-ah-ki. Some time in the future, I determined, when I had done the right thing, she should learn all. Two days later I boarded a train, and in due time arriving in St. Louis put up with genial Ben Stickney of the Planters' Hotel. There I fell in touch with things once more. I met men from Texas and Arizona, from Wyoming and Montana, and we talked of the fenceless land, of the Indians and the buffalo trade, of cattle and miners, and various adventures we had experienced. We would congregate in the lobby of an evening and sit there talking and smoking until long after midnight, or we would go out in a body and see the town in true western style. If we were a trifle hilarious, the police were good, and kindly looked the other way when our sombreroed crowd tramped by, singing, perchance, at the tops of our voices.

"Also, I did not forget Nat-ah-ki. I bought another trunk, and prowling around among the stores picked up various washable things of quaint and pretty pattern, strings of beads, a pair of serpent bracelets, a gold necklace, and various other articles dear to the feminine heart. At last the trunk was so full I could barely lock it, and then, gathering up my things. I boarded a train for Corinne, Wyoming. From there by stage to Helena a week, and on to Fort Benton two days more.

"My first inquiry was for Berry. He was down at the mouth of the Marias, the trader told me, with the Piegans, but his mother and the Crow Woman were living in the little cabin above, and, with a knowing wink, he added that he believed a certain young woman named Nat-ah-ki was with them.

"It was very early in the morning. I hurried out and up the dusty trail. A faint smoke was beginning to rise from the chimney of the little cabin. I pushed open the door and entered. Nat-ah-ki was kneeling before the fireplace blowing the reluctant flame. 'Ah,' she cried, springing up and running to me, 'he has come! My man has come!' She threw her arms around my neck and kissed me, and in another instant she was in the next room crying out: 'Awake, arise; my man has returned!'

"Berry's mother and the Crow Woman hurried out and also embraced and kissed me, and we all tried to talk at once, Nat-ah-ki hanging to my arm and gazing at me with brimming eyes. 'Ah,' she said, over and over, 'they kept telling me that you would not come back, but I knew that they were wrong. I knew that you would not forget me.'

"Truly, these were my people. I had returned to my own. Come what might, I vowed never even to think of leaving the little woman again, and I kept my word. Kept it, say I—I never had cause nor wish to do anything else.

"That was a queer breakfast Nat-ah-ki and I had; in fact, no breakfast at all. We gave up attempting to eat, and she recounted all that had happened during my absence. Then she questioned me: What had I been doing all this time? What had I seen? Was my good mother well? I had nothing to relate. I wanted to hear her talk, to watch her happiness, and in that I was happy, too.

"In due time my trunks were brought over, and handing her the key of one, I said that it and its contents were all hers. What exclamations of surprise, of admiration there were as she unwrapped and unfolded the various things and spread them out here and there on table and couch and chairs. She threw the necklace on over her head, clasped on the bracelets, ran over and gave me a silent kiss, and then laid them away. 'They are too nice, too good,' she said. 'I am not handsome enough to wear them.'

"Then she came back and whispered: 'But all these are too many for me. May I give some of them to my grand-mothers?'—meaning Mrs. Berry and the Crow Woman.

"In the lot there were several quiet dress patterns, a couple of shawls, which I had intended for them, and I said that they would be appropriate gifts for women of advanced age. How happy she was as she picked them up and presented them to the faithful friends. I look back upon that morning as the pleasantest one of my life."[1]

March 16, 1884. Son, Hart Merriam Schultz (Lone Wolf) born. Became a well-known artist.

1902. "We built us a home, Nat-ah-ki and I, in a lovely valley where the grass grew tall and green. We were a long time building it. Up in the mountains where I cut the logs our camp under the towering pines was so pleasant that we could hardly leave it for a couple of days to haul home a wagonload of material. And there were so many pleasant diversions that the ax leaned up against a stump during long, dreamy days while we went trout fishing, or trailed a deer or bear, or just remained in camp listening to the wind in the pine tops, watching the squirrels steal the remains of our breakfast, or an occasional grouse strutting by.

"The years passed happily. We had a growing bunch of cattle. There was little work to do, and we made a trip somewhere every autumn, up to the Rockies with friends, or took a jaunt by rail to some distant point. Sometimes we would take a skiff and idly drift and camp along the Missouri for three or four hundred miles below Fort Benton, returning home by rail. I think that we enjoyed the water trips the most. The shifting, boiling flood, the weird cliffs, the beautifully timbered, silent valley had a peculiar fascination for us such as no place in the great mountains possessed.

"It was during one of these river trips that Nat-ah-ki began to complain of sharp pain in the tips of her righthand fingers. 'It is nothing but rheumatism,' I said, 'and will soon pass away.'

"But I was wrong. The pain grew worse, and abandoning our boat at the mouth of Milk River, we took the first train for the city where our doctor lived. He came, felt her pulse, got out his stethoscope, and moved it from place to place until, at last, it stopped at a point at the left side of the neck, close to the collarbone. There he listened long, and I began to feel alarmed. 'It is not rheumatism,' I said to myself. 'Something is wrong with her heart.'

"The doctor gave some directions to the nurse, then turning to Nat-ah-ki he said, 'Take courage, little friend, we'll pull you through all right.'

"Nat-ah-ki smiled. Then she grew drowsy under the influence of an opiate, and we left the room.

"'Well, old man,' said the doctor, 'I can do little. She may live a year, but I doubt it.'

"For eleven months we did all we could, and then one day my faithful, loving, tender-hearted little woman left me.

"By day I think about her. At night I dream of her.

"I dream of her and of the great, beautiful land where the winds blow free."[1]

1904. Left reservation.

1922. Arrived at Pikuni (Blackfeet) reservation to write *Friends of My Life as an Indian.*

"Journeying up from Los Angeles and delayed by the strike of the railway shopmen, I did not arrive at Glacier Park Station until August 5th. My son had already come on from New York, and rented, for a studio for the summer, a cottage just across the middle fork of the Two Medicine from the huge Glacier Hotel. Night had come. I neared the cottage, and in the yard in front of it saw six lodges redly glowing with the little fires within them. I thought of long-ago nights when I had seen six hundred Pikuni lodges, all of them of new white buffalo leather so glowing. I thought of the sturdy care-free hunters who had lived in them; nearly all had long since gone to the Sand Hills. Of those who survived, only the few here had been able to travel and make camp and await my coming.

"The outer lodge of this little camp was painted with a huge red half-circle rising several feet above the doorway; it was, I knew, the symbol of the Iniskim, the Buffalo Stone medicine, owned by Boy Chief. I neared the lodge, shouting out, 'Nistumo! Ni kauto!' (Brother-in-law! I have come!)

"Out came the old man, shouting to those in the other lodges: 'Itó, anukah kitaiokowow anan!' (Has come, he whom we await!) But they too, had heard my call, and were hurrying out to welcome me—Heavy Eyes, Curly Bear, White Grass, Raven Chief, Many Tail Feathers, White Dog, Short Face, Wonderful Child, young Crow Feathers, and their women; and from the little cottage came my son and his good white wife, Naoma. It was a happy moment to us all. The soft smooth speech of these my Indian friends was pleasant in my ears. I was glad that I had not forgotten one least word of it.

"'But come! Your place awaits you,' Boy Chief presently said to me, and led the way into his lodge.

". . . we formed a complete circle around the little fire. Boy Chief filled his huge long-stemmed black stone pipe and passed it to Raven Chief—also a medicine man—to light. He laid a glowing coal upon the mixture of tobacco and *l'herbe* blew a few whiffs of the sweet-scented smoke to the sky gods and down to Earth Mother, shortly prayed for long life and happiness for us all, and passed the pipe. As it went from one to another around the circle, I was asked about my journey up from the Always-Summer land; and White Grass wanted to know if it were really true, as he had heard, that there snow never fell, and fruits and vegetables ripened every moon of winter.

"'This time I want to write about my friends; they who are living, and those who are gone. I want to make a thick-writing [book] about their life away back in the days before the fire-wagons came, and brought in the multitude of whiteskins who killed off our buffaloes,' I replied.

"'Good! That will be a worth-while writing!' he exclaimed; and the others voiced their approval of it.

"Said Heavy Eyes: 'We go; our knowledge of the great country that once was ours dies with us. Only by reading Apikuni's writings may our children's children, and their children after them, learn how we lived, hunted, kept our enemies out of that country, what were our names for its mountains, lakes, and streams, and why we so named them.'

"'Our children! It is little that they want to know about those far-back days of the buffalo! White teachers and white preachers have ruined their minds! They have no faith in our gods nor any other! They lie, they steal! All that they care for is to wear good clothes and ride crazily about!' Boy Chief exclaimed; and to that there was sad assent.

"'There are many, very many whites who are anxious to learn all that they can about our old-time life; it is for them that I will make this thick-writing.' I said.

"'I for one shall enjoy this work. Thinking and talking about our adventures in the long ago is the one bright part of my old age,' said White Grass.

"My son and Crow Feathers caught up a couple of horses and brought my roll of bedding and other baggage from the railway station. I spread the blankets upon my springy balsam couch. Our friends went to their lodges, and I lay down and was content. I watched the dying fire, listened to the hooting of owls in the pines on the flat, and the mournful howls of a far-off wolf, and soon slept.

"The rumbling of distant thunder awoke me. It came nearer, booming here and there down the mountain-side, and lightning intermittently illuminated the lodge. Suyó-pekina cried out: 'Have pity, Thunder Bird! Do not harm us!' Rain beat heavily upon the lodge, and fierce gusts of wind made its ears flap and snap with reports as loud as pistol shots. A flash of lightning almost blinded us, and, following it, a terrific, deafening crash of thunder broke right above us, Suyópekina shrieked and again begged Thunder Bird to spare us; and successive lightning flashes revealed Boy Chief sitting up and praying as he hurriedly filled his big pipe, lit it, and blew sacrificial smoke into his medicine sacks.

"'O sacred and powerful Buffalo Stone, protect us, drive Thunder Bird away,' he pleaded; and then sang one after another his medicine songs. And suddenly as it had come, the storm passed on, up the ridge to the east, and out upon the plain, and we slept again.

"Crow Feathers, early riser, awakened us: 'You within,' he shouted, 'come out and see what Thunder Bird did last night.'

"We dressed and hurried out, and from the other lodges came our old people in answer to his call. No more than three feet from our doorway was a deep and jagged hole in the ground, as though a blast of giant powder had been exploded there. As we stared at it, White Dog gave a loud cry of astonishment and pointed to the lodge skin, and we saw that it had a black, burned streak running from the narrow space between the ears, down to the edge of the red painted half-circle, the symbol of Boy Chief's medicine.

"Every one gasped, uttered little cries of reverence, and Boy Chief exclaimed: 'O Buffalo Stone! O sacred one! You saved us, you saved us! Far more powerful you than Thunder Bird! He could not make his dreadful fire penetrate our lodge and kill us! When it struck the edge of your red painting, it had to glance off and uselessly tear into the ground.'

"'True! True!'—'Yes! That medicine painting was your shield; it saved you!' the others cried." [James Willard Schultz, *Friends of My Life as an Indian*, Houghton, 1923.[2]]

September 19, 1922. "Yesterday we were all of us sober-faced and quiet when we gathered around the evening fire in Curly Bear's lodge. He filled his big pipe with the fragrant mixture of tobacco and *l'herbe* but, instead of passing it to another to light, as was customary, lit it himself and, after blowing a few whiffs of the smoke to the sky, and down to the ground, he pointed the stem aloft and prayed: 'O Sun! We smoke to you, pity us! With this night, our time of happy together-camping ends. To-morrow we separate; we go our different ways. We are old! Very old! Pity us, Sun! Fully pity us! Help us all to survive the coming winter; let us see the green grass of another summer!'

"Curly Bear handed me a beautiful porcupine-quill embroidered buffalo-leather tobacco pouch, saying: 'Take it. I give it to you. Its contents are very sacred: some of the East-Plant, and a piece of ancient fire-rock.'

"The fire-rock was, of course, a piece of flint. The East-Plant (nahwat' osin) was the narcotic plant which the Blackfeet tribes cultivated and used for smoking before they obtained tobacco from the white traders. It was so named, according to an ancient tradition, because the tribes first got it from a people who lived to the east of their country, then the region of the Great Slave Lake. The Pikuni tribe of the Confederacy had not cultivated it in my time, but I had once smoked some of the plant, given me by Earth Woman, Joseph Kipp's mother, and I remembered that I had found it not to my liking.

"This morning, while the women were taking down the lodges and packing the horses, my son and I had a last smoke with our old friends, and few were our words as the pipe went from hand to hand the round of the circle. At last it was smoked out, and slowly and with pain-staking care Curly Bear knocked the ashes from it, put it in its pouch, and exclaimed: 'Kyi! It is finished, this our happy time together! Now, we go!'

"And at that we all got up, and one by one the old men embraced my son and me, and silently and with bowed heads went to their saddled horses, and their women came and as silently, and some with tears, shook hands with us and turned away. Then, as the little caravan of them started down the valley, Curly Bear turned and came back to us, and said: 'You have the East-Plant that I gave you. Be sure to smoke it now and then in the coming winter, and pray the gods to keep us in health and strength, so that we may at least once more camp together here upon this river.'

"'Yes! We will do that!' my son replied. And as the old man gave his eager horse its head, we heard the rumble of the automobile truck coming to take us and our impedimenta to the studio and the railway station. And as we watched it whiz up past the slow procession of our departing friends, my son exclaimed: 'There's contrast, the travois and the automobiles!'

"'And soon there will be no travois, except here and there one under glass in the museums!'

"'And soon, no more Pikuni! The ruthless white men and their civilization, what haven't they done to these, our people!'

"'That,' said I, 'is the blackest page of American history!'"[2]

June 11, 1947. Died.

FOR MORE INFORMATION SEE: James W. Schultz, *My Life as an Indian,* Doubleday, Page, 1907, reprinted, Fawcett, 1968; Stanley J. Kunitz and Howard Haycraft, editors, *Junior Book of Authors,* Wilson, 2nd edition, 1951.

Constance Lindsay Skinner

SKINNER, Constance Lindsay   1882-1939

PERSONAL: Born in 1882, in British Columbia, Canada; died March 27, 1939, in New York City; daughter of Robert James and Annie (Lindsay) Skinner. *Education:* Attended a private school in Vancouver, British Columbia, and studied under private tutors. *Home:* New York City.

CAREER: Novelist, poet, historian; began writing for newspapers in British Columbia while in her teens, later worked for the Los Angeles *Times,* the Los Angeles *Examiner,* the Chicago *American,* and the *New York Herald Tribune,* serving at various times as political reporter, editorial writer, special features writer, dramatic and musical critic, and book reviewer. *Member:* Women's National Book Association (vice-president).

WRITINGS—Fiction, except as noted: *Good-Morning, Rosamond!* (illustrated by Thomas Fogarty), Doubleday, Page, 1917; *The Search Relentless,* Methuen, 1925, new edition, Coward, 1928; *Silent Scot: Frontier Scout,* Macmillan, 1925; *Becky Landers: Frontier Warrior,* Macmillan, 1926, reprinted, 1967; *The White Leader* (illustrated by Remington Schuyler), Macmillan, 1926; *Roselle of the North* (illustrated by Frank Schoonover), Macmillan, 1927; *The Tiger Who Walks Alone,* Macmillan, 1927; *The Ranch of the Golden Flowers,* Macmillan, 1928; *Andy Breaks Trail,* Macmillan, 1928; *Red Willows,* Coward, 1929; *Red Man's Luck* (illustrated by Caroline Gibbons Granger), Coward, 1930; *Songs of the Coast-Dwellers* (poems), Coward, 1930; *Debby Barnes: Trader* (illustrated by John Rae), Macmillan, 1932; *Rob Roy: The Frontier Twins,* Macmillan, 1934.

Nonfiction: *Pioneers of the Old Southwest: A Chronicle of the Dark and Bloody Ground,* Yale University Press, 1919; *Adventurers of Oregon: A Chronicle of the Fur Trade,* Yale University Press, 1920; (with Clark Wissler and William Wood) *Adventurers in the Wilderness,* Yale University Press, 1925; *Beavers, Kings and Cabins* (illustrated by W. Langdon Kihn), Macmillan, 1933.

Also author of the novel, *Builder of Men,* published in Germany, 1913, and of the play, "David," produced at the Forest Theatre in Carmel, California, 1910. Contributor of stories to *Boys' Life* (Boy Scout magazine) and to *American Girl* (Girl Scout magazine). Editor of the "Rivers of America" series published by Farrar & Rinehart, 1937-39. The series, which continued after Skinner's death, was published in a young readers' edition by Holt, beginning in 1961.

SIDELIGHTS: The Constance Lindsay Skinner Medal was founded in 1939 by the Women's National Book Association. The bronze plaque was designed by Frances O'-Brien Garfield and was first awarded to Anne Carroll Moore in 1940.

FOR MORE INFORMATION SEE: Horn Book, July, 1939; Muriel Fuller, editor, *More Junior Authors,* Wilson, 1963; Obituaries—*New York Times,* March 28, 1939; *Publishers Weekly,* April 1, 1939; *Time,* April 10, 1939; *Library Journal,* April 15, 1939; *Wilson Library Bulletin,* May, 1939.

Jack Sprat could eat no fat. ■ (From *Mother Goose*. Illustrated by E. Boyd Smith.)

SMITH, E(lmer) Boyd 1860-1943

PERSONAL: Born May 31, 1860, in St. John, New Brunswick, Canada; died, 1943. *Education:* Studied art in Paris. *Home:* Wilton, Connecticut.

CAREER: Author and illustrator.

WRITINGS—All self-illustrated: *My Village,* Scribner, 1896; *The Story of Noah's Ark,* Houghton, 1905; *The Story of Pocahontas and Captain John Smith,* Houghton, 1906, *Santa Claus and All about Him,* F. A. Stokes, 1908; *The Circus and All About It,* F. A. Stokes, 1909; *Chicken World,* Putnam, 1910; *The Farm Book: Bob and Betty Visit Uncle John,* Houghton, 1910; *The Seashore Book: Bob and Betty's Summer with Captain Hawes,* Houghton, 1912;

The Railroad Book: Bob and Betty's Summer on the Railroad, Houghton, 1913.

The Early Life of Mr. Man before Noah, Houghton, 1914; *In the Land of Make Believe,* Holt, 1916; *After They Came Out of the Ark,* Putnam, 1918; *The Story of Our Country,* Putnam, 1920; *Fun in the Radio World,* F. A. Stokes, 1923; *The Country Book,* F. A. Stokes, 1924; *Lions 'n' Elephants 'n' Everything,* Putnam, 1929; *So Long Ago,* Houghton, 1944.

Illustrator: Joel Chandler Harris, *Plantation Pageants,* Houghton, 1899, reprinted, Books for Libraries, 1970; Abbie Farwell Brown, *In the Days of Giants: Norse Tales,* Houghton, 1902; Florence Holbrook, *The Book of Nature Myths,* Houghton, 1902; Bidpai, *Tortoise and the Geese*

(From *The Tortoise and the Geese* retold by Maude Barrows Dutton. Illustrated by E. Boyd Smith.)

(retold by M. B. Dutton), Houghton, 1908; Mary Raymond Shipman Andrews, *The Enchanted Forest,* Dutton, 1909; A. F. Brown, *John of the Woods,* Houghton, 1909; Daniel Defoe, *Robinson Crusoe,* Houghton, 1909.

James Fenimore Cooper, *The Last of the Mohicans,* Houghton, 1910; *Aesop's Fables,* Century, 1911; Richard Henry Dana, *Two Years before the Mast,* Houghton, 1911; Frederick Marryat, *Children of the New Forest,* Holt, 1911; James Willard Schultz, *Sinopah, the Indian Boy,* Houghton, 1913; Sir Walter Scott, *Ivanhoe,* Houghton, 1913; Mrs. M. Cary, *French Fairy Tales,* Crowell, 1919; Mother Goose, *The Boyd Smith Mother Goose,* Putnam, 1919; Robert Gordon Anderson, *Seven O'Clock Stories,* Putnam, 1920; Cornelia Lynde Meigs, *Willow Whistle,* Macmillan, 1931.

At these words of the Great Spirit, all the stones before him stirred with life and lifted themselves on many-colored wings. They fluttered away in the sunshine, and the southwind sang to them as they went. ■ (From *The Book of Nature Myths* by Florence Holbrook. Illustrated by E. Boyd Smith.)

STOWE, Harriet (Elizabeth) Beecher 1811-1896
(Christopher Crowfield)

PERSONAL: Born June 13, 1811, in Litchfield, Connecticut; died July 1, 1896, in Hartford, Connecticut; daughter of Lyman (a Congregational minister) and Roxana (Foote) Beecher; sister of Henry Ward Beecher; married Calvin Ellis Stowe (a clergyman), January 6, 1836; children: seven. *Education:* Privately tutored at home; later attended her sister Catherine's school in Hartford, Connecticut.

CAREER: Author, teacher, activist in the movement to abolish slavery. *Awards, honors:* Publication prize from the *Western Monthly* magazine, 1834, for the story "Uncle Lot."

WRITINGS—Novels: *Uncle Tom's Cabin; or, Life among the Lowly* (first published serially in *The National Era,* 1851-52), J. P. Jewett, 1852, new edition, Dodd, 1972 [other editions include those illustrated by George Cruikshank, Cassell, 1852; John Leech, Bogue, 1852; Thomas R. Macquoid and G. H. Thomas, N. Cooke, 1853; Edward W. Kemble, Houghton, 1892; Miguel Covarrubias, Limited Editions Club, 1938]; *Dred: A Tale of the Great Dismal Swamp,* Phillips, Sampson, 1856, reprinted, AMS Press, 1970 (also published as *Nina Gordon: A Tale of the Great Dismal Swamp,* Ticknor & Fields, 1866); *The Minister's Wooing,* Derby & Jackson, 1859, reprinted, Gregg, 1968; *The Pearl of Orr's Island: A Story of the Coast of Maine,* Ticknor & Fields, 1862, reprinted, Scholarly Press, 1970; *Agnes of Sorrento,* Ticknor & Fields, 1862, reprinted, AMS Press, 1971; *Old Town Folks,* Fields, Osgood, 1869, reprinted, AMS Press, 1971; *Our Charley and What to Do with Him,* Lippincott, 1869; *Pink and White Tyranny: A Society Novel,* Roberts Brothers, 1871; *My Wife and I; or, Harry Henderson's History,* J. B. Ford, 1871; *We and Our Neighbors; or, The Records of an Unfashionable Street,* J. B. Ford, 1875; *Poganuc People: Their Loves and Lives,* Fords, Howard, 1878.

Short stories: *The Mayflower; or, Sketches of Scenes and Characters among the Descendants of the Pilgrims,* Harper, 1843, reprinted, Books for Libraries, 1972; *Uncle Sam's Emancipation; Early Care, a Heavenly Discipline; and Other Sketches,* W. P. Hazard, 1853, reprinted, Books for Libraries, 1970; (under pseudonym Christopher Crowfield) *Little Foxes* (first published in the *Atlantic Monthly,* 1865, as part of the series *The Chimney-Corner*), Ticknor & Fields, 1866; (under pseudonym Christopher Crowfield) *The Chimney-Corner* (first published serially in the *Atlantic Monthly,* 1865-66), Ticknor & Fields, 1868, reprinted, Books for Libraries, 1972; *Sam Lawson's Oldtown Fireside Stories,* Houghton, 1872, reprinted, Gregg, 1967; *Betty Bright's Idea; also, Deacon Pitkin's Farm, and The First Christmas of New England,* J. B. Ford, 1875, reprinted, Books for Libraries, 1972; *Regional Sketches: New England and Florida* (edited by John R. Adams), College and University Press, 1972.

Poems: *Religious Poems,* Ticknor & Fields, 1867; *Collected Poems* (edited by John Michael Moran, Jr.), Transcendental Books, 1967.

Harriet Beecher Stowe, 1853.

Nonfiction: *A Key to "Uncle Tom's Cabin,"* J. P. Jewett, 1853, reprinted, Scholarly Press, 1970; *Sunny Memories of Foreign Lands,* Phillips, Sampson, 1854; (under pseudonym Christopher Crowfield) *House and Home Papers,* Ticknor & Fields, 1865; *Queer Little People* (animal stories), Ticknor & Fields, 1867; *Men of Our Times; or, Leading Patriots of the Day,* J. D. Denison, 1868, reprinted, Books for Libraries, 1972, revised edition published as *The Lives and Deeds of Our Self-Made Men* (edited by son Charles E. Stowe), Estes & Lauriat, 1889; *Lady Byron Vindicated,* Fields, Osgood, 1870, reprinted, R. West, 1973; *Palmetto Leaves,* Osgood, 1873, new edition (edited by Mary B. Graff), University Presses of Florida, 1968; *Women in Sacred History,* J. B. Ford, 1874 (also published as *Bible Heroines,* Fords, Howard, 1878); *Footsteps of the Master* (biography of Jesus), J. B. Ford, 1877.

Collections: *The Writings of Harriet Beecher Stowe,* 16 volumes, Riverside Press, 1896, reprinted, AMS Press, 1967.

Also author of *An Elementary Geography,* 1835; *A Geography for My Children,* 1855; *Our Famous Women,* 1884.

ADAPTATIONS—Movies and filmstrips: "Uncle Tom's Cabin" (motion pictures), World Producing Corp., 1914, Famous Players-Lasky Corp., 1918, Universal Pictures, 1927; "My Wife and I" (motion picture), Warner Brothers, 1925; "The Minister's Housekeeper" (motion picture), Time, Inc., 1952. Plus numerous theatrical productions.

SIDELIGHTS: **June 13, 1811.** Born in Litchfield, Connecticut. The seventh of nine children. Father, Lyman Beecher, a leading clergyman of the time. "My earliest recollections of Litchfield are those of its beautiful scenery, which impressed and formed my mind long before I had words to give names to my emotions, or could analyze my mental processes. . . . [It] was a mountain town, where the winter was a stern reality for six months of the year, where there were great winds, drifting snows of a sublime power and magnitude.

"My blessed father, for many years so true an image of the Heavenly Father . . . never seemed to realize that people were unbelievers for any other reason than want of light, and that clear and able arguments would not at once put an end to scepticism.

"[He] was very fond of music, and was susceptible to its influence; and one of the great eras of the family, in my childish recollection, is the triumphant bringing home from New Haven a fine-toned upright piano, which a fortunate accident had brought within the range of a poor country minister's means. The ark of the covenant was not brought into the tabernacle with more gladness than this magical instrument into our abode." [E. C. Wagenknecht, *Harriet Beecher Stowe: The Known and the Unknown,* Oxford University Press, 1965.[1]]

1816. Mother died. "I was between three and four years of age when our mother died, and my personal recollections of her are therefore but few. But the deep interest and veneration that she inspired in all who knew her were such that during all my childhood I was constantly hearing her spoken of, and from one friend or another some incident or anecdote of her life was constantly being impressed upon me.

"Mother was one of those strong, restful, yet widely sympathetic natures in whom all around seemed to find comfort and repose. The communion between her and my father was a peculiar one. It was an intimacy throughout the whole range of their being. There was no human mind in whose decisions he had greater confidence. Both intellectually and morally be regarded her as the better and stronger portion of himself, and I remember hearing him say that after her death his first sensation was a sort of terror, like that of a child suddenly shut out alone in the dark.

"In my own childhood only two incidents of my mother twinkle like rays through the darkness. One was of our all running and dancing out before her from the nursery to the sitting-room one Sabbath morning, and her pleasant voice saying after us, 'Remember the Sabbath day to keep it holy, children.'

"Another remembrance is this: mother was an enthusiastic horticulturist in all the small ways that limited means allowed. Her brother John in New York had just sent her a small parcel of fine tulip-bulbs. I remember rummaging these out of an obscure corner of the nursery one day when she was gone out, and being strongly seized with the idea that they were good to eat, using all the little English I then possessed to persuade my brothers that these were onions such as grown people ate and would be very nice for us. So we fell to and devoured the whole, and I recollect being somewhat disappointed in the odd sweetish taste, and thinking that onions were not so nice as I had supposed. Then mother's serene face appeared at the nursery door and we all ran towards her, telling with one voice of our discovery and achievement. We had found a bag of onions and had eaten them all up.

"Also I remember that there was not even a momentary expression of impatience, but that she sat down and said, 'My dear children, what you have done makes mamma very sorry. Those were not onions but roots of beautiful flowers, and if you had let them alone we should have next summer in the garden great beautiful red and yellow flowers such as you never saw.' I remember how drooping and dispirited we all grew at this picture, and how sadly we regarded the empty paper bag." [Charles Edward Stowe, *Life of Harriet Beecher Stowe: Her Letters and Journals,* Riverside Press, 1889.[2]]

"[Mother's death was] a loss, which I have felt from my earliest childhood every year deeper—the one friend whom God never replaces—whom I never knew personally but yet have always deplored the want of. . . . She was of a temperament peculiarly restful and peace-giving. . . . Her union of spirit with God, unruffled and unbroken even from very early childhood, seemed to impart to her an equilibrium and healthful placidity that no earthly reverses ever disturbed.

Her closest sibling was her brother, Henry, who became a clergyman: "the noblest and most Christlike human being I know . . . he who is to me another self. . . .

"I went to church Sunday morning and heard [him] in one of his happiest moods. Not one of the tearing excited ones, but calm clear bright elevated. The prayer seemed to open a wide and solemn path up into Heaven and to isolate one from earth. I could feel with my eyes shut as if there were such a great upward current as Titian represents in the Assumption of the Madonna. This is just the way the church service always affects me, but how few men—single men—there are with the power of being at the moment more than a whole liturgy. Some times a thought would seem so beautiful so comforting so tenderly and nobly expressed I would say, I will remember that, and write it to the girls but it was just as it was on the sea beaches; one long bright wave effaced the last and so one after another, each bright and making room for another.

"I have so long lived with [my family] that I can scarcely think of a separate mental history."[1]

1821. Attended Litchfield Academy at age twelve. Her essay, "Can the Immortality of the Soul be Proved by the Light of Nature?" was chosen to be read in public: "I remember well the scene at that exhibition, to me so eventful. The hall was crowded with all the literati of Litchfield. Before them all our compositions were read aloud. When mine was read I noticed that father, who was sitting on high . . ., brightened and looked interested, and at the close I heard him ask, 'Who wrote that composition?' 'Your daughter, sir,' was the answer. It was the proudest moment of my life. There was no mistaking father's face when he was pleased and to have interested him was past all juvenile triumphs."[2]

1824. Moved to Hartford, Connecticut where she continued her studies and assisted her eldest sister Catharine as student-teacher at Hartford Female Seminary. Began writing for the *Western Monthly* Magazine, the *New York Evangelist,* and other media. "I am trying to cultivate a general spirit of kindliness toward everybody. Instead of shrinking into a corner to notice how other people behave, I am holding out my hand to the right and to the left, and forming casual or incidental acquaintances with all who will be acquainted with me. In this way I find society full of interest and pleasure—a pleasure which pleaseth me more because it is not old and worn out."[1]

1833. Collaborated with Catharine on a *First Geography for Children* which was very successful.

1834. Visited Niagara Falls. "I have seen . . . [Niagara] and yet live. Oh, where is your soul? Never mind, though. Let me tell, if I can, what is unutterable. . . . It is not *like* anything; it did not look like anything I expected; it did not look like a waterfall. I did not once think whether it was high or low; whether it roared or didn't roar; whether it equaled my expectations or not. My mind whirled off, it seemed to me, in a new, strange world. It seemed unearthly, like the strange, dim images in the Revelation. I thought of the great white throne; the rainbow around it; the throne in sight like unto an emerald; and oh! that beautiful water rising like moonlight, falling as the soul sinks when it dies, to rise refined, spiritualized, and pure. That rainbow, breaking out, trembling, fading, and again coming like a beautiful spirit walking the waters. Oh, it is lovelier than it is great; it is like the Mind that made it: great, but so veiled in beauty that we gaze without terror. I felt as if I could have *gone over* with the waters; it would be so beautiful a death; there would be no fear in it. I felt the rock tremble under me with a sort of joy. I was so maddened that I could have gone too; if it had gone."[2]

January 6, 1836. Married Calvin E. Stowe, a professor and later a distinguished Biblical scholar. Of this marriage there were seven children. "Indeed, . . . I am but a mere drudge with few ideas beyond babies and housekeeping. As for thoughts, reflections, and sentiments, good lack! good lack!

"I suppose I am a dolefully uninteresting person at present, but I hope I shall grow young again one of these days, for it seems to me that matters cannot always stand exactly as they do now.

"Well . . . this marriage is—yes, I will speak well of it, after all; for when I can stop and think long enough to discriminate my head from my heels, I must say that I think myself a fortunate woman both in husband and children. My children I would not change for all the ease, leisure, and pleasure that I could have without them. They are money on interest whose value will be constantly increasing. . . ."[2]

"In thinking how all my life and strength and almost my separate consciousness passed away from me into my children and how they seem to depend on me from day to day for sympathy, I seemed to understand what Christ meant when he spoke of himself as being made bread and giving his flesh and blood as the vital food for his own."[1]

Stowe's house, Brunswick, Maine, where *Uncle Tom's Cabin* was written.

She wrote to her twin girls: "You don't know how I love you—you never will till you love some one as I do you—you have educated me quite as much as I you—you have taught me the love of God, by awakening such love in me. . . . I long to put the experience of fifty years at once into your young hearts to give you at once the key of that treasure chamber every gem of which has cost me tears and struggles and prayers. . . .

"Now, when I think of appealing to you for help in various crises which arise I find you with your own plans all laid—your time divided and your wishes very strong. Tho you always beautifully assent to my wishes yet it is so evident that I break in on your plans and derange them that I often suffer any inconvenience and go far beyond my strength rather than ask one of you to help me.

"Remember my children, nobody can help me who depresses my spirits. My courage, hope and animal spirits are the fund on which I, and you and all depend, and when I feel that all around me are gloomy and depressed, it is a *sorer drain on my vitality than any amount of hard work*. . . . I think my children do not often enough consider my nature, its wants and needs. I am very sensitive, very affectionate. A word spoken harshly by any one *to any other* grates on me—I hear the blame of all. . . . Then too I have so little society. Papa goes off by himself and reads—you and Eliza go by yourselves and talk—I have no companion unless one of my sisters."[1]

And to one son, who, as a youth became a seaman: "Unfortunate is the hen who hatches a duck, but she must make the best of it."[1]

To her traveling husband: "With regard to myself I freely confess that I am constitutionally careless and too impetuous and impulsive easily to maintain that consistency and order which is necessary in a family—that I often undertake more than I can well perform and so come to mortifying failures. I also see *now* plainer than I ever did before that I have felt too little the necessity of conceding to such of your peculiarities as seemed to me unreasonable, and have too often pushed my own purposes without reference to them. . . .

"One thing would make a great difference with me. If when you have said things hastily and unjustly you would only be willing to retract them in calmer moments. This is what you almost never do in any particular case. . . . You leave the poisoned arrow in the wound. Now my nature is such that I *cannot* forget such words—if they are only taken back I get over them directly but if not they remain for months. . . . It does seem to me that with such a foundation for mutual respect and affection as there is in us—with such true and real and deep love, that we might exercise a correcting power over each other—that I might help you to be kind and considerate, you me to be systematic and regular."[1]

1843. Her first book of fiction was published, *The Mayflower: Sketches and Scenes and Characters among the Descendents of the Puritans.* In one of her many letters to George Eliot she wrote: "And is it not true, that what we authors want is not *praise* so much as sympathy? A book is *a hand* stretched forth in the dark passage of life to see if there is another hand to meet it."[1]

1845. "I am sick of the smell of sour milk, and sour meat, and sour everything, and then the clothes *will* not dry, and no wet thing does, and everything smells mouldy; and altogether I feel as if I never wanted to eat again.

". . . I have been called off at least a dozen times; once for the fishman, to buy a codfish; once to see a man who had brought me some barrels of apples; once to see a book agent; then to Mrs. Upham's to see about a drawing I promised to make for her; then to nurse the baby; then into the kitchen to make a chowder for dinner; and now I am at it again, for nothing but deadly determination enables me ever to write; it is rowing against wind and tide."[1]

1846. Went to Brattleboro, Vermont for a health cure. "For this week, I have gone before breakfast to the wave-bath and let all the waves and billows roll over me till every limb ached with cold and my hands would scarcely have feeling enough to dress me. After that I have walked till I was warm, and come home to breakfast with such an appetite! Brown bread and milk are luxuries indeed, and the only fear is that I may eat too much. At eleven comes my douche, to which I have walked in a driving rain for the last two days, and after it walked in the rain again till I was warm. . . . After dinner I roll ninepins or walk till four, then sitz-bath, and another walk till six."[1]

July 26, 1849. During an epidemic, her son died of cholera. "MY DEAR HUSBAND,—At last it is over and our dear little one is gone from us. He is now among the blessed. My Charley—my beautiful, loving, gladsome baby, so loving, so sweet, so full of life and hope and strength—now lies shrouded, pale and cold, in the room below. Never was he anything to me but a comfort. He has been my pride and joy. Many a heartache has he cured for me. Many an anxious night have I held him to my bosom and felt the sorrow and loneliness pass out of me with the touch of his little warm hands. Yet I have just seen him in his death agony, looked on his imploring face when I could not help nor soothe nor do one thing, not one, to mitigate his cruel suffering, do nothing but pray in my anguish that he might die soon. I write as though there were no sorrow like my sorrow, yet there has been in this city, as in the land of Egypt, scarce a house without its dead. This heart-break,

Harriet Beecher Stowe

this anguish, has been everywhere, and when it will end God alone knows."[2]

March 20, 1852. *Uncle Tom's Cabin* published in book form—3,000 copies sold the first day, within a year over 300,000 copies had been issued and sold in the United States. "It has been my earnest desire to address myself to southern minds, for I have always believed that there was slumbering at the South, energy enough to reform its evils, could it only be aroused.

"It has seemed to me that many who have attacked the system, have not understood the southern character, nor appreciated what is really good in it. I think I have, at least I have tried, during this whole investigation, to balance my mind by keeping before it the most agreeable patterns of southern life and character.

"It seems to me that truly noble minds ought to consider that the best friendship which refuses to defend their faults, but rather treats them as excrescences which ought to be severed, and what is true of individuals is true of countries.

"I respect and admire the true chivalric, noble ideal of the southern man, and therefore more indignantly reprobate all that which is no part of him, being the result of an unnatural institution, and which is unworthy of him, and therein, I think, show myself more fully a friend than those who undertake to defend faults and all. . . .

"It was my hope that a book so kindly intended, so favorable in many respects, might be permitted free circulation among the [Southerners] and that the gentle voice of Eva and the manly generosity of St. Clare might be allowed to say those things of the system which would be invidious in any other form. . . .

(From the stage production of "Uncle Tom's Cabin" starring Otis Skinner.)

Yesterday's Authors of Books for Children

"The great error of controversy is, that it is ever ready to assail *persons* rather than *principles*. The slave system as a *system,* perhaps concentrates more wrong than any other now existing, and yet those who live under and in it may be as we see, enlightened, generous, and amenable to reason. If the system alone is attacked, such minds will be the first to perceive its evils, and to turn against it; but if the system be attacked through individuals, self-love, wounded pride, and a thousand natural feelings, will be at once enlisted for its preservation. . . ."[1]

"I am a minister's daughter, and a minister's wife, and I have had six brothers in the ministry (one is in heaven); I certainly ought to know something of the feelings of ministers on this subject. I was a child in 1820 when the Missouri question was agitated, and one of the strongest and deepest impressions on my mind was that made by my father's sermons and prayers, and the anguish of his soul for the poor slave at that time. I remember his preaching drawing tears down the hardest faces of the old farmers in his congregation.

"I well remember his prayers morning and evening in the family for 'poor, oppressed, bleeding Africa,' that the time of her deliverance might come; prayers offered with strong crying and tears, and which indelibly impressed my heart and made me what I am from my very soul, the enemy of all slavery. . . .

"I was married when I was twenty-five years old to a man rich in Greek and Hebrew, Latin and Arabic, and alas! rich in nothing else. When I went to housekeeping, my entire stock of china for parlor and kitchen was bought for eleven dollars. That lasted very well for two years, till my brother was married and brought his bride to visit me. I then found, on review, that I had neither plates or teacups to set a table for my father's family; wherefore I thought it best to reinforce the establishment by getting me a tea-set that cost ten dollars more, and this, I believe, formed my whole stock in trade for some years.

"But then I was abundantly enriched with wealth of another sort.

"I had two little, curly-headed twin daughters to begin with, and my stock in this line has gradually increased, till I have been the mother of seven children, the most beautiful and the most loved of whom lies buried near my Cincinnati residence. It was at his dying bed and at his grave that I learned what a poor slave mother may feel when her child is torn away from her. In those depths of sorrow which seemed to me immeasurable, it was my only prayer to God that such anguish might not be suffered in vain. There were circumstances about his death of such peculiar bitterness, of what seemed almost cruel suffering, that I felt that I could never be consoled for it, unless this crushing of my own heart might enable me to work out some great good to others. . . ."[2]

James Russell Lowell noted in his journal: "How she is shaking the world with [*Uncle Tom's Cabin*]. . . . At one step she has reached the top of the stair-case up which the rest of us climb on our knees year after year."[1]

She wrote to Horace Mann: "Today I have taken my pen from the last chapter of *Uncle Tom's Cabin* and I think you

Harriet Beecher Stowe, 1884.

will understand me when I say that I feel as if I had written some of it almost with my heart's blood. I look upon it almost as a despairing appeal to a civilized humanity—in the close of it I think you may trace the result of some of your suggestions."[1]

1853, 1856 and 1859. Toured Europe. "I am a little bit of a woman,—somewhat more than forty, about as thin and dry as a pinch of snuff; never very much to look at in my best days, and looking like a used-up article now.

"The poor people seem to expect something quite angelic. I wish for their sakes I was rather more than I am. I am sorry to break up their innocent illusions by the vision of a little matter of fact commonplace woman—neither good looking nor accomplished, not even learned . . . and entirely ill adapted to any kind of speech making or show making in any form . . . as beauty has never been one of my strong points, . . . I am open to flattery upon it."[1]

In Europe she encountered Gothic art and architecture. "There are gables, and pinnacles, and spires, and balconies, and buttresses any where and every where, without rhyme or reason; for wherever the poet wanted a balcony, he had it; or wherever he had a fragment of carved stone, or a bit of historic tracery to put in, he made a shrine for it forthwith, without asking leave of any rules.

"If people will make such dismal hobgoblin saints, and such fat virgins and such roystering, blackguard angels, I would much rather have none. There was a crucifix high up in the nave, enough to make one sick to look at it; and on one side of it a virgin, with a gridiron on her head, and on the other a very fat saint, in yellow petticoats."[1]

"Mother! mother! Don't, don't!" said the boy. "They say you's got a good master." ■
(From *Uncle Tom's Cabin* by Harriet Beecher Stowe. Illustrated by James Daughterty.)

Egyptian art she considered horrible, like something that had "floundered up out of Nile mud." So she did not bother to look at it. "But Rubens, the great, joyous, full-souled, all-powerful Rubens!—there he was, full as ever of triumphant, abounding life; disgusting and pleasing; making me laugh and making me angry; defying me to dislike him; dragging me at his chariot wheels; in despite of my protests forcing me to confess that there was no other but he.

"My first sensation was of astonishment, blank, absolute, overwhelming. After all that I had seen, I had no idea of a painting like this. I was lifted off my feet, as much as by Cologne Cathedral, or Niagara Falls, so that I could neither reason nor think whether I was pleased or not. It is difficult, even now, to analyze the sources of this wonderful power. The excellence of this picture does not lie, like Raphael's, in a certain ideal spirituality, by which the scene is raised above earth to the heavenly sphere; but rather in a power, strong, human, almost homely, by which, not an ideal, but the real scene is forced home upon the heart."[1]

1857. Son, Henry, drowned while a student at Dartmouth.

February 12, 1859. To her daughter Georgiana: "Why haven't I written? Because, dear Georgie, I am like the dry, dead, leafless tree, and have only cold, dead, slumbering buds of hope on the end of stiff, hard, frozen twigs of thought, but no leaves, no blossoms; nothing to send to a little girl who doesn't know what to do with herself any more than a kitten. I am cold, weary, dead; everything is a burden to me.

"I let my plants die by inches before my eyes, and do not water them, and I dread everything I do, and wish it was not to be done, and so when I get a letter from my little girl I smile and say, 'Dear little puss, I will answer it'; and I sit hour after hour with folded hands, fact is, pussy, mamma is tired. Life to you is gay and joyous, but to mamma it has been a battle in which the spirit is willing but the flesh weak, and she would be glad, like the woman in the St. Bernard, to lie down with her arms around the wayside cross, and sleep away into a brighter scene.

"Henry's fair, sweet face looks down upon me now and then from out a cloud, and I feel again all the bitterness of the eternal 'No' which says I must never, never, in this life, see that face, lean on that arm, hear that voice. Not that my faith in God in the least fails, and that I do not believe that all this is for good. I do, and though not happy, I am blessed. Weak, weary as I am, I rest on Jesus in the innermost depth of my soul, and am quite sure that there is coming an inconceivable hour of beauty and glory when I shall regain Jesus, and he will give me back my beloved one, whom he is educating in a far higher sphere than I proposed. So do not mistake me,—only know that mamma is sitting weary by the wayside feeling weak and worn, but in no sense discouraged."[2]

1868. "We see nothing unfeminine or improper in a woman's exercising the right of suffrage; we see no impropriety in her pursuing an extended career of study, which shall fit her to be a physician, we think that women may become architects . . . or they may become landscape-gardeners, and find abundant exercise for taste and skill, and healthy, remunerative employment; they may even be teachers of a naval school, and expound to disciples the mysteries of ocean navigation, as a woman at this day is successfully doing—in short, there is no earthly reason why they should not . . . use every advantage which God and nature have put into their hands. . . .

"In this view, we see no impropriety in a woman's becoming a public character, when constitution and genius evidently fit her peculiarly for such a course. No one ever listened to Mrs. Fanny Kemble's public interpretations of Shakespeare and had any doubts of the propriety of her giving them because she was a woman. Anna Dickinson's career has fully shown that the good sense of the community justifies even a young woman in being a public lecturer, who has a gift and genius for oratory. All such instances make their own laws, and the general good sense of mankind admits them."[1]

1870. Her son, Frederick, disappeared in San Francisco, after valiant but vain attempts to rehabilitate himself after his Civil War experiences.

1870's. Began her career as a public reader of her own works. "So far [she wrote her daughters, on November 9, 1872], my health has been better than any autumn for several years. The fatigue of speaking is nothing—the general fatigue of excitement &c lessens as I get accustomed to it and the fatigue of railroad travel seems to do me good. I never sleep better than after a long day's ride."[1]

"One woman, totally deaf, came to me afterwards and said: 'Bless you. I come jist to see you. I'd rather see you than the Queen.' Another introduced her little girl named Harriet Beecher Stowe, and another, older, named Eva. She said they had traveled fifty miles to hear me read. An incident like that appeals to one's heart, does it not?"[2]

"My vocation is simply that of painter, and my object will be to hold up in the most lifelike and graphic manner possible Slavery, its reverses, changes, and the negro character, which I have had ample opportunities for studying. There is no arguing with *pictures,* and everybody is impressed by them, whether they mean to be or not.

"I had planned an article gay sprightly wholly domestic, but as I began and sketched the pleasant home and quiet fireside an irresistible impulse *wrote for me* what followed an offering of sympathy to the suffering and agonized, whose homes have forever been darkened. It is vain to propose and announce subjects from week to week. One must write what one is thinking of. When the mind is full of one thing, why go about to write on another?

"A story *comes,* grows like a flower, sometimes will and sometimes won't, like a pretty woman."[1]

1875. Her brother, Henry, underwent a protracted ordeal of scandal and public notoriety. "[He] has had a degree of worldly success, he has power and wealth and worldly strength, so that a rabble were following him for loaves and fishes using his name to sell quack medicines and him as a speculation. The Lord has lopped away all this worldly growth—none cling to him now but the really good. As to him he was in danger of over self confidence and of wan-

dering into a sort of naturalistic philosophy. The trial has *driven* him to the Bible and Christ as a child clings to its mother. Best of all, I *do* believe that this severe affliction which has been to him a crucifixion has so entirely subdued his will to God's that he is now in that blessed state of rest which comes from having given up self altogether. He has so entirely placed himself in God's hands and God's will has so become his own that he has no care.

"I think I never knew any one so cruelly treated. . . . If he had not the sweetest kindest most patient magnanimous nature to begin with, I don't think even Divine Grace could have led a man to bear what he has borne.

"He is peculiar, in a sort of extreme delicacy of feeling, and an entire and utter inability to talk of what pains him. In the great sorrows of life, the loss of his brother and his little children, he has always shut himself up and been dumb—there is a terrible inward intensity. The trial of this vile story came on him three years ago when first with amazement and disgust and horror he learned that such a thought could enter a human soul with regard to him. Since then he has been busy forgiving—healing restoring returning good for evil and blessing for cursing, and God helping he will carry it through, notwithstanding this vile woman's attempt to tear open old wounds. I who know all and have seen all from the first feel as if I could give my life's blood for him.

"This has drawn on my life [she wrote George Eliot]—my heart's blood. He is myself; I know you are the kind of woman to understand me when I say that I felt a blow at him more than at myself. I, who know his purity, honor, delicacy, know that he has been from childhood of an ideal purity,—who reverenced his conscience as his king, whose glory was redressing human wrong, who spoke no slander, no, nor listened to it. . . . It seems now but a little time since my brother Henry and I were two young people together. . . . I taught him drawing and heard his Latin lessons, for you know a girl becomes mature and womanly long before a boy. I saw him through college, and helped him through the difficult love affair that gave him his wife; and then he and my husband had a real German, enthusiastic love for each other, which ended in making me a wife. Ah! in those days we never dreamed that he, or I, or any of us, were to be known in the world. All he seemed then was a boy full of fun, full of love, full of enthusiasm for protecting abused and righting wronged people, which made him in those early days write editorials, and wear arms and swear himself a special policeman to protect the poor negroes in Cincinnati, where we then lived, when there were mobs instigated by the slaveholders of Kentucky."[1]

August 6, 1886. Husband, Calvin, died.

February 5, 1893. She wrote to her beloved friend, Oliver Wendell Holmes: "I make no mental effort of any sort; my brain is tired out. It was a woman's brain and not a man's, and finally from sheer fatigue and exhaustion in the march and strife of life it gave out before the end was reached. And now I rest me, like a moored boat, rising and falling on the water, with loosened cordage and flapping sail. . . .

"My mental condition might be called nomadic, I have no fixed thoughts or objects. I wander at will from one subject to another. In pleasant summer weather I am out of doors most of my time, rambling about the neighborhood and calling upon my friends. I do not read much. Now and then I dip into a book much as a humming-bird, poised in air on whirring wing, darts into the heart of a flower, now here, now there, and away. Pictures delight me and afford me infinite diversion and interest. I pass many pleasant hours looking over books of pictures."[1]

July 1, 1896. Died of brain congestion complicated by partial paralysis.

FOR MORE INFORMATION SEE: Charles E. Stowe, *The Life of Harriet Beecher Stowe: Compiled from Her Journals and Letters,* Houghton, 1889, reprinted, Gale, 1967; A. C. Crozier, *The Novels of Harriet Beecher Stowe,* 1896, reprinted, Oxford University Press, 1969; Annie A. Fields, *The Life and Letters of Harriet Beecher Stowe,* Houghton, 1897, reprinted, Gale, 1970; C. E. Stowe and Lyman Beecher Stowe, *Harriet Beecher Stowe: The Story of Her Life,* Houghton, 1911; Constance M. Rourke, *Trumpets of Jubilee: Lyman Beecher, Harriet Beecher Stowe, Henry Ward Beecher, Horace Greeley, P. T. Barnum,* Harcourt, 1927; L. B. Stowe, *Saints, Sinners, and Beechers,* Bobbs-Merrill, 1934, reprinted, Books for Libraries, 1970; Catherine Gilbertson, *Harriet Beecher Stowe,* Ryerson, 1937, reprinted, Kennikat, 1968; Forrest Wilson, *Crusader in Crinoline: The Life of Harriet Beecher Stowe,* Lippincott, 1941, reprinted, Greenwood, 1972.

Mary B. Graff, *Mandarin on the St. Johns,* University of Florida Press, 1953; Charles H. Foster, *The Rungless Ladder: Harriet Beecher Stowe and New England Puritanism,* Duke University Press, 1954, new edition, Cooper Square Publications, 1970; John R. Adams, *Harriet Beecher Stowe,* Twayne, 1963; Johanna Johnston, *Runaway to Heaven: The Story of Harriet Beecher Stowe,* Doubleday, 1963; Joseph C. Furnas, *Goodbye to Uncle Tom,* Apollo, 1964; Edward Wagenknecht, *Harriet Beecher Stowe: The Known and the Unknown,* Oxford University Press, 1965; Winifred E. Wise, *Harriet Beecher Stowe: Woman with a Cause,* Putnam, 1965; Noel B. Gerson, *Harriet Beecher Stowe,* Praeger, 1976.

For children: Elizabeth R. Montgomery, *Story behind Great Books,* McBride, 1946; Phyllis W. Jackson, *Victorian Cinderella: The Story of Harriet Beecher Stowe,* Holiday House, 1947; Mabel C. Widdemer, *Harriet Beecher Stowe: Connecticut Girl,* Bobbs-Merrill, 1949, new edition, 1962; Jean Rouverol, *Harriet Beecher Stowe: Woman Crusader,* Putnam, 1968; Laura Benét, *Famous New England Authors,* Dodd, 1970.

WALTER, Villiam Christian
See ANDERSEN, Hans Christian

WHEELER, Captain
See ELLIS, Edward S(ylvester)

WIGGIN, Kate Douglas (Smith)   1856-1923

PERSONAL: Born September 28, 1856, in Philadelphia, Pennsylvania; died August 24, 1923, at Harrow-on-Hill, England; daughter of Robert Noah (a lawyer) and Helen E. (Dyer) Smith; married Samuel Bradley Wiggin, 1881 (died, 1889); married George Christopher Riggs, 1895. *Education:* Graduated from Abbott Academy, Andover, Massachusetts, 1878.

CAREER: Kindergarten teacher; founded and conducted in San Francisco, California, the first free kindergarten on the Pacific Coast, 1878-84; composer and pianist; novelist and writer for children. *Awards, honors:* Litt.D., Bowdoin College, 1906.

WRITINGS—Stories for children, except as noted: *The Story of Patsy: A Reminiscence,* Murdock, 1883; *The Birds' Christmas Carol,* Murdock, 1887, also published as *Carol Bird's Christmas,* Scholastic Service, 1974, other editions illustrated by Katharine R. Wireman, Houghton, 1912, by Helen Mason Grose, 1929, and by Jessie Gillespie, 1941; dramatization by K. D. Wiggin and Helen Ingersoll published as *The Birds' Christmas Carol,* Houghton, 1914; *A Summer in a Canyon: A California Story,* Houghton, 1889; (with sister, Nora Archibald Smith) *The Story Hour: A Book for the Home and the Kindergarten,* Houghton, 1890; *Timothy's Quest: A Story for Anybody, Young or Old, Who Cares to Read It,* Houghton, 1890 [also see below], later edition illustrated by Oliver Herford, 1895; extract from *Timothy's Quest* published as *Finding a Home,* Houghton, 1907; *Polly Oliver's Problem: A Story for Girls,* Houghton, 1893; *The Village Watch-Tower* (short stories), Houghton, 1895, reprinted, Books for Libraries, 1970; (composer) *Nine Love-Songs and a Carol,* Houghton, 1896; *Marm Lisa,* Houghton, 1896.

The Diary of a Goose Girl (illustrated by Claude A. Shepperson), Houghton, 1902; *Half-a-Dozen Housekeepers: A Story for Girls,* in *Half-a-Dozen Chapters* (illustrated by Mills Thompson), Altemus, 1903; *Rebecca of Sunnybrook Farm,* Houghton, 1903, later editions illustrated by Helen Mason Grose, Houghton, 1925, an edition with illustrations from the movie starring Shirley Temple, Random House, 1959, other editions illustrated by Miriam Troop (and abridged by Alice Thorne), Grosset & Dunlap, 1960, illustrated by June Goldsborough, Whitman, 1965, and by Lawrence Beall Smith (with an afterword by Clifton Fadiman), Macmillan, 1962; *Rose o' the River* (illustrated by George Wright), Houghton, 1905 [also see below]; *The Flag-Raising* (short stories), Houghton, 1907; *The Old Peabody Pew: A Christmas Romance of a Country Church,* Houghton, 1907, dramatization by the author published under the same title, Samuel French, 1917; *The New Chronicles of Rebecca* (short stories), Houghton, 1907; *Susanna and Sue* (illustrated by Alice Barber Stephens and N. C. Wyeth), Houghton, 1909 [also see below]; *Homespun Tales: Rose o' the River, The Old Peabody Pew, and Susanna and Sue,* Houghton, 1909.

Mother Carey's Chickens, Houghton, 1911, later edition illustrated by Elizabeth Shippen Green Elliott, 1930, dramatization by K. D. Wiggin and Rachel Crothers published under the same title, Samuel French, 1925; *The Story of Waitstill Baxter* (illustrated by H. M. Brett), Houghton, 1913; *The Romance of a Christmas Card* (illustrated by

Alice Ercle Hunt), Houghton, 1916; *The Writings of Kate Douglas Wiggin* (autograph edition), Houghton, 1917; *Creeping Jenny, and Other New England Stories*, Houghton, 1924; (with Charlotte Thompson) *Rebecca of Sunnybrook Farm: A State o' Maine Play* (four-act; based on *Rebecca of Sunnybrook Farm* and *The New Chronicles of Rebecca*), Samuel French, 1932.

Adult novels, except as noted: *A Cathedral Courtship* [*and*] *Penelope's English Experiences* (illustrated by C. Carleton), Houghton, 1893 [also see below]; *Penelope's Progress*, Houghton, 1898 (later edition illustrated by Charles E. Brock), 1900; *Penelope's English Experiences* (illustrated by Brock), Houghton, 1900; *A Cathedral Courtship* (illustrated by Brock), Houghton, 1901; *Penelope's Irish Experiences*, Houghton, 1901, later edition illustrated by Brock, 1902; (with Mary Findlater, Jane Findlater, and with Charlotte Stewart under pseudonym Allan McAulay) *The Affair at the Inn*, Houghton, 1904; (with M. Findlater, J. Findlater, and A. McAulay) *Robinetta*, Houghton, 1911; *Bluebeard: A Musical Fantasy* (satire), Harper, 1914; *Ladies in Waiting* (short stories), Houghton, 1919; *Love by Express: A Novel of California*, privately printed, 1924; *A Thorn in the Flesh: A Monologue* (adapted from the French of Ernest Legouvé), Samuel French, 1926.

Nonfiction: *The Relation of the Kindergarten to the Public School*, Murdock, 1891; *Children's Rights: A Book of Nursery Logic*, Houghton, 1892, reprinted, Gale, 1971; (editor) *The Kindergarten*, Harper, 1893; (with Nora Archibald Smith) *The Republic of Childhood*, Houghton, 1895-96 (contains *Froebel's Gifts*, *Froebel's Occupations*, and *Kindergarten Principles and Practice*); *A Child's Journey with Dickens*, Houghton, 1912; *The Girl and the Kingdom: Learning to Teach*, [Los Angeles], 1915; *My Garden of Memory: An Autobiography*, Houghton, 1923; *A Thanksgiving Retrospect; or, Simplicity of Life in Old New England*, Houghton, 1928.

Editor—All with Nora A. Smith: *The Golden Numbers: A Book of Verse for Youth*, McClure, Phillips, 1902, reprinted, Books for Libraries, 1970; *The Posy Ring: A Book of Verse for Children*, McClure, Phillips, 1903, reprinted, Books for Libraries, 1970, also published as *Poems Every Child Should Know*, Doubleday, Doran, 1942; *The Fairy Ring*, McClure, Phillips, 1906, later editions illustrated by Elizabeth MacKinstry, Doubleday, Doran, 1934, by Warren Chappell (and revised by Ethna Sheehan), Doubleday, 1967, also published as *Fairy Stories Every Child Should Know* (illustrated by E. MacKinstry), Doubleday, Doran, 1942; *Pinafore Palace: A Book of Rhymes for the Nursery*, McClure, 1907, reprinted, Books for Libraries, 1972; *Magic Casements: A Second Fairy Book*, McClure, 1907; *Tales of Laughter: A Third Fairy Book*, McClure, 1908, later edition illustrated by E. MacKinstry, Doubleday, Page, 1926, also published as *Tales of Laughter Every Child Should Know*, Doubleday, Doran, 1939; *Arabian Nights: Their Best-Known Tales* (illustrated by Maxfield Parrish), Scribner, 1909; *Tales of Wonder: A Fourth Fairy Book*, Doubleday, Page, 1909, also published as *Tales of Wonder Every Child Should Know*, circa 1941; *An Hour with the Fairies*, Doubleday, Page, 1911; *The Talking Beasts: A Book of Fable Wisdom* (illustrated by Harold Nelson), Doubleday, Page, 1911; *Twilight Stories: More Tales for the Story Hour*, Houghton, 1925.

Kate Douglas Wiggin, 1897.

ADAPTATIONS—Movies and filmstrips: "A Bit o' Heaven" (motion picture), adaptation of *The Birds' Christmas Carol*, Frieder Film Corp., 1917; "Rebecca of Sunnybrook Farm" (motion pictures), adaptation of the book of the same title, starring Mary Pickford, Pickford Film Corp., 1917, adaptation of the play of the same title, Fox Film Corp., 1932, adaptation of the book of the same title, starring Shirley Temple, Twentieth Century-Fox Film Corp., 1938; "Rose o' the River" (motion picture), Famous Players-Lasky Corp., 1919; "Timothy's Quest" (motion pictures), Dirigo Films, Inc., 1922, Paramount Productions, Inc., 1936, and Teaching Film Custodians, 1947; "Mother Carey's Chickens" (motion picture), adaptation of the book and the play of the same title, starring Fay Bainter, RKO Radio Pictures, Inc., 1938; "Summer Magic" (motion picture), adaptation of the book *Mother Carey's Chickens*, starring Hayley Mills and Burl Ives, Walt Disney Productions, 1963.

SIDELIGHTS: **September 20, 1856.** Born in Philadelphia. "When I was a little girl! . . . I have said before, . . . that these six words are perhaps the most charming in the language. If you have any doubt of their eloquence, experiment with them upon any group of children, however unsusceptible or undisciplined, and observe their almost hypnotic effect. Breathed even to your own heart in some quiet moment, they have a like influence, sending your thought back to some fragrant memory-garden, some hidden corner of the 'little past,' where you re-live the care-free, eager, impetuous, poignant hours when self was first beginning to be conscious of self, and all you have since become was in the glowing bud." [Kate Douglas Wiggin, *My Garden of Memory,* Houghton, 1923.[1]]

1859. "My very earliest recollections . . . begin in something too fugitive to be called a memory, but I never cease to capture, lose again, and recapture, a moment at a children's party . . . when I could not have been more than two years old. This glimpse—it is nothing more—is of many children, and a man who was the idol of all, the center of attraction, the source of all merriment, the fount of all delight; and, with the picture, a sense of personal pride of possession; for this bewildering being, whom the children followed as they did the Pied Piper of Hamelin, was my very own father, and the feeling in my heart was certainly pride, if the psychologists are willing to admit that a child who has only lately learned to lisp can feel an emotion that ordinarily comes a little later.

"My brilliant, gifted father, a young lawyer, . . . went on a business journey to a Western State and died there shortly after.

"What is [strange], perhaps, is my conscious sense of close kinship with my father. It did not haunt me in childhood, but began when I myself began to 'do things.' I have often finished a book and thought: 'My father would have liked

(From *Rebecca of Sunnybrook Farm* by Kate Douglas Wiggin. Illustrated by Helen Mason Grose.)

that!' or, 'My father would have done this, in something this way, only better.'

"An early recollection in this epoch is my first spanking, and a timid and sentimental effort it was, as was just, perhaps, for my offense was merely against conventions. The kind rector of the Episcopal Church had come to bring me a present and my mother summoned me to the parlor to receive it. The gift, when taken from its wrappings and disclosed to my eager gaze, proved to be a prayer book, and as I took it, I remarked, indiscreetly and ungratefully: 'Thank you ever so much, Mr. F., but I do wish you had given me almost anything else!' The rector departed in a few minutes, and thereupon I was practically (though feebly) introduced to the necessity of concealing one's own feelings if, thereby, one can avoid hurting the feelings of somebody else. The spanking reduced my mother to tears, but, beyond some faint idea that I had annoyed her and been impolite to a clergyman, my sufferings, mental or physical, were infinitesimal."[1]

1863. "Real life, conscious, coherent, continuous, begins with me when I see myself driving from the New England city to the village of Hollis, [Maine] sixteen miles distant,—a rough and dusty, rather hilly, road, two horses, and a huge, heavy, dignified 'carryall' holding four people. My mother, after some years of widowhood, had married a distant cousin, Dr. Albion Bradbury, the beloved physician of a large countryside. [They were now the children of a well-to-do physician.]

"My childish pleasures were many, though so simple that a little girl of to-day would certainly think them woefully dull. We played paper dolls, jackstraws and jackstones. . . . We pulled hairs from the horse's tail and put them in the brook to grow snakes, which, to our surprise and regret, they never did; we waded in the river and ran to and fro on the rafted logs.

"One of our pleasures was a little out of the common. I asked my step-father one day if he would give us a part of the garden brook for our froggery. The garden in question covered an acre or two of ground, with little up-hills and down-dales, while a dashing, tumultuous brook, with here and there a bit of quiet water, ran through it. . . . In one of the deep, quiet pools of the brook, hidden by green alder bushes, my father put pieces of fine wire netting, and so arranged them that the frogs we caught and placed there lived a pleasant and secluded life free from the cares and dangers that we fancied existed in large ponds.

"Here we used to wait for gay young polliwogs to grow into frogs, one leg at a time. Repeated and prolonged observations by the pond never once permitted us to see a leg actually coming out. Nature somehow decreed that it should happen in the night.

"All our frogs had names of their own and we knew them all apart. They always had plenty of fat juicy flies and water-bugs for dinner, and sometimes we put little silver shiners and tiny minnows into the pool. 'They will know now, you see, that there are other things in the world except frogs,' I explained to the Small Sister, who did not favor the idea, principally because she could never lean over the fishy part of the brook to catch minnows without tumbling in head foremost.

(From the film "Rebecca of Sunnybrook Farm," copyright 1938, Twentieth-Century Fox. Starring Shirley Temple, Randolph Scott, and Bill "Bojangles" Robinson.)

At the time of her journey with Dickens.

"We held a frog singing school once a week. It was very troublesome, but exciting. We used to put a nice little board across the pool and then catch the frogs and try to keep them in line with their heads all facing the same way during the brief lesson. They never really caught the idea, and were never in a singing mood until just before our own early bedtime, when the baby frogs were so sleepy that they kept falling from the board into the pool. They could never quite apprehend the difference between school and pool; but at the end of the summer's training we twice succeeded in getting them into line, quiet, docile, motionless, without a hint of the application of force. . . . It was a beautiful sight worth any amount of toil and trouble! Twenty-one frogs in line, for a minute and a half, all graded nicely as to size, all in fresh green suits with white shirtfronts.

"It does not need the prophetic gift of an Amos or an Ezekiel to see in this sort of play a foreshadowing of my future absorbing interest in education. We both read without being taught. No power on earth could have kept us from ferreting out the momentous secrets that lay between the covers of books. We never heard that there was an alphabet that had to be learned before we could read.

"Books, books, books! There was always plenty of time (incredible statement!); therefore books before breakfast, after playtime, before bedtime, between-times. Oh! the unconscious misery, the dullness, the loneliness of the child who does not care for reading! No one pretends that a book is the only open sesame to knowledge, for we learn a thousand things by other means . . . but the book, the dear, enlivening enchanting, stimulating, informing, uplifting book, is the most faithful of all allies, and, after human friendship, the chief solace as well as the most inspiring influence in human life. For periodical literature we read *Harper's* Magazine and *Littrell's Living Age,* faithfully and passionately. No books were too old for us! We not only read *Robinson Crusoe, The Lamplighter, Typee, Scottish Chiefs, Thaddeus of Warsaw, The Minister's Wooing, Undine, Uncle Tom's Cabin,* and such old-fashioned treasures, but Thackeray, Dickens, Scott, Shakespeare, and the Bible. There was, besides, my stepfather's good medical library in the many shelves surmounting a professional cupboard which, when opened, exhaled undesirable perfumes. (I can at any time still call up the repulsive odor of Podophyllin).

"On the two lower shelves were most of the novels of Charles Dickens, more eagerly devoured than all the rest. It seems to me that no child nowadays has time to love an author as the children and young people of that generation loved Dickens; nor do I think that any living author of to-day provokes love in exactly the same fashion. From our yellow dog, Pip, to the cat, the canary, the lamb, the cow, down to all the hens and cocks, almost every living thing was named, sooner or later, after one of Dickens's characters; while my favorite sled, painted in brown, with the title in brilliant red letters, was 'The Artful Dodger.'

"We never read newspapers save the weekly *Portland Transcript,* so that there was a moment of thrilling excitement when my mother, looking up from the *Portland Press,* told us that Mr. Dickens was coming to America. Day of unspeakable excitement!—we learned that he had been prevailed upon to give one reading in Portland, which was only sixteen miles away from our village.

"It chanced that my mother was taking me [on the train] to Charlestown, Massachusetts, to pay a visit to an uncle on the very day after the one appointed for the great event in Portland. When the train stopped for two or three minutes at North Berwick, the people on the side of the car next the station suddenly arose and looked eagerly out at some object of apparent interest. There on the platform stood the Adored One! It was unbelievable, but there he was in the flesh; standing smiling, breathing, like ordinary human beings. It was only a momentary view, for the train started, and Dickens vanished, to resume his place in the car next to ours, where he had been, had I known it, ever since we left Portland.

"When my mother was again occupied with her book, I slipped away, and, borne along by some resistless and hitherto unrecognized force, I entered the next car; . . . and gazed steadily at the famous man, who was chatting busily with [a] Mr. Osgood. I remembered gratefully that my mother had taken the old ribbons off my gray velvet hat and tied me down with blue under the chin, and I thought, if Dickens should happen to rest his eye upon me, that he could hardly fail to be pleased with the effect of the blue ribbon that went under my collar and held a very small squirrel muff in place.

"Half an hour passed, perhaps, and one gentleman after another came from here or there to exchange a word of greeting with the famous novelist, so that he was never for a moment alone, thereby inciting in my breast my first, and about my last, experience of the passion of jealousy. Suddenly, however, Mr. Osgood arose, and with an apology went into the smoking-car. I never knew how it happened; I had no plan; no preparation, no intention, certainly no provocation; but invisible ropes pulled me out of my seat, and, speeding up the aisle, I planted myself breathlessly and timorously down, an unbidden guest, in the seat of honor. I had a moment to recover my equanimity, for Dickens was looking out of the window, but he turned suddenly and said with justifiable surprise:

"'God bless my soul, child, where did you come from?'

"My heart was in my mouth, but there was still room to exercise my tongue, which was generally the case. I was frightened, but not so completely frightened as if I had been meeting a stranger. You see I knew him, even if he did not know me; so I became immediately autobiographical, although palpitating with nervousness. I had to tell him, I thought, where I came from who I was, where I was going, or how could I account for myself and my presence beside him in Mr. Osgood's seat? So I began, stammeringly, to answer his question.

"'I came from Hollis, Maine, and I'm going to Charlestown to visit my uncle. My mother and her cousin went to your reading last night, but of course three couldn't go from the same family, it was so expensive, so I stayed at home. Nora, that's my little sister, is left behind in Hollis. She's too small to go on a journey, but she wanted to go to the reading dreadfully. There was a lady there who had never heard of Betsey Trotwood, and had only read two of your books!'

"'Well, upon my word!' he said; 'you do not mean to say that *you* have read them!'

"'Of course!' I replied; 'every one of them but the two that we are going to buy in Boston, and some of them six times.' 'Of course,' I explained conscientiously, 'I do skip some of the very dull parts once in a while; not the short dull parts, but the long ones.'

"He laughed heartily. 'Now, that is something that I hear very little about,' he said. 'I distinctly want to learn more about those very long dull parts.'

(From the stage production of "Rebecca of Sunnybrook Farm," starring Marion Nixon.)

(From the movie "Mother Carey's Chickens," copyright 1938, RKO Radio Pictures. Starring Fay Bainter and Frank Morgan.)

"And, whether to amuse himself, or to amuse me, I do not know, he took out a notebook and pencil from his pocket and proceeded to give me an exhausting and exhaustive examination on this subject; the books in which the dull parts predominated; and the characters and subjects which principally produced them. He chuckled so constantly during this operation that I could hardly help believing myself extraordinarily agreeable, so I continued dealing these infant blows, under the delusion that I was flinging him bouquets.

"It seems to me, as I look back now, and remember how the little soul of me came out and sat in the sunshine of his presence, that I must have had some premonition that the child, who would come to be one of the least of writers, was then talking with one of the greatest;—talking, too, as it were, of the author's profession and high calling, for were we not discussing books? All the little details of the meeting stand out as clearly as though it had happened yesterday. I can see every article of his clothing and of my own; the other passengers in the car; the landscape through the window; and above all the face of Dickens, deeply lined, with sparkling eyes and an amused, waggish smile that curled the corners of his mouth under his grizzled mus-

tache. A part of our conversation was given to a Boston newspaper next day, by the author himself, or by Mr. Osgood, and was long preserved in our family archives.

"I once kept a journal when I had attained the ripe age of ten summers. I set down in a mottled-covered blank-book daily, for a portion of one season, all the doings of my life in a small New England hamlet. There is not a trace of literary talent in this childish effort, I am ashamed to say.

"The first entry reads as follows: 'March 24th: I got up this morning at twenty minutes past seven; then I went downstairs and dusted the parlor, which took me until breakfast time. After breakfast we read the prayers for the day and two chapters in the Bible. Then Nora [my sister] and I went out to feed the hens. We found one egg. After we got through I put on my things and went for the milk. After I got home we went up to Grandmother's to spend the day—Mother, Cousin E. and all three of us children. [There was a . . . half-brother, Philip, by this time.] I read a little while in the new Harper. The story that I read first was 'My Fathers-in-law.' It was real funny, but it didn't sound true. Then Grandma said she wanted me to help her. Cousin E. went out with me, she mashed turnips, and I

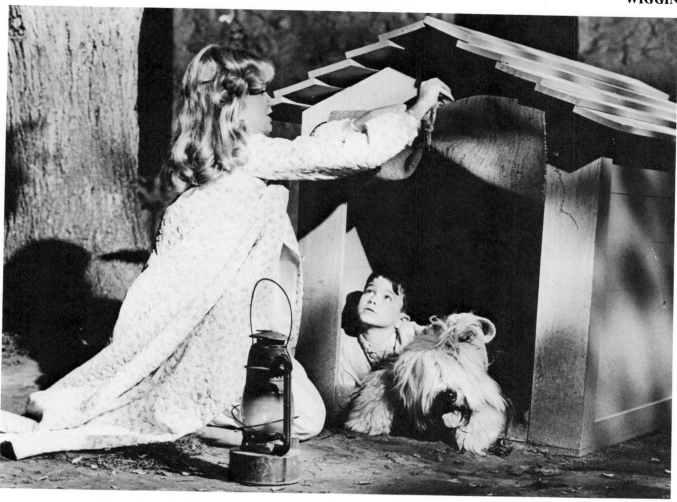

(From the movie "Summer Magic," copyright 1962, Walt Disney Productions. Starring Hayley Mills and Dorothy McGuire.)

pounded beefsteak with a broken plate to make it tender; then I fixed the sausages for dinner, helped set the table; then we sat down. We had a real nice dinner—sausages, beefsteak, pickles, turnips, potatoes, cheese, biscuits; for dessert—pumpkin and apple pies, coffee, apple sauce. After supper I dressed and went to the Bible class. I read once, and answered three or four questions.'

"My sister and I had few playmates, but I cannot remember that we were ever dull, for dullness in a child, as in a grown person, means lack of dreams and visions, and those we had a-plenty.

"School days play an extraordinarily small part in my life. I should probably pass for a fairly well-educated person, so long, at any rate, as I do not frequent the too-intimate society of scholars, or of those human horrors whose conversation resembles a questionnaire, or who presume so confidently on your acquaintance with the Neanderthal Man, Hammurabi, Tiberius Gracchus, or the Venerable Bede . . . W.E.H. Lecky, the Irish historian, once told me about sitting beside a young, charmingly dressed American lady at a dinner where the guests were mostly celebrities in one field or another. She was a stranger and begged him to

identify the principal personages for her delectation. Finally she asked: 'And what do you do, sir?' 'I am a writer,' he replied; 'I suppose I may say I am by way of being an historian; are you by any chance interested in history, Madam?' 'Oh! no, not a bit,' she answered blithely; 'I always say let bygones be bygones!'

"In our early days my sister and I were taught at home under the capable, slightly impatient, somewhat sporadic direction of our busy stepfather, whose large practice distributed over a wide territory did not permit regularity of hours. He was a . . . good teacher, if his pupil answered his questions instantly. My Latin Grammar was much damaged by his irritable pounding of it on the table; while the Small Sister's Greenleaf's Arithmetic was once flung into the orchard when she was particularly and distractingly dense about the multiplication table, which she detested.

"I cannot say just how, when, where, or whether I ever acquired any substantial body of knowledge, or any adequate degree of mental training, for when one's years from seven to sixteen are passed in a small New England village, continuity in education, a rather valuable factor, is almost impossible. A hunger for companionship, and for learning in company with others, led finally to my going to the little district school in a small white building farther down our village street. This school I have somewhat veraciously described in *Rebecca of Sunnybrook Farm,* which book, while wholly fictitious in story, is in background as true as my modest art could make it. Both desks and benches were battered, scarred, cut, and stained by ten or twelve years of use and abuse by badly bored children, who for the most part resisted the acquisition of learning as something wholly outside their idea of the universe.

"A term at the little red-brick schoolhouse across the river in Buxton followed at some time or other, but I can recall nothing about it."[1]

1869. "The next memories are of being a boarding pupil during three terms, from November to June inclusive, at the Gorham Female Seminary eight miles away! I learned little or nothing at the Gorham Female Seminary for some reason or other, although I sometimes wonder just when we really do learn anything."[1]

1873. "The rest of my family left Maine for many a year, and embarked for Santa Barbara, where it was hoped that my [step]father, who had a little weakness of the lungs, might grow stronger in the mild and beautiful climate of California. I, still 'uneducated,' strange to say, having sipped momentarily at five founts of learning, was left behind for six months at Abbot Academy, Andover, Massachusetts, one of the best boarding schools for girls in New England. I was a sore trial to the Faculty, for I was, in a manner of speech, a senior in Literature, a junior in French and Latin, a sophomore in Grammar, a freshman in History, and a poor risk for the preparatory department in Mathematics!

"Now ensued what proved to be the most irresponsible delightful, entirely healthful and enchanting year or two of my life. No words can describe the loveliness of Santa Barbara, with its semi-tropical atmosphere, its luxuriance of foliage and flowers, its lovely semi-circle of mountains, its blue, blue sea!

"I had been used to the deep snows, and late reluctant springs of Maine. In California, when the rains had ceased, April was a revelation of beauty hitherto unimagined. We had a pleasant house, although there were no positively unpleasant ones to be found.

"It was a free, eager, venturesome, joyous life altogether, and if I had a dozen daughters I should like those born in the East to have a breath of the West, while I would send Californian girls to the East for a year or two.

"I had never once heard money matters mentioned in our household from childhood up to this moment; never any talk about income; never a word of debts, credits, hopes, fears, economies, or extravagances. We were never told to save, and never given presents that seemed to indicate riches; the whole subject of finance was left untouched. My mother in her first widowhood had a comfortable living income on which to support herself, my little sister, and me. This inheritance came from her father.

"My stepfather's practice supplied the rest of the annual budget (if there ever was a budget, which I very much doubt), and . . . there was an extraordinary lack of discussion as to ways and means. This may have meant indifference, but it certainly did not imply debts or difficulties, for, when these occur, children can never be kept in ignorance, since the very atmosphere breathes a nameless misery and continual arguement in and out of season.

"Into the hopeful, contented, wholly untrained, and, I fear, unbusinesslike family, there came the death of my stepfather after an illness of only a few months. It occurred when the ebb tide of . . . land speculation was only too obvious, the fortunate and far-seeing buyers having departed with their legitimate gains, while a couple of hundred disappointed ones were left behind to regret their too enthusiastic, ill-selected, and promiscuous purchases. Within a year the growth of the town had veered in an unexpected direction, and we were among those who had not prophesied discreetly.

"To be left with many parcels of unsalable land, all mortgaged, as was the invariable custom, the mortgages to be paid out of the profits that never came; to be left with our own cottage, horses, carriages, harnesses, and household effects in peril because of the lack of income: all this is disagreeable enough; but to be encumbered with a drugstore and two clerks needing continual advice and skilled superintendence as well as salary, this was tragedy. A widow with two youthful daughters and a boy of twelve might well despair, and she did.

"While we were eating up the horses and carriages and harnesses, I wrote a story partially based upon an experience occurring during the time that I was a boarding pupil at the Gorham Female Seminary.

"The thing was called 'Half-a-Dozen Housekeepers,' and was sent as soon as finished to the *St. Nicholas* Magazine in New York. . . . I called daily at the post-office, but was not really surprised that I received no answer. I thought little of the story, and wondered I had had the impertinence to offer it. . . . One dreary day of the first autumn rains I made my usual call at the post-office, feeling a little more grown-up and practical than I had before, for I had heard that morning of an entirely new and unknown fatality called 'taxes.'

"The postmaster handed me an envelope, not knowing that he was a fairy godfather. It had '*St. Nicholas* Magazine, 33 East 17th Street,' printed on it and appeared like any ordinary letter, but on being opened by trembling fingers disclosed an acceptance of 'Half-a-Dozen Housekeepers,' which was to be printed in three installments, and a check fluttered to the ground beside me. I had never seen a check before, but I picked it up and departed eagerly to a secluded spot to find that it appeared to call for a payment of a dollar and fifty cents which I thought was fair value for a first effort, though inadequate for taxes. Concentrated scrutiny gave me the idea after a moment that it was perhaps for fifteen dollars, though that seemed a large amount for my services to art. I continued to study it, arithmetic being my weak point and ciphers particularly distracting, but I could read and understand written words, and my eyes finally slipped to the plain statement that one hundred and fifty dollars was to be paid me by the misguided, the extravagant, the romantic editor of the *St. Nicholas.* (Dear Mary Mapes Dodge, of blessed memory!)

. . . there burst forth a very thick smoke, which obliged him to retire two or three paces back. ■
(From *The Arabian Nights* edited by Kate Douglas Wiggin and Nora A. Smith. Illustrated by Maxfield Parrish.)

Kate Douglas Wiggin with children featured in one of her films.

"I thought quite soberly the rest of the week about the whole affair; the comparatively short time in which I had written the story, its speedy acceptance, its generous recompense. Manifestly the right and obvious thing was to sit down and write another, and then another and maintain my responsibility as the head of the family, but I found to my surprise that I had nothing in particular to write about! No themes, no convictions, no powerful urge to express myself, no background of culture, no experience, no knowledge of human nature! What was there in me, I thought, out of which to make a successful author? Nothing! The right thing for me was to learn to do something well, to have a profession of some sort; not one requiring long study and apprenticeship, for that was impossible under the circumstances, but a modest vocation. What should it be? Teaching of some sort was one of the obvious channels of activity, but how could I teach when I possessed so little knowledge? The younger the children, the less book-learning I should need, but, on the other hand, the more wisdom. How should I gain this indispensable asset?"[1]

Summer, 1877. "At this crucial moment . . . came a remarkable woman to Santa Barbara, Mrs. Caroline M. Severance, of Boston, sometimes called the Mother of Women's Clubs. She interested me greatly in the kindergarten method, which was then gaining ground in Massachusetts under the name of the 'New Education,' and through the efforts of Elizabeth Peabody, who, not long returned from the land of Froebel, was fully assured that she had solved the riddle of the universe. Her brother-in-law, Horace

Mann, had introduced the system into his famous school. If I had been made of tinder and a lighted match had been applied to me, I could not have taken fire more easily when Mrs. Severance told me of this new educational enterprise with young children.

Began training in Los Angeles. "There were only three of us in Miss Marwedel's first training-class, . . . but twenty-five children had been gathered by Mrs. Severance by the day I arrived in Los Angeles, and they were a lovely group from four to seven years old.

"I was in an incredible state of excitement, for I felt that for the first time in my life I was clearly doing something that I was able to do well, perhaps in course of time superlatively well.

"I am very grateful that my first training came from Miss Marwedel. She was not adapted to all pupils, her English not being perfect and her method not systematic. Her feet never trod the solid earth; she was an idealist, a dreamer, and a visionary, but life is so apt to be crammed with Gradgrinds that I am thankful when I come into intimate

As to her hair, the local milliner declared it impossible for Rose Wiley to get an unbecoming hat; that on occasion, being in a frolicsome mood, Rose had tried on all the headgear in the village emporium,—children's gingham "shakers," mourning bonnets for aged dames, men's haying hats and visored caps—and she proved superior to every test, looking as pretty as a pink in the best ones and simply ravishing in the worst.
■ (From *Rose o' the River* by Kate Douglas Wiggin. Illustrated by George Wright.)

contact with a dreamer. Dreamers and visionaries are not always comfortable members of families; that, I allow. They are unpractical, unpunctual, not given to toiling and spinning, prefer sunsets to sewing and poetry to cooking; but, for outside intercourse, give me a dreamer or two to stir the imagination and kindle the heart's desire for noble things. This has been and can be done at the cookstove and in the business office, but candor compels me to state that a sunset, a quiet hour on a hilltop, a 'book of verses underneath the bough,' all prove more serviceable in my experience.

"When Miss Marwedel painted the possibilities of the children with whom we were working, when she recounted Froebel's vision of the future of the race if children from the earliest years could be self-governing and creative, instead of disciplined like soldiers and 'standardized,' I escaped temporarily from a world of rigid realities.

"For my first experiment I rented a most lovely old adobe house in Santa Barbara called 'The Swallow's Nest,' on a quiet street bordered with eucalyptus trees and blooming with rose-gardens. We were a very happy family in 'The Swallow's Nest' that summer, and we taught one another more than any of us realized."[1]

Summer, 1878. "Felix Adler, the noted preacher, teacher, lecturer, author, philanthropist, came to San Francisco . . . and in a brief visit gathered a company of men and women interested in education, forming a board of directors, which raised sufficient money to rent a building and assume the task of opening the first free kindergarten west of the Rocky Mountains. There were but few trained kindergartners from whom to choose and I was called from Santa Barbara to organize the work.

"The building in Silver Street, which I hoped was to be the scene of such beautiful and inspiring doings as had been seldom observed on this planet, was pleasant and commodious.

"'This school,' I thought, 'must not be an exotic, a parasite, an alien growth, a flower of beauty transplanted from a conservatory and shown under glass; it must have its roots deep in the neighborhood life, and there my roots must be also. No teacher, be she ever so gifted, ever so consecrated, can sufficiently influence the children under her care for these few hours a day, unless she can gradually persuade the parents to be her allies.'

"These were early days. The kindergarten theory of education was on trial for its very life. I simply stepped into a cockleshell and put out into an unknown ocean, where all manner of derelicts needed help and succor. It was an experience of which I had heretofore known nothing; with lives miserable, sometimes entirely overburdened, and often criminal.

"My cockleshell managed to escape shipwreck, and took its frail place among the other craft that sailed in its company. I hardly saw or felt the safety of the harbor or the shore for three years, the three years out of my whole life the most wearying, the most heart-searching, the most discouraging, the most inspiring; also, I dare say, the best worth living."[1]

. . . her pencil moved as easily as her tongue, and no more striking simile could be used. ■ (From *New Chronicles of Rebecca* by Kate Douglas Wiggin. Illustrated by F. C. Yohn.)

1880. "Returning in the late autumn with the commendation and approval of the leaders of the movement East and West, I opened . . . my own California Kindergarten Training-School. I took but four pupils the first season, my sister, Nora Archibald Smith, being one of them. She had just returned from a two years' pioneering excursion of her own account, among the Spanish-speaking children of Mexico and Arizona, and was prepared to be one of the torch-bearers of the new training-school.

"The writing and delivery of lectures on kindergarten theory and practice, together with constant study and brief talks at educational conventions here and there, made this a very busy but not at all a monotonous year.

"To take in more of the babies waiting wistfully in the back streets, I tried to replenish our treasury by writing *The Story of Patsy* (1882).

"I was far too close to the life I was picturing to make this book wholly worthy of its subject. I am well aware that it lacks perspective, and that it has more heart than art, but oh! how many kindergartens it brought to places that had never known one; how many girls read it and flew to the nearest training school, unconscious, perhaps, that they were not only being fitted for teaching, but for motherhood and for life in general! It was not published, only privately printed, bound in a paper cover, and sold here and there for twenty-five cents for the benefit of the cause.

"For the same reason, with no special literary impulse or ambition, I later wrote *The Birds' Christmas Carol* (1886), and I remember that the kindly printer remarked casually that, if I gave the profits to the Kindergarten Association, I ought at least to keep the copyright myself. I had no time to look in the dictionary and see exactly what the terms of a copyright might be, but the printer acted in my behalf and went through the necessary legal steps. (I am grateful to him for the suggestion and so, I am sure, are my publishers!)"[1]

December, 1881. "I married an old friend of my early girlhood, Samuel Bradley Wiggin, a young lawyer of Boston and a graduate of Dartmouth College, who had followed me to San Francisco, hopeful that a legal career might open to him in the West. In natural gifts and wide culture, in qualities of mind and heart, he was equal to any good fortune that might await him. Money, or prospects of money, neither of us had at the moment, nor could either of us assure the other of any probable future wealth. Even of health there was no superabundance to give on either side, for I was somewhat nervously exhausted by my three years of exacting labor, and the young partner in our perhaps perilous adventure was not of strong constitution, so that serious illness often disturbed the otherwise even tenor of our few years together; years never marred by difference of aims, ambitions, and ideals, many of them, alas! never to be realized by him!"[1]

About **1884-85.** "I removed to New York with my husband, but I returned to San Francisco each spring for the final lectures to the training-class, the examinations, graduating exercises, and signing of diplomas.

"Each year I took the opportunity to visit the more notable Free Kindergartens and Manual Training-Schools in Chicago, Detroit, St. Louis, Washington, Philadelphia, New York, and Boston, consulting with all the best leaders of the movement and taking back the fruits of my observations and study to the West."[1]

September, 1889. "While I was in California for a necessary stay of several months giving lectures to the Training-School, the end came suddenly to my husband in New York. His death came in a moment, softly, quietly, and without warning, and the whole current of my life was changed.

"I needed rest, recreation, change of climate, change of work, and all of these came to me in the course of a few years, but I returned to San Francisco for several seasons for visits to my dearly loved Training-School during the closing weeks before graduation. There came, alas! a time when it was no longer possible to go back to the dear old spot, for some years later, after my mother and sister had joined me in the East, the San Francisco fire and earthquake destroyed almost the entire quarter surrounding Silver Street, and the place of blessed memories was dynamited to stay the progress of the flames. Not a trace was left of the dear roof that at the height of my activities had sheltered three hundred children.

"Sydney Smith will be recalled as saying that it is a very wise rule in the conduct of the understanding to acquire early a correct notion of your own peculiar constitution of mind, and to become well acquainted, as a physician would say, with your idiosyncrasies. . . . It is a prodigious point gained if any man can find out where his powers lie, and what are his deficiencies—if he can contrive to ascertain what Nature intended for him.

"I am not at all sure even now about the precise quality of such powers as I possess, although I am well aware of my deficiencies as an author. When I recall those marvelous days in California, first with children, their mothers, fathers, and homes, and then with large classes of young women (though many of my pupils were twice my age), and also with many audiences in villages and towns in the vicinity of San Francisco, I half believe that Nature intended me, not for a writer, but for a teacher.

"One rather dreary day in the last years of my work in San Francisco, when I was thinking of my future, I read in a novel these lines: 'There comes a time in most of our lives when in order to make any real progress it seems necessary slightly to change our direction.' I wondered what direction along the life-trail I was best fitted to take, for I felt that it must be changed. I wondered if 'Patsy' and the 'Carol' had really any literary significance or whether they had been bought simply to aid a good cause.

"I had done no writing for several years save on educational subjects and I had not the slightest sense of being an author. I had an ample supply of stories for use in kindergartens, stories that my sister and I had constantly told to the children, also various essays of ours to be collected under one cover and to be called *Children's Rights*, but these two possible volumes existed only in manuscript and were a natural part of my educational work.

"Nobody had ever suggested that I could write; nobody had ever thought of any easier road for me than the one I had traveled; nobody had fancied that I could earn more than twelve hundred dollars or so in any year by any method. It was with no burning ambition, no special belief in myself, no idea of the ultimate outcome, but rather from languid curiosity that I sent the paper-covered 'Carol' to Houghton. . . .

"That it had been printed and sold privately I felt must be, of course, a handicap, and so, indeed, it would generally have been considered. In spite of this drawback, Mr. Henry O. Houghton, the senior member of the firm, took the book home in his pocket and read it aloud to his family on the piazza of their country home. . . . The next morning Mr. Houghton walked into the office of his firm at 4 Park Street, Boston, and said; 'If you folks don't happen to like this book, I do, and I'll publish it on my own account if necessary.'

"The great and unexpected success of this unpretentious Christmas story showed me clearly the new 'direction' in which I was bound to travel; indeed, it left me no choice, for the book cleared the way for me from the first day of publication, 'easing my shoulders from the burden' and 'delivering my hand from making the pots.'

Quillcote

"In spite of these encouraging successes, the early spring of 1890 found me still weary, depressed, and much in need of entire change."[1]

May 24, 1890. "[I sailed with friends] from New York on the Ems, of the North-German Lloyd Line. . . . It was our first journey abroad, so we went where everybody else went, we saw what everybody else saw, and wrote back the same sort of enthusiastic letters to home friends.

"I am glad that I saw all these things with religious fervor, and had my one serious taste of London and its historic past; for in twenty or more subsequent visits in after years I never once went sight-seeing, but settled down into London life as if it were home, as indeed, it always seems to me the moment my feet touch the beloved streets."[1]

1891. Returned to U.S. and began giving readings and lectures across the country. "In quick succession in the early winter of 1892 came two invitations to read at Miss Master's School at Dobbs Ferry and Miss Aiken's at Stamford. The coaxing notes from the girls' English and Composition classes were irresistible, and I read at both schools. It was in this way, even before 'Polly Oliver' and 'Rebecca' were written that my life began continuously to intersect the orbit of youth."[1]

1892-93. She noted in her diary: "'Went to Dr. W.'s private hospital April 11th and left there May 26th for additional period of complete rest at my hotel.'

"I was young and had great recuperative power, so it is not remarkable that I sailed for London on the Etruiria a month later. Before and after that time I was as frequently in a rest-cure as my income would permit, though commonly for brief periods. If any reader of statistical tendencies finds sensational gaps in the records of my activities, he will know that I was probably sojourning in a sanatorium. Quite a number of my more cheerful books have been written in hospitals or health resorts, particularly *Rebecca of Sunnybrook Farm*, all of which was conceived in severe illness and most of the work done at Dansville, New York. My superiors, Robert Louis Stevenson and Mark Twain, wrote many novels in bed. Of course, they constantly smoked cigars or cigarettes, which seem to be a great help in stimulating constructive imagination, but my humble Muse would never lift an eyebrow or condescend to give me an idea in the atmosphere of tobacco smoke.

"The only places where I can write are, first, in an empty room, with a large wooden table; second, in a hospital in moderate pain and with very little sleep; third, in a Pullman car filled with travelers whom I never perceive; then,

. . . as he poured over picture-books, or sat silently by the window, watching the drops chase each other down the pane, his talk was often of heaven and the angels. ■ (From *The Story of Patsy* by Kate Douglas Wiggin.)

fourth, in bed, with the rest of the house shut off and in as reasonable quiet as one can expect nowadays in a noisy, bustling, unreflecting world.

"One cannot see callers, answer the telephone, go to luncheons or dinners, visit the dentist or shoemaker, address charitable organizations in or from a bed; therefore a bed, in my experience, is simply bristling with ideas. I don't know whether any robust person sitting up, in good health and spirits, ever reads my books, but, if any doubting Thomas wishes to find out if I am a favorite among invalids, he can write to thousands of nurses who will say that when they unpack a patient's belongings they invariably find, among the lingerie, photographs of the best beloved, dressing-jackets, and hot-water bottles, a book of mine for emergencies! The pallid sufferer sits on the edge of her cot while the nurse distributes her effects, and says feebly: 'I thought if I happened to live, I might like to read *that*.'

"I arrived in London June 26th of that year, and began my annual frivolities. London for a few years was my only playground, my best source of intellectual stimulation, my chief place for meeting distinguished people representing all the arts. I sailed for New York, arriving October 25th, and the old life of traveling and writing between-times was resumed.

"I distinctly remember one occasion in a theater when I was to appear with Mark Twain. Feeling that no one could be so deliciously funny as he, I wrote a pathetic tale, with glances of humor now and then in the dialogue. He chose a story I had never heard before, however, one simply heartbreaking in its pathos, so that the audience, though interested, was somewhat sad, dejected, and tearful.

"The mood was not quite right, for the preliminary offering on that evening was the reading in very monotonous style of a lengthy poem in perhaps a hundred or a thousand stanzas of ten lines each, semi-historical, with a tropical background of the South Sea Islands. I was extremely bored myself, but very curious as to its unexpected effect upon Mark Twain in the opposite box to mine. He leaned out farther and farther, fixing his eyes intently upon the speaker.

"'The poem must be better than I think,' I kept saying to myself, for Mark Twain's eyes never left the poet's face.

"He explained afterwards, . . . that he kept his eye fixed on the poet for fear that he should go to sleep and tumble over the railing of the box on the stage. ''Livy' (his lovely wife Olivia) 'always hates to have me do that!' he said. 'She is so conventional.''

1893. "If I should tabulate the number of states, cities, towns, and villages in America and the various parts of Europe in which I have lived from six months to several years, it would seem that I must be at least a century old.

"Archimedes said if he only had a spot of firm ground on which to rest his lever he could move the world. [My mother, sister and I] had no special desire to embark upon so large a project, but we longed unspeakably for a home, and a definite place to work.

"My desk in New York has always commanded a view of unanswered letters and household accounts, while the sound of the vacuum cleaner or telephone in the distance, and the ringing of the front doorbell continually break the desired silence. There is generally a glimpse of a lampshade which the housemaid has arranged unsymmetrically, a picture hanging askew on the wall, or a Wedgwood teacup which has had its handle broken off and glued on since I last noted it. In the midst of a fairly good sentence, it is impossible for me to avoid the reflection that the window cleaner must be ordered for the next day.

"We discovered that the only spot where we united in wishing to spend the summer was in Hollis, Maine, where our early childhood had been passed. There my mother and sister preceded me and there I followed them in a sort of bewildered and intoxicated joy at the enterprise. No more crowds, no more big audiences, no more compliments, for they never compliment anybody in Hollis; it is considered weakening to the character of the recipient.

"I was now a house and land leaser, temporary proprietor of ten acres of hayfield, the most beautiful maples and elms in the village, and a more or less defunct apple orchard, seven or eight hundred square feet of leaky roofs on house, shed, and barn, the said barn having sunk two feet off the perpendicular—all acquired at an unrevealed rent, except that it had a four in it. [We named it 'Quillcote.']

"Early summer, 1894, found me on my way to England again. My dear mother was inclined at first to think that these annual journeys across the Atlantic were slightly extravagant. My mother realized before long that the ocean voyages gave me rest after my exhausting winters, and that I always came home rejuvenated in body and mind, with a hundred new impressions valuable in a literary as well as in a financial way.

"Tranquilly I walked up the gangway on that sunny May morning in 1894, looking aloft and waving my hand in answer to the skipper's welcome. I had not the smallest idea that before many days I should be making the most Micawber-like leap of my career, for, standing somewhere on one of the decks, was the man whom I was going to marry.

"I went down to luncheon very late and the people at table had nearly finished the meal. We all made a brief remark or so to one another, with a view to deciding what sort of companionship might be established on a nine days' voyage. . . . The nice chap opposite, named on the list as George C. Riggs, New York City, looked sufficiently the part."[1]

March 30, 1895. "My marriage took place quietly in All Souls' Church . . . a day marvelously like summer, with birds singing in Madison Square and the young leaves as green as if it had been May.

"My husband's business interests were largely in Scotland and Ireland, and for a few years in Germany also, so that we always sailed early in April and generally spent three months on the other side of the Atlantic, mostly in Great Britain.

"England, Scotland, and Ireland became second homes to me, and until the World War, with all its cruel changes, narrowed my list and prevented my annual visits for a time, I had as many acquaintances and friends there as in America.

. . . he was attempting to paint a copy of the aforesaid inscription upon the side of a too patient goat, who saw no harm in the operation. He was alone and very, very happy. ■ (From *A Summer in a Canoe* by Kate Douglas Wiggin. Illustrated by Frank T. Merrill.)

"My habit of work has been, generally speaking, to write what was uppermost in my mind and to stop when I had nothing more to say about it. I have done many wrong things in my life, but I have never done a long thing! This may have been discretion, but it is quite likely that it was lack of matter!

"As I gaze upon these various milestones set along the road of a literary life, I wonder which of them all is dearest to me. The inquiry is, happily, almost out of fashion among readers, although it sometimes occurs in unsophisticated circles of society, where an author is still considered a person of unique powers. It was always a foolish question, and an embarrassing one to answer. No one would ever think of asking a mother which one of her children she regarded as most interesting.

"There is no confusion in my mind as to where any particular book grew into being, although on all other points I have the most treacherous of memories.

"I remember a large bedroom in San Francisco—it overlooked the Golden Gate and the low green slopes of the Marin shore—where I wrote my first book, *The Birds' Christmas Carol.*

"Last comes *Rebecca of Sunnybrook Farm,* which the world doubtless supposes to be the darling of my heart. I am not in the least a psychic person, but Rebecca's origin was peculiar to herself. I was recovering from a long illness and very early one morning I lay in a sort of waking dream. I saw an old-fashioned stage-coach rumbling along a dusty country road lined with maple and elm trees. A kind, rosy-faced man held the reins that guided two lean horses and from the little window of the coach leaned a darkhaired gypsy of a child. I was instantly attracted by her long braids floating in the breeze and by the beauty of the eyes in her mischievous face. She pushed back a funny little hat with an impatient gesture, straightened it on her head with a thump, and, with some wriggling, managed to secure the attention of the driver by poking him with a tiny frilled parasol. That was all. The picture came, and went, and returned, and finally faded away, but it haunted me, and I would recall every detail of it at will. Too weak to write, I wondered who the child was, and whither she was traveling, and whence she came. I could not content myself until I had created answers to my questions and the final answer was, indeed, the book itself.

"The book was begun at a Southern health resort, carried on a little during a make-believe convalescence, and finished in a sanatorium where I persuaded the doctors that the work was better out of my system than in it.

"No room in the world is more vividly remembered than the quiet one looking on to distant hills and mountains, where Rebecca lived with me for a month or more, mitigating my weariness and sense of separation from active life. I could not put all I seemed to know about her into the first volume, and a year or two later wrote the *New Chronicles of Rebecca,* which is not a sequel, but a further 'filling in' of incidents from the child's checkered existence at Aunt Miranda Sawyer's brick house in Riverboro.

"Rebecca somewhat changed the current of my life-stream by bringing me into a wider fellowship and intimacy with girls of all ages. She unconsciously made me a deal of trouble, for she doubled my correspondence as suddenly and efficiently as she had leaned from the stage-window and poked Uncle Jerry Cobb with the ivory knob of her pink parasol. These letters make one glad as well as weary, for, if one cannot do the great, the memorable things in literature, there is something intoxicating in the sensation that one has chanced to create a child who seems real as well as winsome, one that other children recognize as belonging to their favorite circle.

"When I feel a trifle depressed that my audience is chiefly one of girls and women, I re-read an occasional letter from men, who are not copious correspondents!

> Headquarters
> First Japanese Army
> Fen-Wang-Chu
> Manchuria
> May 25th, 1904

Dear Kate Douglas Wiggin:
May I thank you for 'Rebecca?' *Penelopes Experiences* whiled away the hours for me the other day, but they appealed to my head, while Rebecca won my heart. Of course, I have laughed, but I have wept as well. She is real; she lives; she has given me many regrets, but I love her. I would have quested the wide world over to make her mine, only I was born too long ago and she was born but yesterday. Why could she not have been my daughter? Can't I adopt her? And, O, how I envy 'Mr. Aladdin!' Why couldn't it have been I who bought the three hundred cakes of soap? Why, O, why?

> Gratefully yours,
> Jack London

"When the twenty-seventh person (they were none of them names to conjure with) had asked if he or she might send me the 'little play' he or she had made of Rebecca, I began to consider the matter of trying it myself. I felt that I could protect the spirit of my own book, and preserve its simplicity, better than any one else. The result could only be an unpretentious drama, very different from the accepted forms, but it might possibly be an amusing, touching, human sort of thing, pleasing in spite of its slightness.

April, 1909. "My Rebecca play was accepted . . . and produced in November of that same year in Springfield, Massachusetts, remaining on tour for several months and opening in New York, October, 1910." [It was enormously successful.]

"The dramatization of 'Mother Carey's Chickens,' in which I had the cooperation of Miss Rachel Crothers, was my next effort. It had a wonderfully good cast of my own choosing, headed by Edith Taliaferro, the dainty, exquisite little fairy who played my Rebecca all over the United States and in London. My Mother Carey was a beautiful woman, my Osh Popham a genial and delightful comedian, my Cousin Ann perfection; indeed, each player seemed born for his character. The first performance was given in Poughkeepsie, and it played a whole season in the large cities on tour, before opening for a six weeks' engagement at the Cort Theater, New York, in September, 1917.

"An author may forget a book the week after it is published, but a play once produced can never be out of mind for a day until it has finished its prosperous journey, or been peacefully interred in the theatrical storehouse. A book is a solid, corporeal fact, but a play is a quicksilver sort of thing that indulges in sudden unexpected, mysterious, unaccountable changes. It seems to present one aspect in Buffalo, and another in Boston. They may love it in Pittsburgh, and loathe it in Peoria; the critics praise it in Syracuse, and revile it in Schenectady. It seems better than it really is when the players are well, happy, and delighted with their several parts, and worse than it really is when they are not. It is better on Fridays than on Mondays; on Saturday matinees than on Wednesdays; and although it may have faults it is always a perfectly delightful play when the 'Standing Room Only' sign decorates the outside of the theater, giving a style and distinction to the sidewalk that no other placard in the world possesses. And this, mind you, is really not so much because the box-office is prosperous as because it means eager, sympathetic, responsive audiences, who almost make and unmake plays at will."[1]

August 24, 1923. Died at Harrow-on-the-Hill, England, at the age of 66. A few months later her autobiography was published. "I never overrated my work myself, and I never shall! I have a sense of literary values, and a camel sees himself truly when he goes under a mountain. I am much in the company of mountains and they do not encourage vanity. Nevertheless, my books have brought me such joy and such richness of compensation that I can only hope that some of it has overflowed the cup and given pleasure elsewhere, for I should always like to be a 'sharing' sort of a person if I might, believing with. Lowell that the gift without the giver is bare."[1]

FOR MORE INFORMATION SEE: Frederic Taber Cooper, *Some American Story Tellers*, Holt, 1911; Kate Douglas Wiggin, *My Garden of Memory: An Autobiography*, Houghton, 1923; Nora A. Smith, *Kate Douglas Wiggin as Her Sister Knew Her*, Houghton, 1925; G. M. Overton, *Women Who Make Our Novels*, Dodd, 1928; Elizabeth R. Montgomery, *Story behind Great Books*, McBride, 1946; Montgomery, *Story behind Great Stories*, McBride, 1947; L. W. Stebbins, "Kate Douglas Wiggin as a Child Knew Her," *Horn Book*, November, 1950.

Miriam E. Mason, *Yours with Love, Kate*, Houghton, 1952; Helen F. Benner, *Kate Douglas Wiggin's Country of Childhood*, University of Maine Press, 1956; Mason, *Kate Douglas Wiggin, the Little Schoolteacher*, Bobbs-Merrill, 1962; Laura Benét, *Famous Storytellers for Young People*, Dodd, 1968; Brian Doyle, editor, *Who's Who of Children's Literature*, Shocken Books, 1968.

WILLIAMS, Hawley
See HEYLIGER, William

ILLUSTRATIONS INDEX